Dictionary of Literary Biography

Dictionary of Literary Biography Documentary Series

Dictionary of Literary Biography Yearbooks

Concise Series

Concise Dictionary of American Literary Biography, 7 volumes (1988-1999): *The New Consciousness, 1941-1968; Colonization to the American Renaissance, 1640-1865; Realism, Naturalism, and Local Color, 1865-1917; The Twenties, 1917-1929; The Age of Maturity, 1929-1941; Broadening Views, 1968-1988; Supplement: Modern Writers, 1900-1998.*

Concise Dictionary of British Literary Biography, 8 volumes (1991-1992): *Writers of the Middle Ages and Renaissance Before 1660; Writers of the Restoration and Eighteenth Century, 1660-1789; Writers of the Romantic Period, 1789-1832; Victorian Writers, 1832-1890; Late-Victorian and Edwardian Writers, 1890-1914; Modern Writers, 1914-1945; Writers After World War II, 1945-1960; Contemporary Writers, 1960 to Present.*

Concise Dictionary of World Literary Biography, 10 volumes projected (1999-   ): *Ancient Greek and Roman Writers; German Writers; African, Caribbean, and Latin American Writers; South Slavic and Eastern European Writers.*

Dictionary of Literary Biography® • Volume Two Hundred Forty-Three

The American Renaissance in New England
Fourth Series

Dictionary of Literary Biography® • Volume Two Hundred Forty-Three

The American Renaissance in New England
Fourth Series

Edited by
Wesley T. Mott
Worcester Polytechnic Institute

A Bruccoli Clark Layman Book
The Gale Group
Detroit • San Francisco • London • Boston • Woodbridge, Conn.

Printed in the United States of America

The paper used in this publication meets the minimum requirements
of American National Standard for Information Sciences—Permanence
Paper for Printed Library Materials, ANSI Z39.48-1984. ∞™

Library of Congress Cataloging-in-Publication Data

The American renaissance in New England. Fourth series / edited by Wesley T. Mott.
    p. cm.—(Dictionary of literary biography: v. 243)
"A Bruccoli Clark Layman book."
Includes bibliographical references and index.
ISBN 0-7876-4660-1 (alk. paper)
1. American literature—New England—Dictionaries. 2. American literature—19th century—Dictionaries.
3. American literature—New England—Bio-bibliography—Dictionaries. 4. American literature—
19th century—Bio-bibliography—Dictionaries. 5. Authors, American—New England—Biography—
Dictionaries. 6. Authors, American—19th century—Biography—Dictionaries. 7. United States—Intellectual
life—1783–1865—Dictionaries. 8. New England—Biography—Dictionaries. I. Mott, Wesley T. II. Series.

PS243 .A544 2001
810.9'003—dc21   2001031517
[B]

10 9 8 7 6 5 4 3 2 1

To Sandy

Contents

Contents

Plan of the Series

. . . Almost the most prodigious asset of a country, and perhaps its most precious possession, is its native literary product—when that product is fine and noble and enduring.

Mark Twain*

The advisory board, the editors, and the publisher of the *Dictionary of Literary Biography* are joined in endorsing Mark Twain's declaration. The literature of a nation provides an inexhaustible resource of permanent worth. Our purpose is to make literature and its creators better understood and more accessible to students and the reading public, while satisfying the needs of teachers and researchers.

To meet these requirements, *literary biography* has been construed in terms of the author's achievement. The most important thing about a writer is his writing. Accordingly, the entries in *DLB* are career biographies, tracing the development of the author's canon and the evolution of his reputation.

The purpose of *DLB* is not only to provide reliable information in a usable format but also to place the figures in the larger perspective of literary history and to offer appraisals of their accomplishments by qualified scholars.

The publication plan for *DLB* resulted from two years of preparation. The project was proposed to Bruccoli Clark by Frederick G. Ruffner, president of the Gale Research Company, in November 1975. After specimen entries were prepared and typeset, an advisory board was formed to refine the entry format and develop the series rationale. In meetings held during 1976, the publisher, series editors, and advisory board approved the scheme for a comprehensive biographical dictionary of persons who contributed to literature. Editorial work on the first volume began in January 1977, and it was published in 1978. In order to make *DLB* more than a dictionary and to compile volumes that individually have claim to status as literary history, it was decided to organize volumes by topic, period, or

*From an unpublished section of Mark Twain's autobiography, copyright by the Mark Twain Company

genre. Each of these freestanding volumes provides a biographical-bibliographical guide and overview for a particular area of literature. We are convinced that this organization—as opposed to a single alphabet method—constitutes a valuable innovation in the presentation of reference material. The volume plan necessarily requires many decisions for the placement and treatment of authors. Certain figures will be included in separate volumes, but with different entries emphasizing the aspect of his career appropriate to each volume. Ernest Hemingway, for example, is represented in *American Writers in Paris, 1920–1939* by an entry focusing on his expatriate apprenticeship; he is also in *American Novelists, 1910–1945* with an entry surveying his entire career, as well as in *American Short-Story Writers, 1910–1945, Second Series* with an entry concentrating on his short fiction. Each volume includes a cumulative index of the subject authors and articles.

Since 1981 the series has been further augmented by the *DLB Yearbooks*, which update published entries, add new entries to keep the *DLB* current with contemporary activity, and provide articles on literary history. There have also been nineteen *DLB Documentary Series* volumes which provide illustrations, facsimiles, and biographical and critical source materials for figures works, or groups judged to have particular interest for students. In 1999 the *Documentary Series* was incorporated into the *DLB* volume numbering system beginning with *DLB 210, Ernest Hemingway*.

We define literature as the *intellectual commerce of a nation:* not merely as belles lettres but as that ample and complex process by which ideas are generated, shaped, and transmitted. *DLB* entries are not limited to "creative writers" but extend to other figures who in their time and in their way influenced the mind of a people. Thus the series encompasses historians, journalists, publishers, book collectors, and screenwriters. By this means readers of *DLB* may be aided to perceive literature not as cult scripture in the keeping of intellectual high priests but firmly positioned at the center of a nation's life.

DLB includes the major writers appropriate to each volume and those standing in the ranks behind them. Scholarly and critical counsel has been sought in deciding which minor figures to include and how full their entries should be. Wherever possible, useful references are made to figures who do not warrant separate entries.

Each *DLB* volume has an expert volume editor responsible for planning the volume, selecting the figures for inclusion, and assigning the entries. Volume editors are also responsible for preparing, where appropriate, appendices surveying the major periodicals and literary and intellectual movements for their volumes, as well as lists of further readings. Work on the series as a whole is coordinated at the Bruccoli Clark Layman editorial center in Columbia, South Carolina, where the editorial staff is responsible for accuracy and utility of the published volumes.

One feature that distinguishes *DLB* is the illustration policy–its concern with the iconography of literature. Just as an author is influenced by his surroundings, so is the reader's understanding of the author enhanced by a knowledge of his environment. Therefore *DLB* volumes include not only drawings, paintings, and photographs of authors, often depicting them at various stages in their careers, but also illustrations of their families and places where they lived. Title pages are regularly reproduced in facsimile along with dust jackets for modern authors. The dust jackets are a special feature of *DLB* because they often document better than anything else the way in which an author's work was perceived in its own time. Specimens of the writers' manuscripts and letters are included when feasible.

Samuel Johnson rightly decreed that "The chief glory of every people arises from its authors." The purpose of the *Dictionary of Literary Biography* is to compile literary history in the surest way available to us–by accurate and comprehensive treatment of the lives and work of those who contributed to it.

The *DLB* Advisory Board

Introduction

Ralph Waldo Emerson issued a ringing challenge to the literary community of the young nation in his 1837 Harvard Phi Beta Kappa address, "The American Scholar": If American writers were "free and brave," with words "loaded with life," they would usher in a "new age." Emerson looms over that age, whether as an inspiration to reformers and artists of his generation and the next, or as a bugbear to those distrustful of social and institutional change or literary innovation. Never wishing to lead a "party" or to be imitated himself, he always thought it his role (and that of the "scholar") to "provoke" others to discover their own resources of genius and power. The rich literary production in New England during the next quarter century—in many senses a response to Emerson's provocation—constituted what has come to be known as the "American Renaissance."

This third of three *DLB* volumes dedicated to *The American Renaissance in New England* comprises forty-one biographical/bibliographical essays on writers—not associated primarily or exclusively with the Concord or Boston and Cambridge literary communities—who flourished throughout New England in the mid nineteenth century. As late as 1866—a year after the end of the Civil War—the United States produced "scarcely any literature outside of New England," William Dean Howells reflected three decades later. Indeed, Boston—home of *The Atlantic Monthly* and the Old Corner Book Store—was the hub of literary activity, drawing contributions and visits by writers from all over the region. Howells admitted, however, that many writers popularly identified with Boston actually lived in various towns outside the city, and that other communities such as Salem, Portland, and Newport had their own special literary traditions. Each New England state, we now know, produced distinctive writers during this period, and one of the greatest American poets, of course, was living in obscurity in remote Amherst, Massachusetts.

To understand the lively and complex relationships among the writers of this important moment in literary history, readers should consult all three volumes of *The American Renaissance in New England:* Second Series (The Concord Writers), Third Series (Boston and Cambridge Writers), and Fourth Series (Regional Writ-

ers). Geographical categories for careers and residence are, of course, highly fluid. Several Concord and Regional writers, for example, were born or educated in Boston or Cambridge. Writers such as Nathaniel Hawthorne (associated with Salem, Massachusetts) chose to live in Concord because of its congenial setting and literary culture; others, such as Elizabeth Palmer Peabody (who had a long and diverse career in Boston), identified with the Emersonian or Transcendental climate of Concord. Many writers simply took up jobs and residence at several locations in New England and elsewhere and are not easily classified by geography. (The major Transcendentalist reform communities and publications, moreover, though not physically based in Concord, are found in the Concord volume as a convenience and in recognition of their various indebtedness to the Concord writers.)

Together, the three *American Renaissance in New England* volumes supersede the 1978 *DLB 1* volume with the same title, edited by Joel Myerson. A pioneering work in its own right, as well as the inaugural volume in the now-venerable *DLB* series, the 1978 version included ninety-eight biographical/bibliographical essays, some of which were comprehensive master essays but most of which were brief—several only a paragraph in length. The format of the *DLB* entries has evolved over the past twenty-two years. The new three-volume version provides significantly augmented essays, with full primary bibliographies, on most of the figures included in the original work. (George Henry Calvert is included in the new, augmented *Antebellum Writers of New York and the South,* edited by Kent P. Ljungquist; James Marsh and Edwin Percy Whipple, who have substantial essays in, respectively, *DLB 59* and *DLB 64,* do not appear in the new volumes, nor does Samuel Longfellow.) Eleven new figures have been added in response to recent critical reevaluations of New England writers: the rediscovered women writers Lucy Larcom and Harriet Wilson; the Wampanoag William Apess; a neglected poet who bridges Romanticism and modernism, Frederick Goddard Tuckerman; the Vermont historian Abby Maria Hemenway; and various orators and preachers whose published works were also important—Orville Dewey, Charles Follen, John B. Gough, Wendell Phillips,

Charles Sumner, and Henry Ware Jr. Each volume concludes with a secondary bibliography encompassing standard modern studies as well as older titles that, although in many cases superseded by recent scholarship, retain historical value for their treatment of the literature of New England.

F. O. Matthiessen, in his *American Renaissance: Art and Expression in the Age of Emerson and Whitman* (1941), first termed the "half-decade of 1850–55" a national renaissance—not really a "*re-birth,*" he noted, but rather the flowering of "its first maturity . . . in the whole expanse of art and culture." This five-year period produced major works of Ralph Waldo Emerson, Nathaniel Hawthorne, Herman Melville, Henry David Thoreau, and Walt Whitman, which Matthiessen thought unsurpassed in "imaginative vitality" even as they were engaged with distinctly American issues. For all their differences, he maintained, the "one common denominator of my five writers . . . was their devotion to the possibilities of democracy."

Matthiessen's useful and compelling term for the era needs qualification in the context of the work at hand. First, the cast of characters does not neatly fit this regional focus. Emerson, Hawthorne, and Thoreau, of course, were New Englanders born and bred; but Melville (though he wrote *Moby-Dick, or, the Whale* [1851] at Pittsfield, Massachusetts) was first and last a New Yorker, and Whitman (though at crucial stages of his career he came under the influence of Emerson) is associated primarily with New York and New Jersey. Second, the period 1850–1855 is too restrictive to accommodate the many important New England writers, genres, and themes that flourished at midcentury. It has long been customary, in college courses and in monographs, to stretch Matthiessen's term back to 1836, the year Transcendentalism emerged, with books such as Emerson's *Nature* (1836), and ahead to the Civil War, during which event many of the reform issues that preoccupied the antebellum period culminated and by which time certain political, economic, and social developments that were transforming American life had accelerated and many of the leading literary figures of the period had become less productive or had died. Third, in an age of assaults on the traditional nineteenth-century literary canon, Matthiessen's heroes have come to many to seem decidedly too homogenous.

Matthiessen's scheme, however, has proved resilient, solidly endorsed, for example, by Robert E. Spiller's influential *Literary History of the United States* (revised third edition, 1963):

> In quality of style, and particularly in depth of philosophic insight, American literature has not yet surpassed the collective achievement of Emerson, Thoreau, Hawthorne, Melville, and Whitman. Having freed itself in these writers from its earlier tendencies either blindly to imitate or blindly to reject European models, American literature here for the first time sloughed off provincialism, and, by being itself—by saying only what it wanted to say and as it wanted to say it—attained, paradoxically, the rank and quality of world literature, a literature authentic not only in America but everywhere the English tongue is understood.

Matthiessen's monumental work has always invited interpretive refinement and theoretical challenges. But for all the specialized correctives and more broadly conceived cultural canvasses appearing in the past fifty-nine years, Matthiessen is still unsurpassed for the synthetic power of his grasp of the distinctive quality of an age, for the clarity of his expression, and for his own tenacious conviction that literary criticism in a democracy has moral implications.

Social observers of the young republic continually questioned whether these shores would be hospitable to the emergence of a homegrown literary culture. National anxiety marked the first two decades of the nineteenth century in the wake of the French Revolution, aggravated by ongoing tensions with Britain culminating in the War of 1812 and lingering fears about what President James Madison had called the greatest internal threat to democracy—"faction." Americans, moreover, prided themselves on dogged personal independence, preferring practicality to speculation and action to introspection. In "most mental operations each American relies on individual effort and judgment," noted the French social critic Alexis de Tocqueville in *Democracy in America* (volume 2, 1840); thus, he suggested wryly, "of all countries in the world, America is the one in which the precepts of Descartes are least studied and best followed." Yet, in Federalist Boston, efforts to establish an original national culture had begun in earnest early in the new century. For example, *The Monthly Anthology* (1803–1811), forerunner of *The North American Review,* was founded by William Emerson and others to inculcate values of rationality, taste, and civic virtue—all deemed essential to order and stability in a republic—and to engender a sense of pride in New England culture. *The Christian Disciple* was established in 1813 to express and unify the growing spirit of liberal Christianity in Greater Boston; later called *The Christian Examiner,* this journal continued to play a crucial role as a more radical and innovative wing of Unitarianism—Transcendentalism—began to emerge in the 1830s.

In hindsight, these early efforts seem tame, parochial, even strangely in awe of and imitative of British culture. Ralph Waldo Emerson later mocked the labors of his father's generation as "that early ignorant & transitional *Month-of-March,* in our New England culture." By the 1820s the question "What is distinctive about American literature?"—a central question in literary study to this day—became a matter of some urgency as American writers and critics sought their own identity and mission. The call for "literary nationalism" became a refrain as Americans insisted that the United States must cease imitating British and European literary models, that a great nation must have a great literature. As William Ellery Channing declared in his *Christian Examiner* review essay on a "National Literature" (January 1830), "A people, into whose minds the thoughts of foreigners are poured perpetually, needs an energy within itself to resist, to modify this mighty influence, and without it, will inevitably sink under the worst bondage, will become intellectually tame and enslaved." Channing was a nationalist, but he was no jingo. Great literature, he believed, consists of all original writings of "superior minds" that express a "nation's mind" and contribute "new truths to the stock of human knowledge." "We love our country much," he insisted, "but mankind more. As men and Christians, our first desire is to see the improvement of human nature." The special "genius" of the United States, as Channing saw it, was to bear witness to the potential of the unfettered human spirit. Prophetically he declared, "We want a reformation. We want a literature, in which genius will pay supreme, if not undivided homage, to truth and virtue." Emerson's more famous "The American Scholar" (1837) went on to outline the influence on, and duties of, "Man Thinking," leading Oliver Wendell Holmes years later to call this address "Our intellectual Declaration of Independence." Emerson's criticism of our dependence on the culture of other nations was secondary, however, to his radical celebration of the continually active, evolving power of mind, an *organic* process that could never stop to admire itself, to indulge in a sense of national superiority, or to congeal into institutional formalism. In this address, Emerson *was* renewing Channing's call for a national literature that, without being self-congratulatory, would express the potential of democratic culture as a contribution to the world.

The flowering of New England culture—in politics, education, religion, and literature—derives from the emergence of "liberal Christianity," or Unitarianism, in the early nineteenth century. Puritanism, the dominant religious and cultural force in the region since the 1630s, had held, in broadest terms, that man, being depraved, can be redeemed only by God's free grace. In fact, debates had simmered within Puritanism since the Reformation over the role man might play in *responding* to God's offer of grace. Eighteenth-century rationalism—manifest in the documents of the American Revolution—had only advanced the case for the ability of men and women to improve their own political as well as spiritual estates. The election of Henry Ware Sr. as Hollis Professor of Divinity at Harvard in 1805 signaled the arrival of the liberal theology in the halls of power in New England. The generation that came of college age in the 1820s, not satisfied with casting off the vestiges of Puritan theology, began to challenge the rationalist epistemology they associated with such philosophers as John Locke and William Paley, and they eagerly embraced theories maintaining that truth is perceived intuitively. William Ellery Channing's famous declaration in 1828 that self-knowledge is attained through "likeness to God" was the high point of this shift and prepared the way for the Transcendentalist movement that emerged in the mid 1830s. The Unitarians held that self-culture—a continual process of introspection, self-control, and moral growth—was the great project of life. Against this background, the Emersonian concept of *self-reliance*—often misinterpreted as a philosophy of self-absorption—was a profoundly moral stance.

The New England concern with self-culture, with its moral bent, manifested itself more naturally in forms outside merely belletristic kinds of fiction and verse. The archetypal regional genre since the founding of the Massachusetts Bay Colony in 1628 had been the sermon—always on these shores a means not simply to inculcate religious doctrine but also to exhort, to uplift, and to renew communal bonds. Despite the aridness implied by the misleading term "plain style," even Puritan sermons had been, of course, aesthetic performances. As Lawrence Buell and others have shown, the early-nineteenth-century Unitarians, largely freed from doctrinal burdens, exploited "literary" aspects of the genre to appeal to a new generation of parishioners—men and women who were bound less by appeals to authority and more by the power of pulpit eloquence to move intellect and emotion through narrative, dramatic, even "poetic" discourse. Many of the leading Transcendentalists had been trained for the ministry. Some (most dramatically, Emerson) left the pulpit for the lecture hall and the literary life; others continued to preach, some (most emphatically, Theodore Parker) to diverse audiences for whom denominational issues were subordinate to the power of sermons to affect feeling and to address the social concerns of a new age. Emerson's Harvard Divinity School Address (1838) struck many as a heretical challenge to religion; yet, it concludes by reaffirming "the institution of preaching,—the speech of man to men,—essentially the most flexible of all organs, of all forms."

Public eloquence, deriving from a two-hundred-year-old preaching tradition, an admiration for political oratory, and a new craving for information, education, and entertainment, now found an outlet in the lecture hall. Josiah Holbrook founded the first lyceum in Millbury, Massachusetts, in 1826 to satisfy the growing demand for more systematic instruction for working adults, and within a few years the lyceum movement had spread to the Ohio Valley. Figures as diverse as William Andrus Alcott, Frederick Douglass, Emerson, John B. Gough, Elizabeth Oakes Smith, and Thoreau were much anticipated on the lecture circuit. The ultimate extension of New England oral traditions, responding to the highly introspective demands of self-culture, was the Conversation. The most able practitioners of this most ephemeral genre, Bronson Alcott and Margaret Fuller, captivated the attention of select audiences by conducting seemingly spontaneous dialogues on topics ranging across the scholarly, the political, the aesthetic, and the speculative. The journal, a genre owing much to habits of New England spirituality, was practiced even by the nonliterary as a means of self-examination, of measuring growth in self-culture. In the hands of writers such as Emerson and Thoreau, the journal was also used pragmatically as a storehouse of quotations, anecdotes, and spontaneous thoughts, or artistically as a writing laboratory. Emerson called his extensive and carefully indexed journals his "savings bank," and he typically ransacked them for lecture material, and the lectures in turn often were polished into essays later collected in book form.

The deep-seated theological traditions of New England and attendant preoccupation with moral and spiritual development made the region somewhat biased against fiction as a frivolous diversion from the serious purpose of life. In the preface to his last novel, *The Marble Faun; or, The Romance of Monte Beni* (1860), Nathaniel Hawthorne named other cultural barriers to writing in a new land. America—with its materialism and self-confidence, its lack of history and tradition, and its insistence on practicality—failed to provide materials and context for works of the imagination. "No author, without a trial," Hawthorne declared, "can conceive of the difficulty of writing a Romance about a country where there is no shadow, no antiquity, no mystery, no picturesque and gloomy wrong, nor anything but a common-place prosperity, in broad and simple daylight, as is happily the case with my dear native land." Antebellum fiction, dominated by the didactic and the sentimental, was regarded as an appropriate vehicle for providing examples of virtue, heroism, and patriotism; for instructing youth; and for modeling domestic virtues for women. In the case of Louisa May Alcott, however, popular juvenile fiction

became enduring art. *Little Women* (1868–1869), still a perennial favorite of young girls, resonates with themes that engage readers of all ages—home and family as the foundation of virtue, a sense of place, cultivation of personal and social reform, the difficulty of selecting a vocation—notably writing—and especially for a woman, the deepening of idealism that encounters reality, and reconciling the needs for self-reliance and community. Serious adult fiction began to explore such issues as regional history, the abilities of women, and racism. Hawthorne attained international status for tales and romances exploring psychological and tragic dimensions of human nature. New England poetry—seemingly taking its lead from Emerson's injunctions in "The Poet" that "it is not metres, but a metre-making argument, that makes a poem" and that poets are "liberating gods"—was as likely as fiction to aim at elevating language and thought. The best verse of the period, however, is moral in no narrow sense and achieves rich diversity of expression. Regional and national history, legends, and public issues mingled with deeply personal meditations and experiences to convey rich psychological and cultural landscapes. Emerson sought to show the miraculous in the common, speaking in the language of real people. Holmes and James Russell Lowell demonstrated that American poetry could be urbane and witty. John Greenleaf Whittier was the righteous poet as reformer who, in "Snow-Bound," could also win popular acclaim by capturing the post–Civil War elegiac mood, aching for loved ones and a past now lost. Henry Wadsworth Longfellow, steeped in the Romance languages, became the most revered American poet of his day by employing European models and verse patterns to elevate American events and legends to epic status. Emily Dickinson, little known in her own time, is perhaps the most radically innovative of all poets to emerge from this literary renaissance; though not as isolated from nature or society as stereotype has had it, her verse is the boldest exploration of the mind and the imagination.

The "American Renaissance" emerged, however, in a distinctly international context, warranting much of the recent scholarly criticism of the long celebration of American literary "exceptionalism." William Wordsworth, for example, appealed to New England writers with his call for poetry dealing with the commonplace, in language spoken by real people. Sir Walter Scott, for all his exotic and British settings, and Charles Dickens, with his rich evocation of English society and character, remained intimidating models of the great novelist. Samuel Taylor Coleridge and Thomas Carlyle were indispensable for introducing and interpreting Immanuel Kant and other German writers whose commentary on intuition and the workings of the mind fired the imaginations of young Transcendentalists eager to find an alternative to the pragmatic rationalism of Locke. The mystic Emanuel Swedenborg had a major influence not only on New England spirituality but also on theories of the origin and nature of language. Johann Wolfgang von Goethe and Alexander von Humboldt, moreover, were admired as examples of modern renaissance men, accomplished scientists as well as writers.

As Matthiessen knew, however–and depicted graphically in using as his frontispiece to *American Renaissance* a striking daguerreotype of David McKay, builder of the great clipper ship the *Flying Cloud*– the writers of this period shared in large degree the forward-looking spirit of their own nation. Emerson's statement that "Our American literature and spiritual history are, we confess, in the optative mood" (this last phrase provides the title for Matthiessen's first chapter) parallels the egalitarian optimism and the assertive "go ahead" attitude of the entrepreneurial class of the young nation that have come to seem so distinctively American. The Romantic individualism of young intellectuals in New England during the 1830s, however, was frequently at odds with the materialism of commercial and industrial expansion. New England, with its Federalist heritage, was naturally unfriendly turf for the presidency of Andrew Jackson (1829–1837). Although the Transcendentalists shared with Jacksonian democracy a belief in the common citizen and a distrust of big money, they abhorred its crude political leveling with its hypocritical callousness toward slavery, the plight of Native Americans, and principled political dissent. The antislavery activists of the region perceived the expansionist impulse of the nation in the 1840s and 1850s as entangled with imperialism and insidious strategies to expand the slave territory. Thus, they saw the originally idealistic concept of "Manifest Destiny" to be a cynical tool of jingoism, the Mexican War as an excuse for annexing Texas, and the Compromise of 1850–with its Fugitive Slave Law–as Daniel Webster's great moral sellout.

Consequently, even as major New England writers in various ways spoke for their age, an important strain of American literature began to stand in critical, often antagonistic, opposition to national habits and values. With such exuberant hope as that expressed by Channing and Emerson, with such expectations that a distinctive American literature would emerge to give voice to the distinctive genius of the young nation, disappointment and even alienation were perhaps inevitable. The discrepancies between the national "dream" and reality were felt keenly. The reading public has always sought entertainment and reassurance. The major writers of New England refused, however, to

offer easy fair and smooth answers and in both openly defiant and subtle ways increasingly stood at odds with prevailing standards.

If, as Matthiessen thought, the most challenging writers of the age represented a high-water mark of democratic culture, they did so not only by celebrating what the United States had become but also by reminding the nation of what it had yet to become. Emerson's great project was to awaken the nation to its latent "power" and possibilities; yet, he saw that, in the present state of human nature, "A man is a god in ruins." For many writers of the period, the American Revolution was incomplete, its promises not yet realized. "Even if we grant that the American has freed himself from a political tyrant," declared Thoreau in "Life without Principle" (1863), "he is still the slave of an economical and moral tyrant. . . . What is the value of any political freedom, but as a means to moral freedom? . . . With respect to a true culture and manhood, we are essentially provincial still, not metropolitan,– mere Jonathans." Often heard during the literary renaissance of New England is the rhetoric of the jeremiad, a characteristic Puritan mode that in America, as Sacvan Bercovitch has shown, was a powerful means not simply of lamenting the national failings but also of calling for renewal. The antebellum period was the Age of Reform in New England more than in any other region, as citizens sought to redeem the promises of the American Revolution in many crusades–for abolition, woman's rights, and temperance; for education reform, prison reform, and diet reform; for more humane treatment of convicts, the blind, and the insane; for free love and reform of marital laws; and in opposition to forced removal of Native Americans from their ancestral lands and to imperialist aggression toward Mexico. New England writers threw their support behind many such movements.

Racial hypocrisy in the United States was often exposed in terms that forced white Christians to redefine their own religious assumptions. The Wampanoag preacher William Apess in 1833 asked rhetorically, "What is all this ado about missionary societies, if it be not to Christianize those who are not Christians? And what is it for? To degrade them worse, to bring them into society where they must welter out their days in disgrace merely because their skin is of a different complexion." The escaped slave Frederick Douglass testified that Christianity could be a tool to enforce the "peculiar institution" by instilling passivity and acceptance in the slave and that religious conversion could make the slaveholder more self-righteously vicious than he had been in a state of unbelief. Douglass's compelling autobiography is an extraordinary record of the unfolding of a mind gradually becoming aware–

through experiences ranging from violent struggle to subterfuge to an awakening of the power of language—of its potential for integrity, independence, and growth. Even white New England abolitionists, however, were often reviled and abused on their own soil from 1831, when William Lloyd Garrison founded *The Liberator* in Boston, until the Civil War and its aftermath, when the self-aggrandizing myth of Northern moral righteousness became widespread and finally entrenched.

Women in disproportionate numbers were active in the antislavery movement. Many were struck by a stunning irony: they were permitted, even encouraged in certain circles, to agitate on behalf of chattel slaves hundreds of miles away; and yet, they themselves could not vote and did not enjoy legal protection even within matrimony. In *Woman in the Nineteenth Century* (1845) Margaret Fuller observed the dramatic change in women who were "champions of the enslaved African": "this band it is, which, partly in consequence of a natural following out of principles, partly because many women have been prominent in that cause, makes, just now, the warmest appeal in behalf of woman." Fuller had been fortunate in having a father "who cherished no sentimental reverence for woman, but a firm belief in the equality of the sexes." He demanded intellectual development and "addressed her not as a plaything, but as a living mind." What struck too many contemporaries as a threat to "family union" was to Fuller a natural extension of Transcendentalist "self-reliance": "This self-dependence, which was honored in me, is deprecated as a fault in most women. They are taught to learn their rule from without, not to unfold it from within."

Scholarship over the last several decades has stressed the deep cultural divide in the nineteenth century between the masculine world of industry, commerce, and politics, and "woman's sphere"—the home. Women, in this view, had the separate (but indispensable) role of nurturing. As mothers and as wives, their supposedly finer female susceptibility to sentiment, virtue, and piety rendered the domestic scene a realm of education in knowledge, feeling, and behavior—a veritable incubator of civic values crucial to a young republic. Many of the manuals, collections of verse, and novels of the period written by and for women were designed to enhance women's effectiveness in and satisfaction with their important but closely circumscribed "sphere" of activity. Some women writers, however, powerfully showed that domestic "female" virtues need not be cloistered. In that most influential of all American novels, *Uncle Tom's Cabin* (1852), Harriet Beecher Stowe employed "Christian" as well as maternal love in the service of moral suasion to move readers to a felt awareness of the horrors of slavery. The gender of Uncle Tom—and the recent discovery that "feeling" in oratory and literature was also directed at men—should be a reminder of the truth, even in the mid 1800s, of Fuller's claim that "Male and female represent the two sides of the great radical dualism. But, in fact, they are perpetually passing into one another." Indeed, several women writers began to challenge the validity of separate "spheres."

All of this scrutiny of social issues resulted not because New England writers were detached, privileged cultural observers but because they were enmeshed in economic forces transforming the region and the nation. The liberal Christian culture that had shaped nineteenth-century Boston was theologically liberal but politically conservative, and the connections between work, success, and civic virtue had become articles of faith. The population of Boston boomed by 40 percent in the 1820s, but there were causes for worry: economic panics in 1825 and 1837, and the proud shipping industry of Boston already being bested by that of New York City. The thirty years before the Civil War, moreover, ushered in an industrial revolution and market economy that was both exhilarating and threatening. Mills in Lowell and Lawrence, Massachusetts, reorganized patterns of work for thousands to manufacture efficiently raw materials supplied, in many cases, by the South (suggesting, to several writers, one form of Northern complicity in slavery). Symbolic of the new age for the Concord writers was construction of the Fitchburg Railroad by the shores of Walden Pond in 1844; Thoreau, who moved to Walden Woods the next year, announced ambivalently, "So is your pastoral life whirled past and away." In 1849 the California Gold Rush seemed to many writers a destabilizing form of gambling, as dangerous as Wall Street speculation. The emergence of money as the ultimate and pervasive measure of value, altering relationships and personal identity, was troubling. Emerson declared, "Society is a joint-stock company. . . . The virtue in most request is conformity. Self-reliance is its aversion." "This world," said Thoreau in disgust, "is a place of business. . . . It is nothing but work, work, work." Making a living as a writer was, then as now, difficult. Many writers—Emerson the most notable example—spent years traveling the arduous lecture circuit to supplement often meager income from book sales. Thoreau was bitterly disappointed by weak sales of his first book, *A Week on the Concord and Merrimack Rivers* (1849). Margaret Fuller turned to journalism in New York. Authorship in a competitive culture was an uneasy vocational choice for many men, and literary excellence too often was obscured by the marketplace success of hackwork, often sentimental tripe by and for women. Hawthorne had to rely on political patronage and resented the "d____d mob of scribbling women" that he blamed for his own predicament as a struggling author. American writers were as victimized as their English counterparts by the absence (until 1891) of international copyright protection.

If, as Emerson noted, it was "the age of the first person singular," it was also the age of association. Thus, two distinct means for reforming economic and social relationships are generally identified in antebellum New England: the individualistic and the communitarian. Adherents to each alternative agreed that if all people are endowed with intellectual and spiritual capacity for growth, then conditions that thwart such growth must be removed. Unitarian self-culture and Emersonian self-reliance embody the conviction that reform must start with the individual—a stance demanding imaginative if not literal solitude for reflection, balance, and moral integrity; Thoreau's two-year experiment in transcendental economy at Walden is, in this sense, the classic "community of one." Bronson Alcott's Fruitlands and George Ripley's Brook Farm are the most dramatic experiments in New England in group living. These polarities are useful, however, for describing not absolute alternatives but rather tendencies and tensions in reform thinking. Emerson and Thoreau were both interested in communal ventures but for various reasons declined to sign on to new social arrangements; but each demanded that personal character flower in action, and each looked hopefully for signs of social amelioration. Whatever personal and economic forces finally undid Fruitlands and Brook Farm, each in its own way sought (by rearranging and redefining economic relationships) to cultivate *individuals* in a group setting—thus, their wide appeal to writers and the various successes (at Brook Farm, at least) in education and the arts.

"Prophetic" writers of the American Renaissance—those lamenting national failures and disgraces—were often scorned in their own land. Serious writers who were not essentially reformers had other reasons, moreover, for being disaffected with American life. Their forms of literary "subversion" were aimed chiefly not at reforming society but at undermining deeper-seated complacencies about human nature, American self-images, and understandings of the function and purpose of literature itself. Hawthorne, for example, in "Earth's Holocaust" (1844) satirized the passion for reform sweeping his generation. Seeking to start the world anew, freed from all the corruptions and encumbrances of history and tradition, the idealist zealots in the tale toss into a huge bonfire the documents and symbols of virtually every contemporary institution. Watching the proceedings is a "dark-visaged stranger, with a portentous grin"

who announces to the narrator the one fundamental thing not consigned to the "conflagration": "the human heart itself!" The stranger undercuts the myth of American exceptionalism by raising both the immediate specter of European corruptions that Americans prided themselves on having left behind, and the more ancient ghost of post-Edenic sin and evil, concluding, "Oh, take my word for it, it will be the old world yet!" Hawthorne had lived briefly at Brook Farm and initially found it physically and intellectually stimulating. He later satirized both the utopian impulse and his own ambivalent attitude toward reformers in *The Blithedale Romance* (1852), however, and was primarily concerned in his fiction to probe the complexities, contradictions, and hypocrisies of human psychology. Many of his tales and romances were popularly admired for their quaint depictions of colonial history, but his darker insights into human nature were often missed. Indeed, as Melville wrote in what may be the most famous review of one American author by another, "Hawthorne and His Mosses" (1850), "spite of all the Indian-summer sunlight on the hither side of Hawthorne's soul, the other side—like the dark half of the physical sphere—is shrouded in a blackness, ten times black." Like "Shakespeare and other masters of the great Art of Telling the Truth," Hawthorne told the truth, "even though it be covertly, and by snatches." Most readers, Melville held, would not even "discern" the truths of Hawthorne's works, for "some of them are directly calculated to deceive—egregiously deceive, the superficial skimmer of pages." Dickinson, too, knew, in her dazzling, tight, metaphysical verse, that true poetry is not smooth or easy: "Tell all the Truth but tell it slant— / . . . The Truth must dazzle gradually / Or every man be blind—." Even poets lionized in their own time—Longfellow and Whittier, for example—often subtly undercut the worship of progress during the age, with bittersweet verse evoking longing and memory or a cyclical, tragic sense of time and history.

An introduction to the themes and issues that occupied the great writers of New England would be incomplete and misleading if it failed to take note of the rich forms of collaboration and community that invigorated the region at midcentury. The strikingly original, even anticonventional, achievements of the American Renaissance in New England, combined with the tendency to think of writing as a solitary act of genius, obscures that much of the greatest literature of the age was fueled by apprenticeships, friendships, and mentoring—for example, Emerson and Thoreau; Hawthorne and Melville; Emerson and Fuller; Garrison and Douglass; Whittier and Larcom; and Higginson and Dickinson. Key collaborative literary ventures include such periodicals as *The*

Dial and ambitious projects such as Ripley's *Specimens of Foreign Standard Literature* (1838–1842). The proliferation of clubs, beginning with the Transcendental Club (1836) and including the Town and Country Club and the Saturday Club, attest to the intellectual stimulation and fundamental sociability found in gatherings of the like-minded. Many of these groups were male-dominated, but the later growth of grassroots "women's clubs"—several formed by Julia Ward Howe—proved that the club impulse knew no gender.

Besides these smaller personal and social collaborations (and the reform communities of Fruitlands and Brook Farm), New England also produced literary communities within cities and towns. Boston and Cambridge, of course, dominated literary life in antebellum New England—its sheer size and wealth reflected by rich institutions of education, religion, and the arts. Regionally, Salem and New Bedford (Massachusetts), Hartford (Connecticut), Providence (Rhode Island), and Portland (Maine) sustained lively local cultures and produced important writers. Worcester, Massachusetts, a prosperous industrial city that was especially friendly to reform, was home to a particularly vibrant lyceum network that regularly brought leading authors to the platform. Thoreau, who professed disdain for the pretentious institutional and social world of Boston and Cambridge, found a congenial circle of friends in Worcester. The most striking literary community was the town of Concord, founded by Emerson's ancestor the Reverend Peter Bulkeley in 1635. Two hundred years later, Emerson, born and raised in Boston, returned to his ancestral ground, rendering Concord the American example of Romantic rural solitude and contemplation, and by the force of his reputation and personality making the town a mecca for Bronson Alcott, Fuller, Hawthorne, and many lesser figures. Of all the important writers who called Concord home, only Thoreau was a native son. By cultivating the Transcendentalist's heightened awareness of the epic and divine in the microcosmic, Thoreau did more than any other writer to celebrate—in Concord—a sense of place, asserting at once modestly and hyperbolically in *Walden,* "I have travelled a good deal in Concord." Its Revolutionary and literary history have combined to make Concord a living symbol of the American spirit.

A professional and commercial "community" was fostered by the publishing house Ticknor and Fields, which positioned itself as the publisher of leading New England writers, counting within its stable Emerson, Thoreau, Lowell, Longfellow, and Hawthorne. At midcentury, their offices at the corner of Washington and School Streets—the fabled Old Corner Book Store—became a gathering place for authors, and, in the popular mind as well, a virtual literary landmark. Through shrewd marketing, the firm that later evolved into Houghton, Mifflin—though not particularly sympathetic to Transcendentalism—helped create a myth of New England as the cradle of American literary culture.

Even as the literary myth of New England was being established, however, events were transpiring that changed the face of American literary culture. By 1850 New York City had a population of more than 500,000, and Boston, 136,881; the literary center of the nation inexorably shifted to New York as well. The Civil War was, in many ways, the culmination of the spirit of reform generated by the American Renaissance in New England. Julia Ward Howe's "Battle Hymn of the Republic" epitomized the self-image of the North as one of victorious moral righteousness. But the Civil War, with its bloodshed and with the accelerated urbanization, industrialization, political corruption, and national cynicism that followed in its wake, also overwhelmed the prewar moral idealism that had helped define the meaning of the war. The critical fortunes of the writers of the New England renaissance, too, have varied since the Civil War. With the exception of Dickinson, many of the poets of the period have come to be seen as the smug embodiment of Boston Brahmin privilege, exponents of refinement and safe middle-class values. Even Emerson, once deemed radical and dangerous, had become a national icon, his challenging concept of self-reliance safely denatured as an endorsement of industrial and economic growth and manifest destiny. The "Fireside poets" and other canonical figures came to be treasured not for their innovation but as reassuring voices from a seemingly simpler, more bucolic time. The popular image of New England authors gathered sociably at the Old Corner Book Store evoked a still-palpable regional Golden Age. Forgotten in the haze of nostalgia was that the three decades before the Civil War had been a time in New England not of mere pastoral charm but of moral outrage and restless creative energy.

The influence of the American Renaissance in New England, however, has been profound. Antebellum idealism might have begun to seem quaint, but William Dean Howells, the great champion of literary realism, responded to the Transcendentalists' examination of the commonplace and their moral vision and faith in democracy. Modernist poets have been attracted to the Transcendentalists' bold openness of form and embracing of the volatility of truth. Hawthorne was an essential example to later novelists as different as Henry James and William Faulkner. Today

Thoreau exerts unprecedented appeal as a voice for social justice, the founder of American environmentalism, and a master of prose. Fuller is admired as the first and greatest literary feminist. Dickinson is regarded as the finest poetic experimenter. Emerson, for whatever purpose he is invoked, is widely considered the central figure in American culture. The literary canon continues to evolve. But the New England writers are as important as ever for the expression they gave to the possibilities of the American experience.

This volume is indebted not only to a fine group of contributors but also to several others who gave indispensable advice and help. Peggy Isaacson, of the Worcester Polytechnic Institute (WPI) Publications Office, and Ray J. Emerson (WPI '01) offered expert computer assistance. Penny Rock and Margaret Brodmerkle, of the WPI Humanities & Arts Department, provided generous logistical support. For suggesting contributors, I am grateful to Steven C. Bullock, Phyllis Cole, Sterling F. Delano, Brenda Yates Habich, Len Gougeon, Kent P. Ljungquist, Beverly G. Merrick, Joel Myerson, Cameron C. Nickels, David Robinson, and Frank Shuffelton. Every editor should be as fortunate—in working with publishing-house editors—as I have been in working with Penelope M. Hope of Bruccoli Clark Layman, Inc.; she has been efficient, cooperative, scholarly, and professionally skillful at every stage of production. Besides the example of his own pioneering *DLB 1*, which the present volumes augment, Professor Joel Myerson, for two decades my professional colleague and friend, took time from his own daunting scholarly projects to offer guidance at every stage. For years of "provocation" and love, this work is dedicated to my wife, Sandy.

—*Wesley T. Mott*

Acknowledgments

This book was produced by Bruccoli Clark Layman, Inc. Karen L. Rood is senior editor. Penelope M. Hope was the in-house editor.

Production manager is Philip B. Dematteis.

Administrative support was provided by Ann M. Cheschi, Amber L. Coker, and Angi Pleasant.

Accounting supervisor is Ann-Marie Holland.

Copyediting supervisor is Phyllis A. Avant. The copyediting staff includes Brenda Carol Blanton, Brenda Cabra, Allen E. Friend Jr., Thom Harmon, Melissa D. Hinton, William Tobias Mathes, Rebecca Mayo, Nancy E. Smith, and Elizabeth Jo Ann Sumner.

Editorial associates are Andrew Choate and Michael S. Martin.

Database manager is José A. Juarez.

Layout and graphics supervisor is Janet E. Hill. The graphics staff includes Karla Corley Brown and Zoe R. Cook.

Office manager is Kathy Lawler Merlette.

Photography supervisor is Paul Talbot. Photography editors are Charles Mims and Scott Nemzek.

Permissions editor is Jeff Miller.

Digital photographic copy work was performed by Joseph M. Bruccoli.

The SGML staff includes Frank Graham, Linda Dalton Mullinax, Jason Paddock, and Alex Snead.

Systems manager is Marie L. Parker.

Typesetting supervisor is Kathleen M. Flanagan. The typesetting staff includes Jaime All, Patricia Marie Flanagan, Mark J. McEwan, and Pamela D. Norton. Freelance typesetters are Wanda Adams and Vicki Grivetti.

Walter W. Ross did library research. He was assisted by Steven Gross and the following librarians at the Thomas Cooper Library of the University of South Carolina: circulation department head Tucker Taylor; reference department head Virginia W. Weathers; Brette Barclay, Marilee Birchfield, Paul Cammarata, Gary Geer, Michael Macan, Tom Marcil, Rose Marshall, and Sharon Verba; interlibrary loan department head John Brunswick; and interlibrary loan staff Robert Arndt, Hayden Battle, Barry Bull, Jo Cottingham, Marna Hostetler, Marieum McClary, Erika Peake, and Nelson Rivera.

Dictionary of Literary Biography® • Volume Two Hundred Forty-Three

The American Renaissance in New England
Fourth Series

Dictionary of Literary Biography

Jacob Abbott
(14 November 1803 – 31 October 1879)

Christopher L. Nesmith
University of South Carolina

See also the Abbott entries in *DLB 1: The American Renaissance in New England* and in *DLB 42: American Writers for Children Before 1900*.

BOOKS: *The Bible Class Book,* by Abbott and N. W. Fiske (Amherst, Mass.: J. S. & C. Adams, 1828);

Conversations on the Bible, as Erodore (Boston: Massachusetts Sabbath School Union, 1829);

The Little Philosopher, as Erodore (4 volumes, Boston: Carter & Hendee, 1829; 1 volume, London: T. Allman, 1847);

A Lecture on Moral Education, Delivered in Boston, Before the American Institute of Instruction, August 26, 1831 (Boston: Hilliard, Gray, Little & Wilkins, 1831);

A Description of the Mount Vernon School in 1832 (Boston: Peirce & Parker, 1832);

The Young Christian; or, A Familiar Illustration of the Principles of Christian Duty (Boston: Peirce & Parker, 1832; London: L. B. Seeley, 1833); Memorial Edition, with bibliography and biography by Edward Abbott (New York: Harper, 1882);

The Teacher; or, Moral Influence Employed in the Instruction and Government of the Young (Boston: Peirce & Parker, 1833; London: Darton, 1834?);

Early Piety (New York: John S. Taylor, 1834; London: T. Ward, 1835);

Fire-Side Piety; or, The Duties and Enjoyments of Family Religion (New York: Leavitt, Lord / Boston: Crocker & Brewster, 1834; London: T. Allman, 1835);

The Duties of Parents (Boston: Tuttle & Weeks, 1834);

The Corner-Stone; or, A Familiar Illustration of the Principles of Christian Truth (Boston: William Peirce, 1834; London, G. Seeley, 1834);

Right and Wrong, or Familiar Illustrations of the Moral Duties of Children, as Marianne (Boston: William Peirce, 1834);

Every Day Duty, as Marianne (New York: Leavitt, Lord, 1834; London: Allan Bell, 1837);

China and the English; or, The Character and Manners of the Chinese (Boston: Crocker & Brewster / New York: Leavitt, Lord, 1835; London: T. Ward, 1835);

The Little Scholar Learning to Talk. A Picture Book for Rollo (Boston: John Allen, 1835; London: J. S. Hodson, 1836); republished as *Rollo Learning to Talk* (Boston: Weeks & Jordan, 1839);

Rollo Learning to Read; or, Easy Stories for Young Children (Boston: John Allen, 1835; London: J. S. Hodson, 1836);

New England and Her Institutions, anonymous, by Jacob Abbott and John S. C. Abbott (Boston: John Allen, 1835; London: R. B. Seeley & W. Burnside, 1835);

Real Dialogues on the Evidence of Christianity (New York: Leavitt, Lord, 1835);

The Mount Vernon Reader . . . for Middle Classes (Boston: John Allen, 1835; New York: B. & S. Collins, 1835); republished as *Abbott's Reader* (London: J. W. Parker, 1835);

The Family Story Book, volume 2 (Boston: John Allen, 1835);

Sabbath-Day Book for Boys and Girls (Boston: John Allen, 1835);

The Week-Day Book for Boys and Girls (Boston: John Allen, 1835);

The Way for a Child to Be Saved (New York: Leavitt, Lord, 1835; London: T. Allman, 1851?);

The Way of Salvation Explained to a Young Inquirer (New York: Leavitt, Lord, 1835?; London: T. Allman, 1838);

The Way to Do Good; or, The Christian Character Mature (Boston: William Peirce, 1836; London: Allan Bell, 1836);

Rollo at Work; or, The Way for a Boy to Learn to Be Industrious (Boston: T. H. Carter, 1838);

Rollo at Play; or, Safe Amusements (Boston: T. H. Carter, 1838);

The Mount Vernon Reader . . . for Junior Classes (Boston: Otis, Broaders, 1838; Boston: T. H. Carter, 1838);

Hoaryhead and the Vallies Below; or, Truth Through Fiction (Boston: Crocker & Brewster, 1838; London: G. Wightman, 1838);

Rollo at School (Boston: T. H. Carter, 1839; London: J. S. Hodson, 1839);

Rollo's Vacation (Boston: William Crosby, 1839; London: J. S. Hodson, 1840);

Rollo's Experiments (Boston: Weeks, Jordan, 1839);

Rollo's Museum (Boston: Weeks, Jordan, 1839);

McDonner; or, Truth Through Fiction (Boston: Crocker & Brewster, 1839; London: T. Allman, 1839);

republished as *Hoaryhead and M'Donner; Very Greatly Improved* (New York: Harper, 1855);

Caleb in Town, a Story for Children (Boston: Crocker & Brewster, 1839; London: T. Allman, 1840);

Caleb in the Country (Boston: Crocker & Brewster, 1839; London: T. Allman, 1840);

Jonas's Stories Related to Rollo and Lucy (Boston: W. D. Ticknor, 1839);

Jonas a Judge; or, Law among the Boys (Boston: W. D. Ticknor, 1840);

Rollo's Travels (Boston: William Crosby, 1840);

Rollo's Correspondence (Boston: William Crosby, 1840);

A Sermon, Preached on the National Fast, May 14, 1841, Occasioned by the Death of William Henry Harrison (Salem, Mass.: W. Ives, 1841);

The Rollo Code of Morals; or, The Rules of Duty for Children (Boston: Crocker & Brewster, 1841);

Jonas on a Farm in Summer (Boston: W. D. Ticknor, 1842);

Jonas on a Farm in Winter (Boston: W. D. Ticknor, 1842);

Cousin Lucy at Study (Boston: B. B. Mussey, 1842);

Stories Told to Rollo's Cousin Lucy When She Was a Little Girl (Boston: B. B. Mussey, 1842);

Cousin Lucy's Conversations (Boston: B. B. Mussey, 1842);

Cousin Lucy at Play (Boston: B. B. Mussey, 1842);

Cousin Lucy on the Sea-Shore (Boston: B. B. Mussey, 1842);

Cousin Lucy among the Mountains (Boston: B. B. Mussey, 1842);

The Rollo Philosophy, Part I—Water (Philadelphia: Hogan & Thompson / Boston: Gould, Kendall & Lincoln, 1842);

The Rollo Philosophy, Part II—Air (Philadelphia: Hogan & Thompson / Boston: Gould, Kendall & Lincoln, 1842);

The Rollo Philosophy, Part III—Fire (Boston: Otis, Broaders, 1843);

The Rollo Philosophy, Part IV—The Sky (Boston: Otis, Broaders, 1843);

Marco Paul's Travels and Adventures in the Pursuit of Knowledge. City of New York (Boston: T. H. Carter, 1843);

Marco Paul's Travels and Adventures in the Pursuit of Knowledge. The Erie Canal (Boston: T. H. Carter, 1843);

Marco Paul's Adventures in the Pursuit of Knowledge. Forests of Maine (Boston: T. H. Carter, 1843);

Marco Paul's Adventures in the Pursuit of Knowledge. State of Vermont (Boston: T. H. Carter, 1843);

Marco Paul's Adventures in the Pursuit of Knowledge. City of Boston (Boston: T. H. Carter, 1843);

Marco Paul's Adventures in the Pursuit of Knowledge. Springfield Armory (Boston: T. H. Carter, 1843);

The Mount Vernon Arithmetic, by Jacob Abbott and Charles A. Abbott (New York: Saxton & Miles / Collins, 1846, 1847);

A Summer in Scotland (New York: Harper, 1848; Dublin: James M'Glashan, 1849);

The History of King Charles the First (New York: Harper, 1848; London: T. Allman, 1850);

The History of Mary, Queen of Scots (New York: Harper, 1848; London: T. Allman, 1850);

The History of Alexander the Great (New York: Harper, 1848);

The History of Julius Caesar (New York: Harper, 1849; London: T. Allman, 1850);

The History of Hannibal the Carthaginian (New York: Harper, 1849; London: Sampson Low, 1849);

The History of William the Conqueror (New York: Harper, 1849; London: T. Allman, 1850);

The History of King Charles the Second of England (New York: Harper, 1849; London: T. Allman, 1850);

The History of Queen Elizabeth of England (New York: Harper, 1849; London: T. Allman, 1850);

The History of King Alfred of England (New York: Harper, 1849; London: T. Allman, 1850);

The History of Xerxes the Great (New York: Harper, 1850; London: T. Allman, 1851);

The History of Cyrus the Great (New York: Harper, 1850);

The History of Darius the Great (New York: Harper, 1850; London: T. Allman, 1850);

Malleville: A Franconia Story (New York: Harper, 1850; London: T. Allman, 1853);

Mary Bell: A Franconia Story (New York: Harper, 1850; London: T. Allman, 1853);

Wallace: A Franconia Story (New York: Harper, 1850; London: T. Allman, 1853);

Beechnut: A Franconia Story (New York: Harper, 1850; London: T. Allman, 1853);

Mary Erskine: A Franconia Story (New York: Harper, 1850; London: T. Allman, 1853);

The History of Cleopatra, Queen of Egypt (New York: Harper, 1851);

Ellen Linn: A Franconia Story (New York: Harper, 1852; London: T. Allman, 1853);

Rodolphus: A Franconia Story (New York: Harper, 1852; London: T. Allman, 1853);

The History of Romulus (New York: Harper, 1852);

The History of Nero (New York: Harper, 1853);

Stuyvesant: A Franconia Story (New York: Harper, 1853; London: T. Allman, 1853);

Agnes: A Franconia Story (New York: Harper, 1853; London: Ward, 1853);

Caroline: A Franconia Story (New York: Harper, 1853; London: T. Allman, 1853);

The History of Pyrrhus (London: Nathaniel Cooke, 1853; New York: Harper, 1854);

Rollo's Tour in Europe—Rollo on the Atlantic (Boston: W. J. Reynolds, 1853; London: Sampson Low, 1854);

Rollo in Paris (Boston: W. J. Reynolds, 1854; London: Sampson Low, 1854);

Rollo in Switzerland (Boston: W. J. Reynolds, 1854);

Rollo in London (Boston: W. J. Reynolds, 1855);

Rollo on the Rhine (Boston: W. J. Reynolds, 1855);

Bruno; or, Lessons of Fidelity, Patience, and Self-Denial Taught by a Dog (New York: Harper, 1854; London: Darton, 1855);

Willie and the Mortgage: Showing How Much May Be Accomplished by a Boy (New York: Harper, 1854);

Madeline, A Story of the Early Spring-time (London: Routledge, 1854);

The Strait Gate (New York: Harper, 1855);

The Little Louvre; or, The Boys' and Girls' Gallery of Pictures (New York: Harper, 1855);

Prank; or, The Philosophy of Tricks and Mischief (New York: Harper, 1855);

Emma; or, The Three Misfortunes of a Belle (New York: Harper, 1855);

Virginia; or A Little Light on a Very Dark Saying (New York: Harper, 1855);

Timboo and Joliba; or, The Art of Being Useful (New York: Harper, 1855);

Timboo and Fanny; or, The Art of Self-Instruction (New York: Harper, 1855);

The Harper Establishment; or How the Story-Books Are Made (New York: Harper, 1855);

Franklin, The Apprentice Boy (New York: Harper, 1855);

The Studio (New York: Harper, 1855);

The Story of Ancient History; From the Earliest Period to the Fall of the Roman Empire (New York: Harper, 1855);

The Little Learner: Learning to Talk (New York: Harper, 1855);

The Little Learner: Learning to Think (New York: Harper, 1856);

The Little Learner: Learning to Read (New York: Harper, 1856);

The Story of English History; From the Earliest Periods to the American Revolution (New York: Harper, 1856);

The Story of American History; From the Earliest Settlement of the Country to the Establishment of the Federal Constitution (New York: Harper, 1856);

John True; or, The Christian Experience of an Honest Boy (New York: Harper, 1856);

Elfred; or, The Blind Boy and His Pictures (New York: Harper, 1856);

The Museum; or, Curiosities Explained (New York: Harper, 1856);

The Engineer; or, How to Travel in the Woods (New York: Harper, 1856);

Rambles Among the Alps (New York: Harper, 1856);

The Three Gold Dollars; or, An Account of the Adventures of Robin Green (New York: Harper, 1856);

The Gibraltar Gallery; or, Being an Account of Various Things Both Curious and Useful (New York: Harper, 1856);

The Alcove; Containing Some Further Account of Timboo, Mark, and Fanny (New York: Harper, 1856);

Dialogues for the Amusement and Instruction of Young Persons (New York: Harper, 1856);

The Great Elm, or, Robin Green and Josiah Lane at School (New York: Harper, 1856);

Aunt Margaret; or, How John True Kept His Resolutions (New York: Harper, 1856);

Rollo in Scotland (Boston: W. J. Reynolds, 1856);

Rollo in Geneva (Boston: Brown, Taggard & Chase, 1857);

Rollo in Holland (Boston: Brown, Taggard & Chase, 1857);

The Little Learner: Learning About Common Things (New York: Harper, 1857);

The Little Learner: Learning About Right and Wrong (New York: Harper, 1857);

Vernon, or, Conversations about Old Times in England (New York: Harper, 1857);

Carl and Jocko; or, The Adventures of the Little Italian Boy and His Monkey (New York: Harper, 1857);

Lapstone; or, The Sailor Turned Shoemaker (New York: Harper, 1857);

Orckney the Peacemaker; or, The Various Ways of Settling Disputes (New York: Harper, 1857);

Judge Justin; or, The Little Court of Morningdale (New York: Harper, 1857);

Minigo; or, The Fairy of Cairnstone Abbey (New York: Harper, 1857);

Jasper, or The Spoiled Child Recovered (New York: Harper, 1857);

Congo, or Jasper's Experience in Command (New York: Harper, 1857);

Viola and Her Little Brother Arno (New York: Harper, 1857);

Little Paul; or, How to Be Patient in Sickness and Pain (New York: Harper, 1857);

The History of King Richard the First of England (New York: Harper, 1857; London: T. Allman, 1857);

The History of King Richard the Second of England (New York: Harper, 1858; London: T. J. Allman, 1859);

The History of King Richard the Third of England (New York: Harper, 1858; London: T. J. Allman, 1859);

Rollo in Naples (Boston: Brown, Taggard & Chase, 1858);

Rollo in Rome (Boston: Brown, Taggard & Chase, 1858);

The History of Peter the Great (New York: Harper, 1859);

The History of Genghis Khan (New York: Harper, 1860);

Stories of Rainbow and Lucky: Handie (New York: Harper, 1860);

Stories of Rainbow and Lucky: Rainbow's Journey (New York: Harper, 1860);

Stories of Rainbow and Lucky: The Three Pines (New York: Harper, 1860);

Stories of Rainbow and Lucky: Selling Lucky (New York: Harper, 1860);

Stories of Rainbow and Lucky: Up the River (New York: Harper, 1860);

Aboriginal America (New York: Sheldon, 1860);

The Discovery of America (New York: Sheldon, 1860);

The Southern Colonies (New York: Sheldon, 1860);

The Florence Stories: Florence and John (New York: Sheldon, 1860);

The Florence Stories: Grimkie (New York: Sheldon, 1860);

The Florence Stories: Excursion to the Orkney Islands (New York: Sheldon, 1861);

The History of Margaret of Anjou (New York: Harper, 1861);

The Northern Colonies (New York: Sheldon, 1862);

Wars of the Colonies (New York: Sheldon, 1863);

The Rocking Horse; or, The Rollo and Lucy First Book of Poetry (Philadelphia: George W. Childs, 1863);

Carlo; or, The Rollo and Lucy Second Book of Poetry (Philadelphia: George W. Childs, 1864 [i.e., 1863?]);

The Canary Bird; or, The Rollo and Lucy Third Book of Poetry (Philadelphia: George W. Childs, 1863;

The Harlie Stories: The New Shoes; or, Productive Work by Little Hands (New York: Sheldon, 1863);

The Harlie Stories: The French Flower; or, Be Kind and Obliging to Your Teacher (New York: Sheldon, 1863);

The Harlie Stories: Harlie's Letter; or, How to Learn with Little Teaching (New York: Sheldon, 1863);

The Harlie Stories: Wild Peggie; or, Charity and Discretion (New York: Sheldon, 1863);

The Harlie Stories: The Sea-Shore; or, How to Plan Picnics and Excursions (New York: Sheldon, 1863);

The Harlie Stories: Friskie, the Pony; or, Do No Harm to Harmless Animals (New York: Sheldon, 1863);

The Florence Stories: The English Channel (New York: Sheldon, 1863);

The Florence Stories: Visit to the Isle of Wight (New York: Sheldon, 1864);

The Florence Stories: Florence's Return (New York: Sheldon, 1864);

John Gay; or, Work for Boys—Work for Winter (New York: Hurd & Houghton, 1864);

John Gay; or, Work for Boys—Work for Spring (New York: Hurd & Houghton, 1864);

John Gay; or, Work for Boys—Work for Summer (New York: Hurd & Houghton, 1864);

John Gay; or, Work for Boys—Work for Autumn (New York: Hurd & Houghton, 1864);

Revolt of the Colonies (New York: Sheldon, 1864);

War of the Revolution (New York: Sheldon, 1864);

Washington (New York: Sheldon, 1865);

Mary Gay; or, Work for Girls–Work for Winter (New York: Hurd & Houghton, 1865);

Mary Gay; or, Work for Girls–Work for Spring (New York: Hurd & Houghton, 1865);

Mary Gay; or, Work for Girls–Work for Summer (New York: Hurd & Houghton, 1865);

Mary Gay; or, Work for Girls–Work for Autumn (New York: Hurd & Houghton, 1865);

William Gay; or, Play for Boys–Play for Winter (New York: Hurd & Houghton, 1869);

William Gay; or, Play for Boys–Play for Spring (New York: Hurd & Houghton, 1869);

William Gay; or, Play for Boys–Play for Summer (New York: Hurd & Houghton, 1869);

William Gay; or, Play for Boys–Play for Autumn (New York: Hurd & Houghton, 1869);

The Juno Stories: Juno and Georgie (New York: Dodd & Mead, 1870; London: Strahan, 1873);

The Juno Stories: Mary Osborne (New York: Dodd & Mead, 1870; London: Strahan, 1873);

The Juno Stories: Juno on a Journey (New York: Dodd & Mead, 1870; London: Strahan, 1873);

The Juno Stories: Hubert (New York: Dodd & Mead, 1870; London: Strahan, 1873);

Science for the Young–Heat (New York: Harper, 1871);

Science for the Young–Light (New York: Harper, 1871);

Science for the Young–Water and Land (New York: Harper, 1871);

The August Stories: August and Elvie (New York: Dodd & Mead, 1871);

The August Stories: Hunter and Tom (New York: Dodd & Mead, 1872);

Gentle Measures in the Management and Training of the Young; or, Principles on Which a Firm Parental Authority May Be Established and Maintained (New York: Harper, 1872);

The August Stories: The Schooner Mary Ann (New York: Dodd & Mead, 1872; London: Strahan, 1873);

The August Stories: Granville Valley (New York: Dodd & Mead, 1872; London: Strahan, 1873);

Science for the Young–Force (New York: Harper, 1872).

OTHER: John Abercrombie, *Inquiries Concerning the Intellectual Powers,* additions and explanations by Abbott (Hartford: F. J. Huntington, 1833);

John S. C. Abbott, *The Mother's Friend; or, Familiar Directions for Forming the Mental and Moral Habits of Young Children,* edited by Jacob Abbott (New York: Leavitt, Lord / Boston: Crocker & Brewster, 1834);

John Abercrombie, *The Philosophy of the Moral Feelings,* preface and introduction by Abbott (Boston: T. H. Carter, 1836);

The New Testament of Our Lord and Savior . . . with brief Explanatory Notes, notes by Abbott and John S. C. Abbott (Boston: Crocker & Brewster, 1842);

Abbott's Addition Columns, edited by Abbott (New York: Saxton & Miles, 1846);

Mrs. Markham (Mrs. John Penrose), *A History of France,* supplementary chapter and notes by Abbott (New York: Harper, 1848).

Jacob Abbott is remembered today primarily as the author of the "Rollo Books," the most popular fictional series for juveniles in nineteenth-century America. The books, published in two series–fourteen volumes from 1834 to 1842, and a ten-volume series from 1853 to 1858–center on the intellectual and moral development of Rollo Holiday, who became the first truly popular child character in American fiction. Besides the Rollo Books, Abbott created eleven other juvenile-fiction series and wrote or cowrote more than two hundred books in all, including works on popular history, science, education, and child rearing. Before becoming an author, Abbott was a Congregational minister and a pioneer educator, directing a progressive and hugely successful school for girls in Boston from 1829 to 1833. While there he wrote *The Young Christian; or, A Familiar Illustration of the Principles of Christian Duty* (1832), one of the earliest American "best-sellers" to achieve popularity on both sides of the Atlantic. The success of this book and the first Rollo Books led Abbott to pursue writing as a full-time profession in 1835, one of the first American writers able to do so. In addition to fiction, Abbott and his brother John S. C. Abbott wrote for *Harper's New Monthly Magazine,* contributing historical and biographical sketches, as well as travel essays and popular-science pieces. The two brothers also collaborated on a series of historical biographies that came to be known as the "Abbott Histories," one of the first series of its kind to be aimed at a popular reading audience and the one that President Abraham Lincoln credited with providing him "all the knowledge of history which I have." Even as Abbott's career as a writer grew, his interest in the field of education never abated, and he was a primary figure in the American child-nurture movement. One of his last books, *Gentle Measures in the Management and Training of the Young* (1871), emphasizes the sympathetic but firm parental practices advocated throughout his juvenile books. Nearly all Abbott's many books continued to be republished into the early decades of the twentieth century.

Jacob Abbott was born on 14 November 1803 in Hallowell, Maine, a commercial port on the Kennebec River, the second of seven children and the firstborn son of Jacob and Betsey Abbot. Although his father sided with the Unitarians in the schism that divided the

Silhouette of Harriet Vaughan, whom Abbott married in 1828
(from Lyman Abbott, Reminiscences, *1915)*

the Mount Vernon School for Girls. The successful venture outgrew its original quarters within two years. At Mount Vernon, Abbott experimented with progressive educational techniques, advocating student self-government and the use of persuasion rather than punishment in maintaining order. In 1832 Abbott published an account of the Mount Vernon School, republished a year later as a chapter in *The Teacher; or, Moral Influence Employed in the Instruction and Government of the Young* (1833), one of the first books on teacher training published in the United States.

That same year Abbott began work on what became his first major success—and one of the best-sellers of the decade—*The Young Christian*, originally a series of Sunday lectures given at the Mount Vernon School. A Boston firm, Peirce & Parker, published *The Young Christian* in the early summer of 1832, with a first-print run of 3,000 copies. Half the edition was sold by September. The book achieved success throughout the country and even across the Atlantic. In 1833 alone it was reprinted four times, twice in Boston and also in New York and London. In all, *The Young Christian* was reprinted twenty-one times and sold more than 250,000 copies.

Abbott was overwhelmed by the success of the book, but by late 1833 he was at work on another, *The Corner-Stone; or, A Familiar Illustration of the Principles of Christian Truth*, which he finished the following March. Its publication in 1834 was awaited by an eager public and impatient booksellers—one dealer in Philadelphia ordered a thousand copies in advance. But during an era of theological dissension, *The Corner-Stone* met with controversy, especially in England, where John Henry Newman criticized it severely in one of his famous *Tracts for Our Times* for its heretical tendencies. Abbott was shocked by the criticisms, for he considered himself an orthodox Congregationalist. Yet, his Unitarian leaning—which Newman found most objectionable—can be glimpsed in certain passages, where he states that only through self-improvement can one "advance in the attainment of every excellence."

After the success of *The Young Christian*, despite his growing reputation as a progressive educator, Abbott resigned from the Mount Vernon School in 1834 and embarked upon a brief career as the full-time minister of the Eliot Congregational Church in Roxbury, Massachusetts. Later that year he was approached by Thomas Harrington Carter, a Boston publisher, who showed him some engravings he thought might work in a book for juveniles. Abbott began to work and in 1835 produced his first Rollo book, *The Little Scholar Learning to Talk. A Picture Book for Rollo* (1835).

After the initial success of the series Carter's visit inspired, Abbott moved his family back to Maine,

Congregational Church in Abbott's youth, young Jacob was raised in the orthodox Calvinist tradition. He and his four brothers—John, Gorham, Charles, and Samuel—all graduated from Bowdoin College, studied at Andover Theological Seminary, and went on to become educators, ministers, and authors. In 1817 Abbott entered Bowdoin College, where he added another "t" to his last name and excelled in mathematics and the physical sciences. After graduating from Bowdoin in 1820, he taught the following year at Portland Academy, where Henry Wadsworth Longfellow was one of his students. In addition to teaching, Abbott attended Andover from 1821 to 1824, occasionally engaging in amateur belletristic writing as a member of a secret literary society. Abbott joined the faculty at the newly created Amherst College, where he was appointed professor of mathematics and natural philosophy in 1825. While there, he wrote or collaborated on a variety of religious educational books, some under the pen name Erodore, which he had adopted while a member of the Andover literary club.

On 18 May 1828 Abbott married Harriet Vaughan, also of Hallowell. They eventually had four sons: Benjamin Vaughan, Austin, Lyman, and Edward. Soon after their marriage the Abbotts moved to Boston, where Abbott had been hired to direct a new academy, where he tried his hand at writing full time. He lived in Farmington near his parents until 1843, publishing thirty-four books, including twelve more "Rollo" books, and six volumes each of the "Cousin Lucy" series, the "Jonas" series, and the "Marco Paul" series. These books were unusual among American literary productions for juveniles, presenting child characters and adults realistically, in a primarily secular framework. Unlike characters in other writings for children and juveniles at the time, Abbott's characters—including Rollo—were shown to be deeply influenced by parents and adults rather than innately depraved or wicked. All of Abbott's series emphasize his theory of child development: recognizing childhood not as a single phase, but as a succession of progressive steps toward adulthood. A look at the titles of the Rollo Books suggests this sequence, chronicling Rollo's development as he learned to talk, to read, and to write. The early books emphasize the difficulties Rollo encounters as he attempts to learn each new skill, at times leading to obstinate behavior. But Rollo's parents appeal to his reason, rather than resort to discipline, to modify his conduct. Later Rollo books describe his experiences in the wider world—at school, at work, and abroad with his family—learning factual and useful information, rather than developing basic literacy and social skills.

As a writer, Abbott put into practice what he had learned about human nature at the Mount Vernon School, where he had emphasized learning by doing. Some of the later Rollo books were even designed to be used in schools; yet, they employ the same narrative techniques that characterize the Rollo books. Even as Abbott introduced more difficult and abstract concepts—such as the scientific method and reasoning by analogy—into these books, he always portrayed Rollo and his friends realistically and in everyday situations.

This strategy also characterized the later series of Rollo books, "Rollo's Tour in Europe," in which Rollo travels through Europe with his family, spending most of his time with his Uncle George. In this series, Rollo's Uncle George points out in *Rollo in Scotland* (1856): "We are now traveling for improvement, not for play." Indeed, Rollo and the reader are exposed to a great deal of historical and factual information, as Rollo explores the landmarks of Paris, London, and Rome, as well as the Swiss countryside and the Rhine River valley. As the series began with *The Little Scholar Learning to Talk,* the initial phase in the learning process, it ends appropriately with the Grand Tour, the culmination of a young, well-to-do American boy's education.

Abbott did not begin the second Rollo series until he himself had traveled to Europe several times. In the meantime, he inaugurated a new series centering on a character often encountered in the Rollo series,

Abbott, circa 1855

the teenage farmhand Jonas. The "Jonas Books" include *Jonas a Judge; or, Law among the Boys,* published in 1840, which describes how Jonas—too old for the neighborhood school—spends one winter studying and working in the law office of Rollo's Uncle George. Jonas uses the principles of justice he encounters there to settle various disputes among Rollo and his playmates, which Abbott hopes "may be the means of ending or preventing contention among many little circles of brothers and cousins." Abbott believed in the influence and power of role models for children, and all of his books are characterized by at least one older or adult character who exemplifies upstanding moral behavior and who explains the rationale behind good decision making. In 1842 Abbott also began a series for girls, which focused on Rollo's five-year-old cousin, Lucy. The "Cousin Lucy Books," according to Abbott, correspond "in their general style and characteristics with the Rollo Books for boys," but they are "designed more particularly for the other sex." *Cousin Lucy at Study* focuses on Lucy's experiences as a student at a dame school, where she is tutored by the sage and industrious Mary Jay. At home, her father teaches her about money by keeping her allowance on deposit in an account book, so "this was the way in which Lucy got her first regular ideas of money and accounts."

Although Abbott remained prolific throughout his career, this first period of intense production ended in 1843, when Abbott returned from his first trip to Europe to find his wife on her deathbed. After her death Abbott moved to New York City, joining his brothers Gorham and Charles in a new educational enterprise, the popular Abbott Institute. In New York, Abbott finished work on a new series that combined travel literature with his tested juvenile model, the same model he later employed in the series "Rollo's Tour in Europe." In his preface, Abbott wrote that he saw the series "Marco Paul's Adventures in Pursuit of Knowledge" as a means "to communicate . . . as extensive and varied information as possible, in respect to the geography, the scenery, the customs and the institutions of this country."

After the Abbott Institute closed in 1851, Abbott stayed in New York, and he and his brother John began to contribute more steadily to a new periodical begun only months before—*Harper's New Monthly Magazine.* Between 1848 and 1861, the Harpers also published the Abbotts' "Makers of History" series, consisting of thirty-two volumes, twenty-two by Jacob and ten by John. These volumes, bound in red cloth, became known as "Abbott Histories." Shortly before his death, President Abraham Lincoln wrote a letter to the Harpers (often republished in the advertisement pages in the back of Abbott's books), stating,

> I have not education enough to appreciate the profound works of voluminous historians, and, if I had, I have no time to read them. But your Series of Histories gives me, in brief compass, just that knowledge of past men and events which I need. . . . To them I am indebted for about all the historical knowledge I have.

The Abbotts found a wide audience among schoolchildren in England as well as in the United States. Clarence Gohdes, in *American Literature in Nineteenth Century England* (1944), claims that "many an English child first learned of the old monarchs of Britain in Abbott's juveniles. . . . It is doubtful whether many British writers of children's books were more popular in England."

In addition to his interest in history, Jacob Abbott's love of the natural sciences and his scientific background led him to write articles for *Harper's New Monthly Magazine* in a field of knowledge that was experiencing exponential growth. Abbott's gift for finding the proper tone in which to connect with the public allowed the Harpers to present popular science to a rapidly growing and increasingly curious reading public. J. Henry Harper, in his reminiscence *The House of Harper* (1912), wrote that in this new field of popular-science writing, "Jacob Abbott was

the first and most valued contributor." The first article he wrote for the magazine was a description of the "Novelty Iron-Works, in New York City," and many of the articles Abbott contributed throughout the 1850s and 1860s were scientific or industrial in nature, such as "The Armory at Springfield," "Deep Sea Soundings," "Early Aeronautics," "Electric Light," "Negative Photography," and "The Ocean Steamer." Ironically, the industrial character of some of his articles clashed with the rural New England settings of many of his stories for children. His account of the Harper Publishing House (a "factory" in its own right), *The Harper Establishment; or How the Story-Books Are Made* (1855), favorably presented the assembly-line production techniques implemented there. And though Abbott acknowledged that much of the physical labor that went on in the massive seven-story building was hard work, "to those who perform it well, it is an easy and agreeable occupation." Written ostensibly for a juvenile audience, this book remains one of the best accounts of American nineteenth-century book production.

Although Abbott was aware of the swift changes taking place around him, the New England of his own childhood became the scene of the first series he inaugurated while working with the Harpers. The "Franconia Stories," set in the rural New Hampshire village of that name, among the "mountains of the North," were reminiscent of his own New England boyhood. The emphasis on village and domestic life anticipates some of the concerns of the "local color" regionalism that flourished in the last decades of the century. Writing of this particular series, William W. Lawrence, in his article "Rollo and His Uncle George," found them "the most artistic and mature of all his tales for children." In one, *Rodolphus* (1852), which had originally been serialized in *Harper's New Monthly Magazine,* clearly Abbott is speaking as much to parents who might be reading the book as to any child. Rodolphus is described as a clever boy "who generally contrived to have his own way in almost every thing. His mother did not attempt to govern him; she tried to *manage* him; but in the end it generally proved that he managed her." The end of the first chapter, appropriately titled "Bad Training," makes clear that because of "the way in which Rodolphus was brought up in his childhood . . . it is not surprising that he came in the end to be a very bad boy." In an age when children who misbehaved were often thought of as incorrigible delinquents, beyond reform, Abbott made it clear the problem with Rodolphus was his parents.

Although Abbott has been acknowledged for his pioneering child-rearing and educational theories, he has often been grouped with many conservative New

Englanders too slow to act on the issue of slavery. John C. Crandall points out that Abbott "did not permit the disturbing slavery issue to upset the placidity of the rational world of Rollo, Jonas, Caleb and Lucy." But while Abbott did not address the issue directly in his writings for children, he did deal with racial prejudice. Six books between 1857 and 1861 feature an African American child as a major character. In the five-volume series "Stories of Rainbow and Lucky," the title character Rainbow resembles Rollo, Jonas, and Marco Paul, with only one notable difference–he is black. As Mary E. Quinlivan points out, throughout the series Abbott "made the reader aware of the prevalence of racial prejudice in antebellum America. He frequently mentioned the black youngster's fear of rejection at school, at play, in public conveyances, and at public lodging." Through his diligence and good nature, however, Rainbow is able to overcome the prejudices of the white people he encounters. While such conclusions are obviously problematic, Abbott at least confronted the problem of racism in New England, and in his sympathetic understanding of his characters gave many children their first insight into the human side of slavery and racial prejudice.

During the years leading up to the Civil War and in the decades that followed, Abbott often traveled. Professional writing allowed him the income and the freedom to travel, since, according to his son Lyman, he could write as comfortably at the train station as at his desk. He traveled often to Europe and to the Middle East, where he composed a piece titled "Memoirs of the Holy Land," which was serialized in *Harper's New Monthly Magazine* in 1852 and 1853. After he remarried in 1853, he continued to travel to Europe with his new bride, the former Mary (Dana) Woodbury; there he wrote several books for the "Rollo's Tour" series and the "Florence" series. After his second wife's death in 1866, however, Abbott lived in Farmington with his sisters.

According to Lyman Abbott, in his *Silhouettes of My Contemporaries* (1921), one of Jacob Abbott's last works summed up "the philosophical principles upon which all of his children's books were based." *Gentle Measures in the Management and Training of the Young,* published in 1872, was not a children's book but a guide for parents, explaining Abbott's theories of child rearing in a practical format. Abbott embraced the Lockean model of the mind, but he used the notion of a "blank slate" to emphasize parental influence on the future character of their children and as a means to advocate sympathetic understanding and direction rather than harsh discipline. Abbott's lifelong concern for children, still seen at the end of his career, had been established

Illustration from Abbott's Rollo in Scotland *(1856), one of a series of books in which Rollo travels in Europe with his Uncle George*

from even the earliest of his writings. At the end of *The Young Christian,* Abbott said,

> Childhood is a most fertile part of the vineyard of the Lord. The seed which is planted there vegetates very soon, and the weeds which spring up are easily eradicated. It is in fact in every respect an easy and pleasant spot to till, and the flowers and fruits which, with proper effort, will bloom and ripen there, surpass all others in richness and beauty.

Jacob Abbott died on 31 October 1879 at home in Maine after a brief illness, attended by his sisters and two of his sons. His fame as the creator of the Rollo Books has established his importance among literary and cultural historians, but it is only one facet of his career. As one of the first professional writers in the United States and one of the first to attract a large popular audience, Abbott's role in creating and shaping popular reading tastes in travel literature, history, and science needs to be acknowledged and explored. His innovations in juvenile fiction are likewise a neglected subject, for he challenged the contemporary assumptions of race, class, and gender in his day far more often than he succumbed to them. For all of these reasons, as well as for his influence upon American educational and child-development philosophy,

Jacob Abbott deserves attention from students of the American Renaissance.

Bibliographies:

Rollo G. Silver, "Rollo on Rollo: A Bibliography of First Edition 'Rollo Books,'" *Colophon: New Graphic Series, Number Two* (Spring 1939): 5–16;

Carl J. Weber, *A Bibliography of Jacob Abbott* (Waterville, Maine: Colby College Press, 1948).

Biographies:

Edward Abbott, "A Biographical Sketch of Jacob Abbott," in *The Young Christian, Memorial Edition* (New York: Harper, 1882);

Philip Wesley Kendall, "The Times and Tales of Jacob Abbott," dissertation, Boston University, 1968.

References:

Lyman Abbott, *Reminiscences* (Boston & New York: Houghton Mifflin, 1915);

Abbott, *Silhouettes of My Contemporaries* (Garden City, N.Y.: Doubleday, Page, 1921);

Lysla I. Abbott, "Jacob Abbott: A Goodly Heritage," *Horn Book Magazine,* 30 (April 1954): 119–132;

Jani L. Berry, "Discipline and (Dis)order: Paternal Socialization in Jacob Abbott's Rollo Books," *Children's Literature Association Quarterly,* 18 (Fall 1993): 100–105;

John B. Boles, "Jacob Abbott and the Rollo Books: New England Culture for Children," *Journal of Popular Culture,* 6 (Winter 1972): 507–528;

John C. Crandall, "Patriotism and Humanitarian Reform in Children's Literature, 1825–1860," *American Quarterly,* 21 (Spring 1969): 3–22;

Alice M. Jordan, *From Rollo to Tom Sawyer, and Other Papers* (Boston: Horn Book, 1948);

William W. Lawrence, "Rollo and His Uncle George," *New England Quarterly,* 18 (September 1945): 291–302;

Anne Scott MacLeod, *A Moral Tale, Children's Fiction and American Culture 1820–1860* (Hamden, Conn.: Archon, 1975);

Mary E. Quinlivan, "Race Relations in the Antebellum Children's Literature of Jacob Abbott," *Journal of Popular Culture,* 16 (Summer 1982): 27–36;

Mark I. West, "Guilt and Shame in Early American Children's Literature: A Comparison of John S. C. Abbott's *The Child at Home* and Jacob Abbott's Rollo Books," *University of Hartford Studies in Literature: A Journal of Interdisciplinary Criticism,* 18, no. 1 (1986): 1–7;

Bernard Wishy, *The Child and the Republic: The Dawn of Modern American Nurture* (Philadelphia: University of Pennsylvania Press, 1968).

Papers:

There are collections of Jacob Abbott's papers at the Bowdoin College and Colby College libraries.

William Andrus Alcott

(6 August 1798 – 29 March 1859)

Larry A. Carlson
College of Charleston

See also the Alcott entry in *DLB 1: The American Renaissance in New England*.

BOOKS: *Essay on the Construction of School-Houses, To Which Was Awarded the Prize Offered by the American Institute of Instruction, August, 1831* (Boston: Hilliard, Gray, Little & Wilkins, 1832);

A Historical Description of the First Public School in Hartford, Conn. (Hartford: D. F. Robinson, 1832);

On Teaching Penmanship, Addressed to Parents, School Committees, and Teachers (Boston: Lilly, Wait, Colman & Holden, 1833);

The Young Man's Guide to Excellence (Boston: Lilly, Wait, Colman & Holden, 1833; revised and enlarged edition, Boston: T. R. Marvin, 1844);

A Word to Teachers; or, Two Days in a Primary School (Boston: Allen & Ticknor, 1833);

The House I Live In. Part First: The Frame, for the Use of Family and Schools (Boston: Lilly, Wait, Colman & Holden, 1834); enlarged as *The House I Live In; or, The Human Body, for the Use of Family and Schools* (Boston: Light & Stearns, 1837); edited by Thomas C. Girtin (London: J. W. Parker, 1837);

The First Foreign Mission (Boston: Massachusetts Sabbath School Society, 1834);

The Happy Family Made Happier; or, The Resurrection of Lazarus, revised by the Committee of Publication (Boston: Massachusetts Sabbath School Society, 1835);

The Second Foreign Mission (Boston: Massachusetts Sabbath School Society, 1835);

Story of Ruth the Boabitess, revised by the Committee of Publication (Boston: Massachusetts Sabbath School Society, 1835);

Story of the Prodigal, revised by the Committee of Publication (Boston: Massachusetts Sabbath School Society, 1835);

Early Rising (Boston: Light & Stearns, 1836);

The Life of Peter the Apostle, revised by the Committee of Publication (Boston: Massachusetts Sabbath School Society, 1836);

William Andrus Alcott

The Young Mother; or, Management of Children in Regard to Health (Boston: Light & Stearns, 1836);

The Young Wife; or, Duties of Woman in the Marriage Relation (Boston: C. D. Strong, 1837);

The Young Missionary: Exemplified in the Life of Timothy, revised by the Committee of Publication (Boston: Massachusetts Sabbath School Society, 1837);

An Address Delivered before the American Physiological Society, March 7, 1837 (Boston: Light & Stearns, 1837);

Ways of Living on Small Means (Boston: Light & Stearns, 1837);

The Young House-keeper; or, Thoughts on Food and Cookery (Boston: G. W. Light, 1838);

Vegetable Diet; As Sanctioned by Medical Men, and by Experience in All Ages (Boston: Marsh, Capen & Lyon, 1838);

The Mother in Her Family; or, Sayings and Doings at Rose Hill Cottage (Boston: Weeks & Jordan, 1838);

Jesus at Nain; or, the Widow's Son Raised, revised by the Committee of Publication (Boston: Massachusetts Sabbath School Society, 1839);

Stories of Eliot and the Indians, revised by the Committee of Publication (Boston: Massachusetts Sabbath School Society, 1839);

The Young Husband, or, Duties of Man in the Marriage Relation (Boston: G. W. Light, 1839);

Tea and Coffee: Their Physical, Intellectual, and Moral Effects on the Human System (Boston & New York: G. W. Light, 1839; London: Holyoake, 1859; Stoke-upon-Trent: G. Turner, 1859);

Confessions of a School Master (Andover & New York: Gould, Newman & Saxton, 1839; revised edition, Reading, Pa.: H. A. Lantz, 1856);

Sketches of William Penn (Boston: D. S. King, 1839);

Health Tracts, for the Diffusion of Knowledge on the Preservation of Health and the Laws of Human Constitution, nos. 1–12 (Boston: G. W. Light, 1839–1841)—comprises *Dosing and Drugging, How to Prevent Consumption, City and Country, Right Use of Fruits, Thoughts on Bathing, Breathing Bad Air, Clothing and Temperature, Domestic Poisons, Tight Lacing, Abuse of the Eye, Health in Common Schools,* and *Right Use of Physicians;*

The Young Woman's Guide to Excellence (Boston: G. W. Light, 1840);

Travels of Our Saviour, with Some Leading Incidents of His Life, revised by the Committee of Publication (Boston: Massachusetts Sabbath School Society, 1840);

My Progress in Error, and Recovery to Truth; or, A Tour through Universalism, Unitarianism and Skepticism (Boston: Gould & Lincoln, 1841);

The Sabbath School as It Should Be (New York: J. Leavitt / Boston: Crocker & Brewster, 1841; London: Printed for Thomas Tegg, 1842);

The Mother's Medical Guide in Children's Diseases (Boston: T. R. Marvin, 1842);

Paul's Shipwreck, revised by the Committee of Publication (Boston: Massachusetts Sabbath School Society, 1842);

Slate and Black Board Exercises (Hartford: Tyler & Porter / New York: Dayton & Saxton, 1842);

The Story of Ananias and Sapphira, revised and edited by D. P. Kidder (New York: G. Lane & C. B. Tippett for the Sunday School Union of the Methodist Episcopal Church, 1844);

The Use of Tobacco: Its Physical, Intellectual and Moral Effects on the Human System (Boston: G. W. Light, 1844);

The Boy's Guide to Usefulness, Designed to Prepare the Way for the "Young Man's Guide" (Boston: Waite, Peirce, 1844);

The Beloved Physician; or, The Life and Travels of Luke the Evangelist, revised and edited by Kidder (New York: G. Lane & C. B. Tippett for the Sunday School Union of the Methodist Episcopal Church, 1845);

Paul at Ephesus, revised by the Committee of Publication (Boston: Massachusetts Sabbath School Society, 1846);

Water Cure for Debilitated Young Men (Boston: Bela Marsh, 1846);

The Fiery Chariot; or, The Story of Elijah's Ascent into Heaven, revised by the Committee of Publication (Boston: Massachusetts Sabbath School Society, 1846);

The Story of Jeroboam, The Son of Nebat (New York: Carlton & Porter, 1846);

The Voice of Solomon to Young Men (Hartford: Printed by D. B. Moseley, 1846);

Familiar Letters to Young Men on Various Subjects. Designed as a Companion to the Young Man's Guide (Buffalo: G. H. Derby, 1849);

Gift Book for Young Ladies; or Familiar Letters on Their Acquaintances, Male and Female, Employments, Friendships, Etc. (New York: Derby, Jackson, 1849);

Gift Book for Young Men; or Familiar Letters on Self-Knowledge, Self-Education, Female Society, Marriage, Etc. (New York: Derby, Jackson, 1850);

Lectures for the Fireside, Founded on the Ten Commandments (Rochester, N.Y.: E. Darrow, 1850);

Letters to a Sister; or, Woman's Mission. To Accompany the Letters to Young Men (Buffalo: G. H. Derby, 1850);

The Young Woman's Book of Health (Boston: Tappan, Whittemore & Mason, 1850);

Sunday among the Puritans; or, The First Twenty Sabbaths of the Pilgrims of New England (New York: Carlton & Porter, 1851);

Lectures on Life and Health; or, The Laws and Means of Physical Culture (Boston: Phillips, Sampson, 1853);

The Physiology of Marriage (Boston: John P. Jewett, 1856);

The Home-Book of Life and Health; or, The Laws and Means of Physical Culture Adapted to Practical Use (Boston: Phillips, Sampson, 1856);

The Life of Robert Morrison, The First Protestant Missionary to China (New York: Carlton & Porter, 1856);

Tall Oaks from Little Acorns; or, Sketches of Distinguished Persons of Humble Origins (New York: Carlton & Phillips, 1856);

The Laws of Health; or, Sequel to The House I Live In (Boston: John P. Jewett, 1857);

The Moral Philosophy of Courtship and Marriage (Boston: John P. Jewett, 1857);

Forty Years in the Wilderness of Pills and Powders; or, The Cogitations and Confessions of an Aged Physician (Boston: John P. Jewett, 1859).

PERIODICALS EDITED: *American Annals of Education and Instruction,* edited by Alcott and William C. Woodbridge, 1831;
Juvenile Rambler, 1832–1833;
Parley's Magazine, 1833–1837;
The Moral Reformer and Teacher on the Human Constitution, 1835–1836;
The Library of Health, and Teacher on the Human Condition, 1837–1842;
The Teacher of Health, and the Laws of the Human Constitution, 1843.

Largely neglected today in studies of the nineteenth century, William Andrus Alcott was in his time a popular and influential educator, editor, physician, and apostle of dietary and personal health reform. "The least-remembered Alcott," as one twentieth-century scholar has called him, was born 6 August 1798 in Wolcott, Connecticut, the son of Obed and Anna (Andrus) Alcox. His paternal grandfather, John Alcox, first settled the village in 1731, and his mother was a descendant of William Andrus, who was one of the first settlers of neighboring Waterbury. When not pressed for duty on the family farm, William attended the local school with his cousin Amos Bronson Alcott, with whom he altered the family surname. Attending the school was an experience that helped shape both cousins' commitment to educational reform: they disliked the intolerable physical conditions, the limited curriculum, and the rote-learning pedagogy. As an early sign of their mutual interest in self-education, he and Bronson practiced the art of composition by exchanging letters and, with other boys, collected books to form a juvenile library. For a brief period William studied with the parish minister, who kept a kind of high school in the winter months. When he was eighteen, William began a four-year teaching stint in several schools in Litchfield and Hartford Counties. When he was twenty-two, he and Bronson traveled to the South in the hope of finding teaching jobs. Journeying from Charleston, South Carolina, to the state capital in Columbia, and then on to Norfolk, Virginia, they were unsuccessful in their attempt to find employment. The trip had to be aborted when Bronson nearly died of typhoid fever, through which William nursed him and which helped heighten William's awareness of the dangers of illness.

On his return to Connecticut, William took up teaching again, in a district not far from Wolcott, boarding around in various houses of the community, as was often the practice at the time. Now twenty-four, he truly became a professional in his missionary zeal to improve education. Among his reforms to make learning more enjoyable was improving the physical conditions of the school. He added seats with backs to replace the primitive benches that were so uncomfortable for the children. In addition, he imple-

Title page for one of the books in which Alcott urged women to devote their lives to rearing healthy and virtuous families

mented a system of ventilation to help control the quality, temperature, and movement of the air. Alcott's efforts to reach a wider audience in his attempts at such reforms were later published in his *Essay on the Construction of School-Houses, To Which Was Awarded the Prize Offered by the American Institute of Instruction, August, 1831* (1832). He also made the room itself more pleasant by adding curtains to the windows, ornamenting the walls with maps, and bringing in flowers. At this point in his career he began expanding the curriculum—over the years incorporating arithmetic, grammar, and geography. To keep his charges occupied when their individual groups were not being called upon to recite, Alcott introduced slates to encourage them to draw, to spell, and to write. He also became a firm believer in the importance of physical exercise for his students. Supplementing his instruction in the schoolhouse, he also taught the children, as well as their parents, in their own homes. Alcott's struggles with his own hopes and shortcomings as a teacher were published in *Confessions of a School Master* (1839), which, in addition to providing a detailed account of his transition from "plough-boy" to "pedagogue," also offers practical advice for future teachers and useful information for school boards and parents.

So complete was his dedication to his calling that he rose before dawn, often foregoing breakfast, and arrived an hour or two before school opened to sweep the room, start the fire, and prepare the daily lessons. All this enthusiastic activity proved physically and mentally draining, however, and his exhaustion was compounded by ill health. He suffered from indigestion and the premature decay of his teeth; a case of measles permanently weakened his eyes; erysipelas led to facial eruptions and at one point even to the loss of his hair; and most serious of all, he was afflicted with consumption, its worst effects (hectic fever, emaciation, and severe coughing) manifesting themselves throughout his twenties. To understand his own illnesses, especially his tubercular infection, he began studying medicine while teaching in the central school of Bristol in 1824–1825. During the next year he attended Yale Medical School on a regular basis; and in March 1826, having written his thesis on tuberculosis, he earned his diploma, which allowed him to practice medicine and surgery.

With a renewed commitment to teaching, Alcott applied for and received the teaching post at the central school in Wolcott, aspiring to create a model school in his hometown. Exhaustion caused by overwork led to another breakdown. At this point in his life he became an itinerant physician, riding on horseback to make his rounds and spending much time outdoors. Apparently invigorated by the open air, he tried once again to be a schoolmaster, this time in Southington, Connecticut. When he suffered yet a further bout of illness, he despaired of making a career in either teaching or medicine, planning instead to spend the rest of his life farming. When by chance he met the Reverend William C. Woodbridge, however, Alcott took a different path. Woodbridge, who had studied with the noted Swiss educators Johann Heinrich Pestolozzi and Philip von Fellenberg, asked Alcott to help establish a Fellenberg school near Woodbridge's hometown of Hartford. Alcott accepted the offer and began what became a three-decade-long career proselytizing his ideas through print and lecture.

In 1831 he went with Woodbridge to Boston to assist him with editing the *American Annals of Education and Instruction,* and for the next two years Alcott also served as editor of the *Juvenile Rambler,* the first children's magazine in the country. From 1833 to 1837 he held the same position for *Parley's Magazine,* the owner of which, S. G. Goodrich (famous for his "Peter Parley's Tales"), had invited him to assume the editorship. In addition to contributions to *American Annals of Education and Instruction,* Alcott published in the *Recorder,* the *Watchman,* and the *Traveller* of Boston and in the *Boston Medical and Surgical Journal.* In 1835 he founded his own journal, *The Moral Reformer and Teacher on the Human Constitution,* which he continued for nine years under various titles—*The Moral Reformer, The Library of Health,* and *The Teacher of Health.*

While Alcott continued his educational reforms, he also became a major crusader in the popular health movement that began during the Jacksonian era. Few if any pioneers and promoters of the personal health crusade—among them Sylvester Graham, Catharine Esther Beecher, Edward Hitchcock, Orson Fowler, Samuel Wells, Mary Gove Nichols, William Metcalf, Russell Trall, and Joel Shew—could claim the sheer number of books and pamphlets that Alcott eventually wrote on the subject. Many other reformers of the day were engaged in reimagining political, social, and religious institutions in one form or another: Alcott's utopian dreams, by contrast, focused on reclaiming the moral and physiological purity of the soul and the human body—or *The House I Live In* (1834), as he called one of his books on the subject. His prolific efforts in this field are perhaps best understood by appreciating his nearly obsessive drive for "sinless perfection" and his frustrating struggle to deal with what he described as "my diseased and enfeebled frame," caused by his bad health—issues that inform his autobiographical *Forty Years in the Wilderness of Pills and Powders; or, The Cogitations and Confessions of an Aged Physician* (1859). Blaming his parents (and theirs in turn) for a family history of poor dietary and health habits and the medical profession for emphasizing cure over prevention, Alcott sought to empower individuals by sharing his ideas and personal experiences. As he noted in *Forty Years in the Wilderness of Pills and Powders,* "I have probably, during the progress of a long life, made more experiments on myself, both in sickness and in health, than any other existing individual." The republican and practical Alcott found the medical establishment arrogantly elitist and esoteric, hopelessly backward in their attitude toward patients, still prescribing such dubious procedures as dosing, bleeding, and purging advocated by earlier physicians in the century, most notably Benjamin Rush. Better to use nothing at all, Alcott concluded, than to rely on what most doctors routinely prescribed at the time: mercury, calomel, tinctures, quassias, ales, opium or laudanum, nitrate of silver, and carbonate of ammonia.

Central to all his beliefs about health and moral purity (many extreme) is the doctrine that less is best, which he conceptualized in the apt economic metaphor that humans "manufacture" the conditions of their health. He believed that people create either disease or good health. Because they have only a limited supply of "physical capital," he believed that they must avoid "bankruptcy" by resisting the temptation to indulge in bad habits. Saving their "capital" yields the desired payoff of longevity. All diseases, he was certain, are "caused by transgressions of physical and moral law." As he argued in *Vegetable Diet; As Sanctioned by Medical Men, and by Experience in All Ages* (1838)—the first extended plea for vegetarianism by an American—there are nine reasons why the logical starting place for a disease-free life is adopting a diet completely free of animal products and fish: anatomical, physiological, medical, political, economical, millennial, experimental, biblical, and moral. Alcott thought that his own health problems and early bloating were caused by his parents' misguided ideas about child feeding, which led to his being "literally crammed with flesh-meat" from the age of five months to two years. Milk should be replaced by water only; he found cheese indigestible and thus dangerous to the bowels. Bread should be of the unbolted sort advocated by fellow believer Sylvester Graham. Though the scope and rigor of Alcott's total health strategy went well beyond Graham's, Alcott was spared the wrath that butchers and bakers displayed to Graham. In all instances, restraint should be exercised. The "starvation system," as he called his dietary plan, would fend off a vast range of potential illnesses. In addition and of a piece with this line of reasoning, stimulants of any kind should be eschewed. Heading this list were alcohol, tea, coffee, and hot, spicy foods. Tobacco, like alcohol, was deleterious and associated with idleness and even worse behavior and thus should be avoided altogether.

In matters of personal hygiene, Alcott advocated a spartanlike regimen of daily cold baths and vigorous physical exercise in the open air to improve respiration and circulation. Cleanliness and self-control also included, importantly, sexual restraint, preferably abstinence. In a chapter titled "Criminal Behavior" in *The Young Man's Guide to Excellence* (1833), he warned against premarital intercourse and masturbation, which led to insanity, epilepsy, idiotism, paralysis, blindness, hypochondria, consumption, and early death. As perhaps the only male to do so at the time, he addressed the same issue for females in *The Young Woman's Book of Health* (1850). In addition to the problems that males suffer because of "the solitary vice," female masturbators are also susceptible to nymphomania, leucorrhea ("the whites"), sterility, and uterine cancer. For married couples Alcott, in *The Physiology of Marriage* (1856), prescribed rigid guidelines for intercourse: "one indulgence per lunar month," only once or twice during pregnancy, and not at all during lactation. In a rare and curious acknowledgment of the reality of sexual gratification, Alcott pointed out that "the pleasures of

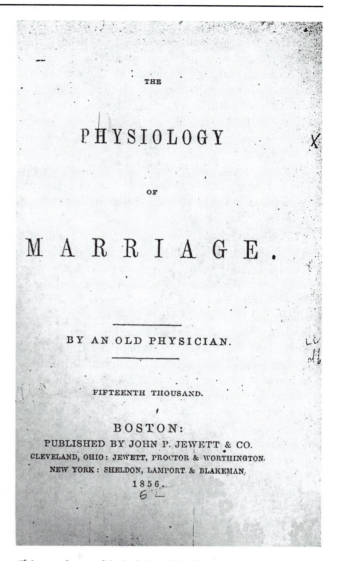

Title page for one of the books in which Alcott advocated sexual restraint

love, no less than the strength of orgasm, are enhanced by their infrequency." In short, as one modern critic has contended, for Alcott the penis, vagina, stomach, anus, and brain had to be subjugated and controlled in order for individuals to be healthy and successful in their province of life. Regulating all functions of the body, Alcott wrote in *The Laws of Health; or, Sequel to The House I Live In* (1857), would become "a means of lifting us toward Eden whence we came."

Alcott's utopian vision of a nation of healthy, productive citizens placed great emphasis on the role of mothers in child rearing. Though physically inferior to men and ideally shunning the activities of men's sphere (here Alcott's social conservatism is quite pronounced), women were naturally nobler and had an enormous opportunity to shape the physical and moral health of future citizens. To fulfill their solemn duties, they should avoid concerts, lectures, the theater, parties, balls, and exhibitions—focusing their efforts and energies instead on making their homes comfortable for their husbands and lovingly raising their children according to the ascetic ideal. As he urged in *The Young Mother; or, Management of Children in Regard to Health* (1836), *The Mother in Her Family; or, Sayings and Doings at Rose Hill Cottage* (1838), *The Young House-keeper; or, Thoughts on Food and Cookery* (1838), and *The Home-Book of Life and Health; or, The Laws and Means of Physical Culture Adapted to Practical Use* (1856), mothers should provide "simple cookery" and be orderly, meticulous organizers, early risers, voices of conscience, and exemplars and promoters of the Christian graces.

Finally, Alcott's holistic approach to a healthy life also included matters of faith. Arguing that "to be healthy we need to be holy," Alcott perceived a direct link between hygiene and religion. Alcott's belief in the importance of self-discipline, rational behavior, and respect for authority is reflected in his own religious experiences. Baptized an Episcopalian, he had at one point in his spiritual travels journeyed to the fringes of liberal Protestantism then spreading across New England. Unlike his Transcendentalist cousin Bronson, however, who wholeheartedly embraced the antinomian "Newness" that grew out of religious progressivism, William found orthodoxy and institutional Christianity indispensable to his physiological-philosophical views. His attitude toward liberal theology is evidenced in the title of his religious autobiography, *My Progress in Error, and Recovery to Truth; or, A Tour through Universalism, Unitarianism and Skepticism* (1841). Too much independence of thought in spiritual matters was as debilitating, he felt, as bodily excesses and indulgences.

Alcott's lifework in print is a testament to his indefatigable commitment to reform. In addition to hundreds of articles, he wrote books and pamphlets— volumes on education, medicine, physical education, and health; volumes for family and school libraries; and volumes for the Sabbath School Library. Many of these works went through multiple editions, thus illustrating his popularity.

Alcott's evangelism was not restricted, however, to editing and writing. He continued his medical practice until he died and maintained his interest in education by site visits to schools and lectures on educational improvements throughout the country. As his schedule permitted, he visited up to a dozen schools a day, perhaps ten thousand in his lifetime, according to one estimate. He helped found the American Physiological Society in 1837 and served as its first president, a position he also held later in the American Vegetarian Society. In addition, he was active in various benevolent groups supporting the Missionary, Bible, and Temperance Societies and aided moral-reform organizations in New York and Boston. On the lecture circuit he traveled throughout New England and into the West.

In 1836 Alcott married Phebe Bronson, of Bristol, Connecticut, by whom he had a daughter and son. His final years were spent in Newton, Massachusetts, where he died of pleurisy on 29 March 1859 and was buried in the town cemetery. William Andrus Alcott's spirit of benevolence and self-sacrifice is succinctly embodied in his dying message to his son, who was at the time a college student: "Tell William to live for others, not for himself."

References:

Amos Bronson Alcott, *New Connecticut* (Boston: Roberts, 1887);

Winston J. Craig, "In the Pink of Health: William Alcott, Sylvester Graham and Dietary Reforms in New England, 1830–1870," *Adventist Heritage,* 14 (Fall 1991): 34–41;

Sidney Ditzion, *Marriage, Morals, and Sex in America: A History of Ideas,* expanded edition (New York: Octagon, 1975), pp. 322–329;

"Dr. William A. Alcott," *American Journal of Education,* 4 (March 1858): 628–656;

Hebbel E. Hoff and John F. Fulton, "The Centenary of the First American Physiological Society Founded at Boston by William A. Alcott and Sylvester Graham," *Bulletin of the History of Medicine,* 5 (October 1937): 687–734;

Paul Mills, "William A. Alcott, M.D. (1798–1859), Pioneer Reformer in Physical Education," dissertation, University of Maryland, 1971;

Samuel Orcutt, *History of the Town of Wolcott (Connecticut) from 1731 to 1874* (Waterbury, Conn.: Press of the American Printing Company, 1874);

Charles E. Rosenberg, "Introduction," *The Physiology of Marriage,* by William Andrus Alcott (New York: Arno, 1972);

Louis B. Salomon, "The Least-Remembered Alcott," *New England Quarterly,* 34 (March 1961): 87–93;

Herbert Thoms, "William Andrus Alcott: Physician, Educator, Writer," *Bulletin of the Society of Medical History of Chicago,* 4 (April 1928): 123–130;

Martin Cornelius Van Buren, "The Indispensable God of Health: A Study of Republican Hygiene and the Ideology of William Alcott," dissertation, University of California, Los Angeles, 1977;

James C. Whorton, "'Christian Physiology': William Alcott's Prescription for the Millennium," *Bulletin of the History of Medicine,* 49, no. 4 (1975): 466–481.

Papers:

No inventory has been undertaken to determine what if any of William Andrus Alcott's private papers exist.

William Apess

(31 January 1798 – 1839)

Michael Berthold
Villanova University

See also the Apess entry in *DLB 175: Native American Writers of the United States.*

BOOKS: *A Son of the Forest: The Experience of William Apess, A Native of the Forest, Comprising a Notice of the Pequot Tribe of Indians* (New York: The author, 1829; revised edition, New York: Printed for the author by G. F. Bunce, 1831);

The Increase of the Kingdom of Christ: A Sermon (New York: Printed for the author by G. F. Bunce, 1831);

The Experiences of Five Christian Indians of the Pequot Tribe (Boston: Printed for the author by James B. Dow, 1833); revised as *Experience of Five Christian Indians of the Pequot Tribe* (Boston: Printed for the publisher, 1837);

Indian Nullification of the Unconstitutional Laws of Massachusetts Relative to the Marshpee Tribe; or, The Pretended Riot Explained (Boston: Jonathan Howe, 1835);

Eulogy on King Philip, as Pronounced at the Odeon, in Federal Street, Boston (Boston: The author, 1836; revised, 1837).

Collection: *On Our Own Ground: The Complete Writings of William Apess, A Pequot,* edited by Barry O'Connell (Amherst: University of Massachusetts Press, 1992).

William Apess

One of the most important Native American writers of the nineteenth century, William Apess has only recently begun to emerge from historical and literary obscurity. His autobiography, *A Son of the Forest: The Experience of William Apess, A Native of the Forest, Comprising a Notice of the Pequot Tribe of Indians* (1829), for example, has come to be recognized as the first extended, written Native American autobiography. While articulating his nuanced sense of what it means to be a "Christian Indian," Apess's writing also provides a scathing and artful critique of the Puritan errand into the wilderness and the construction of empire generally. In rescuing the "native" from invisibility and caricature, Apess in fact underwrites the possibilities for a relegitimized American egalitarianism at once political and religious. As scholarly reconfigurations of the American nineteenth century proceed, Apess's work should emerge as pivotal.

Much of what is known of Apess's actual life derives from his own autobiography. Born on 31 January 1798 in Colrain, Massachusetts, he was the first child of William and Candace Apes. (Apess seemed to favor spelling his last name with a double *s,* although he used "Apes" at times as well; there is no definitive spelling of the name.) Apess's father was half-white and joined the Pequot tribe; Apess claimed his mother was a full-blooded Pequot, although one critic has speculated that she may have been African American. When Apess's parents separated in 1801, Apess went to live with his maternal grandparents in Colchester, Connect-icut. After a beating from his drunken grandmother that left one of his arms broken in three places, the young boy was bound out to a Mr. and Mrs. Furman, and he was later indentured to two other masters; Apess in fact spent more of his formative years in white households than in Indian ones. Amid the many dislocations of his childhood, Apess received only a slight education, attending school during the winter term from the ages of six to twelve.

A Son of the Forest amply reflects Apess's experiences of living between cultures and attempting to judge and mediate them. In part, the autobiography traces Apess's search for an elusive home, a search resolved, if at all, only through his eventual, life-defining conversion to Methodism. Given the limitations of Apess's education, the very production of so skilled a written autobiography is remarkable. The unexplained attainment of not only literacy but also eloquence is in fact one of the most enticing features of the autobiography.

Formally, *A Son of the Forest* can be understood as a conversion narrative, a genre that in its emphasis on its protagonist's spiritual journey from sinfulness to grace was a familiar and malleable species of autobiography in the American nineteenth century. Apess precisely dates his conversion as occurring on "the fifteenth day of March, in the year of our Lord, eighteen hundred and thirteen." Presenting himself as "a lost and ruined sinner" who "throws himself entirely on the Lord," Apess hears a soothing voice forgive him his sins and discovers as a result *perfect freedom* and peace of mind.

Crucial to Apess's conversion experience is the way in which his attainment of a Christian identity affirms his native identity. Evangelical Methodism's welcoming of the marginal and dispossessed spurned by other Christian denominations and its valuing of the "internal" witnessing of Christ as savior had great appeal for Apess; it granted him recognition, authority, and the opportunity to vindicate the "savage" while vilifying the "civilized." In declaring his preference for the *noisy Methodists,* Apess dismisses those nominal Christians who "had deprived me of liberty." The Methodists convince him that "Christ died for all mankind—that age, sect, color, country, or situation made no difference" and "that I was included in the plan of redemption with all my brethren." At the exact moment of his conversion, Apess experiences a "love" that "embraced the whole human family," echoing the introductory insistence in the autobiography that "We are in fact but one family; we are all the descendants of one great progenitor." Apess's conversion to Methodism constitutes a conversion to a kind of ultrademocracy that reimagines the literal American democracy that demeaned him.

His conversion also provides him with a vocation; obtaining "license to exhort," Apess begins his missionary work of spreading the word of the Gospel (he is later officially ordained to preach by the Protestant Methodist Church). His written autobiography, thus, is orally grounded, his public speech prefiguring his published text.

Throughout *A Son of the Forest,* Apess effectively uses particular moments from his life story as registers of larger American injustices. For example, in the unsentimental portrait of his intoxicated, cruel grandmother, Apess unexpectedly recontextualizes the incident to reveal the etiology of the grandmother's "savagery." "I attribute it in a great measure to the whites, inasmuch as they introduced among my countrymen that bane of comfort and happiness, ardent spirits," writes Apess; subsequently, he continues, the whites wronged the natives out of their land, violated their women, and are thus "justly chargeable with at least some portion of my sufferings." Similarly, Apess depicts the effects of racial prejudice on his own self-estimation ("I thought it disgraceful to be called an Indian") and locates his early fear of other Indians and of his own Indianness in the "many stories" that as a boy he was told about Indian cruelty toward whites. "But," adds Apess in the kind of reversal that often characterizes the rhetoric of his autobiography, "the whites did not tell me that they were in a great majority of instances the aggressors," and if they "had told me how cruel they had been to the 'poor Indian,' I should have apprehended as much harm from them."

Although his impassioned religious-social agenda dominates *A Son of the Forest,* Apess does give some expression to what he calls "the varied scenes of my life"—running away from his masters, enlisting in 1813 as a drummer boy in a New York militia unit and seeing action in the battle of Lake Champlain, backsliding from his conversion, and traveling about the northeast as an itinerant worker. Still, Apess has only minimal interest in detailing his personal life or the specificity of the world he inhabited. His wife—Mary Wood of Salem, Connecticut, whom he married in 1821—is mentioned only late in the text and not even named; she is "a woman of nearly the same color as myself" who "bore a pious and exemplary character." Likewise, the couple's offspring (a son and possibly two daughters) are alluded to only as "my little ones." In its deliberate impersonality, the autobiography resists the celebratory individualism often identified as quintessentially American, partaking instead of the Native American ethos that privileged the communal over the subjective. In *A Son of the Forest,* Apess seems intent on constructing a self to transcend that self, to move from "self" to tribe, nation, world, and beyond. The autobiography in fact

Frontispiece from Indian Nullification of the Unconstitutional Laws of Massachusetts Relative to the Marshpee Tribe *(1835),*
a collection of documents from Apess's successful campaign to win the same rights of self-governance for Indians as those
enjoyed by other citizens of Massachusetts

concludes with a long appendix in which Apess dispenses with his own story to survey and quote several white historians (especially Elias Boudinot) to extend his project of justifying the misunderstood native.

Apess's next publication, *The Increase of the Kingdom of Christ: A Sermon* (1831), underlines the deep connections invariably at work for him between speech and print, between preaching and writing. The text of the sermon, Apess's "unwavering confidence in what God has promised for future times" and the "rich glories" of that coming day, is conventional revivalist fare. But the sermon also provides occasions for Apess to adjudicate American abuses of the native population in light of providential destiny: "have not the great American nation reason to fear the swift judgments of heaven on them for nameless cruelties, extortions, and exterminations inflicted upon the poor natives of the forest? We fear the account of national sin, which lies at the doors of the American people, will be a terrible one to balance in the chancery of heaven." In its peroration, the sermon also vividly apostrophizes a white audience, another of Apess's favorite rhetorical tactics, dramatizing for them the conversion of those "red men" who "made their knives keen for the scalp, and sought the

blood of your soldiers, your women, and your children" into devout Christians who must be acknowledged as fellow "heirs of the kingdom of grace."

Published with *The Increase of the Kingdom of Christ* is a separate essay, "The Indians: The Ten Lost Tribes." In this companion piece to the sermon, Apess espouses a favorite hypothesis that the Indians of North America "are indeed no other than the descendants of the ten lost tribes." Through the syncretism of linking Indian history to biblical history, Apess outlines a master narrative favorable to himself and his people. Moreover, he decries the wantonness of historical records that have "blotted out" the records and remnants of those who have been persecuted and conquered, suggesting the recuperative role his own writing might play in the shaping of the annals of American letters.

In *The Experiences of Five Christian Indians of the Pequot Tribe* (1833), as in *A Son of the Forest,* Apess uses autobiography as a means of discarding mere self-expression and entering into other lives and discourses. The text opens with a narration of Apess's own life, Apess casting himself as the first of the five "Christian Indians" of the work and as the "missionary." Significantly, the remaining narratives are given over to four female Christian Indians, making this text the most gender-conscious of Apess's works—although gender has much less ontological force for Apess than religion. His wife, largely absent from *A Son of the Forest,* speaks in the second section of this text. Although still not identified by name (she is the "Missionary's Consort"), Mary Apess is at least assigned authorial credit for the telling of her "experience." Chronicling the spiritual deprivation of her youth and chiding all figurative irreligious parents, Mary Apess's narration, like her husband's, emphasizes the value of "affectionate" exhortation and the welcoming ecumenicalism of Christianity, and her life is exemplary finally for the imperturbability of faith it embodies. The lesson of the next narrative, that of Hannah Caleb, centers on the necessity of the Indian convert's loving white people as well as her own and imagining a reciprocity of that love. But Sally George (Apess's aunt), in the fourth section of the text, emerges as Apess's most heroic female convert. She, most emphatically of Apess's Christian Indians, intuits some fundamental relationship between religion and power. Apess praises her "organic power of communication" and the "free, lively, and animating" nature of her language; "almost a preacher," George occupies a vital public role in her community. Apess admires her, too, for being "no sectarian"; like Hannah Caleb, she possesses that magnanimity of spirit that allows her to feel as much for her white neighbors as for her own kindred. Her "dying bed" provides a particularly "glorious and interesting" tableau for Apess because of the united, emotive tribute both natives and whites pay her. Through her piety and generosity, she achieves a near cross-cultural sainthood, the Indian woman a bold paradigm for some universal Christianity. The final section of *The Experiences of Five Christian Indians of the Pequot Tribe* is most interesting for its brief reproduction of the "broken" speech of Anne Wampy: "Me no like Christians, me hate 'em, hate everybody," she proclaims prior to her conversion; after looking to Jesus, she says "me feel light . . . me love everybody, me want to drink no more *rum*." Her vernacular exhortation of sinners is a striking foil to the more studied eloquence of Apess himself.

The Experiences of Five Christian Indians of the Pequot Tribe concludes with the essay "An Indian's Looking-Glass for the White Man," one of Apess's most brilliant and militant exhortations. He places before the reader the "black inconsistency" of the white man, which is "ten times blacker than any skin that you will find in the universe." Supposing that "each skin had its national crimes written upon it," Apess asks the white man, "which skin do you think would have the greatest?" Jesus himself, Apess reminds his audience, was not a white man. Consistent with the general tenor of his work, however, Apess wishes at the end of the essay

to see the elimination of America's caste system based on race and to behold a just and peaceful union.

In 1833, the year that *The Experiences of Five Christian Indians of the Pequot Tribe* was published, Apess became embroiled in the political controversies of Mashpee, the only surviving Indian town of Massachusetts. His activist struggles for Indian rights are passionately manifest in the time he spent with the Mashpees, who adopted him as one of their own tribe, and in the text that activism yielded, *Indian Nullification of the Unconstitutional Laws of Massachusetts Relative to the Marshpee Tribe; or, The Pretended Riot Explained* (1835). Mashpee autonomy was strangulated by the power of the commonwealth-appointed overseers who could lease out Indian land to whites and even determine who was allowed to enter their town. The Mashpees also had to contend with a Harvard-appointed white minister, Phineas Fish, notoriously unresponsive to their needs. Apess wrote petitions, agitated for the rights of the Mashpees, and brought their struggle into public consciousness—so much so that the Massachusetts governor was prepared to call out troops to quell what in many white minds was a revolt. Marked as the firebrand of the uprising, Apess was arrested (on 4 July), charged with "riot, assault, and tresspass," and made to serve thirty days in jail and pay a substantial fine. But the fomentation continued, and in March 1834 the Massachusetts legislature granted the Mashpees the same rights of self-governance as other citizens of the commonwealth.

Indian Nullification of the Unconstitutional Laws of Massachusetts Relative to the Marshpee Tribe is an amalgamation of texts that Apess superintends. It is composed of letters, notices, and petitions from the actual controversy, as well as newspaper articles on the unfolding drama and Apess's own commentary. At its most powerful, it is stirring and far-seeing protest literature that turns the rhetoric of the founding fathers against itself: "I ask the inhabitants of New England generally," declaims Apess, "how their fathers bore laws, much less oppressive, when imposed upon them by a foreign government." Similarly, in the language of the Mashpee petition to the Massachusetts governor and council, it is resolved that "we, as a tribe, will rule ourselves, and have the right to do so; for all men are born free and equal, says the Constitution of the country." Further contributing to the effectiveness of *Indian Nullification of the Unconstitutional Laws of Massachusetts Relative to the Marshpee Tribe,* the mockery that Apess unleashes throughout is aphoristic, caustic, and witty: "from the year of our Lord, 1656, to the present day, the conduct of the whites toward the Indians has been one continued system of robbery"; "I think that the Indians ought to keep the twenty-fifth of December (Christmas) and the fourth of July as days of fasting and lamentation"; "If an honest white man

Frontispiece from Apess's Eulogy on King Philip *(1836), commemorating the 160th anniversary of the death of the Wampanoag chief known to his people as Metacomet*

could look into our private affairs and know what wrongs we have suffered, it would change his complexion to a hue redder than the Indian's." An article from *The Liberator,* cited in *Indian Nullification of the Unconstitutional Laws of Massachusetts Relative to the Marshpee Tribe,* praises Apess for a "fearless, comprehensive, and eloquent speech"; those adjectives apply equally well to Apess's heroism throughout the Mashpee incident and to *Indian Nullification of the Unconstitutional Laws of Massachusetts Relative to the Marshpee Tribe* itself.

Apess's final work, *Eulogy on King Philip, as Pronounced at the Odeon, in Federal Street, Boston* (1836), is the published version of an oration he gave twice that year in honor of the 160th anniversary of King Philip's death. Consolidating and amplifying his earlier critiques of the arrogance, depravity, and racism behind the European "civilization" of North America, the eulogy makes clear how acts of historicizing and commemoration must intersect with and meliorate present history. As critique, it is as ferocious as anything Apess authored, the baleful "who, my dear sirs, were wanting of the name of savages—whites, or Indians?" of the eulogy, the consummatory interrogation of all his work. The eulogy is particularly adept at exposing the perverse agency of Christianity in the conquest of the native. Apess castigates the missionaries themselves not

only for doing more harm than good but also for the way in which the Europeans "could go to work to enslave a free people and call it religion," rendering "Christianity" and "enslavement" virtual synonyms.

Apess, who in *A Son of the Forest* claimed to be descended from King Philip, unhesitatingly identifies King Philip as "the greatest man that ever lived upon the American shores"; a later assertion of King Philip's superiority to George Washington buttresses Apess's defense. In a particularly ennobling catalogue, Apess finds King Philip "as active as the wind, as dexterous as a giant, firm as the pillows of heaven, and fierce as a lion, a powerful foe to contend with indeed, and as swift as an eagle, gathering together his forces to prepare them for the battle." In quoting a speech by King Philip, Apess makes him out to be as much prophet as warrior, as King Philip forewarns how "these people from the unknown world" will "drive us and our children from the graves of our fathers . . . and enslave our women and children." The eulogy for King Philip functions for Apess as verification of such prophecy, becoming the occasion for a eulogy for the whole race.

By the end of the eulogy, Apess translates the legacy of King Philip for his contemporary America and demands of white people that a "different course must be pursued"—both legally and spiritually. Apess of course wants juster laws to prevail in the nation, but he also wants a new amity between white and Indian. "What do they, the Indians, want?" he asks his white audience—only, like whites themselves, the opportunity to be "good and wholesome citizens." Thus, through the militancy that desires concord, Apess attempts throughout his work to remake America.

Almost nothing is known about Apess after his publication of the eulogy. Obituaries have recently been uncovered that, disconcertingly, record his death from alcoholism in New York in 1839. Perhaps not surprisingly, because of his race and radicalism, Apess has been missing until recently from the American literary canon and American literary histories. At a cultural moment, however, at which critics are increasingly self-conscious about the kinds of questions of race, representation, and subalternity that Apess multifariously raises, he is a figure who will attract significant critical attention as his prescience for a volatile multicultural America is realized.

References:

Carolyn Haynes, "'A Mark for Them All to . . . Hiss At': The Formation of Methodist and Pequot Identity in the Conversion Narrative of William Apess," *Early American Literature*, 31, no. 1 (1996): 25–44;

Arnold Krupat, *Ethnocriticism: Ethnography, History, Literature* (Berkeley & Los Angeles: University of California Press, 1992);

Krupat, *The Voice in the Margin: Native American Literature and the Canon* (Berkeley & Los Angeles: University of California Press, 1989);

Jill Lepore, *The Name of War: King Philip's War and the Origins of American Identity* (New York: Knopf, 1998), pp. 215–226;

David Murray, *Forked Tongues: Speech, Writing and Representation in North American Indian Texts* (Bloomington: Indiana University Press, 1991);

Barry O'Connell, Introduction to *On Our Own Ground: The Complete Writings of William Apess, A Pequot,* edited by O'Connell (Amherst: University of Massachusetts Press, 1992);

A. LaVonne Brown Ruoff, "Three Nineteenth-Century American Indian Autobiographers," in *Redefining American Literary History,* edited by Ruoff and Jerry W. Ward Jr. (New York: MLA, 1990), pp. 251–269;

Karim M. Tiro, "Denominated 'SAVAGE': Methodism, Writing, and Identity in the Works of William Apess, A Pequot," *American Quarterly,* 48 (December 1996): 653–679.

Delia Bacon

(2 February 1811 – 2 September 1859)

Beverly G. Merrick
New Mexico State University

See also the Bacon entry in *DLB 1: The American Renaissance in New England.*

BOOKS: *Tales of the Puritans: The Regicides. The Fair Pilgrim. Castine,* anonymous (New Haven: A. H. Maltby, 1831);

The Bride of Fort Edward, Founded on an Incident of the Revolution (New York: S. Colman, 1839);

The Philosophy of the Plays of Shakspere Unfolded (London: Groombridge, 1857; Boston: Ticknor & Fields, 1857).

Edition: *The Philosophy of the Plays of Shakspere Unfolded* (New York: AMS Press, 1970).

SELECTED PERIODICAL PUBLICATION–UNCOLLECTED: "William Shakspere and His Plays: An Inquiry," *Putnam's Monthly: A Magazine of Literature, Science, and Art,* 7 (January 1856): 1–19.

Delia Salter Bacon—who was a friend of Harriet Beecher Stowe, Ralph Waldo Emerson, and Nathaniel Hawthorne—believed that William Shakespeare's plays were the work of Francis Bacon and his cadre of literary friends. Bacon had some support in her belief. Emerson helped her publish a sketch on the subject in *Putnam's Monthly Magazine,* in January 1856. The editor's note called Bacon's interesting speculations "the result of long and conscientious investigation upon the part of the learned and eloquent scholar." In 1857, with Hawthorne's assistance, she published *The Philosophy of the Plays of Shakspere Unfolded.* The speculative quest Bacon launched has continued to give her theory conversational currency.

As the fourth daughter and the fifth of seven children of former missionaries to the American Indians, Delia Salter Bacon had a difficult young life. She was born in a log cabin, reportedly the first house in Tallmadge, Summit County, Ohio, south of Cleveland. Her father, the Reverend David Bacon, who was related to Oliver Wendell Holmes, established the

Very gratefully yours
Delia Bacon.

First Church in Tallmadge in his home on 22 January 1809. He tried to establish a pioneering utopian farming community in the Western Reserve, based on Connecticut Puritanism, and failed. He returned to his home in Connecticut three years later, a broken man, and he died in 1817, leaving his wife, Alice (Parks) Bacon, deeply in debt and with six children to rear.

Delia was the youngest and most promising of the female offspring. She was only six years old when she became the foster ward of lawyer Thomas Scott Williams of Hartford, who had been a student-at-law when her father was a divinity student. Williams subsequently became chief justice of the Connecticut Supreme Court. His wife, the former

25

Delia Ellsworth, was the daughter of a previous chief justice. Delia Bacon had been named after Ellsworth, who had been a childhood friend of her mother. Even with the support of her foster family, Bacon suffered the same longings of the typical foster child—to be with her own family. Ambition drove her, but she reportedly was known for her mercurial shifts in temperament, driven by religious melancholy.

At about age eleven, Delia Williams gave her namesake a year of schooling. Delia Bacon was enrolled in the Hartford Female Seminary, the celebrated school of Catharine Beecher, sister of Henry Ward Beecher. Catharine Beecher noted that Bacon was a handful, describing her pupil as sincere, impulsive, but possessing "the dangerous power of keen and witty expression." Bacon dutifully received the one year of instruction but was said by Beecher to have been more advanced than her teachers. Beecher also felt that Bacon was intermittently pious. An extracurricular activity—listening to a local resident, Lydia Huntley Sigourney, recite poetry—impressed young Bacon more than her schooling. During this period she also joined the First Congregational Church of Hartford, urging others to profess their faith. Fragile and fiery are adjectives that aptly describe her character.

Bacon soon was entrusted by the parents of her classmates to instruct them. Subsequently, for four years Bacon and a sister tried to establish private schools in Southington, Connecticut; Perth Amboy, New Jersey; Jamaica, on Long Island; and Penn Yan, in western New York. Bacon then began to reevaluate her goal of teaching because of her own and her sister's frail health.

She began to write in a serious vein. In 1831 she published a fictional saga titled *Tales of the Puritans,* including "The Regicides," based on the anecdotal history of the arrivals in New Haven, Connecticut, of several of the judges who had signed the execution order of Charles I of England in 1649. A second tale, "The Fair Pilgrim," is an adaptation based on the fate of Lady Arbella Johnson, the daughter of the earl of Lincoln, who had died at Salem in 1630. The third tale, "Castine," is about Jean-Vincent d'Abbadie, Baron St. Castine, who began a French settlement in the Penobscot. Bacon's work did not credit her with the authorship; the title page carried only the publisher's name—A. H. Maltby, of New Haven.

The year 1831 was productive for Bacon. From the murder of Jane McCrae, she wrote an adaptation called "Love's Martyr," which won a $100 literary prize in a contest sponsored by the Philadelphia *Saturday Courier.* McCrae had been killed by a party of General John Burgoyne's Indians on the way to Fort Edward, a British camp, where she hoped to meet her lover, a loyalist officer. Literary historians have noted that Bacon won out over Edgar Allan Poe, who had entered five stories in the same contest. Bacon used the same incident described in "Love's Martyr" for a dialogue called *The Bride of Fort Edward, Founded on an Incident of the Revolution,* published eight years later in 1839, with an introductory note written by Bacon referring to the historical value of the play.

Following an attack of malaria in 1833, at age twenty-two, Bacon began experimental classes in adult education for ladies, on literature and history, in the home of her brother Leonard, a pastor of the First Church of New Haven. She found some success and a new home. She eventually earned her own living, enjoying an independence almost unknown to women of that period. She was one of the first women to offer such adult classes in America.

Bacon was said to have been able to lecture without notes. Up to a hundred at a time are said to have attended her "Historical Lessons," which gained some renown in Cambridge literary circles, as well as in Boston and New Haven. She lectured on classical antiquity, the Renaissance, and the English language. She soon became known for her intellectual passion and talents for persuasive speech. Her eclectic presentations ranged from lectures to dramatic readings in the disciplines of art, literature, and history. In 1844 she extended her lectures for a new audience, that of married women, a revolutionary concept for that time. She was said to have a real gift of friendship, and the popular lecturer was sought after. Many of those relationships remained constant throughout her life.

At age thirty-five she formed a relationship with the Reverend Alexander MacWhorter, becoming a devoted companion to the theologian and Yale graduate twelve years her junior. Bacon and the young clergyman had met where they resided, in the same boardinghouse. After two years, their growing intimacy became the subject of pervasive gossip, possibly driven by someone she had spurned, a classmate named Robert Forbes, or possibly driven by MacWhorter himself, who had written about their relationship to other church officials and who had hinted that Bacon was pursuing him. Meanwhile, Bacon appears to have backed off, while his affection grew. She left the boardinghouse to get away from him, moving into her brother's home. MacWhorter called on her there, and one popular account reports that she was forced into the position of suing for a proposal of marriage in order to refuse it. Instead, she fled to a family hotel in Brattleboro, Vermont, and he dutifully followed and kept company with her for ten weeks. According to one literary critic, MacWhorter was labeled a "clerical Lothario" by many of his contemporaries. Forbes and his confidantes managed to obtain Bacon's love letters to MacWhorter and made the most of them, to the detriment of the two.

Who wooed whom—and who was ultimately spurned—was a matter of conjecture in the religious society of their time and has remained so in literary circles today. The Congregational Church was drawn into the controversy because MacWhorter was the protégé of Nathaniel William Taylor, professor of Didactic Theology at Yale and one of the most influential figures in New England. Meanwhile, Bacon was a target of gossip because she was a celebrated intellectual and the sister of Taylor's confidant, Leonard Bacon, pastor of the First Church.

In this environment in which clergymen were venerated, those who ascended the pulpit were held to a higher standard of scrutiny than ordinary citizens. MacWhorter did not propose to Bacon officially, even though he had declared his affection for her. Therefore, Leonard Bacon brought charges of misconduct against him in the New Haven Ministerial Association. A hearing was scheduled for November 1847. The resulting ecclesiastical investigation caused a schism in the ranks of the ministerial association.

MacWhorter was acquitted in a thirteen to twelve decision by the ecclesiastic authorities but was instructed "never to do it again." His reputation was damaged severely. Delia Bacon went into seclusion. Three years later Catharine Beecher's book *Truth Stranger Than Fiction: A Narrative of Recent Transactions* (1850) vindicated Delia Bacon, but the affair was not forgotten.

After the publicized affair, Bacon ventured out on her own, leaving the company of friends to seek out the answers to a literary enigma that had been the focal point of many of her "Historical Lessons." Bacon had developed a single-minded belief that the plays attributed to Shakespeare were crafted by a secret society led by Lord Francis Bacon and adherents to his liberal philosophy such as Sir Walter Ralegh and Edmund Spenser. Historical evidence demonstrates that Delia Bacon first proposed this theory in her Cambridge lectures, expounding on it in an 1852 letter to Emerson, who encouraged her to write about "this brilliant paradox." In 1853 her passage to England was paid by an empathetic New York lawyer, Charles Butler. She sailed on the steamer *Pacific,* arriving in Liverpool on Queen Victoria's birthday, 24 May.

At the urging of Emerson, Bacon visited Thomas Carlyle on Cheyne Walk in London; Carlyle, however, called her ideas on Shakespeare quixotic. Carlyle was chagrined to discover that she chose to follow her own methods of intuition rather than his methods of scholarly study to find the answers. Meanwhile, Bacon insisted that Carlyle's belief that Shakespeare was a single author was based on opinion, while hers was based on knowledge. Carlyle never was won over to her way of thinking, but he did admit that Bacon wrote "in a clear, elegant, ingenious and highly readable manner."

While living in destitution in a London garret, Bacon closeted herself, pursuing her research into the hidden meanings of the Shakespearean plays. As the work neared its conclusion, she resolved to see inside Shakespeare's tomb at Stratford's Holy Trinity Church. She believed that significant papers revealing authorship had been interred with the body, but the tomb was not opened to confirm or disprove her belief.

Her subsequent work, *The Philosophy of the Plays of Shakspere Unfolded,* was published in 1857 with the assistance of Emerson and Hawthorne, then the American consul at Liverpool. As has been noted, Emerson's intervention to have an article on Bacon's theory published in the January 1856 issue of *Putnam's Monthly,* then the chief literary magazine in America, helped Bacon get her work published. Hawthorne's preface to the work gave respectability to her theory as well. Hawthorne reportedly gave Bacon his aid because his sister-in-law, Elizabeth Peabody, was one of Bacon's closest friends. In the preface to Bacon's work, Hawthorne calls her theory a demonstration that stimulates the intellect, rather than historical proof. His purpose in writing the preface, he said, was to place his countrywoman upon a ground of amicable understanding with the public. He also wrote favorably about his contact with Bacon in *Our Old Home* (1863), in an essay called "Recollections of a Gifted Woman."

Even so, the work was generally ignored by her contemporaries, dismissed in literary reviews. Bereft, Bacon lingered at Stratford, possessed mentally by the subject of her literary focus. She was briefly confined to the asylum in the Forest of Arden. She finally returned to America, with the assistance of a nephew, in April 1858. Upon her return to the United States, she was brought back to Connecticut by her family, with whom she had once argued bitterly. She was confined there at the Hartford Retreat, reportedly lucid and reconciled to all who knew her. She died a short fifteen months later, on 2 September 1859, at the age of forty-eight. She was buried in Grove Street Cemetery in New Haven.

MacWhorter continued to support her Baconian theory, even as he continued in his ministerial calling. He subsequently married Henrietta Blake, daughter of Eli Whitney Blake, and one of Bacon's nemeses in the whole affair involving himself and Bacon.

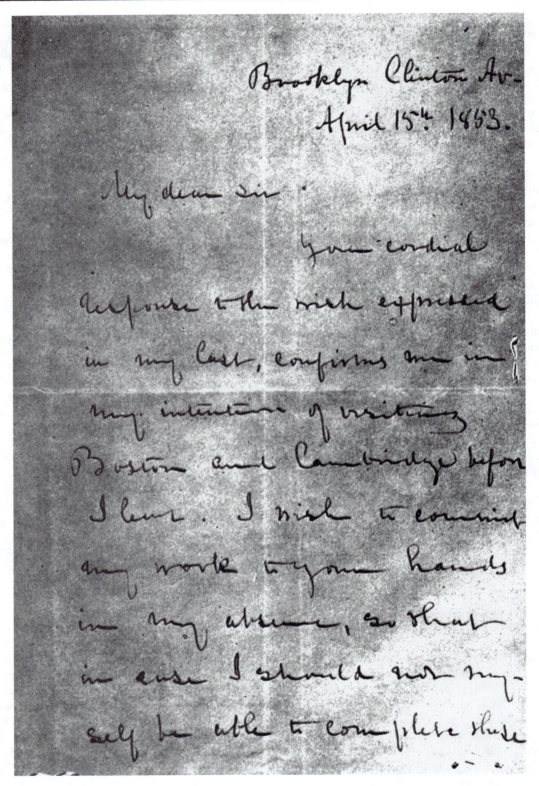

Letter to Ralph Waldo Emerson written about a month before Bacon left for England (in Vivian C. Hopkins,
Prodigal Puritan: A Life of Delia Bacon, *1959)*

Miss Le Kain's Summer Street.
I in Cambridge at Mrs
Francis. I expect now to
~~strike out~~ leave for
England on the 7th of
May, but will wait a
week or two longer if it should
be necessary, to find suitable
company. I shall write
again before I go, to Boston to tell
you just when to expect me.
I'm assured trust.
              Most thankfully your,
                    Delia S Bacon

Mr Emerson —

THE

PHILOSOPHY

OF

THE PLAYS OF SHAKSPERE

UNFOLDED.

BY DELIA BACON.

WITH

A PREFACE

BY

NATHANIEL HAWTHORNE,

AUTHOR OF 'THE SCARLET LETTER,' ETC.

Aphorisms representing A KNOWLEDGE *broken* do invite men to
inquire further.   LORD BACON.
You find not the apostrophes, and so miss the account.
                                                 LOVE'S LABOUR'S LOST.
Untie the spell —PROSPERO.

LONDON:

GROOMBRIDGE AND SONS,

PATERNOSTER ROW.

1857.

*Title page for Delia Bacon's attempt to prove that William
Shakespeare's plays were written by a secret society led
by Francis Bacon (The Joel Myerson Collection of
19th Century American Literature, Special
Collections, Thomas Cooper Library,
University of South Carolina)*

In the late 1800s Ignatius Donnelly—whose research backed up Bacon's findings—called Delia Salter Bacon "the greatest American yet born." His work supporting her thesis was republished in 1888 as *The Great Cryptogram: Francis Bacon's Cipher in the So-Called Shakespeare Plays*—and republished in 1899 as *Cipher in The Plays and on The Tombstone*. Donnelly argued that Shakespeare did not write the plays, just as Delia Bacon had concluded, and furthermore, that Francis Bacon was the real author of the plays, as demonstrated through parallelisms and a cipher of the narratives.

Biographies:
Theodore Bacon, *Delia Bacon: A Biographical Sketch* (Boston & New York: Houghton, Mifflin, 1888);
Vivian C. Hopkins, *Prodigal Puritan: A Life of Delia Bacon* (Cambridge, Mass.: Belknap Press, 1959);
Richard D. Altick, "Delia Bacon," in *Ohio Authors and Their Books: Biographical Data and Selective Biographies for Ohio Authors, Native and Resident, 1796–1950,* edited by William Coyle (Cleveland & New York: World Publishing, 1962).

References:
Martha Bacon, "The Parson and the Bluestocking," in *Puritan Promenade* (Boston: Houghton Mifflin, 1964), pp. 95–118;
Catharine Beecher, *Truth Stranger Than Fiction: A Narrative of Recent Transactions* (Boston: Phillips, Sampson, 1850);
Ignatius Donnelly, *The Great Cryptogram: Francis Bacon's Cipher in the So-Called Shakespeare Plays* (London: Sampson Low, Marston, Searle & Rivington, 1888); republished as *Cipher in The Plays and on The Tombstone* (Minneapolis: Verulam, 1899); republished as *The Great Cryptogram: Francis Bacon's Cipher in the So-Called Shakespeare Plays* (St. Clair Shores, Mich.: Scholarly Press, 1972);
Nathaniel Hawthorne, Preface to *The Philosophy of the Plays of Shakspere Unfolded* (London: Groombridge, 1857);
Alexander Nicholson, *No Cipher in Shakespeare: Being a Refutation of the Hon. Ignatius Donnelly's Great Cryptogram* (London: Unwin, 1888);
Frederick Merrick White, *The Doubting D-[i.e. Ignatius Donnelly] or, A Cranky Cryptogram: A Defence of the Great Bard in Three Fyttes* (London: Sutton, 1888).

Papers:
The papers of Delia Salter Bacon, including letters to and from Ralph Waldo Emerson and Nathaniel Hawthorne, are housed in the Folger Shakespeare Library in Washington, D.C.

George Bancroft

(3 October 1800 – 17 January 1891)

Anne Zanzucchi
University of Rochester

See also the Bancroft entries in *DLB 1: The American Renaissance in New England; DLB 30: American Historians, 1607–1865;* and *DLB 59: American Literary Critics and Scholars, 1800–1850.*

BOOKS: *Prospectus of a School to Be Established at Round Hill, Northampton, Massachusetts,* by Bancroft and Joseph G. Cogswell (Cambridge, Mass.: Hilliard & Metcalf, 1823);

Poems (Cambridge, Mass.: University Press, Hilliard & Metcalf, 1823);

Some Account of the School for the Liberal Education of Boys, Established on Round Hill, Northampton, Massachusetts, by Bancroft and Cogswell (Northampton, Mass., 1826);

An Oration Delivered on the Fourth of July, 1826, at Northampton, Mass. (Northampton, Mass.: Printed by T. Watson Shepard, 1826);

History of the United States from the Discovery of the American Continent to the Present Time, 10 volumes, 1834–1874: volumes 1–2 (Boston: Charles Bowen / London: R. J. Kennett, 1834, 1837); volume 3 (Boston: Little, Brown, 1840); volumes 4–8, 10 (Boston: Little, Brown, 1852–1860, 1874); volume 9 (Boston: Little, Brown / London: Sampson Low, Son, & Marston, 1866); revised as *History of the United States of America from the Discovery of the Continent,* 6 volumes (Boston: Little, Brown, 1876; London: Macmillan, 1876; revised again, New York: Appleton, 1883–1885);

An Oration Delivered before the Democracy of Springfield and Neighboring Towns, July 4, 1836 (Springfield, Mass.: George & Charles Merriam, 1836);

Address at Hartford, before the Delegates to the Democratic Convention of the Young Men of Connecticut, on the Evening of February 18, 1840 (Boston: Office of the Bay State Democrat, 1840);

An Oration . . . Delivered at the Commemoration in Washington of the Death of Andrew Jackson, June 27, 1845 (N.p., 1845);

George Bancroft (photograph by Mathew Brady; Library of Congress)

Literary and Historical Miscellanies (New York: Harper, 1855);

On the Progress of Mankind and Reform (Liverpool: Printed by D. Marples, 1858);

Hon. George Bancroft's Oration, Pronounced in New York, April 25, 1865, at the Obsequies of Abraham Lincoln [and] *The Funeral Ode by William Cullen Bryant* (New York & Philadelphia: Schermerhorn, Bancroft, 1865);

In Memoriam of Abraham Lincoln, the Martyr President of the United States. Oration by the Hon. George Bancroft, the

Historian, at the Request of both Houses of Congress, in the Hall of the House of Representatives of the United States. On Monday, February 12, 1866 (Washington, D.C.: Printed by L. Towers, 1866); republished as *Abraham Lincoln. A Memorial Address, February 12th, 1866* (London: Stevens, 1866); republished as *Memorial Address on the Life and Character of Abraham Lincoln* (Washington, D.C.: Government Printing Office, 1866);

Bancroft's Letter to the Editors of the North American Review (Boston, 1867);

Joseph Reed: A Historical Essay (New York: W. J. Widdleton, 1867);

The History of the Formation of the Constitution of the United States of America, 2 volumes (New York: Appleton, 1882);

A Plea for the Constitution of the United States, Wounded in the House of its Guardians (New York: Harper, 1886);

Martin Van Buren to the End of His Public Career (New York: Harper, 1889);

History of the Battle of Lake Erie, and Miscellaneous Papers (New York: Bonner, 1891).

OTHER: *A Greek Grammar, Principally Abridged from That of Buttmann, for the Use of Schools,* edited by Bancroft (Boston: Cummings, Hilliard / Cambridge, Mass.: University Press, 1824);

The Latin Reader, From the Fifth German Edition. By Frederic Jacobs, edited by Bancroft (Northampton, Mass.: Printed by T. W. Shepard and sold by S. Butler, Northampton; Richardson & Lord, Boston; and Bliss & White, New York, 1825).

TRANSLATIONS: Arnold H. L. Heeren, *Reflections on the Politics of Ancient Greece* (Boston: Cummings, Hilliard / Cambridge, Mass.: University Press, Hilliard & Metcalf, 1824);

Heeren, *History of the States of Antiquity* (Northampton, Mass.: S. Butler / New York: G. & C. Carvill, 1828);

Heeren, *History of the Political System of Europe,* 2 volumes: volume 1 (Northampton, Mass.: S. Butler / New York: G. & C. Carvill, 1828); volume 2 (Northampton, Mass.: S. Butler / Boston: Richardson & Lord / New York: G. & C. Carvill, 1829).

SELECTED PERIODICAL PUBLICATIONS– UNCOLLECTED: "Schiller's Minor Poems," *North American Review,* 16 (October 1823): 268–280;

"Buttmann's *Greek Grammar,*" *North American Review,* 18 (January 1824): 99–105;

"Jacob's *Greek Reader,*" *North American Review,* 18 (April 1824): 280–284;

"Heeren's *Politics of Ancient Greece,*" *North American Review,* 18 (April 1824): 390–406;

"The Value of Classical Learning," *North American Review,* 19 (July 1824): 125–137;

"The Life and Genius of Goethe: Goethe's *Werke,*" *North American Review,* 19 (October 1824): 303–325;

"Herder's Writings," *North American Review,* 20 (January 1825): 138–147;

"Edward Everett's Orations," *New York Review* (25 October 1825): 333–341;

"German Literature," *American Quarterly Review,* 2 (September 1827): 171–186;

"German Literature," *American Quarterly Review,* 3 (March 1828): 150–173;

"German Literature," *American Quarterly Review,* 4 (September 1828): 157–190;

"The Bank of the United States," *North American Review,* 32 (January 1831): 21–64;

"Böckh's *Economy of Athens,*" *North American Review,* 32 (April 1831): 344–367;

"Slavery in Rome," *North American Review,* 39 (October 1834): 413–437;

"On the Progress of Civilization, or the Reasons Why the Natural Association of Men of Letters Is with the Democracy," *Boston Quarterly Review* (October 1838): 389–407;

"William Ellery Channing," *Democratic Review* (May 1843): 524–526;

"The Place of Abraham Lincoln in History," *Atlantic Magazine,* 15 (June 1865): 757–770;

"The Seventh Petition," *New Princeton Review,* 13 (May 1886): 342–345;

"On Self-Government," *Magazine of American History,* 15 (June 1886): 550–554.

George Bancroft is best remembered as a popular nineteenth-century historian. He led a complex life and played an important role in Transcendentalist reform movements. Although never formally part of the Transcendentalist group, he espoused and practiced a similar philosophy. While in college he started to follow in his father's footsteps and planned a career in the ministry. During this time he developed the view that all men can discover God's humanity and have an innate capacity for morality and reason. Although he did not become a clergy member, this sensibility became a part of his writing, teaching, and politics.

Bancroft's life was enriched by opportunities afforded him by his travels and friendships early in life. During his college career in Germany he traveled extensively and met many eminent American and European philosophers, politicians, and authors.

Bancroft's parents, Aaron and Lucretia Chandler Bancroft (from Russel Blaine Nye, George Bancroft: Brahmin Rebel, *1944)*

Soon after his return from Europe, he opened a boy's school based on German and Swiss educational principles. He believed in a child's innate morality, which reveals itself through a teacher's encouragement and guidance. Likewise, he thought that corporal punishment should be abolished because it relies upon external punishment rather than a child's reason and "inner light." Physical exercise and travel were also part of a child's moral education. He encouraged students to think critically and to become interested in a variety of subjects.

After an eight-year commitment to teaching, Bancroft began his long, more successful career as a politician and historian. He continually delivered orations and wrote articles but is perhaps most famous for his *History of the United States* series (1834–1874), which he wrote and revised throughout most of his lifetime. These history books, through an examination of American and colonial history, reflected his ardent belief in the continuity and importance of democracy, as well as his antislavery sentiments. Heavily influenced by German philosophers, Bancroft argued that the will and reason of the people would bring about the progress and unity of a nation. The decidedly American attitude that

progress is natural is a theme in nearly all of his writing. As a member of the Democratic Party he advocated limited government so that individual liberty could thrive. Slavery troubled this viewpoint, for, as Bancroft argued, it contradicted democratic principles and harmed the moral character of the state. Like many other Transcendentalists—such as Amos Bronson Alcott, William Ellery Channing, William Henry Furness, Ralph Waldo Emerson, Theodore Parker, and Henry David Thoreau—Bancroft supported the abolition movement.

George Bancroft was born 3 October 1800 in Worcester, Massachusetts, to the Reverend Aaron and Lucretia (Chandler) Bancroft. He was the eighth of thirteen children. His father was the first president of the American Unitarian Association. In a letter written in 1862 Bancroft reflected that his father's theology was "of New England origin, and, like that of so many others, was a logical consequence of the reaction against the severities of our Puritan fathers." Although Aaron Bancroft wrote more than thirty pamphlets advocating the new Unitarian movement, he was best known for his popular *Life of Washington* (1807).

Bancroft studied at Phillips Exeter Academy for two years before he began his college career at the age of thirteen at Harvard College, where he formed friendships with older, influential members of the university–President John T. Kirkland, Andrews Norton, and his Latin tutor, Edward Everett. Once he graduated from Harvard, Bancroft remained in Cambridge for another year to study theology. His advisers persuaded him to study at the University of Göttingen, Germany, in preparation for a career in the ministry. These men were the principal recipients of Bancroft's letters while he was in Göttingen (1818–1822) and traveling in Europe (1820–1822). Bancroft saw Everett as an intellectual role model, as he was among the first American scholars to travel and study in Germany. Everett, Joseph G. Cogswell, George Ticknor, and later, Bancroft, helped to bring German Romanticism into American Transcendental thinking, particularly the belief that nature offers the knowledge of a connection between the self and God's creations.

At Göttingen, Bancroft became a German scholar while studying philology, theology, and ancient languages such as Hebrew, Syriac, Greek, and Latin. He wrote to President Kirkland during January 1819: "The plan of life, which I have adopted, indicates very clearly that I must become, either an instructor at the University, or a clergyman, or set up a high school." Not surprisingly, Bancroft considered becoming a teacher, since during this time education reform was becoming a topic of debate and concern in the United States. Many reforms were later developed from European pedagogical theories. Bancroft became increasingly drawn toward teaching. In August 1819 he stated, "I would gladly be instrumental in the good cause of improving our institutions of education as it is our schools, which cry out most loudly for reformation."

Bancroft was also in the process of fashioning himself as a literary critic. In December 1818 he commented upon the German influence on American literature: "To think how nobly all good literature would thrive, if we could transport it to America, if we could engraft it on a healthy tree, if we could join it with religion, and at once enlighten and improve the understanding, and purify and elevate the heart." Bancroft valued European literature in terms of its influence on American literature. Later he argued even more stridently that American literature was new and progressing, while British literature was antiquated.

In 1819 Bancroft began to meet eminent Romantic scholars and authors. In October he met Johann Wolfgang von Goethe in Jena, where they discussed George Gordon, Lord Byron; Sir Walter Scott; Samuel Taylor Coleridge; and Immanuel Kant. Bancroft later published a paper in the *North American*

Review, "The Life and Genius of Goethe" (1824), to which Goethe responded by remarking on Bancroft's "youthfully cheerful enjoyment in writing."

Bancroft walked extensively, and he described the landscape of his walks in Romantic terms. These walks were part of a literary exercise of experiencing the sublime, which was probably in anticipation of his first major publication, a book of poems. Eight months after his meeting with Goethe, Bancroft took an expedition through the Harz Mountains. He wrote to Norton, "You may have heard of the Harz as famous for mines, and for picturesque scenery. I found the views often charming, very pleasant, very lovely, but I have not yet seen anything answering my notions of the sublime." His notions of and attention to landscape aesthetics came from his contact with German and British Romantic literature. He desired to transmit these literary values and tropes through his own poetry, or more modestly, through his later translations of German literature.

Bancroft completed his doctorate at Göttingen in 1820. That September he began studies in Berlin for a year with scholars such as George Hegel, Friedrich Wolf, Arnold H. L. Heeren, Gottfried von Herder, and Friedrich Schleiermacher. These scholars emphasized man's inherent goodness and perfectibility, and the will and reason of the people, which would bring about the progress and unity of the state. Bancroft, too, came to describe democracy this way.

Bancroft was increasingly resolved to become a teacher and to reform American educational systems. In November 1820, while in Berlin, he remarked, "At Göttingen the whole tendency of the courses is, to make the students learned, to fill their memories with matters of fact; here the grand aim is to make them think." Reflection and critical thinking, rather than rote memory, became an integral part of Bancroft's educational philosophy. Most likely, his concentration on educational reform came from studying under Schleiermacher, whose educational philosophy emphasized the importance of an academic curriculum as a combination of the arts, science, and physical exercise. Under Schleiermacher's tutelage Bancroft learned the educational philosophy that strongly influenced the 1823 prospectus for his Northampton School venture.

In January 1821 Bancroft's scholarship was renewed, so he remained in Europe for another year, visiting France, Switzerland, and Italy. While in Paris he met Washington Irving, Marquis de Lafayette, and Albert Gallatin. During this time Bancroft began working on his first major publication, *Poems* (1823). This collection represents his only literary venture and is a poetical journal of his European travels.

Round Hill, the school in Northampton, Massachusetts, that Bancroft and Joseph G. Cogswell opened in October 1823

One important influence upon this volume was his meeting with Byron in 1822 at Leghorn, Italy. According to Bancroft's authorized biographer, Mark A. DeWolfe Howe, "The influence of Byron is so apparent in them [Bancroft's poems] that one can hardly help asking whether the young traveler, in his more complacent moments, may not have aspired to become an American Childe Harold." Bancroft and Byron discussed Bancroft's visit with Goethe and the influence of German literature, particularly *Faust* (1808, 1832), upon Romantic poetry. Bancroft later defended Byron as a Christian because it was important to Bancroft that poets be moral and religious.

Religious themes were central to Bancroft's poetry. The opening poem of the book, "Expectation," has the Romantic theme of a traveler who leaves the comforts of home only to discover that his hopes are dashed through life experience: "The visions of young Promise fade; / Ne'er wilt thou find the happy spot, / Where joy her changeless home has made." Discovering that pleasures are not earthly, the traveler thus embarks "Still onward in the search for bliss. / There surely are other worlds than this." Earthly pleasures are fleeting, destructive, and unpromising, whereas the divine offers another world.

The poems written in Switzerland during September 1821 include a series of addresses to various natural and spiritual personae. Some poems are dia-

logues with Mother Nature; others, with the Father in Heaven. Like the traveler in "Expectation," the speaker is generally a weary pilgrim seeking rest, as in "The Valley Above Inden": "Pale Wanderer! hast thou found a friend at last / To give thee shelter, when the tempest blows? / Through pathless skies thy wanderings now are past; / Give Nature thanks; 'tis she that sends repose." In this poem Nature both offers comfort and is the path to the divine, both common Romantic themes.

After writing some verse, in 1821 Bancroft described his poetry as an academic, rather than a literary, exercise. He wrote in December:

> Wrote some verses . . . this I did only as an exercise; and mean often to make verses, though I know they will for the most part be poor ones. But I do it only as a useful task, a good method of gaining command of language and learning to attend to the nice construction of the lines of our harmonious English poets.

Yet, his poetry did make a public appearance. He first read the longest poem of the collection, "Pictures of Rome," to the Phi Beta Kappa Society at Harvard in 1822. A reviewer attributed Bancroft's decision to publish his poems in 1823 to this successful reading.

Indicative of Bancroft's religious beliefs is the "Invocation" of the 1822 series of poems about Italy, in which God and man are spiritually intertwined: "Father and son meld / How mildly beams a father's face! / How true and tender his embrace! / Heaven blends the hearts of sire and son, Their kindred souls are joined in one." These lines about the connected, kindred relationship men have with God are recalled throughout Bancroft's orations and theological arguments.

Most of Bancroft's poems involve religious themes and issues; yet, he grew dissatisfied with the literary exercise, because it did not reflect enough religious devotion. He wrote from Rome on 1 January 1822: "I long to be deeply devout: but the full and internal devotion cannot be fully gained by a wanderer." Bancroft struggled with a paradox: he felt the pressure from home to become a sober, resolute Unitarian clergyman at the same time he realized his own restless aspirations to gain a public, perhaps literary, life.

Soon after its publication *Poems* was reviewed in 1823 by *The Christian Disciple and Theological Review,* a prominent Unitarian journal in which much significant Transcendentalist work was featured. Throughout the review, different qualities of Bancroft's collection are discussed; the reviewer then says, "What we love best, however, to praise in this volume is the moral beauty of it; its pure, affectionate and devout spirit." The reviewer also notes Bancroft's calm contemplation of feelings and contrasts this quiet emotion with the more-passionate qualities of British Romantic poets: "The sentiments are throughout natural and simply expressed without agitation or metaphysics." Bancroft echoes such sentiment in 1827 when he claims that the poet is responsible for seeing "amidst superstition and untruth the nobility of human nature and its connection with God." Although his poetry was well received by his contemporaries, later in life Bancroft made efforts to destroy the remaining copies of *Poems* so that he would be remembered for his prose work.

Just before Bancroft returned to America he remarked, "'Tis but within a few months, that I have learnt 'the necessity of self-reliance.' . . . For our faith and our virtue we must not depend upon any external impulse, but draw it from a source, which is always ours." Although Emerson's famous essay "Self-Reliance" was not published until 1841, Bancroft's sentiment anticipated that particular Transcendental mood of individualism. Bancroft believed in self-culture—an individual's ability to develop spiritual and moral senses internally, rather than from an "external impulse," from which faith and virtue come.

In August 1822 Bancroft returned to the United States to tutor Harvard students in Greek. Also during this time he accepted many invitations to deliver orations throughout Boston. His attempts at preaching lasted only a year. In a few short months he became dissatisfied with tutoring: "For myself, I have found College a sickening and wearisome place. . . . My state has been nothing but trouble, trouble, trouble, and I am so heartily glad that the end of the year is coming so soon." In December he decided to open a school along with another scholar of German, Joseph G. Cogswell. Both Cogswell and Bancroft hoped to instill methods of learning they had been exposed to while in Germany and Switzerland. They opened the school in Northampton, calling it the Round Hill experiment.

At Round Hill, students were encouraged to study foreign languages, to travel, and to exercise. As Cogswell and Bancroft state in their *Prospectus,* "we would encourage them to go abroad and learn to feel the beauty of creation and the benevolence of its Author," an attitude perhaps derivative of Bancroft's own experience abroad at Göttingen. The concept of studying abroad, however, was controversial. In a letter written during February 1765, John Adams had argued that American students who were educated at European universities could "scarcely read" afterward; he defended the innate intelligence of the American people and noted the need for a school in every town. Bancroft was well aware of Adams's influential viewpoint because he had met Adams, through Norton, in 1818 just before leaving for Göttingen. Norton asked Adams what he thought of Bancroft's studying in Germany. Bancroft recalled that Adams "did not omit expressing his opinion dogmatically that it was best for Americans to be educated in their own country." Also, Cogswell and Bancroft knew that the idea of citizenship was tied into these arguments against traveling abroad, so they proposed to "educate not for an ideal world, but for the world as it is. We would make not laborious students only, but faithful and useful citizens."

Bancroft opposed corporal punishment because it relied upon external punishment rather than a student's innate moral sense or reason. He described his discipline methods as parental: "Keeping this principle in mind, we shall endeavour to govern by persuasion and persevering kindness." This principle seeks to bring out a child's innate morality by encouragement. In 1824 Bancroft began writing an article against corporal punishment, never published. He later referred to his background in Germany and the concept of the gymnasium to write an article on the importance of physical exercise in forming a child's moral education.

Although Cogswell's and Bancroft's viewpoints basically came from their experiences in Germany and Switzerland, their ideas were not unlike those of Transcendentalist educational reformers such as

*First page from "Of the Liberal Education of Boys," an unfinished essay Bancroft started while teaching at Round Hill
(New York Public Library, Astor, Lenox and Tilden Foundations)*

Bancroft in his mid fifties (portrait by Samuel Lawrence;
Worcester Art Museum)

Bancroft was a skilled translator and book editor. In 1824 he published a translation of Heeren's *Reflections on the Politics of Ancient Greece*. He also published *A Greek Grammar* (1824) and *The Latin Reader* (1825), and prepared an unpublished German reader (1826). He wrote regularly for the *North American Review,* contributing translations, book reviews, and essays on classical and European scholarship. The *North American Review* featured his controversial paper "The Bank of the United States," in which he supported Andrew Jackson's effort to decentralize the banking system of the United States. Bancroft's supportive essay was so important it was later reprinted as a pamphlet. His marriage to Sarah H. Dwight on 1 March 1827 allowed him to become temporarily involved with her family's business, familiarizing him with banking. "The Bank of the United States" won him the attention of Jackson and several Democratic Party leaders, thus beginning his career in politics. His Jacksonian politics and Transcendentalist beliefs are continuous. Both philosophies advocated limited government, individualism, and the virtues of the common man. Furthermore, Jackson promised a limited government under which individual liberty could thrive.

Jared Sparks, the editor at the time of the *North American Review,* had met Bancroft while at Harvard, and the two maintained a correspondence until 1830. Sparks often disagreed with Bancroft's views, and Bancroft often disagreed with Sparks's editorial license. Although throughout their correspondence Bancroft frequently displayed an unpleasant, fastidious side, Sparks added his own ending to "The Bank of the United States" article. These types of disagreements led by 1834 to the disintegration of their correspondence and the cessation of Bancroft's contributions.

Bancroft's teaching career also disintegrated during this period. After teaching for eight years he abandoned the Round Hill experiment. As he reflected in a letter on 18 January 1832, "It was an unwise thing in me to have made myself a school-master: that was a kind of occupation, to which I was not peculiarly adapted, and in which many of inferior abilities and attainments could have succeeded as well." After his educational experiment, Bancroft moved to the most successful part of his career, politics and history writing.

Bancroft's first published statement against slavery was in his 1831 review of August Böckh's *Public Economy of Athens,* in which he argues that slavery caused the collapse of the city-states. That same year, William Lloyd Garrison founded *The Liberator* in Boston. Bancroft argued in his orations, histories,

Bronson Alcott. Alcott, in his *Observations on the Principles and Methods of Infant Instruction* (1830), also advocated physical exercise: "By encouraging the free and natural activity of the body, the functions on which intellectual energy and happiness depend, are invigorated and most effectively prepared for the lessons of instruction." Like Bancroft, Alcott opposed corporal punishment in favor of appealing to the student's reason and higher moral sense.

During this time as a schoolteacher, Bancroft delivered many orations. His ardent belief in democracy, his antislavery position, and his fierce theological opinions especially came through in his orations. In 1826 Bancroft delivered his first oration at the Northampton Fourth of July celebration and stated, "The government is a democracy, a determined, uncompromising democracy; administered immediately by the people. . . . The popular voice is all powerful with us; this is our oracle; this, we acknowledge is the voice of God." In the popular voice, or the public, is truth.

and miscellaneous essays that slavery undermines progress and democracy.

In 1832 Bancroft published the first volume of the *History of the United States* series. These books were incredibly popular; the first volume was reprinted ten times by 1844. In his histories Bancroft represented the United States as consistently democratic, argued for national centralization, and advocated an antislavery position. He argued that the colonists maintained slavery only for economic and political reasons but were morally opposed to it. England supported the slavery system while "The English continental colonies, in aggregate, were always opposed to the African slave trade." Bancroft believed that slavery opposed progress, challenged national unity, and was economically devastating. His plea to end slavery in the United States was encouraged by the Abolition Act of 1833 in England, which ended slavery in Great Britain.

In 1837 Bancroft's first wife died, never having recovered from her last pregnancy. Leaving his three children with the Dwights and his sister Mary in Springfield, Bancroft made a long trip to Montreal and the mountains of Canada. During the same year the second volume of his history was published. On 16 August 1838 Bancroft, thinking he needed someone to look after his children and his household, married Elizabeth (Davis) Bliss, a widow with two sons. The third volume of his history appeared in 1840. The first three volumes of the series covered colonization. The next several years were absorbed in political activity. Bancroft's next burst of productivity in writing his histories was in the early 1850s.

Despite the popularity of the histories, there were mixed reviews of the volumes. Everett faithfully reviewed the first volume, predicting that it would "last while the memory of America lasts . . . and . . . will instantly take its place among the classics of our language." On 2 October 1837 Emerson remarked on the second volume that one "objection to the book is the insertion of boyish hurra every now & then for each State in turn." Other critics focused upon later editions, which were without footnotes. Thomas Carlyle remarked, "I should say . . . that you [Bancroft] were too didactic, went too much into the origin of things generally known, into the praise of things generally known, into the praise of things only partially praisable, only slightly important." Scholars of today have responses similar to those of John Franklin Jameson, who in 1891 criticized the series for its "exuberant confidence, its uncritical self-laudation, its optimistic hopes." In Bancroft's defense, Jameson suggests that "the historian caught, and with sincere and enthusiastic conviction repeated

to the American people the things which they were saying and thinking concerning themselves."

Bancroft took on an active role in the Democratic Party from 1834 to 1849. He was the editor of a newspaper called the *Baystate Democrat,* a campaigner, and a candidate for the legislature and for governor. He built credibility as a Democratic politician, eventually attaining a position as the Secretary of the Navy in President James Knox Polk's cabinet. Bancroft's most significant accomplishment in this position was to establish the United States Naval Academy at Annapolis. Consistent with his educational philosophy, he also outlawed corporal punishment.

During his political career Bancroft gave speeches expressing his patriotism and ardent belief in democracy. For example, in August 1835 he delivered an oration before the Adelphi Society of Williamstown, "The Office of the People in Art, Government, and Religion." Advocating Herder's philosophy that all men could discover God's humanity, Bancroft argued throughout this oration for man's innate sense of morality and the divine.

The speech opens with an argument for an external and internal sense of the world. This internal sense is one's connection with God and is instinctual. An individual's intuition, rather than study, leads to morality and a sense of the divine. Creative expression also comes from each person's intuition, and artistic capacity derives from everyday life: "The Indian mother, on the borders of Hudson's Bay, decorates her manufactures with ingenious devices and lovely colors, prompted by the same instinct which guided the pencil and mixed the colors of Raphael." Aesthetics and notions of taste come from the public. Bancroft describes the collective as wiser than the learned scholar. As Emerson later argued in *Representative Men* (1850), Bancroft asserts that "Every beneficent revolution in letters has the character of popularity; every great reform among authors has sprung from the power of the people in its influence on the development and activity of mind."

In 1838 Bancroft republished this oration in the October edition of the *Boston Quarterly Review,* titling it "On the Progress of Civilization, or the Reasons Why the Natural Association of Men of Letters Is with the Democracy." In this version he concentrated on describing the emergence of an American literature as opposed to a European one: "The absence of the prejudices of the old world leaves us here the opportunity of consulting the independent truth; and man is left to apply the instinct of freedom to every social relation and public interest." This statement asserts the superiority of American literature, for it is new and progresses, whereas British literature is part of the

Pages from the first draft for Bancroft's History of the United States *(1834–1874) and a secretary's transcription of the original draft with corrections by Bancroft (New York Public Library, Astor, Lenox and Tilden Foundations)*

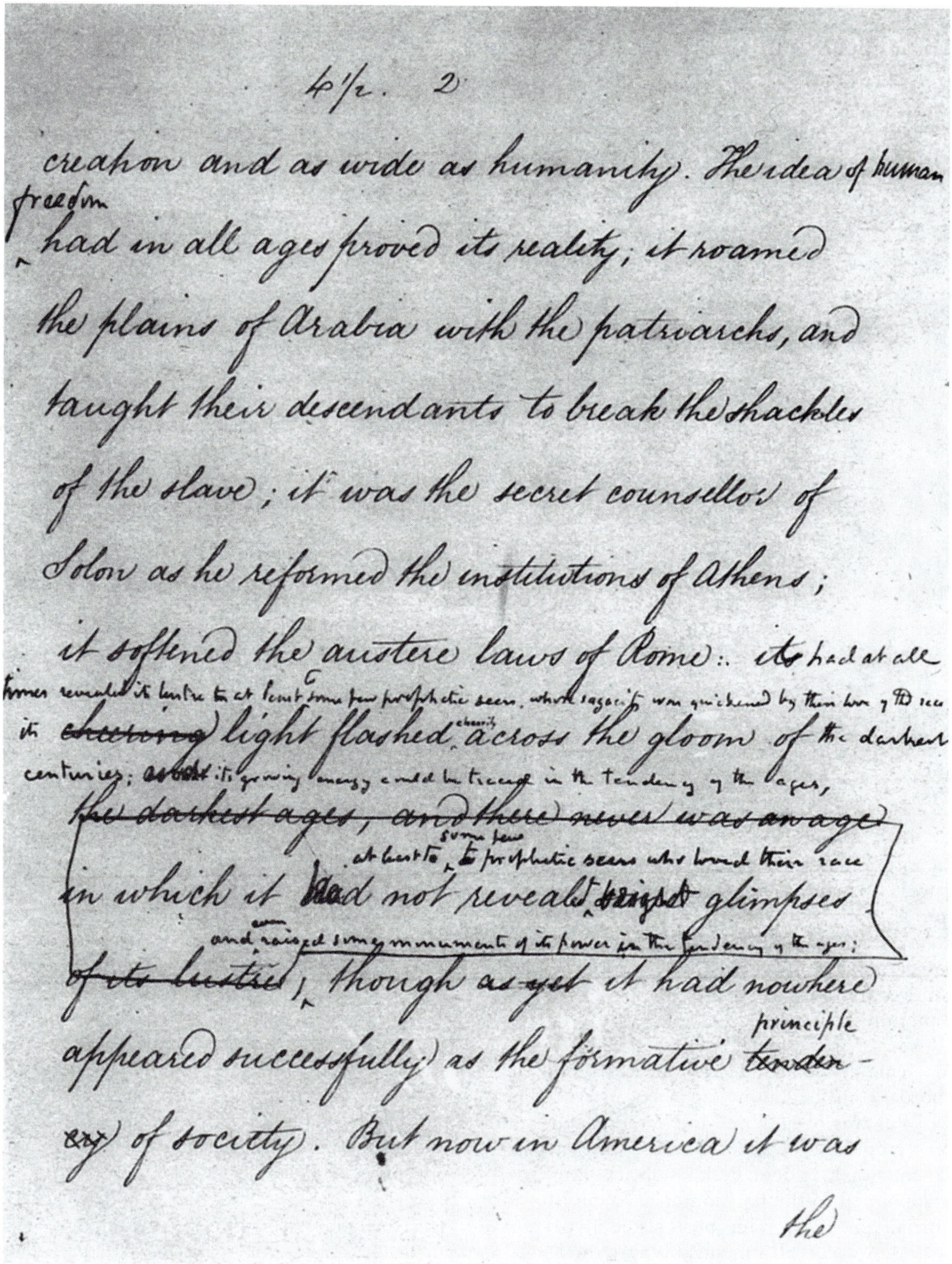

4½.   2

creation and as wide as humanity. The idea of human
freedom
had in all ages proved its reality; it roamed

the plains of Arabia with the patriarchs, and

taught their descendants to break the shackles

of the slave; it was the secret counsellor of

Solon as he reformed the institutions of Athens;

it softened the austere laws of Rome:. its had at all
times revealed it lustre to at least some few prophetic seers, which sagacity was quickened by their love of the race
its ~~shivering~~ light flashed cheerily across the gloom of the darkest
centuries; ~~as well~~ its growing energy could be traced in the tendency of the ages,
~~the darkest ages, and there never was an age~~
                        some few
          at least to, to prophetic seers who loved their race
in which it ~~had~~ not reveald ~~bright~~ glimpses
                atom
          and raised some monuments of its power in the tendency of the ages;
of its ~~lustre~~, though as yet it had nowhere
                                              principle
appeared successfully) as the formative ~~tenden~~ -

cy of society. But now in America it was

                                              the

Bancroft's second wife, Elizabeth Bliss Bancroft, whom he married in 1838 (photograph from the studio of Mathew Brady)

courage and like the republic. A republic or an abyss, no other choice, a republic or civil war: a republic or the ruin of France."

Between 1852 and 1860 Bancroft wrote usually for fourteen hours a day, publishing the five volumes of history that covered the American Revolution. Six years later he published the ninth volume of the series. This prolific period can be attributed to Bancroft's use of British archives during his time as a foreign minister; he had access at that time to significant and otherwise inaccessible accounts of American history.

In 1854 Bancroft delivered an oration to the New York Historical Society, "The Necessity, the Reality, and the Promise of the Progress of the Human Race." This oration reflected his belief in progress and the interconnected relationship between God and man. Throughout the oration he connected the advances in the sciences to moral progress: "The progress of man consists in this, that he himself arrives at the perception of truth. The Divine mind, which is its source, left it to be discovered, appropriated and developed by finite creatures." This moral progress is not dependent upon education but comes from the heart. All men possess reason and are able to perceive truth. God should not be archetypal, abstract, or distant; rather he should be living flesh, "indwelling in man." Bancroft further maintained, "The reciprocal relation between God and humanity constitutes the UNITY of the race."

Bancroft believed ardently in the social progress resulting from democracy. His placement of women in this scheme, however, is fairly conventional. For Bancroft and many others in the nineteenth century women were "emblems of beauty." Their presence "in this briery world is a lily among thorns, whose smile is pleasant like the light of morning, and whose eye is the gate of heaven." Woman is depicted as idealized, moral grandeur, rather than being granted a public role. Although the progress of liberty has "made her less conspicuous," it has "redeemed her into the possession of the full dignity of her nature," which, of course, is in the domestic sphere. Democracy and liberty have placed women even further within the private sphere. Bancroft maintains the separate sphere of philosophy against which many feminists, most notably Margaret Fuller, argued.

In February 1866 Bancroft delivered to Congress his address on Lincoln to Congress, which was an historical account of slavery and President Abraham Lincoln's legacy. Bancroft, like many other Northern Democrats, had been concerned about whether or not Lincoln was equal to the task of abolishing slavery and preserving the Union. Not feeling confident about Lincoln's presidency, Bancroft had

past. Literature may have begun in Britain, but it has moved west to America, for the "mind becomes universal property; the poem, that is invented on the soil of England, finds its response on the shores of lake Erie and the banks of Missouri, and is admired near the sources of the Ganges."

Bancroft was the acting secretary of war in May 1845, during which time he signed the order that allowed General Zachary Taylor to go beyond the Texas border, thus beginning the Mexican War. The Mexican War was not favored in New England, and Bancroft's popularity waned. Because he acted in accordance with President Polk's policies, however, he was appointed to the position of U.S. minister to Great Britain in 1846. This post lasted two short years, with few accomplishments, because the Democrats lost the 1848 presidential election. Once his post in Great Britain ended, Bancroft went to Paris, where he became sympathetic to the Revolution of 1848. This event further confirmed his ardent belief in democracy: "The Bourgeoisie have recovered

Bancroft at home in Washington, D.C., where he lived from 1874 until his death in 1891

written to his wife, Elizabeth, in September of 1861: "We suffer for want of an organizing mind at the head of the government. We have a president without brains, and a cabinet whose personal views outweigh Patriotism." This scathing criticism of Lincoln came from Bancroft's strong desire and impatience to see slavery ended quickly and completely. Bancroft and Lincoln subsequently became acquaintances after Lincoln consulted Bancroft on historical questions. Bancroft's passionate defense of the martyred president dramatically reversed his earlier views of the man.

The opening lines of the *Memorial Address* on Lincoln use natural metaphors to contrast British and American forms of government. Using images of soil and expansive landscape, Bancroft argues that liberty and democracy can take root whereas monarchy and aristocracy cannot. This poetic opening reminds the audience that democracy is natural and divine, a logic resembling that of Manifest Destiny. Yet, slavery disrupted this harmony and natural order: "There remained an unconfessed consciousness that the system of bondage was wrong, and a restless memory that it was at variance with the true American tradition." As in the histories, Bancroft argues that "The monarchy of the English had fastened upon us slavery which did not disappear with independence." Consistent with the natural metaphors to describe democracy, Bancroft characterizes Lincoln as "a child of nature, a child of the West, a

child of America." Lincoln's unfaltering belief in democracy restored the people's faith in democracy and ended slavery.

In 1867 President Andrew Johnson appointed Bancroft the U.S. minister to Prussia. Bancroft and his wife lived in Berlin until 1874. They then settled in Washington, D.C., for the remainder of his life. In 1874, shortly after their return from Berlin, Bancroft completed the tenth, and final, volume of the histories. Following the publication of this volume, he revised and condensed all of the versions into six volumes. This six-volume edition appeared in 1876 and was extremely popular. In 1876 it sold eighteen thousand copies, and four years later, nearly ten thousand. In 1882 Bancroft published a similar series, a two-volume set called *The History of the Formation of the Constitution of the United States of America*.

One of Bancroft's last publications was his 1886 essay "The Seventh Petition" in the *New Princeton Review*. In this essay he revealed his skills as a translator and theologian. He argued over the translation of the phrase "Deliver Us From Evil" in recent versions of the Bible. A contemporary translator had changed this line to read "Deliver us from the evil one." Bancroft was outraged, because for him this word choice was not Christian, but "It is giving up a universal religion, an eternal religion, a religion that dates from the beginning–the Christian religion–for a poor sort of philosophy, which believes in two warring powers eternally ajar, with no decisive superiority on either side." Rather than believing in opposing forces of good and evil, Bancroft, like many other American Transcendentalists, argued for a consistently moral and perfect divinity and humanity.

George Bancroft was a prolific, diligent writer and reformer, even near the end of his life. When Bancroft was close to ninety years old, Oliver Wendell Holmes wrote admiringly, "You must be made of iron or vulcanized india-rubber, or some such compound of resistance and elasticity." After his wife died in March 1886, Bancroft lived with his children in Washington, D.C. When Bancroft died on 17 January 1891, President Benjamin Harrison ordered that the flags in Washington be kept at half-mast until Bancroft's burial in Worcester, Massachusetts.

Letters:

John Spencer Bassett, ed., "The Correspondence of George Bancroft and Jared Sparks, 1823–1832," *Smith College Studies in History,* 2 (January 1917): 67–143.

Biographies:

Mark A. DeWolfe Howe, *The Life and Letters of George Bancroft,* 2 volumes (New York: Scribners, 1908);

Russel Blaine Nye, *George Bancroft: Brahmin Rebel* (New York: Knopf, 1944).

References:

L. H. Butterfield, ed., *Diary and Autobiography of John Adams,* volume 1 (Cambridge, Mass.: Harvard University Press, 1961);

John Franklin Jameson, *The History of Historical Writing in America* (Boston & New York: Houghton Mifflin, 1891);

Orie William Long, *Literary Pioneers; Early American Explorers of European Culture* (Cambridge, Mass.: Harvard University Press, 1935);

Perry Miller, *The Transcendentalists: An Anthology* (Cambridge, Mass.: Harvard University Press, 1950);

Richard C. Vitzthum, *The American Compromise: Theme and Method in the Histories of Bancroft, Parkman, and Adams* (Norman: University of Oklahoma Press, 1974).

Papers:

The Massachusetts Historical Society, the New York Public Library, and the American Antiquarian Society house the major collections of George Bancroft's papers.

Catharine Beecher

(6 September 1800 – 12 May 1878)

Barbara Downs Wojtusik

See also the Beecher entry in *DLB 1: The American Renaissance in New England.*

BOOKS: *Suggestions Respecting Improvements in Education, Presented to the Trustees of the Hartford Female Seminary* (Hartford: Packard & Butler, 1829);

The Elements of Mental and Moral Philosophy, Founded upon Experience, Reason, and the Bible (Hartford, 1831);

Arithmetic Simplified (Hartford: D. F. Robinson, 1832);

Primary Geography for Children, on an Improved Plan, by Catharine Beecher and Harriet Beecher (Cincinnati: Corey & Fairbanks, 1833);

An Essay on the Education of Female Teachers (New York: Van Nostrand & Dwight, 1835);

The Lyceum Arithmetic (Boston: W. Peirce, 1835);

Letters on the Difficulties of Religion (Hartford: Belknap & Hammersley, 1836);

An Essay on Slavery and Abolitionism with Reference to the Duty of American Females (Philadelphia: Henry Perkins / Boston: Perkins & Marvin, 1837);

The Moral Instructor for Schools and Families: Containing Lessons on the Duties of Life, Arranged for Study and Recitation, Also Designed as a Reading Book for Schools (Cincinnati: Truman & Smith, 1838; revised, 1838);

A Treatise on Domestic Economy for the Use of Young Ladies at Home and at School (Boston: Marsh, Capen, Lyon & Webb, 1841; revised edition, Boston: T. H. Webb, 1842);

Letters to Persons Who Are Engaged in Domestic Service (New York: Leavitt & Trow, 1842);

The Duty of American Women to Their Country (New York: Harper, 1845);

The Evils Suffered by American Women and American Children: The Causes and the Remedy (New York: Harper, 1846);

Miss Beecher's Domestic Receipt Book: Designed as a Supplement to Her Treatise on Domestic Economy (New York: Harper, 1846);

An Address to the Protestant Clergy of the United States (New York: Harper, 1846);

Letter to Benevolent Ladies in the United States (New York, 1849);

Catharine Beecher

Truth Stranger than Fiction: A Narrative of Recent Transactions Involving Inquiries in Regard to the Principles of Honor, Truth, and Justice Which Obtain in a Distinguished American University (New York: Printed for the author, 1850; Boston: Phillips, Sampson, 1850);

The True Remedy for the Wrongs of Women (Boston: Phillips, Sampson, 1851);

Letters to the People on Health and Happiness (New York: Harper, 1855);

Physiology and Calisthenics. For Schools and Families (New York: Harper, 1856);

Common Sense Applied to Religion; or, The Bible and the People (New York: Harper, 1857);

An Appeal to the People on Behalf of Their Rights as Authorized Interpreters of the Bible (New York: Harper, 1860);

Religious Training of Children in the School, the Family, and the Church (New York: Harper, 1864);

The American Woman's Home, or Principles of Domestic Science, by Beecher and Harriet Beecher Stowe (New York: J. B. Ford, 1869); revised as *The New Housekeeper's Manual: Embracing a New Revised Edition of the American Woman's Home; or Principles of Domestic Science. Being a Guide to Economical, Healthful, Beautiful, and Christian Homes* (New York: J. B. Ford, 1873);

Principles of Domestic Science; As Applied to the Duties and Pleasures of the Home. A Text Book for the Use of Young Ladies in Schools, Seminaries, and Colleges, by Beecher and Stowe (New York: J. B. Ford, 1870);

Woman Suffrage and Woman's Profession (Hartford: Brown & Gross, 1871);

Woman's Profession as Mother and Educator with Views in Opposition to Woman's Suffrage (Philadelphia & Boston: George Maclean, 1872);

Miss Beecher's Housekeeper and Healthkeeper (New York: Harper, 1873);

Educational Reminiscences and Suggestions (New York: J. B. Ford, 1874).

OTHER: "Fanny Moreland; or, the Use and Abuse of the Risibles," in *Christian Keepsake and Missionary Annual* (Philadelphia: Marshall, 1843);

The Biographical Remains of Rev. George Beecher, Late Pastor of a Church in Chillicote, Ohio, and Former Pastor of a Church in Rochester, New York, edited by Catharine Beecher (New York: Leavitt, Trow / Boston: Crocker & Brewster, 1844).

SELECTED PERIODICAL PUBLICATIONS–UNCOLLECTED: "The Evening Cloud," *Christian Spectator,* 2 (February 1820): 81;

"Female Education," *American Journal of Education,* 2 (April 1827): 219–223, (May 1827): 264–269;

"An Essay on Cause and Effect in Connexion with the Difference of Fatalism and Free Agency," *American Biblical Repository,* 2 (October 1839): 381–408.

Catharine Beecher was one of the first women in America to advocate the acceptance of women as public-school teachers. Through her many books, articles, and lectures, she promoted the position and education of women in the nineteenth century. She proposed that women were intellectually equal and morally superior to men, and more compassionate and understanding than men. Women, said Beecher, have a natural affinity for children. Therefore, she contended that women would be bet-

ter teachers. Once women were properly educated, they could have both a local and a national influence on society. Beecher strongly asserted, however, that women could flourish only through achievements in their own sphere of domesticity. That is, women dominated in the home because of the God-given virtues that characterized them as women. Hence, success in the classroom would be possible only if women created environments based on the conditions of the ideal American home. Furthermore, women must be properly educated on a scale with men. Beecher foresaw the creation of educational facilities for women to equal Harvard, Yale, and Brown. She also expected female teachers to be rewarded with sufficient salaries and professional recognition. Although these goals were not met in her lifetime, her attempts improved public education, produced superior textbooks, and introduced educational innovations such as integrated curriculum, smaller classes, ability grouping, gymnastics, student teachers, guidance programs, and student government.

Catharine Esther Beecher was born into a home already destined for fame. She was the oldest daughter and child of Lyman and Roxana (Foote) Beecher in East Hampton, Long Island, where her father was an extremely successful Calvinist revival preacher. Both parents had been born in Connecticut and were descended from original settlers of the 1630s. When Catharine was nine, the family returned to Connecticut, where Lyman Beecher established a parish in Litchfield, a Federalist stronghold. In 1810 she was enrolled in Miss Pierce's school of Litchfield, one of the most prominent girls' schools in the nation. By 1816 Catharine had seven siblings. Edward and William were the oldest; George was nine years younger than Catharine, followed by Mary, who was five years younger, and then Harriet, Henry Ward, and Charles, who were the babies. A year later, however, Roxana died of consumption, and Catharine withdrew from school in order to help with the children and the home. One year after that Lyman Beecher became engaged and soon married to Harriet Porter of Boston. In 1821 Catharine Beecher accepted a position teaching needlework, drawing, and painting in a female academy located in New London, Connecticut. The following year she became engaged to Alexander Metcalf Fisher, a well-known professor of natural philosophy at Yale. Fisher, however, was killed when a ship upon which he was sailing to England crashed into cliffs on the west coast of Ireland.

The death of Alexander Fisher catapulted Beecher into public attention and inadvertently charted the course of her career. After the death of her fiancé, Beecher was invited by Fisher's family to visit with them in Franklin, Massachusetts. During this time Beecher agreed to tutor Fisher's adult brother Willard. For help in teaching science

Beecher's birthplace in East Hampton, New York

to Willard, Beecher often wrote to her brother Edward at Yale for information. Soon she requested that Alexander Fisher's scientific papers be sent to Franklin as well. Despite the objections of the school, Fisher's things were returned to the family, and Beecher had them at her disposal. Among them she discovered several math books, including one Fisher had written at age eleven. These books whetted her desire for knowledge and encouraged her to attempt methods of imparting knowledge to others, particularly the young. In 1824, with the assistance of her father, she established her first school, the Hartford Female Seminary, in Hartford, Connecticut.

Catharine Beecher's school was an enormous success, enabling her to devote herself to writing articles and books on educational reform. In her first published article, "Female Education" (1827), Beecher proclaimed that women's education had been too much involved with the ornaments of the mind. She asserted, "A lady should study not to *shine* but to *act*." Action was to be the goal of female education, but action beginning in the female spheres of domesticity and proper decorum. Education should, according to Beecher, improve conduct and, therefore, enhance the natural qualities of a woman. Hence, the truly educated woman could be an influence for good in society. In order to train women properly in the use of knowledge, however, reforms in female education

were necessary. Paramount to successful learning were the construction and staffing of facilities and a structured course of study.

In 1831 Beecher stated in *The Elements of Mental and Moral Philosophy, Founded upon Experience, Reason, and the Bible* the three themes that directed her philosophy of female education. These ideas centered on salvation of the soul, reformation of social forms, and women's roles in these activities. In Beecher's perception salvation was the domain of women, who would negate the image of an angry God and replace it with the picture of the loving mother. Women would become the moral leaders, and the home, the center of righteousness. To Beecher good character ensured salvation, and good character was the essence of the properly educated woman. All worthy leaders, in Beecher's view, became so by submerging personal will for the general good. Self-sacrifice was a quality generally associated with women; therefore, women, when properly trained, were born leaders. Overt behavior is often the measure of morality. Hence, the genteel woman was the model of virtue. Her family was the basic unit of society, and the home was the temple of salvation. By the 1840s most Americans shared Beecher's values.

Society accepted that women were the natural heads of the household and moral guides, but Beecher asserted that they needed special education to fulfill these roles. Therefore, she proposed a new school that would embrace

Hartford Female Seminary, the school Beecher founded in 1824

her moral philosophy and offer the proper environment. Instead of a private school for thirty to forty girls, she envisioned an endowed seminary housing 140 young women. Beecher felt that two elements were essential for this facility. First, the educational focus must be on the formation of moral character, with one well-qualified person in charge of that department. Second, a residential dwelling must be built for the students and faculty where they would live in a family atmosphere. At the time no schools supplied housing for their students as it was considered more efficient and less costly to place students in local homes. For this reason—and because Beecher's first choice for school head, Zilpah Grant, the associate principal of Mary Lyon's Ipswich Academy, refused the offer, stating that the endeavor was too worldly—Beecher was unable to raise the $20,000 needed for the school and soon went into a deep depression.

During Beecher's convalescence, her younger sister Harriet took over the leadership of the Hartford Female Seminary. Catharine soon returned, however, to Hartford with new ideas for a school. She planned now to establish a school for young women who upon graduation would begin their own schools dedicated to advancing moral character and the roles of women. She sought teachers who were willing to devote three years of their lives to this cause. In the 1830s teaching was not a female profession. Beecher was the first person to envision teaching as a profession and a respectable and profitable alternative to marriage. As a rapidly expanding population demanded more teachers and a booming industrial economy lured males into higher-wage employment, Beecher's ideas gained more attention. With the expansion of the West, even more schools and teachers were deemed necessary. Beecher thought it was a fortuitous time to take action.

In 1832 Beecher began an educational career in Cincinnati that lasted for more than ten years. In the first two years she established herself in elite society and began her new female seminary, the Western Female Institute. During this period she published little writing but in New York City during the spring of 1835 gave a major address that was subsequently published during the same year as *An Essay on the Education of Female Teachers*. In this speech Beecher called for a corps of women teachers to civilize the children of the West. Beecher described the menace of uneducated people who would destroy democracy with their callowness and decried the lack of education available to many Western children. According to Beecher, one-third of the children had no schools at all. She insisted that ninety thousand teachers were needed and that all of those teachers should be women. Women alone were suited to teaching by disposition, manner, and attitude, and only women would accept the low wages associated with education. Beecher's speech called for the creation of national women's seminaries that would train women to train other women to be teachers. Although initially this plan was to be funded privately, eventually government aid was expected. Despite the general acceptance of the speech in the East, the people of the West, and in particular the gentry of Cincinnati, were not pleased; consequently, funding for the Western Female Institute suffered.

The Beecher family home in Cincinnati

By 1836 Beecher had begun her writings on religious topics. *Letters on the Difficulties of Religion* was an attempt to defend her father by explaining in layman's terms the religious controversies in which her father had become embroiled. This work also reviewed her moral philosophy, which she hoped would help soothe the hostility felt toward her by the people of Cincinnati. The book, like her other religious pieces, was designed to bring unity among differing social and economic classes. *The Moral Instructor for Schools and Families: Containing Lessons on the Duties of Life, Arranged for Study and Recitation, Also Designed as a Reading Book for Schools* (1838) added to the concept an argument for the morality of financial success. Since in the Jacksonian period wealth could swiftly be gained and lost, Beecher asserted that all classes of people should develop standards of economy and self-reliance. When fortune provided the possibility of material pleasures, however, they should be enjoyed as gifts from God, with the realization, nevertheless, that this situation could alter momentarily. Therefore, all Americans, regardless of class, should be fully indoctrinated with the work ethic. In order to be adequately prepared for hard work, their instruction must begin early. Hence, much of *The Moral Instructor for Schools and Families* is concerned with education, child-raising, and the development of the good character essential to Beecher's moral philosophy.

Throughout the spring and summer of 1836 Beecher had toured the East promoting her Cincinnati school. She had been warmly welcomed in this area and had collected the names of more than one hundred young women who were willing to become her missionary teachers to the West. Because of the continuing animosity toward her by the Western populace, however, in 1837 her school failed. In her *An Essay on Slavery and Abolitionism with Reference to the Duty of American Females* (1837) Beecher gave her attention to raising female consciousness concerning politics. In her perspective the horrible race riots of 1836 in Cincinnati were a result of the failure of the male politicians of the city to ensure human rights. Two days of mob violence against free blacks had been the culmination of racial tension, which had been developing for several years. In *An Essay on Slavery and Abolitionism with Reference to the Duty of American Females,* Beecher hoped, by asserting woman's natural moral superiority over men, to create

Beecher at seventy-five

awareness among women of the need for their political action. Women, however, were not to battle men in the public arena but either through their influence in the home or by becoming public-school teachers. In *A Treatise on Domestic Economy* (1841), which she began writing immediately after the publication of *An Essay on Slavery and Abolitionism with Reference to the Duty of American Females,* Beecher discussed this philosophy in detail. These two publications thrust Beecher into national importance as the voice of domestic virtue.

The prominence was short-lived, however, and without a school as a central base or any independent means of financial support, Beecher found herself in a period of economic and physical depression. During the next four years she attempted to create a literary career by writing and marketing with her sister Harriet textbooks on moral instruction for elementary schools. She also wrote arithmetic texts, but a book on domestic economy, *A Treatise on Domestic Economy for the Use of Young Ladies at Home and at School,* became her most significant work. The dismissal of her father from his church and the suicide of her brother George soon erased her good fortune, and further financial problems forced Catharine Beecher into a new

attempt at literary success—fiction. Her first and most popular short story is "Fanny Moreland; or, the Use and Abuse of the Risibles" (1843). She sold the piece to *The Christian Keepsake and Missionary Annual,* a "gift book" designed as a handsomely bound holiday gift book. "Fanny Moreland" is an autobiographical account of Beecher's psychological state and financial woes.

The year 1843 also marked the fourth printing of *A Treatise on Domestic Economy for the Use of Young Ladies at Home and at School* and its adoption into the Massachusetts public-school system as a textbook. The book was initially published by a small Boston firm in 1841, but after she had revised and polished the authoritative tone of the text, Beecher negotiated a new contract for it with Harper, which began publishing the book in 1845. From 1841 until 1856 *A Treatise on Domestic Economy for the Use of Young Ladies at Home and at School* was reprinted nearly every year. In 1846 a receipt book was added and reprinted fourteen times before the ultimate compilation, with Harriet Beecher Stowe, of the enlarged *The American Woman's Home, or Principles of Domestic Science* in 1869. *A Treatise on Domestic Economy for the Use of Young Ladies at Home and at School* marked Beecher as the national authority on the American home; indeed, she explains every aspect of domestic life from house building to table setting. In an attempt to create a servantless household, she supplies designs for labor-saving devices to assist women in managing their own houses. Information on child rearing, gardening, cooking, cleaning, doctoring, and all the other responsibilities of a nineteenth-century homemaker is simply presented. Attention, moreover, is directed toward the psychological, physiological, economic, religious, and political factors of womanhood. Furthermore, Beecher's book not only deals with health, diet, and hygiene but also describes in detail and drawings the human body and its functions. For the first time, a book standardized domestic practices and demonstrated how the system should work.

The success of *A Treatise on Domestic Economy* made Beecher nationally known and allowed her to pursue her educational programs. For the next fifteen years she traveled throughout the country—lecturing, fund-raising, seeking sites for schools, and recruiting teachers. The lectures were designed to clarify her philosophies of education, domesticity, and unification of economic classes. Three of these addresses were subsequently published as *The Duty of American Women to Their Country* (1845), *The Evils Suffered by American Women and American Children: The Causes and the Remedy* (1846), and *An Address to the Protestant Clergy of the United States* (1846). Each of these essays appeals to her audience to facilitate a nation redeemed by women. In order to gain sympathy for her cause, she portrayed the plight of American children as oppressed by cruel, incompetent teachers in cold, dilapidated buildings. To ameliorate this situation, Beecher proposed a national benevolent movement similar to that of the temperance movement to raise money for female teachers and comfortable classrooms. Beecher's plan envisioned an organization for women that would interweave the family, the school, and the church. She expected these women, like Catholic nuns, to practice individual self-denial for the good of the community and to dedicate themselves and their services to education. Her rallying cry was that women must be responsible for saving the country from ignorance, immorality, and factionalism. All women must unite for the good of the country and its people. Beecher was an able publicist and communicator, and her mission was successful. Several schools were initiated, and teaching became the domain of women. As years passed, however, the religious fervor was replaced by an ardent desire to elevate educating to a profession for women.

In 1852 Beecher founded The American Woman's Educational Society with the intention of establishing women's colleges in the West. Through money raised in the East and an arrangement made with Milwaukee businessmen, Beecher was able to open a school in Wisconsin known as the Milwaukee Female College and designed its large, attractive building. In *The True Remedy for the Wrongs of Women* (1851), she presented her new ideas for women's education. Women's colleges, according to Beecher, should be located in large towns and cities. The faculty of these colleges should share equal responsibility for education rather than have principal and subordinate teachers. In addition, beyond the usual curriculum the colleges should offer departments of domestic economy. These colleges, she hoped, would ensure that teaching would become as lucrative a profession for women as the law or medicine was for men. Beecher's hopes for women's education, however, did not materialize, and by 1856 she had ended her relationship with the Milwaukee Female College, resigned from The American Woman's Educational Society, and abandoned her career as an educator.

Beecher's retirement, however, was not without accomplishments. After leaving the West she returned to her sister Harriet and ran her household while Stowe wrote *Uncle Tom's Cabin* (1851–1852). Later, the two sisters collaborated on *The American Woman's Home, or Principles of Domestic Science* (1869). Based on *A Treatise on Domestic Economy,* the book offered some new ideas for efficient household management. While polishing *The American Woman's Home,* Beecher lived with her sister in Nook Farm, Hartford, the famous literary compound whose residents included Mark Twain and Charles Dudley Warner. Stowe's house in the colony became the epitome of Catharine Beecher's concept of the Christian home—a place of worship, a schoolhouse, and a comfortable dwelling, all under one roof and managed by a woman. Beecher's return to Hartford also meant a return to the social life of Hartford and, thereby, an attempt to reestablish the glory of the Hartford Female Seminary with the Beecher sisters in charge. For a year Catharine Beecher lived on campus and directed the curriculum while Harriet Beecher Stowe taught composition and her husband, Calvin, maintained classes on biblical history. After a year the institution was turned over to a cousin, Katy Foote. For the next two years Beecher directed her energies toward fund-raising for new women's universities, one of which became Simmons College in Boston. *Woman's Profession as Mother and Educator with Views in Opposition to Woman's Suffrage* (1872) summarizes these two years and gives a brief argument against the necessity of women's having the vote if they were adequately educated to run the more-important spheres of home and school. In 1874 Beecher published *Educational Reminiscences and Suggestions,* outlining her life's work. Ill health in 1877 sent her to live in Elmira, New York, with her brother Thomas. There she was close to health spas, which she frequented, but also near Elmira College, where she gave lectures and support. Beecher died of a stroke in her sleep the year after moving to Elmira. A few days before her death she had begun a series of letters attempting to arouse further interest in education for women.

References:

Margaret Ward Mahoney, "Catharine Beecher: Champion of Female Intellectual Potential in Nineteenth-Century America," dissertation, Drew University, 1993;

Jo Anne Preston, "Domestic Ideology, School Reformers, and Female Teachers: Schoolteaching Becomes Women's Work in Nineteenth-Century New England," *New England Quarterly,* 66 (December 1993): 531–551;

Kathryn Kish Sklar, *Catharine Beecher: A Study in American Domesticity* (New York: Norton, 1973).

Papers:

Collections of Catharine Beecher's letters and manuscripts are located in the Schlesinger Library at Radcliffe College, the Beinecke Library at Yale University, the Cincinnati Historical Society, the Clements Library at the University of Michigan, the Clifton Waller Barrett Library at the University of Virginia, the Connecticut Historical Society, the Historical Society of Pennsylvania, the Library of Congress, the Massachusetts Historical Society, the New-York Historical Society, the New York Public Library, the Olin Library at Cornell University, the Rutherford B. Hayes Library, the State Historical Society of Wisconsin, the Sterling Memorial Library at Yale University, the Stowe-Day Foundation, the University of Wisconsin–Milwaukee Library, and the Williston Memorial Library at Mount Holyoke College.

Charles Timothy Brooks

(20 June 1813 – 14 June 1883)

Roger Thompson
Virginia Military Institute

See also the Brooks entry in *DLB 1: The American Renaissance in New England.*

BOOKS: *Think on These Things. A Sermon Delivered in the Unitarian Church, Newport, R.I., Sunday, Feb. 28, 1841* (Newport, R.I.: Printed by James Atkinson, 1841);

"Think Soberly." A Sermon on Temperance: Delivered in the Unitarian Church, Newport, R.I. Sunday Evening, February 6, 1842 (Newport, R.I.: James Atkinson, 1842);

The Way, the Truth and the Life (Boston: James Munroe, 1844);

A Poem Pronounced before the Phi Beta Kappa Society, at Cambridge, August 28, 1845 (Boston: Little & Brown, 1845);

Aquidneck; A Poem, Pronounced on the Hundredth Anniversary of the Incorporation of the Redwood Library Company, Newport, R. I. August XXIV. MDCCCXLVII (Providence, R.I.: Charles Burnett Jr., 1848);

The Child's Illustrated Alphabet of Natural History (Newport, R.I.: C. E. Hammett Jr., 1851);

Songs of Field and Flood (Boston: John Wilson, 1853);

The Simplicity of Christ's Teachings, Set Forth in Sermons (Boston: Crosby, Nichols, 1859);

The Christian Minister, the Man of God: A Discourse Delivered before the Graduating Class of the Divinity School in Harvard University, July 15, 1860 (Boston: Walker, Wise, 1860);

Roman Rhymes: Being Winter Work for a Summer Fair. Newport, R.I., August 27, 1869 (Cambridge, Mass.: John Wilson, 1869);

A History of the Unitarian Church in Newport, Rhode Island. Read in the Church, Sunday, January 10, 1875 (Newport, R.I.: Printed by Davis & Pitman, 1875);

William Ellery Channing: A Centennial Memory (Boston: Roberts, 1880);

Augustus Story, A Memorial Paper Read before the Essex Institute. Monday Evening, May 14, 1883 (Salem, Mass., 1883?);

Charles Timothy Brooks

Poems, Original and Translated, with a Memoir by Charles W. Wendte, edited by W. P. Andrews (Boston: Roberts, 1885).

OTHER: *The Controversy Touching the Old Stone Mill, in the Town of Newport, Rhode-Island. With Remarks Introductory and Conclusive,* introductory and concluding remarks by Brooks (Newport, R.I.: C. E. Hammett Jr., 1851);

"Original Hymn," in *Services in Memory of Rev. William E. Channing, D. D. At the Arlington-Street Church, Boston, on Sunday Evening, October 6, 1867* (Boston: John Wilson, 1867), p. 4.

TRANSLATIONS: *William Tell, A Drama in Five Acts. From the German of Schiller* (Providence, R.I.: B. Cranston, 1838);

Songs and Ballads; Translated from Uhland, Körner, Bürger, and other German Lyric Poets (Boston: James Munroe / London: John Green, 1842); republished as *German Lyric Poetry, A Collection of Songs and Ballads, Translated from the Best German Lyric Poets, with Notes* (Philadelphia: Willis P. Hazard, 1863);

Schiller's Homage of the Arts, with Miscellaneous Pieces from Rückert, Freiligrath, and Other German Poets (Boston: James Munroe, 1847);

German Lyrics (Boston: Ticknor, Reed & Fields, 1853);

Faust: A Tragedy Translated from the German of Goethe with Notes (Boston: Ticknor & Fields, 1856);

The Simplicity of Christ's Teachings: Set Forth in Sermons (Boston: Crosby, Nichols, 1859);

Titan: A Romance. From the German of Jean Paul Friedrich Richter, 2 volumes (Boston: Ticknor & Fields, 1862);

The Jobsiad, a Grotesco-Comico-Heroic Poem from the German of Dr. Carl Arnold Kortum (Philadelphia: Frederick Leypoldt / London: Trübner, 1863);

Hesperus or Forty-five Dog-Post-Days, a Biography from the German of Jean Paul Friedrich Richter (Boston: Ticknor & Fields, 1865);

The Layman's Breviary, or Meditations for Every Day in the Year. From the German of Leopold Schefer (Boston: Roberts, 1867);

Puck's Nightly Pranks, Translated from the German of Ludwig Bund, illustrated by Paul Konewka (Boston: Roberts, 1871);

The World Priest. Translated from the German of Leopold Schefer (Boston: Roberts, 1873);

The Convicts and Their Children by Berthold Auerbach (New York: Holt, 1877);

Lorley and Reinhard by Berthold Auerbach (New York: Holt, 1877);

Aloys by Berthold Auerbach (New York: Holt, 1877);

Poet and Merchant, a Picture of Life from the Times of Moses Mendelssohn by Berthold Auerbach (New York: Holt, 1877);

The Wisdom of the Brahmin: A Didactic Poem. Translated from the German of Friedrich Rückert (Boston: Roberts, 1882);

The Invisible Lodge, from the German of Jean Paul Friedrich Richter (New York: Holt, 1883).

Charles Timothy Brooks is best known for his translations of German literature into English, gaining his reputation as an important translator upon the publication of Johann Wolfgang von Goethe's *Faust,* part one (1856). His vocation, however, was that of Unitarian minister, appointed by William Ellery Channing as the pastor of the Unitarian Church of Newport, Rhode Island, where he continued to preach for thirty-five years. Brooks considered himself a poet who was able to transform his poetical talents into eloquent sermons and more accurate and lyrical translations of German literature than others had written. Though both his sermons and his poetry were admired, their range of influence was limited, while his translations helped to stir a growing interest in German literature, theology, and philosophy in a rapidly expanding American intellectual culture. Brooks's translations of *Faust* and Jean Paul Friedrich Richter's *Titan* (1862), in particular, introduced Americans to a German literary culture that was different from traditional visions of it, and the two works, among his other translations, helped to invigorate German studies in America.

Born in 1813 in Salem, Massachusetts, Charles Timothy Brooks was the second child of Timothy and Mary King (Mason) Brooks. Both Charles's father and his mother were descended from old New England Puritan families; his father's family traced to 1649 and his mother's to 1587 and the Reverend Francis Higginson. Charles was a precocious but sensitive child who deeply loved nature and walks in the countryside. He entered Harvard in 1828, where he was both class poet and the head of the Hasty Pudding Club. In 1832, the year Ralph Waldo Emerson preached his resignation sermon "The Lord's Supper," Brooks graduated from Harvard and entered the Harvard Divinity School, from which he graduated in 1835. While at Harvard, Brooks heard both Emerson and Edward Everett speak, took courses from the Henry Wares, and, most important, began his work in German studies under the tutelage of Charles Follen, the premier German scholar of the time. Brooks also became associated with a group of young intellectuals that included John S. Dwight, Oliver Wendell Holmes, Theodore Parker, and Charles Sumner.

On 1 January 1837 Brooks became the first minister of the Unitarian Church in Newport, Rhode Island. In October of that same year he married Harriet Lyman Hazard, the daughter of a Newport legislator, Benjamin Hazard, and in the following year they had the first of their five children. William Ellery Channing conducted the marriage ceremony, and in June of 1837 Channing ordained Brooks in the Newport church, where he remained until poor health forced him to resign his pastorate just before Thanksgiving in 1871. He had a somewhat fragile health,

POEMS,

ORIGINAL AND TRANSLATED,

BY

CHARLES T. BROOKS.

WITH

A Memoir

BY CHARLES W. WENDTE.

SELECTED AND EDITED

BY W. P. ANDREWS.

BOSTON:
ROBERTS BROTHERS.
1885.

*Title page for the posthumously published collection that includes
many of the occasional poems Brooks wrote to commemorate
his connections to important people and events*

both in childhood and as an adult, and illness necessitated several voyages during his lifetime—on two occasions to Mobile, Alabama (1842–1843 and 1851–1852), where he preached to the Unitarian Society, and to Calcutta, India (1853–1854), during which visit he wrote several articles that were published in *Harper's Monthly*. In 1865–1866 he finally made a long-awaited trip to Europe, where he met Thomas Carlyle, some relatives of Richter, William H. Channing, and Elizabeth Gaskell.

Brooks was deeply loved by his parishioners and is praised for his compassion, sincerity, and intellectual acumen as a pastor. His achievement as a preacher is highlighted by the publication of a set of his sermons, *The Simplicity of Christ's Teachings: Set Forth in Sermons* (1859). This set of sermons demonstrates Brooks's fluency with mid-nineteenth-century Unitarian theology as well as his interest in addressing issues such as the rise of the natural sciences and the role of

religious education in a democratic society. Having attended Harvard Divinity School as American Transcendentalism was taking shape and while Unitarianism was enjoying a period of primacy in the religious culture of New England, Brooks displayed in his sermons the integration of diverse fields of knowledge that increasingly characterized Unitarianism and Transcendentalism of the time. Eventually, Brooks composed 1,350 sermons, many lectures, and a large body of religious poetry, though many poems remain unpublished.

Even in his work as a preacher, Brooks viewed himself as a poet, and though neither his sermons nor his poetry has received much critical attention (indeed, almost none), he was a prolific writer. Much of his poetry was published in periodicals of the time, such as a series of "Entomological Alphabet" poems, which appeared in *The Dayspring*. Reflecting the themes of most of his periodical poetry, these alphabetic poems were essentially lessons in moral and religious living. His initial book of poetry, *Songs of Field and Flood* (1853), illustrates the themes of moral living but places them frequently in the frame of occasional poems or nature poems. *Poems, Original and Translated,* published posthumously in 1885 by his biographer, Charles W. Wendte, is the most important collection of Brooks's poetry and reflects his focus on moral instruction. It includes many occasional poems that are important in showing his connection to seminal events and people of the nineteenth century, including ones that commemorate his visit to St. Peter's in Rome, his stays in Alabama, his relationship with Channing, and the death of Jones Very. Images of nature and its power to facilitate the redemption of humankind often drive the religious themes of the poems, suggesting Brooks's interest in some of the central tenets of Transcendentalism. Even so, his poetry, as well as his sermons, remains largely uninvestigated by current scholars, and he remains regarded primarily as a regional poet whose importance rests most significantly in his translations of German poetry.

Brooks's stature as one of the premier translators in New England overshadows his regional reputation as the kindly and pious preacher-poet of Newport. When he first came into contact with German while studying at Harvard under Follen, Brooks expressed an exuberance for German poetry that continued to drive his work until his death. Indeed, Brooks envisioned his poetic ability as well suited to providing more-accurate translations of German lyric poetry than was available at the time, and he saw the entire act of translation as an act of poetry.

His initial translation, *William Tell, A Drama in Five Acts. From the German of Schiller* (1838), came to a public already familiar with the drama, and the importance of the translation is probably as much in its indication of Brooks's own enjoyment of Friedrich von Schiller's work as in its positive reception. Indeed, Brooks's earnestness to translate the lesser-known lyric work of Schiller led to the publication of Schiller's *Homage of the Arts, with Miscellaneous Pieces from Rückert, Freiligrath, and Other German Poets* (1847), in which Brooks began the work of presenting to the American public the German lyrics of Schiller, Friedrich Rückert, and Ferdinand Freiligrath, whom he met in London years later during his voyage to Europe. The work went through three editions and met with considerable public praise.

The initial success of his early translations helped to ensure publication of what came to be regarded as the most important translation of his career, *Faust*. Brooks's translation was the first English version to be published in America, and it solidified his reputation as one of the premier literary translators of the time. Indeed, his translation was the most widely respected until the publication of Bayard Taylor's. Wendte argues that Brooks's might even be a better translation than Taylor's, but that Taylor's translation assumed preeminence because he published the entirety of *Faust,* whereas Brooks published only part one. Regardless, Brooks says in his preface that his goal was the creation of the finest translation of the work, the truest to the poetic qualities of the original German, and the most scholarly.

This goal of a more poetic and true-to-the-original translation undergirds virtually all of Brooks's work, and it suggests his desire to make known the lyrical sophistication of German poetry as well as the lyricism of German prose works. *Titan* was Brooks's first attempt to bring to America the epic work of Richter, for whom Brooks felt a special fondness and whom he called the "Shakespeare of Germany." American literary culture had some familiarity with Richter through Carlyle and through Follen, and probably through the influence of both of these figures Brooks conceived of the importance of Richter, since Follen was Brooks's German instructor and Carlyle was a person whom Brooks greatly admired and later met on his journey to Europe. Brooks's translation of the novel *Titan* and later of *Hesperus or Forty-five Dog-Post-Days, a Biography from the German of Jean Paul Friedrich Richter* (1865), however, were ambitious attempts to introduce Richter's work in its entirety in order to demonstrate its lyrical beauty and moral sense.

The moral qualities of German literature greatly appealed to Brooks and led to his translations of Leopold Schefer's *The Layman's Breviary* (1867) and *The World Priest* (1873). Again, Brooks saw his mission as partly the introduction to America of a lesser-known German poet, but in these two works Brooks illustrates the piety of the German writers as well. *The Layman's Breviary* is essentially a devotional, spun with words of wisdom for the lay people, and *The World Priest* is a collection of verse essays steeped in moral idealism. Both works reflect Brooks's Unitarianism, especially in their appeals to a revelatory human reason, a zeal for liberty, and an embracing of the common and lowly.

The focus on the common and lowly appears with most strength in a series of translations of Berthold Auerbach for the Leisure Hour Series of Henry Holt and Company. *Lorley and Reinhard* (1877), *The Convicts and Their Children* (1877), and *Aloys* (1877) all exhibit the power of virtuous characters to overcome their circumstances and, in the case of *Lorley and Reinhard,* in the power of fate to level those lacking in virtue. In all these works, virtuous characters and virtuous actions are rewarded, and the world is shown as a place for the potential of human goodness. These traits certainly appealed to Brooks and fit well with his Unitarian background.

Brooks's Unitarianism was further reflected in his translation of Rückert's *The Wisdom of the Brahmin* (1882). This translation, dedicated to Frederic Henry Hedge and William Henry Furness, highlights the extent to which Eastern thought had entered American philosophical and literary circles. The poem, subtitled *A Didactic Poem,* abounds in passages of idealism and moralizing piety and illustrates Brooks's continued interest in idealist thought until the end of his life.

Brooks's death, one year after the publication of *The Wisdom of the Brahmin,* was widely reported, and his memorial was attended by such notables as George Bancroft, testifying to his stature in the religious and literary community. *Communications on the Death of Brooks,* a book commemorating his life and achievements, was published in 1884 and includes reflections on his significance to New England culture and to the citizens of Newport by, among others, Charles Wendte and W. P. Andrews. Wendte's more lengthy "Memoir," published as an introduction to *Poems, Original and Translated* (1885), provides a more detailed biography, and from it come most of the descriptions of Brooks and his significance on which late-twentieth-century scholarship still relies. Brooks and his works, however, remain largely unexamined, his translations having only one book-length study dedicated solely to them—Camillo von Klenze's *Charles Timothy Brooks: Translator from the German and the Genteel Tradition* (1937)—and his sermons and poetry are generally dismissed as regional and uninspired, even in scholarship that praises his translations.

Bibliographies:

Bibliography of American Literature, volume 1, compiled by Jacob Blanck (New Haven, Conn.: Yale University Press, 1955);

Charles Timothy Brooks, a Checklist of Printed and Manuscript Works in the Library of the University of Virginia, compiled by Fannie Mae Elliott and Lucy Clark (Charlottesville: University of Virginia Press, 1960).

Biographies:

E. B. Willson, C. W. Wendte, R. S. Rantoul, and W. P. Andrews, *Communications on the Death of Charles T. Brooks, of Newport, R. I.* (Salem, Mass.: Essex Institute, 1884);

Wendte, "Memoir," in *Poems, Original and Translated, with a Memoir by Charles W. Wendte,* selected and edited by Andrews (Boston: Roberts, 1885), pp. 3–114.

References:

Cyrus Hamlin, "Transplanting German Idealism to American Culture: F. H. Hedge, W. T. Harris, C. T. Brooks," in *Translating Literatures, Translating Cultures: New Vistas and Approaches in Literary Studies,* edited by Kurt Mueller-Vollmer and Michael Irmscher (Stanford, Cal.: Stanford University Press, 1998), pp. 107–124;

Camillo von Klenze, *Charles Timothy Brooks: Translator from the German and the Genteel Tradition* (Boston: D. C. Heath, 1937);

Henry A. Pochmann, *German Culture in America: Philosophical and Literary Influences 1600–1900* (Madison: University of Wisconsin Press, 1957);

Stanley M. Vogel, *German Literary Influences on the American Transcendentalists* (Hamden, Conn.: Archon Books, 1970).

Papers:

The major holdings of Charles Timothy Brooks's works and manuscripts are housed in the Andover-Harvard Theological Library, Brown University; Houghton Library at Harvard University; and Barrett Special Collections Library at the University of Virginia.

Orestes A. Brownson

(16 September 1803 – 17 April 1876)

James Emmett Ryan
Auburn University

See also the Brownson entries in *DLB 1: The American Renaissance in New England; DLB 59: American Literary Critics and Scholars, 1800–1850;* and *DLB 73: American Magazine Journalists, 1741–1850.*

BOOKS: *An Address on the Fifty-Fifth Anniversary of American Independence Delivered at Ovid, Seneca Co. N.Y. July 4, 1831* (Ithaca, N.Y.: S. S. Chatterton, 1831);

An Address on Intemperance, Delivered in Walpole, N.H., February 26, 1833 (Keene, N.H.: J. & J. W. Prentiss, 1833);

An Address Delivered at Dedham, on the Fifty-Eighth Anniversary of American Independence, July 4, 1834 (Dedham, Mass.: H. Mann, 1834);

A Sermon Delivered to the Young People of the First Congregational Society in Canton, on Sunday, May 24th, 1835 (Dedham, Mass.: H. Mann, 1835);

New Views of Christianity, Society, and the Church (Boston: James Munroe, 1836);

A Discourse on the Wants of the Times. Delivered in Lyceum Hall, Hanover Street, Boston, Sunday, May 29, 1836 (Boston: James Munroe, 1836);

Babylon Is Falling. A Discourse Preached in the Masonic Temple, To the Society for Christian Union and Progress, on Sunday Morning, May 28, 1837 (Boston: I. R. Butts, 1837);

An Address on Popular Education. Delivered in Winnisimmet Village, on Sunday Evening, July 23, 1837 (Boston: John Putnam, 1837);

An Oration Delivered before the United Brothers Society of Brown University, at Providence, R.I., September 3, 1839 (Cambridge, Mass.: Metcalf, Torry & Ballou, 1839);

The Laboring Classes, An Article from the Boston Quarterly Review (Boston: Benjamin H. Greene, 1840);

Brownson's Defence. Defence of the Article on the Laboring Classes (Boston: Benjamin H. Greene, 1840);

Charles Elwood: Or the Infidel Converted (Boston: Little, Brown, 1840; London: Chapman, 1845);

Oration Before the Democracy of Worcester and Vicinity, Delivered at Worcester, Mass., July 4, 1840 (Boston: E. Littlefield / Worcester: M. D. Phillips, 1840);

The Policy to Be Pursued Hereafter by the Friends of the Constitution, and of Equal Rights (Boston: Benjamin H. Greene, 1841);

A Review of Mr. Parker's Discourse on the Transient and Permanent in Christianity (Boston: Benjamin H. Greene, 1841);

Oration of Orestes A. Brownson, Delivered at Washington Hall, July 5, 1841 (New York: G. Washington Dixon, 1841);

Constitutional Government (Boston: Benjamin H. Greene, 1842);

The Mediatorial Life of Jesus. A Letter to Rev. William Ellery Channing, D.D. (Boston: Little, Brown, 1842);

An Oration on the Scholar's Mission (Boston: Benjamin H. Greene, 1843);

Social Reform. An Address before the Society of the Mystical Seven in the Wesleyan University, Middletown, Conn., August 7, 1844 (Boston: Waite Peirce, 1844);

A Review of the Sermon by Dr. Potts, on the Dangers of Jesuit Instruction, Preached at the Second Presbyterian Church, St. Louis, on the 25th September, 1845 (St. Louis: "News-Letter" Publication Office, 1846);

Essays and Reviews Chiefly on Theology, Politics, and Socialism (New York, Boston & Montreal: D. & J. Sadlier, 1852);

An Oration on Liberal Studies, Delivered before the Philomathian Society, of Mount Saint Mary's College, Md., June 29th, 1853 (Baltimore: Hedian & O'Brien, 1853);

The Spirit-Rapper: An Autobiography (Boston: Little, Brown / London: Charles Dolman, 1854);

The Convert: or, Leaves from My Experience (New York: Edward Dunigan & Brother [James B. Kirker], 1857);

The War for the Union. Speech by Dr. O. A. Brownson. How the War Should Be Prosecuted. The Duty of the Government, and the Duty of the Citizen (New York: George F. Nesbitt, 1862);

The American Republic: Its Constitution, Tendencies, and Destiny (New York: P. O'Shea, 1865);

Conversations on Liberalism and the Church (New York: D. & J. Sadlier / Boston: P. H. Brady, 1870);

An Essay in Refutation of Atheism, edited by Henry F. Brownson (Detroit: Thorndike Nourse, 1882);

Uncle Jack and His Nephew; or Conversations of an Old Fogy with a Young American, edited by Henry F. Brownson (Detroit: H. F. Brownson, 1888);

The Two Brothers; or, Why Are You a Protestant? edited by Henry F. Brownson (Detroit: H. F. Brownson, 1888).

Collections: *The Works of Orestes A. Brownson,* 20 volumes, edited by Henry F. Brownson (Detroit: Thorndike Nourse, 1882–1887);

The Brownson Reader, edited by Alvan S. Ryan (New York: P. J. Kenedy, 1955).

PERIODICALS EDITED: *Boston Quarterly Review,* 1838–1842;

Brownson's Quarterly Review, 1844–1864, 1873–1875.

One of the most prolific American political essayists, lecturers, and religious philosophers of the nineteenth century, Orestes A. Brownson in his early writing and lecturing career, particularly in his role as editor of the *Boston Quarterly Review* (1838–1842), worked at the center of many debates concerning theology, Jacksonian politics, and proto-Marxian labor theory. He became notorious during those same years for his tendencies to change his religious affiliation and his political positions. Following his 1844 conversion to Roman Catholicism, however, he turned his considerable rhetorical skills toward the cause of promoting his new religion, which he hoped would eventually become the dominant religion in the United States, and remained a Catholic for the rest of his life. Although he was an early associate of Henry David Thoreau and Ralph Waldo Emerson and a dominant figure in early Transcendentalism, his conversion to Catholicism—surprising to his associates—led him to a career that is as notable for its increasing obscurity as it is for its deep religious conservatism. As editor and sole contributor for most of the existence of *Brownson's Quarterly Review,* the first important American journal devoted exclusively to philosophy and cultural criticism from a Catholic perspective, Brownson eventually emerged as the leading intellectual proponent of Roman Catholicism during an era when large-scale Irish immigration had begun to alter the religious landscape of the United States.

A Yankee with deep New England roots, Orestes Brownson was a descendent of early settlers of Connecticut and Vermont, including such notables as Thomas Hooker of the Hartford colony (on the paternal side) and *Mayflower* pilgrims (on the maternal side). On 16 September 1803 Orestes Augustus and his twin sister, Daphne Augusta, were born in the village of Stockbridge, Vermont, to Sylvester and Relief (Metcalf) Brownson. Only months after the twins were born, however, Sylvester Brownson died of pneumonia, leaving his impoverished wife alone to care for the twins and the older children—Daniel, Oran, and Thorina. Eventually, the mother decided to accept offers to adopt her twin children, and they were placed in separate adoptive homes. Daphne went to live with neighbors in Stockbridge. Orestes was adopted by an elderly couple in Royalton, Vermont, where they lived on a small farm near the White River, in the foothills of the Green Mountains.

Brownson's adoptive parents were not churchgoers, but they raised him according to the broad principles of their religious tradition, New England Congregationalism. As he wrote in his 1857 autobiography, *The Convert,* they taught him "to be honest, to owe no one anything but good will, to be frugal and industrious, to speak the truth, never to tell a lie under any circumstances, or to take what was not my own, even to the value of a pin; to keep the Sabbath, and never to let the sun go down on my wrath." Raised in relative isolation as an only child, Orestes never attended school during these years but instead turned his energies to reading as a substitute for other youthful interests and activities. Soon, he had read the few books in his stepparents' home and, lacking a library of any kind, began to search out all the books that his village neighbors might have, eventually locating copies of John Locke's *Essay concerning Human Understanding* (1690), Alexander Pope's translation of Homer, volumes on American history and the Indian wars, Daniel Defoe's *Robinson Crusoe* (1719), Isaac Watts's version of the Psalms, and, especially, the King James Bible. Indeed, he turned most enthusiastically as a youngster to the Bible as a source of both literary inspiration and religious teaching. Never able to obtain children's books or other juvenile reading, Orestes strengthened his youthful intellect through this immersion in studying the Bible, "all of which," he later noted, "I had read by the time I was eight, and a great part of which I knew by heart before I was fourteen years of age."

The Brownson family was finally reunited for a few years beginning in 1816, when a legendarily cold and snowy Vermont winter drove Orestes's mother, Relief Brownson, to move to Ballston Spa, Saratoga County, New York. At the academy in Ballston Spa, Orestes had his only year of formal schooling, during which he acquired his first knowledge of the Latin and Greek languages. He obtained work in a busy printer's shop filled with deists, atheists, sectaries, and Universalists, where he first was exposed to the complexities of early-nineteenth-century evangelical discourse, a set of religious controversies that had been superheated during the Second Great Awakening, a religious revival that began in New England in the 1790s. Finally, after a personal spiritual experience at a Presbyterian meetinghouse in Ballston Spa, Orestes decided to be baptized and joined the Presbyterian Church in 1822. Probably also through his connection with the Presbyterian Church he turned from work in the print shop to a new job as schoolteacher in the village of Stillwater, New York.

His position as schoolteacher was soon withdrawn in 1823 when Brownson revealed that he had left Presbyterianism for the Universalist faith—the first in a long succession of religious conversions that ended only with his ultimate conversion to Roman Catholicism in 1844. As a Universalist, in 1824 Brownson moved for a short time to Springwells, Michigan (about eleven miles south of Detroit), and quickly reached the decision to apply for the Universalist ministry and

BROWNSON'S

QUARTERLY REVIEW.

JANUARY, 1844.

ART. I. — INTRODUCTION. — *The Boston Quarterly Review.* — *Greeting to Old Friends.* — *Design of the Work.* — *Change of Views.* — *Eclecticism.* — *Saint-Simonism.* — *German Philosophy.* — *Philosophy of Life.* — *Theology.* — *The Church.* — *Law of Continuity.* — *Ultraists.* — *Conservatism.* — *Constitutionalism.* — *Moral and Religious Appeals.*

AT the close of the volume for 1842, I was induced to merge the Boston Quarterly Review, which I had conducted for five years, in the Democratic Review, published at New-York, on condition of becoming a free and independent contributor to its pages for two years. But the character of my contributions having proved unacceptable to a portion of its ultra-democratic subscribers, and having, in consequence, occasioned its proprietors a serious pecuniary loss, the conductor has signified to me, that it would be desirable for my connexion with the Democratic Review to cease before the termination of the original agreement. This leaves me free to publish a new journal of my own, and renders it, in fact, necessary, if I would continue my communications with the public. I have no fault to find with the conductor of the Democratic Review, Mr. O'Sullivan,—a gentleman for whom I have a very

VOL. I. NO. I.   1

First page from the inaugural issue of the magazine Brownson edited from 1838 to 1842

return to the Northeast. On 18 June 1826, at the age of twenty-two, Brownson was ordained as a Universalist minister in Jaffrey, New Hampshire. He proceeded with his Universalist preaching in New England over the next three years and, during that time, worked as an essayist and editor. Soon, he was editor of the most influential Universalist periodical in the country, *The Gospel Advocate and Impartial Investigator.* He taught school for a few months upon his return to New York, and while teaching in Elbridge, New York, during 1826–1827 met Sally Healy, one of his students, and they were married on 19 June 1827. Cousin of the Honorable John P. Healy–the law partner of Daniel Webster– Sally Healy was an Elbridge native and daughter of a prosperous farmer in Onandaga County.

By 1829 Brownson had resigned his Universalist ministry and turned to writing essays for the *Free Enquirer,* a weekly journal published in New York City by the social reformers Fanny Wright, Robert Dale Owen, and other members of the ultrademocratic Workingmen's Party. He briefly associated with the

Workingmen's Party, during which he also worked as editor of pro-Workingmen papers such as the *Republican and Herald of Reform,* published in Leroy, New York. Brownson remained a contributor to the *Free Enquirer* until the elections of 1830, when, after repudiating all political parties, he returned to the pulpit once again, announcing himself during his first appearance in Ithaca as a self-declared independent preacher.

Brownson became increasingly well known as a fiery platform and lyceum lecturer on a range of issues related to social reform, and as a lecturer Brownson earned the largest part of his income for many years while becoming a public figure on the national stage. Brownson's writings during this period, many of them concerned with describing his own religious experiences, often appeared in his columns in *The Philanthropist,* a short-lived Ithaca weekly that he edited and published until its financial failure in 1832. Embarrassed by his latest venture in publishing, Brownson determined to obtain a position as minister in one of the newly popular Unitarian churches in New England. He left his wife, Sally, and two young sons, Orestes Augustus Jr. (born 18 April 1828) and John Healy (born 14 April 1829), in Ithaca while he spent several months canvassing the Northeast in search of a permanent ministerial position. After a summer of itinerant preaching in New York, Vermont, New Hampshire, and Massachusetts, Brownson finally accepted a contract with the Unitarian parish in Walpole, New Hampshire, where he was installed as minister on 29 October 1832.

Once established in Walpole, Brownson devoted himself to a systematic study of theology and philosophy while maintaining his career as a public speaker. Riding the tide of the popular lyceum movement and the regular demand for his lectures on public holidays and at university commencements, he traveled widely—appearing by invitation in midwestern cities such as St. Louis, Canadian cities such as Montreal and Quebec, and southern cities such as New Orleans and Mobile. Brownson's popularity as a public speaker during his early years as a minister came not only as a result of his rhetorical skill but also from an imposing physical presence that lent considerable authority to his positions on religion, politics, temperance, education, history, literature, and many other controversial topics. His son Henry described him thus:

> Two inches over six feet in height, with broad shoulders and a large frame, his weight was less than 170 pounds. His bodily strength was unusually great, and his vigor was kept up by habitual exercise, both in walking and working in the garden. His hair was black and brushed straight back from his forehead without parting; around his mouth he was shaved, and on the upper part of his cheeks; his eyes seemed black, but were of mixed grey and hazel; his upper lip long, his hands long and broad. His dress, at this time and until he gave up preaching, was broadcloth; he wore a dress coat, what is sometimes called a swallow-tail, at all hours of the day, even in his studies, and a large square white handkerchief folded to a width of three or four inches in front of his neck, crossed behind and tied in front. He slept little, but sat up writing or studying till 2 or 3 o'clock or later. His diet was sparing, his abstinence from wine and spirits total, though he drank strong coffee morning and evening. His total abstinence from alcohol was as much due to taste as to principle, and indeed he never heartily took up the total abstinence fanaticism, though he often addressed temperance societies.

Living in Walpole as a Unitarian minister also gave Brownson the crucial opportunity to associate with many distinguished thinkers who were members of the Boston Unitarian community, thus forging his first links with what became known as the Transcendentalist movement. Moreover, through his essays in popular Unitarian periodicals such as *The Unitarian* and *The Christian Register,* Brownson had already begun to make a name for himself and to draw the attention of such important early Unitarian figures as William Ellery Channing and George Ripley.

Brownson's increasing reputation as a promising young Unitarian minister led to his May 1834 appointment to the Canton, Massachusetts, Unitarian pulpit, where he could remain in closer contact with the leading figures of Massachusetts Unitarianism. The two years Brownson spent in Canton also exposed him directly to the plight of the working classes, many of whom worked in the Canton textile mills and formed the impetus for his famous "Essay on the Laboring Classes" (1840), perhaps his best-known work. In Canton, Brownson also met Henry David Thoreau, who had taken a year off from his studies at Harvard to earn money as a teacher. Brownson was the person who examined Thoreau for competence as a teacher in early 1836 and subsequently invited him to live with the Brownson family for six weeks while tutoring Brownson's sons and teaching at the local school.

In late 1836 Brownson moved once again, this time giving up his pulpit in Canton to move to Chelsea, outside of Boston. Now the father of two more sons, William Ignatius (born 4 January 1834) and Henry Francis (born 7 August 1835), Brownson applied himself to developing a new form of Christian thought based loosely on the French eclectic philosophy of Victor Cousin and the French social reformism of Claude-Henri de Rouvroy Saint-Simon. This new unification of the Christian world—what Brownson called the "Church of the Future"—was intended to erase the differences among the many fragmented sects scattered about the nineteenth-century American religious landscape. Brownson elaborated the complete theory for such a new church in his first published book, *New Views of Christianity, Society, and the Church* (1836), a densely philosophical volume that drew not only on Cousin and Saint-Simon, but also on the work of Benjamin Constant, Heinrich Heine, and Friedrich Schleiermacher. *New Views of Christianity, Society, and the Church* included Brownson's critiques of both Catholicism and Protestantism (for excessive spiritualism and materialism, respectively) and also his view of Jesus as the "mediator" between spirit and matter; the union of the spiritual and the material could thus come about according to the eclectic principle of Cousin, through the reconciling intervention of Jesus.

As he had done in his early radical years, Brownson maintained a ministerial role, now as founder of his Society for Christian Union and Progress (founded 1 July 1836), as well as a publishing role as editor of the influential *Boston Reformer* newspaper. Among the important developments for Brownson during his tenure at the *Boston Reformer* was his new friendship with the eminent historian George Bancroft, who began corresponding with Brownson after Brownson reviewed his work approvingly. Bancroft, a Jacksonian supporter and admirer of Brownson's views on democratic principles, used his own patronage position as collector of the port of Boston to provide Brownson a sinecure as steward of the United States Marine Hospital in Chelsea, a position that carried with it few responsibilities but included a comfortable house and a yearly salary of $1,600–a welcome respite from the depression of 1837–1843.

Relatively free from financial pressures and yet frustrated by the lack of enthusiasm for his Society for Christian Union and Progress, Brownson soon resolved to found a new intellectual quarterly, and by January 1838 the first number of the *Boston Quarterly Review* appeared, establishing the review immediately as one of the preeminent learned journals in America. With this new vehicle for his ideas (for every issue of the *Boston Quarterly Review* was written almost entirely by him), Brownson reenergized his broadest ambitions as a critic. As he noted in a letter to his friend Bancroft, "My design in publishing it is by means of a higher philosophy of man than Reid's or Locke's to christianize democracy and democratize the church." In format, issues of the *Boston Quarterly Review* typically consisted of six review essays, most of them occasioned by recently published European or American books. Although the largest burden of writing was assumed by Brownson himself, contributors to the *Boston Quarterly Review* also included prominent figures associated with the Transcendentalist movement, such as George Bancroft, George Ripley, Margaret Fuller, Theodore Parker,

ESSAYS AND REVIEWS

CHIEFLY ON

THEOLOGY, POLITICS, AND SOCIALISM.

BY

O. A. BROWNSON, LL. D.

NEW YORK:
D. & J. SADLIER & Co. 164 WILLIAM-STREET.
BOSTON:—128 FEDERAL-STREET.
MONTREAL, C. E:
CORNER OF ST. FRANCIS XAVIER AND NOTRE-DAME STREETS.
1852.

Title page for a collection of Brownson's writings on subjects such as Christian socialism

Alexander H. Everett, Sarah Whitman, Elizabeth Peabody, William H. Channing, John S. Dwight, and Albert Brisbane. Two years before the 1840 founding of *The Dial*–the quarterly magazine that eventually became the dominant Transcendentalist periodical under the editorship of Fuller–the *Boston Quarterly Review* provided an early forum for an eclectic range of thought informed by debates about Unitarianism that can be placed under the general rubric of Christian Socialism. Although he usually defended Emerson's ideas and literary achievement against the many attacks made by adversaries in the Unitarian churches, Brownson in his contributions to the *Boston Quarterly Review* was anything but uncritical of the Transcendentalist movement. By the third issue of the magazine, published in October 1838, Brownson had already registered his misgivings about Emerson's perceived move (in his Divinity School Address of 1838) toward the dismantling of traditional religion. Nor did Brownson align himself directly with the more conservative Unitarian religious establishment led by Harvard Divinity School professor Andrews Norton, whose *Evidences of the Genuineness of the Gospels* (volume 1, 1837) Brownson critiqued severely in 1839 for lack of attention to both true spirituality and the needs of working-class persons. Finally, Brownson had attained the centrality and importance for which he had striven from his youth, a position of great intellectual respect in a city known for its writers and thinkers.

At the center of Brownson's intellectual world in the early days of the *Boston Quarterly Review* was the new school of thinkers who came to be known as the Transcendentalists. This young group of writers and ministers, many of them raised as Unitarians and educated at Harvard College, began holding meetings in Boston in 1836, and Brownson—on the verge of founding the *Boston Quarterly Review*—attended four of these sessions, including one Transcendentalist meeting, "Education of Humanity," held at his own home in Chelsea on 18 October 1836. Indeed, for a brief time between 1836 and 1838, Brownson was often mentioned as one of the prime forces in Transcendental thought, along with Parker and Emerson. Almost immediately after aligning himself with the Transcendentalists, however, Brownson began to diverge from their more liberal perspectives on politics, culture, and religion. Emerson, quickly emerging as the crucial theorist of the "new views," also drew sharp criticism from Brownson after the publication of *Nature* (1836) and the Divinity School Address (1838), which Brownson praised for their literary merit but faulted severely for irreligious "worship of the self" and "dispensing with the historical Christ," respectively. Brownson's tireless theoretical and practical writings on behalf of democracy and social justice, which did much to align him with the Transcendentalists, were conjoined with an abiding religious conservatism that made him a provisional Transcendentalist at best. Despite his early work on behalf of the Transcendentalists, Brownson decades later denied that he had ever been a Transcendentalist and lamented the Transcendentalists' liberalizing influence on American culture, even as he acknowledged the tremendous intellectual ferment that characterized the movement.

While Brownson was energized and informed by the early exchanges among the Transcendentalists, and questions of religion and theology dominated much of his career, the largest immediate concerns of his writing in the *Boston Quarterly Review* were strongly political. Brownson's first essay published in the *Boston Quarterly Review*, "Democracy," serves as an emblem of his dominant concern during the years leading up to the pivotal presidential election of 1840. True to his radical democratic roots, Brownson had begun by 1838 to place the full force of his rhetoric behind the idea of popular democracy, and in a way that foreshadowed his single-minded devotion to the cause of Catholicism during his later years: "True and holy for us are the instincts of the masses. . . . We stand in awe of them, and apply ourselves to the work of enabling them to march to the glorious destiny God has appointed them, and to which his hand is leading them." Adding fuel to Brownson's fiery populist rhetoric during these years was the depression of 1837, which led to widespread financial panic and economic crisis.

Brownson's momentous reaction to the twin concerns of economics and democracy, concerns sharpened by the financial crisis and the impending Democratic versus Whig presidential election of 1840, finally culminated in his important essay "The Laboring Classes" (*Boston Quarterly Review,* July 1840; a second essay with the same title appeared in the October issue, responding to criticism of the July essay). The most influential, controversial, and enduring of Brownson's many essays published during his years at the *Boston Quarterly Review,* "The Laboring Classes" appeared in the context of continuing debates about the proper form of democracy for the United States in the wake of Jacksonian politics and precisely at the deepest point of a massive economic depression. Opening with an approving review of "Chartism," Thomas Carlyle's critique of English labor conditions, Brownson's essay went beyond Carlyle's ideas to pronounce—years in advance of Karl Marx—that the end of the oppression of working people "will be found only at the end of one of the longest and severest struggles the human race has ever been engaged in, only by that most dreaded of all wars, the war of the poor against the rich, a war that, however long it may be delayed, will come with all its horrors. The day of vengeance is sure; for the world after all is under the dominion of a Just Providence." Such a class war was thus both desirable and morally justified, since for Brownson, wage laborers toiling in the modern factory system were subject to social conditions even more oppressive than those of slave plantations, the laborers of which were provided some minimal degree of security and shelter. Departing from the rhetoric of antebellum reformers who proposed evangelical Christianity as the solution to social problems, Brownson placed much of the blame for intractable class stratification upon Christian leaders who had failed to preach a true Christianity of equality and social justice. Therefore, the first steps toward economic justice must come in the form of a renewed Christian religion devoted to the cause of human equality. In addition, Brownson proposed sweeping legislative changes, many of them concerned with banking regulations, that would serve the cause of the laboring classes.

Warning of the impending threat of violent insurrection by those who labor at the will of the merchant class, Brownson asserted that the great work of the age was to improve the lot of laborers, to emancipate the industrial proletariat, whose condition under the oppression of wage labor and the factory system he described as more desperate even than that of American slaves. Much of the difficulty in altering the inequalities of the economic system he saw as deriving from a surprising source–organized religion. For all their enthusiasm for social change, Christian reformers of the nineteenth century, according to Brownson's view, had failed miserably at the central moral task of elevating the laboring classes and ameliorating the growing disparity between the rich and poor. But clearly religious change and religious leadership alone would be insufficient to engender the kinds of necessary upheaval called for by the injustice of capitalism and industrialism. Fiercely polemical in tone, "The Laboring Classes" also called for many concrete changes to be implemented in order to avoid what Brownson saw as an imminent worker's revolution by force. First, pointing to the manifest failure of the existing economic system, obvious from the depression of 1837, the essay calls directly for the banking system itself, which represented the interests of employers and merchants, to be completely dismantled so that power could be more fairly distributed among those who had little or no access to the credit economy. Second, and even more radically, Brownson extended his critique of economic power from banking and credit to an even more basic form of monopoly. At the root of the explosive problem of class in the United States–a republic apparently free of aristocratic privilege–lay the modern form of inherited power, the hereditary descent of property. Inherited wealth, another means of solidifying and extending the power of the rich, must also be abolished in order to create a Christian society based on principles of equality.

Reaction to "The Laboring Classes"–most of it furiously opposed to Brownson's argument–came quickly and from many quarters. Apart from arousing opposition in the press, however, the essay also galvanized the Whig Party, which seized on Brownson's radical essay as proof positive that the Democratic Party and its incumbent president, Martin Van Buren, stood for socioeconomic subversion and anarchy. When Van Buren was defeated in November 1840 by William Henry Harrison, Brownson's enraged Democratic colleagues and Van Buren himself accused Brownson of contributing to the Whig victory by his imprudent diatribe against the wealthy classes in America. Twentieth-century opinion, however, has generally pointed to this essay as an example of Brownson's thought at its liberal best, the height of his achievement before the sharp conservative turn that he took upon converting to Catholicism a few years later.

Although he made many visits to the Brook Farm experimental community, founded in 1841 by his friend George Ripley, Brownson began to associate himself less with Transcendentalist thinking over the next few years as he began to consider seriously a conversion to the Catholic Church. The force of Brownson's growing enthusiasm for the Catholic religion was already manifest during his time at Brook Farm, where he played a key role in the eventual conversion of several residents there–most importantly, Isaac Hecker, who converted to Catholicism in early 1844 and subsequently became a Redemptorist priest and later founder of the Paulist Fathers, the first order of American priests. Hecker, a wealthy New Yorker and Democratic partisan whose German immigrant family owned a baking business, probably met Brownson in New York City during one of Brownson's speaking engagements of March 1841. Brownson and Hecker became leading figures in American Catholicism over the next several decades. *Catholic World,* a magazine founded in 1865 by Hecker, eventually became, along with Brownson's own journal, one of Brownson's chief vehicles for publication during the final decade of his life.

Another casualty brought on in part by Brownson's radical and infamous "The Laboring Classes" was the *Boston Quarterly Review,* which had begun to lose many of its subscribers after the Democratic failure in the 1840 elections. Seeing the decline of the *Boston Quarterly Review* and wishing to bolster his own publication, John L. O'Sullivan, editor of the monthly *Democratic Review* in New York and originator of the slogan "Manifest Destiny," invited Brownson to become a contributor on 4 May 1842. In return, Brownson agreed to cease publication of the *Boston Quarterly Review* with the October 1842 issue and merge his subscription list with that of the *Democratic Review.* Despite his enthusiasm for his new work at the high-profile magazine (for which he was to be paid $3.00 per page for at least one fifteen- to twenty-page essay each month), Brownson's tenure at the *Democratic Review* was brief, shortened by disagreements with O'Sullivan about political philosophy. Still reeling from the disappointment of the Democratic failure in the 1840 presidential election, Brownson had begun to question openly, within the Democratic Party's most important journal, the principle of strict majority rule. To the dismay of O'Sullivan, in 1843 Brownson wrote three lengthy essays titled "The Origin and Ground of Government" for the magazine; they amounted to a grave critique–based on a conservative interpretation of the Constitution–of popular democracy itself, with its assertion of sovereignty by absolute majority rule. Above all, according to Brownson's argument, mob rule ran the risk of assigning itself the authority of God, when the true need was for religion to work closely with constitutional law in order to create a just and pious society.

Brownson in 1863 (portrait by George P. A. Healy; from Joseph F. Gower and Richard M. Leliaert, eds. The Brownson-Hecker Correspondence, *1979)*

The prominence that Brownson had attained during the years leading up to the 1840 election and his reputation as a contrarian both fiercely dogmatic in style and yet strangely unsettled in his own beliefs began to deteriorate somewhat, although he remained popular as a lecturer for the rest of his life. In more liberal circles, he had by now become a frequently caricatured figure, one who had ventured far from the mainstream of American thought and religion. A thinker whose quest for intellectual and spiritual truth had made him appear willing to use his formidable syllogistic talents on either side of a given political or theological issue, Brownson found himself admired for his sinewy writing and yet satirized by writers such as James Russell Lowell, whose *Fable for Critics* (1848) concluded,

> The worst of it is, that his logic is so strong,
> That of two sides he commonly chooses the wrong,
> If there *is* just one, why he'll split it in two,
> And first pummel this half, and then that, black and blue;
> That white's white needs no proof, but it takes a deep fellow,
> To prove it jet black, and that jet black is yellow.

Nevertheless, prior to his 1844 conversion, Brownson was known not only for his mercurial beliefs but also for his unsurpassed philosophical learning, which made him one of the leading candidates for a chair in philoso-

phy at Harvard when he was recommended unsuccessfully for the post in 1838 by his friend the famous French philosopher Victor Cousin.

Through all his conversions, Brownson reaffirmed the importance of religion, as with his long letter of June 1842 written to the Unitarian leader William Ellery Channing, which eventually appeared in pamphlet form as *The Mediatorial Life of Jesus* (1842). In that letter, Brownson—by now separating himself entirely from the Emerson of the Divinity School Address—insisted on the centrality of the historical Jesus to modern religion. He wrote retrospectively in his autobiography of 1857 that the real problem lay with Protestantism and its misunderstanding of the need for true communion between God and man through the figure of Christ:

> The error of Protestantism was in that it broke with tradition, broke with the past, and cut itself off from the body of Christ, and therefore from the channel through which the Christian life is communicated. Protestantism was a schism, a separation from the source and current of the divine–human life which redeems and saves the world.

Using his study of French philosophy, notably that of Victor Cousin and Pierre Leroux, Brownson began in *The Mediatorial Life of Jesus* a more resolute turn against Emerson's secular turn and toward systematic religion. (Leroux's writings inspired Brownson to convert to Catholicism and provided him with the notion of "communion with God through nature," which Brownson adapted as communion with God through Christ.) From Protestantism of various kinds, he looked toward a solution to the problems of the modern age—first (like his British contemporary Cardinal John Henry Newman) within what he called a "Catholicity without the Papacy" and eventually (again like Newman) within a full acceptance and defense of Roman Catholicism. Convinced that Roman Catholicism held the answer to his quest for historical authenticity and all-encompassing church authority, and recently inspired by a series of lectures delivered at the Tabernacle in New York City by Bishop John Hughes, Brownson converted to Catholicism. In Boston on 20 October 1844 Bishop John Bernard Fitzpatrick baptized Brownson.

The entire Brownson family followed by converting to Catholicism at about the same time as Orestes himself. According to Brownson, his wife, Sally, had actually converted to Catholicism just before he did, and most of the young children of the family did as well. Only Orestes Jr., who had also spent time at Brook Farm and who at the time was working at sea, was reluctant and delayed his conversion until 1845. Although still enjoying the modest benefits of his patronage position as steward of the Chelsea Marine Hospital, Brownson had increased family and financial responsibilities. In addition to Orestes Jr., John Healy, William Ignatius, and Henry Francis, the family now included Sara Nicolena, born 7 June 1839; George, 20 November 1840; Edward Patrick, 16 October 1843; and Charles Joseph, 15 November 1845. Thus, Brownson continued to lecture widely to provide another important source of income, particularly since the paid circulation of his journal–typically only about a thousand subscribers–was so limited.

No longer welcome as a contributor to the *Democratic Review* because of his attacks on majority rule, Brownson almost immediately–at the urging of his spiritual director, Bishop Fitzpatrick–began publishing the journal that occupied him over the next several decades, *Brownson's Quarterly Review* (1844–1864, 1873–1875). To an even greater extent than the *Boston Quarterly Review,* this new journal consisted almost entirely of Brownson's essays. Wide-ranging in its outlook and devoted to countless debates within politics, theology, economics, literature, and philosophy, *Brownson's Quarterly Review* began not only with essays on the relation between religion and social reform but also with endeavors such as the translation of a great deal of Immanuel Kant's *Critique of Pure Reason* (1781), along with several essays of commentary on Kant's philosophy in which Brownson admired the power of Kant's work but also deplored his atheism and skepticism. Brownson's conversion also occurred at the height of the nativist anti-Catholic movement in the United States, with its riots, convent burnings, and virulent attacks on Catholic immigrants. Because of these nativist pressures, many early essays in his review reflect Brownson's concern for refuting the views of the politically powerful Know-Nothing Party, which had risen to power in many cities by using an anti-Catholic platform.

Surprised and discouraged by the Whig presidential victory of 1840, Brownson nevertheless had continued to study political theory and to write extensively about constitutional government, a project that culminated decades later with the publication of his most comprehensive statement on the subject, *The American Republic: Its Constitution, Tendencies, and Destiny* (1865). But, after the watershed election, the politics of world reform soon gave way to religion as Brownson's primary subject of study, as may be seen with his involvement with the Brook Farm communal experiment in practical Christian living that began in West Roxbury, Massachusetts, under the leadership of Brownson's old friend George Ripley. (Brownson had provided to Ripley much of the early encouragement for Brook Farm, visited the farm often, and also placed his son Orestes Jr. in residency there for a period of time.)

Having newly pledged to use his editorial and rhetorical skill in the defense of his new faith, Brownson continued his interests in philosophy, science, political theory, theology, and literary criticism in *Brownson's Quarterly Review,* but with the crucial difference that his judgments in these areas were now subject to his new commitments to Catholicism. In response to criticism from his Transcendentalist allies, one of Brownson's early essays in his review was "Transcendentalism, or the Latest Form of Infidelity" (1845). Although he had published his theory of communion with Jesus in his *The Mediatorial Life of Jesus* in 1842, his conversion in 1844 brought his views more squarely under the influence of Catholic authorities such as Bishop Fitzpatrick, who monitored and sometimes censored his Catholic apologetical writings to make them conform to official Catholic doctrine. Among the various projects that Brownson undertook during these years were ongoing criticism of Protestant theology, republican political analysis (including strong support for the Union cause, but a reluctance before the Civil War to oppose Southern slaveholding), development of a model of Catholic authorship and literary criticism, and debates with theorists of modern science who followed the evolutionary principles of Charles Darwin and others. Brownson also used *Brownson's Quarterly Review* as a forum for discussing the ideas of John Henry Newman and others affiliated with the English Tractarian controversy and the Catholic Oxford Movement.

Determined though he was to produce an intellectual journal that would fairly represent the most sophisticated American Catholic religious and social thought, Brownson had only a modest success in terms of subscriptions to his review. After several years of struggle to maintain the solvency of the journal, by 1850 there were only 1,400 subscribers, and thus the review proved insufficient as a means of supporting Brownson's large family. So that the journal could remain solvent, Brownson returned to the professional lecture circuit, delivering addresses on Catholicism and civilization to large audiences in eastern cities as well as in St. Louis and New Orleans and in Canada. Although his journal was perennially undersubscribed, there was broad interest in Brownson's lectures, and he seems to have cut an impressive figure at these events, as a typical newspaper report from an 1852 lecture in St. Louis can attest:

His style of lecturing is the perfection of the lecturing style. Calm, massive, unimpassioned, he begins by telling you what he will prove, and he ends by proving it. He looks his audience in the face, and learns from their eyes when they have caught his sense, and whether they are following his chain of reasoning; now he goes back to pull the last link to show that it is strong; now he proceeds rapidly, adding strand after strand to his cord, till no Titan can make it crack; occasionally he rises with his subject to the highest eloquence. From first to last he impresses you with the idea of power; you may not like the goal to which he would take you,

Four of Brownson's children: Henry, Orestes Jr., Edward, and Sara Nicolena

but place yourself once in his hands, and you feel it is vain to resist.

Whatever the inherent quality of Brownson's lecturing during the 1840s and 1850s, his public appearances came during an era when anti-Catholic sentiment had become particularly virulent. Nativist politics and anti-Catholic writers had contributed to a political atmosphere in which Catholicism came to be understood as the religion of immigrants and of those who would subvert, through papal power, the authority of republican government. Brownson, never one to take an easy political path, ultimately outraged both nativist and Catholic groups by arguing in opposition to the racism and discriminatory rhetoric of the nativists, such as those of the anti-Catholic Know-Nothing Party, and at the same time suggesting to the Irish Catholic immigrants that their own political radicalism must be tempered and their Irish customs and habits refined before they could be welcomed fully into the American republic.

Unsettled by the storm of controversy engendered by his involvement in debates about nativism and Irish immigration, and increasingly uneasy with the censorship imposed on his writing by his one-time spiritual guide, Bishop Fitzpatrick of Boston, Brownson decided to leave Boston. By the fall of 1855, he and his family had moved to New York City and soon after to Elizabeth, New Jersey. Frustrated in Boston, Brownson found in New York an opportunity to associate more closely with a range of friends and literary colleagues (including his old companion Isaac Hecker, now a Catholic priest), as well as with New York bishop John Hughes. However, Brownson soon had serious theological conflicts with Hughes, as he had had with Fitzpatrick. Around this time, Brownson figured more prominently as a literary personage, with the publication of his debunking of the spiritualist fad, *The Spirit-Rapper* (1854), and soon after, with the publication of a spiritual autobiography, *The Convert; or, Leaves from My Experience* (1857). Continuing to write prolifically and to lecture widely, by 1862 Brownson had reached such prominence that he ran unsuccessfully for Congress after being nominated as a wartime candidate by the New Jersey Republican Party, which hoped that he would draw support from both Republicans and Catholic Democratic voters.

As the Civil War continued at full strength, the subscriber list of *Brownson's Quarterly Review* was decimated. Moreover, wartime constraints dictated a greatly reduced lecture schedule for Brownson, who had also begun to experience the disabling effects of gout, which inflamed his hands and feet and blinded his eyes for a period. Recognizing Brownson's financial difficulties, Hecker, who by this time had founded the Paulist Fathers in New York City, arranged in 1865 with some

Brownson in later life

other Catholic friends to provide a $1,000 annuity for Brownson, who had served so loyally for decades as the most prominent American Catholic intellectual and publicist. In supplying sufficient funds for his retirement, this annuity also provided Brownson the opportunity to complete his most fully developed treatise on American society and constitutional government, *The American Republic*. In *The American Republic,* published soon after the conclusion of the Civil War and using the familiar rhetoric of manifest destiny, Brownson asserted that the American nation had been Providentially ordained to realize the great ideas of democracy and freedom by balancing the conflicting demands of authority and liberty.

No longer at the helm of his own journal after 1864 (although it was briefly revived from 1873 to 1875), Brownson continued to write about religious issues for other Catholic periodicals—including Hecker's monthly *Catholic World* and the Catholic weekly *Ave Maria,* as well as the New York *Tablet,* for which he served as editor, beginning in 1867. Brownson lectured far less after the Civil War than he had previously and usually close to his home in New Jersey, especially at the Catholic Seton Hall College in South Orange, New Jersey. But after several years of relatively moderate writing activity, Brownson became energized by the public response to his last major book, *Conversations on Liberalism and the Church* (1870), and decided for one last time to revive *Brownson's Quarterly Review* and to resign his positions with the other New York periodicals for which he had been writing. The review continued under Brownson's editorship until 1875, when his declining health led him to close the publication for good and to move from the New Jersey home that he had been sharing with his daughter, Sara Nicolena, to the Detroit home of his son Henry.

Retired completely from his editorial work by 1875 and living in the city to which he had traveled half a century earlier in hopes of finding a job as a teacher, Brownson turned to the task, never completed, of writing his autobiography at the side of his son Henry, who later served as his literary executor. After falling gravely ill during the spring of the next year, Orestes A. Brownson died in Detroit on Easter Monday, 17 April 1876.

At the time of his death, Brownson's daughter Sara Nicolena had already embarked on a career as a novelist, eventually publishing her *Marian Elwood* (1859). His son Henry, who was an attorney, became the author of the first biography of his father and editor of Brownson's posthumous twenty-volume collected works. These volumes, which represent approximately one-third of Brownson's writings, are drawn almost entirely from his work as a Catholic after his 1844 conversion, although volume four includes some of his preconversion essays.

A galvanizing figure in his own day, and especially during his early career as a lecturer on political and social topics, Brownson had far fewer readers and listeners in the decades following his conversion to Catholicism. Even before his conversion, however, he had become for many people an overly dogmatic follower of a succession of contradictory social and religious trends. Nevertheless, he engaged systematically with nearly all of the most important social and religious problems of his time, and so his career marks him as one of the most comprehensive American thinkers of his generation. In an age before the full development of the American university system, with its specialized departments, the self-educated Brownson was able to maintain a significant, ongoing, and often compelling intellectual presence within at least four major discourses during the nineteenth century—philosophy, literary criticism, theology, and political theory. Brownson will likely be remembered longest, however, for the sheer radicalism of his startling polemic "The Laboring Classes," which stands as a key document in the history of American labor politics. As for

larger religious aims, Brownson's attempt to create a politically conservative intellectual foundation for American Catholicism remains striking and stands as a sharp revision of more typical narratives that trace a relatively seamless Protestant genealogy of religiosity and social thought during the American nineteenth century.

Letters:

The Brownson–Hecker Correspondence, edited, with an introduction, by Joseph F. Gower and Richard M. Leliaert (Notre Dame & London: University of Notre Dame Press, 1979).

Biographies:

Henry F. Brownson, *Orestes A. Brownson's . . . Life* (Detroit: H. F. Brownson, 1898–1900);

Thomas R. Ryan, *Orestes A. Brownson: A Definitive Biography* (Hamilton, Ind.: Our Sunday Visitor, 1976).

References:

Leonard Gilhooley, *Contradiction and Dilemma: Orestes Brownson and the American Idea* (New York: Fordham University Press, 1972);

Gilhooley, ed., *No Divided Allegiance: Essays in Brownson's Thought* (New York: Fordham University Press, 1980);

Charles Carroll Hollis, "The Literary Criticism of Orestes Brownson," dissertation, University of Michigan, 1954;

Americo Lapati, *Orestes A. Brownson* (New York: Twayne, 1965);

George Parsons Lathrop, "Orestes Brownson," *Atlantic Monthly,* 77 (1876): 770–780;

R. W. B. Lewis, "The Real Presence: Parker and Brownson," in his *The American Adam: Innocence, Tragedy, and Tradition in the Nineteenth Century* (Chicago: University of Chicago Press, 1955), pp. 174–194;

Arthur M. Schlesinger Jr., *Orestes A. Brownson: A Pilgrim's Progress* (Boston: Little, Brown, 1939);

Per Sveino, *Orestes Brownson's Road to Catholicism* (New York: Humanities Press, 1970).

Papers:

The primary collection of Orestes A. Brownson's unpublished writings is at the Notre Dame University Library. These papers are available on twenty rolls of microfilm and have been catalogued in *A Guide to the Microfilm Edition of the Orestes Augustus Brownson Papers* (Notre Dame, Ind.: University of Notre Dame Archives, 1966).

William Henry Channing

(25 May 1810 – 23 December 1884)

Sandra Harbert Petrulionis
Pennsylvania State University, The Altoona College

See also the Channing entries in *DLB 1: The American Renaissance in New England* and *DLB 59: American Literary Critics and Scholars, 1800–1850.*

BOOKS: *Correspondence and Remarks Relative to the Recent Attempt to Exclude Unitarians from the Young Men's Bible Society* (Cincinnati: John B. Russell, 1841);

A Letter from the Rev. William Channing, to the Unitarian Society of Cincinnati (Cincinnati: Printed by R. P. Brooks, 1842);

A Statement of the Principles of the Christian Union (New York: Press of Hunt's Merchants' Magazine, Printed by George W. Wood, 1843);

The Gospel of To-day: A Discourse Delivered at the Ordination of T. W. Higginson, as Minister of the First Religious Society in Newburyport, Mass., Sept. 15, 1847 (Boston: Crosby & Nichols / Newburyport: A. A. Call, 1847);

The Christian Church and Social Reform: A Discourse Delivered Before the Religious Union of Associationists (Boston: Wm. Crosby & H. P. Nichols, 1848);

The Relations of Great Britain and the United States of America: Their Common Destiny and Duty (Liverpool, 1856);

Lessons from the Life of Theodore Parker: A Discourse Delivered in Hope Street Church, Liverpool, on Sunday Evening, June 10, 1860 (London: E. T. Whitfield, 1860);

The Civil War in America: or, The Slaveholder's Conspiracy (Liverpool: W. Vaughn, 1861 / London: G. Vickers / Manchester: John & Abel Heywood, 1861);

Religions of China: Address Before the Free Religious Association, Boston, May 27, 1870 (Boston: J. Wilson, 1870).

OTHER: Théodore Simon Jouffroy, *Introduction to Ethics, Including a Critical Survey of Moral Systems,* 2 volumes, translated by Channing (Boston: Hilliard, Gray, 1840);

Memoir of William Ellery Channing, with Extracts from His Correspondence and Manuscripts, 3 volumes, edited by Channing (Boston: W. Crosby & H. P. Nichols,

William Henry Channing (Unitarian Universalist Association Archives, Boston)

1848; London: J. Chapman, 1848); abridged as *The Life of William Ellery Channing,* 1 volume (Boston: American Unitarian Association, 1880);

The Memoir and Writings of James Handasyd Perkins, 2 volumes, edited by Channing (Cincinnati: Trueman

& Spofford / Boston: W. Crosby & H. Nichols, 1851);

Memoirs of Margaret Fuller Ossoli, edited by Channing, Ralph Waldo Emerson, and James Freeman Clarke (2 volumes, Boston: Phillips, Sampson, 1852; 3 volumes, London: Bentley, 1852);

William Ellery Channing, *The Perfect Life: In Twelve Discourses,* edited by Channing (Boston: Roberts, 1876).

SELECTED PERIODICAL PUBLICATIONS–
UNCOLLECTED: Review of "An Oration Delivered Before the Phi Beta Kappa Society" by Ralph Waldo Emerson, *Boston Quarterly Review,* 1 (January 1838): 106–120;

"Outrages of Missouri Mobs on Mormons," *Western Messenger,* 7, no. 3 (1839): 209–214;

"Ernest the Seeker, Chapter First," *Dial,* 1 (July 1840): 48–58;

"Ernest the Seeker, Chapter Second," *Dial,* 1 (October 1840): 233–242;

"Charles Fourier," *Present,* 1 (15 September 1843): 28–29;

"Call of the Present.–No. 1.–Social Reorganization," *Present,* 1 (15 October 1843): 37–44;

Review of *Mosses from an Old Manse* by Nathaniel Hawthorne, *Harbinger,* 3 (27 June 1846): 43–44;

Review of *The History of Woman Suffrage* edited by Elizabeth Cady Stanton, Susan B. Anthony, and Matilda Joslyn Gage, *Inquirer* (London, 5 November 1881).

William Henry Channing, the nephew of Unitarian clergyman William Ellery Channing (1780–1842) and cousin of poet and Transcendentalist William Ellery Channing II (1817–1901), was a Unitarian minister, an author, an editor, and an idealistic reformer who assumed a variety of philosophical and religious identities during his life. He has been referred to as "the political conscience of the transcendental movement," but although Channing did initially espouse the tenets of Transcendentalism, he ultimately parted ways with its emphasis on self-culture. Instead, Channing advocated Christian socialism and sought to bring about what he called "the Kingdom of heaven on Earth" through the doctrine of associationism. Channing is important to the American Renaissance primarily as the influential editor of three periodicals—the *Western Messenger,* the *Present,* and the *Spirit of the Age*—publications that featured his own articles on social reform as well as others on literature, philosophy, and religion. Additionally, he compiled and wrote the *Memoir of William Ellery Channing, with Extracts from His Correspondence and Manuscripts* (1848) and a biography of his cousin and fellow editor,

The Memoir and Writings of James Handasyd Perkins (1851); he translated Théodore Simon Jouffroy's *Introduction to Ethics, Including a Critical Survey of Moral Systems* (1840) for George Ripley's *Specimens of Foreign Standard Literature* (1838–1842); and he co-edited, along with James Freeman Clarke and Ralph Waldo Emerson, the *Memoirs of Margaret Fuller Ossoli* (1852). Channing also published pamphlets on political, religious, and social issues, and he participated in many of the reform movements of his era, particularly antislavery and woman's rights.

William Henry Channing was born on 25 May 1810 into two old and prominent Boston families. His mother, Susan Higginson, was the daughter of Stephen Higginson, a member of the Continental Congress; and his father was Francis Dana Channing, a lawyer and the brother of William Ellery Channing. Because Channing's father died the year he was born, his famous uncle filled the role of an influential father figure throughout Channing's formative years. Early-nineteenth-century Boston was home to many of the most-accomplished ministers of America, and the city experienced rapid social changes during these years; it was an exciting place and time for the young and imaginative Channing. Channing's sole biographer, Octavius Brooks Frothingham, describes Boston at this time as "the centre of every movement in intellectual and spiritual life . . . full of the germs of a surprising moral activity." Channing studied at the Lancaster Academy and the Boston Latin School, and he graduated from Harvard University in 1829, in a class that included Oliver Wendell Holmes as well as Channing's close friend James Freeman Clarke. Channing completed Harvard Divinity School in 1833 and became an ordained Unitarian minister in 1835. In December 1836 he married Julia Allen, with whom he had four children.

Frothingham declares that Channing "was predestined to the ministry," but he endured some soul-searching and disappointment before fulfilling this prophecy. After graduating from Harvard Divinity School and preaching at a few local churches in Boston, Channing began to question his Christian faith. He went west for a time, visiting friends in Pennsylvania and then in Cincinnati, Ohio. He toured Europe for a year, and upon returning to America in August 1836 he moved to New York City to pursue a Unitarian "ministry-at-large" among the inner-city poor, a position that first acquainted him with Margaret Fuller, Lydia Maria Child, and Horace Greeley. Walter Donald Kring states that Channing came to realize the inadequacy of his "rather advanced intellectual ideas about religion" in a largely working-class and impoverished area, but Joel Myerson also explains that this time in New York developed the "social reformer" in Channing. An added source of frustration for him was that more than fifty different churches of various denominations were already meeting the religious needs of the urban poor.

Channing soon left New York and set out again for Cincinnati in September 1838, where he joined a group of Transcendentalist "missionaries" and friends—Christopher Pearse Cranch, James Handasyd Perkins, William Greenleaf Eliot, and James Freeman Clarke—in attempting to liberalize the west. Originally, Channing's assignment at Cincinnati's First Congregational Church was to last six months, but the position became permanent in March 1839. Thanks both to his success with the congregation there and to his personal satisfaction with the city, Channing recovered from the spiritual and vocational crisis brought on by his self-perceived failure in New York. Cincinnati in the 1830s and 1840s was considered a more tolerant locale than even the Transcendentalists' native Boston, and at least initially they enjoyed a receptive audience for their philosophical speculation. Channing in fact remarked that Cincinnati "presented a delightful contrast to the frigid and artificial tone of Boston society."

In June 1839 Channing assumed the coeditorship of the *Western Messenger,* a Transcendentalist periodical heretofore edited by Clarke. Channing had been a frequent contributor to the magazine, and under his reign as editor, its previously religious scope broadened, and the magazine featured articles on Johann Wolfgang von Goëthe, Friedrich von Schiller, and Friedrich Ernst Daniel Schleiermacher, among others; contributors included John Quincy Adams, George W. Hosmer, Ephraim Peabody, Ralph Waldo Emerson, Margaret Fuller, and Bronson Alcott. The *Western Messenger* preceded *The Dial* as the first Transcendentalist periodical, but in addition, as Robert D. Habich notes, its breadth encompassed the western expansionist movement, and articles on the frontier ran alongside philosophical writings. After the magazine moved to Cincinnati, the May 1840 issue carried "To Our Friends," an article that included Channing's description of the revised purpose of the magazine. He wrote that the *Western Messenger* would not "be the organ of a sect" but would "preach and practice Christian Eclecticism." Channing explained that the primary purpose of the magazine would be "the inculcation of a spirit of Life—individual and social Life. We would seek to conceive and realise an Ideal of Humanity."

Channing became sole editor of the *Western Messenger* in 1840, but early that year he wrote of his frustrations to Margaret Fuller. By April 1841 the magazine had ceased publication, and Channing experienced a spiritual crisis in which he seriously questioned the divinity of Jesus, a doubt that naturally jeopardized his ability to serve as a Christian minister. Channing described this period as one of uncertainty

about the role of Jesus in an overall conception of the Christian faith: "While admitting to the full, therefore, the profound truth of the words of Jesus, and the surpassing loveliness of his life, I was yet inclined to look upon him rather as a beautiful manifestation of human nature, under uncommon circumstances, than as peculiarly, and in sublime reality, the Son of God." According to Frothingham, Channing now "became a deist" and believed that "Christianity was not a divine institution." Yet, in her examination of Channing's spiritual crisis, Elizabeth R. McKinsey disagrees with Frothingham's assessment of this period in Channing's life. McKinsey argues that Channing "felt Jesus and the Church were not enough. . . . Channing stood for the Heart after all, not the Head," and she believes that when Channing resigned his pulpit in Cincinnati, he "faced an almost complete self-definition." Regardless of what led to this crisis, both McKinsey and Frothingham agree that Channing emerged from it with a renewed faith in Christianity and with a reworked understanding of Jesus' relation to his faith. Frothingham asserts that this foundation provided Channing with the basis for all of the religious and social reformations that followed in his life. This nebulous creed was nondogmatic and general enough to satisfy the shifting theological dimensions of Channing's time and his peers, although Frothingham characterizes it simply as "glorified" Unitarianism. Writing in the *Western Messenger* in 1840, Channing vacillated on accepting the Unitarian label: "We bear indeed the name Unitarian. It is a name, which in the present state of the Christian world, we are bound to wear. But we would gladly change it. . . . We dislike the name Unitarian, because it is a mere scholastic title." He goes on to describe his preference for a simpler, more inclusive religious title, such as "Christian Brethren."

In *Heralds of a Liberal Faith* (1910), Thomas Wentworth Higginson describes Channing as "very eloquent in the pulpit"; throughout his life, admirers spoke of Channing's impassioned and extemporaneous public delivery. Nathaniel Hawthorne's wife, Sophia, described the impact of Channing's pulpit performance: "he was an angel of God, his lips were touched with the fire of sacred love and wisdom, and the grace and power of Jesus Christ were made manifest in him." Yet, Channing's enthusiasms in the pulpit centered on social reform, not on religious conversion. Frothingham claims that Channing was a Unitarian, not from a devotion to its theology but from a belief that it was the "purest" version of Christianity—that it fostered the tolerance and benevolence that Channing believed was essential to effect true social reform.

Channing moved to New York in 1842, preaching first in Brooklyn and then at the Stuyvesant Institute,

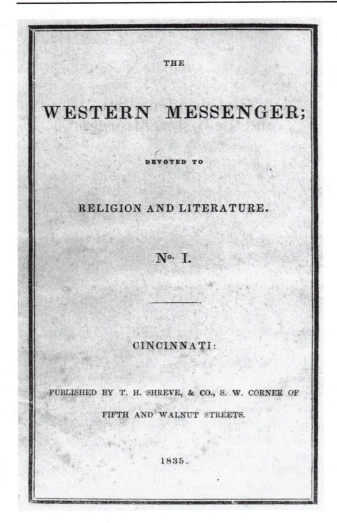

Inaugural issue of the first Transcendentalist periodical

with Henry James Sr. and Horace Greeley often in attendance. On 9 April 1843 he wrote *A Statement of the Principles of the Christian Union,* the first of several attempts to define and legitimize a Christian brotherhood devoted to creating the "church universal." Channing held that an unnatural division among people and an unnecessary mysteriousness separating religious creeds had led the human race to the zealous pursuit of material wealth, a condition that resulted in real poverty for some and spiritual destitution for all. With his New York congregation, Channing intended to foster a Christian community that enabled humanity to realize its true potential. Channing wholeheartedly believed that the timing was right: "a great change is spreading over men's spirits," he wrote. "The era of denial and scoffing has passed . . . there is a new confidence in the universal presence of the Spirit of Truth." Channing asserted that "the peculiar work of the present moment,

it appears to us, is *Union*—the union of those interested in either of the three great reforms we have mentioned, in a oneness of feeling, thought, and action." *A Statement of the Principles of the Christian Union* lays out the premise on which the organization was based:

> But has not the past taught the *insufficiency of individual exertion?* If the eternal law of creation is unity in variety; if the human race is one in many, with one modified life flowing through all; if the Infinite Spirit communicates influences to every soul in proportion to its power and fidelity,—then may we be sure that God reveals himself most fully where men are bound together in mutual sympathy and respect, in justice, truth, and love, in common joy. We live in the lives of our brethren.

Channing admitted to what he regarded as the necessary vagueness of the charter of the Christian Union: "the very confession that we are seeking what we have not found, that we are waiting for a future which, from the past through the present, is tending to fulfillment, is the life of our movement." Many of his friends criticized Channing for what they perceived as his aimlessness— to them, he lacked real purpose. Myerson writes that Child, for example, complained that Channing "had no fixed goal to steer by."

To accompany the initiation of the Christian Union, Channing launched a new periodical. The *Present* commenced on 15 September 1843 and ran until April 1844, ceasing publication at the same time as *The Dial.* The first issue carried Channing's statement of the purpose of the Christian Union, and the magazine routinely published literary, social, philosophical, and religious criticism by such authors as Parke Godwin, Higginson, Fuller, and George W. Curtis. As had the *Western Messenger,* the *Present* ran articles that elaborated on the ideas of French socialist Charles Fourier, whose systematic theory of communal living was later adopted at Brook Farm, largely due to Channing's influence. The *Present* served as an important outlet for the development of Channing's Christian Socialism, and according to Minda Pearson Dorn, it consistently promoted the idea that a revolution in American social policies was essential in order to improve life for the working classes. In the 18 September 1843 issue, Channing commented favorably on a visit from Bronson Alcott and Charles Lane, who had been in New York recruiting for their short-lived utopia, Fruitlands. Channing called them the "Essenes of New England," but while he praised their plan, he doubted its practicality. In his regular column, "Signs of the Times," on 1 March 1844 Channing spoke more optimistically about the success ongoing at Brook Farm: "There can be no doubt that this institution offers an unsurpassed opportunity for a practical manifestation of Association." This article also called attention to the need of Brook Farm for capital, and Channing exhorted his readers to donate generously to the community.

With the last issue of the *Present,* Channing explained that the demise of the magazine resulted from his own need to devote time to collecting and writing the memoirs of the Reverend William Ellery Channing, who had died in 1842. Channing spent the next six years putting together this overwhelming and time-consuming project. The *Memoir of William Ellery Channing* compiles the famous clergyman's private papers, and Channing's biographical commentary is interspersed throughout. In 1880, for the American Unitarian Association, Channing produced a one-volume, condensed version of the *Memoir of William Ellery Channing,* titled *The Life of William Ellery Channing* (1880). Both editions focus on Dr. Channing's popular career as minister at the Federal Street Church in Boston and virtually ignore the heated controversies in which he was involved as the primary spokesman of his era for liberal Unitarianism. As he later did with his editing of Margaret Fuller's memoirs, Channing excised significant portions of his uncle's correspondence and concentrated on presenting his interpretation of Dr. Channing as a learned and impassioned minister.

When George Ripley founded Brook Farm in September 1841, Channing was one of the strongest supporters of and most regular visitors to the community. Although he never lived there for more than a few months, most historians acknowledge that Channing was the spiritual leader—the "unofficial chaplain"—of Brook Farm. He preached eloquent, passionate sermons outdoors at a locale called "Pulpit Rock." In the *Present* and in the pulpit, he was quite vocal in promoting the theories of Fourier, and Channing is generally credited with instigating Brook Farm's transformation to an official Fourierist community in early 1844. Fourier's ideas had come to America initially through Albert Brisbane's *The Social Destiny of Man* (1840). Anne C. Rose in *Transcendentalism as a Social Movement, 1830–1850* (1981) explains the attraction that Fourier held for the Transcendentalists, particularly for those involved in the communal living experiment at Brook Farm. Fourier, like Channing and other Transcendentalists, believed in the innate goodness of the human race, but he held that social and class divisions resulting from unequal economic conditions had subverted humanity's natural propensity to goodness. Fourier had devised an elaborate system of social reorganization based on a series of "phalanxes," buildings in which people would live with, work with, and relate to each other. Channing saw in Fourier's social planning a method for instituting his own plan for a harmonious, universal, and moral soci-

ety. In *The Utopian Alternative: Fourierism in Nineteenth-Century America* (1991), Carl J. Guarneri declares that Channing showed "Brook Farmers [how] to accept Fourierism as an intellectual system." Guarneri explains that "by injecting spiritual regeneration and self-sacrifice into communitarian economic reform, Channing's articles of 1843–1844 led Brook Farmers "to Christianize Fourierism as they adopted it." Richard Francis adds that Channing related Fourierism and Transcendentalism by "superimposing a moral order onto the social structure." Despite the adoption of Fourierism by the Brook Farmers, Channing was still able to enumerate the faults of the community. Writing to a friend shortly after a fire had destroyed its main phalanstery, Channing criticized the facilities, the ill-conceived economic planning, and the substandard work ethic of the inhabitants themselves.

Channing's relationship to the Transcendental movement is a bit problematic because, although Channing belonged to the Transcendental Club and identified with the reformist views and liberal theology of most Transcendentalists, he rejected their emphasis on individualism. Channing stressed the need to reform the entire human race, not the lone human being. In 1852 Channing wrote "A Participant's Definition" of Transcendentalism for inclusion in the memoirs of Fuller, which he co-edited with Emerson and Clarke. With characteristic imprecision he characterized the movement as "an assertion of the inalienable integrity of man." Perry Miller claims that Channing "extracted out of Transcendental metaphysics a program of social regeneration," while Guarneri aligns Channing with Ripley and Orestes Brownson, who, in breaking from Emerson, sought a "Christianized society achieved not through self-reliance but through immersion in the lives of others and ultimately through social reorganization."

On other occasions Channing more clearly articulated his objections to Transcendentalism. As early as January 1838, in a review of Emerson's "American Scholar" address, Channing muted his otherwise largely positive comments with phrases such as this one: "and yet would we see him more fully warmed with the great social idea of our era,—the great idea . . . of human brotherhood." Criticizing a sermon by Theodore Parker, Channing wrote to him in 1842: "the Race is inspired as well as the Individual. . . . Humanity is a growth from a Divine Life as well as Man; and indeed . . . the true advancement of the individual is dependent upon the advancement of a generation." That same year, he voiced the identical complaint more stridently to Emerson: "*You deny the human Race.* You stand, or rather seek to stand, a complete Adam. But you cannot do it." Channing perhaps too narrowly interpreted Emerson's use of the word "self," a word that David Robinson argues Emerson applied broadly to include all individual selves. Robinson postulates that Channing and Emerson agreed on the "nature of the self"; to him, their point of departure "was over the manifestations of the self in society."

Emerson leveled his own criticism at Channing. His 1847 "Ode Inscribed to W. H. Channing" upbraids Channing and other abolitionists for embracing a policy of "disunion," an action that to Emerson would have been a disastrous method for abolishing slavery. The second line of the poem calls Channing "the evil time's sole patriot," a misnomer, since, as Leonard Gougeon has pointed out, advocating disunion was hardly patriotic. In spite of these differences with Emerson, however, Channing valued their friendship. Indeed, Emerson chose Channing to baptize his children—the only minister Emerson felt was "pure" enough to do so, according to Moncure Daniel Conway.

Another Concord Transcendentalist, Henry David Thoreau, did not think much of Channing. After their first meeting in 1843 Thoreau described Channing as somewhat despondent and aloof and declared that "you would like to see him when he has made up his mind to run all the risks." As they became better acquainted, Thoreau modified his initial distaste, however, and came to appreciate Channing, though not what Thoreau referred to as Channing's "schemes."

On 3 January 1847 Channing organized in Boston the Religious Union of Associationists. Also called the First Church of Humanity, this new reform ministry included in its informal congregation many former members of Brook Farm, including Ripley and John S. Dwight, and eventually numbered Peabody, Fuller, and James among its sympathizers. Sterling F. Delano describes the Union as a "direct outgrowth of Channing's earlier ministrations at Brook Farm." Channing served as the spiritual leader to the group and explained that it sought "to devote their lives to the establishment of the Kingdom of God on Earth"; he declared that this church would strive "to introduce upon this planet an era of Universal Unity." Delano states that the Associationists' primary goal was to "reconcile the Christian Church and social reform," while William R. Hutchison viewed it as "a sugar-coating of Christianity to Fourierist ideals." Channing's Associationist ministry was enormously popular. He delivered emotional and erudite sermons that converted large crowds to the cause of Christian Socialism. Conway declared that Channing preached with "a tone of prophetic authenticity," and in *Transcendentalism in New England: A History* (1876), Frothingham describes Channing's appeal: he "burned with a pure enthusiasm that lifted souls into a celestial air and made all possibilities of justice seem practicable." Delano's "A Calendar of Meetings of the 'Boston Reli-gious Union of Associationists'" reveals the breadth of the Associationist gatherings at which, among other topics, Channing addressed "The Kingdom of Heaven at Hand," "The Life of Holiness," "Fraud and Robbery," "prevailing sophistries in relation to social evils," "Universal Selfishness," and "The Unity of the Race."

From June 1845 to June 1847 the *Harbinger* was published as the official organ of Brook Farm; editors were Ripley and Dwight. Its purpose was to set forth the goals of the Associationists, including Fourierism, but it also published a good deal of literary criticism, and Channing contributed several book reviews, including one of Hawthorne's *Mosses from an Old Manse*. After the demise of Brook Farm, the magazine moved in October 1847 to New York, and Channing joined Ripley in editing it there. When the *Harbinger* ceased publication in February 1849, Channing almost immediately conceived of another magazine that would address issues of concern to the Associationists. The *Spirit of the Age* commenced on 7 July 1849 and ran weekly for slightly less than a year until 27 April 1850. Worried about his poor health and overworked by a frenzied schedule that frequently took him out of town, Channing announced the cessation of the publication in the last issue. He said that the *Spirit of the Age* was ending because the editor was "brain-sick—and it does not pay." In June 1850 Channing also bid what he regarded as a temporary farewell to the Religious Union as he left for a summer stay at a Fourierist phalanx in New Jersey, but the Union effectively ended with his departure. After years of perpetual new beginnings, he simply wanted, as he wrote to a friend, "some shelter, where the heart may find refreshment." Eventually Channing took a position at the Unitarian church in Rochester, New York, where he remained until 1854.

In late July 1850 Channing went to New York along with Thoreau to search through the wreckage off Fire Island for the remains and manuscripts of his longtime friend and fellow Transcendentalist Fuller. Fuller, her husband, and their infant son had drowned when the ship bringing them home from Italy wrecked just off the New York coast. To commemorate Fuller's life and present her writings to a wider audience, Channing joined with Emerson and Clarke in editing her memoirs. Robert Richardson Jr. credits Channing with first suggesting publication of the memoirs, and Bell Gale Chevigny raises the possibility that Channing oversaw the entire project. The *Memoirs of Margaret Fuller Ossoli* was published in both England and America in 1852. Each editor combined his recollections of Fuller with her own writings, both published and private, and Channing included in it "A Participant's Definition" of Transcendentalism.

Especially because of the prominence of its editors, the *Memoirs of Margaret Fuller Ossoli* was an enormously influential work. Not until decades later, however, did Fuller's subsequent biographers realize the extent to which Channing, Clarke, and Emerson had censored and assiduously rewritten her work in an effort to present their modified version of the author to the world. Chevigny, in "The Long Arm of Censorship: Myth-making in Margaret Fuller's Time and Our Own" (1976), claims that the editors took it upon themselves to "invent" Fuller; she believes that they felt compelled to "*make over* the moral image" of their subject, particularly as they pored over her often intimate, stridently feminist correspondence. Especially, the editors abridged and routinely "feminized" Fuller's frank discussions of politics and sexuality. Moreover, according to Chevigny, Channing "took the greatest liberties of the three in preparing his section of the Memoirs." Chevigny claims that Channing criticized Fuller's writing far less than Clarke or Emerson did and that his sentimental tone praised Fuller as a woman rather than as a literary figure. Miller includes Channing as one of a number of admirers "who threw themselves (intellectually) at the feet of Margaret Fuller," a conclusion perhaps reflected in Channing's commentary in the *Memoirs of Margaret Fuller Ossoli*. He notes Fuller's "saucy sprightliness" and claims that she was "too *intense* in expression, action, emphasis, to be pleasing." These remarks transform Fuller into a romantic, intellectual freak, although Channing must have intended to be balanced when he characterized her "genius" as the result of the opposing qualities of "feminine receptiveness with masculine energy."

Chevigny's presentation of the excisions and editorial interpolations that Channing made to Fuller's words calls into serious question Channing's ability as an editor to present Fuller on her own terms. Additionally disturbing is that all three of the editors paid little attention to the rigors of careful editing; throughout the *Memoirs of Margaret Fuller Ossoli,* names and dates are often missing or inaccurate, and much information is simply excised. For his part, Emerson recorded in his journal at least one instance of disagreement with Channing during their consultation on the *Memoirs* in the summer of 1851. Channing did not believe that Fuller had indeed married Italian nobleman Giovanni Ossoli because such a legal tie "was contrary to her view of a noble life," but Emerson held that she had. Thirty years later, when Higginson began researching for his own biography of Fuller, Channing admonished him to be true to the essential qualities of Fuller as Channing had been; his interpretation of Fuller, he wrote to Higginson, was "juster, deeper, purer, truer, loftier, than has ever been given elsewhere."

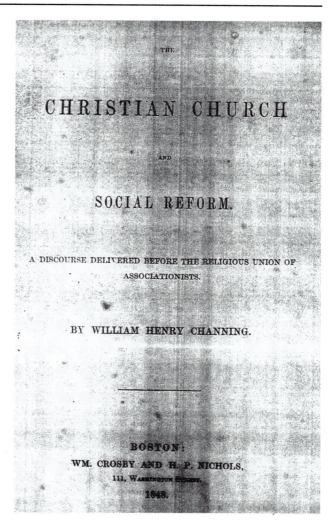

Title page for an address Channing gave before the group he organized "to devote their lives to the establishment of the Kingdom of God on Earth"

Channing's efforts as a social reformer were always an intrinsic aspect of his ministerial and editorial work. He joined the antislavery movement in the 1830s and spoke frequently at abolitionist gatherings, including an August 1846 meeting sponsored by the Concord Female Anti-Slavery Society and held at Thoreau's Walden Pond cabin. Particularly when he lived in Rochester in the years just after the Fugitive Slave Law had passed in 1850, Channing provided aid to fugitive slaves, acts that earned him the praise of Frederick Douglass, a resident of Rochester at that time. Channing also delivered a number of speeches at woman's rights conventions in the early 1850s, and as editor of the *Harbinger* and the *Spirit of the Age,* he published articles on woman's rights, including one by British reformer Harriet Martineau.

In 1854 Channing and his family moved to England, where he accepted the prominent ministry of Renshaw Chapel in Liverpool. In 1857 Channing assumed the pulpit at the Hope Street Chapel in Liverpool, replacing James Martineau. English Unitarians received Channing warmly, and he became more comfortable there with conservative Christian theology and rituals than he had been up to this time in America. His life as an expatriate seems finally to have fulfilled him. Late in life, Channing described having endured religious crises with his idealism intact; in 1882 he wrote that "we are actually living in the Morning of a wholly New Era of . . . *Universal Unity.*"

Channing returned to America to visit in 1861, during which time the Civil War broke out. He decided to remain in the United States and served the Union cause in various capacities from a base in Washington, D.C. He was the minister of the Unitarian Society; he helped to establish the Sanitary Commission; he nursed the wounded in several military camps in the area; and when hospital space was in urgent demand, he transformed his church into an emergency facility for the wounded. In 1863 Channing served as the chaplain to Stanton Memorial Hospital, and from 1863 to 1864 he served as Chaplain to the U.S. Congress. When the war ended in 1865, Channing returned to England and made it his home for the remainder of his life. He returned to America often, however, to visit old friends and associates, including an extended stay in the summer of 1880 when he accepted Alcott's invitation to give a series of lectures on "Oriental Mysticism" at Alcott's School of Philosophy in Concord, Massachusetts.

Many of his contemporaries complained of Channing's inability to lead the movements he began. Parker once remarked that Channing "hit the same nail every time; he hit it hard; but the head was downward; he never drove the iron in." Later writers, such as Lindsay Swift in his study of Brook Farm, have been more severe. Swift determines that Channing "had an over-enthusiasm and lack of definiteness well calculated to wreck any project dependent on him alone to shape its course." Yet, as Frothingham notes, Channing's goal had been to inspire men to aspire to loftier moral and spiritual heights and to educate and expose his peers to new ideas, not necessarily to govern the movements themselves. Frothingham argues that Channing "was a preacher of reconciliation and theological peace." More recently, critics such as Robinson have forgiven Channing's naiveté in favor of assessing the enormous contributions he made to "support a radical political and social transformation in America." Robinson praises Channing's convictions and cites him as the most appropriate exemplar of "transcendental politics,"

although he agrees that Channing's "career leaves us with the sense of enormous talent and energy that never found a satisfactory outlet." Unquestionably, however, William Henry Channing and his millennial mission inspired many, and he wielded considerable influence on fellow reformers, ministers, and Transcendentalists. Channing died in London on 23 December 1884 and is buried in Boston.

Bibliography:

Elizabeth R. McKinsey, "William Henry Channing," *The Transcendentalists: A Review of Research and Criticism,* edited by Joel Myerson (New York: MLA, 1984), pp. 108–111.

Biography:

Octavius Brooks Frothingham, *Memoir of William Henry Channing* (Boston: Houghton, Mifflin, 1886).

References:

Bell Gale Chevigny, "The Long Arm of Censorship: Myth-making in Margaret Fuller's Time and Our Own," *Signs,* 2 (Winter 1976): 450–460;

Moncure Daniel Conway, *Emerson at Home and Abroad* (Boston: Osgood, 1882);

George Willis Cooke, *An Historical and Biographical Introduction to Accompany The Dial,* 2 volumes (New York: Russell & Russell, 1961);

Cooke, *Unitarianism in America: A History of Its Origin and Development* (Boston: American Unitarian Association, 1902);

Charles Crowe, "Christian Socialism and the First Church of Humanity," *Church History,* 35 (March 1966): 93–106;

Edith Roelker Curtis, *A Season in Utopia: The Story of Brook Farm* (Edinburgh, New York & Toronto: Thomas Nelson, 1961);

Sterling F. Delano, "The Boston Union of Associationists (1846–1851): 'Association Is to Me the Great Hope of the World,'" in *Studies in the American Renaissance 1996,* edited by Joel Myerson (Charlottesville: University Press of Virginia, 1996), pp. 5–40;

Delano, "A Calendar of Meetings of the 'Boston Religious Union of Associationists,' 1847–1850," *Studies in the American Renaissance 1985,* edited by Myerson (Charlottesville: University Press of Virginia, 1985), pp. 187–267;

Delano, *The Harbinger and New England Transcendentalism: A Portrait of Associationism in America* (Rutherford, N.J.: Fairleigh Dickinson University Press, 1983);

Minda Ruth Pearson Dorn, "Literary Criticism in the *Boston Quarterly Review,* the *Present,* and the *Massa-*

chusetts *Quarterly Review*," dissertation, Southern Illinois University at Carbondale, 1975;

Richard Francis, "The Ideology of Brook Farm," *Studies in the American Renaissance 1977,* edited by Myerson (Boston: Twayne, 1977), pp. 1–48;

Octavius Brooks Frothingham, *Transcendentalism in New England: A History* (New York: Putnam, 1876);

Clarence L. F. Gohdes, *The Periodicals of American Transcendentalism* (Durham, N.C.: Duke University Press, 1931);

Leonard Gougeon, "The Anti-Slavery Background of Emerson's 'Ode Inscribed to W. H. Channing,'" *Studies in the American Renaissance 1985,* edited by Myerson (Charlottesville: The University Press of Virginia, 1985), pp. 63–77;

Judith A. Green, "Religion, Life, and Literature in the *Western Messenger,*" dissertation, University of Wisconsin, Madison, 1981;

Carl J. Guarneri, *The Utopian Alternative: Fourierism in Nineteenth-Century America* (Ithaca, N.Y. & London: Cornell University Press, 1991);

Robert D. Habich, "The 'Spiral Ascending Path' of William Henry Channing: An Autobiographical Letter," *ESQ,* 30 (First Quarter 1984): 22–26;

Habich, *Transcendentalism and the* Western Messenger: *A History of the Magazine and Its Contributors, 1835–1841* (Rutherford, Madison & Teaneck: Fairleigh Dickinson University Press, 1985);

Walter Harding and Carl Bode, eds., *The Correspondence of Henry David Thoreau* (New York: New York University Press, 1958);

Thomas Wentworth Higginson, "William Henry Channing," *Heralds of a Liberal Faith,* edited by Samuel A. Eliot (Boston: American Unitarian Association, 1910), III: 59–66;

William R. Hutchison, *The Transcendentalist Ministers: Church Reform in the New England Renaissance* (New Haven: Yale University Press, 1959);

Walter Donald Kring, *Liberals among the Orthodox: Unitarian Beginnings in New York City 1819–1839* (Boston: Beacon, 1974);

Elizabeth R. McKinsey, *The Western Experiment: New England Transcendentalists in the Ohio Valley* (Cambridge, Mass.: Harvard University Press, 1973);

Perry Miller, ed., *The American Transcendentalists: Their Prose and Poetry* (Garden City, N.Y.: Doubleday / Anchor, 1957);

Miller, ed., *The Transcendentalists: An Anthology* (Cambridge, Mass.: Harvard University Press, 1950);

Joel Myerson, *The New England Transcendentalists and* The Dial: *A History of the Magazine and Its Contributors* (Rutherford, Madison & Teaneck: Fairleigh Dickinson University Press, 1980);

David Robinson, "The Political Odyssey of William Henry Channing," *Association Quarterly,* 34 (Summer 1982): 165–184;

Anne C. Rose, *Transcendentalism as a Social Movement, 1830–1850* (New Haven: Yale University Press, 1981);

Frank R. Shivers Jr., "A Western Chapter in the History of American Transcendentalism," *Bulletin of the Historic and Philosophical Society of Ohio,* 15 (April 1957): 117–130;

Madeleine B. Stern, "William Henry Channing's Letters on 'Woman in Her Social Relations,'" *Cornell Library Journal,* 6 (Autumn 1968): 54–62;

Lindsay Swift, *Brook Farm: Its Members, Scholars, and Visitors* (New York: Macmillan, 1900);

Walter Samuel Swisher, "William Henry Channing: A Neglected Figure in the History of Unitarianism," *Proceedings of the Unitarian Historical Society,* 6, part 2 (1939): 1–12;

A. G. Thacher Jr., "William Henry Channing and the Spirit of the Age," M.A. thesis, Columbia University, 1941;

W. H. Venable, *Beginnings of Literary Culture in the Ohio Valley: Historical and Biographical Sketches* (Cincinnati: Robert Clarke, 1891).

Papers:

The major collections of William Henry Channing's papers are at the Houghton Library of Harvard University, the Andover-Harvard Theological Library, the Massachusetts Historical Society, and the Boston Public Library.

Lydia Maria Child

(11 February 1802 – 20 October 1880)

Deborah P. Clifford

See also the Child entries in *DLB 1: American Renaissance in New England* and *DLB 74: American Short-Story Writers Before 1880.*

BOOKS: *Hobomok, A Tale of Early Times,* as an American Lady (Boston: Cummings, Hilliard, 1824);

Evenings in New England. Intended for Juvenile Amusement and Instruction, as an American Lady (Boston: Cummings, Hilliard, 1824);

The Rebels, or Boston before the Revolution, as the author of *Hobomok* (Boston: Cummings, Hilliard, 1825);

Emily Parker, or Impulse, Not Principle. Intended for Young Persons, as the author of *Evenings in New England* and editor of *The Juvenile Miscellany* (Boston: Bowles & Dearborn, 1827);

Biographical Sketches of Great and Good Men. Designed for the Amusement and Instruction of Young Persons, as the editor of *The Miscellany* (Boston: Putnam & Hunt / Philadelphia: Thomas T. Ash, 1828);

The First Settlers of New-England: or, Conquest of the Pequods, Narragansets and Pokanokets: As Related by a Mother to Her Children, and Designed for the Instruction of Youth, as a Lady of Massachusetts (Boston: Munroe & Francis / New York: Charles S. Francis, 1829);

The Frugal Housewife. Dedicated to Those Who Are Not Ashamed of Economy, as the author of *Hobomok* (Boston: Marsh & Capen / Carter & Hendee, 1829; revised and enlarged edition, Boston: Carter & Hendee, 1830); republished as *The American Frugal Housewife* (Boston: Carter & Hendee, 1832);

The Little Girl's Own Book (Boston: Carter, Hendee & Babcock, 1831; London: Tegg, 1832; enlarged edition, Boston: Carter & Hendee, 1834);

The Mother's Book (Boston: Carter, Hendee & Babcock / Baltimore: Charles Carter, 1831; London: Tegg, 1832; revised and enlarged edition, New York: C. S. Francis / Boston: Joseph H. Francis, 1844);

The Coronal. A Collection of Miscellaneous Pieces, Written at Various Times (Boston: Carter & Hendee, 1832); republished as *The Mother's Story Book; or Western Coronal. A Collection of Miscellaneous Pieces. By Mrs.*

Lydia Maria Child

Child . . . To Which Are Added a Few Tales, by Mary Howitt, and Caroline Fry (London, Edinburgh, Dublin & Glasgow: T. T. & J. Tegg, 1833);

The Biographies of Madame de Staël, and Madame Roland, volume 1 of *Ladies' Family Library* (Boston: Carter & Hendee, 1832); republished in part as *The Biography of Madame de Staël* (Edinburgh: Thomas Clark, 1836); 1832 edition revised and enlarged as *Memoires of Madame de Staël, and of Madame Roland* (New York: C. S. Francis / Boston: J. H. Francis, 1847);

The Biographies of Lady Russell and Madame Guyon, volume 2 of *Ladies' Family Library* (Boston: Carter &

Hendee, 1832); republished in part as *The Biography of Lady Russell* (Edinburgh: Thomas Clark, 1836);

Good Wives, volume 3 of *Ladies' Family Library* (Boston: Carter, Hendee, 1833); republished as *Biographies of Good Wives* (New York: C. S. Francis / Boston: J. H. Francis, 1846; London: Griffin, 1849); republished as *Celebrated Women; or, Biographies of Good Wives* (New York: Charles S. Francis, 1861); republished as *Married Women: Biographies of Good Wives* (New York: Charles S. Francis, 1871);

An Appeal in Favor of That Class of Americans Called Africans (Boston: Allen & Ticknor, 1833);

The History of the Condition of Women, in Various Ages and Nations, 2 volumes, volumes 4 and 5 of *Ladies' Family Library* (Boston: John Allen, 1835; London, 1835); revised and republished as *Brief History of the Condition of Women, in Various Ages and Nations* (New York: C. S. Francis / Boston: J. H. Francis, 1845);

Anti-Slavery Catechism (Newburyport, Mass.: Charles Whipple, 1836);

The Evils of Slavery, and the Cure of Slavery. The First Proved by the Opinions of Southerners Themselves, the Last Shown by Historical Evidence (Newburyport, Mass.: Charles Whipple, 1836);

Philothea. A Romance (Boston: Otis, Broaders, 1836; New York: C. S. Francis, 1845); republished as *Philothea: A Grecian Romance* (New York: C. S. Francis, 1845);

The Family Nurse; or Companion of The Frugal Housewife (Boston: Charles J. Hendee, 1837);

Letters from New-York [first series] (New York: C. S. Francis / Boston: James Munroe, 1843; London: Bentley, 1843);

Flowers for Children. I. For Children Eight or Nine Years Old (New York: C. S. Francis / Boston: J. H. Francis, 1844); republished as *The Christ-Child, and Other Stories* (Boston: Lothrop / Dover, N.H.: G. T. Day, 1869);

Flowers for Children. II. For Children from Four to Six Years Old (New York: C. S. Francis / Boston: J. H. Francis, 1844); republished as *Good Little Mitty, and Other Stories* (Boston: Lothrop / Dover, N.H.: G. T. Day, 1869);

Letters from New-York. Second Series (New York: C. S. Francis / Boston: J. H. Francis, 1845);

Fact and Fiction: A Collection of Stories (New York: C. S. Francis / Boston: J. H. Francis, 1846; London: William Smith, 1847); republished as *The Children of Mount Ida, and Other Stories* (New York: C. S. Francis, 1871);

Flowers for Children. III. For Children of Eleven and Twelve Years of Age (New York: C. S. Francis / Boston: J. H.

Francis, 1847); republished as *Making Something, and Other Stories* (Boston: Lothrop / Dover, N.H.: G. T. Day, 1869);

Sketches from Real Life. I. The Power of Kindness. II. Home and Politics (Philadelphia: Hazard & Mitchell, 1850; London: Collins, 1850); republished as *The Power of Kindness; and Other Stories* (Philadelphia: Hazard, 1853);

The Children's Gems. The Brother and Sister: And Other Stories, anonymous (Philadelphia: New Church Book Store, 1852);

Isaac T. Hopper: A True Life (Boston: John P. Jewett / Cleveland: Jewett, Proctor & Worthington, 1853 / London: Sampson Low, 1853);

The Progress of Religious Ideas, Through Successive Ages, 3 volumes (New York: C. S. Francis, 1855 / London: Sampson Low, 1855);

A New Flowers for Children. For Children from Eight to Twelve Years Old (New York: C. S. Francis, 1856);

Autumnal Leaves: Tales and Sketches in Prose and Rhyme (New York & Boston: C. S. Francis, 1857);

Correspondence between Lydia Maria Child and Gov. Wise and Mrs. Mason of Virginia (Boston: American Anti-Slavery Society, 1860);

The Right Way The Safe Way, Proved by Emancipation in the British West Indies, and Elsewhere (New York, 1860; enlarged, 1862);

The Duty of Disobedience to the Fugitive Slave Act: An Appeal to the Legislators of Massachusetts (Boston: American Anti-Slavery Society, 1860);

A Romance of the Republic (Boston: Ticknor & Fields, 1867);

An Appeal for the Indians (New York: Wm. P. Tomlinson, 1868).

Collections: *Hobomok and Other Writings on Indians,* edited by Carolyn L. Karcher (Brunswick, N.J.: Rutgers University Press, 1986);

A Lydia Maria Child Reader, edited by Karcher (Durham & London: Duke University Press, 1997).

OTHER: *The Juvenile Souvenir,* edited, with contributions, by Child, as the editor of *The Juvenile Miscellany* (Boston: Marsh & Capen / John Putnam, 1827);

Moral Lessons in Verse, edited by Child, as the editor of *The Juvenile Miscellany* (Cambridge: Hilliard & Brown, 1828);

The Oasis, edited, with contributions, by Child (Boston: Allen & Ticknor, 1834);

Authentic Anecdotes of American Slavery, nos. 1–3, edited anonymously, with contributions, by Child (Newburyport, Mass.: Charles Whipple, 1835–1838);

Child's husband, David Lee Child, whom she married in 1828 (from Helene G. Baer, The Heart Is like Heaven: The Life of Lydia Maria Child, *1964)*

American Anti-Slavery Almanac [for 1843], edited by Child (New York: American Anti-Slavery Society, 1842);

The Patriarchal Institution, As Described by Members of Its Own Family, edited by Child (New York: American Anti-Slavery Society, 1860);

Harriet Jacobs, *Incidents in the Life of a Slave Girl,* edited by Child (Boston: Published for the Author, 1861); republished as *The Deeper Wrong; or, Incidents in the Life of a Slave Girl* (London: Tweedie, 1862);

Looking toward Sunset. From Sources Old and New, Original and Selected, edited, with contributions, by Child (Boston: Ticknor & Fields, 1865);

The Freedmen's Book, edited, with contributions, by Child (Boston: Ticknor & Fields, 1865);

Aspirations of the World. A Chain of Opals, edited, with an introduction, by Child (Boston: Roberts, 1878).

Lydia Maria Child ranks among the most influential of nineteenth-century American women writers. She was renowned in her day as a tireless crusader for truth and justice and a champion of excluded groups in American society—especially Indians, slaves, and women. A writer who early heeded the call for an American literature with American themes, she was a pioneer in several literary genres. She wrote one of the earliest American historical novels, the first comprehensive history of American slavery, and the first comparative history of women. In addition, she edited the first American children's magazine, compiled an early primer for the freed slaves, and published the first book designed for the elderly. Child possessed an uncanny ability for knowing exactly what the American reading public wanted and when they wanted it. She was also gifted at rendering radical ideas, such as the abolition of slavery, palatable for American readers.

Born on 11 February 1802 in Medford, Massachusetts, Lydia Francis (she added Maria when she was rebaptized at nineteen) was the youngest of six children born to Convers and Susannah (Rand) Francis. Bright and imaginative, headstrong and curious, Lydia Francis's early years were marred by an ill, distant mother and a stern, religiously orthodox father. Her mother died when Lydia was twelve, and she spent her adolescent years living in the interior of Maine with a married sister. The relatively open frontier society of Norridgewock gave Lydia a taste for freedom. It also exposed her to the plight of the Native Americans, for she befriended a small community of impoverished Abenaki and Penobscot Indians.

At nineteen Maria moved back to Massachusetts, where she lived with her brother Convers, a scholarly Unitarian minister and the person chiefly responsible for her education. She was twenty-two and still living with her brother in 1824 when she captivated the Boston literary world with *Hobomok, A Tale of Early Times,* her first novel.

Set in the early settlement of Salem, Massachusetts, *Hobomok* breaks away from the traditional Puritan narrative by looking at American history from a feminine point of view. Its heroine, Mary Conant, rebels against the religious and racial bigotry of her father by marrying first an Indian by whom she has a son, and later an Episcopalian. The scandalous subject matter of the novel, interracial marriage, which initially drew fire from the critics, also explains its success. *Hobomok* has the distinction of being the first New England historical novel and includes within its pages many of the Reformist themes found in Francis's later writings.

The patronage of George Ticknor, then a leading member of Boston literary society, launched *Hobomok* and made Francis an overnight celebrity. But she was never entirely comfortable with her position in the aristocratic society of Boston. While she enjoyed the company of cultivated people who appreciated her wit and learning, she also disliked the "stiffened elegance and cold formality" of their world. "My lines are all *straight,*" Maria Child admitted to her friend Sarah Shaw on 11

February 1859, "and they run against a great many corners which graceful sinuousities would avoid."

Francis's first children's book, *Evenings in New England. Intended for Juvenile Amusement and Instruction* (1824), appeared soon after *Hobomok* and comprises a series of educational conversations between Aunt Maria and her two children. The subjects discussed range from history and literature, slavery and Indians, to botany and other sciences. The focus of the book on American issues and its inculcation of American values made it an instant success. Critics hailed it as eminently suited to the children of a democratic republic. By publishing literature designed for American children, Francis discovered that she was not only filling a void but also earning a living.

Francis's second novel, *The Rebels, or Boston before the Revolution* (1825), observes prerevolutionary Boston through the eyes of two women patriots. The heroine of the novel, Lucretia Fitzherbert, is an impetuous, imaginative creature with exalted talents, who learns from her mistakes and is rewarded with marriage to a virtuous and cultivated man. Melodramatic and unfocused, *The Rebels* was not a critical success. The *North American Review* described the author as overwhelmed by her imaginative powers and accused her of filling the pages of her short book with enough plots to serve a dozen novels.

Perhaps because of the poor critical reception of *The Rebels,* Francis did not publish another novel for ten years. Instead, while continuing to write short fiction, she turned her talents in a more lucrative direction by editing the first American children's magazine, *The Juvenile Miscellany* (1826–1834). This little bimonthly included stories and poems, history and biography, and puzzles and conundrums. Though strongly didactic, its nonsectarian approach made it seem liberal for its day. While Francis's promotion of such values as hard work, sobriety, frugality, and productivity ensured the popularity of the magazine, she could not help nudging her readers to accept her dream of racial equality. The *North American Review* recommended *The Juvenile Miscellany,* and Sarah Hale's *Ladies' Magazine* urged every family with children to subscribe. A decided success, *The Juvenile Miscellany* assured its editor a modest but steady income of $300 a year.

In 19 October 1828 Maria Francis threw away all this hard-won financial security by marrying an improvident young lawyer, newspaperman, and aspiring politician named David Lee Child. Child endeared himself to her with his idealism and his enthusiastic promotion of her writings in the columns of his Whig newspaper, the *Massachusetts Journal*. But Maria Child quickly became the couple's chief breadwinner, and despite her best efforts, indebtedness hounded the

Childs throughout most of their married life. They never had any children.

Soon after the Childs' marriage, David turned the literary column of the *Massachusetts Journal* over to his wife. At this time Maria Child also began work on another children's book; it marked her debut as a political writer. Published during the Indian Removal Crisis, *The First Settlers of New-England: or, Conquest of the Pequods, Narragansets and Pokanokets: As Related by a Mother to Her Children, and Designed for the Instruction of Youth* (1829) takes the form of a dialogue between a mother and her two daughters and is set during the Indian wars of the seventeenth century. Instead of providing a patriotic portrait of the European colonists, however, Child focuses on the atrocities committed by the Puritans against the Indians. As in *Hobomok,* Child blames the first white settlers' inhuman treatment of the Native Americans on their religious bigotry and demonstrates once again that all white Americans are guilty of racial prejudice. This revisionist history of the American colonial period, with its endorsement of racial intermarriage, is Child's most radical book. But *The First Settlers of New-England* escaped critical censure, for there were no published reviews. Perhaps fear for her reputation prompted its author to see that this radical publication stayed off the market.

Early in her marriage, Child also began writing successfully for the growing number of women readers. The most popular of these works was a manual called *The Frugal Housewife. Dedicated to Those Who Are Not Ashamed of Economy* (1829). Directed at "middling" and lower-class women who could not afford servants, it was an early attempt to raise domesticity to a level of competence equal to that of other skilled trades. *The Mother's Book* (1831) was aimed at a similar audience and included advice on the rearing of children, particularly girls. Contrary to other domestic manuals of the day, it counseled that girls be educated in a way that would enable them to "support themselves respectably." While contemporary reviewers found *The Mother's Book* dangerously liberal, it met a need and consequently was popular.

Although Child netted $2000 from *The Frugal Housewife* in its first two years of publication, David Child's debts continued to rise and swallow up every penny his wife earned. To add to the couple's troubles, in 1830 David was sent to jail for libel. But Maria Child's writings from this time reveal little of these personal trials and disappointments.

The first three volumes of the *Ladies' Family Library* (1832–1835), for example, idealize marriage and domesticity. They include long and short sketches of notable women, each exemplifying the ideal of republican womanhood. While several of the women in *Good*

Child at age sixty-three

study of that institution in the United States. In this book Child blames the North as well as the South for the existence of the "peculiar institution." She calls for the immediate abolition of slavery and the eradication of all forms of racial discrimination, including laws of antimiscegenation that forbade intermarriage between blacks and whites. Once again she openly defended interracial marriage.

The abolitionists wasted little time in praising *An Appeal in Favor of That Class of Americans Called Africans.* In his review published in *The Liberator* on 10 August 1833, Garrison wrote that any "heart must be harder than the nether mill-stone which can remain unaffected by the solemn truths it contains." Indeed, scholars credit this book with converting more men and women to abolition than any other publication.

But no such accolade came from the American reading public. Old admirers, including the editor of the *North American Review,* quickly denounced Child's *An Appeal in Favor of That Class of Americans Called Africans.* Sales of her books plummeted, and in 1834 canceled subscriptions forced Child to relinquish the editorship of *The Juvenile Miscellany.* Her friend John Greenleaf Whittier later claimed that no other woman had suffered so greatly for principle as Child.

As Child worked actively behind the scenes of the American Anti-Slavery Society, the respect accorded her by Garrison and his friends convinced her that men and women could labor more effectively side by side than in separate organizations. But she participated as well in the women's auxiliary antislavery societies, helping to organize bazaars and other fund-raising events.

In the wake of *An Appeal in Favor of That Class of Americans Called Africans,* Child published four more antislavery works, including *The Oasis* (1834), a gift book including stories, poems, and articles all related in some way to the antislavery cause. Child was the author of most of the selections, but David Child and friends also contributed. Intended for the general reader, the purpose of the book was "to familiarize the public mind with the idea that colored people are *human beings*—elevated or degraded by the same circumstances that elevate or degrade other men." Stories about slaves in *The Oasis,* and in later issues of *The Juvenile Miscellany,* demonstrate Child's pioneering effort to employ fiction as a medium for overcoming racial prejudice. Although Garrison's *The Liberator* greeted *The Oasis* with effusive praise, sales of the gift book were disappointing.

Antislavery themes also pervade Child's *The History of the Condition of Women, in Various Ages and Nations* (1835), her most ambitious work to date. Its two volumes completed her *Ladies' Family Library* and include a wealth of information about the status of women in nations across the globe from biblical times to the mid

Wives (volume 3, 1833) are blessed with unusual learning and talent, all are commended for their piety, their courage, and their patriotism as well as their willing submission to their husbands' wishes. By contrast, Child's *The Biographies of Madame de Staël, and Madame Roland* (volume 1, 1832) projects a more independent and creative role for women. All three volumes received glowing press notices, hailing Child's least original work as her best.

In the early 1830s, just when Child's literary reputation was at its height, she and her husband joined the band of antislavery reformers organizing under the leadership of William Lloyd Garrison. Child later claimed that Garrison's forceful language had won her over to the cause, but she had long been a champion of freedom, and the abolitionist views on the slavery question matched her own. This literary celebrity was considered a great catch for the movement and from the start Child put her talents as a writer to work for the cause.

An Appeal in Favor of That Class of Americans Called Africans (1833) is the first scholarly American overview of the history of slavery and the first major nineteenth century. As in the other writings in this series, Child was careful to avoid offending her readers by speaking directly to feminist issues. While she provides a vast array of facts showing that societies that respect women and allow them to develop and use their talents will prosper, Child provides no analysis of this material. Indeed, her antiracist agenda is far more explicit in this book than her feminist agenda. Yet, as Carolyn L. Karcher has observed in her 1994 biography of Child, within less than a decade of the publication of the history, Sarah Grimké and Margaret Fuller, in their own writings on women, explicitly promoted the ideas Child had merely implied.

By 1835 Child had adjusted to the idea of belonging to a band of social outcasts. Although the loss of so many erstwhile friends and admirers had been a bitter blow, she had the consolation of knowing that her fellow abolitionists shared her passion for truth and freedom and that they were pleased with her work.

Meanwhile, financial troubles continued to plague the Childs' marriage. David Child's law practice had failed, and income from Maria Child's books was at an all-time low. A plan hatched by Garrison and his friends to send the Childs to England as salaried abolitionist agents seemed a solution to the couple's difficulties. But that too fell through. The day their ship was to sail from New York, David Child's legal entanglements led once again to his arrest on 16 August 1835. While soon freed, he was forced to look for other work.

Maria Child spent these months of uncertainty boarding with a Quaker family in New Rochelle, where she consoled herself by completing a work of fiction she had begun five years earlier. *Philothea. A Romance* (1836), her first novel since *The Rebels,* satisfied a longing to escape the world of reform for a romantic and idealistic realm of her own making. While the novel is set in ancient Athens, the political and philosophical preoccupations of its major characters are more reminiscent of nineteenth-century Boston. Pericles, the Athenian statesman, resembles a Jacksonian tyrant, while Anaxagoras (Philothea's father) is a good republican. Philothea, meanwhile, embodies the domestic virtues that Child was trying to cultivate as David Child's wife. Philothea marries an equally virtuous young man, who eventually dies from a debilitating illness. Her foil, Aspasia, personifies the assertive, ambitious, passionate self Child was seeking to repress. Published three weeks before Ralph Waldo Emerson's *Nature* (1836), *Philothea* is above all a fictional exploration of the connection between the material and spiritual worlds, its heroine a woman perfectly in tune with nature and the Divine Mind.

Once published, *Philothea* received wide notice and was generally praised as Child's most distinguished literary work to date. The *North American Review* in January 1837 predicted it would "take a permanent place in our elegant literature." But, while the book was popular in Transcendentalist circles, general sales were disappointing.

In the spring of 1838 the Childs moved to Northampton, Massachusetts, where David Child attempted unsuccessfully to make a living manufacturing beet sugar. Overwhelmed by poverty, loneliness, and isolation, Child stopped writing. Relief came in May 1841 when she was offered $1000 a year to edit the abolitionist *National Anti-Slavery Standard.* Child's exile in Northampton had coincided with mounting divisiveness among Garrison's followers, and during her two years as editor she worked to heal the breach between the warring groups. She also strove to reach a wider audience with the abolitionist message and to refocus her fellow reformers' efforts on their real enemy, slavery. By 1842 Child's editorship of the *National Anti-Slavery Standard* had transformed it from a dry partisan organ into a first-rate "family newspaper." Its circulation now doubled that of *The Liberator,* and even Child's severest critics admitted that the paper was converting many people to the abolitionist cause.

The most popular literary item in the *National Anti-Slavery Standard* was Child's column "Letters from New-York." Critics today agree that these journalistic sketches include some of Child's best and most popular writing. She skillfully combines personal reflection and mystical and poetical musings with social protest. Especially noteworthy and original are those letters depicting the modern city of New York with its heterogeneous and mushrooming population.

Despite her manifest skills as an editor, Child could not meet the demands placed on her by the various antislavery factions. She gave offense if she refused to publish Liberty Party notices and was rebuked by the Garrisonians if she did not print their nonresistant resolutions declaring that upholding manmade law was sinful. In the spring of 1843, after two years as editor of the *National Anti-Slavery Standard,* she resigned. But instead of returning to Northampton, she remained in New York, where she hoped to separate herself from her husband's legal and financial entanglements and devote herself to literature.

The next five years were among the happiest and most productive of Child's literary career. Her first undertaking was the republication of her popular column for the *National Anti-Slavery Standard* in book form, *Letters from New-York* (1843). She underwrote the cost herself, and the risk paid off. After two months the book was selling so well that several publishers offered to bring out a second edition. The popularity of this book did much to restore Child's literary reputation. As

6

If Charles Moulton, of Wayland, Mass—'ts, survives me, I wish my niece, Mrs. Sarah M. Parson's to send $50 annually, for his use, to Mr. Henry Wight, of Wayland, Mass—ts; to be paid, in monthly instalments, to the said Charles Moulton, provided he abstains from intoxicating drinks; but if he does not so abstain, he is to forfeit the annuity.

I hereby declare this to be my Last Will and Testament. In witness whereof I, Lydia Maria Child, the Testator, do hereunto set my hand and seal. January 27th, 1880

Lydia Maria Child.

Signed, sealed, and published, as my Last Will and Testament, in presence of the witnesses whose names are hereunto subscribed, and in presence of the Testator, each and all being present and witnessing the signature of each.

Sarah Shaw Russell.

Maria Russell

Sarah Russell

Last page of Child's will (from Helene G. Baer, The Heart Is like Heaven: The Life of Lydia Maria Child, *1964)* late as 1900, newspaper editors were still praising these essays as examples for young journalists to emulate.

By the spring of 1844 Child had enough offers from booksellers to keep her busy. *Letters from New-York. Second Series* came out in 1845. *Flowers for Children,* three volumes that included old stories from *The Juvenile Miscellany* as well as new compositions, began publication in 1844 and was completed in 1847.

The most noteworthy of Child's writings from this time is a collection of short stories, *Fact and Fiction: A Collection of Stories* (1846). This return to the fictional medium gave her the opportunity to explore aspects of her own life, especially her marriage, that were too painful to confront directly. The most significant aspect of this collection, however, is less its autobiographical strain than its use of fiction as an effective device to gain the sympathies of hostile or indifferent readers for the abolitionist cause. One of the best stories, "Slavery's Pleasant Homes," provides an outspoken critique of plantation life that equates prostitution with the lot of female slaves. The radicalism of many of the stories found in *Fact and Fiction*—particularly their daring celebration of sexual passion—brought silence from the critics, and this reaction had the effect of cooling Child's literary ambitions.

After nearly a decade in New York, Child's years of independence ended. Her unemployed husband rejoined her in the fall of 1849, and the following year David and Maria Child returned to Massachusetts. After renting a hardscrabble farm in Newton, in 1854 they moved in with Child's elderly father, who lived in Wayland, a small village twenty miles from Boston. This rural community remained the couple's home for the rest of their married life.

This time Child's return to a life of domesticity only temporarily put a stop to her writing. In the fall of 1852 she began work on a biography of Isaac Hopper, the reformer who had been her landlord when she first lived in New York. Hopper had played a vital role in the Underground Railroad and in prison reform. Child's lively if disjointed portrait of this Quaker hero, *Isaac T. Hopper: A True Life* (1853), became her most popular antislavery publication. Its completion gave her the strength and courage to resume work on a book she had begun while living in New York.

The Progress of Religious Ideas, Through Successive Ages (1855) is another pioneering work. The product of diligent research on the major religions of the ancient world, its three volumes seek not simply to recount the spiritual progress of humanity but also to promote religious tolerance. As Child explains in the preface, "I wished to show that *theology* is not *religion;* with the hope that I might break down partition walls." Secular themes, such as slavery and the status of women, also pervade the book. Despite her effort to see each religion in its own light, Child left little doubt in her reader's mind about the superiority of Christ's teachings and their influence on human progress.

Child's determination to be impartial was too much for her nineteenth-century critics. The clergy, particularly, were outspoken in their denunciations; the only accolades came from such radicals as Theodore Parker. *The Progress of Religious Ideas* never did have a wide readership.

Since her resignation from the editorship of the *National Anti-Slavery Standard,* Child had largely devoted her life to literature. But her focus changed in the 1850s as she once again embraced the abolitionist cause. Her activism was rekindled partly by her husband's political enthusiasms. But she was also responding to the mounting sectional crisis of the 1850s, particularly the violence erupting in Kansas over the expansion of slavery and the beating of the antislavery Senator Charles Sumner on the floor of the Senate in May 1854.

These events had the further effect of undercutting the nonresistant views shared by Child and the other Garrisonians. For Child, freedom for the slave was always a priority, and if emancipation was only obtainable through force, then force must be used. As always, however, the printed word remained her principal weapon, and Child gave vent to the real anger she nursed over the free-soil issue by writing one of her most influential short stories, "The Kansas Immigrants" (1856). The heroes and heroines of this tale are law-abiding, peace-loving settlers from New England who suffer persecution at the hands of border ruffians from Missouri. The story greatly exaggerates the horrors perpetrated by the Missourians and might be dismissed as a piece of fictional propaganda intended to alert the American public to the horrifying events in Kansas. But Horace Greeley, the editor of the *New-York Tribune,* thought enough of the story to interrupt the serialization of Charles Dickens's *Little Dorrit* and run "The Kansas Immigrants" in its place. Published during the closing days of the fiercely contested presidential campaign between John Fremont and James Buchanan, the story had an enormous readership.

"The Kansas Immigrants" was reprinted in *Autumnal Leaves: Tales and Sketches in Prose and Rhyme* (1857), Child's last published collection of her short fiction. The stories encompass a wide range of social concerns, from slavery and capital punishment to women's rights and religious tolerance. But the theme of sexual passion so prominent in *Fact and Fiction* is absent here, and critics were thus more ready to notice and praise this latest collection.

Maria Child reached her pinnacle of fame as an antislavery activist in the fall of 1859 when John

The graves of David and Lydia Maria Child in Wayland, Massachusetts

Brown's raid on the federal arsenal at Harpers Ferry prompted her to write her most widely circulated antislavery tract, *Correspondence between Lydia Maria Child and Gov. Wise and Mrs. Mason of Virginia* (1860). In it she praised Brown's generous intentions while deploring his methods. But there is no conciliatory rhetoric here. Child warned Southerners that compromise over the slavery issue was no longer possible and challenged Northerners to risk war rather than yield further on the question. The pamphlet had an enormous circulation for those days; more than three hundred thousand copies were distributed throughout the free states. It also enjoyed considerable exposure in the Southern press, which denounced it in scathing terms.

Although isolated in Wayland for much of the Civil War, Child worked hard to ensure that the conflict would result in true liberation for the blacks. Her writings from this time were carefully designed to calm fears on the emancipation question and to prepare her Northern readership gently for the former slaves' eventual acceptance as full-fledged members of a free republic. In the last year before the war, she published two tracts designed to influence the election campaign. *The Right Way The Safe Way, Proved by Emancipation in the British West Indies, and Elsewhere* (1860), intended for Southern readers, was deliberately mild and courteous in its tone. It provided evidence that immediate, unconditional emancipation would contribute to their safety and prosperity. By contrast, *The Patriarchal Institution, As Described by Members of Its Own Family* (1860), a Republican campaign document, is openly sectional and attacks slavery directly.

The most eloquent and powerful of Child's antislavery writings from this time is a small pamphlet directed at the state lawmakers of Massachusetts. *The Duty of Disobedience to the Fugitive Slave Act: An Appeal to the Legislators of Massachusetts* (1860) censured the legislators for their indifference to the plight of the escaped slaves and urged strengthening a recently enacted bill that secured trial by jury for individuals claimed as slaves. Child's concern for the plight of these fugitives had been heightened by editing the memoirs of Harriet A. Jacobs. *Incidents in the Life of a Slave Girl* (1861) describes the sexual oppression Jacobs suffered while a slave and her successful struggle to free herself and her children. Although *Incidents in the Life of a Slave Girl* is now recognized as a major antebellum autobiography of a black woman, the timing of its publication in the months just prior to the Civil War brought it little public notice.

Child's most significant literary contribution to the war effort was a book of readings designed especially for the emancipated slaves. Primer, anthology, history text, and self-help manual, *The Freedmen's Book* (1865) sought above all to counteract the sense of inferiority shared by former slaves. The selections promote both self-respect and self-reliance and include biographical sketches of such prominent African Americans as Frederick Douglass. These sketches were intended to serve both as models for the freedmen to emulate and as sources of racial pride.

In the period of reconstruction following the war, Child worried that former slaves would not achieve true freedom. She worked hard to guarantee the rights of citizenship and suffrage for blacks embodied in the Fourteenth and Fifteenth Amendments. Although Child also supported the idea of enfranchising women, she unhesitatingly favored the male African American population as the group that should come first.

A Romance of the Republic (1867), Child's last published novel, sought to raise public consciousness on the evil legacies of slavery. The story traces the lives of two mulatto sisters, Flora and Rosabelle, from their kindly and sheltered upbringing as slaves in New Orleans, through the trials and sorrows of their early adult life, to their marriage to white men and their eventual acceptance as respectable Boston matrons. Child's intention was to entice her white readers into accepting the idea of a truly egalitarian society. But while *A Romance of the Republic* succeeds in highlighting the social ills of America, particularly its racism, Child was in the end too much a product of her own time to envision any solution other than the ultimate conformity of African Americans to her own white social world.

Child was bitterly disappointed by the critical reception of *A Romance of the Republic,* which she called the child of her old age. Sales of the novel were poor, and notices were brief or nonexistent. Particularly galling was the lack of response from her friends. Apparently, interracial marriage was no less distasteful to many Northerners in 1867 than it had been in 1824, when Child published *Hobomok.* In her despondent mood, however, she failed to notice the gratifying attention the book was getting from her African American friends.

Never again did Child attempt a work of fiction. Instead, she returned to political journalism, contributing regularly to various reformist periodicals on behalf of such crusades as women's suffrage and Indian rights. Her pamphlet *An Appeal for the Indians* (1868), first published in the *National Anti-Slavery Standard,* takes issue with the recommendations of the federal Indian Peace Commission, which had been formed to end the open warfare between the Plains Indians and advancing white settlers. The commission suggested confining the Indians to reservations where benevolent white authorities would firmly induce them to accept white ways. Child's *An Appeal for the Indians* favored a more humane style of acculturation, including an educational program that stressed positive incentives and the use of bilingual school readers. But she had no quarrel with the commissioners' ends, and like other humanitarians, she could imagine no alternative but to civilize these "peoples less advanced than ourselves."

David Child's death in 1874 was a great loss to Child. The couple's last years together had been happy ones; money problems had eased. Now her husband, the chief companion of her old age, was gone. For the remainder of her life she kept the house in Wayland and lived largely as a recluse. Her last book, *Aspirations of the World. A Chain of Opals* (1878), was an anthology of holy writings from various ages and nations. Child called it her "eclectic Bible" and hoped it would show the ordinary reader how much there was about which all mankind could agree. Friends responded warmly to the book, but sales were slow, and critics refused to accept her placement of Christianity on the same footing as other religions. Child lived for another two years. She died quietly in Wayland on 20 October 1880.

At the end of her life Child believed she had outlasted her reputation, and in certain respects she had. While some of her fiction, including her many stories for children, had enjoyed considerable popularity, sales never matched those of more-successful novelists such as Harriet Beecher Stowe. Nor do her stories and novels hold much appeal for the modern reader. Didactic, effusive, at times tedious, they are often too intent on making a point rather than simply telling a good story and telling it well. Child was admittedly adept at creating new literary genres, but she never honed her skills as a writer of fiction.

By contrast, Child's nonfiction still displays considerable power and force. In her journalistic essays and pamphlets she confronted real problems with lucid, lively, hard-hitting prose, and few modern scholars would question the extent of her influence as a social critic. Her writings, too, are wonderful reflections of her age and time, but only the best, such as her *Appeal in Favor of That Class of Americans Called Africans,* transcend these times. In sum, Lydia Maria Child is an historical figure of importance because she put her considerable literary skills in service to the many causes she espoused. No other nineteenth-century American writer personifies as well the link between the world of literature and that of reform.

Letters:

Letters of Lydia Maria Child, with a Biographical Introduction by John G. Whittier and an Appendix by Wendell Phillips, edited by Harriet Winslow Sewall (Boston: Houghton, Mifflin, 1882);

The Collected Correspondence of Lydia Maria Child, 1817–1880, edited by Patricia G. Holland, Milton Meltzer, and Francine Krasno (Millwood, N.Y.: Kraus Microform, 1980);

Lydia Maria Child: Selected Letters, 1817–1880, edited by Holland, Meltzer, and Krasno (Amherst: University of Massachusetts Press, 1982).

Biographies:

Helene G. Baer, *The Heart Is like Heaven: The Life of Lydia Maria Child* (Philadelphia: University of Pennsylvania Press, 1964);

Milton Meltzer, *Tongue of Flame: The Life of Lydia Maria Child* (New York: Crowell, 1965);

Deborah Pickman Clifford, *Crusader for Freedom: A Life of Lydia Maria Child* (Boston: Beacon Press, 1992);

Carolyn L. Karcher, *The First Woman in the Republic: A Cultural Biography of Lydia Maria Child* (Durham & London: Duke University Press, 1994).

References:

Kenneth Cameron, ed., *Philothea, or Plato Against Epicurus: A Novel of the Transcendental Movement in New England,* by Lydia Maria Child, with an Analysis of Background and Meaning for the Community of Emerson and Thoreau (Hartford, Conn.: Transcendental Books, 1975);

Susan Phinney Conrad, *Perish the Thought: Intellectual Women in Romantic America, 1830–1860* (New York: Oxford University Press, 1976);

Edward P. Crapol, "Lydia Maria Child: Abolitionist Critic of American Foreign Policy," in *Women and American Foreign Policy: Lobbyists, Critics, and Insiders,* edited by Crapol (Westport, Conn.: Greenwood Press, 1987), pp. 1–18;

Blanche Glassman Hersh, *The Slavery of Sex: Feminist Abolitionists in America* (Urbana: University of Illinois Press, 1978);

Thomas Wentworth Higginson, "Lydia Maria Child," in his *Contemporaries,* volume 2 of *Writings of Thomas Wentworth Higginson* (Boston: Houghton, Mifflin, 1900), pp. 108–141;

Kirk Jeffrey, "Marriage, Career, and Feminine Ideology in Nineteenth-Century America: Reconstructing the Marital Experience of Lydia Maria Child, 1828–1874," *Feminist Studies,* 2 (1975): 113–130;

Carolyn L. Karcher, "Censorship American Style: The Case of Lydia Maria Child," *Studies in the American Renaissance 1986,* edited by Joel Myerson (Charlottesville: University Press of Virginia, 1986), pp. 283–303;

William S. Osborne, *Lydia Maria Child* (Boston: Twayne, 1980);

Robert E. Streeter, "Mrs. Child's 'Philothea'—A Transcendentalist Novel?" *New England Quarterly,* 16 (December 1943): 648–654;

Jean Fagan Yellin, *Women & Sisters: The Antislavery Feminists in American Culture* (New Haven: Yale University Press, 1989), pp. 53–76.

Papers:

Manuscripts and letters by Lydia Maria Child may be found in the Lydia Maria Child Papers, Anti-Slavery Collection, Rare and Manuscript Collections, Cornell University; the Lydia Maria Child Papers, New York Public Library; and the Francis Alexander Family Papers, Schlesinger Library, Radcliffe College. Locations of uncollected letters may be found on pp. 770–772 of Carolyn L. Karcher's biography of Child.

Christopher Pearse Cranch

(8 March 1813 – 20 January 1892)

Mathew David Fisher
Ball State University

See also the Cranch entries in *DLB 1: The American Renaissance in New England* and *DLB 42: American Writers for Children Before 1900.*

BOOKS: *A Poem Delivered in the First Congregational Church in the Town of Quincy, May 25, 1840, the Two Hundredth Anniversary of the Incorporation of the Town* (Boston: James Munroe, 1841);

Poems (Philadelphia: Carey & Hart, 1844);

Address Delivered before the Harvard Musical Association, in the Chapel of the University at Cambridge, August 28, 1845 (Boston: S. N. Dickinson, 1845);

The Last of the Huggermuggers, a Giant Story (Boston: Phillips, Sampson, 1856); republished in *Giant Hunting; or, Little Jacket's Adventures* (Boston: Mayhew & Baker, 1860);

Kobboltzo: A Sequel to the Last of the Huggermuggers (Boston: Phillips, Sampson, 1857); republished in *Giant Hunting; or, Little Jacket's Adventures;*

Satan: A Libretto (Boston: Roberts, 1874);

The Bird and the Bell, with Other Poems (Boston: Osgood, 1875);

Ariel and Caliban with Other Poems (Boston & New York: Houghton, Mifflin, 1887);

Three Children's Novels by Christopher Pearse Cranch, edited by Greta D. Little and Joel Myerson (Athens: University of Georgia Press, 1993).

Collection: *Collected Poems of Christopher Pearse Cranch,* edited by Joseph M. De Falco (Gainesville, Fla.: Scholars' Facsimiles & Reprints, 1971).

OTHER: *The Aeneid of Virgil Translated into English Blank Verse,* translated by Cranch (Boston: Osgood, 1872);

"The Poetical Picnic," in *Sketches and Reminiscences of the Radical Club,* edited by Mary E. Sargent (Boston: Roberts, 1880), pp. 405–407;

"Personal Reminiscences," in *In Memoriam. Memorial to Robert Browning* (Cambridge, Mass.: Printed for the Browning Society by the University Press, 1890), pp. 48–53.

Christopher Pearse Cranch

SELECTED PERIODICAL PUBLICATIONS–
UNCOLLECTED: "To my Sister M., with Wordsworth's Poems," *Western Messenger,* 4 (February 1838): 375–376;

"Transcendentalism," *Western Messenger,* 8 (January 1841): 405–409;

"Ralph Waldo Emerson," *Unitarian Review,* 20 (July 1883): 1–19;

"Emerson's Limitations as a Poet," *Critic,* new series 17 (27 February 1892): 129.

Minister, musician, poet, and painter, Christopher Pearse Cranch spent most of his long life eking out a modest living in a variety of professions. Many scholars of the period dismiss Cranch as merely a dabbler who pursued these professions with only meager levels of skill. Ralph Waldo Emerson, however, believed that Cranch's problem was that he was in fact too creative—that if the range of his expressive power had been more focused, it would have been stronger. Like his fellow Transcendentalists, Cranch published several essays on the intellectual climate of the day and translated a handful of foreign texts, but his most lasting literary contribution is his poetry. Published in such journals as *The Western Messenger, The Dial,* and *The Atlantic Monthly,* Cranch's verse places him along with Emerson, Henry David Thoreau, and Jones Very as important Transcendentalist poets.

Cranch was the tenth of thirteen children born to William Cranch and Anna (Greenleaf) Cranch. William Cranch was an important judicial figure, having been appointed to the circuit court in the District of Columbia by President John Adams. The Cranch family resided in Alexandria, Virginia, where Christopher showed an early proficiency at sketching and drafting. He attended Columbian College (modern Georgetown University) and then Harvard Divinity School, from which he graduated in 1831. His classmates at the Divinity School included such Transcendentalist luminaries as Theodore Parker and his good friend John Sullivan Dwight. On graduation Cranch was assigned by the Unitarian Association to become a roving Unitarian preacher, filling pulpits in Andover, Portland, and Bangor, Maine. He also served congregations in Washington, Richmond, Cincinnati, Louisville, and St. Louis. While he was in St. Louis, Cranch read Emerson's *Nature* (1836) and from that point became embroiled in the controversy that shook the very foundation of the Unitarian faith. Much impressed with Emerson's application of French and German philosophy and theology to Unitarian principles, Cranch adopted the Transcendental position in his preaching.

In Louisville he filled James Freeman Clarke's pulpit and edited *The Western Messenger* in November 1837 and in December 1838. He began to contribute poetry and essays to the journal. The poems Cranch submitted, often mined from earlier creative efforts, include sonnets glorifying the Unitarian faith and stylized romantic visions of nature in poems such as "To a Hummingbird." During his stay in Louisville, he and Clarke also entertained themselves with a series of "comic illustrations of some of Emerson's quaint sentences." Cranch's rendering of Emerson as a transparent eyeball in top hat and waistcoat promenading across "a bare Common" is perhaps the most famous of these.

In 1839 Cranch returned from the West. Now at the height of his social powers, he had a fine baritone voice, was usually pressed to play any one of several musical instruments at parties, and was an engaging, if not brilliant, conversationalist. Revisiting old acquaintances and classmates such as Theodore Parker showed Cranch that his budding liberality ran parallel to that of the leading Transcendentalist figures of the time. He continued to preach, filling the pulpit at the South Boston Church, and for a time substituting for Frederic Henry Hedge in Bangor, Maine. Cranch also submitted several poems to Emerson for the first volume of *The Dial.* Of these, "Enosis" is the most consistent with the Transcendental agenda of the journal:

> Only when the sun of love
> Melts the scattered stars of thought;
> Only when we live above
> What the dim-eyed world hath taught;
> Only when our souls are fed
> By the Fount which gave them birth,
> And by inspiration led,
> Which they never drew from earth,
> We like parted drops of rain
> Swelling till they meet and run,
> Shall be all absorbed again,
> Melting, flowing into one.

Certain that word of his Transcendentalist leanings would alarm his conservative father, Cranch wrote a letter defending his views on 11 July 1840, in which he attempted to divorce himself from the Transcendentalism of "Kant, Fichte, Hegel, Schelling, etc.," but to align himself with Victor Cousin, who to Cranch "seems to stand between both Locke and Kant, the two extremes." This letter was published in the January 1841 issue of *The Western Messenger.*

In 1840 he wrote the 200th-anniversary poem for Quincy, Massachusetts, which traces the history of the town in language evoking William Wordsworth rather than Emerson:

> O then, my Country, when thy tribes shall fill
> Each flowery valley and each wild green hill,
> When wealth hath purchased wisdom—when thy soil
> Lies all in bloom beneath the land of toil,—
> When the bright chain of love, that God hath given,
> Extends from heart to heart, and thence to Heaven—
> And all that souls prophetic dream of thee
> Is ripening in the smile of Liberty—
> O then, America, thy name shall shine
> Written in glory by a hand divine [.]

The next year, Cranch was introduced to George Ripley's community at Brook Farm. Cranch was predictably sympathetic with the design of Brook Farm, and though he never became a member, he was a regular

Cranch's best-known caricature of Ralph Waldo Emerson, drawn after Cranch read Emerson's 1836 essay Nature
(Houghton Library, Harvard University)

visitor. A period of depression descended upon him during the next three years. While visiting family in Washington, D.C., however, he discovered that painting with oils seemed to soothe his nerves. Later that year he met Elizabeth De Windt, a cousin. After a year of courtship, the two were married on 10 October 1843. They took residence in New York, where Cranch attempted to earn a living painting landscapes.

Carey and Hart published Cranch's first volume of poetry, *Poems,* in 1844. This volume includes early poems such as "College Lyfe," written in 1833, and the poems that had previously been published in *The Western Messenger,* the *Southern Literary Messenger, The Atlantic Monthly,* and elsewhere. Edgar Allan Poe reviewed Cranch's work in *Godey's Lady's Book,* focusing on several poems from this volume. Among other characteristically droll observations, Poe identified Cranch as the "least intolerable of the school of Boston transcendentalists" and praised the poet for his "unusual vivacity of fancy and dexterity of expression." Many of the poems in this volume, which was dedicated to Emerson, attempt to flesh out the abstraction of Transcendental philosophy. In "The Ocean," for instance, Cranch supplies readers with a workable poetical explanation of Emerson's concept of the Oversoul:

> Tell me, brother, what are we?–
> Spirits bathing in the sea
> Of Deity!
> Half afloat and half on land,
> Wishing much to leave the strand,–
> Standing, gazing with devotion,
> Yet afraid to trust the Ocean–
> Such are we.

Other poems, such as "Field Notes," decry the crass materialism of the age in contrast to more natural, idealistic notions:

> Grumbling little merchant man,
> Deft Utilitarian,
> Dunning all the idle flowers,
> Short to him must be the hours,
> As he steereth swiftly over
> Fields of warm sweet-scented clover.

The five hundred copies of *Poems* proved to be more than enough as sales were disappointingly low. In the meantime, Cranch resolved to hone his painting skills, and to that end, in 1846, with some financial assistance from his wife's father, Cranch and his wife departed for Italy.

The Cranches spent the first two of these three Italian years in Rome, the last in various cities–Florence, Naples, and Sorrento. In Italy they had no shortage of company from New England. George Wil-

liam Curtis, whom Cranch had first met at Brook Farm, traveled with them in Europe. Margaret Fuller met the Cranches in Italy, where she introduced them to Robert and Elizabeth Barrett Browning. Cranch and Robert Browning struck up a close relationship based on a mutual appreciation of poetry, music, and painting. In fact, Joseph M. De Falco points out in the preface to *Collected Poems* (1971) that Browning advised Cranch during the revision of his long poem, "The Bird and the Bell." Though much of his time was consumed with painting during these years, Cranch continued to write poetry. Physically removed from the narrow concerns of New England culture, Cranch in his poems shows the effects of a broadening experience. Poems from this period, for instance, argue against the strict authority of Italian culture and especially the Roman Catholic Church. In "The Bird and the Bell" the bird, representative of transcendent, natural deity, is the

> blithe remembrancer of field and grove,
> Dropping thy fairy flute-notes from above,
> Fresh message from the Beauty Infinite
> That clasps the world around and fills it with delight!

This image stands in opposition to the bell, representative of the authoritarian Catholic Church:

> What was it jarred the vision and the spell,
> And brought the reflux of the day and place?
> Athwart the bird's song clanged a brazen bell
> . . . .
> That domineering voice; and in the race
> Of rival tongues the Bell outrang the Bird,–
> The swinging, clamoring brass which all the city heard.

The couple, now in company with their first two children, George William and Leonora–both born in Italy–returned to America in 1849. Though Cranch had been unable to sell enough of his art in European markets to sustain his growing family, he opened a studio in New York when they returned. For the next four years, the family remained in New York where Cranch's landscapes earned him a solid though unremarkable reputation but little increase in income. Still relying on family and friends to remain financially afloat, Cranch took his family to Paris in 1853. The sculptor William Wetmore Story, with whom Cranch had spent a great deal of time during his previous visit to Europe, wrote Cranch in 1850, offering his financial assistance:

> I want to ask you truly how you get along, and whether the wheels turn easily or not, and whether I can do anything for you. You know, or ought to know, that you ought never to need when I can help you. My purse, my dear friend, is ever at your service. Let us

Cranch's lampoon of the passage in The American Scholar *(1837) where Emerson lauds the Transcendental individualist who looks into "his privatest, secretest presentiment" to find universal truths and realizes: "This is my music; this is myself" (Houghton Library, Harvard University)*

spend together and make life as happy as we can. You will not be vexed at this suggestion, I feel. I don't know why there should ever be any shamefacedness about such matters. If fortune has been better friends with me than you, she makes me her agent to give to those whom I love. . . .

Though they intended to stay in Paris for a year, the Cranches remained in Paris and in Italy until 1863, living as they had previously, on sales of Cranch's painting and occasional publication and on the generosity of family and friends such as Story. During this second European excursion, Cranch was introduced to James Russell Lowell, and the two became lifelong friends. Of course, the Cranches rekindled their relationship with the Brownings and other friends from the European art world.

Cranch tried his hand at children's literature in 1856, publishing *The Last of the Huggermuggers,* an allegorical story about giants and dwarves that was surprisingly successful. The publishers of *The Last of the Huggermuggers* paid Cranch $500 for the sequel, *Kobboltzo* (1857), and Cranch was working on a third volume when the international depression of 1857 struck and the publishers lost interest. Though *The Last of the Huggermuggers* and *Kobboltzo* went through several subse-

quent editions, the two volumes failed to make a significant contribution to the genre. These two stories, along with *The Legend of Doctor Theophilus; or, the Enchanted Clothes,* were published in *Three Children's Novels by Christopher Pearse Cranch* in 1993.

In 1863 Cranch and his family returned home. His Italian paintings were more sought after than ever before. He became modestly respected in American art circles and adequately well off. The next year Cranch was appointed a National Academician and a member of the Water-Color Society. Around this time he also began, as an amusement, a translation of Virgil's *Aeneid* in blank verse. Much to his surprise, it was quite good. Encouraged by his colleagues, and with Lowell's editing help, Cranch published it in 1872. He continued to contribute his poetry to journals such as *The Atlantic Monthly* during this time, and by 1873 he had completely abandoned his painting. In 1874 he published *Satan: A Libretto,* a poem dedicated to Transcendentalist concerns. Though the poem itself raised no critical hackles, the Transcendental theme had long been played out; it generated nearly no sales. Cranch revised the poem, changing its title to "Omuzd and Ahriman" for his last volume of poetry, *Ariel and Caliban with Other Poems* (1887).

William Wetmore Story's sketch of Cranch in the year of his marriage (Collection of Robert D. Habich)

In 1873 Cranch moved his family to Cambridge, Massachusetts. Along with many of his aging Transcendentalist friends, he was a regular member of the Radical Club. He contributed poetry consistently to *The Atlantic Monthly, The Independent,* and *Dwight's Journal of Music.* Cranch collected many of these pieces in 1875 for his largest volume of poetry, *The Bird and the Bell, with Other Poems,* which included as the title poem the piece written in Italy so many years before. The first sixty-five poems in this volume were written over the span of more than twenty years, and so this volume was plagued by the same inconsistency in theme and quality that critics complained of in his earlier *Poems.* Included in this section of *The Bird and the Bell* are occasional poems, such as those written commemorating James Russell Lowell's fiftieth birthday, and wry observations in lines such as these from "Cornucopia":

> There's a lodger lives on the first floor;
> (My lodgings are up in the garret;)
> At night and at morn he taketh a horn,
> And calleth his neighbors to share it,–
> A horn so long and a horn so strong,
> I wonder how they can bear it.

The second section of *The Bird and the Bell* consists of a series of eleven sonnets, four of them dedicated to

friends such as Curtis, Story, and Octavius Brooks Frothingham. The final chapter in the volume is titled "Poems of the War." Here Cranch includes staunchly pro-Northern poems such as "The Burial of the Flag" and the ballad "The Rose of Death." He memorializes Abraham Lincoln in "The Martyr" and vilifies slavery in poems such as "The Abolitionists."

The Cranches lost both of their sons–George to a fever in 1867 and Quincy to a shipping accident in 1876. In 1880 Cranch ventured once more to Europe– at least in part to foster the budding artistic talents of his daughter, Caroline, who showed signs of becoming an accomplished portrait artist. The family remained in Europe for two years.

In the summer of 1882 Cranch returned to America and to his home and studio in Cambridge. In her account of her father's last years, his daughter Leonora Cranch Scott wrote,

He was seen to best advantage in his Cambridge study, which also did duty as a studio. Here, with soft-tinted walls, an open Franklin grate for cheer, his armchair at a convenient angle, his favorite books near, and most suggestive studies from Nature, a portrait of his friend, William Wetmore Story, by May, and his own copy of one of Ziem's Venices, on the walls, studies from the Forest of Fontainebleau, the little Mont Blanc sunrise that was poetical, and photographs of his dear ones on the mantel—he was in his best element.

Scott's list of visitors to the Cambridge studio shows the level of respectability to which Cranch had risen late in his life—Dwight, Hedge, John Holmes, Frank Boott, and William James.

Cranch's last volume of poetry, *Ariel and Caliban with Other Poems,* collected most of the poems written in the twelve years since the publication of *The Bird and the Bell. Ariel and Caliban* includes some of Cranch's most polished verse—fifty-seven sonnets, many written to old friends and heroes: Lowell, Curtis, John Greenleaf Whittier, Holmes, and Ripley. Cranch himself referred to this volume as "the best and maturest work I have done in verse." In a letter to his friend, Curtis offered praise for the volume: "Then how beautiful and tender are the sonnets. In your first slight volume which I have, I remember also the sonnets and how they enchanted me. But this last sheaf has your golden grain, and I shall say so aloud."

Complaining to friends about "dyspepsia," Cranch rapidly deteriorated in the winter of 1891 and died on 20 January 1892. His friend George William Curtis wrote in his piece for the "Easy Chair" series in *Harper's New Monthly Magazine* a reminiscence of Cranch that has served to define the poet's character:

> Cranch followed the leading of his temperament and talent in becoming an artist. He was, indeed, an artist in various kinds. The diamond which the good genius brought to his cradle, it broke into many parts. He was poet, painter, musician, student, with a supplement of amusing social gifts, and chief of all was the freshness of spirit which kept him always young.

Bibliography:

DeWolfe F. Miller, "Christopher Pearse Cranch: New England Transcendentalist," dissertation, University of Virginia, 1942, pp. 404–414.

Biography:

Leonora Cranch Scott, *The Life and Letters of Christopher Pearse Cranch* (Boston: Houghton Mifflin, 1917).

References:

Francis B. Dedmond, "Christopher Pearse Cranch: Emerson's Self-Appointed Defender Against the Philistines," *Concord Saunterer,* 15 (Summer 1980): 6–19;

DeWolfe F. Miller, *Christopher Pearse Cranch and His Caricatures of New England Transcendentalism* (Cambridge, Mass.: Harvard University Press, 1951).

Papers:

Christopher Pearse Cranch's papers are housed in various manuscript collections, including those at the Massachusetts Historical Society, Harvard University, the Boston Public Library, the Andover-Harvard Theological Library, and the University of Wyoming.

Orville Dewey

(28 March 1794 – 21 March 1882)

Susan L. Roberson
Alabama State University

BOOKS: *On the Duties of Consolation, and the Rites and Customs Appropriate to Mourning* (New Bedford: Book and Tract Association, 1825);

The Unitarian's Answer; or, A Brief and Plain "Answer to Any That Ask a Reason" of Our Attachment to Unitarianism, Considered as a System Both of Doctrine and Instruction (New Bedford: Printed by B. Lindsey, 1825);

The Claims of Puritanism. A Sermon Preached at the Annual Election, May 31, 1826. Before His Excellency, Levi Lincoln, Governor. The Honorable Council, and the Legislature of Massachusetts (Boston: Printed by True & Greene, 1826);

On the Religious Phraseology, of the New Testament, and of the Present Day (Boston: I. R. Butts, 1826);

Two Discourses: Designed to Illustrate in Some Particulars, the Original Use of the Epistles of the New Testament, Compared with Their Use and Application at the Present Day (Boston: I. R. Butts, 1827);

On Tests of True Religion (Boston: Bowles & Dearborn, 1828);

Letters of an English Traveller to His Friend in England, on the "Revivals of Religion" in America (Boston: Bowles & Dearborn, 1828);

The Deep Things of the Gospel: A Discourse Delivered at the Ordination of the Rev. George Putnam, as Colleague Pastor with Rev. Eliphalet Porter, D.D., over the First Church and Religious Society in Roxbury. July 7, 1830 (Boston: Gray & Bowen, 1830);

An Oration Delivered at Cambridge Before the Society of the Phi Beta Kappa, August 26, 1830 (Boston: Gray & Bowen, 1830);

The Pulpit, as a Field of Exertion, Talent and Piety. A Sermon Delivered at the Installation of the Rev. Edward B. Hall, as Pastor of the First Congregational Society in Providence (New Bedford: Printed by B. Lindsey, 1832);

A Sermon on the Moral Uses of the Pestilence, Denominated Asiatic Cholera: Delivered on Fast-day, August 9, 1832 (New Bedford: Printed by Benjamin T. Congdon, 1832);

On Erroneous Views of Death (Boston: C. Bowen, 1833);

Discourses on Various Subjects (New York: D. Felt, 1835; London: C. Fox, 1835);

A Brief Statement and Explanation of the Unitarian Belief (Boston: American Unitarian Association, 1835);

On the Preaching of Our Saviour: A Sermon Delivered at the Ordination of Joseph Angier as Pastor of the First Congregational Church in New-Bedford, May 20, 1835 (New Bedford: Benjamin T. Congdon, 1835);

On the Unitarian Belief (New York: D. Felt, 1835);

A Review on the Calvinistic View of Moral Philosophy (New York: D. Felt, 1835);

A Discourse on Miracles, Preliminary to the Argument for a Revelation: Being the Dudleian Lecture Delivered Before Harvard University, May 14th, 1836 (Cambridge: Folsom, Wells & Thurston, 1836);

On Profession of Religion (Boston: J. Munroe, 1836);

A Sermon on Occasion of the Late Fire, in the City of New York (New York: D. Felt, 1836);

A Sermon Preached in the Second Unitarian Church, in Mercer Street: on the Moral Importance of Cities, and the Moral Means for Other Reformation, Particularly on a Ministry for the Poor in Cities (New York: D. Felt, 1836);

The Old World and the New; or, A Journal of Reflections and Observations Made on a Tour in Europe (New York: Harper, 1836; London & Belfast: Simms & M'Intyre, 1844);

An Address Delivered before the Members of the American Institute, in the City of New-York (New York: Printed for J. Van Norden, 1837);

Moral Views of Commerce, Society, and Politics, in Twelve Discourses (London: Fox, 1838; New York: D. Felt, 1838);

A Discourse Delivered at the Dedication of the Church of the Messiah, in Broadway, New-York (New York: Stationers' Hall Press, 1839);

On Reading. A Lecture Delivered before the Mechanics' Library Association in New York (Cambridge, Mass.: Metcalf, Torry & Ballou, 1839);

Remarks on the Sacred Scriptures and on Belief and Unbelief (Boston: J. Munroe, 1839);

Discourses and Discussions in Explanation and Defence of Unitarianism (Boston: J. Dowe, 1840);

Discourses on Human Life (New York: D. Felt, 1841; London: J. Green, 1842);

On the Uses of the Communion (Boston: American Unitarian Association, 1841);

Two Discourses on the Nature and Province of Natural, Revealed and Experimental Religion (New York: D. Felt, 1841);

On Experimental Religion (Boston: J. Munroe, 1842);

On the Nature and Province of Natural and Revealed Religion (Boston: J. Munroe, 1842);

A Discourse on the Character and Writings of Rev. William Ellery Channing, D.D. (New York: C. S. Francis, 1843); republished as *A Memorial Discourse on the Life and Writings of Rev. William Ellery Channing, D.D.: Reprinted as Originally Delivered in the Church of the Messiah, New York, in 1843, the Year Following Dr. Channing's Death* (New York: James Miller, 1880);

The Law of Retribution (Boston: J. Munroe, 1843);

The Appeal of Religion to Men in Power: A Sermon on Occasion of the Late Calamity at Washington (New York: C. S. Francis, 1844);

A Discourse on Slavery and the Annexation of Texas (New York: C. S. Francis, 1844);

A Sermon Preached in the Church of the Messiah, Nov. 24, 1844, On the Character and Claims of Seamen (New York: American Seamen's Friend Society, 1844); republished as *The Character and Claims of Sea-faring Men: A Sermon* (New York: C. S. Francis, 1845);

On American Morals and Manners (Boston: W. Crosby, 1844);

Rights, Claims, and Duties of Opinion. An Address Delivered before the Berry St. Ministerial Conference, May 28, 1845 (Boston: Crosby & Nichols, 1845);

Discourses and Reviews upon Questions in Controversial Theology and Practical Religion (New York: C. S. Francis, 1846);

The Voices of the Dead (Boston: Crosby & Nichols, 1846);

Discourses on Human Nature, Human Life, and the Nature of Religion (New York: C. S. Francis / Boston: J. H. Francis, 1847);

An Address Delivered before the American Peace Society, Boston, May 1848 (Boston: American Peace Society, 1848);

Anniversary Address before the American Unitarian Association (Boston: Crosby & Nichols, 1848);

Discourses on the Nature of Religion, and on Commerce and Business; with Some Occasional Discourses (New York: C. S. Francis, 1848);

A Discourse on Obedience, Preached in the City of Washington, June 27, 1852 (New York: C. S. Francis, 1852);

The Laws of Human Progress and Modern Reforms. A Lecture Delivered Before the Mercantile Library Association of the City of New York (New York: C. S. Francis / Boston: Crosby & Nichols, 1852);

Sin and its Consequences (Boston: American Unitarian Association, 1854);

An Address Delivered under the Old Elm Tree in Sheffield, With Remarks on the Great Political Question of the Day (New York: C. S. Francis, 1856);

On Patriotism: The Condition, Prospects, and Duties of the American People, a Sermon Delivered on Fast Day at Church Green, Boston (Boston: Ticknor & Fields, 1859);

On the Alleged Decay of Faith (Albany: Printed by Weed, Parsons, 1860);

A Sermon, Preached on the National Fast Day, at Church Green, Boston (Boston: Ticknor & Fields, 1861);

A Talk with the Camp (New York: A. D. F. Randolph, 1863);

The Problem of Human Destiny; or, The End of Providence in the World and Man (New York: J. Miller, 1864);

The Two Great Commandments: Sermons (New York: J. Miller, 1876);

Autobiography and Letters of Orville Dewey, D.D., edited by Mary E. Dewey (Boston: Roberts, 1883).

Edition and Collections: *The Works of the Rev. Orville Dewey* (1 volume, London & Belfast: Simms &

M'Intyre, 1844; 3 volumes, New York: C. S. Francis, 1848–1852);

The Works of Orville Dewey, D.D., With a Biographical Sketch, New and Complete Edition (Boston: American Unitarian Association, 1883);

"On the Uses of the Communion," in *An American Reformation: A Documentary History of Unitarian Christianity,* edited by Sydney E. Ahlstrom and Jonathan S. Carey (Middletown, Conn.: Wesleyan University Press, 1985), pp. 256–266.

SELECTED PERIODICAL PUBLICATIONS—
UNCOLLECTED: "The Rite of the Lord's Supper a Symbolical Language," *Christian Examiner and Theological Review,* 5 (May and June 1828): 203–208;

Review of "The Bravo: A Tale," *Christian Examiner and General Review,* 19 (March 1832): 78–90;

"Dignity of the Clerical Office," *Christian Examiner and General Review,* 19 (July 1832): 349–375;

"Dr. Channing's Writings," *Christian Examiner and General Review,* 20 (March 1833): 54–84;

"On the Signs and Prospects of the Age," *Christian Examiner and Religious Miscellany,* fourth series, 1 (January 1844): 7–23.

As Lawrence Buell has pointed out in an article for *ESQ* (1987), there is a close connection between American Unitarianism and the American literary renaissance of the nineteenth century, both aesthetically and genealogically, for many of the renowned writers of the period were connected to the Unitarian Church in some way and modeled their discourses on and found their subjects from similar influences. A powerful voice during his time, Orville Dewey was one of the most successful Unitarian ministers of nineteenth-century America. Known for his eloquence, he was, according to Octavius Brooks Frothingham, "perhaps the greatest" preacher of the Unitarian community. In a tribute to Dewey's life, the Reverend Henry Whitney Bellows called Dewey "the most truly human of our preachers" and claimed that he was "the founder and most conspicuous example of what is best in the modern school of preaching," practical preaching. The pastor of the Unitarian church in New Bedford, Massachusetts, and later of the Church of the Messiah in New York City, Dewey succeeded in strengthening the congregations of these churches and making them centers of liberal religion. A popular speaker, Dewey was called upon to give such lectures as the Phi Beta Kappa Address at Harvard in 1830, the 1836 Dudleian Lecture, and an 1851 course of lectures on "The Problem of Human Destiny." In addition, he was a frequent contributor to *The Christian Examiner* and *The North American Review.* As

one of the foremost men of his religion, Dewey was connected to people such as William Ellery Channing; Ralph Waldo Emerson, to whom he was an early benefactor; Catharine Maria Sedgwick; Henry and William Ware; and William Cullen Bryant.

Born 28 March 1794 in Sheffield, Massachusetts, in the Housatonic valley, to Silas and Polly (Root) Dewey, Orville Dewey spent his early years helping his father on the family farm and attending the common district school until the age of sixteen. After preparing intensely for a year or two under William H. Maynard and Elisha Lee of Sheffield, Orville went to Williams College, from which he graduated in 1814 at age twenty. In his autobiography Dewey relates two significant events of his college career—"the loss of sight, and the gain . . . of insight." During his junior year, his eyes were weakened by an attack of measles, and he was compelled to think rather than just study, finding in his meditations the call to the ministry. He then attended Andover Theological Seminary until 1819. During his study for the ministry he began to doubt the Orthodox system in which he was raised. Consequently, he declined ordination after his graduation from Andover and took a year to preach throughout Massachusetts for the American Education Society and another year to supply the pulpit for the Congregational church in Gloucester. After much thought, he adopted Unitarian views and was invited to assist William Ellery Channing at the Federal Street Church of Boston for two years. From that time on, he was a close friend of Channing. On 26 December 1820 Dewey married Louisa Farnham, a cousin of Ralph Waldo Emerson.

Upon Channing's return to his pulpit in the autumn of 1823, Dewey accepted the call from the Congregational Church of New Bedford and was ordained on 17 December, with Dr. Joseph Tuckerman giving the ordination sermon. At first a small congregation with many members from the Society of Friends, the New Bedford church became one of the wealthiest and most liberal societies in the country. Led by Mary Rotch, a New Light advocate, a group of Quakers had separated from their own congregation and had joined Dewey's congregation, where they were to influence Dewey's thinking. From the Friends' reverence for the Light Within as the authority for religion and their lessened respect for historical Christianity, Dewey learned the value of original intuitions of inward light even as he preached that "Christ's teaching and living and dying were the most powerful appeal and help and guidance to the inward nature, to the original religion of the soul." Overcome, however, by the ardors of his pastoral duties and his almost constant contributions to *The Christian Examiner,* the leading Unitarian periodical, Dewey suffered a "nervous disorder of the brain" from overwork. Emerson, who had preached from Dewey's New Bedford pulpit in November 1827 when he was just beginning his own short career as a Unitarian minister, again filled the pulpit in November of 1833 while Dewey traveled abroad in Europe to regain his health, where he joined Johnathan Phillips and Tuckerman on a tour of the Rhine River and Switzerland. The literary result of Dewey's yearlong sojourn abroad, *The Old World and the New; or, A Journal of Reflections and Observations Made on a Tour in Europe,* was published in 1836.

As a memorial to his New Bedford congregation, Dewey published a collection of his sermons, *Discourses on Various Subjects* (1835). A gathering of eighteen sermons, the volume evidences Dewey's belief as he stated it in an article in 1833 for *The Christian Examiner and General Review:* "all deep preaching . . . must come from deep thinking. It requires keen discrimination, a well-considered order of thought, and a fertile imagination, as well as deep feeling." The volume also demonstrates Dewey's interpretation of natural theology, for it celebrates the majesty of the external universe and the inner powers of humans to understand it as well as to work out their salvation rationally. As a Unitarian, Dewey saw more of human goodness than weakness, though his view of human potential was more balanced than that of Channing, whom he criticized for not adequately acknowledging human frailty. Guided by the conscience, "the government that God has set within" the self, and engaged in a "fearful contest between good and evil," humans, according to Dewey, attain virtue through effort and self-denial; from power to do wrong they gain "*the power to do right.*" Like other Unitarians Dewey contended that "Life is . . . the education of the soul, the discipline of conscience, virtue, piety" and that religious sensibility is to be cultivated rationally through meditation, reading, and prayer. Even though he preached a practical and rational religion, Dewey also recognized the importance of feeling–of awe at the splendors of the "vast universe" given forth to show "the majesty and love of God" and of preaching to "our *whole* nature." Though Dewey criticized the emotional excesses of revivalism, he also warned against a lukewarm religion, asserting that reason and feeling are "intimately connected." Indeed, he argued in "Dignity of the Clerical Office" (*Christian Examiner and General Review,* July 1832) that the best sermons come from the ministers' "own hearts" and that the power of rituals such as the Lord's Supper, as he had argued in an earlier piece for *The Christian Examiner and Theological Review* (May and June 1828), lies in their ability as symbols and "solemn mementos" to quicken and touch the hearts of believers. Dewey's ability to practice what he preached is attested to by the many acclamations of his "great depth and strength of feeling," even his "rare

MORAL VIEWS

OF

COMMERCE, SOCIETY AND POLITICS,

IN TWELVE DISCOURSES,

BY

ORVILLE DEWEY.

NEW-YORK:
DAVID FELT & CO. STATIONERS' HALL.
1838.

Title page for the American edition of a collection of sermons that reveal the practical side of Dewey's theology

dramatic talent," in combination with an "extraordinary intellectual ability."

After his return from Europe, Dewey was invited by the Second Congregational Church in New York to preach to them, and a year later on 8 November 1835 he took on full pastoral duties. When the church building at the corner of Mercer and Prince Streets burned on 16 November 1837, the congregation rebuilt on Broadway as the Church of the Messiah. In this church he gained a national reputation as a great preacher. Among his parishioners in this wealthy and influential congregation were Peter Cooper, William Cullen Bryant, and Charles Curtis, a civic leader and the father of George William Curtis, an important political leader. In addition to writing the weekly sermon, a task that bore heavily on him, Dewey also held weekly evening meet-

The Church of the Messiah on Broadway in New York City, where Dewey established his national reputation as a great preacher

ings in the church library and attended to the emotional needs of his congregation. During his tenure at the Church of the Messiah, the Sunday School membership doubled, and he was instrumental in forming the Unitarian Association for the State of New York. The strain of pastoring, however, again took its toll, and in 1841 Dewey again retreated to Europe with his family for a two-year sabbatical. After his return to the United States, he plunged once more into Unitarian activities, serving as president of the American Unitarian Association from 1845 to 1847 and writing tracts for it. He also became involved in the controversy surrounding Theodore Parker's sermon "The Transient and the Permanent in Christianity" (1841) and the question of Parker's exclusion from the Boston Unitarian Association. Addressing the Berry Street Conference in May 1845, Dewey argued that freedom of thought does not imply an inalienable right to utter, without any risk of censure, what others regard as pernicious untruth, claiming, "We preach an authoritative and miracle-sanctioned Christianity."

Before his second retreat to Europe, Dewey had gathered another collection of sermons—*Discourses on Human Life* (1841)—this time in honor of his New York congregation. The sermons in this volume illustrate the closeness of his theology to Transcendentalist philosophy and art. Lawrence Buell remarks that Emerson's essay "Circles" looks as if Dewey's "Everything in Life is Moral" had been rewritten in prose run mad, and Buell also claims that Dewey's "The Religion of Life" is Emersonian in its diversity of examples centered on a single spiritual idea. In this volume Dewey speaks of the "secret intimations" and "inscrutable *mysteries*" of the grand omnipotence of the infinite that come to us in the form of the small and finite forms of life, like the "spire of grass." Nature, he writes, is a book of God's making and an oracle for each to hear. In a later article on Unitarianism for Samuel Johnson's *Oriental Religions and Their Relation to Universal Religion. China* (1877), Dewey made clear the connection with nature: " . . . the stand taken by Unitarianism is for nature, for human nature, for every thing that God has made, as the manifestation of His will as truly as any thing written in the Bible." Dewey's sermons further illustrate the link with Transcendentalist ideas when he argues that the mind, not external evidences or experiences, constitutes reality: "Life . . . takes its coloring from our own minds; . . . the archetypes, the ideal forms of things without . . . they exist within us. The world is the mirror of the soul." Given the power of the individual mind to color reality, Dewey preaches its power to form the individual character. Seeing life as a period of probation, Dewey encourages his congregation to "moral and spiritual learning." He preaches that "Life . . . like nature, is a system of checks and balances" between good and evil, but that the Unitarian religion is based on the belief that God, and hence humankind, is good. In a passage that illustrates the compounding and cataloguing of examples that Buell has identified as Transcendentalist aesthetic practice, Dewey identifies religion and the moral sentiment with nature, goodness, and a good life: "Religion–the beauty of the world–that which mingles as their pervading spirit with the glory of the heavens and the loveliness of nature–that which breathes in the affections of parents and children and in all the affections of society–that which ascends in humble penitence and prayer to the throne of god–this is no mystic secret." Passages such as this one illustrate Dewey's eloquence and the freedom with which he mingles sacred and secular subjects, characteristics of the new mode of homiletics developing in the nineteenth century among liberal Congregationalist and then Unitarian ministers, with the encouragement of Harvard professors of rhetoric. As the reviewer of another volume of Dewey's sermons said, "the peculiar charm of Dr. Dewey's style . . . lies in the remarkable combination of colloquial ease with depth of thought, and frequent pathos and solemnity."

In addition to the two volumes of sermons dedicated to his New Bedford and New York congregations, Dewey published three volumes of discourses in 1846–1848 through the C. S. Francis publishing house of New York. *Discourses and Reviews upon Questions in Controversial Theology and Practical Religion* (1846) includes a valuable discussion of what constitutes Unitarianism, clarifying its distinction from Trinitarianism. Dewey explains that Unitarians interpret the Scripture just as they would any other book and that they believe in the unity of God, seeing Jesus as God's Son and messenger. "On the Original Use of the Epistles of the New Testament" demonstrates the influence of the higher criticism on Dewey's biblical exegesis as he reminds his congregation that the New Testament passages concerning the Last Supper were written for Christians in a pagan world and that they were "peculiar to the times."

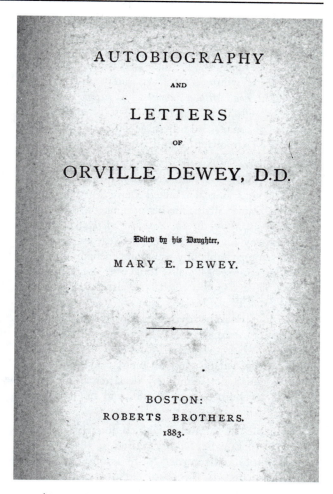

AUTOBIOGRAPHY

AND

LETTERS

OF

ORVILLE DEWEY, D.D.

Edited by his Daughter,

MARY E. DEWEY.

BOSTON:
ROBERTS BROTHERS.
1883.

Title page for Dewey's posthumously published memoir, which he began writing after his retirement in 1862

Dewey's 1836 Dudleian Lecture at Harvard University, "On Miracles, Preliminary to the Argument for a Revelation" (also reprinted in this volume), argues that Christianity is "a special revelation, an authoritative record of God's will" that is attested to not by rationality or moral philosophy but by miracle. In another essay, he defines faith as "a believing with the heart, a principle that works by love." *Discourses on Human Nature, Human Life, and the Nature of Religion* (1847) includes twenty-four sermons meant "to quicken and direct [readers'] efforts to attain the Christian character, the true spiritual life." The third volume, *Discourses on the Nature of Religion, and on Commerce and Business; with Some Occasional Discourses* (1848), which may be a reprint of *Moral Views of Commerce, Society, and Politics, in Twelve Discourses* (London, 1838), expands pulpit subject matter by including lectures on the moral laws of trade, contracts, accumulation, and labor, as well as some on freedom and political morality under the conviction that the minister should address the public mind in all its moral and religious duties and dangers. These discourses also demonstrate the practical side of Dewey's theology and his understanding of the material realities of modern life. All three volumes were separately and favorably reviewed in *The Christian Examiner and Religious Miscellany* (1847), though the third reviewer took exception to Dewey's "visionary and unwise scheme" to educate and free the slaves in order to send them to California.

Though Dewey was adamantly opposed to slavery, his position on gradual emancipation was criticized, and Emerson in his journal rebuked Dewey, along with the Reverend Daniel Sharp, for his position on the Fugitive Slave Law of 1850. In *On American Morals and Manners* (1844) Dewey questioned how the Negroes, "separated from us by impassable physical, if not mental barriers . . . refused intercourse as equals," could ever rise. His sermon "On the Slavery Question" (1843), also reviewed in *The Christian Examiner and Religious Miscellany* (1844), was apparently misinterpreted as advocating slavery when in fact his comments focused on the annexation of Texas and "whether it is right to legalize slavery anew" rather than on the problem of what to do with the slaves already legally held. He ended the sermon by declaring himself to be "fanatical for human brotherhood, and not for human bondage!"

Unable to regain his health completely, even after his retreat to Europe, Dewey retired in 1848 from his pastoral duties and returned to the family seat in Sheffield, Massachusetts. Even so, he spent the winter of 1850–1851 writing a course of lectures for the Lowell Lecture series, "Lectures on the Problem of Human Destiny," which he first delivered in Boston in the autumn of 1851 and repeated for four or five years thereafter in various places. An erudite and ambitious undertaking, the series attempted to trace the role of Providence in the world from the beginning of time to the present. Heavily weighted with references to history, the ancients, and philosophy, the series lacks the spark and eloquence of his sermons. In the lectures Dewey argues that "The world is constructed to be the abode of human life," that in his wisdom God created evil in the world as part of his providential plan for the improvement of humankind, and that indeed, the human race has progressed during time. Dewey ends the series by asserting that "progress redeems all [the barbarity of the past], pays for all; shows that in all things, however dark and mysterious, there has been a good intent and tendency, a good Providence, ruling all. . . ." As the Lectures demonstrate, Dewey tended to adapt Unitarian faith in the goodness of God and humankind in his reading of ancient and contemporary historical and political matters, celebrating progress and overlooking the costs to those who pay for it.

Dewey spent the next several years in temporary positions—filling the Unitarian pulpit in Albany, New York, for a year; serving as Chaplain of the U.S. Navy in 1851; and serving as supply preacher in Charleston, South Carolina, during the winter of 1856–1857. In 1858 he became the pastor for the New South Church in Boston, remaining for four years. In 1862 he retired permanently to his farm in Sheffield, lecturing and preaching occasionally. He also took the time to write his autobiography. He died 21 March 1882 at the age of eighty-seven. His daughter, Mary E. Dewey, subsequently edited her father's autobiography along with selected letters.

References:

Lawrence Buell, "The Literary Significance of the Unitarian Movement," *ESQ,* 33 (1987): 212–223;

Buell, *Literary Transcendentalism: Style and Vision in the American Renaissance* (Ithaca, N.Y.: Cornell University Press, 1973), pp. 24, 28–29, 47, 108, 114–115, 117, 125, 130, 157;

Buell, "The Unitarian Movement and the Art of Preaching in Nineteenth Century America," *American Quarterly,* 24 (May 1972): 166–190;

Kenneth Walter Cameron, ed., *Research Keys to the American Renaissance. Scarce Indexes of The Christian Examiner, The North American Review, and The New Jerusalem Magazine for Students of American Literature, Culture, History, and New England Transcendentalism* (Hartford, Conn.: Transcendental Books, 1967).

Papers:

The Andover-Harvard Theological Library has a collection of Orville Dewey's manuscripts, including lectures and correspondence. The Massachusetts Historical Society has some of his letters.

Emily Dickinson

(10 December 1830 – 15 May 1886)

Sarah Ann Wider
Colgate University

See also the Dickinson entry in *DLB 1: The American Renaissance in New England.*

BOOKS*: *Poems by Emily Dickinson,* edited by Mabel Loomis Todd and T. W. Higginson (Boston: Roberts, 1890; London: Osgood, McIlvaine, 1891);

Poems by Emily Dickinson, Second Series, edited by Higginson and Todd (Boston: Roberts, 1891);

Letters of Emily Dickinson, edited by Todd (2 volumes, Boston: Roberts, 1894; enlarged edition, New York: Harper, 1931);

Poems by Emily Dickinson, Third Series, edited by Todd (Boston: Roberts, 1896);

The Single Hound: Poems of a Lifetime, edited by Martha Dickinson Bianchi (Boston: Little, Brown, 1914);

Further Poems of Emily Dickinson, edited by Bianchi and Alfred Leete Hampson (Boston: Little, Brown, 1929; London: Secker, 1929);

Unpublished Poems of Emily Dickinson, edited by Bianchi and Hampson (Boston: Little, Brown, 1935);

Bolts of Melody: New Poems of Emily Dickinson, edited by Todd and Millicent Todd Bingham (New York & London: Harper, 1945; London: Cape, 1946);

Emily Dickinson's Letters to Dr. and Mrs. Josiah Gilbert Holland, edited by Theodora Van Wagenen Ward (Cambridge, Mass.: Harvard University Press, 1951);

The Poems of Emily Dickinson, 3 volumes, edited by Thomas H. Johnson (Cambridge, Mass.: Harvard University Press, 1955);

The Letters of Emily Dickinson, 3 volumes, edited by Johnson and Ward (Cambridge, Mass.: Harvard University Press, 1958);

The Complete Poems of Emily Dickinson, edited by Johnson (Boston: Little, Brown, 1962);

The Manuscript Books of Emily Dickinson, 2 volumes, edited by R. W. Franklin (Cambridge, Mass.: Harvard University Press, 1981);

*Letters volumes are listed because they include poems.

Emily Dickinson in 1847 or 1848

Emily Dickinson's Open Folios, edited by Marta L. Werner (Ann Arbor: University of Michigan Press, 1995);

Open Me Carefully: Emily Dickinson's Intimate Letters to Sue, edited by Martha Nell Smith and Ellen Louise Hart (Ashfield, Mass.: Paris Press, 1998);

The Poems of Emily Dickinson, Variorum Edition, 3 volumes, edited by Franklin (Cambridge, Mass.: Harvard University Press, 1998).

A poet who took definition as her province, Emily Dickinson challenged the existing definitions of poetry and the poet's work. Like writers such as Ralph Waldo Emerson, Henry David Thoreau, and Walt

Dickinson's parents, Edward and Emily Norcross Dickinson (portraits by O. A. Bullard, 1840; Houghton Library, Harvard University)

Whitman, she experimented with expression in order to free it from conventional restraints. Like writers such as Charlotte Brontë and Elizabeth Barrett Browning, she crafted a new type of persona for the first person. The speakers in Dickinson's poetry, like those in Brontë's and Browning's works, are sharp-sighted observers who see the inescapable limitations of their societies as well as their imagined and imaginable escapes. To make the abstract tangible, to define meaning without confining it, to inhabit a house that never became a prison, Dickinson created in her writing a distinctively elliptical language for expressing what was possible but not yet realized. Like the Concord Transcendentalists whose works she knew well, she saw poetry as a double-edged sword. While it liberated the individual, it as readily left him ungrounded. The literary marketplace, however, offered new ground for her work in the last decade of the nineteenth century. When the first volume of her poetry was published in 1890, four years after her death, it met with stunning success. Going through eleven editions in less than two years, the poems eventually extended far beyond their first household audiences.

Emily Elizabeth Dickinson was born in Amherst, Massachusetts, on 10 December 1830 to Edward and Emily (Norcross) Dickinson. At the time of her birth, Emily's father was an ambitious young lawyer. Edu-

cated at Amherst and Yale, he returned to his hometown and joined the ailing law practice of his father, Samuel Fowler Dickinson. Edward also joined his father in the family home, the Homestead, built by Samuel Dickinson in 1813. Active in the Whig Party, Edward Dickinson was elected to the Massachusetts State Legislature (1837–1839) and the Massachusetts State Senate (1842–1843). Between 1852 and 1855 he served a single term as a representative from Massachusetts to the U.S. Congress. In Amherst he presented himself as a model citizen and prided himself on his civic work—treasurer of Amherst College, supporter of Amherst Academy, secretary to the Fire Society, and chairman of the annual Cattle Show. Comparatively little is known of Emily's mother, who is often represented as the passive wife of a domineering husband. Her few surviving letters suggest a different picture, as does the scant information about her early education at Monson Academy. Academy papers and records discovered by Martha Ackmann reveal a young woman dedicated to her studies, particularly in the sciences.

Dickinson herself has given critics the greatest impetus for questioning the characterizations of her parents. In one of her first letters to Thomas Wentworth Higginson, she spoke cryptically of both parents, describing them in far from complimentary terms: "My Mother does not care for thought—and Father, too busy with his Briefs—to notice what we do—He buys me many Books—but begs me not to read them—because he fears they joggle the Mind." This image of two individuals indifferent to and wary of intellectual freedom has long governed the understanding of Dickinson's parents. Her representation of her parents is far different from their early self-representations. As young adults they traded comments on their books, encouraging each other to share their reading. Writing to Emily Norcross shortly before their marriage, Edward Dickinson praised Catharine Sedgwick's recent novel *Hope Leslie* (1827). The author was firmly committed to "liberal Christianity"—the Unitarianism of William Ellery Channing and the testing ground for Emerson. Emily Norcross and Edward Dickinson's endorsement is thus all the more challenging to the established perceptions of them. Both were firmly rooted within a Calvinist tradition that found the free inquiry and self-culture of Unitarianism highly suspect. Both nonetheless praised a book in which the protagonists are defined by the importance of principled action, even when such action entails breaking the law.

Sedgwick ends her novel with the characters' marriage. Little is learned of them after that change in their individual lives. For Edward and Emily Norcross Dickinson, marriage meant a pattern in which the individual's interests were subordinated to the general good of family and community. The experimentation open to them in late adolescence was foreclosed; as husband and wife, father and mother, they faced the pressing responsibility of representing moral character and forming it within their children.

By the time of Emily's early childhood, there were three children in the household. Her brother, William Austin Dickinson, had preceded her by a scant year and a half. Her sister, Lavinia Norcross Dickinson, was born in 1833. All three children attended the one-room primary school in Amherst and then moved on to Amherst Academy, the school out of which Amherst College had grown. The brother and sisters' education was soon divided. Austin was sent to Williston Seminary in 1842; Emily and Vinnie continued at Amherst Academy. By Emily Dickinson's account, she delighted in all aspects of the school—the curriculum, the teachers, the students. The school prided itself on its connection with Amherst College, offering students regular attendance at college lectures in all the principal subjects—astronomy, botany, chemistry, geology, mathematics, natural history, natural philosophy, and zoology. As this list suggests, the curriculum reflected the nineteenth-century emphasis on science. That emphasis reappeared in Dickinson's poems and letters through her fascination with naming, her skilled observation and cultivation of flowers, her carefully wrought descrip-

tions of plants, and her interest in "chemic force." Those interests, however, rarely celebrated science in the same spirit as the teachers advocated. In an early poem, she chastised science for its prying interests. Its system interfered with the observer's preferences; its study took the life out of living things. In "'Arturus' is his other name" she writes, "I pull a flower from the woods— / A monster with a glass / Computes the stamens in a breath— / And has her in a 'class!'" At the same time, Dickinson's study of botany was clearly a source of delight. She encouraged her friend Abiah Root to join her in a school assignment: "Have you made an herbarium yet? I hope you will, if you have not, it would be such a treasure to you." She herself took that assignment seriously, keeping the herbarium generated by her botany textbook for the rest of her life. Behind her school botanical studies lay a popular text in common use at female seminaries. Written by Almira H. Lincoln, *Familiar Lectures on Botany* (1829) featured a particular kind of natural history, emphasizing the religious nature of scientific study. Lincoln was one of many early-nineteenth-century writers who forwarded the "argument from design." She assured her students that study of the natural world invariably revealed God. Its impeccably ordered systems showed the Creator's hand at work.

Lincoln's assessment accorded well with the local Amherst authority in natural philosophy. Edward Hitchcock, president of Amherst College, devoted his life to maintaining the unbroken connection between the natural world and its divine Creator. He was a frequent lecturer at the college, and Emily had many opportunities to hear him speak. His emphasis was clear from the titles of his books—*Religious Lectures on Peculiar Phenomena in the Four Seasons* (1861), *The Religion of Geology and Its Connected Sciences* (1851), and *Religious Truth Illustrated from Science* (1857). Like Louis Agassiz at Harvard, Hitchcock argued firmly that Sir Charles Lyell's belief-shaking claims in the *Principles of Geology* (1830–1833) were still explicable through the careful intervention of a divine hand.

Dickinson found the conventional religious wisdom the least compelling part of these arguments. From what she read and what she heard at Amherst Academy, scientific observation proved its excellence in powerful description. The writer who could say what he saw was invariably the writer who opened the greatest meaning to his readers. While this definition fit well with the science practiced by natural historians such as Hitchcock and Lincoln, it also articulates the poetic theory then being formed by a writer with whom Dickinson's name was often linked later. In 1838 Emerson told his Harvard audience, "Always the seer is a sayer." Acknowledging the human penchant for classification,

The Dickinson house, the Homestead, in Amherst, Massachusetts

he approached this phenomenon with a different intent. Less interested than some others in using the natural world to prove a supernatural one, he called his listeners and readers' attention to the creative power of definition. The individual who could say what *is* was the individual for whom words were power.

Although an early connection with Emerson is tempting to imagine, envisioning Dickinson as a keenly interested adolescent reader of the first editions of the *Essays, First and Second Series* (1841, 1844), she did not become one of his readers until her adulthood. The first work of Emerson known certainly to have been in Dickinson's possession is a copy of his 1847 *Poems*. It was given to her in 1850 by Benjamin Newton, whom she later considered one of her first "preceptors"; she described Emerson's poetry as "very pleasant" to her.

Their contemporaneity was surely something she would not have found in any of the literature read at Amherst Academy. In keeping with the educational philosophy of the day, literary works were carefully chosen for their "moral value." Considering its orthodox bent, Amherst Academy may well have been more cautious than most. It kept to the religious poets of the seven-

teenth and eighteenth centuries–John Milton, Isaac Watts, William Cowper, and Edward Young. Hitchcock considered even Alexander Pope too "wanton," and William Shakespeare himself came under fire for the "libertine" elements in his character. Newton, an individual who had not attended college, might well choose the new poetry in favor of the scholar's paradigm.

While the strength of Amherst Academy lay in its emphasis on science, it also contributed to Dickinson's development as a poet. The seven years at the academy provided her with her first "Master," Leonard Humphrey, who served as principal of the academy from 1846 to 1848. Although Dickinson undoubtedly esteemed him while she was a student, her response to his unexpected death in 1850 clearly suggests her growing poetic interest. She wrote Abiah Root that her only tribute was her tears, and she lingered over them in her description. She will not brush them away, she says, for their presence is her expression. So, of course, is her language, which is in keeping with the memorial verses expected of nineteenth-century mourners.

Humphrey's designation as "Master" parallels the other relationships Emily was cultivating at school. At the academy she developed a group of close friends within and against whom she defined her self and its written expression. Among these were Abiah Root, Abby Wood, and Emily Fowler. Other girls from Amherst were among her friends–particularly Jane Humphrey, who had lived with the Dickinsons while attending Amherst Academy. As was common for young women of the middle class, the scant formal schooling they received in the academies for "young ladies" provided them with a momentary autonomy. As students, they were invited to take their intellectual work seriously. Many of the schools, like Amherst Academy, required full-day attendance, and thus domestic duties were subordinated to academic ones. The curriculum was often the same as that for a young man's education. At their "School for Young Ladies," William and Waldo Emerson, for example, recycled their Harvard assignments for their students. When asked for advice about future study, they offered the reading list expected of young men. The celebration in the Dickinson household when Austin completed his study of David Hume's *History of England* (1762) could well have been repeated for daughters, who also sought to master that text. Thus, the time at school was a time of intellectual challenge and relative freedom for girls, especially in an academy such as Amherst, which prided itself on its progressive understanding of education. The students looked to each other for their discussions, grew accustomed to thinking in terms of their identity as scholars, and faced a marked change when they left school.

Dickinson's last term at Amherst Academy, however, did not mark the end of her formal schooling. As was common, Dickinson left the academy at the age of fifteen in order to pursue a higher, and for women, final, level of education. In the fall of 1847 Dickinson entered Mount Holyoke Female Seminary. Under the guidance of Mary Lyon, the school was known for its religious predilection. Part and parcel of the curriculum were weekly sessions with Lyon in which religious questions were examined and the state of the students' faith assessed. The young women were divided into three categories: those who were "established Christians," those who "expressed hope," and those who were "without hope." Much has been made of Emily's place in this latter category and in the widely circulated story that she was the only member of that group. Years later fellow student Clara Newman Turner remembered the moment when Mary Lyon "asked all those who wanted to be Christians to rise." Emily remained seated. No one else did. Turner reports Emily's comment to her: "'They thought it queer I didn't rise'–adding with a twinkle in her eye, 'I thought a lie would be queerer.'" Written in 1894,

shortly after the publication of the first two volumes of Dickinson's poetry and the initial publication of her letters, Turner's reminiscences carry the burden of the fifty intervening years as well as the reviewers and readers' delight in the apparent strangeness of the newly published Dickinson. The solitary rebel may well have been the only one sitting at that meeting, but the school records indicate that Dickinson was not alone in the "without hope" category. In fact, thirty students finished the school year with that designation.

The brevity of Emily's stay at Mount Holyoke–a single year–has given rise to much speculation as to the nature of her departure. Some have argued that the beginning of her so-called reclusiveness can be seen in her frequent mentions of homesickness in her letters, but in no case do the letters suggest that her regular activities were disrupted. She did not make the same kind of close friends as she had at Amherst Academy, but her reports on the daily routine suggest that she was fully a part of the activities of the school. Additional questions are raised by the uncertainty over who made the decision that she not return for a second year. Dickinson attributed the decision to her father, but she said nothing further about his reasoning. Edward Dickinson's reputation as a domineering individual in private and public affairs suggests that his decision may have stemmed from his desire to keep this particular daughter at home. Dickinson's comments occasionally substantiate such speculation. She frequently represents herself as essential to her father's contentment. But in other places her description of her father is quite different (the individual too busy with his law practice to notice what occurred at home). The least sensational explanation has been offered by biographer Richard Sewall. Looking over the Mount Holyoke curriculum and seeing how many of the texts duplicated those Dickinson had already studied at Amherst, he concludes that Mount Holyoke had little new to offer her. Whatever the reason, when it came Vinnie's turn to attend a female seminary, she was sent to Ipswich.

Dickinson's departure from Mount Holyoke marked the end of her formal schooling. It also prompted the dissatisfaction common among young women in the early nineteenth century. Upon their return, unmarried daughters were indeed expected to demonstrate their dutiful nature by setting aside their own interests in order to meet the needs of the home. For Dickinson the change was hardly welcome. Her letters from the early 1850s register dislike of domestic work and frustration with the time constraints created by the work that was never done. "God keep me from what they call *households*," she exclaimed in a letter to Root in 1850. While she complained about her domes-

Emily, Austin, and Lavinia Dickinson in 1840 (portrait by O. A. Bullard; Houghton Library, Harvard University)

tic duties, she also spoke indirectly about what she would rather be doing:

> The circumstances under which I write you this morning are at once glorious, afflicting, and beneficial. . . . On the lounge asleep, lies my sick mother . . . *here* is the *affliction*. I need not draw the *beneficial* inference—the good I myself derive, the winning the spirit of patience, the genial house-keeping influence stealing over my mind, and soul, you know all these things I would say, and will seem to suppose they are *written,* when indeed they are only *thought.*

Particularly annoying were the number of calls expected of the women in the Homestead. Edward Dickinson's prominence meant a tacit support within the private sphere. The daily rounds of receiving and paying visits were deemed essential to social standing. Not only were visitors to the college welcome at all times in the home, but also were members of the Whig Party or the legislators with whom Edward Dickinson worked. Emily Norcross Dickinson's retreat into poor health in the 1850s may well be understood as one response to such a routine.

For Dickinson, the pace of such visits was mind-numbing, and she began limiting the number of visits she made or received. She baked bread and tended the garden, but she would neither dust nor visit. There

was one other duty she gladly took on. As the elder of Austin's two sisters, she slotted herself into the expected role of counselor and confidante. In the nineteenth century the sister was expected to act as moral guide to her brother; Dickinson rose to that requirement—but on her own terms. Known at school as a "wit," she put a sharp edge on her sweetest remarks. In her early letters to Austin, she represented the eldest child as the rising hope of the family. She promoted two virtues, only one of which was central to the moral guide's provenance. From Dickinson's perspective, Austin's safe passage to adulthood depended on two aspects of his character. With the first she was in firm agreement with the wisdom of the century: the young man should emerge from his education with a firm loyalty to home. The second was Dickinson's own invention: Austin's success depended on a ruthless intellectual honesty. If he borrowed his ideas, he failed her test of character. There were to be no pieties between them, and when she detected his own reliance on conventional wisdom, she used her language to challenge what he had left unquestioned.

In her letters to Austin in the early 1850s, while he was teaching and in the mid 1850s during his three years as a law student at Harvard, she presented herself as a keen critic, using extravagant praise to invite him to question the worth of his own perceptions. She positioned herself as a spur to his ambition, readily reminding him of her own work when she wondered about the extent of his. The variety of her different epistolary voices is well demonstrated in a letter from June 1851. It begins with the voice of the solicitous sister who also recognizes that a brother who is not at home may well be a brother too busy to bother with letters: "At my old stand again Dear Austin, and happy as a queen to know that while I speak those whom I love are listening, and I am happier still if I shall make *them* happy." She trusts he is "listening" to her words and implies a return action for her labors—that his response will reflect his acknowledgment of her concern. She advocates temperance, but in this case, her warning ends with an injunction against ice cream. During a spell of abominably hot weather she suggests caution: "I hope you're very careful working, eating and drinking when the heat is so great—there are temptations there which at home you are free from—beware the juicy fruits, and the cooling ades, and cordials, and do not eat *ice-cream,* it is so very *dangerous.*" While the cordials and ades are not omitted, the identification of the most "dangerous" element pokes fun at the moralizing expected from a dutiful sister. When she positions herself at her "old stand" of letter writing, she is happy to remind her "listener" that the conventional wisdom she needs to impart is finally the least part. In this letter, as is typical of the letters to Austin, the greatest part of the discourse is centered in a challenge: Will Austin rise to his own best intellectual work?

To that end Dickinson plays her own progress off against his, creating a staccato rhythm in which her praise turns to criticism, his criticism turns back against himself, and both correspondents are tacitly urged to continue their work as sparring partners. Dickinson first praises the humor of Austin's last letters, but even here the underlined emphasis suggests that the laughter might have been misplaced: "it's *so* funny—we have all been laughing till the old house rung again at your delineations of men, women, and things." The final element in that list ends the praise on a deflating note, and Dickinson's next remarks continue to shape praise into its opposite. She turns to his remarks about her letters. He has complained that her style is too complex: "you say you don't comprehend me, you want a simpler style." His request is not quite her command. She continues in the vein of praise for Austin, but the tone turns mock heroic and the mocking encompasses both brother and sister:

> *Gratitude* indeed for all my fine philosophy! I strove to be exalted thinking I might reach *you* and while I pant and struggle and climb the nearest cloud, you walk out very leisurely in your slippers from Empyrean, and without the *slightest* notice request me to get down! As *simple* as you please, the *simplest* sort of simple—I'll be a little ninny—a little pussy catty, a little Red Riding Hood, I'll wear a Bee in my Bonnet, and a Rose bud in my hair, and what remains to do you shall be told hereafter.

Representing Austin as the very image of the Victorian father, she says that if he plays that part, she will play hers—the child woman whose life is framed by the domestic world with its fairy tales and romances. Her combination of images, however, suggests just how subversive such a part can be. As she remarks, her next work is beyond his ken: "what remains to do you shall be told hereafter."

After this warning, Dickinson returns to praise. She again commends his letters—"your letters are richest treats"—but suggests his reliance on humor is superficial. She comments, "the only 'diffikilty' [is] they are so very *queer,* and *laughing* at such hot weather is *anything* but *amusing.* A little more of earnest, and a little less of jest until we are out of August."

Dickinson's 1850s letters to Austin are marked by an intensity that did not outlast the decade. As Austin faced his own future, most of his choices defined an increasing separation between his sister's world and his. Initially lured by the prospect of going West, he decided to settle in Amherst, apparently at his father's urging.

Not only did he return to his hometown, but he also joined his father in his law practice. Austin Dickinson gradually took over his father's role: He too became the citizen of Amherst, treasurer of the College, and chairman of the Cattle Show. In only one case, and an increasingly controversial one, Austin Dickinson's decision offered Dickinson the intensity she desired. His marriage to Susan Gilbert brought a new "sister" into the family, one with whom Dickinson felt she had much in common. That Gilbert's intensity was finally of a different order Dickinson learned over time, but in the early 1850s, as her relationship with Austin was waning, her relationship with Gilbert was growing. She would figure powerfully in Dickinson's life as a beloved comrade, critic, and alter ego.

Born just nine days after Dickinson, Susan Gilbert entered a profoundly different world from the one she would one day share with her sister-in-law. The daughter of a tavern keeper, Sue was born at the margins of Amherst society. Her father's work defined her world as clearly as Edward Dickinson's did that of his daughters. Had her father lived, Sue might never have moved from the world of the working class to the world of educated lawyers. Sue's mother died in 1837; her father, in 1841. After her mother's death, she and her sister Martha were sent to live with their aunt in Geneva, New York. They returned periodically to Amherst to visit their older married sister, Harriet Gilbert Cutler. Sue, however, returned to Amherst to live and attend school in 1847. Enrolled at Amherst Academy while Dickinson was at Mount Holyoke, Sue was gradually included in the Dickinson circle of friends by way of her sister Martha.

The end of Sue's schooling signaled the beginning of work outside the home. She took a teaching position in Baltimore in 1851. On the eve of her departure, Amherst was in the midst of a religious revival. The community was galvanized by the strong preaching of both its regular and its visiting ministers. The Dickinson household was memorably affected. Emily Norcross Dickinson's church membership dated from 1831, a few months after Emily's birth. By the end of the revival, two more of the family members counted themselves among the saved: Edward Dickinson joined the church on 11 August 1850, the day that Susan Gilbert also became one of the fold. Vinnie Dickinson delayed some months longer, until November. Austin Dickinson waited several more years, joining the church in 1856, the year of his marriage. The other daughter never made that profession of faith. As Dickinson wrote to her friend Jane Humphrey in 1850, "I am standing alone in rebellion."

To gauge the extent of Dickinson's rebellion, consideration must be taken of the nature of church mem-

Amherst Academy (at left), the school Dickinson attended from 1840 through 1847

bership at the time as well as the attitudes toward revivalist fervor. As shown by Edward Dickinson's and Susan Gilbert's decisions to join the church in 1850, church membership was not tied to any particular stage of a person's life. To be enrolled as a member was not a matter of age but of "conviction." The individuals had first to be convinced of a true conversion experience, had to believe themselves chosen by God, of his "elect." In keeping with the old-style Calvinism, the world was divided among the regenerate, the unregenerate, and those in between. The categories Mary Lyon used at Mount Holyoke ("established Christians," "without hope," and "with hope") were the standard of the revivalist. But unlike their Puritan predecessors, the members of this generation moved with greater freedom between the latter two categories. Those "without hope" might well see a different possibility for themselves after a season of intense religious focus. The nineteenth-century Christians of Calvinist persuasion continued to maintain the absolute power of God's election. His omnipotence could not be compromised by an individual's effort; however, the individual's unquestioning search for a true faith was an unalterable part of the salvific equation. While God would not simply choose those who chose themselves, he also would only make his choice from those present and accounted for—thus, the importance of church attendance as well as the centrality of religious self-examination. Revivals guaranteed that both would be inescapable.

As Dickinson wrote in a poem dated to 1875, "Escape is such a thankful Word." In fact, her references to "escape" occur primarily in reference to the soul. In her scheme of redemption, salvation depended upon freedom. The poem ends with praise for the "trusty word" of escape. Contrasting a vision of "the savior" with the condition of being "saved," Dickinson says there is clearly one choice: "And that is why I lay my Head / Upon this trusty word." She invites the reader to compare one incarnation with another. Upending the Christian language about the "word," Dickinson substitutes her own agency for the incarnate savior. She will choose "escape." A decade earlier, the choice had been as apparent. In the poems from 1862 Dickinson describes the soul's defining experiences. Figuring these "events" in terms of moments, she passes from the soul's "Bandaged moments" of suspect thought to the soul's freedom. In these "moments of escape," the soul will not be confined; nor will its explosive power be contained: "The soul has moments of escape— / When bursting all the doors— / She dances like a Bomb, abroad, / And swings upon the Hours."

Like the soul of her description, Dickinson refused to be confined by the elements expected of her. The demands of her father's, her mother's, and her dear friends' religion invariably prompted such "moments of escape." During the period of the 1850 revival in Amherst, Dickinson reported her own assessment of the circumstances. Far from using the language of "renewal" associated with revivalist vocabulary, she described a landscape of desolation darkened by an affliction of the spirit. In her "rebellion" letter to Humphrey, she wrote,

How lonely this world is growing, something so desolate creeps over the spirit and we don't know it's name, and it won't go away, either Heaven is seeming greater, or Earth a great deal more small, or God is more "Our Father," and we feel our need increased. Christ is calling everyone here, all my companions have answered, even my darling Vinnie believes she loves, and trusts him, and I am standing alone in rebellion, and growing very careless. Abby, Mary, Jane, and farthest of all my Vinnie have been seeking, and they all believe they have found; I can't tell you *what* they have found, but *they* think it is something precious. I wonder if it *is?*

As the one who stood outside the conversion experience, she saw loneliness in the place of church fellowship. Where others rejoiced in the workings of the spirit, she assessed the desolation it created and wondered over the believers' assumptions. Is their faith well-founded? While they esteem their findings "precious," she cannot help but wonder doubly about their conclusion. Is it worth what they hope, and is its existence sure? She asks, "I wonder if it *is?*"

Dickinson's question frames the decade. Within those ten years she defined what was incontrovertibly precious to her. Not religion, but poetry; not the vehicle reduced to its tenor, but the process of making metaphor and watching the meaning emerge. As early as 1850 her letters suggest that her mind was turning over the possibility of her own work. Extending the contrast between herself and her friends, she described but did not specify an "aim" to her life. She announced its novelty ("I have dared to do strange things—bold things"), asserted her independence ("and have asked no advice from any"), and couched it in the language of temptation ("I have heeded beautiful tempters"). She described the winter as one long dream from which she had not yet awakened. That winter began with the gift of Emerson's *Poems* for New Year's. Her letters of the period are frequent and long. Their heightened language provided working space for herself as writer. In these passionate letters to her female friends, she tried out different voices. At times she sounded like the female protagonist from a contemporary novel; at times, she was the narrator who chastises her characters for their failure to see beyond complicated circumstances. She played the wit and sounded the divine, exploring the possibility of the new converts' religious faith only to come up short against its distinct unreality in her own experience. And

finally, she confronted the difference imposed by that challenging change of state from daughter/sister to wife.

Lacking the letters written to Dickinson, readers cannot know whether the language of her friends matched her own, but the freedom with which Dickinson wrote to Humphrey and to Fowler suggests that their own responses encouraged hers. Perhaps this sense of encouragement was nowhere stronger than with Gilbert. Although little is known of their early relations, the letters written to Gilbert while she was teaching at Baltimore speak with a kind of hope for a shared perspective, if not a shared vocation. Recent critics have speculated that Gilbert, like Dickinson, thought of herself as a poet. Several of Dickinson's letters stand behind this speculation, as does one of the few pieces of surviving correspondence with Gilbert from 1861—their discussion and disagreement over the second stanza of Dickinson's "Safe in their Alabaster Chambers." Writing to Gilbert in 1851, Dickinson imagined that their books would one day keep company with the poets. They will not be ignominiously jumbled together with grammars and dictionaries (the fate assigned to Henry Wadsworth Longfellow's in the local stationer's). Sue and Emily, she reports, are "the only poets."

Whatever Gilbert's poetic aspirations were, Dickinson clearly looked to Gilbert as one of her most important readers, if not the most important. She sent Gilbert more than 270 of her poems. Gilbert may well have read most of the poems that Dickinson wrote. In many cases the poems were written for her. They functioned as letters, with perhaps an additional line of greeting or closing. Gilbert's involvement, however, did not satisfy Dickinson. In 1850–1851 there had been some minor argument, perhaps about religion. In the mid 1850s a more serious break occurred, one that was healed, yet one that marked a change in the nature of the relationship. In a letter dated to 1854 Dickinson begins bluntly, "Sue—you can go or stay—There is but one alternative—We differ often lately, and this must be the last." The nature of the difference remains unknown. Critics have speculated about its connection with religion, with Austin Dickinson, with poetry, with their own love for each other. The nature of that love has been much debated: What did Dickinson's passionate language signify? Her words are the declarations of a lover, but such language is not unique to the letters to Gilbert. It appears in the correspondence with Fowler and Humphrey. As Carroll Smith-Rosenberg has illustrated in *Disorderly Conduct: Visions of Gender in Victorian America* (1985), the passionate nature of female friendships is something the late twentieth century was little prepared to understand. Modern categories of sexual relations, finally, do not fit neatly with the verbal record of the nineteenth century. "The love that dare not speak

Page from the summer 1861 letter to Sue Gilbert Dickinson in which Dickinson included the poem published in the Springfield Daily Republican
(1 March 1862) as "The Sleeping" (Houghton Library, Harvard University)

its name" may well have been a kind of common parlance among mid-nineteenth-century women.

Dickinson's own ambivalence toward marriage—an ambivalence so common as to be ubiquitous in the journals of young women—was clearly grounded in her perception of what the role of "wife" required. From her own housework as dutiful daughter, she had seen how secondary her own work became. In her observation of married women, her mother not excluded, she saw the failing health, the unmet demands, the absenting of self that was part of the husband-wife relationship. The "wife" poems of the 1860s reflect this ambivalence. The gold wears away; "amplitude" and "awe" are absent for the woman who meets the requirements of wife. The loss remains unspoken, but, like the irritating grain in the oyster's shell, it leaves behind ample evidence.

> She rose to His Requirement—dropt
> The Playthings of Her Life
> To take the honorable Work
> Of Woman, and of Wife—
>
> If ought She missed in Her new Day,
> Of Amplitude, or Awe—
> Or first Prospective—Or the Gold
> In using, wear away,
>
> It lay unmentioned—as the Sea
> Develope Pearl, and Weed,
> But only to Himself—be known
> The Fathoms they abide—

Little wonder that the words of another poem bound the woman's life by the wedding. In one line the woman is "Born—Bridalled—Shrouded."

Such thoughts did not belong to the poems alone. Writing to Gilbert in the midst of Gilbert's courtship with Austin Dickinson, only four years before their marriage, Dickinson painted a haunting picture. She began with a discussion of "union" but implied that its conventional connection with marriage was not her meaning. She wrote, "Those unions, my dear Susie, by which two lives are one, this sweet and strange adoption wherein we can but look, and are not yet admitted, how it can fill the heart, and make it gang wildly beating, how it will take *us* one day, and make us all it's own, and we shall not run away from it, but lie still and be happy!" The use evokes the conventional association with marriage, but as Dickinson continued her reflection, she distinguished between the imagined happiness of "union" and the parched life of the married woman. She commented, "How dull our lives must seem to the bride, and the plighted maiden, whose days are fed with gold, and who gathers pearls every evening; but to the *wife,* Susie, sometimes the *wife forgotten,* our lives perhaps seem dearer than all others in the world; you have seen flowers at morning, *satisfied* with the dew, and those same sweet flowers at noon with their heads bowed in anguish before the mighty sun." The bride for whom the gold has not yet worn away, who gathers pearls without knowing what lies at their core, cannot fathom the value of the unmarried woman's life. That remains to be discovered—too late—by the wife. Her wilted noon is hardly the happiness associated with Dickinson's first mention of union. Rather, that bond belongs to another relationship, one that clearly she broached with Gilbert. Defined by an illuminating aim, it is particular to its holder, yet shared deeply with another. Dickinson represents her own position, and in turn asks Gilbert whether such a perspective is not also hers: "I have always hoped to know if you had no dear fancy, illumining all your life, no one of whom you murmured in the faithful ear of night—and at whose side in fancy, you walked the livelong day." Dickinson's "dear fancy" of becoming poet would indeed illumine her life. What remained less dependable was Gilbert's accompaniment.

That Susan Dickinson would not join Dickinson in the "walk" became increasingly clear as she turned her attention to the social duties befitting the wife of a rising lawyer. Between hosting distinguished visitors (Emerson among them), presiding over various dinners, and mothering three children, Susan Dickinson's "dear fancy" was far from Dickinson's. As Dickinson had predicted, their paths diverged, but the letters and poems continued. The letters grow more cryptic, aphorism defining the distance between them. Dickinson began to divide her attention between Susan Dickinson and Susan's children. In the last decade of Dickinson's life, she apparently facilitated the extramarital affair between her brother and Mabel Loomis Todd. Regardless of outward behavior, however, Susan Dickinson remained a center to Dickinson's circumference. In her 1854 letter Dickinson had envisioned herself as a solitary singer, a departing bird who nonetheless returns with "melody new." In a palindromic sentence, Dickinson divides the two fellow travelers, yet plays the ambiguity into a decisive singularity: "Perhaps this is the point at which our paths diverge—then pass on singing Sue, and up the distant hill I journey on." At first reading, each part of the sentence describes a different person. Sue passes on, singing, while Dickinson journeys up the distant hill. At second glance, the entire phrase may well belong to Dickinson. She travels up that hill, the poet whose subject is sharply defined.

As the relationship with Susan Dickinson wavered, other aspects in Dickinson's life were just coming to the fore. The 1850s marked a shift in her friendships. As her school friends married, she sought

The Evergreens, home of Dickinson's brother, Austin, and his family

new companions. Defined by the written word, they divided between the known correspondent and the admired author. No new source of companionship for Dickinson, her books were primary voices behind her own writing. Regardless of the reading endorsed by the master in the academy or the father in the house, Dickinson read widely among the contemporary authors on both sides of the Atlantic. Among the British were the Romantic poets, the Brontë sisters, the Brownings, and George Eliot. On the American side was the unlikely company of Longfellow, Thoreau, Nathaniel Hawthorne, and Emerson. With a knowledge-bound sentence that suggested she knew more than she revealed, she claimed not to have read Whitman. She read Thomas Carlyle, Charles Darwin, and Matthew Arnold. Her contemporaries gave Dickinson a kind of currency for her own writing, but commanding equal ground were the Bible and Shakespeare. While the authors were here defined by their inaccessibility, the allusions in Dickinson's letters and poems suggest just how vividly she imagined her words in conversation with others.

Included in these epistolary conversations were her actual correspondents. Their number was growing. In two cases, the individuals were editors; later generations have wondered whether Dickinson saw Samuel Bowles and Josiah Holland as men who were likely to help her poetry into print. Bowles was chief editor of the *Springfield Republican;* Holland joined him in those duties in 1850. With both men Dickinson forwarded a lively correspondence. To each she sent many poems, and seven of those poems were printed in the paper— "Sic transit gloria mundi," "Nobody knows this little

rose," "I Taste a liquor never brewed," "Safe in their Alabaster Chambers," "Flowers—Well—if anybody," "Blazing in gold and quenching in purple," and "A narrow fellow in the grass." The language in Dickinson's letters to Bowles is similar to the passionate language of her letters to Susan Gilbert Dickinson. She readily declared her love to him; yet, as readily declared that love to his wife, Mary. In each she hoped to find an answering spirit, and from each she settled on different conclusions. Josiah Holland never elicited declarations of love. When she wrote to him, she wrote primarily to his wife. In contrast to the friends who married, Mary Holland became a sister she did not have to forfeit.

These friendships were in their early moments in 1853 when Edward Dickinson took up residence in Washington as he entered what he hoped would be the first of many terms in Congress. With their father's absence, Vinnie and Emily Dickinson spent more time visiting—staying with the Hollands in Springfield or heading to Washington. In 1855 after one such visit, the sisters stopped in Philadelphia on their return to Amherst. Staying with their Amherst friend Eliza Coleman, they likely attended church with her. The minister in the pulpit was Charles Wadsworth, renowned for his preaching and pastoral care. Dickinson found herself interested in both. She eventually deemed Wadsworth one of her "Masters." No letters from Dickinson to Wadsworth are extant, and yet the correspondence with Mary Holland indicates that Holland forwarded many letters from Dickinson to Wadsworth. The content of those letters is unknown. That Dickinson felt the need to send them under the covering hand of Holland suggests an intimacy critics have long puzzled over. As with Susan Dickinson, the question of relationship seems finally irreducible to familiar terms. While many have assumed a "love affair"—and in certain cases, assumption extends to a consummation in more than words—there is little evidence to support a sensationalized version. The only surviving letter written by Wadsworth to Dickinson dates from 1862. It speaks of the pastor's concern for one of his flock: "I am distressed beyond measure at your note, received this moment,—I can only imagine the affliction which has befallen, or is now befalling you. Believe me, be what it may, you have all my sympathy, and my constant, earnest prayers." Whether her letter to him has in fact survived is not clear. There are three letters addressed to an unnamed "Master," but they are silent on the question of whether or not the letters were sent and if so, to whom. The second letter in particular speaks of "affliction" through sharply expressed pain. This language may have prompted Wadsworth's response, but there is no conclusive evidence.

Edward Dickinson did not win reelection and thus turned his attention to his Amherst residence after his defeat in November 1855. At this time Edward's law partnership with his son became a daily reality. He also returned his family to the Homestead. Emily Dickinson had been born in that house; the Dickinsons had resided there for the first ten years of her life. She had also spent time at the Homestead with her cousin John Graves and with Susan Dickinson during Edward Dickinson's term in Washington. It became the center of Dickinson's daily world from which she sent her mind "out upon Circumference," writing hundreds of poems and letters in the rooms she had known for most of her life. It was not, however, a solitary house but increasingly became defined by its proximity to the house next door. Austin Dickinson and Susan Gilbert married in July 1856. They settled in the Evergreens, the house newly built down the path from the Homestead.

For Dickinson, the next years were both powerful and difficult. Her letters reflect the centrality of friendship in her life. As she commented to Bowles in 1858, "My friends are my 'estate.' Forgive me then the avarice to hoard them." By this time in her life, there were significant losses to that "estate" through death—her first "Master," Leonard Humphrey, in 1850; the second, Benjamin Newton, in 1853. There were also the losses through marriage and the mirror of loss, departure from Amherst. Whether comforting Mary Bowles on a stillbirth, remembering the death of a friend's wife, or consoling her cousins Frances and Louise Norcross after their mother's death, her words sought to accomplish the impossible. "Split lives—never 'get well,'" she commented; yet, in her letters she wrote into that divide, offering images to hold these lives together. Her approach forged a particular kind of connection. In these years, she turned increasingly to the cryptic style that came to define her writing. The letters are rich in aphorism and dense with allusion. She asks her reader to complete the connection her words only imply—to round out the context from which the allusion is taken, to take the part and imagine a whole. Through her letters, Dickinson reminds her correspondents that their broken worlds are not a mere chaos of fragments. Behind the seeming fragments of her short statements lies the invitation to remember the world in which each correspondent shares a certain and rich knowledge with the other. They alone know the extent of their connections; the friendship has given them the experiences peculiar to the relation.

At the same time that Dickinson was celebrating friendship, she was also limiting the amount of daily time she spent with other people. By 1858, when she solicited a visit from her cousin Louise Norcross, Dickinson reminded Norcross that she was "one of the ones from whom I do not run away." Much, and in all likelihood too much, has been made of Dickinson's decision to restrict her visits with other people. She has been termed "recluse" and "hermit." Both terms sensationalize a decision that has come to be seen as eminently practical. As Dickinson's experience taught her, household duties were anathema to other activities. The visiting alone was so time-consuming as to be prohibitive in itself. As she turned her attention to writing, she gradually eased out of the countless rounds of social calls. Sometime in 1858 she began organizing her poems into distinct groupings. These "fascicles," as Mabel Loomis Todd, Dickinson's first editor, termed them, comprised fair copies of the poems, several written on a page, the pages sewn together. By 1860 Dickinson had written more than 150 poems. At the same time, she pursued an active correspondence with many individuals. For Dickinson, letter writing was "visiting" at its best. It was focused and uninterrupted. Other callers would not intrude. It winnowed out "polite conversation." The correspondents could speak their minds outside the formulas of parlor conversation. Foremost, it meant an active engagement in the art of writing. If Dickinson began her letters as a kind of literary apprenticeship, using them to hone her skills of expression, she turned practice into performance. The genre offered ample opportunity for the play of meaning.

By the late 1850s the poems as well as the letters begin to speak with their own distinct voice. They shift from the early lush language of the 1850s valentines to their signature economy of expression. The poems dated to 1858 already carry the familiar metric pattern of the hymn. The alternating four-beat/three-beat lines are marked by a brevity in turn reinforced by Dickinson's syntax. Her poems followed both the cadence and the rhythm of the hymn form she adopted. This form was fertile ground for her poetic exploration. Through its faithful predictability, she could play content off against form. While certain lines accord with their place in the hymn—either leading the reader to the next line or drawing a thought to its conclusion—the poems are as likely to upend the structure so that the expected moment of cadence includes the words that speak the greatest ambiguity. In the following poem, the hymn meter is respected until the last line. A poem built from biblical quotations, it undermines their certainty through both rhythm and image. In the first stanza Dickinson breaks lines one and three with her asides to the implied listener. The poem is figured as a conversation about who enters Heaven. It begins with biblical references, then uses the story of the rich man's difficulty as the governing image for the rest of the poem. Unlike Christ's counsel to the young man, however, Dickinson's images turn decidedly secular. She places the reader in a world of commodity with its brokers and discounts, its dividends and costs. The neat financial transaction ends on a note of incompleteness created by rhythm, sound, and definition. The final line is truncated to a single iamb, the final word ends with an open double *s* sound, and the word itself describes uncertainty:

> You're right—"the way *is* narrow"—
> And "difficult the Gate"—
> And "few there be"—Correct again—
> That "enter in—thereat"—
>
> 'Tis Costly—so are *purples*!
> 'Tis just the price of *Breath*—
> With but the "Discount" of the *Grave*—
> Termed by the *Brokers*—"*Death*"!
>
> And after *that*—there's Heaven—
> The *Good* man's—"*Dividend*"—
> And *Bad* men—"go to Jail"—
> I guess—

The late 1850s marked the beginning of Dickinson's greatest poetic period. By 1865 she had written nearly 1,100 poems. Bounded on one side by Austin and Susan Dickinson's marriage and on the other by severe difficulty with her eyesight, the years between held an explosion of expression in both poems and letters. Her own stated ambitions are cryptic and contradictory. Later critics have read the epistolary comments about her own "wickedness" as a tacit acknowledgment of her poetic ambition. In contrast to joining the church, she joined the ranks of the writers, a potentially suspect group. Distrust, however, extended only to certain types. If Dickinson associated herself with the Wattses and the Cowpers, she occupied respected literary ground; if she aspired toward Pope or Shakespeare, she crossed into the ranks of the "libertine." Dickinson's poems themselves suggest she made no such distinctions—she blended the form of Watts with the content of Shakespeare. She described personae of her poems as disobedient children and youthful "debauchees."

The place she envisioned for her writing is far from clear. Did she pursue the friendships with Bowles and Holland in the hope that these editors would help her poetry into print? Did she identify her poems as apt candidates for inclusion in the "Portfolio" pages of newspapers, or did she always imagine a different kind of circulation for her writing? Dickinson apologized for the public appearance of her poem "A Narrow Fellow in the Grass," claiming that it had been stolen from her, but her own complicity in such theft remains unknown. Her April 1862 letter to the well-known literary figure Thomas Wentworth Higginson certainly suggests a particular answer. Written as a response to his *Atlantic*

Monthly article "Letter to a Young Contributor"—the lead article in the April issue—her intention seems unmistakable. She sent him four poems, one of which she had worked over several times. With this gesture she placed herself in the ranks of "young contributor," offering him a sample of her work, hoping for its acceptance. Her accompanying letter, however, does not speak the language of publication. It decidedly asks for his estimate; yet, at the same time it couches the request in terms far different from the vocabulary of the literary marketplace:

> Mr. Higginson,
> Are you too deeply occupied to say if my Verse is alive?
> The Mind is so near itself—it cannot see, distinctly—and I have none to ask—
> Should you think it breathed—and had you the leisure to tell me, I should feel quick gratitude—
> If I make the mistake—that you dared to tell me—would give me sincerer honor—toward you—
> I enclose my name—asking you, if you please—Sir—to tell me what is true?
> That you will not betray me—it is needless to ask—since Honor is it's own pawn—

Higginson's response is not extant. It can only be gleaned from Dickinson's subsequent letters. In them she makes clear that Higginson's response was far from an enthusiastic endorsement. She speaks of the "surgery" he performed; she asks him if the subsequent poems that she has sent are "more orderly."

Higginson himself was intrigued but not impressed. His first recorded comments about Dickinson's poetry are dismissive. In a letter to *Atlantic Monthly* editor James T. Fields, Higginson complained about the response to his article: "I foresee that 'Young Contributors' will send me worse things than ever now. Two such specimens of verse as came yesterday & day before—fortunately *not* to be forwarded for publication!" He had received Dickinson's poems the day before he wrote this letter. While Dickinson's letters clearly piqued his curiosity, he did not readily envision a published poet emerging from this poetry, which he found poorly structured. As is made clear by one of Dickinson's responses, he counseled her to work longer and harder on her poetry before she attempted its publication. Her reply, in turn, piques the later reader's curiosity. She wrote, "I smile when you suggest that I delay 'to publish'—that being foreign to my thought, as Firmament to Fin." What lay behind this comment? The brave cover of profound disappointment? The accurate rendering of her own ambition? Sometime in 1863 she wrote her often-quoted poem about publication with its disparaging remarks about reducing expression to a market value. At a time when slave auctions were palpably rendered for a Northern audience, she offered another example of the corrupting force of the merchant's world. The poem begins, "Publication–is the Auction / Of the Mind of Man" and ends by returning its reader to the image of the opening: "But reduce no Human Spirit / To Disgrace of Price–."

While Dickinson spoke strongly against publication once Higginson had suggested its inadvisability, her earlier remarks tell a different story. In the same letter to Higginson in which she eschews publication, she also asserts her identity as a poet. "My dying Tutor told me that he would like to live till I had been a poet." In all likelihood the tutor is Ben Newton, the lawyer who had given her Emerson's *Poems*. His death in 1853 suggests how early Dickinson was beginning to think of herself as a poet, but unexplained is Dickinson's view on the relationship between being a poet and being published. When she was working over her poem "Safe in their Alabaster Chambers," one of the poems included with the first letter to Higginson, she suggested that the distance between firmament and fin was not as far as it first appeared. As she reworked the second stanza again, and yet again, she indicated a future that did not preclude publication. She wrote to Sue, "Could I make you and Austin–proud–sometime–a great way off–'twould give me taller feet." Written sometime in 1861, the letter predates her exchange with Higginson. Again, the frame of reference is omitted. One can only conjecture what circumstance would lead to Austin and Susan Dickinson's pride. That such pride is in direct relation to Dickinson's poetry is unquestioned; that it means publication is not. Given her penchant for double meanings, her anticipation of "taller feet" might well signal a change of poetic form. Her ambition lay in moving from brevity to expanse, but this movement again is the later reader's speculation. The only evidence is the few poems published in the 1850s and 1860s and a single poem published in the 1870s.

This minimal publication, however, was not a retreat to a completely private expression. Her poems circulated widely among her friends, and this audience was part and parcel of women's literary culture in the nineteenth century. She sent poems to nearly all her correspondents; they in turn may well have read those poems with their friends. Dickinson's poems were rarely restricted to her eyes alone. She continued to collect her poems into distinct packets. The practice has been seen as her own trope on domestic work: she sewed the pages together. Poetry was by no means foreign to women's daily tasks–mending, sewing, stitching together the material to clothe the person. Unremarked, however, is its other kinship. Her work was also the minister's. Preachers stitched together the pages of their sermons, a task they apparently undertook themselves.

Gilbert, Dickinson's favorite nephew, who died in 1883

When future minister William Channing Gannett was born, his grandfather's gift to him was a case containing needle and thread with which he could sew together his future sermons.

Dickinson's comments on herself as poet invariably implied a widespread audience. As she commented to Higginson in 1862, "My Business is Circumference." She adapted that phrase to two other endings, both of which reinforced the expansiveness she envisioned for her work. To the Hollands she wrote, "*My* business is to love. . . . *My* Business is to *Sing*." In all versions of that phrase, the guiding image evokes boundlessness. In song the sound of the voice extends across space, and the ear cannot accurately measure its dissipating tones. Love is idealized as a condition without end. Even the "circumference"–the image that Dickinson returned to many times in her poetry–is a boundary that suggests boundlessness. As Emerson's essay "Circles" may well have taught Dickinson, another circle can always be drawn around any circumference. When, in Dickinson's terms, individuals go "out upon Circumference," they stand on the edge of an unbounded space. At the same time, that circumference gives definition to what is inside it.

Dickinson's use of the image refers directly to the project central to her poetic work. It appears in the structure of her declaration to Higginson; it is integral to the structure and subjects of the poems themselves. The key rests in the small word *is*. In her poetry Dickinson set herself the double-edged task of definition. Her poems frequently identify themselves as definitions: "'Hope' is the thing with feathers," "Renunciation—is a piercing Virtue," "Remorse—is Memory—awake," or "Eden is that old fashioned House." As these examples illustrate, Dickinsonian definition is inseparable from metaphor. The statement that says "is" is invariably the statement that articulates a comparison. "We see—Comparatively," Dickinson wrote, and her poems demonstrate that assertion. In the world of her poetry, definition proceeds via comparison. One cannot say directly what is; essence remains unnamed and unnameable. In its place the poet articulates connections created out of correspondence. In some cases the abstract noun is matched with a concrete object—hope figures as a bird, its appearances and disappearances signaled by the defining element of flight. In other cases, one abstract concept is connected with another, remorse described as wakeful memory; renunciation, as the "piercing virtue."

Comparison becomes a reciprocal process. Dickinson's metaphors observe no firm distinction between tenor and vehicle. Defining one concept in terms of another produces a new layer of meaning in which both terms are changed. Neither hope nor birds are seen in the same way by the end of Dickinson's poem. Dickinson frequently builds her poems around this trope of change. Her vocabulary circles around transformation, often ending before change is completed. The final lines of her poems might well be defined by their inconclusiveness: the "I guess" of "You're right—'the way *is* narrow'"; a direct statement of slippage—"and then—it doesn't stay"—in "I prayed, at first, a little Girl." Dickinson's endings are frequently open. In this world of comparison, extremes are powerful. There are many negative definitions and sharp contrasts. While the emphasis on the outer limits of emotion may well be the most familiar form of the Dickinsonian extreme, it is not the only one. Dickinson's use of synecdoche is yet another version. The part that is taken for the whole functions by way of contrast. The specific detail speaks for the thing itself, but in its speaking, it reminds the reader of the difference between the minute particular and what it represents.

Opposition frames the system of meaning in Dickinson's poetry: the reader knows what is, by what is not. In an early poem, "There's a certain Slant of light," Dickinson located meaning in a geography of "internal difference." The following poem demonstrates precisely the lay of this land:

It was not Death, for I stood up,
And all the Dead, lie down—
It was not Night, for all the Bells
Put out their Tongues, for Noon.

It was not Frost, for on my Flesh
I felt Siroccos—crawl—
Nor Fire—for just my marble feet

Could keep a Chancel, cool—
And yet, it tasted, like them all,
The Figures I have seen
Set orderly, for Burial,
Reminded me, of mine—

As if my life were shaven,
And fitted to a frame,
And could not breathe without a key,
And 'twas like Midnight, some—

When everything that ticked—has stopped—
And space stares all around—
Or Grisly frosts—first Autumn morns,
Repeal the Beating Ground—

But, most, like Chaos—Stopless—cool—
Without a Chance, or Spar—
Or even a Report of Land—
To justify—Despair.

In this description of a particular unnameable yet experienced state of consciousness, the speaker relies first on negative definition. The series of "it was not" creates images that extend far beyond their individual lines. The various evocative parts add up to many related yet distinct situations—the dead in their graves, the clattering bells of noon that nonetheless ring with a force of Judgment Day (figured in the synecdochical "tongues"), the climatic condition in which the spring wind announces both extremes of temperature, the warmth exchanged for the cool surface of marble. The images are distinctly separated by syntax yet united by overlapping connections. The reference to death in the first line never disappears: It is heard in the knell-like sound of the bells, felt in the crawling flesh, seen in the marble statue of the chancel.

The next two stanzas continue this comparison with death. Whatever this condition is, its most remarkable equivalent lies in the images of the grave, a kind of live burial in which the life is reshaped to the coffin's dimensions. The image leads to suffocation (line 15) and then abruptly changes to a different point of comparison. Confined space gives way to time, the dividing line between day and night–connecting both, yet part of neither. The comparison with midnight in turn gives rise to other images in which distinctions blur: The dark of midnight is figured in the invisible face of unbounded space. In the end, however, the comparison returns to an unsettling admission that negative definition is the only approach to this powerful, unnameable experience. The final stanza opens with a direct comparison. This state of being is like "chaos," the state defined by its absence of definition. Unbounded by limits of time ("stopless") or space ("Without . . . report of Land"), it leaves the reader in a place where even the strongest emotion is denied. "Despair" is meaningless without prospect of hope.

In its dynamics of loss, this poem takes comparative definition to its chilling conclusion. The extremes of opposition point to the bleak experience of the individual observer. Knowledge proceeds by negation. One cannot hold onto its objects. They slip from possession. One knows something most distinctly precisely because one does not have it. Time and again Dickinson describes knowledge by its unattainable nature: "Success is counted sweetest / By those who ne'er succeed"; "'Tis beggars–Banquets–best define" ("I should have been too glad, I see"); "Bread is that Diviner thing / Disclosed to be denied" ("The Begger at the Door of Fame"); "To disappear enhances." In Dickinson's economy imagination remains its own best reward and want is elemental to desire's perfection:

> Who never wanted–maddest Joy
> Remains to him unknown–
> The Banquet of Abstemiousness
> Defaces that of Wine–
>
> Within it's reach, though yet ungrasped
> Desire's perfect Goal–
> No nearer–lest the Actual–
> Should disenthrall thy soul–

Little wonder that Dickinson equated Susan Gilbert Dickinson with imagination and turned the distance in their relationship into the internal difference where meanings lie.

Uniting the differences within the poems themselves are the distinct voices of Dickinson's speakers. Even in the poems with no "I" present, the lines speak in the strong tones of an orator. Clearly influenced by a culture that acclaimed its speakers–both secular and religious–Dickinson transferred the force of spoken eloquence to her written lines. The personae are several: There is the unfaltering voice that makes authoritative statements in the third person ("Two swimmers wrestled on the spar," "This World is not conclusion"; "These are the Signs to Nature's Inns"); the third-person voice that gives way to an editorial *we* ("The Bustle in a House"); the child whose literal rendering of figurative meaning exposes the poverty of such meaning ("What is–'Paradise,'" "There's been a Death, in the Opposite House"), the wife ("I'm 'wife'–I've finished that," "A wife–at Daybreak, I shall be"), the mourner ("It dont sound so terrible–quite–as it did," "The last Night that She lived"), and the dying and dead ("'Twas just this time, last year, I died," "I heard a Fly buzz–when I died"). When the "I" is given no bodied character, it serves as a solitary observer whose commentary ranges from intoxicating celebration ("I taste a liquor never brewed") to grim despair ("I like a look of Agony," "I reason Earth is short"). When the first person governs the poem, the "I" is compelling. Readers readily conflate the writer with her created speakers, but as Dickinson reminded Higginson, "When I state myself, as the Representative of the Verse–it does not mean–me–but a supposed person."

Nowhere has this first person created more confusion than in a group of three letters known as the "Master letters" (letters 187, 233, and 248), so named for their salutation. Written to an unknown correspondent–the extant manuscripts give no clear indication as to whether these words were ever sent or whether a real recipient was ever intended. Charles Wadsworth has been identified as the most likely candidate, given the secretive correspondence facilitated by Mary Holland. His surviving letter to Dickinson with its concern over her "affliction" has been read as a noteworthy moment in their growing intimacy; so have his unexpected visits and her cryptic language about him. Other critics have argued for Bowles, considering her warm expressions of love for him and her unexplained address of two poems to him: "Two swimmers" and "Title divine." At the same time, Dickinson also sent "Title divine" to Susan Dickinson. The language of the Master letters is reminiscent of the despairing letters to Susan Dickinson. Both rely upon extreme statement as the only just way to express heightened emotion. To her "Master" Dickinson wrote, "If you saw a bullet hit a Bird–and he told you he wasn't shot–you might weep at his courtesy, but you would certainly doubt his word. One drop more from the gash that stains your Daisy's bosom–then would you *believe?* Thomas' faith in Anatomy, was stronger than his faith in faith." To Sue, Dickinson wrote, "my heart bleeds so frequently that I shant mind the hemorrhage, and I only add an agony to several previous ones, and at the end of day remark–a bubble burst!" A marked difference, however, separates this language of extremity. In the letters to Susan Dickinson,

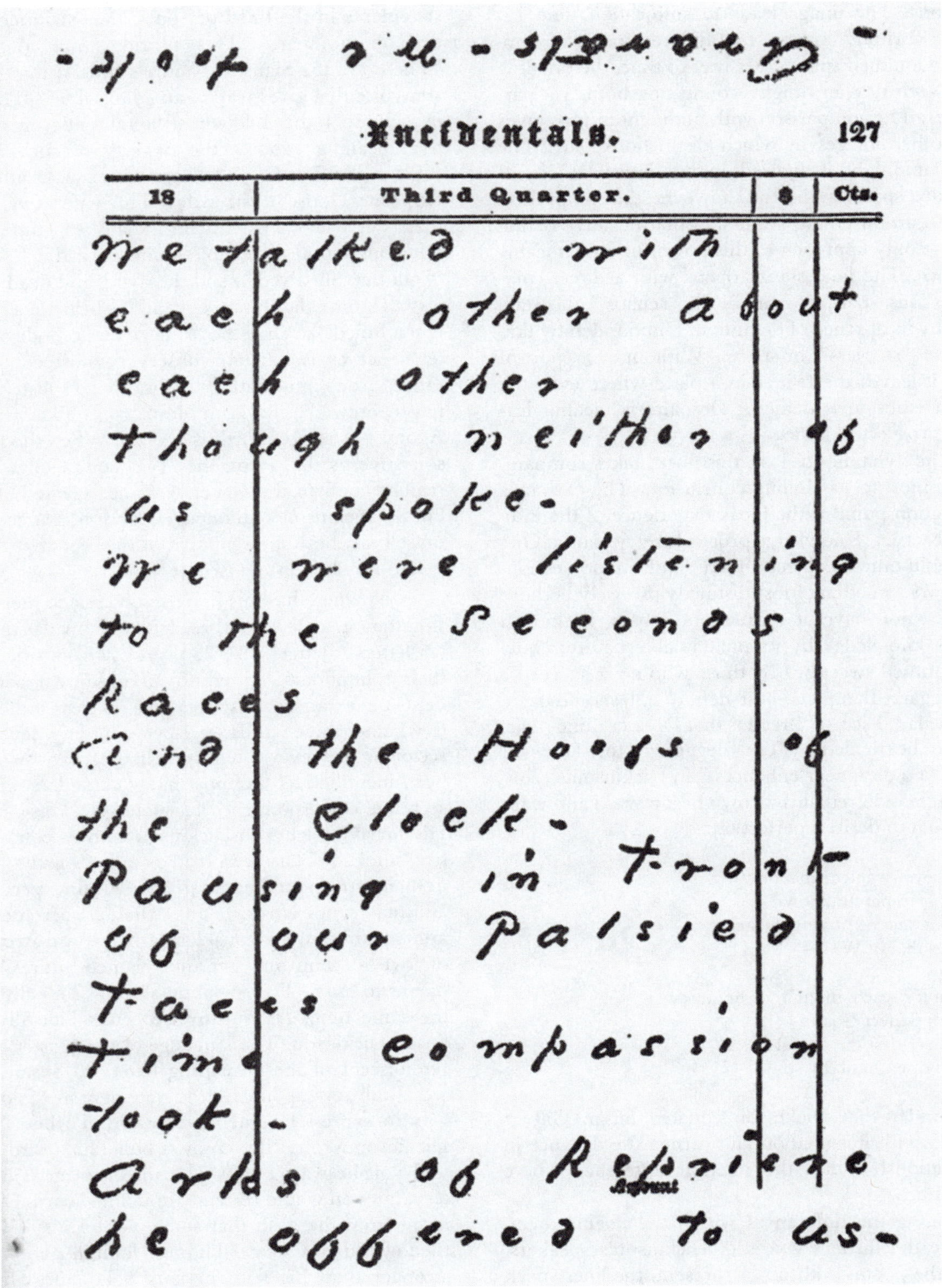

Incidentals. 127

18	Third Quarter.	8	Cts.

We talked with
each other about
each other
though neither of
us spoke.
We were listening
to the seconds
Races
and the Hoofs of
the Clock.
Pausing in front
of our palsied
faces
time compassion
took.
Arks of Reprieve
he offered to us.

Manuscript for a poem that remained unpublished until 1945 (Houghton Library, Harvard University) she is unequivocally her equal. In contrast, Dickinson positions herself as a child in the Master letters; she is the young student in need of the Master. She imagines herself kneeling at his knee or sitting upon it. That this language was commonly used by women during courtship is well worth noting, as is its infrequency in Dickinson's letters. She sometimes played the child, but she most often adopted that role without diminution, appropriating the truth-saying power of the innocent to frame her own comments. While in sections, the Master letters certainly sound "authentic," as if written to a real recipient, not an imagined one; their incomplete nature as well as their slight number leaves open the possibility that these were personae Dickinson tried out and rejected. As she commented to Susan Dickinson, "Such incidents would grieve me, when I was but a child . . . but eyes grow dry sometimes, and hearts get crisp and cinder, and had as lief burn." That she was far distant from the child's perspective she had no doubt; the childlike "Daisy" of the Master letters apparently met the same fate.

Whatever the Master letters reveal about Dickinson's life, the extremity of the language does fit with her own description of an emotional crisis that culminated in 1862. In her first letter to Higginson, she described this crisis as a "terror" lasting six months. Other critics have lengthened it to include the late 1850s, tying her movement toward solitude as the indication of mental disease. That the times—both private and public—were tumultuous is certain. As the 1860s began, so too did a series of deaths. In the first case, the loss was purely familial. In 1860 her mother's sister Lavinia Norcross, the aunt to whom Dickinson was closest, died. The ending marked a beginning: With the death of the aunt, Dickinson turned her attention to the surviving children, Louise and Fanny Norcross. For the next twenty-five years of her life, she corresponded with them faithfully. First positioning herself as comforter, then moving closer to the mother role, she mediated a deeply affectionate relationship that became one of her most abiding. In the case of the other deaths, there was little prospect of new life. With the advent of the Civil War, the loss of Amherst sons was inescapable. Dickinson recorded these deaths in both letters and poems, writing the war into her many poems on death. For many readers, shaped by the expectation of the known "literary" Civil War—Herman Melville's poems, Whitman's poetry and prose, Stephen Crane's later fictional assessment—Dickinson's abstractions seem far removed from the battleground. Recent critics, however, have offered a different perspective, calling upon the difference of women's experience of the war. In Dickinson's burst of creative activity in the early 1860s and in her

concentration on death as a subject, she registered the poet's response to the senseless destruction of war.

In 1864 Dickinson developed serious difficulty with her eyesight. The nature of the problem remains unknown, but for several months in 1864 and again in 1865, she lived with the Norcross cousins while undergoing treatment in Boston. After returning home from her second series of treatments in 1865, she took no trips away from Amherst. Invited by Higginson in 1869 to visit him and his wife in Boston, she responded with a counter invitation: "Could it please your convenience to come so far as Amherst I should be very glad, but I do not cross my Father's ground to any House or town." A year earlier she had ceased her regular visits to Austin and Susan Dickinson's house. Whether the deciding factor was the increased tensions within the marriage or the couple's increasing social involvement in Amherst life remains unrecorded. She received their visits but made few of her own.

While Dickinson chose not to leave the house, she nonetheless continued to solicit a few select visitors. In 1870 Higginson responded to her request that he come to Amherst. He recorded the visit in a letter to his wife and drew upon that record later in one of his first published essays about Dickinson. He found the visit draining. Using the language of the day, he told Mary Higginson, "I never was with anyone who drained my nerve power so much." He reported as much of Dickinson's conversation as he could remember. His reminiscence reveals her well-known definition of poetry ("If I read a book [and] it makes my whole body so cold no fire ever can warm me I know *that* is poetry. If I feel physically as if the top of my head were taken off, I know *that* is poetry"). His description as well provides the long-lasting image of Dickinson as the perpetual child: "A step like a pattering child's in entry. . . . She came to me with two day lilies which she put in a sort of childlike way into my hand & said These are my introduction in a soft frightened breathless childlike voice–& added under her breath Forgive me if I am frightened; I never see strangers & hardly know what I say." By this point, Higginson was long accustomed to the "child-scholar's" voice he had learned from the letters. The actual person neatly, perhaps too neatly, matched his expectation. Higginson visited Dickinson one more time, in 1873. Their correspondence continued, but Dickinson had long ceased to consult him about her poetry.

The poems themselves were written at a more measured pace, although to assess their number accurately is difficult, given the reliance on handwriting as the primary source of dating. As Higginson's role as "preceptor" waned, two individuals came to fill the place she had once assigned to him. In Helen Hunt Jackson, Dickinson found the strongest supporter of her poetry. Jackson, the author of highly acclaimed poetry

Dickinson's friend and correspondent Judge Otis Phillips Lord in 1883

seemed not to believe me." The letter is doubly interesting. Not simply is Dickinson's diffidence toward publishing a curiosity, but Dickinson's further request to Higginson reads his own advice cruelly back against him: "if you would be willing to give me a note saying you disapproved it, and thought me unfit, she would believe you." The man who had counseled Dickinson fourteen years earlier to delay publication is asked to repeat that counsel. His own response is burdened with a peculiar misunderstanding. Assuming the volume was to be a collection of stories, he seemed nonplussed when thinking about Dickinson as a purveyor of narrative fiction. He commented, "it would not seem to me to be in your line." That he still saw Dickinson's poetic work as patently flawed may well be borne out by his later diffidence toward the poems when Vinnie Dickinson suggested their publication after Dickinson's death. But whatever his position, Jackson would not be swayed. She repeated the request until finally "Success is counted sweetest" was published in the Roberts Brothers volume *A Masque of Poets* (1878). The reviewer for the *Literary World,* trying to guess the identity of the author, assumed the words were Emerson's.

At this point in her writing, Dickinson's interest lay in a far different audience from the one targeted by publishers. In her correspondents, she had created her audience of faithful readers. She continued to include poems with her letters and increasingly turned her poems into an inseparable mix of prose and verse. In many cases, she did not send separate poems as enclosures. They were integral to her expression, written into the body of the letters. Such was the case with Otis Phillips Lord, the correspondent who became one of the most important figures to her in her later years. Although she had long known Lord, a prominent Massachusetts judge, their relationship was little more than acquaintance until his wife's death in December 1877. Their correspondence began in 1878, a venture once again into passionate language, but this time, apparently reciprocated. They exchanged weekly letters, or attempted to honor the weekly promise. Dickinson's words speak directly and sensually of her love. In a letter dated by handwriting to 1878, she writes, "Dont you know you are happiest while I withhold and not confer—dont you know that 'No' is the wildest word we consign to Language? . . . to lie so near your longing—to touch it as I passed, for I am but a restive sleeper and often should journey from your Arms through the happy night, but you will lift me back, wont you, for only there I ask to be." As with all Dickinson's language, critics have puzzled over its literal meaning as well as the unlikely pairing of the worldly Judge Lord and the intensely private Emily Dickinson. Sewall speculates that Lord's firm support for intellectual activity

as well as the novel *Ramona* (1884) and a staunch advocate for an end to the abusive policies toward Native Americans, was an Amherst native. Born in the same year as Dickinson, she had not attended school with her, having been sent to a variety of boarding schools known for their stricter discipline. Jackson's own literary career was firmly forwarded by Higginson, and it was he who shared Dickinson's poems with her. Jackson copied them into her own "manuscript volume" of admired poems. Writing to Dickinson in 1876, she praised Dickinson's work and chided her for not pursuing publication: "I have a little manuscript volume with a few of your verses in it—and I read them very often— You are a great poet—and it is a wrong to the day you live in, that you will not sing aloud." Dickinson's response is unknown, but when Jackson urged Dickinson to contribute to a volume of poems to be published anonymously, Dickinson hesitated. She explained the situation to Higginson: "I told her I was unwilling, and she asked me why?—I said I was incapable and she and his fascination with abstract thought appealed to Dickinson. In a eulogy, Lord praised the deceased for "the incessant activity of his intellect . . . the highest condition of mental activity." For Dickinson, such activity defined the meaningful life. She was as restive in sleep as in waking, writing poems such as "They shut me up in Prose," "The Brain, within it's Groove," "If ever the lid gets off my head," "The Brain—is wider than the sky," "You'll know Her—by Her Foot," "I felt a clearing in my Mind," and "Severer Service of myself" to describe the ceaseless activity of the brain.

While the 1870s brought new and profoundly satisfying relationships, there were also losses. Edward Dickinson died in 1874 while at work in Boston. Dickinson felt his death profoundly. Her letters on the subject are defined by brevity, an economy of language designed to contain an overpowering grief. Writing to her cousins, she describes the effect of her father's death as one of self-alienation. "I cannot recall myself," she remarked. A year later her mother suffered a stroke that left her paralyzed. For the remaining seven years of her life, she was taken care of by her older daughter. In the midst of these two life-altering events, Susan and Austin Dickinson's youngest son, Gilbert, was born. He soon became the beloved nephew, greeted with an even greater tenderness than had embraced his two older siblings. That tenderness was relatively short-lived. A tragedy shook both the Homestead and the Evergreens: Gilbert died of typhoid fever when he was eight years old.

The 1880s were marked by more deaths. Charles Wadsworth died in April 1882; Dickinson's mother died seven months later. Gilbert died in 1883; Judge Lord, in 1884. In the same year, Dickinson experienced her first attack of "faintness," the onset of the illness that eventually ended with her own death. The one contrast appeared in the arrival of a new friend, one who became important in the life of the Dickinson households as well as in the future of Dickinson's poetry. Mabel Loomis Todd arrived in Amherst in 1881. Wife of the newly hired astronomy professor at Amherst College, David Todd, she was quickly incorporated into the social events at the Evergreens. At first the primary friendship was between Susan Dickinson and Mabel Todd. Emily Dickinson added Mabel Todd to her list of correspondents. The first extant letter is a curious two lines, noting Mabel Todd's departure for a Washington visit: "The parting of those that never met, shall it be delusion, or rather, an unfolding snare whose fruitage is later?" In September 1882 Mabel Todd and Austin Dickinson crossed their private "Rubicon" and entered into a passionate love affair that lasted until Austin Dickinson's death in 1895. The affair was no secret. It understandably created an unbridgeable abyss between Susan Dickinson and Mabel Todd; it was apparently countenanced by both Emily and Vinnie Dickinson. Dickinson's letters indicate knowledge; her allusions pointedly meet the situation—comments on "an adjourning Heart," references to Antony and Cleopatra and the "Criterion Lover."

Throughout her life Dickinson had looked for unexpected connections—between individuals, between ideas and images, between the knowledge one has and the knowledge one wants. Her final written words suggest the power she imagined could rest within her hands. She sent one last message to her beloved Norcross cousins. A simple few words, they announced her death with the allusive wit that had marked her life. Hours before she lapsed into unconsciousness, Dickinson wrote to Fanny and Lou, "Little Cousins, Called Back. Emily." The phrase she chose for her death was also the title of a popular occult novel. In an undated poem, she had remarked on the strange power of words. In contrast to the Christian "word made flesh" who did indeed die, language itself offered an unbroken path to immortality. "A Word that breathes distinctly," she had written "has not the power to die."

Dickinson's words have not had the power to die. Although she instructed Vinnie to burn all her papers, the younger sister could not obey the dying sister's command. She destroyed the letters Dickinson had kept; she would not touch the poetry and eagerly sought its publication. She first asked Susan Dickinson to serve as editor. She expressed interest, but not in the manner Lavinia Dickinson had envisioned. Thinking first to publish several of the poems separately, Susan Dickinson sent a poem "on the 'Wind'" to Richard Gilder, then editor at *Century Magazine*. It was not accepted. Vinnie Dickinson found this approach limiting and far too slow. She envisioned volumes of her sister's verse and turned instead to Mabel Loomis Todd and Thomas Wentworth Higginson. Higginson hesitated, unsure whether enough excellent poems could be found. Todd was much more enthusiastic and in fact did most of the editorial work. She transcribed the poems and arranged them into three categories—those she thought best, those of flawed excellence, and those of lesser quality.

In 1890, four years after Dickinson's death, the first volume of her poetry appeared. It was published by Roberts Brothers, whose editor Thomas Niles had overseen *A Masque of Poets* and who at that time had suggested a volume to Dickinson. He was not as enthusiastic at this 1890 prospect as his 1870s interest might have suggested, but the publishing house was clearly made glad by his decision. The edition of 500 copies sold out in a matter of weeks. Another, larger run was immediately prepared. In one year, 4,500 copies were sold; by

Binding for the first collection of Dickinson's poems (1890), edited by Mabel Loomis Todd and Thomas Wentworth Higginson, who changed Dickinson's punctuation and altered her rhymes and meters to make her poems seem more conventional than she had intended

the end of the second year, 11 editions of the first volume had appeared. The poetry that Higginson had found "spasmodic" and "uncontrolled" had become the fascination of the last decade of the nineteenth century. Arranged under headings such as "Love," "Nature," "Time and Eternity," the poems were presented in a format appealing to genteel readers. Todd and Higginson agreed that Dickinson's irregular meter and rhyme should be altered for publication, thus tempering the effect of her poems. Even with these changes, the reviewers remarked on her "strangeness." The comment was not unfavorable, playing into a fin-de-siècle sense of the outré.

With the success of the first volume, Vinnie urged Mabel to prepare a second. *Poems, Second Series* appeared in 1891. In her preface to this volume, Todd attempted to disband notions of the growing Dickinson myth: Her "reclusiveness" was chosen; her poetry was not the product of a broken heart. Todd wrote, "She was not an invalid, and she lived in seclusion from no love-disappointment." From the poetry, Todd turned to the letters, editing a two-volume collection in 1894. She then edited a third volume of the poetry, published in 1896. By this time, the Dickinson

"fad" was nearing its end, and Todd had exhausted the supply of poems in her upper two categories. In 1896 Lavinia Dickinson filed suit against the Todds in a dispute over land. The lawsuit ended the possibility of Mabel's editing future volumes, as did the unlikely exchange of poems from Susan Dickinson to Mabel Todd. Many poems were still held by Susan Dickinson, who published a few in various literary journals such as *Scribner's* and *The Independent*. At her death in 1899 Vinnie Dickinson left the remaining manuscripts to her niece Martha Dickinson Bianchi, Susan and Austin Dickinson's daughter, but no further editions appeared until 1914, the year after Susan Dickinson's death. Bianchi prepared five different collections between 1914 and 1937. In 1945 Millicent Todd Bingham, Mabel Todd's daughter, produced a volume of six hundred previously unpublished poems. Its appearance signaled the need for a complete edition of Dickinson's poetry. Although Bianchi had titled her 1924 edition *The Complete Poems of Emily Dickinson,* the further editions gave a strange definition of completeness. And with the manuscripts still divided between two households, a complete edition was divided as well. With Bianchi's death, the poems in her possession went to Harvard. Harvard claimed the rest, a claim eventually denied, and the manuscripts held by Mabel Todd and Millicent Todd Bingham were deposited at Amherst.

In 1955 Thomas H. Johnson published a three-volume variorum edition, *The Poems of Emily Dickinson*. A one-volume reader's edition appeared in 1960. The questions of editing, however, were not over. Dickinson's poems present a distinct difficulty to the editor. Since Dickinson herself never prepared her poems for print, her "final intention" is unclear. For many of the poems, the manuscript is a draft version, not a fair copy. These versions frequently include a list of alternate words, with no indication of choice. That she would have made any such choice is also uncertain. Given her inclusion of the same poem to different correspondents, the changes may well reflect her sense of their occasional nature. Her manuscripts offer little help to the individual looking for a "final" form. There are also questions of physical reproduction. As R. W. Franklin observed, "printing is itself a misrepresentation of the texts as they exist in manuscript." Her irregularities of capitalization, her unconventional use of punctuation, and the difficulty of her handwriting itself leave the editor with a wealth of unsettled questions.

Franklin's early dissatisfaction continued as feminist critics reevaluated the ideology behind editorial practice. As Susan Howe commented, "the issue of editorial control is directly connected to the attempted erasure of antinomianism in our culture." Editing "regularizes" and "normalizes"—a process that may well diminish the lawbreaking practiced by unconventional writers. A standard edition is hardly commensurate with Dickinson's shape-shifting poetics. Acknowledging the difficulty of the editorial task, Franklin argued that the poems in Johnson's one-volume edition were misleading. They presented the reader with the appearance of final versions, when Dickinson rarely "finished" a poem. Looking at the variety of alternates she allowed to stand, he suggested that each version could be considered a separate poem. In his 1967 *The Editing of Emily Dickinson,* he called for a "new editorial procedure." Toward this end, he published *The Manuscript Books of Emily Dickinson* in 1981, the forty fascicles and an additional fifteen sets of poems Dickinson apparently placed together but did not sew. A facsimile edition, it prints the poems in the groupings Dickinson created. While the use of facsimile obviates the need for editorial intrusion, it also makes reading difficult for the unpracticed eye and excludes poems not part of either the fascicles or the sets. Franklin's print edition of the poems, *The Poems of Emily Dickinson, Variorum Edition,* appeared in 1998. Franklin's variorum differs from Johnson's three-volume edition by printing "a separate text for each known manuscript." Rather than listing the alternatives in critical apparatus and choosing one version of the poem to represent the different poems Dickinson produced from it, Franklin prints the different manuscript versions. He comments, "Since nearly every text differs in some respect from all others, each has been presented individually, gathered within a single entry." His further comment about his own principles of inclusion are interesting, considering the approaches to Dickinson's poetry they suggest: "Principal representation implies choice for a particular purpose: an edition of the fascicles would have to choose those manuscripts, an edition of poems sent to a particular recipient, those. The aim of this edition is a comprehensive account, not a selection for a specific end." As scholars have recently argued, readers of Dickinson's poetry are well advised to remember the particular audience of a poem and look carefully at the poems as they were sent to their individual recipients. Franklin also suggests new dating for many of the poems, based on work that postdated Johnson's edition.

Franklin largely respects the conventions of print, retaining a standard stanzaic form for most poets. Martha Nell Smith and Ellen Louise Hard and Marta Werner's editions of Dickinson's poems, letters, and letter poems to Sue Dickinson and Smith and Hart's edition of forty of Dickinson's late drafts and fragments attempt to reproduce in print a much closer version to what Dickinson wrote on the page. In *Open Me Carefully: Emily Dickinson's Intimate Letters to Susan Huntington Gilbert,* Dickinson's words scroll down the page in short lines with often no more than one word to a line. Werner

reproduces forty pieces of Dickinson's late writing in facsimile with "typed transcriptions that display as fully as possible her compositional process." In *The Manuscript Books* (1981), Franklin reproduced only the poems collected into fascicles. Werner takes the reader into the late words of Dickinson, where she apparently abandoned a book-like structure for her poems. In *Open Folios* (1995) Werner comments, "In the 1870s and 1880s the leaves of the folios lie scattered: the end of linearity is signaled not in their apparent disorder but, rather, in their apprehension of multiple or contingent orders. No longer marking a place in a book, the loose leaves of stationery and scraps of paper are risked to still wilder forms of circulation."

Reminding the reader precisely how inadequate the medium of print is for Dickinson's writing, the collaborators on the *Dickinson Electronic Archives* emphasize Dickinson's method of publication: her widespread and extensive correspondence. They note the importance of the physical object itself–the handwritten poems, letters, assembled manuscript books–an importance virtually lost in any printed version. Headed by Smith, Hart, and Werner, the Dickinson Editing Collective has undertaken the ambitious project of making photographic reproductions of Dickinson's writings, as well as writings by Dickinson family members and correspondents, electronically available. Readers will thus be able to study Dickinson's poems and letters in a visual form much closer to the one in which they were written. In her description of the archives in *The Emily Dickinson Handbook,* Smith notes, "the *Dickinson Electronic Archives* is not an ultimately 'authoritative' edition but serves as a valuable resource for exploring theoretical implications of the material structures of Dickinson's texts (both individual documents and the organization of their relationships to one another." The Editing Collective's work charts the course for twenty-first century interpretations of Dickinson.

Because of the complexity of the manuscripts, the "editing of Emily Dickinson" will never be complete. Dickinson's will always be the last word. In a poem first published in 1914, undated by either Johnson or Franklin, Dickinson articulated the rich dilemma facing the poet. To settle on a particular word limits meaning, but choice itself is quickly set aside in favor of endless exploration:

> To tell the Beauty would decrease
> To state the spell demean–
> There is a syllable less Sea
> Of which it is the sign
> My will endeavors for it's word
> And fails, but entertains
> A Rapture as of Legacies–
> Of introspective Mines–

Letters:

Letters of Emily Dickinson, edited by Mabel Loomis Todd (2 volumes, Boston: Roberts, 1894; enlarged edition, New York: Harper, 1931);

Emily Dickinson's Letters to Dr. and Mrs. Josiah Gilbert Holland, edited by Theodora Van Wagenen Ward (Cambridge, Mass.: Harvard University Press, 1951);

The Letters of Emily Dickinson, 3 volumes, edited by Thomas H. Johnson and Ward (Cambridge, Mass.: Harvard University Press, 1958);

The Master Letters of Emily Dickinson, edited by R. W. Franklin (Amherst: Amherst College Press, 1986);

Open Me Carefully: Emily Dickinson's Intimate Letters to Sue, edited by Martha Nell Smith and Ellen Louise Hart (Ashfield, Mass.: Paris Press, 1998).

Electronic Resources:

Dickinson Editing Collective (Martha Nell Smith, Ellen Louise Hart, and Marta Werner, gen. eds.), *Dickinson Electronic Archives* <http://jefferson.village.virginia.edu/dickinson/>

Bibliographies:

Willis Buckingham, *Emily Dickinson: An Annotated Bibliography: Writings, Scholarship, Criticism and Analysis, 1850–1968* (Bloomington: Indiana University Press, 1970);

Annual bibliographies in *Dickinson Studies* (1978–1993);

Joseph Duchac, *The Poems of Emily Dickinson: An Annotated Guide to Commentary Published in English, 1890–1977* (Boston: G. K. Hall, 1979);

Joel Myerson, *Emily Dickinson: A Descriptive Bibliography* (Pittsburgh: University of Pittsburgh Press, 1984);

Karen Dandurand, *Dickinson Scholarship: An Annotated Bibliography, 1969–1985* (New York: Garland, 1988);

Duchac, *The Poems of Emily Dickinson: An Annotated Guide to Commentary Published in English, 1978–1989* (New York: G. K. Hall, 1993);

Myerson, "Supplement to *Emily Dickinson: A Descriptive Bibliography,*" *Emily Dickinson Journal,* 4, no. 2 (1995): 87–128.

Biographies:

George Whicher, *This Was a Poet: A Critical Biography of Emily Dickinson* (New York: Scribners, 1938);

Thomas H. Johnson, *Emily Dickinson: An Interpretive Biography* (Cambridge, Mass.: Harvard University Press, 1955);

Jay Leyda, *The Years and Hours of Emily Dickinson,* 2 volumes (New Haven: Yale University Press, 1960);

John Cody, *After Great Pain: The Inner Life of Emily Dickinson* (Cambridge, Mass.: Harvard University Press, 1971);

Richard B. Sewall, *The Life of Emily Dickinson,* 2 volumes (New York: Farrar, Straus & Giroux, 1974);

Barbara Mossberg, *Emily Dickinson: When a Writer Is a Daughter* (Bloomington: Indiana University Press, 1982);

Jerome Loving, *Emily Dickinson: The Poet on the Second Story* (Cambridge: Cambridge University Press, 1986);

Cynthia Griffin Wolff, *Emily Dickinson* (New York: Knopf, 1986);

Alfred Habegger, *My Wars Are Laid Away in Books: The Life of Emily Dickinson* (New York: Random House, 2001).

References:

Charles Anderson, *Emily Dickinson's Poetry: Stairway of Surprise* (New York: Holt, Rinehart & Winston, 1960);

Annual review essays in *American Literary Scholarship* (1963–   );

Christopher Benfey, *Emily Dickinson and the Problem of Others* (Amherst: University of Massachusetts Press, 1984);

Paula Bennett, *Emily Dickinson: Woman Poet* (Iowa City: University of Iowa Press, 1990);

Millicent Todd Bingham, *Ancestors' Brocades: The Literary Debut of Emily Dickinson* (New York: Harper, 1945);

Willis Buckingham, *Emily Dickinson's Reception in the 1890s: A Documentary History* (Pittsburgh: University of Pittsburgh Press, 1989);

Buckingham, "Poetry Readers and Reading in the 1890s: Emily Dickinson's First Reception," in *Readers in History: Nineteenth-Century American Literature and the Contexts of Response,* edited by James L. Machor (Baltimore: Johns Hopkins University Press, 1993), pp. 164–179;

Edwin H. Cady and Louis J. Budd, eds., *On Dickinson: The Best From American Literature* (Durham: Duke University Press, 1990);

Sharon Cameron, *Lyric Time: Dickinson and the Limits of Genre* (Baltimore: Johns Hopkins University Press, 1979);

Jack L. Capps, *Emily Dickinson's Reading, 1836–1886* (Cambridge, Mass.: Harvard University Press, 1966);

Joanne Feit Diehl, *Dickinson and the Romantic Imagination* (Princeton: Princeton University Press, 1981);

Joanne Dobson, *Dickinson and Strategies of Reticence: The Woman Writer in Nineteenth-Century America* (Bloomington: Indiana University Press, 1989);

Jane Donahue Eberwein, *Dickinson, Strategies of Limitation* (Amherst: University of Massachusetts Press, 1985);

Eberwein, ed., *An Emily Dickinson Encyclopedia* (Westport, Conn.: Greenwood Press, 1998);

The Emily Dickinson Journal (1992–);

Judith Farr, *The Passion of Emily Dickinson* (Cambridge, Mass.: Harvard University Press, 1992);

Paul Ferlazzo, ed., *Critical Essays on Emily Dickinson* (Boston: G. K. Hall, 1984);

R. W. Franklin, *The Editing of Emily Dickinson: A Reconsideration* (Madison: University of Wisconsin Press, 1967);

Albert J. Gelpi, *Emily Dickinson: The Mind of the Poet* (Cambridge, Mass.: Harvard University Press, 1965);

Sandra Gilbert and Susan Gubar, *The Madwoman in the Attic: The Woman Writer and the Nineteenth Century Literary Imagination* (New Haven: Yale University Press, 1979);

Grabher Gudrun, Roland Hagenbüchle, and Cristanne Miller, eds., *The Emily Dickinson Handbook* (Amherst: University of Massachusetts Press, 1998);

Jeanne Holland, "Scraps, Stamps, and Cutouts: Emily Dickinson's Domestic Technologies of Publication," in *Cultural Artifacts and the Production of Meaning: The Page, the Image and the Body,* edited by J. M. Ezell and Katherine O'Keeffe (Ann Arbor: University of Michigan Press, 1994), pp. 139–181;

Margaret Homans, *Women Writers and Poetic Identity: Dorothy Wordsworth, Emily Brontë, and Emily Dickinson* (Princeton: Princeton University Press, 1980);

Susan Howe, "These Flames and Generosities of the Heart: Emily Dickinson and the Illogic of Sumptuary Values," in her *The Birth-Mark: Unsettling the Wilderness in American Literary History* (Hanover, N.H.: University Press of New England, 1993), pp. 131–153;

Suzanne Juhasz, *The Undiscovered Continent: Emily Dickinson and the Space of the Mind* (Bloomington: Indiana University Press, 1983);

Juhasz, ed., *Feminist Critics Read Emily Dickinson* (Bloomington: Indiana University Press, 1983);

Juhasz, Cristanne Miller, Martha Nell Smith, eds., *Comic Power in Emily Dickinson* (Austin: University of Texas Press, 1993);

Karl Keller, *The Only Kangaroo Among the Beauty: Emily Dickinson and America* (Baltimore, Md.: Johns Hopkins University Press, 1979);

Benjamin Lease, *Emily Dickinson's Readings of Men and Books: Sacred Soundings* (New York: St. Martin's Press, 1990);

Mary Loeffelholz, *Dickinson and the Boundaries of Feminist Theory* (Urbana: University of Illinois Press, 1991);

Wendy Martin, *An American Triptych: Anne Bradstreet, Emily Dickinson, Adrienne Rich* (Chapel Hill: University of North Carolina Press, 1984);

Cynthia MacKenzie, *Concordance to the Letters of Emily Dickinson* (Boulder: University of Colorado Press, 2000);

Jerome McGann, *Black Riders: The Visible Language of Modernism* (Princeton: Princeton University Press, 1993);

Cristanne Miller, *Emily Dickinson: A Poet's Grammar* (Cambridge, Mass.: Harvard University Press, 1987);

Domhnall Mitchell, *Emily Dickinson: Monarch of Perception* (Amherst: University of Massachusetts Press, 2000);

Dorothy Oberhaus, *Emily Dickinson's Fascicles: Method and Meaning* (University Park: Pennsylvania State University Press, 1994);

Martin Orzeck and Robert Weisbuch, eds., *Dickinson and Audience* (Ann Arbor: University of Michigan Press, 1996);

Vivian Pollak, *Dickinson: The Anxiety of Gender* (Ithaca, N.Y.: Cornell University Press, 1984);

David Porter, *Emily Dickinson, the Modern Idiom* (Cambridge, Mass.: Harvard University Press, 1981);

Adrienne Rich, "Vesuvius at Home: The Power of Emily Dickinson," in her *On Lies, Secrets, and Silence: Selected Prose, 1966–1978* (New York: Norton, 1979), pp. 157–183;

S. P. Rosenbaum, *A Concordance to the Poems of Emily Dickinson* (Ithaca, N.Y.: Cornell University Press, 1966);

Martha Nell Smith, *Rowing in Eden: Re-Reading Emily Dickinson* (Austin: University of Texas Press, 1992);

Barton Levi St. Armand, *Emily Dickinson and Her Culture: The Soul's Society* (New York: Cambridge University Press, 1984);

Robert Weisbuch, *Emily Dickinson's Poetry* (Chicago: University of Chicago Press, 1975);

Marta L. Werner, ed., *Emily Dickinson's Open Folios: Scenes of Reading, Surfaces of Writing* (Ann Arbor: University of Michigan Press, 1995);

Shira Wolosky, *Emily Dickinson: A Voice at War* (New Haven: Yale University Press, 1984).

Papers:

Emily Dickinson's manuscripts are located in two primary collections: the Amherst College Library and the Houghton Library of Harvard University. The poems that were in Mabel Loomis Todd's possession are at Amherst; those that remained within the Dickinson households are at the Houghton Library.

Frederick Douglass
(February 1818 – 20 February 1895)

Patricia Dunlavy Valenti
University of North Carolina at Pembroke

See also the Douglass entries in *DLB 1: The American Renaissance in New England; DLB 43: American Newspaper Journalists, 1690–1872; DLB 50: Afro-American Writers Before the Harlem Renaissance;* and *DLB 79: American Magazine Journalists, 1850–1900.*

BOOKS: *Narrative of the Life of Frederick Douglass, an American Slave, Written by Himself* (Boston: Anti-Slavery Office, 1845; Dublin: Webb & Chapman, 1845; Wortley, U.K.: Printed by J. Barker, 1846);

American Slavery. Report of a Public Meeting Held at Finsbury Chapel, Moorfields, to Receive Frederick Douglass, the American Slave, on Friday, May 22, 1846. Joseph Sturge, Esq., in the Chair (London: Printed by C. B. Christian, 1846);

Farewell Speech of Mr. Frederick Douglass: Previously to Embarking on Board the Cambria, upon His Return to America, Delivered at the Valedictory Soiree Given to Him at the London Tavern, on March 30, 1847 (London: Ward, 1847);

Abolition Fanaticism in New York. Speech of a Runaway Slave from Baltimore, at an Abolition Meeting in New York, Held May 11, 1847 (Baltimore, 1847);

A Letter from Frederick Douglass to His Old Master, Written on the Anniversary of His Liberation from Slavery (Warrington: Printed at the Oberlin Press, 1848?; London: Printed by H. Armour, 1848?);

Address by Frederick Douglass, Formerly a Slave to the People of the United States of America (Edinburgh: H. Armour, 185?);

Lectures on American Slavery. . . . Delivered at Corinthian Hall, Rochester, N.Y. (Buffalo, N.Y.: G. Reese, 1851);

Oration, Delivered in Corinthian Hall, Rochester . . . , July 5th, 1852 (Rochester, N.Y.: Printed by Lee, Mann, 1852);

The Claims of the Negro Ethnologically Considered: An Address Before the Literary Societies of Western Reserve College, at Commencement, July 12, 1854 (Rochester, N.Y.: Printed by Lee, Mann, 1854);

Address by Frederick Douglass. Poem by A. C. Hills: Delivered at the Erection of the Wing Monument, at Mexico,

Frederick Douglass during the 1840s (National Portrait Gallery, Smithsonian Institution)

Oswego Co., N.Y., September 11th, 1855 (Syracuse, N.Y.: J. G. K. Truair, 1855);

The Anti-Slavery Movement: A Lecture by Frederick Douglass Before the Rochester Ladies' Anti-Slavery Society (Rochester, N.Y.: Printed by Lee, Mann, 1855); republished as *The Nature, Character, and History of the Anti-slavery Movement: A Lecture Delivered Before the Rochester Ladies' Anti-Slavery Association* (Glasgow, Scotland: G. Gallie, 1855);

My Bondage and My Freedom (New York & Auburn, N.Y.: Miller, Orton & Mulligan, 1855);

Two Speeches by Frederick Douglass; One on West India Emancipation, Delivered at Canandaigua, Aug. 4th, and the Other on the Dred Scott Decision, Delivered in New York, on the Occasion of the Anniversary of the American Abolition Society, May 1857 (Rochester, N.Y.: Printed by C. P. Dewey, 1857);

Eulogy of the Late Hon. Wm. Jay: Delivered on the Invitation of the Colored Citizens of New York City, in Shiloh Presbyterian Church, New York, May 12, 1859 (Rochester, N.Y.: A. Strong, 1859);

The Constitution of the United States: Is It Pro-Slavery or Anti-Slavery? (Halifax, U.K.: Printed by T. & W. Birtwhistle, 1860?);

U. S. Grant and the Colored People. His Wise, Just, Practical, and Effective Friendship Thoroughly Vindicated by Incontestable Facts in His Record from 1862 to 1872. Words of Truth and Soberness! He Who Runs May Read and Understand!! Be Not Deceived, Only Truth Can Endure!!! (Washington, D.C., 1872);

Address Delivered by Hon. Frederick Douglass, at the Third Annual Fair of the Tennessee Colored Agricultural and Mechanical Association, on Thursday, September 18, 1873, at Nashville, Tennessee (Washington, D.C.: New National Era and Citizen, 1873);

Oration by Frederick Douglass, Delivered on the Occasion of the Unveiling of the Freedmen's Monument in Memory of Abraham Lincoln, in Lincoln Park, Washington, D.C., April 14th, 1876 (Washington, D.C.: Printed by Gibson, 1876);

Speech on the Death of William Lloyd Garrison, at the Garrison Memorial Meeting in the 15th Street Presbyterian Church, Monday, June 2, 1879 (Washington, D.C.? 1879?);

Life and Times of Frederick Douglass, Written by Himself. His Early Life as a Slave, His Escape from Bondage, and His Complete History to the Present Time, Including His Connection with the Anti-slavery Movement (Hartford, Conn.: Park, 1881; London: Christian Age Office, 1882; revised and enlarged edition, Boston: DeWolfe, Fisk, 1892);

John Brown. An Address by Frederick Douglass, at the Fourteenth Anniversary of Storer College, Harper's Ferry, West Virginia, May 30, 1881 (Dover, N.H.: Morning Star Job Printing House, 1881);

Address . . . , Delivered in the Congregational Church, Washington, D.C., April 16, 1883, on the Twenty-first Anniversary of Emancipation in the District of Columbia (Washington, D.C., 1883);

Three Addresses on the Relations Subsisting Between the White and Colored People of the United States (Washington, D.C.: Printed by Gibson, 1886);

The Nation's Problem: A Speech Delivered by Hon. Frederick Douglass, Before the Bethel Literary and Historical Society in Washington, D.C., April 16, 1889 (Washington, D.C.? 1889?);

The Race Problem: Great Speech . . . Delivered Before the Bethel Literary and Historical Association, in the Metropolitan A. M. E. Church, Washington, D.C., October 21, 1890 (Washington, D.C.? 1890?);

Lecture on Haiti. The Haitian Pavilion Dedication Ceremonies Delivered at the World's Fair, in Jackson Park, Chicago, Jan. 2d, 1893 (Chicago, 1893);

Address . . . , Delivered in the Metropolitan A. M. E. Church, Washington, D.C., Tuesday, January 9th, 1894, on the Lessons of the Hour. In Which He Discusses the Various Aspects of the So-called, but Miscalled, Negro Problem (Baltimore: Press of Thomas and Evans, 1894);

A Defense of the Negro Race: An Address Delivered at the Annual Meeting of the American Missionary Association in Lowell, Mass., 1894 (New York: American Missionary Association, 1894);

The Frederick Douglass Papers, edited by John W. Blassingame and others: *Series I: Speeches, Debates, and Interviews*, 5 volumes (New Haven: Yale University Press, 1979–1992); *Series II: Autobiographical Writings*, 3 volumes projected (New Haven: Yale University Press, 1999–); *Series IV: Published Editorials and Essays*, 4 volumes projected (New Haven: Yale University Press, forthcoming).

OTHER: "The Heroic Slave," in *Autographs for Freedom*, edited by Julia Griffiths (Boston: J. P. Jewett, 1853; London: Sampson Low, 1853).

PERIODICALS EDITED: *North Star*, 3 December 1847–May 1851;
Frederick Douglass' Paper, 1851–1860;
Douglass' Monthly, January 1859–August 1863;
New National Era, 8 September 1870–22 October 1874.

SELECTED PERIODICAL PUBLICATIONS–UNCOLLECTED: "Reconstruction," *Atlantic Monthly*, 18 (December 1866): 761–765;
"Lynch Law in the South," *North American Review*, 155 (July 1892): 17–24.

Born Frederick Augustus Washington Bailey, a slave, Frederick Douglass went on to become a leading abolitionist orator, writer, and public figure whose life spanned most of the nineteenth century, though the work for which he is best known was published during the American Renaissance. The two autobiographies he published during that period are premier examples of the slave narrative so significant in mid-nineteenth-century American literature. These works situate Douglass among other authors who stressed the importance of individual experience and moral conviction. Douglass's escape from slavery was only the beginning of his acquisition of

Anna Murray Douglass, whom Douglass married in 1838 (Prints and Photographs Collection, Moorland-Spingarn Research Center, Howard University)

freedom from other forms of white paternalism and control, and he developed into a leader in the fight for abolition of slavery, black enfranchisement, and equal rights.

Frederick Douglass was born in February 1818 at Tuckahoe near Easton, Talbot County, Maryland. The month and year of birth have been fixed by historians, even though Douglass believed himself to have been born a year earlier. During his first six years of life, he lived with and obtained emotional sustenance from his grandparents Betsy and Isaac Bailey. Isaac Bailey occupied an anomalous position as a free woodcutter in a rural portion of a slave state. Betsy Bailey—a competent, bright, physically fit woman—was a clever farmer, an expert fisher, and the caretaker of Bailey children. She was given unusual liberty in the management of her affairs, even though she was a slave. Isaac and Betsy's daughter Harriet Bailey, who worked on the Tucka-hoe farms for Aaron Anthony, was Douglass's mother. Although the farms were not a great distance from the Baileys' cabin, Harriet visited her son rarely. Douglass never remembered seeing his mother before he was six years old, and he claimed to have reacted to the news of her death, when he was only seven, without emotion. He later came to understand that this emotional distance between himself and his mother was a result of the institution of slavery. Of Douglass's father, the only fact known with certainty is that he was white. It was hinted that Douglass's father was his mother's master, a term that would have applied to several men—a Mr. Stewart, a man to whom Harriet had been hired out; Aaron Anthony, the manager of the Tuckahoe farms and the Wye House estate; Edward Lloyd, the owner of Wye House and its large, surrounding plantation; and Thomas Auld, the man to whom Douglass most often referred as his master and who was also Anthony's son-in-law.

In August of 1824, without any explanation, Betsy Bailey left young Frederick at Wye House. There Douglass observed in close proximity the many offenses of the slave system. The owners lived in the luxury of their immense wealth while the slaves suffered the indignities of poverty and servitude. Douglass recalled eating mush with a shingle as his only utensil and awakening regularly to the screams of slaves being beaten. On this plantation Douglass lived in the home of Thomas and Lucretia Auld. Lucretia Auld could not have been ignorant that both her father and her husband had been rumored to be Douglass's father, something that may have affected the Aulds's complex relationship to Douglass. Later in his life, Douglass saw in Thomas and Lucretia Auld the embodiment of the evils of slavery, but Thomas and Lucretia Auld were also the people who identified Douglass's remarkable intellect. Their sending him to Baltimore to live with Thomas's brother Hugh and his wife, Sophia, may have been prompted by their desire to provide Douglass with greater opportunity.

In the Auld household in Baltimore, Douglass learned to read, at first through the efforts of Sophia, whose tutelage was soon curtailed by her husband's prohibition. Douglass later quoted Hugh Auld as saying, "'Learning would *spoil* the best nigger in the world. Now,' said he, 'if you teach that nigger (speaking of myself) how to read, there would be no keeping him. It would forever unfit him to be a slave.'" Auld's remark about the consequences of literacy had a perverse truth, for learning to read was perhaps the most decisive event in Douglass's youth and the beginning of his long career as a man of letters. Although Sophia Auld obeyed her husband and refused to continue teaching Douglass to read, the

Douglass's daughter, Rosetta, and second son, Frederick Jr. (left: Anacostia Neighborhood Museum, Smithsonian Institution; right: Prints and Photographs Collection, Moorland-Spingarn Research Center, Howard University)

seed of literacy had been planted. Douglass pored over the Aulds's books, notably Caleb Bingham's *The Columbian Orator* (1797), and he tricked literate white boys into furthering his mastery of words and letters. Such rebelliousness prompted Hugh and Sophia Auld to return Frederick to Thomas and Lucretia Auld in March 1833.

In January 1834 the Aulds hired out Douglass to Edward Covey, a man attempting to build a farm for himself out of rented land; he, as Douglass recorded later, was reputed to be a "nigger-breaker." Strong, deceitful, and violent, Covey clashed with Douglass. Douglass sought refuge with his only possible protector, Thomas Auld, but was sent back despite Douglass's well-founded fears that Covey might kill him. In a fight that assumed mythic dimensions in Douglass's retelling of it, Douglass used all his physical strength and mental endurance to conquer a foe who represented the evils of institutional-

ized slavery. In his 1845 autobiography, Douglass interpreted the meaning of this fight thus: "You have seen how a man was made a slave; you shall see how a slave was made a man."

Motivated by his newly acquired sense of manhood, Douglass attempted unsuccessfully to escape, whereupon Thomas Auld sent him back to his brother in Baltimore. Douglass was hired out as an apprentice caulker in a Baltimore shipyard; there he discovered what his wages might obtain for him, had he been allowed to keep them. Coupled with this newly acquired sense of economic potential was his burgeoning cultural awareness; Douglass learned to play the violin. He also made the acquaintance of Anna Murray, a free black woman. Five years older than Douglass, Anna was illiterate and remained so all her life. Douglass felt that he was ready to marry and begin a family, but his sense of financial and cultural potential contrasted painfully with the ever increasing injustices

*Douglass in 1856 (University Art Museum, University
of New Mexico, Albuquerque)*

of slavery, whetting his desire to escape to the North. Thus, on 3 September 1838, disguised as a sailor, he jumped aboard a train heading toward Wilmington, Delaware. There he boarded a steamboat for Philadelphia and then proceeded to New York City, where he adopted the last name Johnson. Anna Murray joined him, and the two were married.

Douglass and his wife soon left for New Bedford, Massachusetts. That port city had a reputation for friendliness to African Americans, and Douglass found employment on the wharf; he also found that the name Johnson was extremely common, and he adopted a suggestion to take a name drawn from Sir Walter Scott's *Lady of the Lake* (1810), which he did without verifying spelling. Henceforth, the escaped slave was known as Frederick Douglass. In New Bedford, Anna bore a daughter, Rosetta, in 1839 and a son, Lewis Henry, in 1840; Douglass was attempting to start life anew as a family man and laborer, forgetting the horrors of slavery that he had escaped. On 12 March 1839 Douglass was at a church meeting during a debate over shipping slaves to Africa. Douglass was moved by the discussion to make his first speech, in which he condemned the practice of colonization. Informing his auditors of the evils of sla-

very that he had endured, Douglass made the strong claim for the immediate freeing of all slaves in America. William Lloyd Garrison noted this speech in his anti-slavery newspaper, the *Liberator*. Pleased by this notice, Douglass was drawn to hear Garrison himself speak at Mechanics Hall on the night of 16 April 1839. Not long after, Douglass traveled to Nantucket for the meeting of the Massachusetts Anti-Slavery Society. On 16 August 1841, stirred by others' speeches, Douglass himself felt called to speak. Drawing deeply from the spring of his youthful learning, his knowledge of *The Columbian Orator* served him well, and his audience was mesmerized. Garrison hired Douglass as a speaker, and the anti-slavery movement found in this runaway slave its most eloquent rhetorician in the war of moral suasion.

In 1842 Anna gave birth to a second son, Frederick Jr., and in 1844 the couple's third son, Charles Remond, named after Douglass's friend the abolitionist, was born. During this same two-year period, Douglass was often away from home. Traveling the abolitionists' circuit as their leading orator in states such as New York, Ohio, Vermont, and Pennsylvania, Douglass began to discover the tensions and paradoxes inherent in his position as the most conspicuous spokesman for a nonviolent movement led by whites. In September 1843 he took part in a meeting of abolitionists at a church in Indiana. The meeting turned violent, and Douglass was injured, but he was saved from greater peril by William A. White, a graduate of Harvard, who thereby gained Douglass's lifelong affection. No less problematic than avoiding violence was Douglass's maintaining autonomy in a movement in which whites remained the organizers and the dominant force and in which blacks sometimes experienced the condescension of their white protectors and standard-bearers.

In 1844, at the urging of Wendell Phillips and other antislavery leaders, Douglass began to write the story of his life in slavery and his escape from it. Though nothing in his extant correspondence documents the process of writing about these events, *Narrative of the Life of Frederick Douglass, an American Slave, Written by Himself,* published by the Anti-Slavery Office in Boston in June 1845, recounts in the same detail and in the same language the story that Douglass had told through his powerful oratory. This consistency between the oral and written accounts of Douglass's experiences was used to counter charges that such a work could never have been the product of a former slave, and authentication of Douglass as author was the purpose of William Lloyd Garrison's "Preface" and Wendell Phillips's "Letter," both of

Douglass's first son, Sergeant Major Lewis Henry Douglass, and his third son, Private Charles Remond Douglass, during their service in the Fifty-fourth Massachusetts Volunteers, the Union regiment commanded by Colonel Robert Gould Shaw (Prints and Photographs Collection, Moorland-Spingarn Research Center, Howard University)

Cedar Hill, the house in the Anacostia neighborhood of Washington, D.C., that Douglass bought in 1878 (National Park Service, Frederick Douglass National Historic Site)

which were printed at the beginning of *Narrative of the Life of Frederick Douglass.* Widely circulated and enthusiastically received by abolitionists during the three years immediately following its publication, the narrative sold eleven thousand copies in the United States and went through nine English editions.

Narrative of the Life of Frederick Douglass, a scant 125 pages, is now arguably the best-known example of that indigenously American genre of autobiography, the slave narrative. Like other works of that genre—such as William Wells Brown's *Three Years in Europe* (1852), Henry Bibb's *Narrative of the Life and Adventures of Henry Bibb: An American Slave* (1849), and Harriet A. Jacobs's *Incidents in the Life of a Slave Girl* (1861), to name but three slave narratives of the many that flourished during the mid nineteenth century—Douglass's narrative functioned as both historical document and autobiography, even though

detractors immediately questioned its authenticity and veracity.

Specifically in the case of Douglass's narrative, abolitionists pointed to the quality of its writing to demonstrate—to those who needed such demonstration—the intellect of an author who could not be regarded as "chattel" possession but who must be recognized as a rational human being and one capable of highly intelligent thought. Reflecting the literary influence of the range of reading material available in plantation households, from the Bible to William Shakespeare to sentimental domestic fiction, *Narrative of the Life of Frederick Douglass* conveys the story of brutal beatings and servitude in eloquent figurative language, brilliantly balanced sentences, and vividly detailed and highly emotional scenes. Douglass asserted that nothing in *Narrative of the Life of Frederick Douglass* was fabricated or falsified; rather, he claimed to have omitted details that might have

Frederick and Helen Pitts Douglass during their honeymoon trip to Niagara Falls, 1884
(National Park Service, Frederick Douglass National Historic Site)

pushed his autobiography past the pale of credibility for his Northern audience. Nonetheless, Douglass's skillfully detailed writing was used by doubters of the authenticity of the work to argue that it could not have been produced by one whose origins should have prohibited his literacy, never mind his capacity as a powerful rhetorician. A. C. C. Thompson, one of the immediate and most vociferous detractors of *Narrative of the Life of Frederick Douglass,* printed his view in the *Delaware Republican* that the work was a complete fraud. Southerners generally wished to promulgate the position that allegations of brutality on plantations were simply lies, even though Douglass's book was replete with specific names and places, a daring level of realism in writing for one who was still legally a runaway slave.

With the publication of the Webb and Chapman edition of *Narrative of the Life of Frederick Douglass* in Dublin, Douglass obtained an international audience and the impetus for a speaking tour in the British Isles at a moment when leaving the country seemed a wise decision for one who had gained such

notoriety as a runaway slave. In the fall of 1845 Douglass departed aboard the *Cambria* with James Buffum, a successful white businessman. Because Douglass was denied a cabin, the two companions were relegated to steerage. In Cork, Douglass and Buffum were guests of Thomas and Ann Jennings, whose affection Douglass won, although he antagonized many others during this sojourn. Richard D. Webb, the Dublin publisher of *Narrative of the Life of Frederick Douglass,* perceived Douglass to be rude and arrogant. In Edinburgh, Douglass discomfited his hosts by chiding them for failing to disavow their Presbyterian slaveholding brethren in the American South. Together with Garrison in London, Douglass attempted to link the plight of the poor workers in Europe, Britain, and America with the poor workers in the American South, referring metaphorically to the slavery of the wage laborer in this industrializing nation. Douglass also garnered some antagonists within the antislavery movement by allowing Anna Richardson, an English Quaker, to purchase his freedom from Thomas Auld for £150 in 1846. His safe return to the United States was thereby assured, but some abolitionists considered the purchase of another human being for whatever motive a type of slave traffic. In addition to his ability to return home a legally free man, two significant results of this first trip across the Atlantic for Douglass were his decision to found his own newspaper upon returning to America and his meeting Julia Griffiths in Newcastle in December 1846.

In 1847 Douglass moved with his family to Rochester, New York, where he began his own antislavery newspaper, the *North Star,* which, along with other publications at this time, signaled his separation from Garrison's organization, a necessary step in Douglass's independence from the subtler forms of white control. Funds for the *North Star* had been donated by British friends. Douglass was no longer the white man's icon for the antislavery movement; he was in his own right a leader who championed causes without the blessing of Garrison or Phillips. In the summer of 1848 Douglass was the only man at Elizabeth Cady Stanton's Woman's Rights Convention in Seneca Falls, New York, who supported the right of women to vote. On the tenth anniversary of his escape in September 1848 Douglass was emboldened to publish in the *North Star* an eight-page diatribe against Thomas Auld, asserting that Douglass's own children now freely attended a white school—though he failed to mention that Rosetta was not permitted to enter the classroom with the other children because of her race. Though the practices of slave owners such as Auld were not allowed in Northern cities, Douglass was all too aware of the racism in the North, which prevented black citizens from being truly free and equal.

Griffiths arrived in Rochester in 1849, the same year that Douglass's youngest child, Annie, was born. Douglass frequently traveled to fulfill speaking engagements, and the *North Star* sorely needed someone to attend to its business, a need Griffiths happily addressed. Her attention to the details of the newspaper was matched by her personal attentiveness to Douglass, and their close friendship became a continuing source of rumors. In June 1851 the *North Star* changed its name to *Frederick Douglass' Paper*. In 1852 Griffiths, in her capacity as secretary for the Rochester Anti-Slavery Society, devised a plan to raise money for the movement. Various notables in the cause were asked to produce antislavery statements, followed by facsimiles of their autographs, which were printed in *Autographs for Freedom* (1853), edited by Griffiths. Douglass contributed to this endeavor his only work of fiction, the novella "The Heroic Slave," which had already been published in *Frederick Douglass' Paper* in March 1853. "The Heroic Slave" represents a turning point in African American literature as its first work of fiction, thereby departing from the scrupulously guarded practice of factual reporting that had characterized African American autobiography. The novella also embodies Douglass's evolving belief that African Americans would have to become the architects of their own liberation.

The heroic slave of the novella is Madison Washington, a character based upon an historical figure of the same name who had led a revolt in 1841 aboard the *Creole* as it was bound for New Orleans. But unlike Nat Turner, whose revolt a decade earlier had resulted in a massacre, Washington had managed a mutiny and diverted the ship to Nassau, where the slaves were liberated while he maintained control and won the admiration, if reluctant, of those whose lives had been spared when he had the power not to spare them. Douglass recasts this story in a four-part fiction. The novella opens with Washington's apostrophe (overheard by a visitor to the state of Virginia), despairing of life without liberty. The eloquence of Washington's rhetoric and the legitimacy of his claim obtain the admiration of his listener, Mr. Listwell, who thenceforth is converted to the cause of abolition. In part 2 the escaped Washington finds himself in Ohio, where, by coincidence, he is aided by Mr. Listwell, who gives him a place to rest in his own home and assists Washington's escape to Canada. In part 3 Washington has returned to Virginia, unable to live in freedom without his wife, whom he hopes to help escape. Frustrated in this effort, Washington is captured. He is sold and about to be sent to New Orleans aboard the *Creole* when Listwell once again encounters him, apparently unable to do anything to alter Washington's fate. Part 4 takes place some months after the mutiny and recounts its events through the conversation of one of the mates of the *Creole*. Tom Grant points out that Washington's eloquence as much as his strength made him a leader among the slaves. Douglass consciously associates his fictional character and the real-life figure with the founding fathers of the United States, thus reinforcing the legitimacy of the claim for freedom. Douglass also clearly identifies with Washington, who, like himself, can use words to compel admiration and action. If the white characters depicted in "The Heroic Slave" have redeeming qualities absent in the whites portrayed in Douglass's *Narrative of the Life of Frederick Douglass,* one can attribute this shift to Douglass's increased awareness of his white audience's needs. The Fugitive Slave Law of 1850 had made any citizen in the North or the South legally bound to capture slaves. Grimly aware of this law, Douglass created white characters with attitudes he would have liked white citizens to emulate, while at the same time making Madison Washington the sole agent of freedom for himself and his fellow slaves.

On 5 July 1852 in the Corinthian Hall in Rochester, Douglass issued a personal declaration of independence in a speech that he had been asked to give to mark the birth of the nation. Although he accepted the invitation, he would not deliver the speech on 4 July. Incensed by the Fugitive Slave Law, Douglass declared that the existence of slavery deprived him, and by implication all African Americans, of any ability to celebrate Independence Day. Douglass was unafraid to be combative. Maturing as a speaker and a writer, he had begun to realize, as he stated in his second autobiography, that his escape from slavery in the South had been only the beginning of his achievement of full liberty as an equal citizen of the United States.

Douglass grappled with these issues in *My Bondage and My Freedom*, published in 1855 with Griffiths's encouragement and editorial help. This second life story is much longer than the first, not only because it includes events that had transpired since the writing of *Narrative of the Life of Frederick Douglass*, including an account of his twenty-one-month sojourn in Great Britain, but also because it augments with additional detail and analysis incidents previously recounted. In addition to its greater length, it is a more substantial autobiography, demonstrating Douglass's ability to exercise his own will freely. His separation from Garrison and the American Anti-Slavery Society and his association with rival parties in the abolitionist movement were announced by the inclusion of an introduction to *My Bondage and My Freedom* by one of Garrison's vehement detractors, James McCune Smith. By including this introduction, Douglass not only liberated himself from white paternalism, but he also placed himself alongside men such as Henry David Thoreau, Ralph Waldo Emerson, and Walt Whitman, whose writings during the 1850s also affirmed the validity of the first-person narrative voice as both the individual and the representative expression of identity. *My Bondage and My Freedom* thus claims the place of the first African American autobiography that reached beyond the narrative of a slave's life.

The schisms within the antislavery movement and the increased combativeness of Douglass's tone were among the many signs of national tension as the Civil War approached. Moral suasion was losing ground to violence as a means to end slavery. In 1856 John Brown engaged in his first act of violence

in the territory of Kansas, savagely killing three pro-slavery men—a father and his two sons. In 1857 the Dred Scott decision polarized the pro- and antislavery forces even further by preventing Congress from prohibiting slavery in the territories. Although to endorse violence was not characteristic of Douglass, he nonetheless joined his wealthy abolitionist friend Gerrit Smith and others in suggesting that their followers send guns to abolitionists in Kansas. Douglass had met Brown in 1848 and was affected by Brown's charisma and the warmth Brown felt for African Americans; moreover, Douglass had maintained contact with Brown throughout the 1850s. On 16 October 1859 Brown led a small band in a failed attempt to seize the arsenal at Harpers Ferry for the purpose of obtaining weapons for a slave revolt. Because of Douglass's association and correspondence with Brown, Douglass was charged with inciting insurrection as one of Brown's allies.

Douglass had earlier announced in *Douglass' Monthly,* a publication that had begun as a supplemental journal for *Frederick Douglass' Paper* but that by January 1859 was being published separately, that he was planning a tour of Europe. The end of 1859 was clearly the moment to begin that tour, and in November Douglass departed for the safety of England. He renewed his friendship with Griffiths, now Julia Griffiths Crofts, and spent Christmas in Yorkshire with her and her husband of only several months. In January 1860 Douglass traveled to Edinburgh, then to Glasgow, where news of his daughter Annie's death reached him. He curtailed further travel and returned to the United States. In Rochester by April, Douglass continued the publication of *Douglass' Monthly*. His safe return to the United States was facilitated by the termination of congressional inquiry into any possible accomplices in the Harpers Ferry raid and by Northern acceptance of John Brown as a martyr to the cause of abolition. Abraham Lincoln took the oath of office in March 1861, and the following month the firing on Fort Sumter, South Carolina, began the Civil War.

On 1 January 1863 Abraham Lincoln signed the Emancipation Proclamation, which freed slaves. Douglass celebrated the significance of this event with an emotionally charged speech the following 6 February at Cooper Union in New York. With joy and triumph Douglass announced to his audience that forevermore African Americans' Independence Day would be 1 January 1863. Douglass saw this date not as the end to the great struggle for the abolition of slavery but as yet another beginning. That African Americans were free was not enough; they must be equal, and joining the ranks of the soldiers fighting in

Letter to the secretary of state written soon after President Benjamin Harrison appointed Douglass minister and consul to Haiti (National Archives, Washington, D.C.)

the people among whom he would
send the.

I therefore feel it my duty to
accept the mission thus tendered me
by His Excellency, the President of the
United States, under the conditions
expressed in your note _as_ to the time
of going.

A note from you will bring
me to the State Department at
any time that may suit your
convenience.

I am dear Sir
Very Respectfully Yours

Frederick Douglass,

Douglass with his grandson Joseph, who became a concert violinist

black communities in this regiment that Lewis and Charles Douglass joined were led by Colonel Robert Gould Shaw, a staunch abolitionist and member of an aristocratic New England family. In May 1863 the regiment departed for the Sea Islands off the coast of South Carolina. Charles Douglass was among a group of recruits unable to accompany his regiment because of illness. Lewis Douglass, a sergeant major in the regiment, fought with his comrades in the battle at Fort Wagner, which resulted in an overwhelming and bloody defeat for the Union. Robert Gould Shaw was one of more than 1,500 men in the Fifty-fourth killed; Lewis Douglass was one of the few fortunate soldiers who somehow managed to survive. Frederick Douglass continued his efforts in the North to encourage blacks to enlist, efforts that were complicated by the sentiments of Northerners who believed that blacks should be fighting their own battle but who resented the ability of wealthy whites (Shaw had been a notable exception) to buy their way out of conscription. Anticipating a commission as the first black officer in the Union Army, Douglass stopped publication of *Douglass' Monthly* in the summer of 1863, but the commission never materialized.

Douglass's own posture regarding the causative factors in societal change had continued to evolve. He no longer depended upon the efficacy of individual moral belief, and he increasingly espoused the need for governmental agency in societal amelioration. In a speech at Cooper Union in February 1864 titled "The Mission of War," Douglass announced to the Women's Loyal League that this great war must not only accomplish the abolition of slavery but also the enfranchisement of blacks, a position he later conveyed to President Lincoln. At the close of the war, Douglass labored passionately for the enfranchisement of blacks. In Baltimore on 29 September 1865 Douglass spoke at the dedication of the Douglass Institute, a center founded for the cultural enrichment of African Americans of that city, and his theme was enfranchisement. Douglass saw little real significance to emancipation without enfranchisement and sometimes found himself at odds with advocates of the vote for women, who were competing for the same right, a competition that caused a rift between former allies. Susan B. Anthony, for example, made the assertion that white women were more deserving of the vote than black men. Republicans, on the other hand, failed to support women's enfranchisement. In 1870, with the ratification of the Fifteenth Amendment to the Constitution, guaranteeing the right to vote regardless of "race, color, or previous condition of servitude," Douglass called for the enfranchisement of women.

the Civil War was one of the ways blacks could demonstrate their equality with whites while simultaneously earning the respect of their white counterparts. Though of an age still young enough to become an active combatant, Douglass chose to fight through words, as he had for more than two decades. Through speeches and his writing in *Douglass' Monthly,* he exhorted other black men to enlist, despite the realistic counsel of Thomas Wentworth Higginson—the Massachusetts clergyman, man of letters, and colonel of the black regiment of the First South Carolina Volunteers—who warned that blacks taken prisoner in the South could be sold into slavery. Notwithstanding the great risks for black combatants, Douglass published a particularly eloquent appeal, "Men of Color to Arms," in March of 1863. Among the men who heeded Douglass's call to arms were two of Douglass's own sons, Lewis and Charles.

Immediately after the Emancipation Proclamation, Massachusetts governor John A. Andrew called for volunteers in what became the Fifty-fourth Massachusetts Volunteers. Recruits from many Northern

Douglass became dissatisfied with post–Civil War president Andrew Johnson. The Freedmen's Bureau Act of 1865 required that land abandoned by white farmers that was being successfully cultivated by former slaves must remain the property of these freed slaves. Johnson, however, pardoned Confederate landowners and returned their land to them, thereby augmenting possibilities for white supremacy in Southern states. The briefly discussed opportunity for Douglass to become head of the Freedmen's Bureau did nothing to improve Douglass's judgment of Johnson. Douglass turned his energies elsewhere, in 1870 becoming an editor once again, this time of the *New National Era,* formerly the *National Era,* a newspaper he renamed upon his purchase of a half interest.

In 1872 Douglass's home in Rochester was destroyed by fire. He was in Washington at the time, and though none of his family members was injured, their personal losses were great, as was the loss to posterity of many of Douglass's papers. Letters and the only complete runs of his journals—*North Star, Frederick Douglass' Paper,* and *Douglass' Monthly*—were destroyed. The destruction of his home in Rochester spurred his permanent relocation to Washington, where in 1878 he purchased Cedar Hill, his home in Anacostia.

In 1874 Douglass became president of the Freedman's Savings and Trust Company, also known as the Freedman's Bank, which had been founded when the Freedmen's Bureau Act had been passed. After almost a decade of bad loans, the Freedman's Bank was insolvent. Douglass's less than careful attention to the details of the business of the bank did nothing to restore its financial viability. Only a few months after assuming its presidency, Douglass voted with the trustees of the Freedman's bank to close it. He was thus at liberty to accept political appointments. In 1877 President Rutherford B. Hayes appointed Douglass United States Marshall for the District of Columbia; in 1881 President James A. Garfield appointed him Recorder of Deeds for the District of Columbia; and in 1889 President Benjamin Harrison appointed him to the post of minister and consul to Haiti.

Anna Murray Douglass's death in 1882 was followed by Douglass's own ill health and depression the following year. In 1884, to the great consternation of his children, Douglass married the white woman he had hired two years earlier as his secretary. Helen Pitts was forty-five when she wed the sixty-six-year-old Douglass. After the wedding the couple traveled to Niagara Falls; two years later, sailing from New York on the *City of Rome,* the couple occupied a stateroom (a decidedly different crossing from Douglass's first transatlantic voyage with James

Buffum when steerage was the only accommodation permitted). Helen and Frederick Douglass toured the great cities of Europe as well as Egypt and other areas of Northern Africa.

Not long after their return to the United States Douglass began his two-year mission in Haiti, but not without the objections of some who feared for Douglass's safety in the troubled regime of President Florvil Hyppolite. Two decades earlier Douglass had espoused President Ulysses S. Grant's desire to annex the neighbor of Haiti, the Dominican Republic, a policy long since abandoned. The United States did, nonetheless, aspire to establish a naval base on Haiti, recognizing the strategic importance of this Caribbean nation, but Douglass anticipated the negative outcome of his negotiations on behalf of his country. Both Helen and Frederick wanted to stand as equals with President Hyppolite, and they failed to recognize him for the tyrant he was. On 28 May 1891 the uprising against Hyppolite's government turned into a massacre of the insurgents, led by President Hyppolite himself. Helen Douglass was seriously ill during the spring of 1891, and soon thereafter, Douglass resigned his post.

In an effort to keep the nation from forgetting the story of slavery, in 1881 Douglass published his third autobiography, *Life and Times of Frederick Douglass, Written by Himself.* The work was revised and republished in 1892. Neither of these editions was received with the accolades that had greeted his first, or even his second, autobiography. In the 1881 edition Douglass recounted his observations on those events that had occurred since his publication of *My Bondage and My Freedom* in 1855. Longtime friend and colleague Ottilia Assing suggested that Douglass might write about Brown and other notable figures who had come into Douglass's orbit during the Civil War, but he was unable or unwilling to shift his focus away from himself. The addition of more than one hundred pages to his 1892 edition did not improve the reception of the book or Douglass's satisfaction with it. It seemed that neither the black nor the white citizens of the nation wanted to reflect upon that pernicious institution that it had so recently abolished. But Douglass's insistence upon remembering where he had come from and what he had accomplished demonstrates forcibly how tied he was to his roots, notwithstanding the place he held in the society of whites. Frederick Douglass died of a heart attack in his home in Washington, D.C., on 20 February 1895.

Letters:

*A Black Diplomat in Haiti: The Diplomatic Correspondence of
    U.S. Minister Frederick Douglass from Haiti, 1889–*

1891, 2 volumes, edited by Norma Brown (Salisbury, N.C.: Documentary Publications, 1977).

Bibliography:

Library of Congress, Manuscript Division, *Frederick Douglass: A Register and Index of His Papers in the Library of Congress* (Washington, D.C.: Library of Congress, 1976).

Biographies:

Charles W. Chesnutt, *Frederick Douglass* (Boston: Small, Maynard, 1899);

Benjamin Quarles, *Frederick Douglass* (Washington, D.C.: Associated Publishers, 1948);

Philip Foner, *The Life and Writings of Frederick Douglass,* 5 volumes (New York: International Publishers, 1950–1975);

William S. McFeely, *Frederick Douglass* (New York: Norton, 1991).

References:

William L. Andrews, Introduction to *My Bondage and My Freedom* (Urbana: University of Illinois Press, 1987);

Andrews, *To Tell a Free Story: The First Century of Afro-American Autobiography, 1760–1865* (Urbana: University of Illinois Press, 1986);

Andrews, ed., *Critical Essays on Frederick Douglass* (Boston: G. K. Hall, 1991);

Houston A. Baker Jr., Introduction to *Narrative of the Life of Frederick Douglass, an American Slave* (New York: Viking, 1982);

David W. Blight, *Frederick Douglass' Civil War: Keeping Faith in Jubilee* (Baton Rouge: Louisiana State University Press, 1989);

Ronald K. Burke, *Frederick Douglass: Crusading Orator for Human Rights* (New York: Garland, 1996);

David B. Chesebrough, *Frederick Douglass: Oratory from Slavery* (Westport, Conn.: Greenwood Press, 1998);

Gregory P. Lampe, *Frederick Douglass: Freedom's Voice, 1818–1845* (East Lansing: Michigan State University Press, 1998);

Bill E. Lawson and Frank M. Kirkland, eds., *Frederick Douglass: A Critical Reader* (Malden, Mass.: Blackwell, 1999);

William W. Nichols, "Individualism and Autobiographical Art: Frederick Douglass and Henry Thoreau," *CLA Journal,* 16 (December 1972): 145–158;

William L. Petrie, ed., *Bibliography of the Frederick Douglass Library at Cedar Hill* (Fort Washington, Md.: Silesia, 1995);

Alan J. Rice and Martin Crawford, eds., *Liberating Sojourn: Frederick Douglass & Transatlantic Reform* (Athens: University of Georgia Press, 1999);

Eric J. Sundquist, ed., *Frederick Douglass: New Literary and Historical Essays* (Cambridge & New York: Cambridge University Press, 1990).

Papers:

The Frederick Douglass Collection at the Library of Congress, Washington, D.C., houses the vast majority of Frederick Douglass's manuscripts, which are available on fifty-two reels of microfilm.

Octavius Brooks Frothingham

(26 November 1822 – 27 November 1895)

Nancy Craig Simmons
Virginia Polytechnic Institute and State University

See also the Frothingham entry in *DLB 1: The American Renaissance in New England.*

BOOKS: *The New Commandment: A Discourse Delivered in the North Church, Salem, on Sunday, June 5, 1854* (Salem, Mass.: Printed at the Observer Office, 1854);

Colonization, Anti-Slavery Tracts, no. 3 (New York: American Anti-Slavery Society, 1855);

The Eternal Life: A Discourse Delivered in the North Church, Salem, April 15, 1855 (Salem, Mass.: Printed at the Observer Office, 1855);

Speech of the Rev. O. B. Frothingham, Before the American Anti-Slavery Society, in New York, May 8th, 1856 (New York: American Anti-Slavery Society, 1856);

The Last Signs. A Sermon Preached at the Unitarian Church in Jersey City, on Sunday morning, June 1, 1856 (New York: J. A. Gray, 1856);

The Gospel of the Day (Albany: Ladies' Religious Publication Society, 1858);

The Christian Consciousness, Its Elements and Expression: A Discourse Delivered at the Installation of J. K. Karcher as Pastor of the Spring Garden Unitarian Church, October 5, 1859 (Philadelphia: T. B. Pugh, 1859);

The Paternal Aspect of Providence: A Sermon Preached in His Church on Fortieth Street Between Fifth and Sixth Avenues, New York (New York: D. G. Francis, 1859);

Theodore Parker: A Sermon Preached in New York, June 10, 1860 (Boston: Walker, Wise, 1860);

The Let-Alone Policy: A Sermon . . . June 9, 1861 (New York: Published at no. 5 Beekman Street, 1861);

Seeds and Shells: A Sermon Preached in New York, Nov. 17, 1861 (New York: Wynkoop, Hallenbeck & Thomas, 1862);

Words Spoken at the Funeral of Robert F. Denyer, Oct. 19th, 1862 (New York? 1862);

The Birth of the Spirit of Christ: A Sermon (New York: Anti-Slavery Office, 1863);

The Morality of the Riot: Sermon at Ebbitt Hall, Sunday, July 19, 1863 (New York: D. G. Francis, 1863);

Stories from the Lips of the Teacher. Retold by a Disciple (Boston: Walker, Wise, 1863);

Stories of the Patriarchs (Boston: Walker, Wise, 1864);

Childhood and Manhood of the Spirit in Jesus, and New Year's Gifts of the Spirit: Two Discourses (New York: D. G. Francis, 1865);

The Unitarian Convention and the Times: A Palm Sunday Sermon (New York: C. M. Plumb, 1865);

The Ministries of Pestilence: A Sermon, Sunday, July 1, 1866 (New York: J. Miller, 1866);

Binding and Loosing: Two Sermons (New York: J. Miller, 1867);

The Inward Guide: A Sermon (New York: J. Miller, 1868);

Radical Work: A Sermon (New York: D. G. Francis, 1868);

Reasonings about Faith: A Sermon (New York: James Miller, 1868);

A Sermon Delivered Before the Graduating Class at the Fifty-second Annual Visitation of the Divinity School of Harvard University (Cambridge, Mass.: J. Wilson, 1868);

The Weightier Matters of the Law: A Sermon (New York: J. Miller, 1868);

What Is It to Be a Christian?: A Sermon (New York: D. G. Francis, 1868);

The Worship of Tools: A Sermon (New York: James Miller, 1868);

The Eternal Gospel: A Sermon at Lyric Hall (New York: D. G. Francis, 1869);

Liberty and License: A Sermon Spoken in Lyric Hall, New York (New York: D. G. Francis, 1869);

The Living Spring of Water: A Sermon (New York: D. G. Francis, 1869);

The Foes of Society: A Sermon . . . Preached at Lyric Hall (New York: D. G. Francis, 1869);

The Infernal and the Celestial Love: A Sermon Preached at Lyric Hall (New York: D. G. Francis, 1869);

Elective Affinity: A Sermon Preached . . . in Lyric Hall . . . December 19, 1869 (New York: D. G. Francis, 1870);

Taking God's Name in Vain: A Sermon . . . Preached in Lyric Hall, February 6, 1870 (New York: D. G. Francis, 1870);

The "Many Mansions": A Sermon, Preached Oct. 2, 1870 (New York: D. G. Francis, 1870);

The Dying and the Living God: A Sermon, Preached . . . in Lyric Hall (New York: D. G. Francis, 1870);

The Issue with Superstition: A Sermon Preached . . . in Lyric Hall (New York: D. G. Francis, 1870);

Personal Independence: A Sermon . . . Preached in Lyric Hall, Sixth Avenue, Between Forty-first and Forty-second Streets, October 30, 1870 (New York: D. G. Francis, 1870);

The Radical Belief: A Discourse . . . Spoken in Lyric Hall (New York: D. G. Francis, 1870);

The Sin Against the Holy Ghost: A Sermon Preached . . . in Lyric Hall (New York: D. G. Francis, 1870);

Beliefs of the Unbelievers: A Lecture . . . Read in Boston, January 8, 1871 (New York: D. G. Francis, 1871);

Prayer: A Sermon . . . Preached in Lyric Hall, January 29, 1871 (New York: D. G. Francis, 1871);

Sowing and Reaping: A Sermon . . . Preached in Lyric Hall, February 12, 1871 (New York: D. G. Francis, 1871);

Faith and Morals: Two Sermons . . . Preached in Lyric Hall, March 5th & 12th, 1871 (New York: D. G. Francis, 1871);

Comfort and Inspiration: A Sermon . . . Preached in Lyric Hall, March 19, 1871 (New York: D. G. Francis, 1871);

The Immortalities of Man: A Discourse . . . Preached in Lyric Hall, April 9th, 1871 (New York: D. G. Francis, 1871);

God Is Spirit: A Sermon . . . Preached in Lyric Hall, April 9, 1871 (New York: D. G. Francis, 1871);

The Gospel of To-day: A Sermon . . . Preached in Lyric Hall, Sixth Avenue, Between Forty-first and Forty-second Streets, April 16th, 1871 (New York: D. G. Francis, 1871);

Living Faith: A Sermon . . . Preached in Lyric Hall (New York: D. G. Francis, 1871);

The Overruling God: A Sermon . . . Preached in Lyric Hall, November 12, 1871 (New York: D. G. Francis, 1871);

Christmas Eve: A Sermon . . . Preached in Lyric Hall, December 24, 1871 (New York: D. G. Francis, 1871);

Sentimental Religion: A Sermon . . . Preached in Lyric Hall, Jan. 14, 1872 (New York: D. G. Francis, 1872);

The Victory over Death: A Sermon . . . Preached in Lyric Hall, March 31st, 1872 (New York: D. G. Francis, 1872);

Letter and Spirit: A Sermon . . . Preached in Lyric Hall, April 7th, 1872 (New York: D. G. Francis, 1872);

Wheat and Tares: A Sermon . . . Preached in Lyric Hall, May 12th, 1872 (New York: D. G. Francis, 1872);

The Scientific Aspect of Prayer: A Sermon . . . Masonic Temple, September 22, 1872 (New York: D. G. Francis, 1872);

Visions of Heaven: A Sermon . . . Preached in Lyric Hall, October 27, 1872 (New York: D. G. Francis, 1872);

Visions of Judgment: A Sermon . . . Preached in Lyric Hall, November 10th, 1872 (New York: D. G. Francis, 1872);

Crime and Punishment: A Sermon . . . Preached in Lyric Hall, December 8th, 1872 (New York: D. G. Francis, 1872);

The Present Heaven: A Discourse (Toledo, Ohio: Index Association, 1872);

The Faith in Immortality: A Sermon . . . Preached in Lyric Hall, Dec. 15, 1872 (New York: D. G. Francis, 1873);

The Religion of Humanity: An Essay (New York: D. G. Francis, 1873);

The Naked Truth: A Sermon . . . Preached in Lyric Hall, January 16th, 1873 (New York: D. G. Francis, 1873);

The Joy of a Free Faith: A Sermon . . . Preached in Lyric Hall, Jan. 26, 1873 (New York: D. G. Francis, 1873);

Ebb and Flow of Faith: A Sermon . . . Preached in Lyric Hall, February 2nd, 1873 (New York: D. G. Francis, 1873);

God's Fellow Workers (New York, 1873?);

The Radical's Root: A Sermon . . . Preached in Lyric Hall, April 27th, 1873 (New York: D. G. Francis, 1873);

Flowers and Graves: A Sermon . . . Preached in Lyric Hall, May 25, 1873 (New York: D. G. Francis, 1873);

Religion, the Poetry of Life: A Sermon . . . Preached in Lyric Hall, June 1st, 1873 (New York: D. G. Francis, 1873);

Modern Idolatry: A Sermon . . . Preached in Lyric Hall, September 28th, 1873 (New York: D. G. Francis, 1873);

The Catholic Revival. A Sermon . . . Preached in Lyric Hall, Sixth Avenue, Between Forty-first and Forty-second Streets, October 5th, 1873 (New York: D. G. Francis, 1873);

The Protestant Alliance: A Sermon . . . Preached in Lyric Hall, October 12th, 1873 (New York: D. G. Francis, 1873);

Religion and a Religion: A Sermon . . . Preached in Lyric Hall, October 19th, 1873 (New York: D. G. Francis, 1873);

The Soul of Goodness: A Sermon . . . Preached in Lyric Hall, November 2d, 1873 (New York: D. G. Francis, 1873);

The Power of the Word Made Flesh: A Sermon . . . Preached in Lyric Hall, Nov. 16th, 1873 (New York: D. G. Francis, 1873);

The Sacraments of Home: A Sermon Preached in Lyric Hall, December 7th, 1873 (New York: D. G. Francis, 1873);

The Puritan Spirit. A Sermon, Preached in Lyric Hall, Sixth Avenue, Between Forty-first and Forty-second Streets, December 21st, 1873 (New York: D. G. Francis, 1873);

The Hidden Life: A Sermon . . . Preached in Lyric Hall, January 25th, 1874 (New York: D. G. Francis, 1874);

Belief and Practice: Sermon . . . Preached in Lyric Hall, Sixth Avenue, Between Forty-first and Forty-second Streets, February 1st, 1874 (New York: D. G. Francis, 1874);

Why Go to Church?: A Sermon . . . Preached in Lyric Hall, February 8th, 1874 (New York: D. G. Francis, 1874);

The Suppression of Vice: A Sermon . . . Preached in Lyric Hall, Feb. 15th, 1874 (New York: D. G. Francis, 1874);

The Revival of Religion: A Sermon . . . Preached in Lyric Hall, March 1st, 1874 (New York: D. G. Francis, 1874);

Saintliness: A Sermon . . . Preached in Lyric Hall, March 22nd, 1874 (New York: D. G. Francis, 1874);

The Agony of the Son of Man: A Sermon . . . Preached in Lyric Hall, March 29th, 1874 (New York: D. G. Francis, 1874);

Resurrection of the Son of Man: A Sermon . . . Preached in Lyric Hall, April 5th, 1874 (New York: D. G. Francis, 1874);

The Law of Habit: A Sermon . . . Preached in Lyric Hall, April 19th, 1874 (New York: D. G. Francis, 1874);

The Disposal of Our Dead: A Sermon . . . Preached in Lyric Hall, May 3d, 1874 (New York: D. G. Francis, 1874);

Spiritual Force and its Supply: A Sermon . . . Preached in Lyric Hall, Sixth Avenue, Between Forty-first and Forty-second Sts., September 20th, 1874 (New York: D. G. Francis, 1874);

The Spirit of Truth, the Comforter: A Sermon . . . Preached in Lyric Hall, Sixth Avenue, Between Forty-first and Forty-second Sts., September 27th, 1874 (New York: D. G. Francis, 1874);

Quality and Quantity of Life: A Sermon . . . Preached in Lyric Hall, October 4th, 1874 (New York: D. G. Francis, 1874);

The Holy Ghost, Lord and Giver of Life: A Sermon . . . Preached in Lyric Hall, October 11, 1874 (New York: D. G. Francis, 1874);

Goodness and Happiness: A Sermon . . . Preached in Lyric Hall, October 18th, 1874 (New York: D. G. Francis, 1874);

The Unseen Sources of Character: A Sermon . . . Preached in Lyric Hall, October 25th, 1874 (New York: D. G. Francis, 1874);

Charity and the Poor: A Sermon . . . Preached in Lyric Hall, November 29th, 1874 (New York: D. G. Francis, 1874);

Theodore Parker: A Biography (Boston: Osgood, 1874);

The Safest Creed and Twelve Other Recent Discourses of Reason (New York: A. K. Butts, 1874);

Character, its Friends and Foes: A Sermon . . . Preached in Lyric Hall, November 15, 1874 (New York: D. G. Francis, 1875);

The Divorce Between Creed and Conduct: A Sermon . . . Preached in Lyric Hall, January 24th, 1875 (New York: D. G. Francis, 1875);

The Struggle for Supremacy over Conscience: A Sermon . . . Preached in Lyric Hall, January 31st, 1875 (New York: D. G. Francis, 1875);

The Devout Life: A Sermon . . . Preached in Lyric Hall, February 14th, 1875 (New York: D. G. Francis, 1875);

Paying Debts: A Sermon . . . Preached in Lyric Hall, Sixth Avenue, Between Forty-first and Forty-second Streets, March 28th, 1875 (New York: Putnam, 1875);

The Cardinal's Berretta: A Sermon . . . Preached in Masonic Temple, May 2nd, 1875 (New York: Putnam, 1875);

Pharisees: A Sermon . . . Preached in Masonic Temple, May 9th, 1875 (New York: Putnam, 1875);

The Dimensions of Life: A Sermon . . . Preached in Lyric Hall (New York: D. G. Francis, 1875);

The Great Hope: A Sermon . . . Preached in Lyric Hall (New York: Putnam, 1875);

Interests Material and Spiritual: A Sermon (New York: Putnam, 1875);

Reasonable Religion: A Sermon . . . Preached in Masonic Hall (New York: Putnam, 1875);

Allegiance to Faith: A Sermon . . . Masonic Temple, Oct. 10th, 1875 (New York: Putnam, 1875);

Thoughts about God: A Sermon . . . Masonic Temple, Oct. 31st, 1875 (New York: Putnam, 1875);

Clogs and Opportunities: A Sermon . . . Masonic Temple, Dec. 5th, 1875 (New York: Putnam, 1875);

New Wine in Old Bottles: A Sermon . . . Masonic Temple, Dec. 12th, 1875 (New York: Putnam, 1875);

Knowledge and Faith: A Sermon . . . Preached in Masonic Temple, Dec. 19th, 1875 (New York: Putnam, 1875);

Infidelity: A Sermon . . . Masonic Temple, Jan. 9th, 1876 (New York: Putnam, 1875 [i.e., 1876]);

Religion and Childhood: A Sermon . . . Masonic Temple, Jan. 16th, 1876 (New York: Putnam, 1876);

The Sermon on the Mount: A Sermon . . . Masonic Temple, Jan. 23d, 1876 (New York: Putnam, 1876);

Materialism: A Sermon . . . Masonic Temple, Jan. 30th, 1876 (New York: Putnam, 1876);

Irreverence: A Sermon . . . Masonic Temple, Feb. 6th, 1876 (New York: Putnam, 1876);

Rights and Duties: A Sermon . . . Masonic Temple, Feb. 27th, 1876 (New York: Putnam, 1876);

Authority and Religion: A Sermon . . . Masonic Temple, March 5th, 1876 (New York: Putnam, 1876);

Moral Narcotics: A Sermon . . . Masonic Temple, April 2d, 1876 (New York: Putnam, 1876);

The Glorified Man: A Sermon . . . Masonic Temple, April 16th, 1876 (New York: Putnam, 1876);

The Natural Man: A Sermon . . . Masonic Temple, April 20, 1876 (New York: Putnam, 1876);

Forgiveness: A Sermon . . . Masonic Temple . . . May 7th, 1876 (New York: Putnam, 1876);

The Golden Rule: A Sermon . . . Masonic Temple, May 28, 1876 (New York: Putnam, 1876);

The Spirit of the New Faith: A Sermon . . . Masonic Temple, Oct. 8th, 1876 (New York: Putnam, 1876);

Beliefs of the Unbelievers and Other Discourses (New York: Putnam, 1876);

Knowledge and Faith, and Other Discourses (New York: Putnam, 1876);

Transcendentalism in New England: A History (New York: Putnam, 1876);

The Perfect Life: A Sermon . . . Masonic Temple, Nov. 5th, 1876 (New York: Putnam, 1876);

The Festival of Joy: A Sermon . . . Masonic Temple, Dec. 24th, 1876 (New York: Putnam, 1876);

A Hundred Years: A Sermon . . . Masonic Temple, Dec. 31st, 1876 (New York: Putnam, 1876);

Waste and Saving of Providence: A Sermon . . . Masonic Temple, December 17th, 1876, reported by Edward F. Underhill (New York: Putnam, 1877);

Life's Test of Creed: A Sermon . . . Masonic Temple, reported by Underhill (New York: Putnam, 1877);

The Cradle of the Christ. A Study in Primitive Christianity (New York: Putnam, 1877);

Prayer and Work: A Sermon . . . Masonic Temple, Jan. 14th, 1877 (New York: Putnam, 1877);

Wisdom a Loving Spirit: A Sermon . . . Masonic Temple, Jan. 21st, 1877 (New York: Putnam, 1877);

Creed and Conduct: A Sermon . . . Masonic Temple, Jan. 28, 1877 (New York: Putnam, 1877);

The Responsibility for Disbelief: A Sermon . . . Masonic Temple, Feb. 4, 1877 (New York: Putnam, 1877);

Modern Irreligion: A Sermon . . . Masonic Temple, Feb. 11th, 1877 (New York: Putnam, 1877);

The Whole Duty of Man: A Sermon . . . Masonic Temple, Feb. 25th, 1877, reported by Underhill (New York: Putnam, 1877);

Duties and Dreams: A Sermon . . . Masonic Temple, March 4th, 1877 (New York: Putnam, 1877);

Dreams and Duties: A Sermon . . . Masonic Temple, March 11th, 1877 (New York: Putnam, 1877);

The Prophetic Soul: A Sermon . . . Masonic Temple, March 18th, 1877 (New York: Putnam, 1877);

The Martyrdom of Man: A Sermon . . . Masonic Temple, March 25th, 1877, reported by Underhill (New York: Putnam, 1877);

The Power of the Immortal Hope: A Sermon . . . Masonic Temple, April 1st, 1877 (New York: Putnam, 1877);

The Threefold Radicalism: A Sermon . . . Masonic Temple, April 22nd, 1877 (New York: Putnam, 1877);

The Three Pentecosts: A Sermon . . . Masonic Temple, May 20th, 1877 (New York: Putnam, 1877);

Creed and Conduct and Other Discourses (New York: Putnam, 1877);

The Mission of the Radical Preacher: A Sermon . . . Masonic Temple, June 10th, 1877 (New York: Putnam, 1877);

The Spirit of the New Faith: A Series of Sermons (New York: Putnam, 1877);

The Rising and the Setting Faith: A Sermon . . . Masonic Temple, September 16th, 1877 (New York: Putnam, 1877);

The Unbeliefs of the Believers: A Sermon . . . Masonic Temple, September 23d, 1877, reported by Underhill (New York: Putnam, 1877);

The Popular Religion: Its Prevalence: A Sermon . . . Masonic Temple, September 30th, 1877, reported by Underhill (New York: Putnam, 1877);

The Higher Sentiments: A Sermon . . . Masonic Temple, December 9th, 1877, reported by Underhill (New York: Putnam, 1878);

Attitudes of Unbelief: A Sermon . . . Masonic Temple, reported by Underhill (New York: Putnam, 1878);

The New Song: A Sermon . . . Masonic Temple (New York: Putnam, 1878);

The Demand of Religion on the Age: A Sermon . . . Masonic Temple (New York: Putnam, 1878);

The Rising and the Setting Faith, and Other Discourses (New York: Putnam, 1878);

The Practical Value of Belief in God: A Sermon . . . Masonic Temple, reported by Underhill (New York: Putnam, 1878);

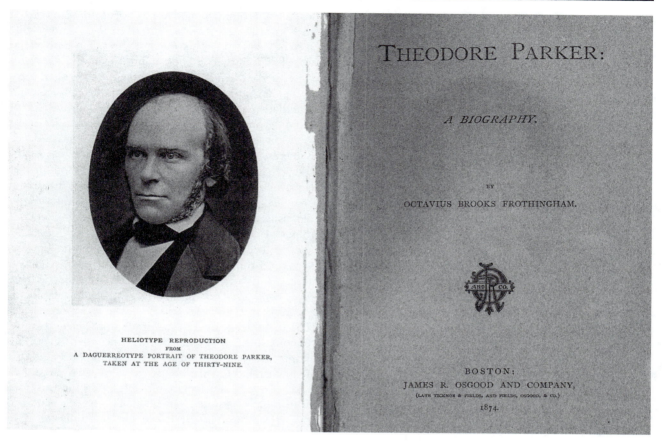

Title page for Frothingham's biography of the man he called "one of the nation's true prophets"

Gerrit Smith: A Biography (New York: Putnam, 1878; revised, 1879);

The Assailants of Christianity: A Lecture (New York: Putnam, 1879);

New Articles of Faith: A Sermon . . . Masonic Temple, reported by Underhill (New York: Putnam, 1879);

Visions of the Future and Other Discourses (New York: Putnam, 1879);

George Ripley (Boston & New York: Houghton, Mifflin, 1882);

Memoir of William Henry Channing (Boston & New York: Houghton, Mifflin, 1886);

Boston Unitarianism, 1820–1850: A Study of the Life and Work of Nathaniel Langdon Frothingham (New York & London: Putnam, 1890);

Recollections and Impressions, 1822–1890 (New York & London: Putnam, 1891);

Francis Parkman: A Sketch (Boston: Wilson, 1894);

Corner Stones: A Sermon . . . Masonic Temple, Nov. 12, 1876 (New York: Putnam, 1897).

Editions: *Transcendentalism in New England: A History,* introduction by Sydney E. Ahlstrom (New York: Harper, 1959);

George Ripley (New York: AMS Press, 1970);

Boston Unitarianism 1820–1850 (Hicksville, N.Y.: Regina Press, 1975);

The Religion of Humanity: An Essay, introduction by William R. Hutchison (Hicksville, N.Y.: Regina Press, 1975).

OTHER: Ernest Renan, *Studies of Religious History and Criticism,* translated, with a biographical introduction, by Frothingham (New York: Carleton, 1864);

A Child's Book of Religion. For Sunday Schools and Homes, compiled by Frothingham (Boston: Walker, Fuller; New York: J. Miller, 1866; revised edition, New York: D. G. Francis, 1871);

Emile Honoré Cazelles, *Outline of the Evolution-Philosophy. By Dr. M. E. Cazelles,* translated by Frothingham (New York: Appleton, 1875);

"Prayer" and "Twenty Years of an Independent Ministry," in *Proceedings at a Reception in Honor of the Rev. O. B. Frothingham . . . April 27, 1879* (New York: Putnam, 1879), pp. 69–71, 73–89;

"Henry Wadsworth Longfellow. A Sketch," in *The Complete Prose Works of Henry Wadsworth Longfellow, with*

His Later Poems, volume 3 of *The Poetical Works of Henry Wadsworth Longfellow,* includes a biographical sketch by Frothingham (Boston: Houghton, Mifflin, 1883);

Samuel Johnson, *Oriental Religions and Their Relation to Universal Religion. Persia,* introduction by Frothingham (Boston & New York: Houghton, Mifflin, 1885);

David A. Wasson, *Wasson's Essays: Religious, Social, Political,* edited, with a biographical sketch, by Frothingham (Boston: Lee & Shepard, 1889).

SELECTED PERIODICAL PUBLICATIONS—
UNCOLLECTED: "Theodore Parker," review of *Life and Correspondence of Theodore Parker,* by John Weiss, *North American Review,* 98 (April 1864): 305–342;

"The Drift Period in Theology," *Christian Examiner,* 79 (July 1865): 1–27;

"Theodore Parker," *Radical,* 6 (August 1869): 89–112;

"Henry Wadsworth Longfellow," *Atlantic Monthly,* 49 (June 1882): 819–829;

"Criticism and Christianity," *North American Review,* 136 (April 1883): 396–407;

"Some Phases of Idealism in New England," *Atlantic Monthly,* 52 (July 1883): 13–23;

"Democracy and Moral Progress," *North American Review,* 137 (July 1883): 28–39;

"The Philosophy of Conversion," *North American Review,* 139 (October 1884): 324–334;

"Why Am I a Free Religionist?" *North American Review,* 145 (July 1887): 8–16;

"Memoir of Rev. James Walker," *Proceedings of the Massachusetts Historical Society,* second series, 6 (May 1891): 443–468;

"Francis Parkman; A Sketch," *Proceedings of the Massachusetts Historical Society,* second series, 8 (May 1894): 520–562;

"Memoir of George Edward Ellis," *Proceedings of the Massachusetts Historical Society,* second series, 10 (May 1895): 207–255.

During his lifetime, Octavius Brooks Frothingham was known as a popular New York City preacher, writer, and promoter of radical or free religion. Eloquent and inspiring, as an orator and teacher he was often compared to Ralph Waldo Emerson, while many considered him Theodore Parker's heir as the champion of free religion. In his last twenty years, he wrote frequently on historical-biographical subjects related to New England Unitarianism and Transcendentalism.

Despite his extensive publication (fourteen books and hundreds of sermons and articles), his modern reputation rests primarily on *Transcendentalism in New England: A History* (1876). Defining Transcendentalism as a philosophical system, a "spiritual" or "intuitive phi-

losophy," Frothingham focused on its European context and roots, described its "tendencies," and wrote sketches of some of its major figures, most of whom were still living. The book stands in the middle of his New England trilogy. He explores the American roots of the movement in a book about his father's and grandfather's generations, *Boston Unitarianism, 1820–1850: A Study of the Life and Work of Nathaniel Langdon Frothingham* (1890), and he points out subsequent developments in his autobiographical *Recollections and Impressions, 1822–1890* (1891). In this trilogy Frothingham constructs his experience as representative of the shift in New England religious and intellectual culture from old-fashioned Unitarianism through Transcendentalism to post–Civil War scientific naturalism.

Except for some letters, no personal papers survive, and the only modern comprehensive scholarly study, J. Wade Caruthers's *Octavius Brooks Frothingham, Gentle Radical* (1977), is "an intellectual biography rather than a study of a man's personal life." The subtitle points to contradictions (also labeled "inconsistencies") many found between Frothingham's aristocratic, conservative demeanor and his democratic, reformist bent. He was a "high-bred radical," a "patrician agitator." Defending his position, Frothingham pointed out that "The freedom of *religion* is the aim, not freedom without religion. The supremacy of *character* is the object, not *absence* of character; creedlessness, not unrighteousness."

Not a great original thinker, Frothingham kept up with new intellectual currents. He embraced an evolutionary pantheism, accommodated Darwinian thinking into his Unitarian-Transcendentalist framework of belief, and accepted the social scientist's view of knowledge and thought as socially constructed, while he remained convinced of "the essential spirituality of man" and saw his role as a "public teacher" of religion— broadly defined as "the best dream of the soul of Humanity of its possible attainment."

Frothingham grew up in the comfortable, genteel, conservative world of Unitarian Boston. His father, Nathaniel Langdon Frothingham, served as minister of the First Church until 1850. In the Summer Street parsonage where the Emerson family had once lived, Octavius Brooks, second of five children, was born 26 November 1822. His mother, Ann Gorham (Brooks) Frothingham, came from a prominent, wealthy, and well-connected Boston merchant family. In his memoirs Frothingham summed up his inheritance: "The dream of a nobler age for literature, art, science, humanity, came directly from my father. The desire to make the dream an actual fact, to prove myself as of some service in the world, came from my mother." His father was dignified, cultured, a gentleman-scholar, socially conservative but "liberal" in the old-fashioned sense of believing in "mental emancipation" rather than reform as the means to improving society. A typical minister's wife, his mother was practical, speculative, and devoted to her family, parishioners, and nature.

Octavius's education was typical of his social class. At age twelve he entered Boston Latin School, and in 1839 he went on to Harvard College in nearby Cambridge, along with Samuel Longfellow (brother of the poet) and Thomas Wentworth Higginson. Graduating near the top of his class in 1843, he immediately began Divinity School at a time when radical thinking had created a ferment in the Unitarian religious establishment.

Frothingham later described himself as conservative at Harvard, holding fast to "old-fashioned" Unitarianism and opposed to "the spiritual philosophy; Strauss was a horror; Parker was a bugbear; Furness seemed an innovator; Emerson was a 'Transcendentalist,' a term of immeasurable reproach." Frothingham's closest Harvard friends, Longfellow and Samuel Johnson, however, were considered "radicals." An antislavery hymn Frothingham wrote in 1846 suggests he may have been inspired by Henry Wadsworth Longfellow's poems on slavery, published in 1842. This little collection, Frothingham remembered, attracted a "new class" of "refined, conservative people" to the slavery issue and "gave poetic dignity to a struggling cause." In his memoir of William Henry Channing, Frothingham mentions hearing this "apostle" of social reform and humanitarianism during this period. The notes of a student in Frothingham's Bible study class at Salem in 1845 and 1846 indicate, Caruthers says, that Frothingham was already a "religious radical in the Transcendentalist tradition," free to consider the Bible as not an inspired but a literary text. Two early publications in the official Unitarian *Christian Examiner* also suggest an inquiring mind. Thus, although Frothingham may have remained outwardly conservative, he was incubating radical ideas throughout his Harvard years.

Soon after graduation from Divinity School in 1846, Frothingham was called as minister to the North Church (Unitarian) of Salem, Massachusetts, where he was ordained on 10 March 1847. Two weeks later he married Caroline Elizabeth Curtis, daughter of a prosperous Boston merchant. The couple had one daughter, Elizabeth (Bessie), born in 1850, and a son who died soon after his birth in 1858. Though the first years of his ministry were "pleasant and tranquil," the young minister felt increasingly isolated. He had plenty of time to read and prepare weekly sermons and lectures and run the Sunday School, and he and his wife contributed to the civic and cultural life of Salem. In 1853, in ill health, he took a six-month leave of absence and traveled alone in Europe.

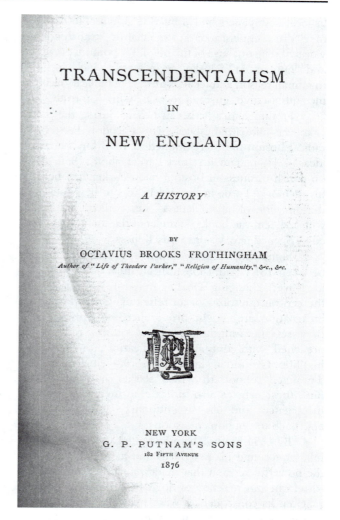

TRANSCENDENTALISM

IN

NEW ENGLAND

A HISTORY

BY

OCTAVIUS BROOKS FROTHINGHAM

Author of "Life of Theodore Parker," "Religion of Humanity," &c., &c.

NEW YORK
G. P. PUTNAM'S SONS
182 FIFTH AVENUE
1876

Title page for the book in which Frothingham traced the development of "intuitive philosophy" from its German roots to the ideas of New Englanders such as Ralph Waldo Emerson, Bronson Alcott, Margaret Fuller, Theodore Parker, and George Ripley

The turning point in Frothingham's career occurred on 4 June 1854, when he preached a sermon titled "The New Commandment"–his outraged response to the capture and re-enslavement of Anthony Burns in Boston two days earlier–and declined to administer communion because it would be a "mockery." In the sermon, he lashed out at so-called Christians whose failure even to attempt to rescue Burns represented failure to practice Jesus' "new commandment," "that ye love one another." "The Christian Church universal of this country . . . is blind and indifferent to the most hideous Institution now existing under the sun; an institution which, on an enormous scale, outrages human rights and crushes human nature," he charged. Contemporary Christianity had become a "system of metaphysics" in which belief was more important than deeds. Reported in local newspapers and printed as a pamphlet, the sermon drew criticism of Frothingham's "transcendental views of religion," use of the pulpit for political purposes, and "humanized" antislavery message, which appealed to human reason and feelings instead of biblical "facts" as the authoritative source of revealed Christian truth.

Frothingham's "crisis in belief" during the Salem years was influenced especially by Theodore Parker–the radical Boston minister shunned in 1843 for "heretical" ideas. Frothingham first met Parker about 1850, while on parish business in Boston. Soon Parker had become his mentor: "To be in his society was to be impelled in the direction of all nobleness," he recalled. "He talked with me, lent me books, stimulated the thirst for knowledge, opened new visions of usefulness."

Some articles published in the *Christian Examiner* between 1851 and 1855 indicate how Frothingham's ideas were changing. Dealing in naturalistic ways with the central questions of all religions–God, revelation, incarnation, atonement, providence, and immortality–they set the foundation of the radical religion he preached, with continued modification, for the rest of his life. Grounded in the biblical criticism of the Tübingen school, to which Parker had introduced him, these articles also indicate an increasing interest in science and an evolutionary and humanistic approach to religious questions.

By 1854 Frothingham had outgrown his Unitarian inheritance, and his new ideas and feelings exploded in the powerful sermon that made public his commitment to reform and rejection of dogma that hobbled genuine religion. Its consequences were swift and clear: the gulf between minister and many of his congregation became obvious; the church became divided; and on 15 April 1855 he delivered his farewell sermon. His next ministry was to a new Unitarian Society in Jersey City, New Jersey, where he remained for four years.

In later years Frothingham said little about his New Jersey experience except to commend his flock for its liberal view of communion, which he dropped. A few publications suggest the direction of his thought at this time. Most significantly, he continued his antislavery activity. In the tract *Colonization* (1855), he carefully argued that the real goal of returning freed slaves to Africa was preservation of the slave system by both Northern and Southern interests. The next year an angry, hard-hitting speech before the annual meeting of the American Anti-Slavery Society in New York charged that the movement had failed to produce action because the vast majority of Americans were "compromisers" or *"Palterers"*: they paid lip service to the cause while preserving the status quo. Soon, on 1 June 1856, he was preaching to his own congregation on the evils of slavery, in a sermon titled *The Last Signs*. After Henry Bel-

lows, minister of the All Souls (Unitarian) Church, arranged for him to lead a new "uptown" Unitarian society in New York, he began his twenty-year ministry in the commercial capital of the nation.

Frothingham's life and work in New York can be conveniently divided in terms of the locations of his evolving ministry. From 1859 to 1863 his newly formed Third Unitarian Society met in a rented hall on 40th Street between Fifth and Sixth Avenues. In 1863 the society moved into its new church nearby. Dissatisfied with the acoustics and traditional church design of this building, in 1869 Frothingham moved his services to the Lyric, a music and dance hall on Sixth Avenue between Fortieth and Forty-first Streets–following the lead of Parker, who had preached to crowds in the Melodeon Theatre in Boston. By 1875 he had changed the name of the society to the Independent Liberal Church and had begun holding services in the more comfortable Masonic Temple at Sixth Avenue and Twenty-third Street, used through his retirement in 1879.

His first decade in New York was marked by Parker's death, the antislavery movement, the Civil War, early reconstruction, and his new role in a new congregation. In the years before moving to Lyric Hall, he published some twenty sermons, tracts, and other addresses, and dozens of articles and reviews in *The Christian Examiner,* the *North American Review,* and the *Nation* (founded in 1865). These works reveal his continued interest in theology, biblical criticism, and antislavery, as well as the arts and social issues, including public education and women's and children's rights.

Less than a week after learning of Parker's death in Italy in May 1860, Frothingham preached a memorial sermon, the first of many efforts–in sermons, discourses, articles, and books–to wrestle with Parker's meaning. As Frothingham foresaw, he was just beginning to understand the significance of Parker's death. "There are men whose loss cannot be estimated in many days. It grows with time. It breaks on mankind in successive shocks." Four years later, his important review of John Weiss's *Life and Correspondence of Theodore Parker* (1864) called Parker a "moral force, . . . a character, . . . a noble human soul" immortalized in the lives of those he had touched.

An early popular sermon, *Seeds and Shells* (delivered in 1861, published in 1862), shows how Frothingham grounded his spiritual message in nature while addressing a contemporary issue, the moral necessity of the war. "These are the great resurrection days of American character; and there is no resurrection without a grave," he counseled. Shells die; young men were dying; so too must outdated institutions and customs die to produce new life. In richly poetic language, he showed how the "regenerating principle" embodied in Jesus had hardened in the "mighty shell of the Church"–a "mammoth institution" whose natural decay released the principles of "modern civilization" and "modern humanity." "There is no exception to this law of moral growth. No institution that man can devise . . . is anything more than a pod, fashioned to protect a living seed." Doctrines, rites, slavery: all were pods whose death would release the seed of the "Spirit of Liberty." Two years later another sermon protested a recent violent antidraft riot in which African Americans and abolitionists were blamed for the war.

Speaking of some articles in the *Christian Examiner,* Stow Persons concluded that Frothingham's real service was introducing the liberal American clergy to contemporary European biblical criticism. The article "The Drift Period in Theology" (*Christian Examiner,* July 1865) indicates where his study was leading. Ostensibly a review of three books by women on religious faith, the piece uses a geological metaphor to account for change in religion and spirituality. Unlike more "volcanic" intellectual revolutions, "Drift" is quieter, yet more massive, stimulated by vast social changes, including popular education and the modern industrial system. Advancing "with spontaneous and unpremeditated power," "Drift" "exhibits the process of becoming," leading to *universal* change and affecting mental activity. Its destination is unclear, though Frothingham rejects spiritualism, theism, and atheism, concluding that the modern "tendency" is toward "an undefined Pantheism." Near the end of the essay he rejects the notion in Transcendentalism of the "divine authority of the individual conscience" in favor of a "general conscience," produced by the laws of society, as revealed by "social science." At the same time, he retains the faith of Transcendentalism in the "perfection of the individual man"—the substitute in the new theology for the older doctrine of the "salvation of the soul."

Several books published during Frothingham's first New York years (and frequently reprinted) reveal his lifelong interest in children's religious education. In *Stories from the Lips of the Teacher. Retold by a Disciple* (1863), he liberally rewrites eleven of Jesus' parables in simple modern language. In *Stories of the Patriarchs* (1864) he rewrites tales from the Hebrew Bible in the same manner. Introducing the first book, he emphasizes the universality of religion and the cultural construction of texts in times and places now lost to the reader: "if they are not so fresh and vivid to you, it is because you are little Americans, and not little Jews; because you live in the United States, and not in Palestine; and because you are alive now, and not when Jesus was, nearly two thousand years ago." He aimed to enable these old texts to speak to modern children. In *A Child's Book of Religion. For Sunday Schools and Homes* (1866) he gathered inspiring poems, Bible passages, parables, stories, and hymns for use in "Sunday Schools and Homes."

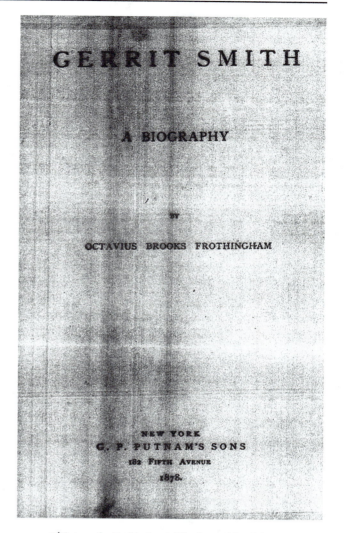

Title page for Frothingham's life of a wealthy abolitionist

Beginning in 1867 Frothingham served for eleven years as president of the Free Religious Association (FRA) he had helped organize. This association broke away from more conventional Unitarians after they organized the National Conference of Unitarian Churches in 1866. Unable to accept the insistence of the National Conference on the "obligations of all disciples of the Lord Jesus Christ," members of the FRA aimed to "promote the interest of pure religion, to encourage the scientific study of theology, and to increase fellowship in the spirit"—or, as Frothingham also put it, to "substitute the universality of religion for the one faith of Christendom." As leader and chief spokesman for a diverse group of freethinking men and women of all ages, Frothingham served extremely well. At frequent national and regional conventions he spelled out principles and goals of the rational religion he hoped to popularize, in addresses on topics such as "What is Free Religion?" and "Beliefs of the Unbelievers." Between 1870 and 1877 Frothingham also published in almost every issue of the *Index,* a weekly periodical closely related to the FRA.

Frothingham's last decade in New York, the 1870s, when he preached in the Lyric and Masonic Halls, is the period of his greatest fame. On Sundays he addressed audiences ranging from six hundred to a thousand. Some 150 discourses were printed and distributed as tracts, newspapers regularly published reports of his services, and out-of-town visitors made special efforts to attend. In addition to at least seven collections of discourses, in this decade he published five significant books: *The Religion of Humanity: An Essay* (1873), *Theodore Parker: A Biography* (1874), *Transcendentalism in New England: A History* (1876), *The Cradle of the Christ. A Study in Primitive Christianity* (1877), and *Gerrit Smith: A Biography* (1878). Each book marks an important element of Frothingham's eclectic thinking on matters of religion, and together they represent the fruit of his reading, writing, thinking, speaking, and publishing since finishing at Harvard in 1846.

The Religion of Humanity packaged his "religious system" in convenient form. It has been called "the principal manifesto of advanced religious thinkers in the postwar decade" and Frothingham's "major religious work." In Hegelian fashion, it describes a modern zeitgeist that identifies the meaning of the age with its "interior spirit," or the spirit of God, while recognizing the role of social forces in determining the form of any moment in history; it offers naturalistic explanations and understanding of myth, and applies Darwinian laws of heredity and environment to the development and growth of human thought and character. Since God works in and through everyday human nature and is not shut up in official "scriptures," attending to the soul's intuition of spiritual things is important.

At almost six hundred pages, *Theodore Parker: A Biography* is Frothingham's fullest account of his mentor. Calling Parker "one of the nation's true prophets," Frothingham hoped to produce something more popular and more personal than Weiss's study. Caruthers praised Frothingham's deft handling of narrative descriptive history, especially his reconstruction of the intellectual milieu, but regretted his complete omission of himself from the work. The biography was generally well received, going through five more editions by 1890, and earned Frothingham a reputation as the authority on Parker.

Transcendentalism in New England, published in connection with the centennial of the American Revolution, was Frothingham's next venture into recent religious history. He traced the development of the "intuitive philosophy" from its German beginnings and subsequent European thought through its manifestation in antebellum New England. Individual chapters focus on practical, reform, religious, and literary tendencies, as well as on several important figures, or types of thinkers—Emerson ("The Seer"), Bronson Alcott ("The Mystic"), Margaret Fuller ("The Critic"), Parker ("The Preacher"), and George Ripley ("The Man of Letters"). Another chapter briefly discusses nine men he calls "Minor Prophets."

Frothingham concluded that "Transcendentalism was an episode in the intellectual life of New England; an enthusiasm, a wave of sentiment, a breath of mind that caught up such as were prepared to receive it, elated them, transported them, and passed on,—no man knowing whither it went." It powerfully influenced all areas—religion, literature, law, social institutions, and reform movements. "New England character received from it an impetus that never will be spent."

In 1959 Sydney Ahlstrom called Frothingham "the only discerning, sensitive, and critical writer who has turned his hand to writing an integrated account of the Transcendental movement" and the book an "unduplicable account that speaks from within the Transcendental impulse." It was Frothingham's "most significant literary achievement"; even the "inclusive final chapter . . . becomes a symbol of the Transcendental crisis and a major commentary on his state of mind." Still, Ahlstrom faulted Frothingham for his inability to relate Transcendentalism to "subsequent developments." That Frothingham's lifework did relate it to those developments, however, is a possible argument.

Contemporary criticism of *Transcendentalism in New England* was less positive. Best known is the witty and acerbic review by Frothingham's cousin, diplomat, and cultural historian Henry Adams. Though he found Frothingham "well fitted" to discuss his subject and agreed that Transcendentalism "represents a part of the eternal fluctuation of human thought," Adams disputed most of Frothingham's "estimates, personal and general," of the significance of the movement, which he mocked, finding Emerson the only "so-called Transcendentalist" worth remembering. The *Nation* reviewer similarly dismissed Transcendentalism as anything more than a passing superstition, though he found the book better written than Frothingham's turgid *Religion of Humanity.* Higginson thought Frothingham was neither close enough to the movement to be truly sympathetic nor far enough removed to be impartial.

In the first chapter of *The Cradle of the Christ,* Frothingham called this study of the New Testament a summary of years of reading and reflection, recorded over many years in notebooks, and revised, tested, and reduced to system. (A five-page list of his "Authorities" concludes the book.) Frothingham's radical summa in the area of scientific and literary biblical scholarship is addressed to an intelligent, popular audience. Describing himself as "no friend to the christian system, [though] a friend of spiritual beliefs," he aimed to show that the text is a "natural product of the Hebrew genius," a work of literature, not divine inspiration.

The biography of Gerrit Smith (who died in 1874) is an anomaly. Possibly Frothingham knew Smith, who was active in the antislavery movement when Frothingham moved to Jersey City. Probably Smith's widow asked Frothingham to undertake the task of writing her husband's life, using his papers. (Caruthers reports that the second edition of the book reflects her insistence that Frothingham revise his statements about Smith's involvement in John Brown's raid at Harpers Ferry.) In the biography Frothingham sought to understand the motives and significance of this controversial, wealthy New York state humanitarian (whom many considered insane), who moved from abolition to philanthropy in the decade following the Civil War.

Frothingham's conclusion to the Smith biography indicates the importance of theoretical frameworks. Unwilling to estimate the "value" of Smith's life to society, he offers three perspectives. A Darwinian social scientist would conclude that Smith's philanthropy was harmful, since giving money to the poor and oppressed made them dependent and idle. An orthodox Christian would find Smith's love for his oppressed brethren a sign of obedience to God's will and Jesus' teachings. The third perspective, not labeled, is that of Transcendentalists and other "disciples and apostles of Individualism in its spiritual form." From this perspective Smith was a success: He stimulated and promoted nobleness, justice, and love.

A long sketch by New York journalist, critic, and man of letters Edmund C. Stedman, published in the *Galaxy* magazine in 1876, contributed to the growing image of Frothingham as a successful, popular metropolitan preacher. Enlarged, it was soon republished as *Octavius Brooks Frothingham and the New Faith* (1876). Stedman, a member of Frothingham's congregation, explained that he was responding to increased interest in "Radical ideas" and offered Frothingham as the principal American "representative and apostle" of the new faith. Describing Frothingham's "devotional philosophy," oratorical style, and major ideas from the discourses of the previous winter in the Masonic Temple, Stedman sought to dispel misconceptions about the man and his Independent Liberal Church, which also sponsored musical and dramatic performances, readings, and other social gatherings.

Frothingham's sermons combined spirituality with practicality; the task of the "public teacher," he stated in an 1878 sermon, was to deal with "live topics," those that were "active and burning in the public

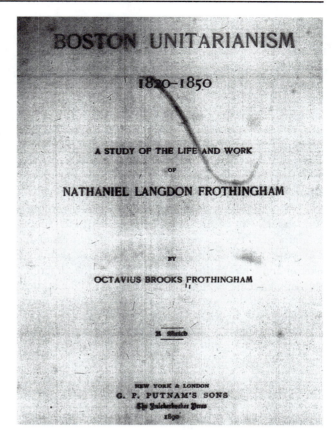

Title page for Frothingham's book about his father

mind, teasing and agitating it." His approach appealed to "eager, restless, unsatisfied spirits, attracted by the originality and boldness of the preacher's [his] views." Frothingham called his congregants "Unitarians, Universalists, 'come-outers,' spiritualists, unbelievers of all kinds, anti-slavery people, reformers generally"; former Catholics, Protestants, Jews, "some of no religious training whatever, materialists, atheists, secularists, positivists—always thinking people. . . . It was a church of the unchurched." The Sunday morning atmosphere was casual and friendly, with "throngs" arriving during breaks in the service before the discourse and many leaving before the closing music and benediction.

The nonsectarian service reflected Frothingham's aesthetic tastes and belief that all natural and human productions are equally valuable revelations of the divine. The aim of religious worship was to stimulate the mind and move feelings in the direction of ideal thought, goodness, and beauty. After music, readings from world scriptures, and a celebratory "prayer," Frothingham delivered his discourse, holding his audience spellbound for an hour or more.

The most successful liberal preacher of his day, Frothingham was graceful, poetic, and "intellectual." His polished style appealed to his audience's reason and was closer to the classical mode of his uncle Edward Everett than to the sentimental, evangelical style of popular preachers such as Henry Ward Beecher. Stedman claimed no living preacher was "more eloquent and imaginative" or demanded such "attention and exercise of mental powers," including the "perceptive, reasoning, and aesthetic faculties." He found Frothingham's language as "compact" and wise as Emerson's, but his discourses clearer and more logical.

By this time Frothingham was preaching without a written text—or even notes or outline. He simply announced a theme, subdivided it, and addressed the topics spontaneously. Many accounts of these seemingly extemporaneous performances survive. One described the simple theme as growing in the course of the address "like a river fed by invisible tributaries. It taxes the mind; it enchains the attention. . . . Grand things drop from the speaker's lips as he stands there, without book or paper, speaking out of a fulness that seems to increase faster than it overflows in the choicest words." Stedman felt he was seeing the speaker's "intellect" at work; Higginson emphasized the power that resulted from Frothingham's understated, classical, unornamented delivery: "the illustrations came as something inevitable; and the most daring iconoclastic thoughts were presented with a frankness which disarmed. It seemed for the moment as if there were no other thoughts supposable."

Although approximately three hundred sermons were published, they cannot capture the oratorical power of a gifted speaker such as Frothingham, and even the source of the printed texts is uncertain. Stedman claimed they were "stenographically reported from week to week" for immediate, free distribution. Josiah Quincy, however, stated that Frothingham delivered 1,311 sermons or discourses during his career. Whether his precise number comes from a preaching record or from manuscripts is unknown, as is whether or not Frothingham corrected or revised the transcriptions before they were printed. Still, the New York sermons articulate the tenets of the "religion of humanity," as Caruthers shows by analyzing the weekly discourses into twelve categories, ranging from the status of Christianity to evolution and human nature, concepts of God, and sin and social ethics.

In February 1879 Frothingham announced his retirement. His pace for more than a decade had been exhausting, and in the past year his speech and handwriting had deteriorated, early signs of the paralyzing neurological disorder (later diagnosed as spinal sclerosis) that crippled him in his last years. Following a huge farewell celebration, with speeches and tributes by a distinguished group of associates and friends, the Frothinghams sailed in April 1879 for Europe, where they remained until September 1881.

Frothingham's farewell sermon, "Twenty Years of an Independent Ministry," a succinct statement of his beliefs and predictions for the future of the "movement," provoked widespread discussion in the popular and religious press. Had he "recanted" his radical views, rejected Transcendentalism, and admitted the "death of liberalism" and failure of his life's work? The controversy continued for several years; in some articles in the *North American Review* in 1883 and 1884, Frothingham tried to clarify his position. Though some believe these questions remain unanswered, the same apparent contradictions appeared in his published writings long before 1879. Caruthers believes Frothingham had always "doubted as he believed," always subjected his beliefs "to the scrutiny of his own skepticism." Put another way, freedom of belief implied freedom to change as conditions changed.

Despite some improvement in his health, by 1880 Frothingham had decided not to resume preaching after his return to New York. Instead, he planned a new career as a man of letters, beginning with a biography of George Ripley, organizer of the Transcendentalist-socialist Brook Farm community. Having completed the Ripley biography in 1882, he began work on a memoir of William Henry Channing, social reformer and "the fervent apostle of every humane idea." In 1884 the Frothinghams moved back to Boston.

Caruthers wrote that Frothingham spent his last decade on "well-worn topics and memorializing deceased comrades." Linking these projects was the essay "Some Phases of Idealism in New England" (*Atlantic Monthly,* July 1883). Inspired by twelve names listed under the heading "Transcendentalism," found among Ripley's papers (the list included his own father, Ripley, Frederic Henry Hedge, James Walker, William Ellery and William Henry Channing, Emerson, and Parker), Frothingham concluded that the common element was "idealism" as a "mode of speculative thought," not a "definite or fixed system." He showed how each man had contributed to the movement and concluded, "Thus philosophy and faith, thought and feeling, literary and poetic fervor, united to produce that singular outburst of idealism which has left so deep an impression on the New England intellect. The circumstances of the time determined the form it assumed."

He also wrote biographical and critical introductions to works by Samuel Johnson and Henry Wadsworth Longfellow, and memorials of James Walker, Francis Parkman, and George E. Ellis. His study of his father's generation and his own memoirs completed his portrait of the era through which he had lived. Each represents the insider's view at the same time that all exhibit his "characteristically uncompromising way [of] dealing frankly and critically" with his subjects.

Frothingham's view of "historical reality," Ahlstrom explained, rested on the sense of the "spiritual dimension of human history." Influenced by Hegelian thought, Frothingham's "prime category was not Being, but Becoming." To this belief he added sociological Darwinism. "Continuity, process, struggle, environment, and the evolutionary concept of social progress became tools of interpretation." A cardinal principle remained the interconnection of history and ideas. As he had said in 1873, "the thought of a period represents the life of the period and affects that life by its reaction on it," and in 1887 he said, "Every organization is as much the creature as the creator of its period." In all of his biographical work, Frothingham presented individual men as representatives of important intellectual currents as he continued to explore his own religious and cultural roots.

Increasingly disabled and in pain, Frothingham accomplished little in his last year. His death in Boston came one day after his seventy-third birthday; his funeral and cremation were consistent with his liberal beliefs. Eulogies and tributes agreed in their estimation of the man. All stressed, according to Caruthers's summary, Frothingham's "brilliance, his oratorical powers, his bold radicalism, his militancy balanced by gentleness toward his adversaries, his undogmatic mind"; "all saw him as the pessimistic-optimist, the conservative-radical, the warmhearted man with a thin layer of ice, the genial but austere personality, and the man with many associates but few close friends."

References:

Sydney E. Ahlstrom, Introduction to *Transcendentalism in New England: A History* (New York: Harper, 1959);

J. Wade Caruthers, "Octavius Brooks Frothingham," in *The Transcendentalists: A Review of Research and Criticism,* edited by Joel Myerson (New York: Modern Language Association, 1984), pp. 171–174;

Caruthers, *Octavius Brooks Frothingham, Gentle Radical* (University: University of Alabama Press, 1977);

Caruthers, "Who Was Octavius Brooks Frothingham?" *New England Quarterly,* 43 (December 1970): 631–637;

Free Religious Association, *Prophets of Liberalism. Six Addresses before the Free Religious Association, Thirty-Third Annual Convention, June 1, 1900* (Boston: James West, 1900);

Paul Revere Frothingham, "Octavius Brooks Frothingham," in *Heralds of a Liberal Faith,* 3 volumes, edited by Samuel A. Eliot (Boston: American Unitarian Association, 1910), III: 120–127;

Thomas Wentworth Higginson, "Octavius Brooks Frothingham," *New World,* 5 (March 1896): 1–9;

William R. Hutchison, Introduction to *The Religion of Humanity: An Essay* (Hicksville, N.Y.: Regina Press, 1975);

New York Ethical Culture Society, *Memorial Exercises in Honor of Octavius Brooks Frothingham,* series 2, no. 10, December 1895 (Philadelphia: S. Burns Weston, 1895);

New York Independent Liberal Church, *Proceedings at a Reception Given in Honor of Rev. Octavius Brooks Frothingham . . . , Union League Theater, April 22, 1879* (New York: Putnam, 1879);

Stow Persons, *Free Religion: An American Faith* (New Haven: Yale University Press, 1947);

Josiah P. Quincy, "Memoir of Octavius Brooks Frothingham," *Proceedings of the Massachusetts Historical Society,* second series 10 (March 1896): 507–539;

Edmund C. Stedman, "Octavius Brooks Frothingham: A Sketch," *Galaxy,* 22 (October 1876): 478–488;

Stedman, *Octavius Frothingham and the New Faith* (New York: Putnam, 1876);

Conrad Wright, Introduction to *Boston Unitarianism 1820–1850* (Hicksville, N.Y.: Regina Press, 1975);

Edward J. Young and James Ford Rhodes, "Remarks on the Death of O. B. Frothingham," *Proceedings of the Massachusetts Historical Society,* second series 10 (December 1895): 363–369.

Papers:

Few personal papers of Octavius Brooks Frothingham survive. Scattered letters are in the Houghton Library of Harvard University, Massachusetts Historical Society, Library of Congress, and Peabody-Essex Institute (Salem, Massachusetts), among other collections.

Samuel Griswold Goodrich
(Peter Parley)
(19 August 1793 – 9 May 1860)

Larry R. Long
Harding University

See also the Goodrich entries in *DLB 1: The American Renaissance in New England; DLB 42: American Writers for Children Before 1900;* and *DLB 73: American Magazine Journalists, 1741–1850.*

SELECTED BOOKS*: *The Child's Arithmetic, Being an Easy and Cheap Introduction to Daboll's, Pike's, White's, and Other Arithmetics* (Hartford: S. G. Goodrich, 1818);

Blair's Outline of Chronology, Ancient and Modern, Embracing Its Antiquities (Boston: S. G. Goodrich, 1825);

The Tales of Peter Parley about America (Boston: S. G. Goodrich, 1827);

The Child's Botany (Boston: S. G. Goodrich, 1828);

Tales of Peter Parley about Europe (Boston: S. G. Goodrich, 1828; London: Tegg, 1834);

A Geographical View of the United States. Embracing Their Extent and Boundaries, Government, Courts and Laws (New York: W. Reed, 1829);

Peter Parley's Method of Telling about Geography to Children (Hartford: H. & F. J. Huntington, 1829);

Stories about Captain John Smith, of Virginia; for the Instruction and Amusement of Children (Hartford: H. & F. J. Huntington, 1829);

A System of School Geography, Chiefly Derived from Malte-Brun, and Arranged According to the Inductive Plan of Instruction (Boston: Carter & Hendee, 1830);

Atlas, Designed to Illustrate the Malte-Brun School Geography (Boston: Carter & Hendee, 1830);

Peter Parley's Tales about Asia (Boston: Gray & Bowen, 1830; London: Allman, 1839);

*Because he also published books by other writers under the pseudonym Peter Parley, many books have been falsely attributed to Goodrich. This list includes only works that can be attributed to Goodrich with some certainty.

Samuel Griswold Goodrich (photograph by Mathew Brady)

Peter Parley's Tales of Animals; Containing Descriptions of Three Hundred Quadrupeds, Birds, Fishes, Reptiles, and Insects (Boston: Carter & Hendee, 1830; London: Tegg, 1832);

Peter Parley's Winter Evening Tales (Boston: Carter & Hendee, 1830);

Tales of Peter Parley about Africa (Boston: Gray & Bowen, 1830);

The Child's Book of American Geography (Boston: Waitt & Dow, 1831);

The First Book of History. For Children and Youth (Boston: Richardson, Lord & Holbrook, 1831);

Peter Parley's Tales about the Islands in the Pacific Ocean (Boston: Gray & Bowen, 1831);

Peter Parley's Tales about the Sun, Moon, and Stars (Boston: Gray & Bowen / Carter & Hendee, 1831; London: Tegg, 1836);

Peter Parley's Tales of the Sea (Boston: Gray & Bowen, 1831);

Peter Parley's Tales about South America (Baltimore: Jewett, 1832);

Peter Parley's Method of Telling about the History of the World to Children (Hartford: F. J. Huntington, 1832);

Peter Parley's Tales about Ancient and Modern Greece (New York: Collins & Hannay, 1832);

A System of Universal Geography, Popular and Scientific, Comprising a Physical, Political, and Statistical Account of the World and Its Various Divisions (Boston: Carter & Hendee, 1832);

The Second Book of History, Including the Modern History of Europe, Africa, and Asia (Boston: Carter & Hendee, 1832);

Peter Parley's Tales about the State and City of New York (New York: Pendleton & Hill, 1832);

Peter Parley's Tales about Great Britain, including England, Wales, Scotland, and Ireland (Baltimore: Jewett, 1832);

Peter Parley's Method of Teaching Arithmetic to Children (Boston: Carter & Hendee, 1833);

Peter Parley's Tales about Ancient Rome, with Some Account of Modern Italy (Boston: Carter & Hendee, 1833);

The Every Day Book for Youth (Boston: Carter & Hendee, 1834);

Peter Parley's Short Stories for Long Nights (Boston: Allen & Ticknor, 1834);

The Third Book of History, Containing Ancient History in Connection with Ancient Geography (Boston: Carter & Hendee, 1834);

The Benefits of Industry. An Address Delivered Before the Inhabitants of Jamaica Plain, July 4, 1835 (Boston: Ticknor, 1835);

The Story of Captain Riley and His Adventures in Africa (New York: Peaslee, 1835);

The Story of La Peyrouse (New York: Peaslee, 1835);

Bible Gazetteer, Containing Descriptions of Places Mentioned in the Old and New Testament (Boston: Otis, Broaders, 1836);

The Outcast, and Other Poems (Boston: Russell, Shattuck & Williams, 1836);

Peter Parley's Bible Dictionary (Philadelphia: Tower, 1836);

Peter Parley's Dictionary of the Animal Kingdom (New York: Hunt, 1836);

Peter Parley's Dictionary of Astronomy (New York: Hunt, 1836);

A Present from Peter Parley to All His Little Friends (Philadelphia: Pomeroy, 1836);

Peter Parley's Arithmetic (Boston: Hendee, 1837);

Peter Parley's Method of Telling about the Geography of the Bible (Boston: American Stationers' Company, 1837);

Fireside Education (New York: Colman, 1838; London: Smith, 1839);

Five Letters to My Neighbor Smith, Touching the Fifteen Gallon Jug (Boston: Weeks, Jordan, 1838);

Peter Parley's Cyclopedia of Botany (Boston: Otis, Broaders, 1838);

The First Reader for Schools (Boston: Otis, Broaders, 1839);

The Second Reader for Schools (Louisville: Morton & Griswold, 1839);

The Third Reader for the Use of Schools (Boston: Otis, Broaders, 1839);

The Fourth Reader for the Use of Schools (Boston: Otis, Broaders, 1839);

Peter Parley's Farewell (New York: Colman, 1840);

Peter Parley's Wonders of the Earth, Sea, and Sky (New York: Colman, 1840);

A Pictorial Geography of the World, Comprising a System of Universal Geography, 10 parts (Boston: Otis, Broaders / New York: Tanner & Disturnell, 1840);

Sketches from a Student's Window (Boston: Ticknor, 1841);

The Story of Alexander Selkirk (Philadelphia: Anners, 1841);

A Pictorial Natural History; Embracing a View of the Mineral, Vegetable, and Animal Kingdoms (Boston: Munroe, 1842);

The Young American; or, Book of Government and Law (New York: W. Robinson, 1842);

Make the Best of It; or, Cheerful Cherry, and Other Tales (New York: Wiley & Putnam, 1843); republished as *Cheerful Cherry; or, Make the Best of It* (London: Darton & Clark, 1843?);

A Tale of Adventure; or, The Siberian Sable-Hunter (New York: Wiley & Putnam, 1843); republished as *Persevere and Prosper; or, The Siberian Sable-Hunter* (London: Darton, 1843);

What to Do and How to Do It (New York: Wiley & Putnam, 1844);

Fairy Land, and Other Sketches for Youth (Boston: Munroe, 1844);

Peter Parley's Little Leaves for Little Readers (Boston: Munroe, 1844);

THE

TALES OF PETER PARLEY,

ABOUT AMERICA.

CHAPTER I.

Parley tells about Himself, about Boston, and about the Indians.

1. HERE I am! My name is Peter Parley! I am an old man. I am very gray and lame. But I have seen a great many things, and had a great many adventures, and I love to talk about them.

2. I love to tell stories to children, and very often they come to my house, and they get around me, and I tell them stories of what I have seen, and of what I have heard.

3. I live in Boston. Boston is a large

Pages from the 1827 book in which Goodrich introduced his popular persona Peter Parley

Wit Bought; or, The Life and Adventures of Robert Merry (New York: Wiley & Putnam, 1844; London: Cassell, Petter & Galpin, 1844);

Dick Boldhero; or, A Tale of Adventure in South America (Philadelphia: Sorin & Ball, 1845; London: Darton, 1846);

A Home in the Sea; or, The Adventures of Philip Brusque; Designed to Show the Nature and Necessity of Good (Philadelphia: Sorin & Ball, 1845);

A Tale of the Revolution, and Other Sketches (Philadelphia: Sorin & Ball, 1845);

The Truth-Finder; or, The Story of Inquisitive Jack (Philadelphia: Sorin & Ball, 1845);

A National Geography, for Schools (New York: Huntington & Savage, 1845);

Right is Might, and Other Sketches (Philadelphia: Sorin & Ball, 1846);

Tales of Sea and Land (Philadelphia: Sorin & Ball, 1846);

A Primer of Geography (New York: Huntington & Savage, 1850);

Take Care of Number One; or, The Adventures of Jacob Karl (New York: Huntington & Savage, 1850);

A Comprehensive Geography and History, Ancient and Modern (New York: Huntington & Savage, 1850);

Poems (New York: Putnam, 1851);

Faggots for the Fireside; or, Fact and Fancy (New York: Appleton, 1855; London: Griffin, 1855);

The Wanderers by Sea and Land, with other Tales (New York: Appleton, 1855; London: Darton, 1858);

A Winter Wreath of Summer Flowers (New York: Appleton, 1855; London: Trübner, 1855);

The Balloon Travels of Robert Merry and His Young Friends over Various Countries in Europe (New York: J. C. Derby / Boston: Phillips, Sampson, 1855; London: Blackwood, 1857);

The Travels, Voyages, and Adventures of Gilbert Go-Ahead in Foreign Parts (New York: Derby, 1856);

Recollections of a Lifetime; or, Men and Things I Have Seen: In a Series of Familiar Letters to a Friend, Historical, Biographical, Anecdotal, and Descriptive, 2 volumes (New York & Auburn: Miller, Orton & Mulligan, 1856);

Illustrated Natural History of the Animal Kingdom, 2 volumes (New York: Derby & Jackson, 1859).

OTHER: *The Token,* edited by Goodrich (Boston: Goodrich, 1828; Boston: Carter & Hendee, 1830; Boston: Gray & Bowen, 1831–1833; Boston: Charles Bowen, 1834–1837; Boston: American Stationers'

Cover for the inaugural issue of Goodrich's first children's magazine

Company, 1838; Boston: Otis, Broaders, 1839, 1840; Boston: W. D. Ticknor, 1841);

The Token and Atlantic Souvenir, edited by Goodrich (Boston: David H. Williams, 1842);

Parley's Cabinet Library, 20 volumes, edited by Goodrich (Boston: Bradbury, Soden, 1843–1845).

PERIODICALS EDITED: *Parley's Magazine,* 1833–1834;

Robert Merry's Museum, 1841–1854.

Samuel Griswold Goodrich was a prolific author, editor, and publisher of children's books and periodicals, the best known of which were issued under the name of Peter Parley. Goodrich himself estimated that seven million of the Peter Parley books had been published by 1856, and as many as twelve million volumes were published in total. The popularity of his texts allowed him to feed the appetite of his young readers for informative, educational materials from a thor-

oughly, if parochial, American point of view. In addition, Goodrich published *The Token,* a major gift book or annual, that associated him with several significant contemporary authors, including Nathaniel Hawthorne, who was involved in various literary ventures with Goodrich.

Born 19 August 1793 in Ridgefield, Connecticut, Samuel Griswold Goodrich was the son of Samuel and Elizabeth (Ely) Goodrich, both from prominent Connecticut families. His father was a Congregationalist minister, and Goodrich grew up as a well-disciplined young man on his parents' farm. His early education was limited, and at fifteen he went to clerk for his brother-in-law Amos Cooke, a merchant in Danbury. Goodrich began a personal reading course and studied manners in an attempt at self-improvement to counter his lack of formal advanced education. After serving in the army but not seeing action in the War of 1812, Goodrich began his ventures in publishing, including the publication of British works without pay-

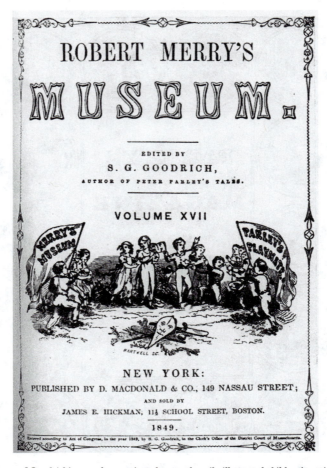

Cover for an issue of Goodrich's second magazine, the most heavily illustrated children's periodical of its time

ing royalties. Despite the difficulties of the industry, Goodrich worked diligently at his publishing enterprises and was especially interested in the publication of American works. In 1820 he published the works of Revolutionary War poet John Trumbull and lost money. He married Adeline Gratia Bradley of Warminster on 2 February 1818, but she died 24 June 1822. By late 1823 Goodrich was on his way to Europe, a trip that changed his direction in life. While touring and meeting authors such as Sir Walter Scott, Goodrich visited Hannah More at Barleywood, near Bristol. The well-known British playwright, pamphleteer, and author of tracts on morality inspired him to enter the field of children's literature in an effort to instill values in literature. Later, in his *Fireside Education* (1838), Goodrich wrote that a child should be "taught the principles of obedience, the habit of bowing to duty, of subjecting his will to the authority of a guide, of yielding his heart up to the rule of right." He also campaigned against Mother Goose, describing her works as "revolting," "shocking," and "deeply painful." By

October 1826 Goodrich had moved his headquarters from Connecticut to Boston, where his business eventually occupied the entire second floor of the Old Corner Book Store at the corner of Washington and School Streets. The first floor was the location of the well-known publisher William D. Ticknor.

On 2 January 1826 Goodrich married his second wife, Mary Booth, and they had six children. Mary Booth's English parents objected to their daughter's marriage to a Yankee, but they later accepted both Goodrich and the success he earned with the help of Peter Parley. Goodrich hosted many gatherings at Rockland, his residence in Jamaica Plain, just outside of Boston, built to reflect his status as a successful publisher. The guests included Daniel Webster, the poet John Brainard (who wrote a special song, "Seabird," in honor of Mary Goodrich), Hawthorne, and Nathaniel Parker Willis.

In 1827 the first of the Peter Parley books, *The Tales of Peter Parley about America,* appeared. Peter Parley introduces himself as "an old man very gray and lame . . . [who has] seen a great many things, and had a great many adventures." Parley adds, in an understatement, "I love to talk about them." According to the account of his daughter Emily, Goodrich stumbled on his pseudonym by absently conjugating the French verb *parler* and suddenly realizing that Peter Parley, Peter the Talker, would appropriately characterize the figure he had in mind. Pictured as a white-haired old gentleman with a cane and knee breeches or with crutches and a gouty foot or wearing a broad-brimmed black hat, Parley became an icon among thousands of children. Goodrich capitalized on the visual details as part of the technique that made his books and stories effective and made Peter Parley a close companion and mentor for his readers. Some children were so convinced they knew Peter Parley that, on growing up and meeting Goodrich, they were intensely disappointed. Peter Parley's ubiquitous presence is illustrated by Ralph Waldo Emerson's self-deprecating comment in 1845 that his lectures were "a kind of Peter Parley's story of Uncle Plato," simplifying Transcendental notions for the public. Because of his obvious appeal to the imagination of his young audience and his subsequent almost universal name recognition, Peter Parley, the character and narrator, is credited with the broad success of Goodrich's texts.

In *Tales about America,* as in the subsequent Peter Parley works, Parley plays the double role of omniscient narrator, often talking directly to his readers, and active participant in some of the incidents. He thereby encourages a close relationship between himself and his readers and takes advantage of this opportunity to promote his values, including some religious and political prejudices. Although he claims to have had no overriding philosophy except to imagine himself sitting on the floor talking with children, in *Peter Parley's Tales about the Sun, Moon, and Stars* (1831) Goodrich notes his purpose: "I have sought to give you pleasure, but I am more anxious that you should be wise and good. I have not forgotten that you have a life to live here and hereafter, and I hope you will never forget that happiness is the lot of the virtuous, and misery the certain doom of the wicked."

Goodrich's Peter Parley books manifested many of the trends of publication and education of the day. For example, they emphasized the use of questions to aid young readers in remembering the information. They also promoted the use of woodcuts as illustrations to help the readers visualize the places and scenes described. Often, on the other hand, the books were colored by melodrama, coincidence, and, despite Goodrich's pronounced emphasis on facts, many inaccuracies.

The books were, nonetheless, popular. Goodrich claimed that in 1856 three hundred thousand were being released annually and that he had written or edited 170 books, 116 of them under the Peter Parley pen name. There is some debate over the physical possibility of his having written all that he claimed, especially since Goodrich admitted that his failing eyesight forced his wife to serve as his amanuensis. In addition to Hawthorne, other writers, such as Samuel Kettell, were also employed to write for Goodrich. Regardless of whether or not Goodrich actually wrote all the Peter Parley books himself, their success led to Goodrich's being dubbed "the most prodigious literary hack of his day" by *The Cambridge History of American Literature* (1919).

In 1827 Goodrich also started *The Token,* one of the earliest and best-known gift books in America. Goodrich edited thirteen of the fifteen issues. Most famous among the writers included in *The Token* were Hawthorne—many of whose *Twice-Told Tales* (1837) first appeared there: Henry Wadsworth Longfellow, N. P. Willis, Lydia Sigourney, Lydia Maria Child, William Cullen Bryant, Jared Sparks, Catharine Maria Sedgwick, J. O. Sargent, Grenville Mellen, Hannah Gould, and Oliver Wendell Holmes. Goodrich himself contributed more than fifty pieces, mostly poetry of questionable quality.

Goodrich contacted Hawthorne after reading his first novel, *Fanshawe* (1828). Their association lasted for several years and included some ambiguous feelings. Hawthorne saw Goodrich as one who exploited the talents of the more gifted authors he hired, although Hawthorne also admitted feeling kindly toward Goodrich. In fact, Goodrich encouraged Hawthorne to collect the stories in *Twice-Told Tales* and helped to get the volume published, joining with Horatio Bridge without Hawthorne's knowledge to get the guarantee that the publisher demanded. Hawthorne eventually contributed more than twenty-five tales and sketches to *The Token,* for which, despite his reservations, Hawthorne was probably paid at about the going rate for a relatively unknown author of the time.

Later Goodrich hired Hawthorne to edit the *American Magazine of Useful and Entertaining Knowledge* from March to August 1836, and in the same year Hawthorne and his sister Elizabeth prepared copy for *Peter Parley's Universal History, on the Basis of Geography* (1837). Their pay of approximately $100 was not in line with the book's success. Hawthorne's relationship with Goodrich can be summed up as uneasy. Goodrich was one of the first to recognize Hawthorne's ability, assisted the publication of *Twice-Told Tales,* and provided hackwork to give Hawthorne both work and money, although not too much of the latter.

RECOLLECTION

OF

A LIFETIME,

OR

MEN AND THINGS I HAVE SEEN:

IN A SERIES OF

FAMILIAR LETTERS TO A FRIEND,

HISTORICAL, BIOGRAPHICAL, ANECDOTICAL, AND
DESCRIPTIVE.

BY S. G. GOODRICH.

VOL. I.

NEW YORK AND AUBURN:
MILLER, ORTON AND MULLIGAN.
New York, 25 Park Row:—Auburn, 107 Genesee-st.
M DCCC LVI.

Title page for Goodrich's rambling autobiography, which includes accounts of his experiences in publishing

In 1833 Goodrich entered the children's periodical market with *Parley's Magazine,* which he sold one year later. In 1841 Goodrich initiated his second major children's periodical, *Robert Merry's Museum,* for the edification and entertainment of the whole family. Like his predecessor Peter Parley, Merry had a distinct personality, admitting to having led a problematic youth and spending time in prison before his travels and his current retirement in New England as an old bachelor storyteller. Both Parley and Merry loved children, were practical, and emphasized the intellectual and moral education of their readers. Reflecting changing attitudes about young people, the periodical tried to prepare its readers for citizenship by presenting stories about places around the world for their education and for the improvement of society. It emphasized the virtues of self-control, moderation, responsibility, and hard work.

As do his other writings, Goodrich's *Robert Merry's Museum* stood against slavery from the position of not extending its evils rather than abolishing the practice immediately. Most likely, *Robert Merry's Museum* was the first American children's periodical to print letters from subscribers and is considered the most heavily illustrated children's periodical of the time. Eventually Goodrich even resurrected Peter Parley (who had "died" in 1841 according to *Robert Merry's Museum*) to serve as co-editor and to engage in conversations with Robert Merry. Goodrich seemed to identify with Parley more than Merry, since Parley's character was absent from the magazine after Goodrich went to Paris to be U.S. consul. Goodrich was associated with the periodical until 1854, and among its later "real" editors was Louisa May Alcott.

Goodrich also produced great quantities of children's textbooks from 1830 to 1850, including a set of five *Goodrich Readers.* In addition to teaching reading skills, Goodrich planned the books to promote the retention of cultural, moral, and intellectual ideas in his audience. Although plagued by occasionally problematic vocabulary, the readers maintained popularity by referring to Peter Parley, emphasizing a New England background for their largely Eastern audience, and offering a broad variety of articles to lessen boredom. As with his other texts, Goodrich's geographies often generalized simplistic descriptions of foreign countries to aid the readers' memories but provided global maps, not the more typical sectioned ones.

Goodrich seemed to relish most his role as historian, and in the history volumes he added sparks of the Parley-like storyteller. He also strayed from a strict chronological pattern in his histories, preferring to start with contemporary events to catch the interest of his young readers before tracing out the history of the places being studied. An important element in his *The First Book of History. For Children and Youth* (1831) was the antislavery commentary inserted throughout the text. *Peter Parley's Universal History, on the Basis of Geography,* actually written by the Hawthornes, was noteworthy for its more violent and gory descriptions when contrasted with other Goodrich histories, even though it did include some of Peter Parley's comments to lighten the tone. In addition to becoming an astute businessman capable of developing favorable contracts, Goodrich created his own library series when neither Massachusetts nor Connecticut school boards adopted his texts. His other textbooks included books on civics, arithmetic, and one on zoology commended by Louis Agassiz.

Goodrich's success was obvious. The *Philadelphia Saturday Courier* (17 September 1842) proclaimed, "Is there a reader in the United States who has not read some of the productions of Peter Parley? . . . Few men of any age have done so much real good towards facilitating the easy acquirement of useful knowledge, as our much esteemed friend, Mr. S. G. Goodrich."

The price of such popularity was the battle against pirated editions published by others using the Peter Parley name, and even Peter Parley impersonators. Among the most egregious of these fraudulent texts was one that converted Parley into an old British sailor who praised the queen—a far cry from Goodrich's uncontrolled nationalism. Goodrich eventually placed and won a suit against one publisher, but there is no indication that he collected on the ruling. These controversies on protecting his authorship plagued him throughout his life.

Although Goodrich held staunchly conservative opinions about civic matters, he was not much of a public figure until 1836, when he was chosen for the state legislature from Roxbury and the next year elected to the state senate. In 1851 President Millard Fillmore appointed Goodrich to the post of U.S. consul in Paris. Goodrich did a good enough job to receive the commendation of Webster and to be the subject of a highly supportive though unsuccessful petition by the American residents in Paris when a change in administration forced Goodrich to relinquish his post. Before his departure in the summer of 1853, he was awarded an honorary medallion embossed with a portrait of himself.

Goodrich remained in Europe until the middle of 1855. Back home, Goodrich continued to pursue his business interests. In 1856 he published his autobiographical *Recollections of a Lifetime; or, Men and Things I Have Seen: In a Series of Familiar Letters to a Friend, Historical, Biographical, Anecdotal, and Descriptive,* a rambling overview of his values and opinions on various topics, his experiences in the publishing world, his acquaintances, and some details about his life. Despite its limitations, it remains a useful and often entertaining source for information about the period.

Goodrich moved in 1858 to a house in Southbury, Connecticut, where his status as Peter Parley earned him the position of community patriarch. While in New York on business, Goodrich died on 9 May 1860; his funeral was on 13 May 1860 at his home.

In his time Goodrich was a prolific author and publisher of juvenile literature that influenced thousands of young people. But no one reads Peter Parley's works today. In history, therefore, Goodrich's place is defined by his general connection with the literary world, his specific association with Hawthorne and other major writers, and the insights his career sheds on America in the nineteenth century.

References:

Helen S. Canfield, "Peter Parley," *Horn Book Magazine,* 46 (April, June, August 1970): 135–141, 274–282, 412–418;

Patricia Ann Pflieger, "A Visit to 'Merry's Museum'; or, Social Values in a Nineteenth-Century American Periodical for Children," dissertation, University of Minnesota, 1987;

Daniel Roselle, *Samuel Griswold Goodrich, Creator of Peter Parley* (Albany: State University of New York Press, 1968).

John B. Gough

(22 August 1817 – 18 February 1886)

John W. Crowley
Syracuse University

BOOKS: *An Autobiography* (Boston: Gough, 1845); republished as *The Hand of Providence Exemplified in the History of J. B. Gough* (London: Darton, 1846); expanded as *The Autobiography of John B. Gough: With a Continuation of His Life to the Present Time* (London: W. Tweedie, 1859);

A Reply to Rev. Mr. Pond's "Echo" (Boston: Haliburton & Dudley, 1845);

Mr. Gough's Account of His Relapse (Leeds?, U.K.: F. R. Lees? 1845?);

Habit (London: J. Nisbet, 1853);

An Address to Children (London, 1854);

Address to the Working Classes (London, 1854);

An Address to Young Men . . . Delivered in Exeter Hall, May 10th, 1854 (London, 1854);

Are They All Fools, Who Become Drunkards? An Oration (London, 1854);

The Evil of Drunkenness: An Oration (London, 1854);

Importance of Female Influence . . . Address . . . April 28th, 1854, in Willis's Rooms (London, 1854);

The Liquor Traffic. An Oration (London, 1854);

The Tide of Drunkenness Rolled Back by the Adoption of the Total Abstinence Principle. With a Critique on Mr. Gough as an Orator (Edinburgh: W. F. Cutthbertson, 1854);

Mr. Gough's Address to the Ladies of Glasgow (Glasgow, 1854);

Our Duty in Regard to the Intemperate . . . Oration Delivered at Exeter Hall, May 11th, 1854 (London, 1854);

Who Is My Neighbour? An Oration (London, 1854);

Man and His Masters. A Lecture Delivered in Exeter Hall, December 12, 1854 (London: J. Nisbet, 1855);

Cause and Effect. An Oration (London, 1857);

Christian Liberty. John B. Gough's Oration. Delivered at Exeter Hall, on Tuesday, August 25th, 1857 (London: Printed by R. Barrett, 1857);

Social Responsibilities. A Lecture (London: J. Nisbet, 1857);

Orations, Delivered on Various Occasions, By John B. Gough (London: W. Tweedie, 1859);

The Farewell Oration of John B. Gough, in Exeter Hall (London: W. Tweedie, 1860);

John B. Gough

Speech . . . at the Reception Meeting at Tremont Temple, Boston, Sept. 17, 1860 (Boston: Printed by J. Wilson [1860]);

The Power of Example. A Lecture Delivered, Before the Young Men's Christian Association, in Exeter Hall, on Feb. 14, 1860 (London: J. Nisbet, 1860?);

Autobiography and Personal Recollections of John B. Gough, With Twenty-Six Years' Experience as a Public Speaker (Springfield, Mass.: Bill, Nichols, 1869);

An Oration on Temperance. By John B. Gough. Delivered in New York on Thursday, May 6th, 1875 (London: W. Tweedie [1875]);

First Four Orations, Delivered in London . . . 1878 (London: Morgan & Scott, 1878);

The Only Remedy (New York: American Temperance Publishing House, 1879);

Temperance Lectures (New York: American Temperance Publishing House, 1879);

Sunlight and Shadow; or, Gleanings from My Life Work (Hartford, Conn.: A. D. Worthington, 1880; London: Hodder & Stoughton, 1882);

Platform Echoes; or, Leaves from My Note-Book of Forty Years, with an introduction by Lyman Abbott (Hartford, Conn.: A. D. Worthington, 1885; London: Hodder & Stoughton, 1885);

John B. Gough: His Anniversary Addresses Before the National Temperance Society, with a biographical sketch by T. L. Cuyler and J. Cook (New York: The National Temperance Society and Publishing House, 1886).

Edition: *Drunkard's Progress: Narratives of Addiction, Despair and Recovery,* edited by John W. Crowley (Baltimore: Johns Hopkins University Press, 1999).

OTHER: *The Works of George Cruikshank in Oil, Water Colors, Original Drawings, Etchings, Woodcuts, Lithographs, and Glyphographs,* collected by John B. Gough (Boston: Club of Odd Volumes, 1890).

John B. Gough (pronounced *Goffe*) was the most powerful and popular temperance orator in America during the mid nineteenth century. Dubbed the "Demosthenes of total abstinence," Gough was gifted with a mellifluous voice, a genius for mimicry, and a charismatic presence. Edward A. Rand, in an early biography, *A Knight That Smote the Dragon; or, The Young People's Gough* (1892), describes Gough as a speaker:

He is of slight build, has flashing eyes set in a sad, thin face, and he has a nervous, intense manner. His voice has great range of expression. It can flame out in a righteous indignation or soften to those inimitable tones of pathos, subduing and melting the hearts of his hearers. Does he need the help of satire? His tongue can hiss out a sharp invective. Would he make his hearers see any of life's humorous sides? He can imitate the fuss and fret of the fat old farmer geeing to his oxen that lazily pull on the old wood-sled, act the marvel-loving sailor spinning a yarn in the forecastle when winds are

fair, or the Yankee trader driving in a rural district a prudent bargain.

Such versatile and compelling performances mesmerized audiences and moved large numbers to take the temperance pledge. Gough, who kept punctilious records of his travels, boasted that during the course of his career he had delivered more than 9,600 lectures to more than 9,000,000 people; his lifetime harvest of converts far exceeded the 140,000 souls whose pledges he could document. In addition to celebrity throughout the United States, Gough enjoyed renown in his native England, where he launched successful tours in 1854, 1857, and 1878. Over the years he added other homiletic topics to his platform repertoire. But, as Frederick Douglass observed in his *Life and Times of Frederick Douglass* (1892), Gough's slogan was, "Whatever may be the title, my lecture is always on Temperance." All of Gough's books derived, in fact, from his platform appearances. Gough's 1845 *An Autobiography,* his major work, was an elaboration of his temperance stump speech, which traced a Dantean journey from Inferno (drunken damnation) to Purgatorio (redemption by the pledge) to Paradiso (justification as a temperance speaker).

In his *Autobiography* Gough begins the story of his hellish descent with a heavenly evocation of Sandgate, the coastal English village in Kent where he was born John Bartholomew Gough on 22 August 1817, the only son of Jane and John Gough, the village schoolmistress and a retired soldier. An exacting father and indulgent mother raised Gough to love reading and righteousness. As a precociously bookish child, he briefly attended a private seminary, where he was entrusted to instruct other boys in spelling and arithmetic. He also came to the attention of the famed abolitionist William Wilberforce, who rewarded the youth's reading skills with an autographed volume. Gough's prospects were nearly extinguished when his skull was accidentally split open by the sharp edge of a workman's shovel. Although he managed to survive this trauma, he was beset for the rest of his life by throbbing headaches, often triggered by the fervor of his oratory.

Young Gough's parents encouraged him to rise above their own station by seeking his fortune in the United States, where he arrived at the age of twelve in the company of English neighbors, the David Mannerings, to whom he had been apprenticed. In 1831, after working two years on the Mannerings' farm near Utica, New York, Gough sought release from his indentures and moved to New York City to learn the bookbinding trade. Having earlier converted to Methodism, he found steady work there at the Methodist Book Store, and he dutifully saved passage money for the rest of his

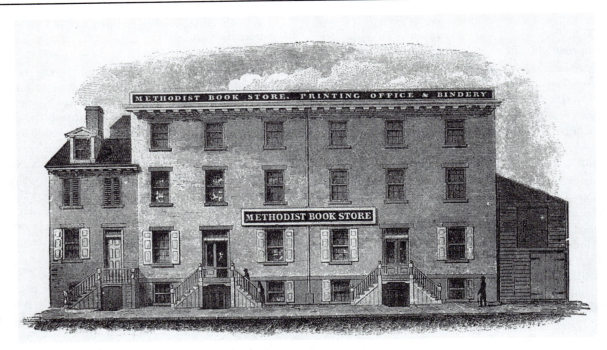

The bookstore on Crosby Street in New York City, where Gough found work as a bookbinder in 1831

family. Gough's mother and his sister, Mary, arrived in New York two years later–his father stayed in England to secure his military pension–and despite hard economic times and a harsh winter, the reunited family endured until Jane Gough died suddenly in 1834.

The grief-stricken Gough then parted company with his sister and fell into dissipation. Seduced by the spiritous camaraderie of city life, he was especially lured by the theater, and for several years, as he drifted about New England, he worked intermittently as a comic actor. But Gough's talent on the boards proved to be better suited to the barrooms, where his high jinks earned him a steady supply of drams. Habitually drunk and often destitute, he also suffered the torments of delirium tremens.

In an effort to pull himself together, Gough decided to start his own bookbinding shop in Newberryport, Massachusetts; after his marriage to Lucretia Fowler on 18 December 1839, he did appear to be settling down. All the while, however, Gough kept drinking himself deeper into intemperance, willfully blind to his own deterioration. "And yet, at this time, I did not consider myself to be what in reality I was–a drunkard," he wrote in his *Autobiography*. "I would frame many excuses for myself–plead my own cause before myself, as judge and jury, until I obtained, at my own hands, a willing acquittal." Gough spun down and down, losing everything he valued along the way–jobs, friends, family (his wife and newborn daughter died

unattended during one of his binges), and also decency, dignity, and any claim to human society. "I was debased in my own eyes, and, having lost my self-respect, became a poor, abject being, scarcely worth attempting to reform." A failure, Gough lived now only to drink.

What saved him, finally, was the compassion of Joel Stratton, a waiter in a temperance hotel, who extended a hand of friendship and induced Gough to take the pledge. With support from Jesse W. Goodrich, Moses Grant, and other members of the Washington Temperance Society of Worcester, Massachusetts, Gough managed to quit drinking in October 1842. When he relapsed five months later, he immediately repented, retook the pledge, and resumed his oratorical career; for despite Gough's backsliding, he was still in great demand as a temperance speaker. He claimed to have traveled more than twelve thousand miles in his first two years on the platform and to have obtained nearly thirty-two thousand signatures to the total-abstinence pledge. The enduring popularity of Gough's *Autobiography* was enhanced by his preeminence on the lecture circuit.

An Autobiography is a defining example of the "temperance narrative"–a genre, akin to the slave narrative and the conversion narrative, in which inebriates recounted their enslavement to alcohol and their miraculous emancipation. Temperance narratives first appeared during the 1840s as a by-product of the revolutionizing of antidrink reform by the Washington Temperance

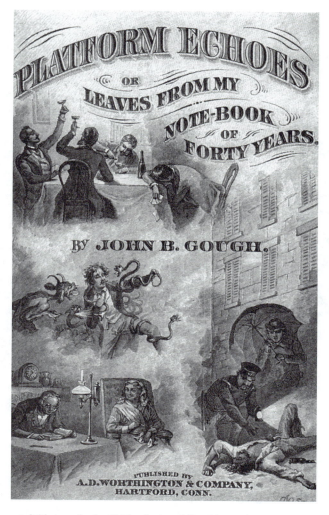

Decorated title page for the 1885 collection of Gough's popular temperance lectures

Society. From its origins late in the eighteenth century, the temperance campaign had been led by a respectable New England establishment of clergymen, lawyers, merchants, and physicians. As temperance became a national movement during the 1820s and 1830s, it spread to the middle and lower classes, which embraced sobriety as a means to self-perfection and upward mobility. These bourgeois improvers, more uncompromising than the Yankee founders, denounced the consumption of *any* alcoholic beverages—including wine, the drink favored by the upper classes, which had been excepted from the pledge in its original form. The new pledge of teetotalism acquired so many advocates that *temperance* was redefined, in practice, as *abstinence;* and leaders increasingly demanded a halt to the liquor traffic by means of prohibition.

At first, temperance reformers were intent on shattering the myth of "moderate" drinking and rescuing potential inebriates from the brink of self-destruction. Confirmed drunkards, thought to be past saving, were expected to drink themselves to death and thus to obviate the social problem of dealing with them, except as transient denizens of the poorhouses and lock-ups. When the Washington Temperance Society was founded in 1840 by six Baltimore artisans who pledged teetotalism, vowed mutual assistance, and recruited other inebriates to their meetings, the focus shifted suddenly to drunkards themselves. The Washingtonians proved that even hopeless cases could get sober through the empathy of reformed drunkards. They built their fellowship around confessional experience meetings, at which reformed drunkards told riveting tales of their battles with the bottle and their deliverance from Demon Rum.

Several of the Washingtonian testimonies, including Gough's, ultimately came to be written down and

Gough in later years

printed, often in small, local editions. The transformation of speech into writing was characteristic also of slave narratives, such as *Narrative of the Life of Frederick Douglass,* published the same year as Gough's *Autobiography.* Because temperance narratives, like slave narratives, were sometimes produced collaboratively, charges of authorial inauthenticity were routinely preferred. In response to such charges, Gough later confessed that he had, indeed, dictated his *Autobiography* to an amanuensis; the book, he remonstrated, was his own work, nevertheless, written almost entirely in his own words. *An Autobiography* first appeared in a self-published edition of one thousand copies; there were a dozen printings (for a total of thirty-two thousand copies) from 1845 through 1853, as well as several issues in England. An expanded (but narratively more diffuse) version, first published in 1869 as *Autobiography and Personal Recollections of John B. Gough, With Twenty-Six Years' Experience as a Public Speaker,* circulated widely as a subscription book, as did two later miscellanies of Gough's lecture material, *Sunlight and Shadow; or, Gleanings from My Life Work* (1880) and *Platform Echoes; or, Leaves from My Note-Book of Forty Years* (1885). Several Gough titles were published independently in London to capitalize on his triumphal tours of England and Scotland.

Gough prospered from his lecture fees, much to the chagrin of his initial Washingtonian sponsors, some of whom questioned the rectitude and magnitude of his earnings. Gough's reputation was sullied by controversy in 1845, when Jesse D. Pond, a minister, and other enemies accused him of slandering the Mannerings, the family that had brought him to the United States. A far more lurid scandal erupted after Gough's spectacular relapse later that same year, when after disappearing for a week in New York, he was found in a brothel, recovering from a binge. According to Gough, he had been drugged and then duped into inebriation by those seeking to embarrass the temperance movement. He had unwittingly fallen among prostitutes, he insisted, in a drunken daze. Although Gough was exculpated by his church and defended by most temperance leaders, his story was widely disbelieved, and he was lampooned in the temperance press. Gough's own statement about the incident was added as a "Supplement" to his *Autobiography,* beginning in late 1845. The anti-Gough position was articulated by a former Washingtonian protégé in *Goffiana* (1846).

Gough eventually broke with the Washingtonians, who were in decline by 1845, over their hostility toward organized religion and their tactical emphasis on the moral suasion of drunkards rather than the legal coercion of drunkard-makers. Once he had joined the temperance mainstream as an (albeit reluctant) advocate of prohibition, he became a truly national and international figure. Although he rigorously abstained from alcohol after 1845, his controversial past made him vulnerable to attacks on his sobriety and integrity. New charges surfaced in 1857, during Gough's second tour abroad, when he became entangled inadvertently in a dispute between suasionist and prohibitionist wings of the English temperance movement. In a private letter of 23 March 1856 he had bemoaned to an English friend the recent defeats of the antidrink crusade: "The cause in this country is in a depressed state; the Maine law [the first enactment of, and the model legislation for, prohibition at the state level] is a dead letter everywhere—more liquor sold than I ever knew before, in Massachusetts,—and in other States it is about as bad." The gloomy tenor of this letter, which was printed without Gough's permission, prompted vicious attacks from English prohibitionists. After one antagonist, F. R. Lees, publicly alleged that Gough was still drinking, and eating opium as well, Gough sued for libel and won a virtually uncontested judgment in June 1858.

During his later years, long since happily remarried (to Mary Whitcomb, on 23 November 1843) and ensconced at the Hillside, his country estate five miles from Worcester, Gough continued to tramp the lecture trail, keeping to an arduous itinerary. His life ended, as he might well have wished, on stage. In his sixty-ninth year, he collapsed from a stroke during an appearance in Frankfort, Pennsylvania, and died three days later on 18 February 1886.

Gough's fame, dependent as it was on his personal vitality, did not long outlast him. Although a decade later H. P. Lovecraft, a pioneering writer of science fiction, was inspired (at the tender age of five) to become an ardent, lifelong Dry by reading *Sunlight and Shadow*, Gough's posthumous influence was rare. By the 1920s, as the noble experiment of Prohibition came and went, he had faded into obscurity—just another name in the dim annals of a reform movement thought risible by the bathtub-gin generation. Although Gough's 1845 *Autobiography*, on which his literary reputation hinges, enjoyed more contemporary popularity than its slave-narrative counterpart, *Narrative of the Life of Frederick Douglass*, Gough never became a canonical author. No modern biography exists, and the *Autobiography* was out of print for a century and a half before its recent republication in abridged form in John W. Crowley's *Drunkard's Progress: Narratives of Addiction, Despair and Recovery* (1999).

Biographies:

W. H. Daniels, ed., *The Temperance Reform and Its Great Reformers* (New York: Nelson & Phillips, 1878), pp. 109–190;

Edward A. Rand, *A Knight That Smote the Dragon; or, The Young People's Gough* (New York: Hunt & Eaton, 1892);

Carlos Martyn, *John B. Gough: The Apostle of Cold Water* (New York: Funk & Wagnalls, 1894);

Honoré W. Morrow, *Tiger! Tiger!: The Life Story of John B. Gough* (New York: Morrow, 1930);

Mark Edward Lender, *Dictionary of American Temperance Biography* (Westport, Conn.: Greenwood Press, 1984), pp. 199–200.

References:

John W. Crowley, "Slaves to the Bottle: Gough's *Autobiography* and Douglass's *Narrative*," in *The Serpent in the Cup: Temperance in American Literature*, edited by David S. Reynolds and Debra J. Rosenthal (Amherst: University of Massachusetts Press, 1997), pp. 115–135;

Crowley, ed., *Drunkard's Progress: Narratives of Addiction, Despair and Recovery* (Baltimore: Johns Hopkins University Press, 1999);

Goffiana; A Review of the Life and Writings of John B. Gough (Boston: Ruggles, 1846);

John Marsh, *Temperance Recollections, Labors, Defeats, Triumphs: An Autobiography* (New York: Scribners, 1866);

Jesse D. Pond, *The Echo of Truth to the Voice of Slander; or, John B. Gough's Early History* (New York: Stanford & Swords, 1845).

Papers:

The bulk of John B. Gough's papers are at the American Antiquarian Society, Worcester, Massachusetts. This collection, which includes diaries, travel records, letters, lectures, clippings, and testimonials, copiously documents Gough's long public career; but it offers little material of a personal nature.

Sarah Josepha Hale

(24 October 1788 – 30 April 1879)

Patricia Okker
University of Missouri, Columbia

See also the Hale entries in *DLB 1: The American Renaissance in New England; DLB 42: American Writers for Children Before 1900;* and *DLB 73: American Magazine Journalists, 1741–1850.*

BOOKS: *The Genius of Oblivion; and Other Original Poems,* as a Lady of New-Hampshire (Concord, N.H.: Jacob B. Moore, 1823);

Northwood; A Tale of New England, 2 volumes (Boston: Bowles & Dearborn, 1827); republished as *Sidney Romelee, A Tale of New England* (London: A. K. Newman, 1827); revised and enlarged as *Northwood; or, Life North and South: Showing the True Character of Both* (New York: H. Long & Brother, 1852);

Sketches of American Character (Boston: Putnam & Hunt / Carter & Hendee, 1829);

Conversations on the Burman Mission, as a Lady of New Hampshire (Boston: Printed by T. R. Martin for the Massachusetts Sabbath School Union, 1830);

Poems for Our Children: Designed for Families, Sabbath Schools, and Infant Schools. Written to Inculcate Moral Truths and Virtuous Sentiments . . . Part First (Boston: Marsh, Capen & Lyon, 1830);

The School Song Book. Adapted to the Scenes of the School Room. Written for American Children and Youth . . . (Boston: Allen & Ticknor, 1834); republished as *My Little Song Book* (Boston: James B. Dow, 1841);

Traits of American Life (Philadelphia: E. L. Carey & A. Hart, 1835);

The Good Housekeeper, or, the Way to Live Well and to Be Well While We Live (Boston: Weeks, Jordan, 1839);

Keeping House and House Keeping. A Story of Domestic Life (New York: Harper, 1845);

Alice Ray: A Romance in Rhyme (Philadelphia, 1845);

"Boarding Out." A Tale of Domestic Life, as the author of "Keeping House and Housekeeping" (New York: Harper, 1846);

Three Hours; or, The Vigil of Love: and Other Poems (Philadelphia: Carey & Hart, 1848);

Harry Guy, The Widow's Son. A Story of the Sea (Boston: B. B. Mussey, 1848);

The Ladies' New Book of Cookery: A Practical System for Private Families in Town and Country (New York: H. Long, 1852); enlarged as *Mrs. Hale's New Cook Book* (Philadelphia: T. B. Peterson, 1857);

Woman's Record; or, Sketches of All Distinguished Women from 'The Beginning' till A.D. 1850 . . . (New York: Harper, 1853; revised and enlarged edition, New York: Harper, 1855; revised and enlarged again, New York: Harper, 1870);

The New Household Receipt-Book (New York: H. Long, 1853); revised and enlarged as *Mrs. Hale's Receipts for the Million* (Philadelphia: T. B. Peterson, 1857);

Liberia; or, Mr. Peyton's Experiments (New York: Harper, 1853);

Manners; or, Happy Homes and Good Society All the Year Round (Boston: J. E. Tilton, 1868);

Love: or, Woman's Destiny. A Poem in Two Parts: With Other Poems (Philadelphia: Duffield Ashmead, 1870).

OTHER: *Flora's Interpreter: or, The American Book of Flowers and Sentiments,* edited by Hale (Boston: Marsh, Capen & Lyon, 1832); republished as *Flora's Interpreter, and Fortuna Flora* (Boston: Benjamin B. Mussey, 1849);

Tales for Youth: Selected from the Juvenile Miscellany, edited by Hale (Boston: J. Hancock, 1835);

The Ladies' Wreath; A Selection from the Female Poetic Writers of England and America, edited by Hale (Boston: Marsh, Capen & Lyon, 1837; revised and enlarged edition, Boston: Marsh, Capen, Lyon & Webb, 1839);

The Lady's Annual Register, and House-Wife's Almanac, edited anonymously by Hale (Boston: William Crosby, 1842);

The Little Boys' and Girls' Library, 10-volume series, edited by Hale (New York: Edward Dunigan, circa 1842);

The Opal: A Pure Gift for the Holy Days, edited, with contributions, by Hale (New York: J. C. Riker, 1845);

The Opal: A Pure Gift for the Holy Days, edited, with contributions, by Hale (New York: J. C. Riker, 1848);

The Opal: A Pure Gift for All Seasons, edited, with contributions, by Hale (New York: J. C. Riker, 1849);

Mary Hughs, *Aunt Mary's New Stories for Young People,* edited by Hale (Boston: James Munroe, 1849);

The Crocus: A Fresh Flower for the Holidays, edited by Hale (New York: Edward Dunigan, 1849);

The Poets' Offering: For 1850, edited by Hale (Philadelphia: Grigg, Elliot, 1850); republished as *A Complete Dictionary of Poetical Quotations* (Philadelphia: Lippincott, Grambo, 1850); republished as *The Poets' Offering: For 1851* (Philadelphia: Lippincott, Grambo, 1851);

The White Veil: A Bridal Gift, edited, with contributions, by Hale (Philadelphia: E. H. Butler, 1854);

The Bible Reading-Book: Containing Such Portions of the History, Biography, Poetry, Prophecy, Precepts, and Parables, of the Old and New Testaments, edited by Hale (Philadelphia: Lippincott, Grambo, 1854);

The Letters of Madame de Sévigné, to Her Daughter and Friends, edited by Hale (New York: Mason, 1856; revised edition, Boston: Roberts, 1869);

The Letters of Lady Mary Wortley Montagu, edited by Hale (New York: Mason, 1856; revised edition, Boston: Roberts, 1869);

Elizabeth Ioceline, *The Mothers Legacie, to Her Unborne Childe,* edited by Hale (Philadelphia: Duffield Ashmead, 1871).

SELECTED PERIODICAL PUBLICATIONS–UNCOLLECTED: "Ormond Grosvenor; A Tragedy," *Godey's Lady's Book,* 16 (January, February, April 1838): 33–40, 49–53, 145–152;

"The Judge; A Drama of American Life," *Godey's Lady's Book,* 42 (January–May 1851): 21–26, 88–93, 154–159, 237–245, 298–301.

An accomplished editor and author whose career spanned more than five decades, Sarah Josepha Hale was a successful and influential figure in the antebellum literary world. For more than four decades she edited *Godey's Lady's Book,* the most popular magazine in the United States before the Civil War, and she used *Godey's Lady's Book* both to promote her views on contemporary women's issues and to influence popular literary standards. Hale was a prolific author as well–publishing novels, collections of short fiction, poetry, books on cooking and housekeeping, edited collections, and an ambitious nine-hundred-page reference work about women in history. Two plays and countless poems, short stories, and essays appeared in the pages of her magazines and in many of the most popular gift books and anthologies of the period.

Born on 24 October 1788 to Gordon and Martha (Whittlesey) Buell, Sarah Josepha Buell grew up on a farm in Newport, New Hampshire. Despite the limited formal education available to her, Sarah received an excellent education. She credited her mother with inspiring her love of reading, which included the works of John Milton, William Shakespeare, and Alexander Pope. She later identified the Bible and John Bunyan's *Pilgrim's Progress* (1678, 1684) as her favorite books as a child. Suggesting her lifelong interests in women writers and patriotic causes, Hale also described Ann Radcliffe's *Mysteries of Udolpho* (1794) and David Ramsay's *History of the American Revolution* (1789) as particularly influential. After Sarah's older brother Horatio entered Dartmouth College, he tutored her each summer in Latin, Greek, philosophy, English grammar, rhetoric, geography, and literature. Through self-education and assistance from her family, then, Sarah was able to receive the equivalent of a college education.

In October 1813 Sarah Buell married David Hale, a New Hampshire lawyer. According to Sarah Hale, she and her husband spent several hours each evening reading and studying; he also encouraged her to write. David Hale died suddenly in September 1822, shortly before the birth of their fifth child. Soon afterward, Sarah Hale turned to writing–publishing her first

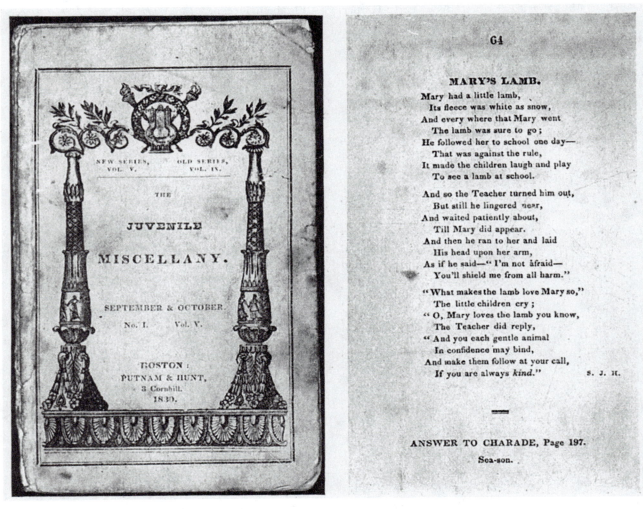

Cover and text page from the issue of the popular children's magazine in which Hale published her best-known poem, collected in Poems for Our Children *(1830)*

volume of poetry, *The Genius of Oblivion; and Other Original Poems,* in 1823. She also began contributing to periodicals. In 1827 Hale furthered her reputation with the publication of *Northwood; A Tale of New England,* a novel that explores contrasts between American life in the North and South. Soon after *Northwood* appeared, Hale was offered a position as editor of the new *Ladies' Magazine,* which was published in Boston, beginning in January 1828. Editing the first few issues of the magazine from her home in Newport, Hale soon moved to Boston, where she continued to edit the magazine for nine years.

Though the *Ladies' Magazine* was not the first American magazine edited by a woman nor the first devoted to women readers, Hale's editorial policies were certainly innovative. Unlike earlier magazines for women, which emphasized entertainment and fashion, Hale's *Ladies' Magazine* was designed to be educational

and literary. Essays on women's education and biographical sketches of famous women were particularly common in the magazine and helped Hale fulfill her promise that the magazine would "accelerate the progress of mental improvement." Hale's editorial policies regarding literature were also unconventional. While other magazines of the period relied on reprinted material from other sources (mostly British), Hale insisted on original material, and the fiction in the magazine featured American settings and characters.

Though Hale wrote a considerable amount of the contents of the magazine, she continued to publish outside of her own magazine during this period. This body of writing attests to her productivity and diversity during her entire career. Some of the material she published during these nine years was compiled from her magazine. *Sketches of American Character* (1829) and *Traits of American Life* (1835), for example, were initially published as series in the *Ladies' Magazine*. Though neither book focused, as did much of the magazine itself, on women's issues, the two series—and the subsequent books—were consistent with the emphasis of the magazine on American subjects. As the preface to *Sketches of American Character* suggests, the focus was on "the minds, manners, and habits of the citizens of our republic."

In addition to publishing prose in book form during her editorship of the *Ladies' Magazine*, Hale also pursued her interest in poetry. *Poems for Our Children: Designed for Families, Sabbath Schools, and Infant Schools. Written to Inculcate Moral Truths and Virtuous Sentiments*, published in 1830, featured religious and moral poetry for children, which Hale wrote herself and which could be set to music and used in school. The poem now known as "Mary Had a Little Lamb" was included, as was a paraphrase of the Lord's Prayer. Hale's poetry for children proved popular, prompting her to issue a second volume of children's verse in 1834, titled *The School Song Book*, which was republished as *My Little Song Book* in 1841. Her brief editorship of the children's magazine *Juvenile Miscellany* similarly suggests her interest in educational and moralistic literature for children. Hale's collection *Flora's Interpreter: or, The American Book of Flowers and Sentiments* (1832) was another popular book of the period. Presenting types of flowers in alphabetical order, with scientific names and poetry associated with the flowers, the collection went through many editions and revisions.

Hale's career took an important turn in January 1837, when she accepted the position as editor of the *Lady's Book*. Though the title of the magazine later changed to *Godey's Lady's Book*, Hale and Louis Godey continued to refer to the magazine as the *Lady's Book*. Begun in 1830 by the Philadelphia publishing entrepreneur Louis A. Godey, the *Lady's Book* was, prior to Hale's arrival, more like other early women's magazines than was Hale's *Ladies' Magazine*. While the *Ladies' Magazine* had featured intellectual topics and original literature, the *Lady's Book* relied heavily on fashion and reprints from British periodicals. Hale's motives in accepting Godey's offer are not certain, but the *Ladies' Magazine* apparently faced financial difficulties. Hale may also have accepted the new position because Godey agreed to let her remain in Boston, where her youngest son attended Harvard. She did not move to Philadelphia until 1841, when her son graduated.

Hale did not abandon her innovative editorial policies when she joined forces with Louis Godey. In fact, Hale and Godey worked to create a magazine that featured both fashion and literature, entertainment and education. Godey continued to feature elaborate engravings and fashion plates, many of them hand-painted in color, while Hale infused into the magazine a strongly literary and intellectual focus. With Hale as editor the magazine began emphasizing original rather than reprinted contents, and Hale added literary reviews and more essays on women's education. She also continued to use her editorial columns to support a variety of causes, including the establishment of Mount Vernon as a national landmark, the founding of Vassar College, and the establishment of Thanksgiving as a national holiday. By all accounts, the new focus of the *Lady's Book* proved wildly successful, and throughout its long history the magazine retained its character as a miscellany. Tales, novels, poetry, essays, music, fashion, book reviews, recipes, needlework and sewing patterns, and even architectural designs all appeared regularly in the *Lady's Book*. Although many magazines attempted to replicate the format of the magazine, the *Lady's Book* prevailed, offering readers some of the most important and most popular writers of the period—including Harriet Beecher Stowe, William Gilmore Simms, Lydia Sigourney, and Edgar Allan Poe—and the *Lady's Book* boasted the highest circulation rates of any American magazine before the Civil War.

The reputation of the *Lady's Book* has varied considerably in the twentieth century. In part because many twentieth-century readers were unfamiliar with the miscellaneous nature of many nineteenth-century literary magazines, they often focused almost entirely on the "embellishments"—the engravings and fashion plates—thus characterizing it as a quaint Victorian women's magazine without any intellectual or literary substance. Others have denounced the literature of the magazine as little more than "sentimental trash." Efforts by late-twentieth-century scholars to reassess sentimental literature, however, have led to a renewed interest in the influence of the magazine on nineteenth-century literary culture. For example, scholars have shown that by refusing to publish reprints, by paying its authors well, and by urging readers to support American writers, the magazine helped establish authorship as a viable profession in the United States.

Hale's interest in supporting American authors is not surprising considering that, while editing the magazine, she continued to write as well—publishing poetry, fiction, and occasional drama. "Ormond Grosvenor; A Tragedy," for example, appeared in the *Lady's Book* in 1838 and illustrated what Hale herself described as the "spirit of the American Revolution; or the struggle between the principles of civil Liberty" and "the prescriptive privileges of aristocratic domination in the old world." Another play, "The Judge; A Drama of American Life," which appeared in 1851, featured a melodramatic plot of romance, corruption, and concealed identity.

LONDON & PARISIAN FASHIONS.
"Look here, upon this picture!"

The first fashion plate Hale published in Ladies' Magazine *(November 1830), the periodical she edited from 1828 until 1837*

Hale's presence in the *Lady's Book* was most felt, however, in her editorial essays. While the topics ranged widely during her forty years with the magazine, Hale repeatedly returned to favorite topics, especially those focusing on women's role in society. Hale was a passionate supporter of improved education for women and more opportunities for women to work, but she opposed women's right to vote, explaining that women already influenced politics by their influence on men in their families. As she explained in an April 1852 editorial, American women already vote "by [their] proxies. This is the way American women should vote, namely, by influencing rightly the votes of men."

While some twentieth-century scholars have characterized Hale, a woman of considerable public influence, as hypocritical for refusing to support women's suffrage, more recent scholarship has placed her stance in the context of theories of gender popular at the time. Like many Victorians, Hale frequently attested to the inherent differences between men and women. As she explained in her inaugural editorial for the *Lady's Book,* "The strength of man's character is in his physical propensities—the strength of woman lies in her moral sentiments." Believing in such an absolute sexual difference, Hale endorsed the idea that men and women inhabit "separate spheres." Thus, while Hale was constantly trying to extend the range of women's influence, she never abandoned the idea that women's moral sentiments made them ill-suited for particular public arenas—including politics.

While Hale never accepted the idea that women would have any direct involvement in national politics, she did occasionally use her writings, as did many other authors of the day, to influence American attitudes. In 1852–shortly after Harriet Beecher Stowe's *Uncle Tom's Cabin* became extremely popular–Hale revised and republished her novel *Northwood* as *Northwood; or, Life North and South: Showing the True Character of Both,* with two new chapters that focus specifically on the moral dilemma over slavery. A year later she published her book *Liberia; or, Mr. Peyton's Experiments,* which supports the American Colonization Society.

As the preface to the revised *Northwood* makes clear, maintaining the Union was a central and primary concern for Hale. "The great error of those who would sever the Union rather than see a slave within its borders," she insists, "is, that they forget the *master* is their brother, as well as the *servant;* and that the spirit which seeks to do good to all and evil to none is the only true Christian philanthropy." Hale's willingness to engage in political subjects and her devotion to maintaining the Union are also demonstrated by her efforts during the political upheaval of the 1850s to establish Thanksgiving as a national holiday. Believing that a nation that shared a meal together would come together as a family rather than divide itself, Hale wrote essays in the *Lady's Book,* urging readers and public officials to join her cause. In November 1859, for example, she asked readers, "If every State should join in union thanksgiving on the 24th of this month, would it not be a renewed pledge of love and loyalty to the Constitution of the United States, which guarantees peace, prosperity, progress, and perpetuity to our great Republic?"

Hale's political writings represent a small fraction of her writings. Much more typical of her book publications during the forty years she edited the *Lady's Book* were her literary productions. In addition to her own volumes of poetry–including *Alice Ray: A Romance in Rhyme* (1845), *Three Hours; or, The Vigil of Love: and Other Poems* (1848), and *Love: or, Woman's Destiny. A Poem in Two Parts: With Other Poems* (1870)–Hale proved tireless in editing collections of poetry. Many of these collections–such as *The Ladies' Wreath; A Selection from the Female Poetic Writers of England and America* (1837; revised, 1839) and *The Opal: A Pure Gift for All Seasons* (1845, 1848, 1849)–were so-called gift books as well, collections designed to be given as gifts, often for particular holidays. Hale was a frequent contributor to gift books–some edited by herself and some by others.

Hale's editorship of many gift books demonstrates the extent to which she established herself as a capable editor both in the book-publishing industry and in periodicals. In general, each of Hale's edited texts focuses on one or more of her interests. Without ever

Louis A. Godey, publisher of Lady's Book *magazine, which Hale edited from January 1837 until December 1877*

interrupting her editorship of the *Lady's Book,* for example, she edited many texts for children, including a ten-volume series published in the 1840s titled *The Little Boys' and Girls' Library,* a collection of Mary Hughs's tales titled *Aunt Mary's New Stories for Young People* (1849), and *The Bible Reading-Book* (1854). Hale's lifelong commitment to women writers is similarly demonstrated by her editorship of *The Letters of Madame de Sévigné, to Her Daughter and Friends* (1856) and *The Letters of Lady Mary Wortley Montagu* (1856).

Similarly, Hale's interest in domestic arts–seen throughout the *Lady's Book*–is evident by the publishing of her popular cookbooks and housekeeping manuals, including *The Ladies' New Book of Cookery: A Practical System for Private Families in Town and Country* (1852) and *Mrs. Hale's Receipts for the Million* (1857). In these books and the magazine Hale repeatedly portrayed women's domestic work as complex and important. In *Mrs. Hale's Receipts for the Million,* for example, she provided instruction on cooking, beekeeping, quilting, and dairy management, and she argued that the health of the nation was dependent on women's expertise in cooking. Hale also repeatedly sought to improve the status of women's domestic work–characterizing cooking and needlework, for example, as arts.

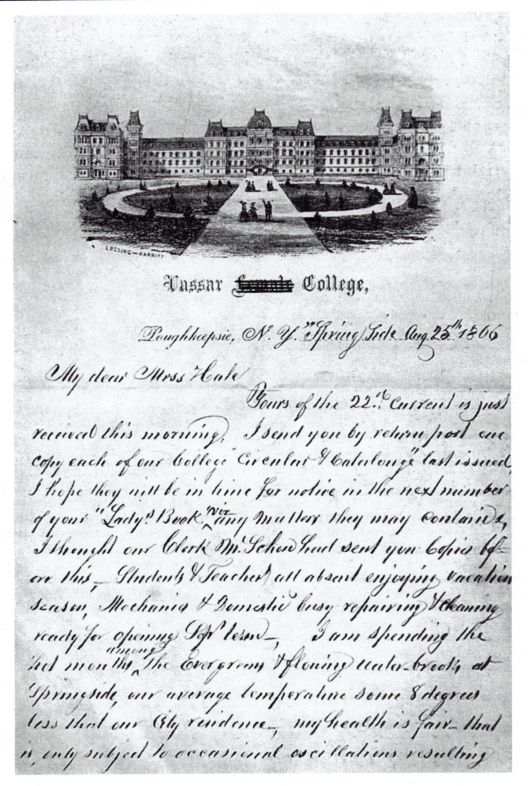

First page of a letter from Matthew Vassar, whose college for women was endorsed by Hale. Her objections to the word female
in the original charter of the institution influenced Vassar to change the name (Vassar College)

One of Hale's most ambitious projects outside of the magazine was the publication of *Woman's Record; or, Sketches of All Distinguished Women from 'The Beginning' till A.D. 1850* (1853). As its subtitle suggests, this nine-hundred-page reference work provided readers with biographical sketches on and often excerpts of writing from more than 1,600 women, ranging from Sappho and Cleopatra to Emma Willard and Hale herself.

Hale's diverse accomplishments as both an editor and an author can perhaps help explain the occasional confusion about her precise contribution to certain texts. Late in her life Hale was accused of plagiarizing "Mary Had a Little Lamb," though she and her children passionately defended her authorship of the poem. More recently scholars continue to describe Hale as the author of *My Cousin Mary; or The Inebriate* (1839) and *The Lecturess; or Woman's Sphere* (1839). Bibliographic experts, however, have argued persuasively that Hale contributed only the preface to *My Cousin Mary*.

The quantity and quality of Hale's writings both within and outside the *Lady's Book* earned her the respect of her peers, and she was included in most of the important literary anthologies of her day. Hale's productivity as a writer and editor continued almost until her death. Her last editorial appeared in December 1877, when, at the age of eighty-nine, she and her longtime publisher, Louis Godey, announced their respective retirements. Though the magazine survived until 1898, its quality suffered after the loss of Hale and Godey. Hale herself died on 30 April 1879, little more than a year after her retirement. Obituaries remembered her as an important and influential member of American literary life, a "venerable authoress and editress."

Biographies:

Ruth E. Finley, *The Lady of Godey's: Sarah Josepha Hale* (Philadelphia: J. B. Lippincott, 1931);

Norma R. Fryatt, *Sarah Josepha Hale: The Life and Times of a Nineteenth-Century Career Woman* (New York: Hawthorn, 1975);

Sherbrooke Rogers, *Sarah Josepha Hale: A New England Pioneer, 1788–1879* (Grantham, N.H.: Tompson & Rutter, 1985).

References:

Barbara A. Bardes and Suzanne Gossett, "Sarah J. Hale, Selective Promoter of Her Sex," in *A Living of Words: American Women in Print Culture,* edited by Susan Albertine (Knoxville: University of Tennessee Press, 1995), pp. 18–34;

Bardes and Gossett, "Women and Political Power in the Republic: Two Early American Novels," *Legacy,* 2 (Fall 1985): 13–30;

Nina Baym, "Onward Christian Women: Sarah J. Hale's History of the World," *New England Quarterly,* 63 (June 1990): 249–270;

Isabelle Webb Entrikin, *Sarah Josepha Hale and "Godey's Lady's Book"* (Philadelphia: University of Pennsylvania, 1946);

Nicole Tonkovich Hoffman, "*Legacy* Profile: Sarah Josepha Hale," *Legacy,* 7 (Fall 1990): 47–55;

Patricia Okker, *Our Sister Editors: Sarah J. Hale and the Tradition of Nineteenth-Century American Women Editors* (Athens & London: University of Georgia Press, 1995);

Nicole Tonkovich, *Domesticity with a Difference: The Nonfiction of Catharine Beecher, Sarah J. Hale, Fanny Fern, and Margaret Fuller* (Jackson: University Press of Mississippi, 1997).

Papers:

Sarah Josepha Hale's papers are scattered in many libraries. The Pierpont Morgan Library in New York, the Henry E. Huntington Library in California, Harvard University, Vassar College, and the Historical Society of Pennsylvania have the largest collections of Hale's letters.

Isaac Thomas Hecker

(18 December 1819 – 22 December 1888)

Patricia Dunlavy Valenti
University of North Carolina at Pembroke

See also the Hecker entry in *DLB 1: The American Renaissance in New England.*

BOOKS: *Questions of the Soul* (New York: Appleton, 1855);

Aspirations of Nature (New York: James B. Kirker, 1857);

An Exposition of the Church in View of Recent Difficulties and Controversies, and the Present Needs of the Age (London: Basil Montagu, 1875);

The Catholic Church in the United States. Its Rise, Relations with the Republic, Growth, and Future Prospects (New York: Catholic Publication Society, 1879);

Catholics and Protestants Agreeing on the School Question (New York: Catholic Publication Society, 1881);

Martin Luther. Protestantism vs. The Church. Luther and the Diet of Worms (New York: Catholic Publication Society, 1883);

The Church and the Age; An Exposition of the Catholic Church in View of the Needs and Aspirations of the Present Age (New York: Catholic Publication Society, 1887);

Isaac T. Hecker: The Diary: Romantic Religion in Ante-bellum America, edited by John Farina (New York: Paulist Press, 1988).

OTHER: *The Young Converts; or, Memoirs of the Three Sisters, Debbie, Helen and Anna Barlow,* as compiled by a lady, edited by Hecker (New York: P. O'Shea, 1861);

Juliana Anchoret, *Sixteen Revelations of Divine Love,* preface by Hecker (Boston: Ticknor & Fields, 1864);

Cattaneo Marabotto, *Life and Doctrine of St. Catherine of Genoa,* edited, with preface and introduction, by Hecker, translated by Sophia Ripley (New York: Catholic Publication Society, 1874).

SELECTED PERIODICAL PUBLICATIONS–
UNCOLLECTED: "The Present and Future Prospects of the Catholic Faith in the United States of North America," *Freeman's Journal* (12, 19, 26 December 1857; 2 January 1858);

Isaac Thomas Hecker (portrait by George P. A. Healy; Paulist Center, Boston)

"The Transcendental Movement in New England," *Catholic World,* 23 (July 1876): 528–537;

"The True and False Friends of Reason," *Catholic World,* 33 (June 1881): 289–298;

"What Does the Public-School Question Mean?" *Catholic World,* 34 (October 1881): 84–90;

"Catholic Musings on Tennyson's 'In Memoriam,'" *Catholic World,* 34 (November 1881): 205–211;

"The Liberty and Independence of the Pope," *Catholic World,* 35 (April 1882): 1–10;

"Protestantism vs. the Church," *Catholic World,* 38 (October 1883): 1–13;

THE

CATHOLIC WORLD.

VOL. I, NO. 1.—APRIL, 1865.

From Le Correspondant.

THE PROGRESS OF THE CHURCH IN THE UNITED STATES.

BY R. RAMEAU.

[THE following article will no doubt be interesting to our readers, not only for its intrinsic merit and its store of valuable information, but also as a record of the impressions made upon an intelligent foreign Catholic, during a visit to this country. As might have been expected, the author has not escaped some errors in his historical and statistical statements—most of which we have noted in their appropriate places. It will also be observed that while exaggerating the importance of the early French settlements in the development of Catholicism in the United States, he has not given the Irish immigrants as much credit as they deserve. But despite these faults, which are such as a Frenchman might readily commit, the article will amply repay reading.—ED. CATHOLIC WORLD.]

AFTER the Spaniards had discovered the New World, and while they were fighting against the Pagan civilization of the southern portions of the continent, the French made the first [permanent] European settlement on the shores of America. They founded Port Royal, in Acadia, in 1604, and from that time their missionaries began to go forth among the savages of the North. It was not until 1620 that the first colony of English Puritans landed in Massachusetts, and it then seemed not improbable that Catholicism was destined to be the dominant religion of the New World; but subsequent Anglo-Saxon immigration and political vicissitudes so changed matters, that by the end of the last century one might well have believed that Protestantism was finally and completely established throughout North America. God, however, prepares his ways according to his own good pleasure; and he knows how to bring about secret and unforeseen changes, which set at naught all the calculations of man. The weakness and internal disorders of the Catholic nations, in the eighteenth century, retarded only for a moment the progress of the Catholic Church; and Providence, combining the despised efforts of those who seemed weak with the faults of those who seemed strong, confounded the superficial judgments of philosophers, and prepared the way for a speedy religious transformation of America.

This transformation is going on in our own times with a vigor which seems to increase every year. The

First page of the inaugural issue of a magazine Hecker helped to found

"Dr. Brownson and the Workingman's Party Fifty Years Ago," *Catholic World,* 45 (May 1887): 200–207;

"Dr. Brownson's Road to the Church," *Catholic World,* 46 (October 1887): 1–11;

"Dr. Brownson and Catholicity," *Catholic World,* 46 (November 1887): 222–235;

"Race Divisions and the School Question," *Catholic World,* 46 (March 1888): 736–742;

"The Things that Make for Unity," *Catholic World,* 47 (April 1888): 102–109.

Born into an immigrant family of successful bakers, Isaac Hecker was motivated by the dual desires to cultivate personal, mystical experience and to ameliorate social problems. The attempt to synthesize these somewhat disparate longings took him on a journey through eclectic political and religious movements. He participated briefly in the experimental utopian communities of Brook Farm and Fruitlands, where he examined Transcendentalism before his conversion to Roman Catholicism. He quickly joined the priesthood, first as a member of the Belgian order of Redemptorists and then as the founder of the Paulist Priests, a group that has become a leader in Catholic publication in America.

On 18 December 1819, Isaac Thomas Hecker was born to John and Caroline (Freund) Hecker, who had wed in 1811. Natives of Prussia, the Heckers had

Chapel of the Redemptorist novitiate at St. Trond, Belgium, where Hecker studied for the priesthood (Paulist Archives, Washington, D.C.)

arrived in New York City before the turn of the century and had four other children by the time of Isaac's birth: John (1812), a second son who died as an infant, Elizabeth (1816), and George (1818). By 1830 the elder John Hecker had abandoned his family. Brothers John and George Hecker became successful in the baking business with their respective inventions, a machine that mixed the ingredients for bread into a dough ready for the oven and a floating grain elevator. These wealthy brothers, particularly George, supported Isaac in his many ventures.

Caroline Hecker was a significant force in her son Isaac's religious formation. As a member of the Methodist Forsythe Street Church, she took Isaac to services with her. Caroline Hecker was tolerant of other religions, though she herself subscribed to the perfectionist movement, which held that holiness could be attained by the common person through everyday experience as well as through specific beliefs and moral actions. Opposing belief in the depravity of human nature and

the doctrine of election espoused by the Calvinists, the Methodist position provided a groundwork for Hecker's religious thought.

Hecker recounted later in his life that as early as age twelve he desired to know the truth and to do good. This quest was abetted by several eclectic political and religious movements in addition to the early influence of his mother's Methodism. During the financially turbulent 1830s Hecker became interested in the Equal Rights, or Loco Foco, Party, which, with its distrust of the banking system and its Jacksonian support of hard currency, was gaining ever increasing support from the common citizen. During the crash of 1837 when the cost of necessities rose precipitously, the "flour riots" spurred the younger John Hecker into joining the Loco Focos. After that party disbanded, he continued his political activism as the Free-Soil Party candidate for congress in 1850 and the Citizen's Association candidate for mayor of New York in 1865. Significant to the development of Isaac Hecker's religious thought was that the Loco Focos absorbed the principles of Christian Democracy, which stressed the application of Christian ideals to the solution of societal problems.

With the dissolution of the Loco Foco Party, Hecker began to examine the ideas of various contemporary religious thinkers. Hecker attended the church of Orville Dewey, a Unitarian minister who rejected both the impersonal God of the Deists and the wrathful God of the Calvinists. Through Dewey, Hecker encountered once again the notion that spiritual enlightenment could be found in every activity, no matter how mundane. Maintaining his interest in the uses of religion for societal amelioration and political reform, Hecker was thus attracted to Joseph Smith's doctrines, which he studied with a Mormon teacher, Parley S. Pratt. The "United Order" was the term used by the Mormons to designate a social order intended to abolish poverty and achieve social equality. Members of this United Order were expected to adhere to thirteen ordinances that coincided with the ascetic regime Hecker himself practiced.

The most significant person Hecker met during this period of intense religious inquiry was Orestes Brownson. Also a seeker of religious truth and spiritual enlightenment, Brownson had made his own ideological journey through Presbyterianism, Universalism, agnosticism, Unitarianism, and Transcendentalism. When Hecker encountered him in 1841, Brownson had begun the process of examining Roman Catholicism, the religion to which he adhered as a major American spokesman for the rest of his life. Brownson, like Hecker and his brothers John and George, was deeply concerned with questions of social reform, and the Hecker brothers eagerly attended Brownson's lecture

"The Democracy of Christ" in February 1841. So affected were the Heckers by this lecture that they arranged to have Brownson give a series of lectures in July 1841 and January 1842, the moment when Brownson was most ready to articulate his evolving ideas on Christian Democracy. Isaac Hecker became Orestes Brownson's apt pupil, and Brownson introduced Hecker to the works of Johann Gottlieb Fichte and Immanuel Kant, philosophers who precipitated Hecker's questioning the validity of his subjective experience of God.

As Hecker sought to respond to the demands of his inner life, he became increasingly fatigued by the stress of poising such a life within the worldly demands of the baking business, and 1842 became a year of crisis. Hecker experienced a series of disturbing dreams, the most intense of which he identified as not a dream at all, since he was seated beside his bed in July 1842 when it occurred. In what he described as a vision, Hecker saw an angelic being beside him who exuded celestial happiness; both he and the angel inhabited unclothed, luminous bodies, and Hecker's sense of unity with this angelic being infused his conscious life with an unsatisfied ideal. Hecker now desired unconditional commitment to a religious life, and at Brownson's suggestion Hecker sought out Brook Farm as a possible means to that end.

With a letter of introduction from Brownson, Hecker arrived at George Ripley's West Roxbury community on 4 January 1843 for his first experience of communal life. Hecker was impressed with the way in which members of Brook Farm engaged in manual labor together, regardless of their status or former livelihood, and other members of the commune were likewise impressed with the affable young man who brought to their establishment much needed expertise as a breadmaker, in addition to the $5.50 he paid weekly for full board. Brook Farm also provided Hecker with the opportunity for formal study of philosophy, in which he engaged with moderate diligence. Although Brook Farm offered Hecker an environment that addressed his interest in social amelioration through the application of philosophical and religious principles, the community did not satisfy his need for spiritual enlightenment.

Within six months Hecker found Brook Farm to be insufficiently rigorous, and he departed for Fruitlands, where he hoped that the radical aspect of Bronson Alcott's experiment would better answer his needs. There Hecker believed that what he characterized as the self-centered, self-indulgent negativity of Brook Farm would be replaced by true interdependence and generosity fostered by Alcott's goal of a self-sufficient community and more disciplined per-

Clarence Walworth, who accompanied Hecker to Europe to study at the novitiate in Belgium (Paulist Archives, Washington, D.C.)

sonal life. The library at Fruitlands made a wide variety of texts available to Hecker, from the works of François de Salignac de La Mothe-Fénélon and Emanuel Swedenborg typically found in mid-nineteenth-century collections to works by Catholic writers and mystics such as Julian of Norwich, St. Brigit of Kildare, Francis of Sales, and Thomas à Kempis. Shortly after his arrival Hecker engaged in a discussion with Sam Larned, Charles Lane, and Alcott himself on the topic of the "Highest Aim." Hecker contributed the notion that the highest aim in life was "Harmonic Being," something that he shortly realized he would not find at Fruitlands, so after only two weeks Hecker departed. At Fruitlands as at Brook Farm, Hecker did not find the answers to the gnawing spiritual questions he was asking, and he turned to the Catholic Church.

*George Deshon, Augustine Hewit, and Francis Baker, who with Hecker were the first members of the Congregation of the Missionary Priests of St. Paul
the Apostle (Paulist Archives, Washington, D.C.)*

The Paulist Fathers' first chapel and living quarters on West 59th Street, New York (Paulist Archives, Washington, D.C.)

Hecker's neglect of philosophical study at Brook Farm had been a facet of his growing distrust—in Emersonian fashion—of the thought of others as the key to his spiritual life. Hecker was drawn to Quietism and mystical experience generally. Yet, he could not accept the Transcendentalists' faith in radical individuality or the Emersonian affirmation of idealism as the sole authority for his inner experience, and he became increasingly persuaded by Brownson's position regarding the necessity for a mediating institution that could validate personal religious experience. Upon returning to New York City, Hecker deliberated about joining the Anglican Church or the Roman Catholic Church while he continued with both his strict discipline and his socially responsible practices. He became a vegetarian, and he started a reading room for employees of the bakery. Eventually he came to believe that in the Roman Catholic Church subjective mystical experience and objective authoritative affirmation could coexist. On 2 August 1844, after six weeks of instruction based upon the *Catechism of the Council of Trent,* a work that became Hecker's lifelong favorite textbook, Bishop John McCloskey received Hecker into

the Catholic Church at the old St. Patrick's Church on Mott Street in New York City.

Hecker and all those associated with the process of his conversion realized that the lay life would be insufficient to satisfy his religious aspirations. Thus, he turned to the priesthood and began a course of study in the Redemptorist novitiate at St. Trond in Belgium. He was accompanied there by two recent Episcopalian converts to Catholicism, James McMaster and Clarence Walworth. McMaster soon abandoned the Redemptorists, but Walworth—a superior student, who had been born in 1820 in Saratoga, New York, to a distinguished family—was ordained in 1845. Hecker, a lackluster student, was not ordained until 23 October 1849, but he became imbued with Catholic thought by reading John of the Cross, Catherine of Genoa, and Louis Lallemant, all the while keeping in touch with American religious issues by reading the *Brownson Quarterly Review.*

Slightly more than a year after his ordination, Hecker returned with Walworth to the United States, where the men were joined by Augustine Francis Hewit, also a convert and the son of a Congregationalist minister from Bridgeport, Connecticut. Hewit had been educated at Philips Andover and Amherst. Hecker, Walworth, and Hewit became part of the Redemptorists' initiative to provide missions to English-speaking parishes, the first of which took place on 6 April 1851. The Redemptorists believed that their purpose in the United States was to sustain the faith of Roman Catholics, who were a minority in a mission land where they were often immigrants and just as often despised, not only because of their faith but also because of their poverty, their cultural differences, and their social practices. Walworth, Hewit, and Hecker formed a complementary and highly effective unit that could claim that their missions contributed to the improved behavior, and thus improved acceptance, of the Catholics they addressed. Hewit brought dignity and refinement to the trio; Walworth brought oratorical powers; and Hecker proved an adept teacher.

During 1854 Hecker turned his instructional gifts to writing *Questions of the Soul,* which was published in the summer of 1855. This book brought Hecker to national attention as an apologist for Roman Catholicism while situating his doctrinal presentation within the ideology of self-culture so central to contemporary American Transcendentalists. For Hecker the choice of Catholicism was inextricably bound to the indigenously American right to live out the consequences of one's own thought and insight. Deploying a logic akin to the one Emerson had announced in "Self-Reliance," Hecker espoused the American right to follow one's own lights in matters of religion, free from the fetters of historical precedent. The mind desires truth and the heart good, he asserted (indeed, he claimed that as a boy of twelve he had sought these qualities), and he used as evidence of this desire the utopian experiments in which he had participated more than a decade earlier. The Roman Catholic Church, Hecker claimed, was the most complete and satisfactory answer to the questions of the soul. The book garnered favorable notices from many quarters—Catholic and non-Catholic alike. Brownson was, of course, fulsome in his praise, as was George Bancroft, who found that the book articulated the significant issues of the era.

Pleased with the success of *Questions of the Soul,* Hecker in 1857, with George Ripley's help, published *Aspirations of Nature.* Hecker attempted to argue the reasonableness of Catholic belief amidst a new wave of anti-Catholic sentiment in the form of the Know Nothing movement. This second, more controversial book did not enjoy an enthusiastic response, even from Brownson, who thought the timing of Hecker's presentation ill-advised and distrusted Hecker's endorsement of the Transcendental belief in the natural inclination of human beings toward the divine.

Meanwhile, Hecker and his band of priests had continued their missions, expanding their audiences to include non-Catholics. The first such event took place in Norfolk, Virginia, in March 1856, the year that George Deshon and Francis Baker joined what had formerly been a group of three. Deshon had been raised as a Congregationalist and had graduated from West Point in the same class with Ulysses S. Grant; Baker, a highly effective preacher, was a convert from Episcopalianism. Hecker now aspired to convert America to his religion, but the Redemptorist officials continued to define their mission as ministering to the needs of Catholics, specifically the German-speaking immigrants. Thus, by the end of 1856, Hecker and his band of four other priests found themselves at odds with their Redemptorist superior, Father George Ruland. Hecker and his cohorts decided that he should travel to Rome to seek sanction for their work from Father Nicholas Mauron, the Redemptorist superior there—an action specifically forbidden by Ruland. George Hecker financed his brother Isaac's trip, and in Rome, Mauron expelled Hecker from the order for insubordination.

Hecker then sought an audience with the Pope, Pius IX, and attempted to clarify perhaps the central issue in nineteenth-century American Catholicism—its allegiance to the Vatican in a country founded upon principles of religious freedom and growing pluralism. He wrote a series of articles for the *Civiltà Cattolica.* He won the favor of the influential officials Cardinal Barnabò and Archbishop Bedini. Hecker also converted to Catholicism George Loring Brown, a painter and member of the community of American expatriate artists in Rome; thus, Hecker emphasized his efficacy in attracting non-Catholic Americans to the Catholic Church. Hecker was received by the Pope in March 1858 and obtained his blessing to become a missionary in the United States, something that could best be accomplished outside of the Redemptorist order. By July 1858 Hewit, Deshon, and Baker (Walworth was not a signator), led by Hecker, signed a governing rule and constitution for the Congregation of the Missionary Priests of St. Paul the Apostle, a group of native-born American priests. The Paulists, as they were henceforth known, demonstrated through their various works the possibility of being both an American and a Catholic. Devoted to the dual ends of the sanctity of its members through a common life and the effort to save others, the Paulists differed from other religious orders by not requiring permanent vows of its members and by de-emphasizing the vow of obedience, thereby institutionalizing Hecker's belief that the individual's fidelity to the leadings of the spirit would inevitably conform with the will of the Church.

With Hecker's return to the United States, the order grew, although it was faced with a shortage of priests because of the death or defection of members, a fact that contributed to Hecker's ill health and depression. In the first years of the order only converts were drawn to become Paulists. In 1872 Adrian Rosecrans, the son of one of Deshon's classmates at West Point, became the first man born to the Catholic religion admitted to the order. Hecker had purchased land in New York City and formed St. Paul's parish, which became known for the quality of its priests' oratory. Hecker himself became a compelling speaker who, like his Protestant counterparts Henry Ward Beecher and Phillips Brooks, sought to apply Christian principles to contemporary conditions. In 1868 James Parton announced in *The Atlantic Monthly* that Hecker was thrusting America into a new era. Although Hecker wished for the Paulists to create a model parish, the order achieved lasting renown primarily for their publications.

Hecker became the spiritual adviser for Jane King, who had been a member of James T. Fields's staff at the *Atlantic Monthly*. In his extensive correspondence with her, Hecker articulated fundamental principles of his religious thought—that the Spirit directs the soul, that goodness is to be found in all creation, and that perfection can be acquired through all activity. Hecker discussed with King the mystical writings of Julian of Norwich, Francis of Sales, Catherine of Genoa, and Lallemant, among others, and he realized that there was no Catholic publication that could readily bring these discussions to the American public.

In 1865 Hecker formulated plans to publish a monthly magazine, *The Catholic World,* with the backing of his brother George's money. *The Catholic World* provided Brownson with a vehicle for expression— the *Brownson Quarterly Review* having ceased publication because of the controversies surrounding Brownson's positions. Hecker remained on good terms with Brownson though the two grew apart ideologically, Brownson viewing Hecker as too liberal and accepting of positions outside the Catholic Church. At first *The Catholic World* culled material from other publications, but by 1866 it had begun printing original material. In 1866 Hecker founded the Catholic Publication Society with the intention of spreading Catholic doctrine beyond the confines of religious institutions, reaching those in the armed forces, prisons, and hospitals. One of the earliest efforts of the Catholic Publication Society was the *Young Catholic,*

Hecker, circa 1870, the year in which he started his Young Catholic *magazine (Paulist Archives, Washington, D.C.)*

begun in 1870; in 1874 the society published *Life and Doctrine of St. Catherine of Genoa.* Sophia Ripley, who herself had become a Catholic convert and who had, with her husband, George, been one of the founders of Brook Farm, translated Cattaneo Marabotto's *Vita della beata Catherina Adorni da Genoua* (1589). Hecker supplied the preface to this work, which he was delighted to publish because of Protestant interest in Catherine of Genoa (also known as Catherine Adorna), a laywoman who exemplified the attainment of perfection in daily life.

Hecker had clearly reached the pinnacle of his career. As a leading spokesman for American Catholicism, he was invited to Malines, Belgium, as vice president at the International Catholic Congress, which he attended in the fall of 1867. Hecker also attended the First Vatican Council in Rome, where he was among those who believed that promulgating the doctrine of the infallibility of the Pope was inopportune, a position that did not prevail. Disheartened by this turn of events, at the breaking point in his relation with Brownson, and at odds with members of his own community, Hecker became depressed and ill as he had at moments of stress earlier in his life. Enthusiasm for his lifelong work diminished, and he traveled extensively, seeing firsthand in Egypt religions extremely different from his own. He did not believe diverse nations should forfeit their cultures when they acquired Christianity. During 1874, as his health and circumstances allowed, he worked on "The Church and Europe, with a Glance at the Future," a title he changed to *An Exposition of the Church in View of Recent Difficulties and Controversies, and the Present Needs of the Age* (1875). Although Hecker had been assured permission to publish, that permission was withdrawn by Roman authorities. After much reflection Hecker published *An Exposition of the Church in View of Recent Difficulties and Controversies, and the Present Needs of the Age* without hierarchical sanction with Basil Montagu Company in London and then in the *Catholic World*. *An Exposition of the Church in View of Recent Difficulties and Controversies, and the Present Needs of the Age* was published again, basically unchanged, as the first chapter of Hecker's last book, *The Church and the Age,* published in 1887. *An Exposition of the Church in View of Recent Difficulties and Controversies, and the Present Needs of the Age* was a call to renewal and trust in the Spirit as the source for individual and societal remedy.

When Hecker returned from his travels in 1875, he resided with his brother George for four years. His prolonged absences from community life as well as his bouts of illness caused a faction within the Paulists to attempt unsuccessfully to have him removed from his position as their superior. Hecker's acceptance of these events at this phase of his life was paralleled by a simi-

lar lack of contentiousness in other areas. He continued to prefer stressing commonalities between Christian denominations rather than their differences. Isaac Hecker died in the New York City community of Paulist priests on 22 December 1888.

Letters:

Joseph F. Gower and Richard M. Leliaret, eds., *The Brownson-Hecker Correspondence* (South Bend, Ind.: Notre Dame University Press, 1979).

Biographies:

Walter Elliott, *The Life of Father Hecker* (New York: Columbus, 1891);

David O'Brien, *Isaac Hecker: An American Catholic* (New York: Paulist Press, 1992).

References:

John Farina, *An American Experience of God: The Spirituality of Isaac Hecker* (New York: Paulist Press, 1981);

Farina, ed., *Hecker Studies: Essays on the Thought of Isaac Hecker* (New York: Paulist Press, 1983);

Joseph McSorley, *Father Hecker and His Friends* (St. Louis: B. Herder, 1952); republished as *Isaac Hecker and His Friends* (New York: Paulist Press, 1972).

Papers:

The largest single repository of Isaac Thomas Hecker materials, the Isaac T. Hecker Papers in forty-seven boxes, is at the Paulist Archives in Washington, D.C. The University of Notre Dame Archives at South Bend, Indiana, house the Brownson-Hecker correspondence.

Frederic Henry Hedge

(12 December 1805 – 21 August 1890)

Guy R. Woodall
Tennessee Technological University

See also the Hedge entries in *DLB 1: The American Renaissance in New England* and *DLB 59: American Literary Critics and Scholars, 1800–1850.*

BOOKS: *A Sermon Preached Before the Ancient and Honorable Artillery Company, on their CXCVIth Anniversary, June 2, 1834* (Boston: J. H. Eastburn, 1834);

An Introductory Lecture, Delivered at the Opening of the Bangor Lyceum, Nov. 15th, 1836 (Bangor: Nourse & Smith / Duren & Thatcher, 1836);

An Oration, Pronounced Before the Citizens of Bangor, on the Fourth of July, 1838 (Bangor: Samuel S. Smith, 1838);

Practical Goodness the True Religion. A Sermon, Preached at Union-Street Church, March 1, 1840 (Bangor: Samuel S. Smith, 1840);

A Discourse on the Death of William Henry Harrison, Ninth President of the United States. Delivered Before the Independent Congregational Society, on the Day of the National Fast, May 14, 1841 (Bangor: Samuel S. Smith, 1841);

A Sermon on the Character and Ministry of the Late Rev. William Ellery Channing, D.D. Preached in the Independent Congregational Church, Bangor, at the Annual Thanksgiving, Nov. 17th, 1842 (Bangor: Samuel S. Smith, 1842);

Conservatism and Reform. An Oration Pronounced Before the Peucinian Society, Bowdoin College, September 5, 1843 (Boston: Little, Brown, 1843);

Christianity Confined to No Sect. A Sermon Preached at the Dedication of the Church, Presented to the Town of Stetson, by the Hon. Amasa Stetson of Dorchester, Mass. February 22, 1844 (Bangor: Samuel S. Smith, 1844);

Gospel Invitations (Boston: Crosby, Nichols, 1846);

The Leaven of the Word. A Sermon Preached at the Ordination of Rev. Joshua Young, as Pastor of the New North Church in Boston, Thursday, Feb. 1, 1849 (Boston: Dutton & Wentworth, 1849);

An Address Delivered Before the Graduating Class of the Divinity School in Cambridge, July 15, 1849 (Cambridge: John Bartlett, 1849);

Frederic Henry Hedge

A Sermon Preached to the Independent Congregational Society, March 3d, 1850, by Frederic H. Hedge, on Closing His Pastoral Connexion with that Society (Bangor: Samuel S. Smith, 1850);

Conscience and the State. A Discourse, Preached in the Westminster Church, Sunday April 27, 1851 (Providence: Joseph Knowles, 1851);

Christian Liturgy. For Use of the Church (Boston: Crosby, Nichols, 1853);

On the Use of the Word "Evangelical." A Discourse, by the Pastor of the Westminster Congregational Society (Providence: Knowles, Anthony, 1854);

The Atonement in Connection with the Death of Christ (Boston: American Unitarian Association, 1856);

An Address Delivered at the Funeral of Mrs. Hannah B. Stearns, of Brookline, on Sunday, Nov. 8th, 1857 (Boston: David Clapp, 1857);

Seventeen Hundred Fifty-Eight and Eighteen Hundred Fifty-Eight. A New Year's Discourse, Preached at Brookline, on the first Sunday in January, 1858 (Boston: Phillips, Sampson, 1858);

Oration Delivered at the Schiller Festivity on the 10th of November 1859, in the Boston Music Hall (Boston: H. Vossnack, 1859);

The National Weakness: A Discourse Delivered in the First Church, Brookline, on Fast Day, Sept. 26, 1861 (Boston: Walker, Wise, 1861);

Old Age and Its Lessons. A Sermon Preached in the Church of the First Parish in Brookline, on the Sunday Succeeding the Death of Mr. Benjamin Goddard, November 3, 1861 (Boston: H. W. Dutton, 1861);

The Sick Woman. A Sermon for the Time (Boston: Prentiss & Deland, 1863);

The National Entail. A Sermon Preached to the First Congregational Church in Brookline, on the 3d July, 1864 (Boston: Wright & Potter, 1864);

Discourse on Edward Everett, Delivered in the Church of the First Parish, Brookline, on the Twenty-Second, January, 1865 (Boston: George C. Rand & Avery, 1865);

Reason in Religion (Boston: Walker, Fuller, 1865);

Memoir of Nathaniel Langdon Frothingham, D.D. (Boston: John Wilson, 1870);

The Primeval World of Hebrew Tradition (Boston: Roberts, 1870);

A Sermon Preached at the Ordination of Mr. Francis T. Washburn as Associate Pastor of the First Congregational Parish in Milton, on Thursday, March 2, 1871 (Boston: Alfred Mudge, 1871);

Shall the Nation by a Change in Its Constitution, Proclaim Itself Christian? A Sermon Preached in the First Parish Church in Brookline, on February 25, 1872 (Cambridge: John Wilson, 1872);

German Prepositions (Cambridge: Charles W. Sever, 1875);

Ways of the Spirit, and Other Essays (Boston: Roberts, 1877);

Theological Progress During the Last Half-Century. A Sermon (Providence, R.I.: Knowles, Anthony, 1878);

Atheism in Philosophy, and Other Essays (Boston: Roberts, 1884);

Hours with German Classics; Masterpieces of German Literature Translated into English (Boston: Roberts, 1886);

Personality and Theism. Two Essays (Cambridge: John Wilson, 1887);

Martin Luther and Other Essays (Boston: Roberts, 1888);

Christmas Hymn (San Francisco: Channing Auxiliary, 1888);

Sermons (Boston: Roberts, 1891);

The Atonement in Connection with the Death of Christ (Boston: American Unitarian Association, n.d.);

The Regent God (Boston: American Unitarian Association, n.d.).

OTHER: *The Prose Writers of Germany,* edited, with translations, by Hedge and others (Philadelphia: Carey & Hart, 1848);

Hymns for the Church of Christ, edited by Hedge and Frederic Dan Huntington (Boston: Crosby & Nichols, 1853);

Recent Inquiries in Theology, By Eminent English Churchmen; Being "Essays and Reviews," edited by Hedge (Boston: Walker, Wise, 1861);

Johann Wolfgang von Goethe, *Faust: A Tragedy, Part I,* edited and annotated by Hedge (New York: T. Y. Crowell, 1882);

Metrical Translations and Poems, by Hedge and Annis Lee Wister (Boston & New York: Houghton, Mifflin, 1888).

SELECTED PERIODICAL PUBLICATIONS–UNCOLLECTED: Review of *Biographia Literaria, The Poetical Works of S. T. Coleridge, Aids to Reflection . . . ,* and *The Friend,* by Samuel Taylor Coleridge, *Christian Examiner,* 14 (March 1833): 108–129;

"Emanuel Swedenborg," *Christian Examiner,* 15 (November 1833): 193–218;

Review of *The Life of Friederich Schiller,* by Thomas Carlyle, *Christian Examiner,* 16 (July 1834): 365–392;

"The Art of Life, the Scholar's Calling," *Dial,* 1 (1840): 175–182;

Review of *Writings of Ralph Waldo Emerson, Christian Examiner,* 38 (January 1845): 87–106;

"Natural Religion," *Christian Examiner,* 52 (January 1852): 117–136;

Review of *The Life and Works of Goethe,* by G. H. Lewes, *North American Review,* 82 (April 1856): 564–568;

Review of "Brooks's *Faust," Christian Examiner,* 63 (January 1857): 1–18;

Review of *Pre-Raffaellitism; or, A Popular Inquiry into Some Newly Asserted Principles Connected with the Poetry, Philosophy and Religion, and Revolution of Art,* by Edward Young, *Christian Examiner,* 63 (September 1857): 290–291;

"Antisupernaturalism in the Pulpit," *Christian Examiner,*
77 (September 1864): 145–159;
"University Reform," *Atlantic Monthly,* 18 (September
1866): 296–307;
"The Destinies of Ecclesiastical Religion," *Christian
Examiner,* 82 (January 1867): 1–15;
"Characteristics of Genius," *Atlantic Monthly,* 21 (February 1868): 150–159;
"The Broad Church," *Christian Examiner,* 69 (July
1869): 53–66;
"Irony," *Atlantic Monthly,* 24 (October 1870): 414–428;
"The Idealist and the Realist," *Unitarian Review,* 9
(March 1878): 320–328;
"Emerson the Philosopher and the Poet," *Literary World,*
25 May 1882, pp. 176–177;
"The Steps of Beauty," *Unitarian Review,* 18 (December
1882): 481–493;
"Classic and Romantic," *Atlantic Monthly,* 57 (March
1886): 309–316;
"Review of *A Memoir of Ralph Waldo Emerson,* by James
Elliot Cabot," *Unitarian Review,* 28 (November
1887): 416–425;
"Nature: A Problem," *Unitarian Review,* 29 (March
1888): 193–197.

The Reverend Frederic Henry Hedge was an important figure in the cultural history of nineteenth-century America. As a Unitarian minister, theologian, professor of divinity, and language scholar, he exerted a significant influence upon the philosophical, aesthetic, and theological thought of his time. His literary output was formidable. He published more than forty books and pamphlets and sixty-five articles in leading periodicals on a wide range of subjects, as well as many fugitive poems and travel letters, and joint editions. His areas of expertise were language, literature, history, religion, and philosophy. On these subjects he also lectured widely. He was an active member of the American Unitarian Association, Massachusetts Historical Society, Transcendental Club, Town and Country Club, Radical Club, and Examiner Club. As a scholar he was a pioneer in the introduction of German metaphysics, aesthetics, and higher criticism in America. He was a founding figure in the New England Transcendental movement in the first half of the nineteenth century and as a churchman was a precursor of the Broad Church and Social Gospel movements in the last half of the century.

Frederic Henry Hedge was born 12 December 1805 in Cambridge, Massachusetts, to Levi and Mary Kneeland Hedge. His father, a respected professor of logic at Harvard, sent his precocious thirteen-year-old son to Germany in June 1818 under the care of George Bancroft (later an historian) to prepare him for

college. In Germany, Hedge studied the German language and literature in the gymnasia at Göttingen, Ilfeld, and Schulforta. Bancroft, himself only eighteen years old, pursued his own studies and monitored Hedge's progress. Between 1818 and 1822 Hedge began to form Transcendental beliefs as he immersed himself in the works of Immanuel Kant and post-Kantian philosophers. He likewise cultivated an appreciation for the prose of Martin Luther and a passion for the poetry of Friedrich von Schiller and Johann Wolfgang von Goethe.

After returning from Germany in late 1822, Hedge entered Harvard College with advanced standing. He graduated with distinction in 1825. He was the poet of the Hasty Pudding Club and in July 1825 delivered the valedictory poem, "The Student." He was chosen poet of the Phi Beta Kappa Society in 1828. After he received his baccalaureate degree, Harvard offered him an instructorship to teach German, but he refused it in order to continue his studies in theology at the Divinity School. He finished the prescribed course of studies in 1828, but the Divinity School granted no degrees at the time. One of the most enduring friendships that Hedge formed at the Divinity School was with Ralph Waldo Emerson, who, though not formally enrolled, was there preparing for the ministry. Hedge did not influence Emerson's thought, but he did encourage Emerson to publish some of his early lyric poems and to cultivate his intellectual gifts. Hedge attempted, without success at first, to interest Emerson in the German language and German literature. Later, however, with Hedge's help, Emerson gained some proficiency in German. At Harvard, Hedge continued in his own German studies under the tutelage of his early adviser, Edward Everett, who had returned from Germany to teach at his alma mater, and George Ticknor (schooled in Germany), who taught the basics of German higher criticism.

After completing his studies at the Divinity School, Hedge, then nineteen years old, was ordained in May 1829 as pastor in the West Cambridge (now called Arlington) Congregational Church, which at the time was moving into the Unitarian ranks. The Reverend Convers Francis of Watertown, a friend and intellectual companion, preached the ordination sermon, "The Kingdom of God Is Within You" (Luke 17:21), which had a distinctively transcendental sound. Hedge's salary was set at $800 per annum. His ministry at West Cambridge lasted until 1835, during which time he earned a reputation as a scholarly pastor. Hedge once remarked that he sought to reach people through the head rather than through the heart. Wherever he preached he was popular with people from all walks of life, but as a learned preacher he appealed more to the well-educated. On 7 September 1830 Hedge married Lucy Pierce, daughter of the Reverend John Pierce, the respected minister of the First Parish in Brookline, Massachusetts, and a close friend of Margaret Fuller. The marriage was solemnized by the Reverend Convers Francis. To Hedge and his wife were born two children—a son, Frederic Henry Jr., on 15 June 1831, and a daughter, Charlotte, on 21 March 1834. While at West Cambridge, Hedge's intellectual horizons widened as he formed closer connections with Fuller, Convers Francis, Emerson (then pastor at the Second Church in Boston), and George Ripley (pastor at the Purchase Street Church in Boston). These friends often met at Elizabeth Peabody's bookstore in Boston, browsed through books and foreign periodicals, and discussed current issues.

At West Cambridge, Hedge established himself as an author of scholarly theological and metaphysical works. In 1833 and 1834 he published five articles in the *Christian Examiner,* the leading Unitarian organ of the time. His review of Samuel Taylor Coleridge's *Biographia Literaria* (1817) in the March 1833 *Examiner* was one of the earliest introductions to America of the metaphysical thought of the German philosophers whose intuitive epistemology was embraced by the American Transcendentalists. In the article Hedge analyzed and endorsed much of the thought of Kant, Johann Gottlieb Fichte, and Friedrich Wilhelm Joseph von Schelling, who had greatly influenced Coleridge. In November 1833 Hedge published a favorable article in the *Examiner* on the work of Emanuel Swedenborg and then one in July 1834 praising the work of Schiller. On reading the reviews of the works of Coleridge and Swedenborg, Emerson wrote his brother Edward on 22 December 1833, "Henry Hedge . . . has just written the best pieces that have appeared in the Examiner; one was a living, leaping Logos, & he may help me." The Boston Transcendentalists found in Hedge's expositions strong support in their struggle against the Lockean sensual philosophy that dominated the theology and aesthetics of the time. In his late years Hedge wrote to Caroline Dall (on 1 February 1877) that these earlier *Examiner* pieces were reactions to the orthodoxy of the Harvard Divinity School. Despite Hedge's great influence in the embryonic stage of the Transcendental movement, he never made Transcendentalism a basis for radical religious or aesthetic reform, but he did remain a Transcendentalist throughout his life.

Hedge's pastorate of seven years at West Cambridge was troubled by dissent among factions of the Universalists, orthodox Congregationalists, and Unitarians. After having established Unitarianism firmly at West Cambridge, however, Hedge moved to Bangor, Maine, to preach for the Independent Congregational (Unitarian) Society. The move affected his career profoundly. As early as 1833 the church in Bangor had asked him through John Gorham Palfrey to preach for them, but Hedge did not give serious consideration to a move until Emerson, on 12 July 1834, recommended the place to him, telling him of the highly intellectual and cultured membership of the congregation there. Hedge told Fuller in a letter on 17 November 1834 that he was reluctant to leave the congenial intellectual climate of Cambridge and Boston for the remote parish in Bangor. When he was offered the editorship of the *Christian Examiner* in January 1835, he debated further about moving, but after careful consideration rejected the editorship. Because of the factionalism in the West Cambridge church, his salary had averaged less than $600 per annum in his last three years; so, driven by financial exigency, he resigned at West Cambridge on 26 February. The church in Bangor issued a formal call on 20 March 1835, which was made irresistible by a handsome salary offer of $1,500 per annum. Hedge preached his farewell sermon at West Cambridge on 12 April and in May 1835 moved to Bangor.

He served the Bangor congregation for fifteen years. He returned to Cambridge and Boston as often as possible to visit family and friends, and he kept in touch with activities back home through a lively correspondence with intimates such as Fuller and Francis. One of the strongest cultural and intellectual ties that he maintained with the Boston and Cambridge area for the first few years after his move was with the Transcendental Club. This club was founded by Hedge, several young Unitarian ministers, and, as Hedge later said, "a few select ladies." Bronson Alcott, the educator-philosopher, was also in the original group. They purposed to meet informally to discuss new ideas in theology, art, philosophy, and literature. In time seventeen Unitarian ministers and five women met with the group. Most shared a common interest in German literature and placed a great deal of faith in the philosophy of intuition, but they were not bound together by any common doctrine or formal rules. The Transcendental Club went by several names, but since it met most frequently when Hedge was back visiting from Bangor, Emerson called it "Hedge's club." Hedge attended at least twenty-three of the thirty meetings of the club between September 1836 and September 1840. His intimates in the Transcendental Club were Emerson, Ripley, Alcott, Francis, Fuller, Caleb Stetson, Cyrus Bartol, James Freeman Clarke, and Theodore Parker. Hedge's interest in the Transcendentalist movement gradually waned because of the increasing radicalism of Emerson, Parker, and Alcott, who repudiated historical Christianity. In the early 1840s Hedge spoke candidly in letters to Fuller and Francis about not wanting to be identified with

Frontispiece and decorated title page for the first American English-language anthology of German prose fiction and criticism (1848), edited, with translations, by Hedge

Alcott, Emerson, and Parker because of their heretical tendencies. A noticeable indication of his desire to distance himself from them was his failure to give more than minimal support to *The Dial* (1840–1844), the organ of the Transcendentalists. He published only four articles in it, a disappointing number to Emerson and Fuller, the editors. A further indication that Hedge wanted to avoid being stigmatized by the heterodoxy of Emerson and Parker was his refusal to let them preach in his pulpit. Hedge, however, continued to exchange pulpit favors with his close friend, the less reform-minded minister Francis. In a letter to Francis, Hedge confided that Francis and Stetson were the only ones of his old friends with whom he felt an affinity. Notwithstanding the theological differences that sometimes tried their patience with one another, Hedge and the radical Transcendentalists enjoyed a lifelong friendship and even outspoken mutual admiration. He, for example, collaborated with both Ripley and William H. Furness on German translations. In 1880 and 1881 Hedge lent his support to Alcott's Concord School of Philosophy; and at Emerson's death in April 1882, Emerson's widow invited Hedge, as her husband's friend, to speak at Emerson's funeral, but an accident prevented him from doing so. In a memorial address on 30 May 1882 Hedge called Emerson a "philosophical essayist" and "lyric poet," praising him as the head of American literature.

Hedge shared a faith in philosophical idealism and intuition with the reformers, but unlike them his theology was that commonly held by most Unitarians: he accepted the fatherhood of God, the divinity of Jesus, and the inspiration and the miracles of the Bible. Hedge was not disposed to reject the past and never felt the need to discard the traditional forms and framework in the church. Evolutionary rather than revolutionary change, he always felt, was better. He was always able to balance comfortably an intellectual radicalism with ecclesiastical conservatism. In his 1841 Phi Beta Kappa oration at Harvard, "Conservatism and

Reform," he pleaded for "an enlightened conservatism." He explained that the current Transcendental philosophy was neither the panacea that its advocates suggested nor the evil force its enemies claimed; it was but another philosophy in the progress of human culture. In a letter to Dall on 1 February 1877, Hedge said of his early connection with the Transcendental movement, "It has no importance, except in so far as I was the first in this country, to the best of my knowledge, to move in that direction."

One major publication that occupied a great deal of his time in Bangor was his *Prose Writers of Germany* (1848), the first American anthology of prose fiction and criticism by German writers. The collection treated twenty-eight prose masters, among whom were Luther, Gotthold Effraim Lessing, Christoph Martin Wieland, Johann Gottfried von Herder, Schiller, and Goethe. The book, widely praised as the best introduction to German prose literature in English up to that time, firmly established Hedge's reputation as the foremost authority in the country on German literature. In Bangor, Hedge also translated and critiqued the German poets for the *New England Magazine, Boston Quarterly Review,* and *Christian Examiner.* From time to time he also issued collections of his translations done in collaboration with some of his old friends in the Transcendentalist circle: Ripley's *Specimens of Foreign Standard Literature* (1838–1842); *Schiller's Song of the Bell, A New Translation by W. H. Furness, with Poems and Ballads from Goethe, Schiller, and Others, by F. H. Hedge* (1850); and *Gems of German Verse* (1851), by W. H. Furness. He personally translated many individual poems of Karl Theodor Körner, Johann Ludwig Uhland, Luther's "Eine feste Burg ist unser Gott" (A Mighty Fortress Is Our God), and works of Goethe, his favorite poet. From the last he translated "Geistes-Gruss" (The Spirit's Salute), passages from *Faust, Erlkonig* (The Erlking), "Urworte, orphisch" (Primeval Word-Orphic), "An ein goldnes Herz, das er am Halse trug" (To a Golden Heart, That He Wore around His Neck), "Der Fischer" (The Fisher), and "Der Sänger" (The Singer).

Exhausted from his labors on *Prose Writers of Germany,* Hedge embarked upon a trip to England and the Continent on 5 June 1847. Bearing a letter of introduction from Emerson, he visited Thomas Carlyle in England. Emerson told Carlyle: "Henry Hedge is a recluse but catholic scholar in our remote Bangor who reads German and smokes in his solitary study through nearly eight months of snow in the year. . . . Hedge has a true and mellow heart . . . and I hope you will like him." In a letter to Emerson on 31 August 1847, Carlyle gave his impression of his visitor: "Hedge is one of the sturdiest little fellows I have come across for many a day. A face like a rock, a voice like a howitzer, only his

honest gray eyes reassure you a little. . . . We may have met only once, but hope (mutually, I flatter myself) it may be often by and by." Leaving England, Hedge traveled through Belgium, Germany, Austria, and Italy, where he visited his old friend Margaret Fuller, now the wife of the Marchese Angelo Ossoli. Along the way he reported on his trip in public letters home to the *Christian Register,* and the *Bangor Daily Whig* and *Bangor Courier.* On the journey he wrote poems in German and translated from the German authors. He returned home in December 1849 and soon thereafter submitted his resignation to the Bangor church.

Hedge preached his farewell sermon in Bangor on 3 March 1850 and moved to Providence, Rhode Island, to become pastor of the Westminster Congregational Society, where he served until 1857. He was not long at Providence before Harvard conferred upon him the D.D. degree in 1852. His ministry at Providence was a productive time for him as an author. In 1853 he published *Christian Liturgy. For Use of the Church* and, in collaboration with Frederick D. Huntington, *Hymns for the Church of Christ,* which included his popular translation of Luther's "Eine feste Burg ist unser Gott."

At Providence, Hedge also wrote about a dozen articles for the *Christian Examiner, North American Review,* and *Atlantic Monthly.* Among these articles was an appreciative review of George Henry Lewes's *Life and Works of Goethe* (1855), which appeared in the *North American Review* in April 1856. In an age in which biographers and critics generally excoriated Goethe, Hedge was pleased to find that Lewes had written a favorable account of his favorite writer's life and commended particularly Lewes's candid treatment of *Faust,* which Hedge held as "the greatest composition since Hamlet." Hedge wrote another article at Providence that drew much favorable critical attention, his 1857 review for the *Christian Examiner* of Charles Timothy Brooks's translation of *Faust* (1856). Hedge lauded *Faust* as "the consummate flower of the Gothic mind" and Charles Timothy Brooks as the premier translator of German lyrics in America.

Hedge continued to rise in the New England intellectual and cultural circles when in 1857 he accepted an invitation from the First Parish Congregational Church in Brookline, Massachusetts, to become their pastor. He was delighted with the opportunity to fill the pulpit that for many years had been held by his late father-in-law, the Reverend John Pierce, but was more pleased with the prospect of once again being close to Boston and Cambridge. In 1857, soon after moving to Brookline, he joined the Harvard Divinity School faculty as a professor of ecclesiastical history, a post he held until 1878. Hedge's sphere of influence in the Unitarian Church increased greatly when in 1857 he became editor of the *Christian Examiner,* a position he had been unable to accept when it had first been offered to him in 1835. On 16 May 1858 he wrote to his friend Henry W. Bellows of his aspirations for the *Examiner:*

> I have endeavored to make it a condign organ for the best thought of the country and to attract the best thinkers to it by giving them the assurance of good company. We have certainly had some excellent articles, and in the *resume* of current literature we excel, I think, all American Periodicals. I take very little credit to myself for all this. My work has been to organize the journal, to lay down the paradigm, and to exercise a negative control, keeping out and staving out, as well I could, the crude stuff and multitudinous inanity that seeks admission into every periodical, appealing to editorial good nature. My hardest labor has been reading foul *mss,* and saying no! to people whom I wish to oblige. One weak and puerile . . . article does a journal more harm than two good articles can neutralize.

Hedge conducted the *Examiner* successfully, mainly because he refused to align himself with any faction in the Unitarian Church. He relinquished the editorship in 1866.

During Hedge's years at Brookline and Cambridge, his reputation and influence as a churchman grew. He published *Recent Inquiries in Theology, By Eminent English Churchmen; Being "Essays and Reviews"* (1861) to further liberal Christianity and to correct the negative spirit of John Locke's sensual philosophy in religion. Hedge was president of the American Unitarian Association (A.U.A.) from 1859 to 1863. In an assessment of Hedge's tenure as president, Raymond William Adams said that at a time when there was much internal discord in the Unitarian ranks, Hedge was welcomed by all to head the organization. Adams said further that while Hedge was "bold and daring" in his own thinking, he was cautious about accepting new theories in the church. Unitarian Church historian George Willis Cooke, in his *Unitarianism in America* (1900), asserts that "Hedge did more than any other man to give Unitarianism a consistent philosophy and theology." An important work prepared while Hedge was administratively involved with the A.U.A. was his *Reason in Religion* (1865), an important exposition of liberal Christianity that further enhanced Hedge's reputation as an American churchman. To Henry Wadsworth Longfellow the book was Hedge's "Holy Grail," and to a modern scholar it was a "classic statement of Transcendental Christianity." In 1870 Hedge made a rare excursion into Old Testament history and exegesis with his *The Primeval World of Hebrew Tradition.*

Several of Hedge's publications in his later life dealt primarily with aesthetics and literary criticism. These theories appeared mainly in essays and book reviews in the *Christian Examiner, North American Review, Atlantic Monthly,* and *Unitarian Review.* His criticism was generally appreciative, but he was candid in citing faults in the works even of his close friends, such as Emerson, James Russell Lowell, and Oliver Wendell Holmes. In a review of Edward Young's *Pre-Raffaellitism* (1857), Hedge said that the essential qualifications of a critic are "calmness, candor, tolerance, and truth." He embraced these principles as his own. A few of the authorities to whom he appealed in his criticism were the Scots Archibald Alison and Dugald Stewart; the Germans Kant, August Wilhelm and Friedrich von Schlegel, Goethe, and Schiller; and the Englishmen Coleridge and Thomas De Quincey. In an essay, "Classic and Romantic" (1886), he elucidated the idea that "Classicism gives perfection of form, but romanticism fills the spirit," noting that both are necessary to produce a literary masterpiece. In "Irony," an essay in the *Atlantic Monthly* (1870), he wrote appreciatively of irony, which is found in abundance in the Bible and the works of most literary giants, such as John Milton and Goethe. In "The Steps of Beauty," in the *Unitarian Review* (1882), his most extensive excursion into aesthetics, Hedge dissented from Kant, saying that rules set forth by critics can improve taste: "The sense of beauty is wanting in none, but no faculty is less perfect by nature. The germ only is given, the rest is discipline."

Hedge's ability to communicate effectively as a writer was complemented by his proficiency as a platform speaker. He was instrumental in founding the Lyceum in Bangor and delivered its opening lecture on 15 November 1836 and afterward often lectured there. In the winter of 1841 he delivered a highly successful course of lectures on "The Philosophy of Literature" and "Shakespeare" before the Boston Society for the Diffusion of Useful Knowledge, which he repeated later before various Lyceum groups; and in the winter of 1842 he delivered at the Lowell Institute in Boston another series, "Medieval History," which he also repeated on later occasions. On 10 November 1859 he delivered the principal address at the Schiller Centennial in the Music Hall in Boston. In it he praised Schiller's genius, calling him the national consciousness and heart of the German people. Schiller, he said, gave him at an early age his first poetic revelations. In "University Reform," a major address delivered before the Harvard alumni in July 1866, he advocated radical changes in American education, such as an elective system that would allow students more freedom in choosing professors and courses. He believed that mathematics and the classics should be mastered before students entered college, allowing undergraduates more time to study modern literature, science, philosophy, and history. He called for a

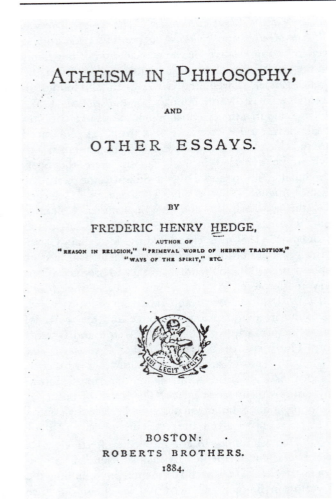

ATHEISM IN PHILOSOPHY,

AND

OTHER ESSAYS.

BY

FREDERIC HENRY HEDGE,

AUTHOR OF

"REASON IN RELIGION," "PRIMEVAL WORLD OF HEBREW TRADITION,"
"WAYS OF THE SPIRIT," ETC.

BOSTON:
ROBERTS BROTHERS.
1884.

Title page for a collection of Hedge's religious essays

kinder education—encouraging that inspiration, not coercion, should be the motivating force in instruction. To celebrate the German effort in the Franco-Prussian War, he spoke in German on 27 July 1870 to an appreciative audience of German citizens at Faneuil Hall in Boston. On 17 April 1877 in New York City he delivered the principal address before the Goethe Club, in which he shared honorary membership with many of the most popular contemporary poets of America. In 1882 he delivered eulogies following the deaths of two old friends, Emerson and Bellows. In September 1882 he spoke on Martin Luther at the Ministers' Institute in Lowell, Massachusetts. Hedge's last major speaking engagement was on 10 November 1883 before the Massachusetts Historical Society at the celebration of the four hundredth anniversary of Luther's birth. This lecture was remarkable because it lasted for an hour and a half, and Hedge, at age seventy-eight, delivered it from memory without a pause.

In 1872 Hedge resigned his pulpit in Brookline and moved to Cambridge to become professor of German language and literature at Harvard, a position he held until February 1881. His superb qualifications as a language scholar and lecturer on literature were never criticized, but his ability as an instructor of elementary German was. There were complaints of his "being the worst teacher of German that ever lived," his being a "testy and fussy old gentleman," and one "who did not suffer fools gladly." In a letter to Dall on 23 March 1881, he said, "I think old men should retire before they become actually superannuated and make way for younger talent and fresh powers"; but this statement notwithstanding, he continued to teach on and off until 1884. In recognition of his nine years of service and contributions to Harvard, President Charles W. Eliot remembered Hedge with appreciation in his annual report in 1881, recalling "Dr. Hedge's service as a teacher, and . . . his established reputation and influence as a student of language, history, and philosophy, and . . . master of style." Concurrent with his teaching German, Hedge kept busy as a writer, publishing *German Prepositions* (1875), considered by many scholars of the time to be a useful book, and *Ways of the Spirit, and Other Essays* (1877), which dealt with historical Christianity, theism, atonement, and Christian evidences. Intermittently between 1879 and 1887 he lectured at Alcott's Concord School of Philosophy.

Old age hardly abated Hedge's literary activities. He edited and annotated *Faust: A Tragedy, Part I* in 1882. *Hours with German Classics; Masterpieces of German Literature Translated into English* (1886) was a critical anthology said by critics to be the most thorough treatment of German literature by an American up to that time. At its two hundred and fiftieth anniversary in 1886 Harvard University honored Hedge with an LL.D. In his waning years Hedge published several significant religious works: *Atheism in Philosophy, and Other Essays* (1884); *Personality and Theism. Two Essays* (1887); and *Martin Luther and Other Essays* (1888). Hedge's final book in his lifetime, published in collaboration with Annis Lee Wister, was *Metrical Translations and Poems* (1888). It included many of his translations as well as some of his own original poems. Hedge made his final public appearance in May 1888 at the Unitarian Festival of Anniversary Week in Boston.

Hedge's mind remained active until he died, but in the two years preceding his death he suffered from eczema and paralysis. He died in Cambridge on 21 August 1890. *Sermons,* published posthumously in 1891, included selected sermons and orations that dealt with Hedge's wide-ranging views on the nature of life, the soul, and human and divine authority. In these sermons readers are encouraged to look within, to trust intuition, and to believe in the natural goodness of mankind. These sermons were consistent with his faith in intuition, biblical revelation and miracles, the progress of mankind, and free inquiry.

Hedge was in the forefront of a group of early-nineteenth-century American scholars schooled in Europe who introduced and popularized German language and literature in America. Especially through his scholarly expositions of Kant, Schelling, Fichte, and their disciple Coleridge, he, more than any other of his contemporaries, introduced the Transcendental philosophy to a coterie of scholars in New England who applied it in religion and literature. Whether Hedge moved away from the New England Transcendental movement or it moved away from him has been debated, but that he was one of the principal founders of the movement is indisputable. No one before him wrote so clearly and appreciatively about the major German prose writers and poets and made their masterpieces more accessible to an American reading public. As a literary critic he was in no way innovative; rather he was essentially judicious, applying old tested and tried rules, but he did influence American criticism toward a kinder and more appreciative tone. He was a force for liberalizing change in the Unitarian religion and Protestantism in general in America; but as a self-proclaimed "enlightened conservative" he sought to effect change slowly rather than by revolution. In the latter part of his career he became an ecumenicist, believing in "unity in diversity"; and as an advocate of practical religion, he became a precursor of the Social Gospel movement in America.

Biographies:

Orie W. Long, *Frederic Henry Hedge: A Cosmopolitan Scholar* (Portland, Maine: Southworth-Anthoensen, 1940);

Bryan F. LeBeau, *Frederic Henry Hedge, Nineteenth Century American Transcendentalist: Intellectually Radical, Ecclesiastically Conservative* (Allison Park, Pa.: Pickwick, 1985).

References:
Doreen Hunter, "Frederic Henry Hedge, What Say You?" *American Quarterly,* 32 (Summer 1980): 160–201;

Joel Myerson, "Frederic Henry Hedge and the Failure of Transcendentalism," *Harvard Library Bulletin,* 23 (October 1975): 396–410;

Leonard Neufeldt, "Frederic Henry Hedge," *The Transcendentalists: A Review of Research and Criticism,* edited by Myerson (New York: Modern Language Association, 1984), pp. 189–194;

Ronald Vale Wells, *Three Christian Transcendentalists: James Marsh, Caleb Sprague Henry, and Frederic Henry Hedge* (New York: Columbia University Press, 1943);

George H. Williams, *Rethinking the Unitarian Relationship with Protestantism: An Examination of the Thought of Frederic Henry Hedge (1805–1890)* (Boston: Beacon, 1949);

Guy R. Woodall, "The Record of a Friendship: The Letters of Convers Francis to Frederic Henry Hedge in Bangor and Providence (1835–1850)," in *Studies in the American Renaissance 1991,* edited by Myerson (Charlottesville: University Press of Virginia, 1991), pp. 1–57.

Papers:
Frederic Henry Hedge's correspondence and miscellaneous documents may be found in at least thirty different libraries and depositories, but the largest collections are at the Bangor Historical Society; the Andover-Harvard Theological Library and the Houghton Library at Harvard University; and the Schlesinger Library, Radcliffe College.

Abby Maria Hemenway

(7 October 1828 – 24 February 1890)

Deborah P. Clifford

BOOKS: *The Mystical Rose; or, Mary of Nazareth, the Lily of the House of David,* as Marie Josephine (New York: D. Appleton, 1865);

Rosa Immaculata, or, the Tower of Ivory, in the House of Anna and Joachim, as Marie Josephine (New York: P. O'Shea, 1867);

The House of Gold and the Saint of Nazareth. A Poetical Life of Saint Joseph, as Marie Josephine (Baltimore: Kelly, Piet, 1873);

Clarke Papers: Mrs. Meech and Her Family (Burlington, Vt., 1878);

Fanny Allen, the First American Nun (Boston: Thomas B. Noonan, 1878).

OTHER: *Poets and Poetry of Vermont,* edited by Hemenway (Rutland, Vt.: George A. Tuttle, 1858; revised, Boston: Brown, Taggard & Chase, 1860);

Songs of the War, edited by Hemenway (Albany, N.Y.: J. Munsell, 1863);

Vermont Historical Gazetteer, edited by Hemenway (volume 1, Burlington, Vt., 1868; volume 2, Burlington, Vt., 1871; volume 3, Claremont, N.H., 1877; volume 4, Montpelier, Vt., 1882; volume 5, Brandon, Vt., 1891).

Abby Maria Hemenway (Collection of David Hemenway)

Abby Maria Hemenway is remembered chiefly for her editorship of the *Vermont Historical Gazetteer,* a five-volume compendium of the state's local history, published between 1860 and 1891. As far as historians know, no one else in the whole United States attempted to do what she did—to single-handedly collect and publish the history of every community in her state. Over the course of her years as editor of the *Vermont Historical Gazetteer,* Hemenway, who never married, engaged hundreds of men and women to write the histories of their towns, churches, businesses, and schools. Hundreds more contributed memoirs of the early days of white settlement or provided sketches of forebears who had braved the terrors of the wilderness to build the first log cabins in their communities. Hemenway accomplished compiling all this material despite innumerable obsta-cles placed in her path, from money and legal troubles to floods and conflagrations.

Abby Maria Hemenway was the fourth of nine children born to Abigail and Daniel Sheffield Hemenway on their farm in the hills above Ludlow, a town in southeastern Vermont. Abby's family on both sides came from hardy pioneer stock, having moved to Vermont in the late eighteenth century. Her mother, Abigail Dana Barton (a distant relative of the Civil War nurse Clara Barton), had been born and raised in the adjacent town of Andover. Besides raising a large family, she gained a considerable local reputation as a poet. Her husband, Daniel, a Ludlow native, struggled to eke a living out of their rocky hillside acres.

Abby Maria inherited her mother's intellectual bent. An avid reader from childhood, Abby acquired much of her early learning at home, although she also attended district school. At age fourteen she began teaching school, and by age eighteen she had saved enough from her meager earnings to enroll at Ludlow's Black River Academy. There she received a classical training, which she later put to use both as a teacher and as a writer. In one way or another the education she obtained at Black River, combined with the support and encouragement she received from her mother and other family members, led young Abby Hemenway to imagine that a literary career was not only appealing but also within her reach.

Hemenway's first major literary effort was a long poem about the Virgin Mary, which she began writing as a young schoolteacher. *The Mystical Rose; or, Mary of Nazareth, the Lily of the House of David* was not published until 1865, but the inspiration for this work can be traced to Hemenway's decision to become a Baptist and to a series of visions of "Mary Mother," which prompted that conversion. By her own account the early scenes in *The Mystical Rose* were written before she had any knowledge of Mary apart from the gospel stories. Thus, she had to rely largely on her youthful imagination—often drawing on her own experience—to amplify and enrich her life of the Virgin Mary.

In 1852 Hemenway concluded her studies at Black River Academy, and after teaching for a year or so in Vermont, she headed west to the newly settled state of Michigan. Little is known of Hemenway's four years in the West except that they were not happy ones. She particularly disliked the get-rich-quick atmosphere that she found there. "The Muses sing not to me in this land of realities," she wrote back home in 1854.

Hemenway was twenty-nine when she rejoined her family in Ludlow in 1857. Soon after her return she began work on a collection of Vermont verse, *Poets and Poetry of Vermont* (1858). Exactly where the inspiration for this project came from, Hemenway does not say. Yet, there seems little question that her years in Michigan had inspired a profound nostalgia for the culture and traditions of her native state.

Poets and Poetry of Vermont was a different sort of collection from most anthologies published at that time. The volume included not only the leading Vermont poets but also many who were unknown. Hemenway wanted, as she phrased it, to give voice to "those who claim no poetic name." She saw poetry, particularly in its oral form, as the traditional way of passing down the values and folkways of northern New England culture. Thus, a love of history prompted Hemenway's effort more than a desire to uncover literary genius.

To ensure as wide and representative a sample as possible, Hemenway sent out notices to the various county newspapers in Vermont asking for submissions. Three thousand pages of verse poured in from every corner of the state. From these pages the works of 110 poets were selected for inclusion, men and women from all walks of life—lawyers and doctors, farmers and housewives, clergymen and newspaper editors.

Poets and Poetry of Vermont was greeted with generally favorable reviews. One Vermont paper, the *Middlebury Register,* hailed it on 15 December 1858 as "a treasury of bright thoughts" in which the "peculiar genius and spirit of our people" are exemplified. The book was successful enough from the start to send Hemenway back to work almost immediately on a second edition.

The success of *Poets and Poetry of Vermont* encouraged Hemenway to embark on another editorial venture, one that celebrated the history as well as the literature of her native state. She was thirty-one when she embarked on this work of gathering and preserving the history of every Vermont village and town. The year was 1859, a time when regional and local identities were competing with an emerging national identity. Moreover, most of those people with memories of the founding and early years of the state had died, and Hemenway came to see her mission as one that preserved the heritage of even the smallest village in the state. Her high purpose was to unite her fellow Vermonters through their shared recollections of the past and to give them a pride in their towns and state, and in themselves as a people.

Hemenway's original plan was to publish a series of fourteen quarterlies, one for every Vermont county, including the history of each town in that county. She expected the whole project to take four years; in the end it took a lifetime.

At the end of her life Hemenway recalled her early editorial adventures in an idiosyncratic periodical, *Notes by the Path of the Gazetteer* (1886–1889). These adventures began in Addison County. There, thanks to the efforts of the Middlebury Historical Society, several town histories were already being written. But the members of this society—several of whom were professors at Middlebury College—made it clear that they regarded Hemenway's whole plan as "an impracticality . . . not a suitable work for a woman. How could one woman," they demanded, "expect to do what forty men had been trying for sixteen years and could not?" She would break down, they predicted, before she had toured half the county.

But Abby Hemenway was not one to be put off by such dismissals. Instead, she started out on her own, visiting all the towns in the county. The job was not an easy one. In almost every community she met resistance from men who agreed that history was not suitable work for a woman. But Hemenway's powers of persuasion were formidable, and in all but three of the towns she visited she found someone to write, or at least collect, the local history of the community. She also engaged in each town "lady assistants," whose job was to sell subscriptions to the *Vermont Quarterly Gazetteer*. When Hemenway returned to Middlebury at the end of this county tour and asked once more for help from the historical society there, its members were impressed enough by her remarkable success to give in with good grace and assist her.

The Addison County number was duly published on 4 July 1860, "a patriotic work; dated for a patriotic day," Hemenway later remembered. "It was the morning of local history in Vermont."

Despite this auspicious beginning, the second number of the *Vermont Quarterly Gazetteer,* covering most of the towns in Bennington County, was not published until October 1861, and so it went. In this way what Hemenway thought at the beginning might be a four-year project became a lifelong endeavor.

A principal reason for these delays was that, while Hemenway was extremely successful in generating historical material for the *Vermont Quarterly Gazetteer,* she was less adept at obtaining the needed funds to publish it. Her plan was to raise money through subscriptions, but she consistently overestimated the number of Vermonters who might be willing to pay for her magazine.

The longest break in the publication of the *Vermont Quarterly Gazetteer* came during the Civil War, when Vermont's heavy financial commitment to the war effort, combined with rising inflation, meant that subscriptions failed to keep up with printing costs. In 1863, perhaps as a money-raising effort, Hemenway compiled a book of patriotic verse, *Songs of the War*. This small paperbound volume is comprised of, as its editor describes them, seventy-three of the most popular war songs.

Despite the patriotic fervor exhibited in this collection, little of it can rightly be called poetry. "Rhymed propaganda ground out for the home front," is how critic Daniel Aaron describes most Civil War verse, and the depiction fits here as well. True, some nationally known poets are represented, including Henry Wadsworth Longfellow, Oliver Wendell Holmes, and Thomas Bailey Aldrich. But with the possible exception of Longfellow's rousing verses on the ramming of the *Cumberland* by a Confederate ironclad, none of the poems in *Songs of the War* have made their way into modern collections of verse.

By 1864 production of the *Vermont Quarterly Gazetteer* had ground to a complete halt, and Hemenway had little choice but to acknowledge at least the temporary demise of her magazine. In partial compensation for this great vacuum in her life, Hemenway turned her energies to spiritual matters. During this difficult time she chose to leave the Baptist church of her childhood and become a Roman Catholic, a decision prompted in part by her research on the life of the Virgin Mary and other reading she did for the *Vermont Quarterly Gazetteer*.

Hemenway's religious fervor as a newly baptized Catholic is reflected in her long poem *The Mystical Rose,* published under the pseudonym Marie Josephine, her baptismal name. *Fervent* is the word that best describes this work. Enthusiastic piety spills out onto almost every one of the nearly three hundred pages of the work. Fortunately, such effusions are offset in part by the grounding of the narrative in a wealth of sources, from ecclesiastical histories and biblical dictionaries to the American writer Bayard Taylor's account of his travels in Syria and Palestine.

The central character of the work is the Virgin Mary, about whom there is little historical information. Thus, most of the material that Hemenway drew on for *The Mystical Rose* is rooted in legend, passed down orally for centuries. She believed that such "remote testimonies" and "traditional stories" would enhance the reception of her book by "the curious, the liberal, and the candid" reader. A similar instinct prompted her to charge her *Vermont Quarterly Gazetteer* historians to enrich their town histories with legendary lore.

While *The Mystical Rose* received little or no attention in Vermont newspapers, it was favorably noticed in the Catholic press and later provided Hemenway with an entrée into Catholic literary circles. Over the course of the next decade she wrote two more books in the same vein. A second volume, *Rosa Immaculata, or, the Tower of Ivory, in the House of Anna and Joachim,* published in 1867, recounts the life of the Virgin Mary from her birth to the incarnation, adding richly imagined vignettes of her saintly parents. The third and last volume, *The House of Gold and the Saint of Nazareth. A Poetical Life of Saint Joseph,* came out in 1873 and is essentially more of the same. Neither of these accounts added much to what Hemenway had already written.

At the end of the war Abby Hemenway was thirty-six, without a settled future and as yet with no prospect of resuming the editorship of the *Vermont Quarterly Gazetteer*. In the spring of 1865 she went west to Notre Dame, Indiana, hoping to find a job at the small Catholic college there. Her timing was propitious, for during the month of her arrival at Notre Dame, a new, and ultimately long-lived, Catholic weekly, *Ave Maria,* dedicated to the Virgin Mary, began publication.

If Hemenway hoped to be given a post on the magazine's editorial staff, she was disappointed, but for the next decade or so her religious poetry did appear now and again in the magazine, under the pseudonym Marie Josephine. Also, for two years beginning in September 1865, she contributed a children's column to the weekly. On this same trip west Hemenway visited Chicago, although she did not find a job there either, and in the late summer she returned home to Ludlow.

The following year, 1866, Hemenway suffered the loss of her mother, the human being who had been most dear to her. Seeking the solace of the Catholic community in Burlington, Vermont, Hemenway headed north late in the fall of 1866. For the next twelve years the bustling little city on the shores of Lake Champlain was home.

At first she found a room in St. Joseph's Convent, where to ease her loneliness and sorrow she began writing her second volume of religious poetry, *Rosa Immaculata*. With the coming of winter Hemenway's fortunes improved. One Sunday after mass at St. Mary's she was introduced to Lydia Clarke Meech, an elderly widow and fellow convert. The younger woman needed a home and the elder woman needed a companion. Sometime in late December 1866, Hemenway moved into the Meech house on Pearl Street for the winter. But what began as a temporary expedient was soon accepted as permanent. From the start Lydia Meech treated her new boarder like her own child, and Hemenway lived with the widow until Meech's death in 1874.

By the spring of 1867 the various pieces of Hemenway's life had finally fallen into place. She had a new mother and a new home, and this measure of security allowed her to resume her editorship of the *Vermont Quarterly Gazetteer.*

The exact status of the work during the long hiatus between the appearance of the sixth number of the *Vermont Quarterly Gazetteer* in August 1863 and resumption of publication four years later in August 1867 remains unknown. When work was halted in 1864, five additional issues of the magazine besides the six already published had been set into type. J. Munsell, Hemenway's printer in Albany, New York, had been sitting on them ever since. All Hemenway needed, apparently, was sufficient money to pay off her debts to the firm, and the remaining town histories of Chittenden County, together with those of Essex County, could be published. Whether Hemenway obtained the necessary funds from loans or gifts, by the late summer of 1867 five issues were finally in print.

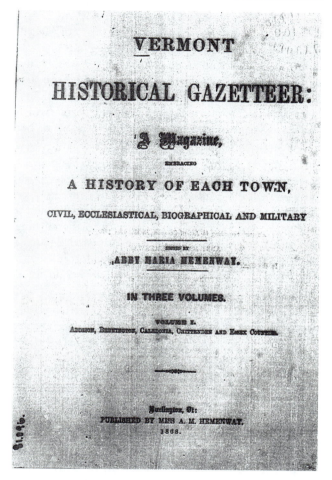

Title page for the first volume of Hemenway's attempt to publish the histories of every community in her home state

The first of the five bulky volumes of the *Vermont Historical Gazetteer* was published early in 1868. Volume one comprises all the issues of the *Vermont Quarterly Gazetteer* published thus far—the histories of the towns in Addison, Bennington, Caledonia, Chittenden, and Essex Counties.

The appearance of this hefty book, with its 1,200 pages packed with Vermont history, solidified Hemenway's reputation as an editor. Up until that time she had published a half dozen individual magazines of approximately 130 pages each, and these had appeared so sporadically as to inspire little confidence that she would ever complete the work. The publication of so many issues of the *Quarterly* under one cover, however, convinced Hemenway's readers that completion was indeed possible. The volume was praised both inside and outside Vermont, and support for Hemenway's *Vermont Historical Gazetteer* was also apparent at the local level, as town after town agreed to prepare its history.

This brief period of happiness and relative prosperity came to an end in 1874 with the death of Meech. The loss for Hemenway was a devastating one. She was alone once again, and alone in a world that was, if anything, more wary than ever of the unattached spinster. Her uncomfortable position as a single woman had been further aggravated by her Catholicism, which erected a social barrier between her and many of her fellow Vermonters.

While Lydia Meech had provided for Hemenway by leaving her a life interest in the Pearl Street house, early in 1875 the dead woman's will was contested. For the next four and a half years Hemenway devoted a good portion of her time and energies to the ensuing court battles. In the end the case was settled out of court in Hemenway's favor, but she was forced to part with the Pearl Street house in order to pay her litigation expenses.

Meanwhile, financial problems continued to plague her publication of the *Vermont Historical Gazetteer*. By the late 1870s Hemenway was so deeply in debt to her printer that she was forced to ask for state aid to continue publication. While she did receive a few hundred dollars from the lawmakers, this amount was not enough to keep the work solvent. Then in the winter of 1882, shortly after the publication of volume four of the *Vermont Historical Gazetteer*, Hemenway discovered that several hundred copies of the volume had missing pages. When her printer insisted that she pay for the defective copies since she owed him money anyway, Hemenway refused. He then confiscated all of the copies of volume four in her possession, claiming they were his property until she paid her printing bills. But she retaliated a few nights later by sneaking into the building where the volumes were housed and reclaiming the confiscated books. This action only led to more trouble. Hemenway was forced to mortgage the fourth volume to help cover her debts and never did regain ownership of it.

Meanwhile, Hemenway's health was deteriorating. In the spring of 1885, on her doctor's orders, she left Vermont for what was originally intended as a four-month vacation. She ended up in Chicago and decided to settle there, finding the atmosphere more congenial than her home state, where she was being hounded by creditors. For the next five years she continued her work for the *Vermont Historical Gazetteer* (she had a printer set up in her room) and supported herself by selling bound copies of individual town histories. She died of a stroke in 1890. She was sixty-one and had continued working to the end.

At the time of Abby Hemenway's death four volumes of the *Vermont Historical Gazetteer* had been pub-

lished. One more, including the town histories of Windham County, appeared in 1892. But the manuscripts of Windsor histories (including her hometown of Ludlow), which were destined for volume six, were destroyed in a fire in North Carolina in 1911.

In recent years respect for the singularity of the *Vermont Historical Gazetteer* as a work of local history has been growing. Where else in the mass of published town histories in this country are found so many firsthand accounts garnered directly from the people who participated in the events they describe? Or so many stories passed down by early settlers to their descendants? Where else, too, is found so much material on the lives and contributions of women to the history of their state?

Abby Hemenway saw her history as uniting Vermonters, not dividing them. Each town in its individuality was part of a larger whole. In this way she nourished a communal pride. Towns, not the state, came first, and even the smallest, poorest community had something to contribute to the whole. The *Vermont Historical Gazetteer* gave Vermonters a newfound pride in their local places and their local people.

Biographies:

Marion P. Hemenway, "Abby Maria Hemenway," paper presented for the D.A.R., Ludlow, Vermont, 1917 (copy in Brigham Index, Vermont Historical Society, Montpelier, Vt.);

Frances Harriet Babb, "Abby Maria Hemenway (1828–1890), Historian, Anthologist, and Poet," M.A. thesis, University of Maine, 1939;

Deborah P. Clifford, "Abby Hemenway's Road to Rome," *Vermont History,* 63 (Fall 1995): 197–213;

Clifford, *The Passion of Abby Hemenway: Memory, Spirit, and the Making of History* (Montpelier, Vt.: Vermont Historical Society, forthcoming 2001).

References:

Brenda Morrissey, ed., *Abby Hemenway's Vermont: Unique Portrait of a State* (Brattleboro, Vt.: Stephen Greene, 1972);

David J. Russo, *Keepers of Our Past: Local Historical Writing in the United States, 1820s–1930s* (New York: Greenwood Press, 1988).

Papers:

Abby Maria Hemenway's extant correspondence is limited to a hundred or so letters scattered among a variety of public and private archives. The public archives include the Vermont Historical Society; the University of Vermont; the Sheldon Museum in Middlebury, Vermont; and the University of Notre Dame.

Thomas Wentworth Higginson

(23 December 1823 – 9 May 1911)

Judy Logan
Eastern Washington University

See also the Higginson entries in *DLB 1: The American Renaissance in New England* and *DLB 64: American Literary Critics and Scholars, 1850–1880.*

BOOKS: *A Sermon: Preached at the Pleasant Street Church, Newburyport, Thanksgiving Day, (Nov. 30, 1848) . . . "Man Shall Not Live by Bread Alone"* (Newburyport: Huse & Bragdon, Advertiser Press, 1848); revised as *"Man Shall Not Live by Bread Alone." A Thanksgiving Sermon: Preached in Newburyport, Nov. 30, 1848* (Newburyport: Charles Whipple / Boston: Crosby & Nichols, 1848);

The Tongue: Two Practical Sermons (Newburyport: A. Augustus Call, 1850);

Mr. Higginson's Address to the Voters of the Third Congressional District of Massachusetts (Lowell: Printed by C. L. Knapp, 1850);

The Birthday in Fairy-Land: A Story for Children (Boston: Crosby & Nichols, 1850);

Merchants: A Sunday Evening Lecture (Newburyport: A. A. Call, 1851);

Things New and Old: An Installation Sermon (Worcester: Printed for the Worcester Free Church Society by Earle & Drew, 1852);

Woman and Her Wishes: An Essay Inscribed to the Massachusetts Constitutional Convention (Boston: Wallcut, 1853; London: Chapman, 1854);

The Unitarian Autumnal Convention, A Sermon (Boston: Mussey, 1853);

Massachusetts in Mourning. A Sermon, Preached in Worcester, on Sunday, June 4, 1854 (Boston: Munroe, 1854);

Scripture Idolatry. A Discourse (Worcester: John Keith, 1854);

Does Slavery Christianize the Negro? (New York: American Anti-Slavery Society, 1855);

A Ride Through Kanzas (New York, 1856);

The New Revolution: A Speech before the American Anti-Slavery Society, at Their Annual Meeting in New York, May 12, 1857 (Boston: Wallcut, 1857);

The Rationale of Spiritualism. Being Two Extemporaneous Lectures Delivered at Dodworth's Hall, December 5, 1858,

Thomas Wentworth Higginson, 1857

recorded by T. J. Ellinwood (New York: Ellinwood, 1859);

The Results of Spiritualism, A Discourse, Delivered at Dodsworth's Hall, Sunday, March 6, 1859 (New York: Munson, 1859);

Out-door Papers (Boston: Ticknor & Fields, 1863);

Malbone: An Oldport Romance (Boston: Fields, Osgood, 1869; London, 1869);

Memoir of Thaddeus William Harris (Boston: Boston Society of Natural History, 1869);

Ought Women to Learn the Alphabet? (Boston: Sold by C. K. Whipple, 1869; Manchester, U.K., 1873);

Army Life in a Black Regiment (Boston: Fields, Osgood, 1870);

The Sympathy of Religions. An Address, Delivered at Horticultural Hall, Boston, February 6, 1870 (Boston: Reprinted from the *Radical*, 1871; London, 1872; revised and enlarged edition, Boston: Free Religious Association, 1876);

Atlantic Essays (Boston: Osgood, 1871);

Higher Education of Woman. A Paper Read . . . Before the Social Science Convention, Boston, May 14, 1873 (Boston: Woman's Journal Office, 1873);

Oldport Days (Boston: Osgood, 1873);

Young Folks' History of the United States (Boston: Lee & Shepard / New York: Lee, Shepard & Dillingham, 1875; London: Sampson Low, 1875);

English Statesmen, volume 1 of *Brief Biographies of European Public Men*, edited by Higginson (New York: Putnam, 1875);

Free Religious Association, 1875. Introductory Address (N.p., 1875);

The Inter-Collegiate Literary Association, Its History, Aims and Results (N.p., 1879?);

Short Studies of American Authors (Boston: Lee & Shepard / New York: Dillingham, 1880; enlarged, 1888);

Common Sense About Women (Boston: Lee & Shepard / New York: Dillingham, 1882; London: Sonnenschein, 1882);

Wendell Phillips (Boston: Lee & Shepard / New York: Dillingham, 1884);

Margaret Fuller Ossoli (Boston & New York: Houghton, Mifflin, 1884);

The Young Men's Party (New York: New York Evening Post, 1884);

A Larger History of the United States of America to the Close of President Jackson's Administration (New York: Harper, 1886 [i.e., 1885]; London: Sampson Low, 1885); expanded as *History of the United States from 986 to 1905*, by Higginson and William Macdonald (New York: Harper, 1905);

The Monarch of Dreams (Boston: Lee & Shepard, 1887);

Unsolved Problems in Woman Suffrage (New York, 1887);

Hints on Writing and Speech-Making (Boston: Lee & Shepard / New York: Dillingham, 1887);

Women and Men (New York: Harper, 1888);

Travelers and Outlaws: Episodes in American History (Boston: Lee & Shepard / New York: Dillingham, 1889);

The Afternoon Landscape: Poems and Translations (New York & London: Longmans, Green, 1889; London: Longmans, Green, 1889);

Life of Francis Higginson, First Minister in the Massachusetts Bay Colony, and Author of "New England's Plantation" (1630) (New York: Dodd, Mead, 1891);

The New World and the New Book. An Address Delivered before the Nineteenth Century Club of New York City, Jan. 15, 1891, With Kindred Essays (Boston: Lee & Shepard, 1892);

Concerning All of Us (New York: Harper, 1892);

A World Outside of Science (N.p., 1892?);

English History for American Readers, by Higginson and Edward Channing (New York: Longmans, Green, 1893); republished as *English History for Americans* (New York: Longmans, Green, 1894; revised editions, 1896, 1897, 1902);

Such As They Are: Poems, by Higginson and Mary Thacher Higginson (Boston: Roberts, 1893);

Book and Heart: Essays on Literature and Life (New York: Harper, 1897);

The Procession of Flowers and Kindred Papers (New York, London & Bombay: Longmans, Green, 1897);

Cheerful Yesterdays (Boston & New York: Houghton, Mifflin, 1898; London: Gay & Bird, 1898);

Tales of the Enchanted Islands of the Atlantic (New York & London: Macmillan, 1898; London: Macmillan, 1898);

Old Cambridge (New York & London: Macmillan, 1899);

Contemporaries (Boston & New York: Houghton, Mifflin, 1899);

The Alliance Between Pilgrim and Puritan in Massachusetts: An Address Delivered before the Old Planters Society . . . in Jacob Sleeper Hall, Boston University, June 9th 1900 (Salem, 1900);

American Orators and Oratory, Being a Report of Lectures Delivered by Thomas Wentworth Higginson at the Western Reserve University, Under the Auspices of the Western Reserve Chapter of the Daughters of the American Revolution (Cleveland: Printed by the Imperial Press, 1901);

Henry Wadsworth Longfellow (Boston & New York: Houghton, Mifflin, 1902);

John Greenleaf Whittier (New York & London: Macmillan, 1902);

A Reader's History of American Literature, by Higginson and Henry W. Boynton (Boston, New York & Chicago: Houghton, Mifflin, 1903);

Part of a Man's Life (Boston & New York: Houghton, Mifflin, 1905; London: Constable, 1905);

Life and Times of Stephen Higginson, Member of the Continental Congress (1783) and Author of the "Laco" Letters, Relating to John Hancock (1789) (Boston & New York: Houghton, Mifflin, 1907);

Edward Atkinson (Boston, 1907?);

Things Worth While (New York: Huebsch, 1908);

Religious Progress in the Last Two Generations: An Address (Chicago: Unity Publishing, 1908);

Carlyle's Laugh, and Other Surprises (Boston & New York: Houghton Mifflin, 1909);

Descendants of the Reverend Francis Higginson, First "Teacher" in the Massachusetts Bay Colony of Salem, Massachusetts and Author of "New-Englands Plantation" (1630) (Boston: Privately printed, 1910).

Higginson's parents, Louisa and Stephen Higginson (from Mary Thacher Higginson, Thomas Wentworth Higginson: The Story of His Life, *1914)*

Collection: *The Writings of Thomas Wentworth Higginson,* 7 volumes (Boston & New York: Houghton, Mifflin, 1900).

OTHER: *Thalatta: A Book for the Sea-side,* edited by Higginson and Samuel Longfellow (Boston: Ticknor, Reed & Fields, 1853);

The Works of Epictetus, translated, with an introduction, by Higginson (1 volume, Boston: Little, Brown, 1865; revised, 2 volumes, 1890);

Harvard Memorial Biographies, 2 volumes, edited, with a preface, by Higginson (Cambridge, Mass.: Sever & Francis, 1866);

Brief Biographies of European Public Men, 4 volumes, edited by Higginson (New York: Putnam, 1875–1876);

A Book of American Explorers, edited by Higginson (Boston: Lee & Shepard / New York: Dillingham, 1877);

Poems by Emily Dickinson, edited by Higginson and Mabel Loomis Todd (Boston: Roberts, 1890; London: Osgood, McIlvaine, 1891);

Poems by Emily Dickinson, Second Series, edited by Higginson and Todd (Boston: Roberts, 1891);

Massachusetts in the Army and Navy during the War of 1861–65, 2 volumes, edited by Higginson (Boston: Printed by Wright & Potter, 1895, 1896).

Thomas Wentworth Higginson—reformer, militant abolitionist, politician, religious radical, advocate of equality for blacks and women, speaker, literary critic, military man, and author of everything from sermons and essays on nature to history, biography, short stories, and a novel—was highly regarded by most of his contemporaries during the latter half of the nineteenth century and the beginning of the twentieth. He published more than five hundred titles in a variety of genres, including more articles in the *Atlantic* than anyone other than James Russell Lowell and Oliver Wendell Holmes. Yet, within fifty years after his death he had plummeted headlong into obscurity, all of his books out of print. In the late twentieth century he was perhaps best known as Emily Dickinson's "Preceptor," but with the new millennium, his book about his experience as leader of the first freed-slave regiment of the Civil War is gaining him new prominence and appreciation.

In many ways Higginson is a conundrum; he refuses to fit neatly into any convenient boxes. While he played a pivotal role in the struggles for black and female suffrage, was injured while attempting to free an escaped slave, dared to support John Brown's plans to transport slaves to Canada, was an outspoken advocate of the Free Church movement, argued for open immi-

Higginson's birthplace on Kirkland Street in Cambridge, Massachusetts

gration, and championed the much-maligned Catholics and Jews, he is frequently perceived as a representative of the stuffy genteel tradition in American letters, the man who supposedly stifled Dickinson's hopes of publication during her lifetime and regularized the life out of her syntax and rhymes after her death, the man who said of Walt Whitman that having written *Leaves of Grass* (1855) was not a discredit to him—the shame was in not having burned it afterward. Higginson's political alignment after the Civil War migrated from radical Republican to mugwump to anti-imperialist to Progressive. While critics today praise him for his support of the oppressed, they often fault him for his beliefs about what he saw as the inherent physical and psychological limitations of women and blacks, as well as minorities such as the Irish and Roman Catholics. In the final analysis Higginson was a man both ahead of and bound by his times.

Thomas Wentworth Higginson spent most of his life in Cambridge, Massachusetts, where he was born into a well-established family. His first American ancestor to come to America, the Reverend Francis Higginson, arrived in 1629 at the invitation of the Massachusetts Bay Company. Francis Higginson's oldest son, John, followed his father into the ministry, eventually earning the title "Nestor of the New England Clergy" and speaking out against the slave trade before his death at ninety-two. Wentworth Higginson's paternal grandfather, Stephen Higginson, was an influential shipowner

and politician who served in the Continental Congress and spoke out against the impotence of the Confederation, arguing the need for a strong federal government to put down rebellions, and served in the Department of the Navy during the first Adams administration. Stephen Higginson married three times: his first wife produced nine children, including Wentworth's father, before her death; when his second wife died, he married her sister and outlived her.

This family tendency toward large families continued into Wentworth Higginson's generation. Born 23 December 1823, he was the tenth and last child of his mother, Louisa (Storrow) Higginson; his father, Stephen, had five children from a previous marriage as well. On his mother's side, Higginson was descended from the Appletons and Wentworths of New Hampshire; the family tree boasted a royal governor, and Wentworth's maternal grandfather was an English officer at St. Andrews, Scotland, in 1786. Wentworth's decision to enter Harvard was a given: his father served as bursar at the college, directed the Harvard Divinity School, and planted the great elms in Harvard Yard. When Wentworth was ten, his father died. At age thirteen Wentworth was admitted to Harvard as the youngest member of his class. Named to Phi Beta Kappa, he graduated second in his class in 1841.

Transcendentalism became the popular movement at Harvard during Higginson's undergraduate years, and Ralph Waldo Emerson and Theodore

Parker were major influences on his thinking. Later, in *Contemporaries* (1899), Higginson wrote of encountering Emerson's ideas: "in the comparative conventionalism of the literature of that period it had the effect of a revelation." The "Newness," as Transcendentalism was known, overturned previous notions about the importance of tradition, reason, and logic, and stressed the exigencies of the moment, intuition, subjective feeling, and the power of the will. The Transcendentalists' rejection of religious orthodoxy was comparatively easy for Higginson to embrace because his upbringing had been relatively free of traditional religious teachings. "Greatly to my bliss," he observed in *Cheerful Yesterdays* (1898), "I escaped almost absolutely all those rigors of the old New England theology which have darkened the lives of so many. I never heard of the Five Points of Calvinism until maturity; never was converted, never experienced religion."

Following his graduation, Higginson was introduced firsthand to the radical abolitionist movement when he heard William Lloyd Garrison and Wendell Phillips speak in Boston. So inspired that he almost made a speech himself, Higginson quickly immersed himself in antislavery arguments and became an outspoken abolitionist. But meanwhile he was faced with the question of his future. Was he to be a poet or a preacher? The life of a poet, while it appealed greatly to him, was too solitary to satisfy his newly fired Transcendentalist need to be in the business of reforming men; yet, traditional religion with its dogmatic doctrines and forms did not interest him. Emerson himself had found even Unitarianism too constricting.

While Higginson pondered, he visited Brook Farm during the period when Nathaniel Hawthorne was in residence. Higginson's initial positive impressions later faded; like Hawthorne, he concluded that shoveling manure was unlikely to result in transcendence, but throughout his life Higginson remained influenced by most of the ideals of the movement. Believing that ideas apart from action were sterile, eventually he decided that as a minister he could possibly devote himself to reform movements, and he returned to Harvard for divinity school. He felt, he wrote to his mother in November 1844, that he might do the most good for humanity by "guiding, governing, pointing out the true course to those who cannot find it unaided—& adding to this the moral force of a disinterested philanthropy." Before long the failure of the divinity school to follow up talk with action caused him to drop out, but he soon re-enrolled, determined to finish.

After he graduated from Harvard Divinity School, Higginson was called to preach by the First Religious Society of Newburyport, Massachusetts. His new wife, Mary Elizabeth (Channing) Higginson, whom he married in September 1847, accompanied him to his first post. Conservative Newburyport, with its businessmen and ship captains formerly engaged in the slavery trade, was unprepared for its unconventional new minister. Higginson's abolitionist sermons and outspoken views on temperance, the Mexican War, organized labor, women's suffrage, and materialism offended many of his flock. Their disenchantment with their minister's radicalism came to a boil in 1848 when he became a candidate for Congress for the Free Soil Party, and he resigned under pressure, even though he lost the election. For the next several years he supported his family by lecturing.

When the Fugitive Slave Law was passed in 1850, Higginson again ran for Congress for the same party, agreeing with Henry David Thoreau's statement in "Civil Disobedience" that one must "yield to a higher law" by refusing to catch or return escaped slaves. In his address to the voters he urged them to disobey the law and then to "show our good citizenship by taking the legal consequences!" Although he hated violence, he said that in "terrible times" to speak of bloodshed became "necessary." The Newburyport paper excoriated him for urging the "nullification of the laws of the land, when they do not correspond with his individual opinions." Undaunted, Higginson continued to speak out against the law.

The Free Church of Worcester liked what they heard and called Higginson as their minister. He went, continuing his outspoken advocacy of the same social and political issues, and emphasizing man's intuitive apprehension of the "great Law of Nature," the humanity of Jesus, and the love of God. Continuing his active involvement in social causes, Higginson managed to incite anger even among radicals. The World Temperance Convention exploded in an uproar when, as one of its organizers, he appointed feminist radical Susan B. Anthony to a committee. Higginson led a walkout, announcing that he could not be associated with a group that excluded half of the human race. He then helped to convene a second meeting, the "*Whole* World's Temperance Convention," supported by some of the foremost names of the radical abolitionist and feminist movements, and was unanimously elected chairman.

Higginson seized the case of Anthony Burns, an escaped slave, as his opportunity to act on his ideals. Higginson instigated a rescue attempt, and, although he had intended to remain on the sidelines, he was swept up by the moment and led a group armed with axes and pistols to the courthouse in Boston. He was slashed in the face by a defender's sword, and the attempt failed when a guard was killed, but Higginson termed the raid "the greatest step in Anti-Slavery which Massachusetts has ever taken."

*Higginson in 1846, during his final year at
Harvard Divinity School*

Higginson was viewed as a hero by those who abhorred the new law. Richard Henry Dana Jr. expressed the reaction of many who knew Higginson: "I knew his ardor and courage, but I hardly expected a married man, a clergyman, and a man of education to lead the mob." Higginson's sermon the following Sunday declared his total commitment to radical action in defense of escaped slaves. He was never prosecuted for his actions. By this time Higginson had concluded that the slave states should be expelled from the Union; slavery should not be countenanced within its borders.

Higginson's next foray into abolitionist activity was occasioned by the Free Soiler immigrants' problems in Kansas, a perfect example of why the slave states should no longer be allowed to remain in the Union. Some who favored the expansion of slavery into the new state were harassing the Free Soilers, and Higginson not only spoke out on their behalf in his "Letters from Kansas," but he went so far as to serve as a guard on a wagon train bound for Topeka. At this point Higginson resigned his pulpit, assembled the State Disunion Convention in Worcester, and preached

revolution and the dissolution of the Union over the slavery issue.

The notoriety Higginson gained from his Kansas exploits and fiery speeches made him the focus of an appeal by John Brown, as he sought funds to finance his scheme to help fugitive slaves escape to Canada. As one of the "secret six"—the others were Samuel Gridley Howe, Theodore Parker, Frank Sanborn, Gerrit Smith, and G. L. Stearns—Higginson was involved with raising money for Brown. When Brown's attack on the arsenal at Harpers Ferry in October 1859 failed, the other conspirators—with the exception of Smith, who was declared insane—fled the country, leaving Higginson to face the music. He pushed a plan to rescue Brown, but Brown demurred and was tried and hanged. Once again, Higginson was never charged nor even called upon to testify, even though his part in the plot was common knowledge.

In January 1862 Higginson received an enigmatic response to his "Letter to a Young Contributor" article in the *Atlantic*. The letter was his first communication with Emily Dickinson. Encouraged by his call for new writers, Dickinson sent him four of her poems and asked him if they "breathed" and what was "true." She had interpreted his remarks about abolitionism as a renunciation, something she could identify with, and she admired his essays and commitment to an unorthodox version of Christianity. He replied promptly, cementing an odd relationship that did not end even with her death.

When war broke out between North and South, Higginson vacillated about how to respond. Believing as he did in excluding the slave states from the Union, he could see little reason for forcing them to remain a part of it. His wife, Mary, was an invalid, dependent upon his care, and both his age, thirty-seven, and his position as a minister could have excused him from active service. Eventually, however, Higginson chose to act. In 1862 he raised a group of volunteers and was appointed captain, but the government in Washington had other plans for him. He was asked to organize and train a group of eight hundred freed slaves into a fighting unit, the first of its kind in the Union. This assignment was an unlikely one for a minister with no military training or experience, but perhaps the U.S. Army, aware of Higginson's reputation as a firebrand and his contributions to the abolitionist cause, felt that he was the ideal man to lead such a regiment. The First South Carolina Volunteers, under his leadership, made forays up the St. Mary's, St. John, and Edisto Rivers.

Later Higginson told the story of how the regiment came to be formed, its training, and its missions in *Army Life in a Black Regiment* (1870). The book detailed the everyday life of the camp and recorded the comments of the men. Many in the North had expressed doubts about the blacks' fitness for military training and exploits; their success under fire and Higginson's book demonstrated that these men were not only patriots and fine soldiers but also an invaluable weapon for the Union. When Southern leaders learned that a regiment of freed slaves would be occupying Jacksonville with the aim of arming the slaves of the area, they were wild with fears that once Southern slaves came into contact with those who had experienced freedom, they would rise up, and the Southern system would be doomed.

Jacksonville was taken without a shot's being fired; its defenders were completely surprised. Once the city was in Northern hands, however, Higginson had his hands full keeping it there. With only nine hundred men at his command, he was forced into maneuvering designed to deceive the enemy as to the size of his force. Another concern was the discipline of the men; because they were originally from Florida, retaliation against their former masters was a real possibility, especially since they were essentially fighting under a death sentence: any former slaves captured by the Confederates were assured of a speedy execution. "'Dere's no flags ob truce for us,'" the men often said. But the lack of revenge on the part of these black soldiers surprised the officers. Higginson's life was on the line as well; white officers over these men were condemned to death in the event of capture, according to an act of the Confederate Congress.

Higginson was convinced from the beginning of the worth of these soldiers, but his sentiments were not shared by all of those in the North. When they enlisted, the men were promised the same pay as the white soldiers received, but soon an attempt was made to give them only half pay. A furious Higginson reacted with a barrage of letters to congressmen, newspapers, and abolitionists. He wrote Senator Charles Sumner that this reversal would "be the greatest blow ever struck at successful emancipation in the Department of the South, for it will destroy all confidence in the honesty of the government." His letter to the *New York Times* argued, "we presume too much on the supposed ignorance of these men. I have never yet found a man in my regiment so stupid as not to know when he was cheated. If fraud proceeds from the government itself, so much the worse, for this strikes at the foundation of all rectitude, all honor, all obligation." His campaign to secure justice for his men was successful; in 1865 full pay was restored to them.

Soon the regiment received orders to abandon the town, and as they were leaving, a fire deliberately set by some of the troops destroyed several dozen buildings, but none of the former slaves was involved in the inci-

Higginson in 1862, during his service as colonel of the First South Carolina Volunteers, one of the black regiments in the Union Army

dent. Following the withdrawal from Jacksonville, Higginson's command was involved in many raids to free slaves, to destroy bridges, railroad tracks, and other fortifications, and to forage for supplies. On one such raid near Beaufort, South Carolina, Higginson was wounded in the side by a ball. Although his clothing was not torn by the contact, he suffered partial paralysis that made standing difficult. After a too-brief convalescence, Higginson attempted to return to duty and suffered a relapse. He was forced to resign his commission in May 1864, and he returned home an invalid.

Higginson's book, published in 1870, was designed to correct the misconceptions of whites about the blacks' fitness for soldiering. He himself admitted to having fears about their ability to hold up under extreme pressures, but the suffering they had undergone as slaves prepared them for the rigors of army life, and they had an added incentive to fight, since their aim was the destruction of the system that had enslaved them and still enslaved thousands of their fellows, including, in many cases, their wives and children. Some of the most fascinating sections of the book describe Higginson's expectations of his men and his surprised reactions both to how they differed from his preconceptions and how strange their habits and culture seemed to him.

He had viewed them as resembling "grown-up children" and assumed that they would be simple, docile, and affectionate. All looked alike to him at first. As his experience with his soldiers expanded, he realized they were all individuals just as whites were. They approached hard work and deprivation with a cheerfulness expressed in singing and a fortitude formed under their former servitude, and they were genuinely patriotic: "'We'll neber desert de ole flag, boys, neber; we hab lib under it for *eighteen hundred sixty-two years,* and we'll die for it now.'" He was surprised that they had not simply risen up and overpowered their masters; he was sure he would have done so had the tables been reversed. He concluded that the explanation was a combination of the inherent docility of their race, their religious training, and the patience ingrained in them by generations of slavery. What good would rebellion have done them, he realized, without weapons, money, organization, leadership, and most of all, confidence in one another?

Their Stoicism and patience in adversity he attributed to their religious training and upbringing, and he considered it a drawback to their becoming successful soldiers, but this background was tempered by their hardiness and willingness to take incredible chances. His only disappointment with his troops concerned their inability to withstand bad weather and illness. They were generally in poor physical condition, probably because of malnutrition during their years of servitude, and they succumbed to disease and fatigue more frequently than did their better-fed white counterparts. He was surprised at how much thought they had given to their current situation. While they appreciated the aid of whites in training them to fight, they realized that the "white men cannot stay and be their leaders always and that they must learn to depend on themselves, or else relapse into their former condition."

Higginson was struck by the domestic habits of his men, their food preferences, and methods of food preparation. They preferred pork, oysters, sweet potatoes, rice, hominy, cornbread, and pancakes concocted of corn and pumpkins. He was also impressed by the spiritual life of his troops, and he recorded thirty-six of their spirituals, taking care to reproduce as closely as possible their dialect. Most, he noted, expressed the need for patience in this world and the expectation of triumph in the next.

Following his discharge, Higginson and his wife, Mary, returned to Newport, Rhode Island, the home of many who shared his literary and political views, including Helen Hunt Jackson and Julia Ward Howe. He served as school committee chairman and worked to integrate the schools; he also promoted the extension of suffrage to the former slaves. During Reconstruction he became disillusioned about the hardness of heart and mind displayed by his countrymen. "We can make," he wrote, "no sudden changes in the constitution of men either at the North or South. I do not look to see in this generation, a race of Southern white men who shall do justice to the Negro." So bleak was the outlook that he eventually concluded that rather than push for the vote, blacks would be better served to be patient; "centuries of time" rather than "special legislation" would be necessary to change men's hearts.

As he sadly turned away from the cause of black suffrage, Higginson immersed himself in writing. He had intended to involve himself in the women's suffrage movement but was discouraged by the conflict within the movement between those who favored tying advances in women's rights to those of blacks and those who refused to do so. He had fought enough battles at this point that he did not wish to enmesh himself in one that seemed so riven by its own adherents. During this period he produced essays, short stories, and a novel, as well as biographies and histories. But even his choice of what translations to do was guided by his interest in emancipation. He wrote to a friend, "I am translating Epictetus . . . because the philosophy of that Roman slave argued irresistibly the 'inevitable laws of retribution'" that pointed ultimately toward restoration of human freedom.

Over the next few years all of this writing produced success—first with the publication in 1866 of *Harvard Memorial Biographies,* which he edited. Commissioned by Harvard, these brief biographies commemorated the young Harvard men who gave their lives for the Union cause during the Civil War. Higginson wrote twelve of them himself. In and around his other writing Higginson was writing his first and only novel, *Malbone: An Oldport Romance,* published in 1869. He enjoyed working on it so much that he longed to give it all of his attention, but he could not. "For the first time perhaps," he wrote, "I have something to write which so interests me it is very hard to leave it even for necessary exercise. I hate to leave it for a moment . . . this Romance is in me like the statue in the marble, for every little while I catch glimpses of parts of it here and there. I have rather held back from it, but a power within steadily forces me on; the characters are steadily forming themselves more and more. . . ." His models were Jane Austen and Hawthorne. He thought Austen's drawing rooms and witty conversation could be successfully evoked in the Newport society of the years before the Civil War. The age of Realism had not yet begun, and he appreciated what he viewed as Hawthorne's spiritual idealism and use of symbolism to cut to the quick of human weaknesses. *Malbone* was originally published serially in the *Atlantic* between January and June 1869; it appeared in book form the same year.

Philip Malbone, the protagonist, was based on William Hurlbert, whom Higginson had known at Harvard Divinity School. Hurlbert had a charismatic personality, great personal charm, and good looks, and Higginson was drawn under his spell for some time before Hurlbert's weaknesses caught up with him and the waste of his many talents and gifts became evident. Higginson said of Hurlbert that he was "so handsome in his dark beauty that he seemed like a picturesque oriental," and "Almost all women loved him, because he loved all; he never had to assume an ardor, for he always felt it." But Hurlbert was ultimately brought down by social scandal, debt, and questionable legal dealings. Malbone, too, is a witty, romantic cad; he has an affair with his fiancée Hope's sister until Hope catches them in the act. Emilia, the sister, who is said to be based on Margaret Fuller, is then conveniently drowned at sea while sailing toward her former lover, with whom she had planned to elope. Malbone, disgraced, retreats in shame to Europe.

Higginson uses the book to present some of his ideas about American writers, politicians, and businessmen, and, in the tradition of the sentimental domestic novel, he provides an epilogue that holds forth hope of a heaven—or a sequel—for the bereaved Hope, who has lost both Malbone and her sister. But critics quickly destroyed all hopes of a sequel. Unfortunately for the author, they agreed, he had aimed for romance and hit melodrama. The book was criticized as too didactic and "very thin." Another wrote that Malbone might have been "delightful if the speeches had not the air of having been studied overnight for the effect." Others said the book read as if it had been written by a woman for women and that it was too heavily laden with morality. Much of the criticism concerning morality centered on the character of Hope, who was entirely too perfect to be human. Idealized throughout the book, she bears her burdens like a saint. And Higginson does not allow the reader to like Malbone for a moment, for while the man combines good and bad traits, the reader is constantly reminded that he is a scoundrel and a cad.

Despite the creaky sentimental framework and one-dimensional characters, Higginson managed to employ a generous amount of satire focused on his depiction of social life in Newport. He was adept at his portrayal of the manners and customs of the wealthy with their snobbishness and pretentiousness. He explored what he viewed as the miseducation of young women as well, pointing out how ill equipped they were by their governesses and coming-out parties to do anything worthwhile. Higginson also targeted the anti-intellectualism of the wealthy and socially conscious who have no use for literature. When Malbone complains that most Americans have no knowledge of, interest in, or appreciation of authors of the caliber of Hawthorne and Thoreau, he seems to be voicing Higginson's thoughts. But stung by the negative response to *Malbone*, Higginson never again ventured another long fictional work. He said of himself in 1900 that he was rather relieved that he had "never shared, on any larger scale, either the disheartening discouragements or the more perilous successes of the novelist."

The year 1870 was important in Higginson's life. *Army Life in a Black Regiment* was published, and on 15 August of that year he journeyed to Amherst to meet a young poet named Emily Dickinson with whom he had been corresponding since 1862. His initial reaction to her (expressed in a letter to his wife), when she greeted him with two daylilies as her "introduction," was that her intensity drained him and that he was glad he did not live much closer to her, for such intensity would have been too much for his "nerve power." "Without touching her, she drew from me," he wrote.

If Higginson had originally envisioned a paternal relationship with this strange young woman in which he would guide her in the craft of poetry, this image vanished as they continued to correspond. Even as she continued to call him "master" and "preceptor" and refer to herself as his "scholar," "pupil," and "gnome," she ignored his advice on regularizing her rhymes and punctuation and puzzled him with her dazzling flashes of insight. He simply did not know what to make of statements such as how she recognized true poetry. Poetry, she said, made her "whole body so cold no fire" could ever "warm" her, and it made her "feel physically as if the top" of her "head were taken off." She simply spoke a language he, despite all of his experience as writer and critic, did not speak. He was shocked at what seemed to him "wantonness of overstatement." Tilden G. Edelstein, in his book *Strange Enthusiasm: A Life of Thomas Wentworth Higginson* (1968), has summarized Higginson's befuddlement with his protégée: Higginson "failed to understand that it was possible to conceive of poetic statements as normal, and logical ones as fantastic." He did not visit Dickinson again for three years; his "pupil" was clearly beyond his understanding. He referred to Dickinson in a 12 September 1890 letter to Mabel Loomis Todd as his "eccentric poetess" and read her poetry to a group of Boston ladies because, he said, it seemed strange.

Following the publication of *Army Life in a Black Regiment*, Higginson once again involved himself in the women's suffrage movement, despite its internal wranglings, this time putting the labor movement on the back burner until women secured the vote. He refused to support radical feminists such as Victoria Hull, but he co-edited and frequently wrote for the *Woman's Journal* for fourteen years. Despite his disappointment with long fiction, Higginson did not wish to give up on fiction entirely and turned to shorter fictional pieces.

In 1873 he published *Oldport Days,* a collection of seven local-color sketches originally published in the *Atlantic* between 1867 and 1873. In them Higginson depicted life in the town where he lived from 1864 to 1878. He enjoyed the summer atmosphere of social rivalry between the representatives of high society from cities as diverse as Boston, New York, and Philadelphia when their paths crossed at this summer watering hole for the wealthy. While each family had a certain standing in the town it hailed from, meeting on common ground neutralized and leveled them, he thought.

But most of all, Higginson celebrated life during the off-season. The wharves, the water, the flora and fauna, the changing of the seasons, the various inhabitants and their daily occupations are painted with a sure hand reminiscent of Harriet Beecher Stowe's in *Oldtown Folks* (1869). Particularly well-realized chapters are "Oldport Wharves," "A Driftwood Fire," "Moonlight," and "In a Wherry": All capture the scene in the best local-color tradition. The book is filled with meditations on nature and its correspondences to spiritual truths that remind the reader of essays by Emerson and Thoreau; many were more popular with the public than Thoreau's. He told Harriet Prescott: "These essays on Nature delight me so infinitely that all other themes seem tiresome beside them; I am sure that I have never come so near to Nature. . . ." Writing from pure enjoyment, he said he spent "days and weeks on single sentences."

Other projects included what he hoped would be his "magnum opus," "The Intellectual History of Woman," which remained unfinished at his death, and three books for children—*Young Folks' History of the United States* and *English Statesmen,* both published in 1875, and *A Book of American Explorers,* published two years later. He later published adult versions of his histories—*A Larger History of the United States* in 1885, *English History for American Readers* in 1893, and *Reader's History of American Literature* in 1903. His juvenile books were his first foray into writing for children and were suggested by Boston educator George B. Emerson. In writing *Young Folks' History of the United States,* Higginson stated in the preface that he had omitted "all names and dates not really needful" and made "liberal use of the familiar traits and incidents of everyday." He filled his books with quotations, anecdotes, and illustrations; their aim was not only to teach history but also to instill a love for and pride in one's country. Unlike most histories, he continued, his did not emphasize wars and battles and

avoided statistics. These events and their analysis, he felt, were of "little value" and "apt to make us forget that the true glory of a nation lies after all, in orderly progress. Times of peace, the proverb says, have few historians; but this may be more the fault of the historians than of the times." Higginson shared Ralph Waldo Emerson's conception of history as "the lengthened shadow of one man"; history and biography should be inseparable and never dull. "History written as it should be," Higginson opined in issue 46 of the *Atlantic* in 1905, "is all Swiss Family Robinson."

As an historian, Higginson does not rank high, having made "no original scholarly contribution," according to professional historians. In addition, he pronounces moral judgments on historical figures in accordance with his views and prejudices, a practice considered anathema by professionals. Higginson declared Andrew Jackson, for instance, to be narrow, ignorant, violent, and unreasonable in his use of the spoils system, commenting: "It is easier for the demagogue than for anyone else to pose for a time as a reformer, and even be mistaken for one." When Higginson was under consideration for an appointment to the history faculty at Harvard, a retired Harvard professional historian reported that members of the department thought he belonged in the English department rather than the history department and agreed to "keep him at arm's length" if he were to receive the appointment. He did not.

Higginson plainly never thought of himself as a professional historian. Instead, he sought to popularize history for students and the average reader. Despite the derivative nature of his histories in the eyes of professionals, his works were exceedingly popular because they brought to life what had formerly been, in general, dull and dry; he infused history with color and dramatic interest for young people and nonspecialists. So successful were these books (*Young Folks' History* alone sold two hundred thousand copies and was Higginson's best-selling work) that they were credited with being the catalyst for "a new era in writing history for children." The books were eventually translated into French, German, Italian, and Braille and were used in schools for decades.

The question of a teaching post at Harvard was not the only evidence of interest in Higginson by people in higher education. He was considered as a possible president of Harvard, and he was offered the presidency of the University of Nebraska, which he declined. He was a popular lecturer all over the country, and he particularly enjoyed small towns in the West.

Higginson's invalid wife, Mary, died in 1877; he married again six months later to Mary Thacher, a

Higginson and his daughter, Margaret, in 1885 (from Howard N. Meyer, Colonel of the Black Regiment: The Life of
Thomas Wentworth Higginson, *1967)*

niece of Henry Wadsworth Longfellow's first wife. Higginson was fifty-five, and his new wife was thirty-three. "Minnie" Higginson soon produced a daughter, Margaret Waldo, the delight of the formerly childless Higginson. In 1880 he was elected to a two-year term in the Massachusetts State Legislature. During his abolitionist years he had eschewed political office, saying that men of principle could not take part in the compromises required of politicians. But by the time of the election, his remarks comparing his own political philosophy to that of his opponent, Abby Kelley Foster, revealed a softening of his former hard-line stance: "Probably I belong by temperament to the half-loaf party and she to that which will accept nothing short of the whole." While he still favored immigration, his sentiments had changed somewhat. His opposition to admitting New Mexico to the union was based on the argument that the majority of its people did not speak English and would be unable to vote intelligently; immigrants must be assimilated before they would be ready for citizenship. Personal freedom, he felt, "is an absolute right," while "suffrage is a relative right, belonging to a certain stage of human progress."

While in office he supported legislation on political and economic rights for women and the poor; however, he voted against a bill that would have extended the ten-hour work law for women and children into the nonmanufacturing sector. He favored bills that extended religious freedom, fought anti-Catholic prejudice, and encouraged the newly established parochial schools. He urged public schools to counter the exodus of students to these Catholic schools by offering a superior education. When asked whether he thought the state should interfere if private schools distorted historical material, he replied, "Heaven forbid!" He also argued against the virulent anti-Semitism of the day, which was shared by many other men of letters, arguing that there was little drunkenness among the Jewish immigrants. Higginson stood with neither those who believed in the melting-pot theory nor those who feared that the immigrants would flood the country and forever remain unassimilated. He spoke positively of his belief that newcomers would become good citizens but would always retain marks of their origins. He thought this "multi-culturalism" a good thing, arguing that each group brought innate temperaments and strengths that would blend with those of other groups to the ultimate benefit of the country.

During this period Higginson was still involved in the women's movement as an editor of the *Woman's Journal* from 1870 to 1884. He asserted that women deserved the vote because it would assure them self-respect and self-protection, not because they were equal to men. He believed women had innate physical and psychological limitations and that although women should not be kept out of the workforce, their responsibilities to their families should come first. Eventually he began to view the issue of the female vote in the same light that he did that of voting rights for former slaves. During the 1883 election debates he advocated pushing civil service reform—he had become sympathetic to the mugwump movement in 1876—rather than women's suffrage. That movement, he had decided, "must be more matured in the public mind before it can wisely be submitted to an ordeal of battle." Unsurprisingly, such statements were viewed as a betrayal by many. The Massachusetts woman's rights association removed him as vice-president, and he was attacked both in print and in public.

Politics had not eclipsed authorship during this period. He published *Short Studies of American Authors* in 1880, just one of about a dozen critical works in addition to many essays on American, English, and European authors and their writings.

In 1884, hoping to push harder for civil service reform, he urged other Republicans to shift support away from candidate James G. Blaine to Grover Cleveland, the Democratic nominee. That same year, while his political views were stirring up the feminists, Higginson published the first of a series of biographies of American authors with one of Margaret Fuller. Having grown up in the same town with Fuller and feeling that she had influenced him more than anyone except Emerson and Parker, Higginson was drawn to sketch her life and believed he could do her life and accomplishments more justice than had earlier biographers. Emerson, William Henry Channing, and James Freeman Clarke had published *Memoirs of Margaret Fuller Ossoli* in 1852, and Julia Ward Howe had published a brief biography on Fuller in 1883. But Higginson based his book on previously unpublished and untapped manuscripts that yielded a fresh look at Fuller's life. Available to Higginson were five volumes of material kept by her family; her letters to Emerson, Channing, and others; her diary for 1844; her travel diary for England and Scotland; a diary of Bronson Alcott's; and a translation of Fuller's correspondence with her husband.

While the book is a traditional biography, Higginson focused particular attention on Fuller's centrality to and contributions to the Transcendentalist movement—her "Conversations" with women in Boston and Cambridge and the two years in which she edited *The Dial,* the primary voice of the Transcendentalist movement. He singled out her writings on Johann Wolfgang von Goethe, Robert James Mackintosh, and "Modern British Poets" for praise. Included are reviews of her books and other writings. She outshone her Transcendentalist colleagues, he felt, in two ways: she had the gift of "lyric glimpses" (the ability to put high thoughts into words) and talent as a literary critic. Higginson concluded that *Woman in the Nineteenth Century* (1845) and *Papers on Literature and Art* (1846) entitled Fuller to a high niche in the pantheon of American writers. His sympathetic view of her life and accomplishments went far beyond anything previously written about her; the book is among his best biographies.

Higginson returned to writing history in 1885, this time for adults. He enlarged the scope of his earlier history by beginning *A Larger History of the United States of America to the Close of President Jackson's Administration* (1885) with the Viking exploration and continuing down to the Jackson administration. The work was sketched out by Higginson's nephew Edward Channing, a Harvard historian, and Higginson reworked and polished it. His theme was the special and unusual nature of the founding and history of America. Higginson was reacting to complaints by James Fenimore Cooper, Hawthorne, and Lowell that America had nothing to offer to the writer; its history was too prosaic and unpoetic. Once again Higginson infused the book with life—this time by focusing on the extraordinary lives and times of many Americans. Two years later he published *Hints on Writing and Speech-Making* (1887).

Higginson's longtime correspondent, Emily Dickinson, died in 1886. They had met only twice in their twenty-four-year acquaintance, but she had sent him more than one hundred of her poems. He traveled to Amherst for her funeral and read Emily Brontë's "Last Lines" in honor of "that rare and strange creature," as he called Dickinson in his diary for 17 May.

Following Grover Cleveland's victory, Higginson was nominated for Congress by the Democrats in 1888 as a result of his support of their candidate. He ran on a platform of civil service reform and tariff reduction but was sharply criticized for his statements about blacks. All of his past service in their behalf was forgotten; what was foremost in the voters' minds now was that he had denied the injustices of Reconstruction and stated that there was as much prejudice in the North as in the South. Southern blacks, he had argued, had voluntarily chosen to de-emphasize politics by putting the getting of an education and rising financially before getting the vote, and the race riots were the result of this decision rather than of injustice. As he looked back on his days as an implacable abolitionist, he stated that he had been too hasty, too intolerant, too lacking in understanding for the situation of Southern whites; in many ways they had been powerless to deal with the slavery question.

Higginson was roundly attacked by former abolitionists, including Frederick Douglass. Higginson's candidacy was also assailed by labor and farm interests, which were angered by his failure to support their side in more than seven hundred strikes the previous year or in the horsecar strikes of 1888. Not one to avoid a battle, Higginson boarded one of the horsecars, now driven by nonunion "scabs," and rode through the picket line, despite a barrage of rocks. When the Haymarket anarchists were convicted and sentenced to death, Higginson approved. These reformers, he concluded, had pushed too hard and stirred up too much strife; they were a threat to peace, stability, and individualism. Higginson's gradualist response also did nothing to enhance his status with labor; he published a poem in the *Nationalist,* "Heirs of Time," that once again urged patience and predicted that eventually the poor would be rewarded.

Higginson had come to side with businessmen, especially those whom he believed to have their workers' interests at heart. For thirty years he had repeatedly delivered his "Aristocracy of the Dollar" lecture, in which he hailed socially responsible businessmen. Andrew Carnegie, with his "Gospel of Wealth," welcomed Higginson as an ally. Shorn of black, labor, and much female support, Higginson's candidacy went down to defeat.

Higginson is perhaps best known today for his part in publishing Emily Dickinson's poetry. He did not take the initiative, however, to see her poems in print. Mabel Loomis Todd, wife of a professor at Amherst and the lover of Dickinson's brother, contacted Higginson in November 1889, seeking his aid in editing the poems for publication. Hesitant to tackle the work because of his health, other projects, and his fears that her work was too odd to please the public, he agreed to help if Todd would do most of the work. His part was to be the final editing, the preface, publishing arrangements, and publicity. His position as a greatly respected man of letters with wide contacts and respect made him a valuable ally for Todd.

Most Dickinson scholars have concluded that Higginson was responsible for altering and regularizing many of Dickinson's rhymes and replacing her dashes with commas and periods. Thomas H. Johnson, in his edition of Dickinson's poems, takes the traditional view, attributing most of the changes to Higginson. In his introduction Johnson writes that Todd and Higginson selected the 115 poems for the first edition (they did not realize at the time that there would be a second collection) and that Higginson "undertook to smooth rhymes, regularize the meter, delete provincialisms, and substitute 'sensible' metaphors. Thus 'folks' became 'those,' 'heft' became 'weight,' and occasionally line arrangement was altered." Anna Mary Wells in her 1963 biography *Dear Preceptor: The Life and Times of Thomas Wentworth Higginson* challenges this view. Wells argues that Todd tinkered with Dickinson's poems, that Higginson was working not from Dickinson's originals but from copies made—and already altered—by Todd.

The evidence suggests that Wells is at least partially correct. Todd did the preliminary editing, and Higginson's reaction when he received the poems Todd had chosen for the book—poems he previously had been unaware of—is enlightening: "I can't tell you how much I am enjoying these poems. There are many new to me which take my breath away & which also have *form* beyond most of those I have seen before. . . . My confidence in their *availability* is greatly increased." As Tilden Edelstein points out, for Higginson, *form* "meant maximum revision by the poet to conform to accepted literary standards." Higginson's own poems clung tenaciously to accepted standards; he viewed Dickinson's spurning of these standards as odd and an almost insurmountable obstacle to publication, as he had told her regarding the first poems she sent him. What impressed him about the new poems was undoubtedly the editing that Mrs. Todd had done.

Higginson, however, appears to have done at least some of the tinkering himself. On 28 August 1890 he wrote to A. Higginson about some specific changes that he had made in the poems. Objecting to "The grass so little has to do / I wish I were a hay," he declared, "It cannot go in so, everybody would say that *hay* is a collective noun requiring the definite article. Nobody can call it *a* hay!" Higginson changed the offending word to "the hay." His sensibilities also stumbled over her alliteration in "And what a Billow be," changing the line to "And what a wave must be." Higginson's most egregious act of alteration, according to Dickinson purists, occurred in "Because I could not stop for death." He titled the poem "The Chariot," changed some of the words, and left out one stanza completely—the one that describes the speaker in her wedding finery, traveling to her wedding with God:

Or rather—He passed Us—
The Dews drew quivering and chill—
For only Gossamer, my Gown—
My Tippet—only Tulle—

The line "The Cornice—in the Ground" was altered to "The cornice but a mound." Edelstein speculates that Higginson completely missed the coexistence of mortality and immortality in the poem, the "simultaneous existence of mortal remains and immortal soul," and changed the poem to reflect his notion of it as merely a view of the soul's ascension to heaven.

The article Higginson published in the *Christian Union* prior to the advent of the publication of the book of poems suggests that he was convinced that Dickinson had told him the truth when she wrote him that for her, publication was as far removed as "firmament from fin." He had asked her repeatedly for poems to publish and had been rebuffed. She was one of those poets, he said, who wrote "for the relief of their own mind and without thought of publication." Because Dickinson destroyed most of Higginson's letters to her, however, there is no way of ascertaining whether he did in actuality express the desire to publish her work. In the article Higginson describes her poetry as "plucked up by the roots, with earth, stones, and dew adhering—it was wayward and unconventional in the last degree; defiant of form, measure, rhyme, and even grammar. . . ." He hoped readers would overlook these defects for the power of the work. Considering what is known of Higginson's reactions to Dickinson's unorthodox style and his published views on other innovators of his day, Higginson probably did much "repair work" on her poems and was pleased by any alterations Todd had done.

In his preface to the first edition Higginson took a different tack than he had in the *Christian Union* article. He wrote that Dickinson had no choice in how she wrote; she was simply a passive receptor of flashes of original and profound insight into nature and life. He asserted that the poems were "published as they were written, with very few superficial changes."

Before the book came out, Higginson expressed doubts that it should have been published at all, but the public loved the collection. The first edition of five hundred was soon followed by three more editions and, within a year, a second series. Todd then published a third series on her own. Higginson's culpability in the alterations of the first collection is clear in his suggestion to Mrs. Todd when she mentioned the possibility of putting out a second series: "Let us alter as little as possible now that the public ear is opened." This collection received much less editing.

Perhaps spurred by the work with Dickinson's poetry, Higginson published an edition of his own and his wife's work in 1893. His title, *Such As They Are: Poems,* reflects his awareness of his own limitations as a poet. While he believed poetry to be the highest kind of literature and thought it was more capable than the novel or essay of transporting the mind to new heights,

he was a sensitive enough critic to gauge the worth of his own efforts. As one would expect from his criticisms of Dickinson's poems, he did not experiment with nontraditional forms. He generally used conventional meters and verse forms for his lyrics. The majority are iambic pentameter with alternating rhymes in stanzas of four lines. During his early years he had written poems echoing his various reform sentiments, and he continued to write on this theme as he aged, many times in poems dedicated to particular writers he admired. He celebrated John Greenleaf Whittier and Helen Hunt Jackson for their contributions to the abolitionist cause and Edward Bellamy for his concern for the working poor. Most popular with the public were his Civil War poems—"Waiting for the Bugle" among them. The final lines read, "Though the sound of cheering dies down to a moan / We shall find our lost youth when the bugle is blown."

After the Civil War most of his poems focused on domestic themes. His young daughter, Margaret, provided inspiration for many. This poem, published earlier in *The Afternoon Landscape* (1889), is typical of his poetry about her:

> Joy of the morning,
>   Darling of the dawning,
> Blithe, lithe little daughter of mine!
>   While with thee ranging
>   Sure I'm exchanging
> Sixty of my years for six years like thine.

True to his Transcendentalist roots, some of his poems describe his response to nature. In "Sea-Gulls at Fresh Pond," also from the earlier collection, Higginson reveals his frustrations as a poet:

> I am no nearer to those joyous birds
>   Than when, long since, I watched them as a child;
>   Nor am I nearer to that flock more wild,
> Most shy and vague of all elusive things,
>   My unattainable thoughts, unreached by words.
>   I see the flight, but never touch the wings.

In 1895 he compiled *Massachusetts in the Army and Navy during the War of 1861–65.* The volumes included a comprehensive overview of the contribution of the state to the Union cause, a history of its regiments and their major battles, a list of officers, and the names of those killed in battle. He also included a section on "Massachusetts Women in the War," the only contemporary account of the war that honored women's efforts to save the Union.

He took an autobiographical look backward in *Cheerful Yesterdays,* originally serialized in the *Atlantic Monthly* in 1896 and then published in book form in 1898. The book is unusual for the genre: it is relatively free of egotism. Higginson displays astonishing humility and a surprising capacity for self-assessment in the face of his popularity; he knew that he did not possess great talent. His reminiscences over seventy years reflect the sweetness and generosity of temperament that drew so many to him. His lifetime spanned many great happenings in which he was near the epicenter—Transcendentalism, abolition and the black and women's suffrage movements, the Civil War, the rise of organized labor and socialism, and controversies over imperialism, to name a few. He was acquainted with, fought alongside, and shared platforms with most of the greatest names of his day, and his work appeared in the most prestigious journals. Howard Mumford Jones considered *Cheerful Yesterdays* a neglected masterpiece.

Looking backward did not keep Higginson from involvement in current problems. The gradualist view of progress continued to be his philosophy, although he found himself allied with many who were far more radical than he. In 1895 he declared that he was sixty percent socialist; the movement offered answers to many social ills. But he did not favor nationalization of all industry or the socialist plan to equalize white- and blue-collar workers; this desire ignored the necessity for highly trained leaders. Even though he had great compassion for the suffering of the working poor, he did not think capitalism was totally irresponsible. In 1896, in response to the antitrust movement, he wrote, "Corporations do not pay salaries of twenty thousand dollars because it amuses them. . . . We have to deal with a world where certain men are born with certain gifts."

As America began to involve itself in the affairs of other countries around the globe, Higginson spoke out against imperialism and the imposition of American culture on other peoples. While he desired to aid other countries toward self-determination, he feared that the situation with Cuba would end in war; too many people in the United States seemed to be spoiling for a fight. He wrote, "war is sweet to those who have never tried it." With other famous authors of the day and others, he founded the Anti-Imperialist League in 1898.

As his concern about imperialism grew, he began to reconsider the plight of blacks in the South. For years he had thought the problem lay with carpetbagging Northerners; now he began to suspect white Southerners had been the problem. While nominally free, blacks did not enjoy true freedom. For answers Higginson turned to Booker T. Washington and his policy of accommodation rather than to W. E. B. Du Bois, the choice of most of his anti-imperialist colleagues. He still believed the answer lay in education rather than confrontation: "I constantly urge my colored friends to be peaceful & hopeful & leave the future to settle matters for itself under the influence of higher education all

Higginson in 1903 (Library of Congress)

around." Although he had argued for giving blacks the vote earlier, he now believed that granting blanket voting rights to groups had proved counterproductive and had greatly increased friction between the races and had hurt those it was intended to help.

In his final years Higginson turned his attention to biographies of Longfellow and Whittier, both for the *American Men of Letters* series. Unlike his earlier biography of Margaret Fuller, neither the Longfellow nor the Whittier book brought to the world any new information or sources. As always, Higginson emphasized the "ideal" qualities of his subjects—their generosity, humor, philanthropy, and humanitarian impulses. He also published biographies of his ancestors Francis and Stephen Higginson in 1891 and 1907, respectively. In addition to these full-length biographies he also wrote short biographical essays on a score of contemporary figures—Emerson, Alcott, Whitman, Lanier, and some of the reformers. While intended as brief biographies filled with personal reminiscences, these works included criticism of the subjects' works. Not surprisingly, he lauded those who agreed with his aesthetics and moral idealism and downplayed those who did not. What he prized most was the combination of well-formed style and themes of social liberalism and spiritual idealism. He prized rich, metaphorical language, elevated diction, and rhetorical grace.

Higginson also published collections of essays—*Book and Heart: Essays on Literature and Life* in 1897 and *Carlyle's Laugh, and Other Surprises* in 1909. These works joined a plethora of earlier forays into criticism and other thoughts on art and literature, such as "Literature As an Art" (1867), "Youth and the Literary Life" (1892), and "Literature As a Pursuit" (1905). He deplored what he called the "literary pendulum" that swings back and forth with popular taste. Urging readers to rise above this preference for the merely popular as opposed to the classical, he praised Hawthorne as an author whose work would stand the test of time, one whose work would survive the current onslaught of realism, which Higginson did not favor for the most part, because it elevated the actual above the ideal. Like Matthew Arnold he sought the best rather than the faddish. Cosmopolitanism held no charms for him; he preferred literature based upon the ideals of his country, works that "declared the essential dignity and value of the individual man." Unlike Cooper, Hawthorne, and Henry James, he thought the American scene was filled with potential for writers—a fresh perspective resulting from the history and social order of the country would yield the originality Emerson had called for in his 1837 address "The American Scholar."

Higginson thought the majority of American poets too tame, without sufficient "fire in the blood." He thought that Whitman, on the other hand, displayed not fire but coarseness. Higginson urged fire with a certain "delicacy." With his preference for the ideal, he had little sympathy for the Art for Art's Sake movement; art, he felt, should elevate and promote traditional American morality, not undermine it. He was ambivalent about the local-color movement: Sarah Orne Jewett's people were sometimes too sentimental; Mary Wilkins Freeman's characters, too grim. Higginson saw little in Mark Twain beyond his humor, and he could not agree with James that one should judge the author solely on his treatment of his subject, not on the subject itself. He thought James's characters too "thin" and lamented his lack of local color, but he judged James's best short stories, such as "Madame de Mauves," the best in modern literature. He was shocked by James's satire on the New England character in *The Europeans* (1878) and the women's suffrage movement in *The Bostonians* (1886). The work of William Dean Howells, despite his commitment to Realism over Idealism, was more to Higginson's taste, especially the novels that reflect Howells's socialist humanitarian concerns. Edith Wharton's *The House of Mirth* (1905)

seemed to Higginson "to stand at the head of all American Fiction, save Hawthorne alone." With the exception of Stephen Crane, Higginson had, predictably, little praise for the Naturalists. Crane's *Red Badge of Courage* (1895) recalled for Higginson his own war service. In *Book and Heart* he called Crane's novel "A Bit of War Photography." Through the years, most critics have pointed out both Higginson's astuteness and his limitations as a critic. Unable to see beyond his time, his background as an idealistic minister, and his own personal views on art, he assumed that Longfellow would live forever and Whitman would sink into oblivion.

Harvard honored Higginson on several occasions, awarding him an honorary LL.D. degree in 1898. In 1906 he led the Phi Beta Kappa procession and heard a black graduate deliver the address "Colonel Higginson and the First Colored Regiment." Higginson learned that he had also made his mark at Columbia University. He was told that his *Atlantic Essays* (1871) were studied in class with the essays of Benjamin Franklin, Emerson, Thoreau, and Francis Parkman. The way Higginson was viewed by his contemporaries is perhaps best suggested by his placing fourth among forty candidates in a public poll conducted by *Literary Life* magazine, aimed at choosing an Academy of Immortals from among living Americans; only Thomas Alva Edison, Twain, and Carnegie received more votes. In the same poll Higginson was voted best essayist. Today he is ranked with the exemplars of the Genteel Tradition—Thomas Bailey Aldrich, E. C. Stedman, and Hamilton Wright Mabie—a victim of the pendulum swings of literary taste.

When Higginson died 9 May 1911 at the age of eighty-seven, he was celebrated as a reformer, soldier, author, critic, biographer, poet, historian, and friend and colleague of many of the great leaders and thinkers of his day. He could perhaps be viewed as "cursed with versatility," as he said of himself; he tried many things and so truly excelled at none. "The trouble with me," he wrote, "is too great a range of tastes and interests. I love to do everything, to study everything, to contemplate and to write. . . . I need either two lives or forty-eight hours in the day to do it all." But despite having had only one life of twenty-four-hour days, Higginson still somehow managed to write and edit more than thirty-five books and publish hundreds of articles and essays. At his funeral, tribute was paid to his service with his black regiment when a group of black soldiers sounded muffled drums as the Loyal Legion Post named for him conducted military honors, and the worn flag of the First South Carolina Volunteers draped his coffin.

While Higginson is today ranked as a writer and critic of the second order, he was a remarkable man.

James W. Tuttleton's estimate of him is valid: "A man of high moral principle, a gentleman, a man without meanness or rancor, high-minded, devoted to literature and culture in the Arnoldian sense of the best that had been thought and said, a defender of human dignity and of the respect due the individual–whatever his or her race, creed, sex, politics, or national origin–committed to action in behalf of social democracy, preeminently a man of character and personal integrity, of deep compassion and wide sympathies–Wentworth Higginson is a memorable example of what an American man of letters in the nineteenth century could be."

Best remembered today as the man who did not appreciate Emily Dickinson's eccentric genius, he did correspond with his "cracked poetess," as his wife referred to Dickinson, for almost twenty-five years and worked hard to bring her work to public notice. Without his influential backing, her poems might never have been printed. Of his own work, his *Army Life in a Black Regiment* is receiving renewed critical appreciation, and *Cheerful Yesterdays* has received praise as an outstanding example of what autobiographical writing can be. His nature essays have received renewed scrutiny, with some critics viewing them as equal to Thoreau's and as links to the later work of John Muir and John Burroughs. Howard W. Hintz has called Higginson's nature studies "comparable with the best American writing that has been done in this form."

The ultimate judgment on Higginson will probably rest most favorably upon how he lived his life rather than on his writings. As a reformer, he lived to see many of his ideals realized; yet, he knew much remained to be done. He was full of hope for the future. The closing words of *Cheerful Yesterdays,* borrowed from French iconoclast Pierre Joseph Proudhon, delineate what Higginson considered to be the most important thing he could say of his own life: "Let my memory perish, if only humanity may be free."

Letters:

Letters and Journals of Thomas Wentworth Higginson, 1846–1906, edited by Mary Thacher Higginson (Boston & New York: Houghton Mifflin, 1921).

Bibliographies:

Winifred Mather, *A Bibliography of Thomas Wentworth Higginson* (Cambridge, Mass., 1906);

Mary Thacher Higginson, bibliographical appendix to *Thomas Wentworth Higginson: The Story of His Life* (Boston & New York: Houghton Mifflin, 1914);

Howard N. Meyer, "Thomas Wentworth Higginson," in *The Transcendentalists: A Review of Research in Criticism,* edited by Joel Myerson (New York: Modern Language Association, 1984), pp. 195–203;

Meyer, "Thomas Wentworth Higginson Checklist," *Higginson Journal,* 43 (1985): 42–44.

Biographies:

Th. Bentzon (Marie Therese De Solms Blanc), *A Typical American: Thomas Wentworth Higginson,* translated by E. M. Waller (London: Bell, 1902);

Mary Thacher Higginson, *Thomas Wentworth Higginson: The Story of His Life* (Boston & New York: Houghton Mifflin, 1914);

Anna Mary Wells, *Dear Preceptor: The Life and Times of Thomas Wentworth Higginson* (Boston: Houghton Mifflin, 1963);

Howard N. Meyer, *Colonel of the Black Regiment: The Life of Thomas Wentworth Higginson* (New York: Norton, 1967);

Tilden G. Edelstein, *Strange Enthusiasm: A Life of Thomas Wentworth Higginson* (New Haven: Yale University Press, 1968).

References:

Geoffrey T. Blodgett, "The Mind of the Boston Mugwump," *Mississippi Valley Historical Review,* 48 (1962): 614–634;

Van Wyck Brooks, "The Twilight of New England," in his *Sketches in Criticism* (New York: Dutton, 1932), pp. 211–217;

K. W. Cameron, "Higginson on Poetry," *Emerson Society Quarterly,* no. 29 (1962): 40–42;

Tilden G. Edelstein, "Emily Dickinson and Her Mentor in Feminist Perspective," in *Nineteenth-Century Women: Writers of the English Speaking World,* edited by Rhoda Nathan (Westport, Conn.: Greenwood Press, 1986), pp. 37–43;

Scott Giantvalley, "'Strict, Straight Notions of literary Propriety': Thomas Wentworth Higginson's Gradual Unbending to Walt Whitman," *Walt Whitman Review,* 4 (Spring 1987): 17–27;

Howard W. Hintz, *Thomas Wentworth Higginson: Disciple of the Newness* (New York: Graduate School of New York University, 1939);

William R. Hutchison, *The Transcendentalist Ministers: Church Reform in New England* (New Haven: Yale University Press, 1959);

Howard Mumford Jones, Introduction to *Army Life in a Black Regiment* (East Lansing: Michigan State University Press, 1960);

Joseph Katz, "The 'Preceptor' and Another Poet: Thomas Wentworth Higginson and Stephen Crane," *Serif,* 5 (1968): 17–21;

Elizabeth Lawson, "God as an 'Eclipse,'" *Dickinson Studies,* 61 (1987): 23–26;

Kent P. Ljungquist and Anthony Conti, "'Near My Heart' After Fifty Years: Thomas Wentworth

Higginson's Reminiscence of Worcester," *Concord Saunterer,* new series 3 (Fall 1995): 120–131;

Christopher Looby, "Flowers of Manhood: Race, Sex, and Floriculture from Thomas Wentworth Higginson to Robert Mapplethorpe," *Criticism: A Quarterly for Literature and the Arts,* 37 (Winter 1995): 109–156;

John Mann, "Dickinson's Letters to Higginson," in *Approaches to Teaching Dickinson's Poetry,* edited by Robin Riley Fast and Christine Mack Gordon (New York: Modern Language Association, 1989), pp. 39–46;

Raymond Mazurek, "'I Have no Monarch in My Life': Feminism, Poetry, and Politics in Dickinson and Higginson," in *Patrons and Protegées: Gender, Friendship, and Writing in Nineteenth-Century America,* edited by Shirley Marchalonis (New Brunswick, N.J.: Rutgers University Press, 1994), pp. 122–140;

Edgar L. McCormick, "Higginson, Emerson, and a National Literature," *Emerson Society Quarterly,* no. 37 (1964): 71–73;

McCormick, "Thomas Wentworth Higginson, Poetry Critic for the Nation, 1877–1903," *Serif,* 2 (1965): 14–19;

George Monteiro, "Emily Dickinson's Business," *Literature and Belief,* 10 (1990): 24–42;

Larry Olpin, "In Defense of the Colonel: Col. Higginson & a Problem of Literary Evaluation," *Higginson Journal,* 42 (June 1985): 3–14;

John M. Picker, "The Union of Music and Text in Whitman's *Drum-Taps* and Higginson's *Army Life in a Black Regiment,*" *Walt Whitman Quarterly Review,* 12 (Spring 1995): 230–245;

Benjamin Quarles, *The Negro in the Civil War* (Boston: Little, Brown, 1953);

Jerrald Ranta, "Dickinson's 'Alone and in a Circumstance' and the Theft of Intellectual Property," *ESQ: A Journal of the American Renaissance,* 41 (1995): 65–95;

Katherine Rodier, "'What Is Inspiration?': Emily Dickinson, T. W. Higginson, and Marin White Lowell," *Emily Dickinson Journal,* 4 (1995): 20–43;

Barton Levi St. Armand, "Fine Fitnesses: Dickinson, Higginson, and Literary Luminism," *Prospects,* 14 (1989): 141–173;

Maude L. Stevens, "Colonel Higginson and His Friends in Newport," *Newport Historical Society Bulletin,* 49 (April 1924): n. pag.;

James W. Tuttleton, *Thomas Wentworth Higginson,* edited by David Nordloh (Boston: Twayne, 1978);

Anna Mary Wells, "Note on Higginson's Reputation," *Dickinson Studies,* 51 (1984): 20–21;

Wells, "The Soul's Society: Emily Dickinson and Colonel Higginson," in *Nineteenth-Century Women Writers of the English-Speaking World,* edited by Rhoda B. Nathan (New York: Greenwood Press, 1986), pp. 221–229;

F. E. White, "Thomas Wentworth Higginson's Idea of Democracy," *Negro Historical Bulletin,* 6 (1942): 55–71;

D. H. Williams, "Thomas Wentworth Higginson on Thoreau and Maine," *Colby Library Quarterly,* 7 (1965): 29–32.

Papers:
Houghton Library at Harvard University houses more than 1,300 letters and 50 volumes of Thomas Wentworth Higginson's journals. The Boston Public Library has a significant collection, and other manuscripts are owned by the American Antiquarian Society, Yale University, the Huntington Library, the Massachusetts Historical Society, the University of Virginia, and the Pilgrim Society Library (in the Marston Watson Papers).

Samuel Johnson

(10 October 1822 – 19 February 1882)

Alan D. Brasher
East Georgia College

See also the Johnson entry in *DLB 1: The American Renaissance in New England.*

BOOKS: *The Crisis of Freedom. A Sermon Preached at the Free Church, in Lynn, on Sunday, June 11, 1854* (Boston: Crosby, Nichols, 1854);

A Discourse Preached on the Day of the National Funeral of President Lincoln, Wednesday, April 19, 1865 (N.p., 1865);

The Religion of a Free Church. A Discourse Delivered at the Opening of a Free Chapel, by the Independent Religious Society at Lynn, on Sunday, June 10, 1866 (Lynn, Mass.: W. W. Kellogg, 1866);

The Worship of Jesus in Its Past and Present Aspects (Boston: William V. Spencer, 1868);

A Ministry in Free Religion. A Discourse Delivered on the Occasion of Resigning this Relation, to the Free Church at Lynn, on Sunday, June 26, 1870 (Boston: Rand, Avery & Frye, 1870);

Labor Parties and Labor Reform (Boston, 1871);

Oriental Religions and Their Relation to Universal Religion. India (Boston: Osgood, 1872);

A Memorial of Charles Sumner. A Discourse Delivered at the Parker Memorial Meeting-House, to the Twenty-eighth Congregational Society, Boston, on Sunday, March 15, 1874 (Boston: A. Williams, 1874);

Oriental Religions and Their Relation to Universal Religion. China (Boston: Osgood, 1877);

Lectures, Essays, and Sermons, edited, with a memoir, by Samuel Longfellow (Boston & New York: Houghton, Mifflin, 1883);

Oriental Religions and Their Relation to Universal Religion. Persia (Boston: Osgood, 1885);

Theodore Parker: A Lecture, edited by John H. Clifford and Horace L. Traubel (Chicago: Charles H. Kerr, 1890);

Hymns (Andover, Mass.: Andover Press, 1899).

Collection: *Selected Writings of Samuel Johnson,* edited by Roger C. Mueller (Delmar, N.Y.: Scholars' Facsimiles & Reprints, 1977).

Samuel Johnson, 1843 (portrait by Charles Osgood; Essex Institute, Salem, Massachusetts)

OTHER: *A Book of Hymns for Public and Private Devotion,* edited by Johnson and Samuel Longfellow (Cambridge, Mass.: Metcalf, 1846);

Hymns of the Spirit, edited by Johnson and Longfellow (Boston: Ticknor & Fields, 1864).

SELECTED PERIODICAL PUBLICATIONS–
UNCOLLECTED: "Bond or Free," *Radical,* 1 (October 1865): 49–59;

"Discourses Concerning the Foundations of Religious Belief": I. "Past and Present," *Radical,* 1 (November 1865): 73–85; II. "Real and Imaginary

The Reverend Samuel Longfellow, Johnson's collaborator on two hymnbooks (Essex Institute, Salem, Massachusetts)

Authority," *Radical,* 1 (December 1865): 113–126; III. "The Fallacies of Supernaturalism," *Radical,* 1 (January 1866): 154–168; IV. "The Adequacy of Natural Religion," *Radical,* 1 (March 1866): 233–246; V. "Spiritual Needs and Certainties," *Radical,* 1 (May 1866): 313–325; VI. "Naturalism," *Radical,* 1 (July 1866): 401–413.

A second-generation Transcendentalist, Samuel Johnson is best known as an orientalist. Though generally dismissed for their reliance on texts in translation, the three volumes of Johnson's *Oriental Religions and Their Relation to Universal Religion* (1872–1885) represent a significant step in the field of comparative religions. His theory moves beyond the nineteenth-century notion of Christianity as the true religion toward which other major religions are progressing–suggesting, instead, that all major religions, Christianity included, are evolving toward a universal religion. Often overlooked are Johnson's "Discourses Concerning the Foundations of Religious Belief" and "Transcendentalism," important periodical publica-

tions offering clear and logical accounts of his transcendental philosophy.

The son of a physician, Dr. Samuel Johnson, and a descendant of an old Salem family, Anna (Dodge) Johnson, Samuel Johnson grew up with the wealth of a busy seaport town and the conservatism of a community wishing to protect its way of life. As the eldest of eleven children, four of whom died before he reached the age of fourteen, Johnson developed a sense of responsibility to his younger siblings, but not to the point of sacrificing his own childhood; he was a vigorous and enthusiastic boy, good at sports and various games. His love of books, as well as his indoctrination into Unitarianism, developed in his parents' home. The museum of the East India Marine Society in Salem seems the most likely point of origin for Johnson's interest in the Orient; it housed treasures from India and China, two of the three nations to which Johnson later devoted a full volume of his three-volume series *Oriental Religions and Their Relation to Universal Religion.*

At sixteen, Johnson entered Harvard, where, according to D. H. Jaques, a classmate, he applied himself faithfully to his courses, even those he was not naturally inclined toward. Likewise, he attended the college chapel with "unfailing punctuality," rarely missing services or morning and evening prayers. Johnson's discipline, however, did not commit him to sensationalism or formal Unitarianism; after college he forged his own beliefs, arguing against Lockean empiricism and for the universality of religions. In his memoir Samuel Longfellow described Johnson as a "transcendentalist by nature." In a passage from his diary dated 1843, Johnson declares that his "highest intuitions are not things of argument." Chosen by his graduating classmates to give the class oration, Johnson characterized as heroic the ongoing efforts to reform the Unitarian Church.

Despite having informed his pastor upon entering Harvard that he would not continue in the Harvard Divinity School after his graduation, he did enroll there in the fall of 1842. Though ill health caused him to leave the divinity school in May 1844, he returned in 1845 and was graduated July 1846. During his years at the divinity school, Johnson was among the young scholars who rebelled against the conservative position of the church. Unwilling to assent to the reconciliation of reason to revelation, a tenet espoused by the Unitarian Church, Johnson nevertheless applied himself to his work with characteristic devotion, hoping to accomplish reform from within the church. As was customary, Johnson began to preach in local churches during his senior year. These sermons were an unremunerated apprenticeship, thereby avoiding competition for jobs between recent graduates and the senior class. One of his earliest sermons was delivered in West Roxbury, the pulpit recently vacated by Theodore Parker, a radical reformer whose later influence on Johnson was profound; Johnson visited Parker's grave in Florence, Italy, shortly after his death in 1860, planting an ivy vine alongside it. Johnson's own radicalism later outreached Parker's as the former pursued a universal religion and the latter a purer Christianity.

In 1846, before Johnson's graduation from Harvard Divinity School, Johnson and Samuel Longfellow compiled *A Book of Hymns for Public and Private Devotion* (1846) to replace the antiquated one that Frank Appleton, a former schoolmate, found inadequate. The hymnbook proved to be surprisingly traditional, with many hymns referring to Christianity and the divinity of Christ. Longfellow claimed that the inclusion of standard hymns had been his own doing, admitting that Johnson had been "generally a little in advance in his theology." Parker adopted the book for his congregation, then meeting at the Music Hall in Boston, because, despite its orthodox references to Christ, it forwarded the transcendental premise that the Holy Spirit not only exists but is present in the human soul. Though in eighteen years a second compilation was necessary to produce a collection of hymns devoid of Christian orthodoxy, Johnson's influence produced a hymnbook that served the reform movement rather than the conservative Unitarians. The compilers accomplished this goal by taking liberties with the hymns they chose, amending many of them. Hymnists included Ralph Waldo Emerson, Parker, Harriet Beecher Stowe, and Henry Wadsworth Longfellow, as well as both editors. The hymnal proved popular, going into a second printing when the first five hundred copies sold out in four months.

After his graduation from the divinity school, Johnson began "candidating" in various Unitarian pulpits. His sermons found more favor with the younger parishioners than the elder. Johnson was charged with being a Deist, mixing politics with religion, and trying to break up churches. Offers of a permanent position did not come. Though he preached for more than a year to the newly formed Harrison Square congregation in Dorchester, they never extended him a call to permanent ministry. The Harrison Square church asked Johnson not to bring politics into his sermons, and he responded in a letter of January 1849, insisting on the "freedom of the pulpit." Johnson's stance on politics in the pulpit locates him in the heart of the developing Unitarian reform movement. Eschewing the notion that a minister's job is to make his parishioners comfortable, Johnson declared that to include issues of politics, commerce, and custom in his sermons was his duty. He strove not to supplant religion with these forces but to demonstrate the primacy of Christian principles over them.

In 1853 Johnson received a call to minister to a new society in Lynn, Massachusetts. The group had formed

Johnson in middle age (Essex Institute, Salem, Massachusetts)

as a Unitarian society, but their new minister refused ordination into that denomination or any other. Conditions of Johnson's acceptance of the pulpit included the reorganization of the group as an independent congregation, with no ties to the Unitarian Church. He must never administer the sacraments and must accept no fees levied to support the church. On 7 August 1853 the Lynn Free Church was formed, with Johnson as minister; he retired from the Lynn Free Church on 26 June 1870. Johnson supplemented his income as a lecturer—addressing abolition, temperance, women's suffrage, and eastern religions. He also addressed labor reform in an essay published in the November 1871 issue of *The Radical*, "Labor Parties and Labor Reform."

In May 1859 Johnson introduced John Brown to a group meeting at the Lynn church, and Brown stirred in him the same admiration and awe that others of the Transcendentalist group felt on first encountering Brown. Describing Brown in his journal entry of 1 June as a "genuine old Revolutionist" and "old warrior," Johnson found inspiration in Brown's "devotion to the slave" despite the sacrifices he had made in his crusade against slavery: one of Brown's sons had been killed and another driven mad. Like Parker, Emerson, and Henry David Thoreau, Johnson embraced Brown's conviction, at least initially,

The Johnson family homestead in North Andover, Massachusetts, where Johnson lived from 1876 until his death in 1882
(Essex Institute, Salem, Massachusetts)

even though Johnson would not shed blood in the name of the causes he championed. Johnson's immediate response to Southern secession was that the slaveholding states should be permitted to withdraw from the Union; however, he ultimately felt that the Union must be preserved with the abolition of slavery enforced throughout. Transcendental optimism, the belief that present events, no matter how dark they may appear to participant and bystander, are part of a universal evolution, informed Johnson's view of the war and helped him reconcile himself to its horrors.

Hymns of the Spirit (entered into the Library of Congress in 1864) was a revision of Johnson and Longfellow's *A Book of Hymns for Public and Private Devotion*. The new collection was compiled by the editors during a yearlong European tour beginning in the summer of 1860, undertaken for Johnson's recuperation from the chronic intestinal troubles he had suffered since college. The preface to the revised edition makes clear the intent of the revision. The new hymnbook proclaims "God as the Present Spirit and Indwelling Life of all . . . Nature as His outward manifestation . . . human Spirit as His more intimate revealer,

and its experiences as the steps of its growth in union with Him." Johnson and Longfellow rearranged and altered the contents of *A Book of Hymns for Public and Private Devotion* so considerably that *Hymns of the Spirit* is only a distant cousin to the original hymnbook. The new edition, dedicated to a more radical Christianity, was made necessary by Johnson's inability to utter the theological sentiments in almost fifty of the hymns in his first collection.

In the fall of 1861 Johnson returned to the Lynn Free Church, where he remained for the next nine years. During the last half of his ministry Johnson published several articles and letters in the Transcendentalist periodical *The Radical*. One of his most noteworthy contributions to the journal was "Bond or Free," from the October 1865 number. In "Bond or Free," Johnson criticizes James Freeman Clarke's remarks on the need for unity within the denomination as an attempt to calm the radical faction of Unitarians who had objected to the statement of belief using the term "Lord Jesus Christ." Clarke responded in a letter to the editor of *The Radical* and set in motion a series of letters and articles through which each man attempted to set the other straight. Clarke argued from the more orthodox perspective, believing in the divinity of Christ and authenticity of miracles, while Johnson granted final authority to individual intuition. Johnson's responses to Clarke pointed to the contradictions of a creed acknowledging the authority of both intuition and institution.

Between November 1865 and July 1866, in the first volume of *The Radical,* Johnson published a series of articles, "Discourses Concerning the Foundations of Religious Belief." This six-part series formulates the transcendental religious theory that underlies his work on oriental religions. "Past and Present" concludes that humankind must find its own divine lessons in the present rather than depending upon the teachings from the past. "Real and Imaginary Authority" finds spiritual authority in the individual self, asserting that God could not be in Jesus unless he is in every human being. "The Fallacies of Supernaturalism" argues against the possibility of miraculous, supernatural events and against the infallibility of humans. "The Adequacy of Natural Religion" locates the source of spiritual growth in the individual character rather than traditional theologies or church dogmas. "Spiritual Needs and Certainties" defines true religion as a living faith devoted to reality, committed to righteous acts, and loyal to its own "spiritual nature." "Naturalism" exalts thought, liberty, and progress as the natural elements of true religion. Taken together, these essays delineate a theory of American Transcendentalism often touched on or hinted at but seldom so clearly defined.

When Johnson resigned his ministry of the Lynn Free Church on 26 June 1870, he did so with the intention of devoting more time to his work on Oriental religions, work which he had begun in the 1850s. His introduction to the Orient certainly dates to his youth in Salem, but his scholarly interest in Oriental religions seems a natural outgrowth of his liberalism. For Transcendentalists the sanctity of the intuition arose from the divine spark present in each human soul. Since this spark allows the individual to intuit truths beyond the proofs of science or religious institutions, granting ascendancy to one faith over another represents an unnecessary limitation of one's spiritual progress. In 1871 Clarke published *Ten Great Religions,* in which he argues for the universality of Christianity. Ultimately, Clarke asserts that the great religions of the world include Truths, but that Christianity is the one religion that includes all Truths. While Clarke's view suited the tastes of many of the radical Unitarians, it was not palatable to Johnson. For him Christianity was merely one among many religions evolving toward a universal one.

The first volume of Johnson's *Oriental Religions and Their Relation to Universal Religion,* subtitled *India,* was published by James R. Osgood and Company in 1872. Because of Johnson's relegation of Christianity to equal

Photograph of Johnson's library taken in March 1882, shortly after his death, with the manuscript for his unfinished book on Persia lying on his desk (Essex Institute, Salem, Massachusetts)

footing with Hinduism and Buddhism and his polemical tone, Osgood required Johnson to pay the stereotyper out of his own pocket (Roberts Brothers had turned down the manuscript for these same reasons). The critical response was generally unfavorable. The most persistent criticism of Johnson's oriental scholarship has been grounded in his inability to read any of the primary sources in their original languages, relying instead on translations into English, French, and German, as well as on questionable or out-of-date texts. Working from translations left Johnson open to attack for taking things "at second hand." According to Samuel Longfellow, however, "Had he given the needed time to them, we should never have had his books. His years were not enough for the work, as it was." Longfellow goes on to defend Johnson's approach on the grounds that "the most learned linguist may well be wanting in the philosophic and spiritual insight which Johnson possessed." In the end, however, scholars were unaccepting of Johnson's work. Carl T. Jackson has suggested that Johnson's work fell somewhere between the popular and the scholarly markets; the volumes were too large and cumbersome for the general public because of footnotes that reflected Johnson's solid grounding in the scholarship of the day; yet, the books fell short of the scholarly rigor applied by leading orientalists and scholars of comparative religion in the late nineteenth century. The volumes subtitled *China* (1877) and *Persia* (1885, unfinished at the time of Johnson's death and published posthumously) were also popular failures, despite garnering a few positive notices.

Johnson's methodology required that each culture he studied had followed a religion that had grown naturally from the "distinctive mind" of its people. In his introduction to the volume on India, he argues that each of the major religions aspires to the divine but that each describes this force differently according to its own dominant tendencies. Johnson may have forced himself into overgeneralization, asserting (also in the India volume) that the Hindu mind is "cerebral" because its tendencies are toward the "subtle introversive, and contemplative," the Chinese mind is "muscular" because of its efficiency "in the world of concrete facts and uses," and the Persian mind is "nervous" because of its tendency toward bringing speculation into practice and then spinning new speculations out of that practice. Probably the most damaging aspect of his approach, however, was his criticism of the Christian claim to primacy. Johnson proclaims the "Christian ideal . . . but a single force among others, all equally in the line of movement." He contends that Christians disparage older religions, designating them "heathen" and merely natural, while holding Christianity as the true spiritual religion. In this scheme, other religions may be seen to progress toward Christianity; yet, Johnson insists that Christianity is progressing alongside these religions toward something greater and truly universal.

In each of his volumes Johnson addresses the spiritual evolution of humankind in order to demonstrate the organicism of each culture's major religion. Johnson finds the force behind spiritual evolution in a major tenet of Transcendentalism—the pervasive "universal Spirit" of Emerson's *Nature* (1836). In the volume on Persia, Johnson argues that when humans see themselves as "centres of productive force" and believe in an "unseen and unattained," they develop a personal will. Religions grow out of this personal will, which depends on the ability of the individual to distinguish him- or herself from the "world of forces, natural and human, into which we are born." The move toward universal religion, then, will come when humans move beyond the religions that develop out of personal will, and seek unity with the Universal Spirit, which is finally recognized as the author of personal will.

"Transcendentalism," an essay by Johnson, was published in the November 1877 number of the *Radical Review*, the same year the second volume of *Oriental Religions* was published. In it Johnson argues for the interdependence of modern science and transcendental philosophy. Distinguishing between transcendental intuition and theological inspiration, he chides scientists for grouping the two simply because they center on something beyond physical experience. While inspiration denies the universality of natural law, transcendental intuition acknowledges these laws but looks to the observer as well as the observed. Johnson finds in the individual's relationship to the physical world a relation to the infinite—since the universe is infinite—that connects the scientist probing the unfathomable to the transcendentalist intuiting the unknowable. Finally, he declares all "universal and invariable" laws transcendental, since no string of consistent experiences can dictate the outcome of the next. By nature, then, science and transcendentalism are idealistic endeavors, searching for the Truth that unifies all.

During the composition and publication process of *Oriental Religions*, Johnson's health deteriorated. After the death of his father in 1876, he took up residence in the ancestral homestead in North Andover. There he set up a study for writing but also began gardening, taking over the family farm. His friend Samuel Longfellow observed that the labor improved his health somewhat. Nonetheless, Johnson continued to be plagued by intestinal trouble and lower-body stiffness. He died at midnight, 19 February 1882. Funeral services were held at the Unitarian Church in North Andover on 23 February. His body was interred in the family plot in Harmony Grove Cemetery in North Salem.

Bibliography:

Roger C. Mueller, "Samuel Johnson," in *The Transcendentalists: A Review of Research and Criticism,* edited by Joel Myerson (New York: Modern Language Association of America, 1984), pp. 204–206.

Biographies:

Samuel Longfellow, "Memoir," in *Lectures, Essays, and Sermons,* edited by Longfellow (Boston & New York: Houghton, Mifflin, 1883), pp. 1–142;

Roger C. Mueller, "Samuel Johnson, American Transcendentalist: A Short Biography," *Essex Institute Historical Collections,* 115 (January 1979): 9–67.

References:

Carl T. Jackson, "The Orient in Post-Bellum American Thought: Three American Popularizers," *American Quarterly,* 12 (Spring 1970): 68–72;

Jackson, *The Oriental Religions in American Thought* (Westport, Conn.: Greenwood Press, 1981).

Papers:

Samuel Johnson's papers—including correspondence, sermons, and diaries—are at the Essex Institute in Salem, Massachusetts.

Sylvester Judd

(23 July 1813 – 26 January 1853)

Richard D. Hathaway
State University of New York at New Paltz

See also the Judd entry in *DLB 1: The American Renaissance in New England.*

BOOKS: *A Young Man's Account of His Conversion from Calvinism. A Statement of Facts,* anonymous, American Unitarian Association Tracts, first series no. 128 (Boston: Munroe, 1838);

The Little Coat: A Sermon, Unitarian Sunday-School Society Tract Series, no. 14 (Boston: American Reform Tract and Book Society, ca. 1840);

The Beautiful Zion. A Sermon . . . Preached July 4, 1841 (Augusta, Me.: Printed by Severance & Dorr, 1841);

A Moral Review of the Revolutionary War, or Some of the Evils of that Event Considered. A Discourse Delivered at the Unitarian Church, Augusta, Sabbath Evening, March 13th, 1842. With an Introductory Address, and Notes (Hallowell, Me.: Printed by Glazier, Masters & Smith, 1842);

A Discourse Touching the Causes and Remedies of Intemperance. Preached February 2, 1845 (Augusta, Me.: Printed by Wm. T. Johnson, 1845);

Margaret. A Tale of the Real and Ideal, Blight and Bloom; Including Sketches of a Place Not Before Described, Called Mons Christi, anonymous (1 volume, Boston: Jordan & Wiley, 1845; revised edition, 2 volumes, Boston: Phillips, Sampson, 1851; London: Ward, Lock, 1874);

Philo: An Evangeliad. By the Author of 'Margaret; A Tale of the Real and Ideal' (Boston: Phillips, Sampson, 1850);

The True Dignity of Politics. A Sermon: By the Rev. Sylvester Judd, Preached in Christ Church, Augusta, May 26, 1850 (Augusta, Me.: Printed by William T. Johnson, Printer to the State, 1850);

Richard Edney and the Governor's Family. A Rus-Urban Tale, Simple and Popular, Yet Cultured and Noble, of Morals, Sentiment, and Life, Practically Treated and Pleasantly Illustrated Containing, Also, Hints on Being Good and Doing Good. By the Author of "Margaret," and "Philo" (Boston: Phillips, Sampson, 1850);

Sylvester Judd

The Birthright Church: A Discourse by the Late Rev. Sylvester Judd . . . Designed for "Thursday Lecture" in Boston, Jan. 6, 1853, edited by Joseph H. Williams (Boston: Crosby, Nichols, 1853);

The Church: In a Series of Discourses, edited by Williams (Boston: Crosby, Nichols, 1854).

EDITION: *Margaret: A Tale of the Real and Ideal, Blight and Bloom* (Upper Saddle River, N.J.: Gregg Press, 1968).

OTHER: "Worth of the Soul," in *Sermons on Christian Communion, Designed to Promote the Growth of the Religious Affections, by Living Ministers,* edited by Thomas R. Sullivan (Boston: Crosby & Nichols, 1848), pp. 24–37.

SELECTED PERIODICAL PUBLICATIONS–UNCOLLECTED: "Truth," *Yale Literary Magazine,* 1 (June 1836): 129–131;

"The Outlaw and His Daughter," *Yale Literary Magazine,* 1 (June 1836): 155–161;

"The Dramatic Element in the Bible," *Atlantic Monthly,* 4 (August 1859): 137–153.

Sylvester Judd's *Margaret. A Tale of the Real and Ideal, Blight and Bloom; Including Sketches of a Place Not Before Described, Called Mons Christi* (1845) was hailed by James Russell Lowell in *A Fable for Critics* (1848) as "the first Yankee book / With the *soul* of Down East in't." In his article "Longfellow's *Kavanagh:* Nationality in Literature," for *The North American Review* (July 1849), Lowell called *Margaret* "the most emphatically *American* book ever written," and in his review of the novel for the *National Anti-Slavery Standard* (24 January 1850) Lowell called it "one of the most original books yet written in America." As might be expected from the author of *The Biglow Papers* (1848 and 1862), Lowell was primarily interested in the colorful New Englandness of the novel and in its homespun language; today, however, the novel, while also valued for those qualities, is known chiefly for its Emersonian overtones. Lydia Maria Child's *Philothea* (1836), the only other Transcendentalist novel, is set in ancient Athens and does not have the down-to-earth quality that Lowell prized, the "smack of the soil" that Ralph Waldo Emerson advocated. *Margaret* does. Contemplating the rose-gold of a rhubarb root in the spring, Margaret says, "Children that germinate with a plenty of mother earth about them, come out in the fairest hues." The colloquial warmth in "a plenty of" adds flavor to the idealism. One thinks of Emerson's "I expand and live in the warm day like corn and melons," criticized by Harvard teacher Francis Bowen as deficient in propriety. Judd's diction, condemned by such genteel critics, went far beyond these mild examples, far beyond anything Emerson wrote.

Judd was born in Westhampton, Massachusetts, on 23 July 1813, the second child of Apphia (Hall) Judd and Sylvester Judd II (1789–1860). Magnified in the memory of Westhampton orators fifty years later was the awesome brow of young Sylvester's grandfather, "Squire" Sylvester Judd (1752–1832)–farmer, number-one citizen, and administrator of justice in the town. Westhampton was a tiny village in the hills near Northampton, and in both towns, indeed throughout the Connecticut Valley, Jonathan Edwards still ruled. That fact was determinative. *Margaret* reflects Judd's love of the natural environment and people of Westhampton, and his rejection of their Calvinism. Judd's father–self-taught at Latin, Spanish, Greek, poetry, and historical research–failing at storekeeping and farming, took his still-growing family to Northampton in 1822. There he became editor of the influential *Hampshire Gazette* and also began jotting down facts–everything from genealogies and local history to temperature changes and spring sproutings. His *History of Hadley* (1863) and his many thousands of manuscript pages are still important for any study of his time and place. He passed on to his son his habit of close observation; *Margaret* is a veritable junk shop of miscellaneousness–flowers, bird calls, unusual dialect words, cracker-barrel aphorisms, folk superstitions, scraps of Latin, and the reiterative litanies of town gossips.

Judd the father, though outwardly orthodox and Federalist, like nearly everyone else in Northampton and Westhampton, was no bigot–indeed, he was too rationalistic ever to undergo the conversion experience necessary to his joining the church. Counting among his friends historian and cosmopolite George Bancroft–a Democrat and a Unitarian–he became too liberal to continue as chief journalist of Hampshire County. In 1835 at the age of forty-six he retired permanently, with a wife and six children, capital of less than $5,000, and his son Sylvester in his junior year at Yale College. No wonder that one of young Sylvester's earliest poems was an impassioned protest against poverty and that his undecorated childhood homes led him to write, in both *Margaret* and *Richard Edney and the Governor's Family. A Rus-Urban Tale, Simple and Popular, Yet Cultured and Noble, of Morals, Sentiment, and Life, Practically Treated and Pleasantly Illustrated Containing, Also, Hints on Being Good and Doing Good. By the Author of "Margaret," and "Philo"* (1850), rags-to-riches plots that ended in celebrating the virtues of beautiful interiors, filled with art and music.

In Northampton and Westhampton the chief events of the 1820s were sensational episodes of religious controversy. The Unitarian heresy had come into the open in 1815, and the towns in the solidly Calvinist Connecticut Valley rallied to resist it. They began ecclesiastical trials of garden-variety sinners and rooted out heretics with loyalty oaths, administering the Creed. In Westhampton this method worked; Unitarianism never had a chance. But in Northampton the one church, Congregationalist, split into four pieces. As the Unitarians seceded in the spring and summer of 1824, the sixty-four-year-old bell in the church steeple suddenly cracked. A new one was ordered, but that one did not please, and then it cracked, too. The fragments–Unitarian, Episcopal, and Baptist; Federalist and Democratic–

had nostalgic memories of a unified past, bitter memories of recent and continuing quarrels.

Westhampton was not spared. The trouble there came not from liberals but from a traveling revivalist, John Truair, who was both a compelling preacher and an accomplished singer. Solid, safe, dull Enoch Hale, who had been the one minister of the town since its founding in 1789, accepted Truair as assistant pastor but swiftly regretted the move when in 1829 the Truairites split off from the church. Young Judd, who in 1826 had been caught up in revivalist enthusiasm in Northampton, returned in the winter of 1828–1829 to his grandfather's house. He was just in time to see the climax of the Westhampton story—the church, across the street, burned down. Some said the destruction of the church was a judgment of God for permitting Truair to preach there; others said that the Truairites had burned it.

In the winter of 1830–1831 Judd returned to Westhampton. He had been on good enough terms with Truair to receive and keep one of his sermons, and Truair's perfectionism and millennialism perhaps modulated into Judd's later utopianism; but even if Judd did not dare mingle with the Truairites, he could hear them down the street, in an ecstasy of midnight meetings, singings in the streets, wallowings on the floor, and holy kisses—behavior hitherto unheard of in staid Westhampton and now leading to serious conflict even between leading citizen Dr. William Hooker and his Truairite wife. Judd remembered all these events, and when he had finally had enough of revivals and Calvinism, he took pains to include in *Margaret* dramatizations of both a revival meeting and a drunken brawl, which, as Judd presented them, had much in common.

The Truairite revival was soon followed by Judd's conversion in the summer of 1831 at the Congregational church in Northampton. His father now heeded his pleas for a liberal education, and after completing his preparation at the nearby Hadley Academy, Judd enrolled at Yale College, graduating in 1836. His family and his other sponsors understood that Judd had not only a hope of salvation but a call to the orthodox ministry. The plan went astray. Judd, who was intense about other people's salvation, proved unable to take care of his own. The "New-School" Calvinism that was emanating from Nathaniel W. Taylor of Yale Divinity School placed the justification for damnation not in some remote transaction in the sky but in the observed fact that everyone sinned, including children too young to understand theology and ethics. The argument, in Judd's mind, came down, as in *Margaret,* to the question of what was the nature of children and what sort of nature did a just and loving God in fact intend to create in children. Indeed, the argument came down to a ques-

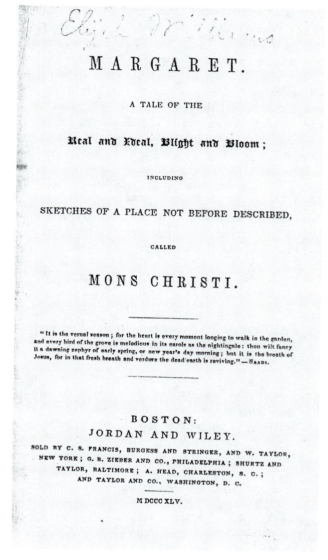

MARGARET.

A TALE OF THE

Real and Ideal, Blight and Bloom;

INCLUDING

SKETCHES OF A PLACE NOT BEFORE DESCRIBED,

CALLED

MONS CHRISTI.

"It is the vernal season ; for the heart is every moment longing to walk in the garden, and every bird of the grove is melodious in its carols as the nightingale : thou wilt fancy it a dawning zephyr of early spring, or new year's day morning ; but it is the breath of Jesus, for in that fresh breath and verdure the dead earth is reviving."—SAADI.

BOSTON:
JORDAN AND WILEY.

SOLD BY C. S. FRANCIS, BURGESS AND STRINGER, AND W. TAYLOR, NEW YORK ; G. B. ZIEBER AND CO., PHILADELPHIA ; SHURTZ AND TAYLOR, BALTIMORE ; A. HEAD, CHARLESTON, S. C. ; AND TAYLOR AND CO., WASHINGTON, D. C.

M DCCC XLV.

Title page for the novel James Russell Lowell called "the most emphatically American book ever written" (Special Collections, Thomas Cooper Library, University of South Carolina)

tion of whether or not a just God could damn Judd's six-year-old sister Peninnah, who was brimming with love and kisses but who had no observable signs of religious conversion. Gradually driven to his knees and almost into despair by his theological doubts, Judd took refuge in deception and, before graduating from Yale, wrote, produced, and directed a poetic drama called "The Deception," a tragedy, in which he played the leading role. In the first volume of the *Yale Literary Magazine* appeared Judd's essay "Truth" and a short story, "The Outlaw and His Daughter," a crude but romantic precursor of *Margaret*.

After his graduation ceremony, at which he delivered the English oration, Judd received an offer of a professorship at Miami College, an old-school Presbyterian college in Ohio, but decided not to accept it. Instead, he went to Templeton, Massachusetts, to teach in a private school. In the spring of 1837 his crisis of faith reached a climax: "I have been employed by the Orthodox party; but, alas for me! I am too liberal," he wrote on the last day of February 1837; and when spring came, he resigned. The structure of orthodoxy was crumbling around him, as well as inside him. Lyman Beecher, one of the leaders of New-School Calvinism and father of Harriet Beecher Stowe and Henry Ward Beecher, was tried in 1837 for heresy, and the whole Presbyterian Church was in a furor that split it down the middle before the year was out. That spring, the orthodox minister in Templeton was forced out for five times secretly drawing liquor from a cask in a public store, not the first of his indiscretions. The shibboleths that Calvinists and Unitarians hurled at each other about "observed facts of human nature," "moral tendency," and "the practical tendency of Calvinism" were taking on a wry, humorous twist. Three months earlier, Judd's childhood minister, Enoch Hale, whose mind had collapsed years before, died.

Even Judd's favorite aunt, Arethusa Hall (nine years older than Judd), who had lived with the family, had helped his mother raise him, and who later became his disciple and biographer, felt she would rather see him dead than become a Unitarian. He was driven at first to despair but then to a characteristic state of ecstatic affirmation as he declared himself. The twenty-four-year-old Unitarian convert was welcomed royally by the Unitarian minister of Templeton and the sophisticated Unitarians in Northampton, who helped him on to Harvard Divinity School. Judd arrived there in late August 1837, just in time to hear Emerson deliver his epoch-making Phi Beta Kappa address, "The American Scholar." Within the week Judd was echoing the rhythms and phrases of that address in letters to his mother and Aunt Arethusa. In March 1838 Judd achieved notoriety—his account of his conversion, developed from a private apologia presented to his family, was published as a Unitarian tract. The doors of Boston swung open to him; he walked the deep carpets of the wealthy and drank tea with them. To Judd's father, steeped in the history of the period 1774 to 1800 (the period Judd later chose for *Margaret*), tea-drinking was British and quaintly unpatriotic. That was not the last of the British things Judd did. A few years later, in Augusta, he was in close relationships with Episcopalians, celebrating Christmas and hanging greens in the church (anathema to Puritans), and climaxing *Margaret* with a vision of an ideal, universal church—with bishops—in which sectarianism vanished.

Judd, now the apostle of light and love, got a full dose of sectarian conflict. In July 1838 he heard Emerson deliver his Divinity School Address. Then the Unitarian conservatives, particularly Andrews Norton, erupted in anger. Emerson's naturalism, his denial of biblical miracles in this speech, gave the Unitarian case away by fulfilling the predictions of the orthodox, who had said all along that Unitarianism was sliding away from Christianity into infidelity. Judd, as can be inferred from his later sermons and from *Margaret*, was basically on Emerson's side in this quarrel. Under Judd's influence, Arethusa Hall began reading Emerson, and his father became absorbed in the works of Thomas Carlyle, though he never accepted Unitarianism. Judd taught himself German and, alone among his classmates, studied the philosophical foundations of Transcendentalism in Immanuel Kant, Friedrich and August Schlegel, Friedrich Wilhelm Joseph von Schelling, and Friedrich Schleiermacher. Judd's best friend at the Harvard Divinity School was Robert Waterston, scion of a wealthy Boston family; Waterston published a Transcendentalist pamphlet in 1836 and was one of the seniors who requested for publication the manuscript of Emerson's Divinity School Address. Another friend of Judd's at the divinity school was Emerson's "brave saint," Jones Very. Judd kept three manuscript poems that Very gave him and memorialized one of his and Very's conversations by writing down some of Very's oracular, hyper-Transcendentalist pronouncements—for example, "You think you see me, but you do not. You can only see me by finding me in yourself. And if you find me in yourself, you will not wish to see me."

At Harvard, Judd was imbibing other radical philosophies besides Transcendentalism. In June 1839 he wrote to his brother Hall that "our whole school, with scarcely an individual exception, sustains the position that all war, offensive and defensive, is inconsistent with the spirit of Christianity. . . . Unitarianism is most peculiarly fitted for such a conclusion." Judd was also ready for abolitionism. The divinity school students, restive and radical, wanted to invite an abolitionist speaker in May 1838, but President Josiah Quincy, Dean John Gorham Palfrey, and the faculty asked them not to do so. With Judd, in a dramatic last-minute switch, casting the deciding vote, the students resolved to go ahead anyway. Apparently the speaker never came, but Judd himself delivered antislavery lectures in Northampton and Hartford a few months later, following up on his success at filling the Northampton town hall in January 1838 with his lecture on "Childhood." Judd's argument for abolition spurned all appeals to expediency to anything less than pure principle. Then, after a year or two of observing abolitionists—such as Child, who lived in

Northampton and who spoke in a letter of 28 July 1838 about a "pious old thief" and "Judas" next door, a former slave auctioneer–Judd had second thoughts. Truth, he said in a sermon of November 1840, had to be uttered in love, not rancor: "And when you have knocked a man down, and bruised his character, and thrust your feet upon his motives, he will be slow to believe you when you tell him you love him, and only wish his good." All his life Judd continued to insist that love and peace were the primary values, that abolitionist and temperance reformers had to act in that spirit. Though he portrayed the evils of demon rum in *Margaret* and *Richard Edney,* his sermon on temperance (1845) said prophetically that the prohibition law about to be adopted in Maine would prove unworkable.

Following his graduation in July 1840, Judd preached for a few weeks in Augusta, Maine, then for a month in Deerfield, Massachusetts. Both churches offered him permanent positions. He chose Augusta, largely because of his attraction to the Williams family.

Judd was not a particularly tactful man. Scarcely settled, he naively embarked on a series of sermons that could not help but embarrass his hearers. Their style was reminiscent of Emerson's. On 18 October 1840 he preached on "Political Strife"; he was against it. In this sermon he said, "We are false at the caucus, we are hypocrites in the drawing room. . . . Ridicule and denunciation shuffle into every man's hands brickbats and clubs. . . . In Mexico they have learned to ballot with balls." Probably among the listeners to this sermon was Governor John Fairfield, who at that moment was anxiously awaiting the results of a recount that resulted in his defeat by fewer than a hundred votes. Judd followed up his sermon on "Political Strife" with one the next week on "Social Strife." He was against it, too. Particularly he was against clans, coteries, and friendship clubs. Augusta society was especially characterized by clans and coteries, and the Williams clan was at the pinnacle.

On 31 August 1841 Judd married Jane Elizabeth Williams, twenty-one years old, who had five sisters, three of them married, and an unmarried brother. Her father, Reuel Williams, was a self-made man, the wealthiest one in Augusta, and at the time a United States senator from Maine. Williams was a Unitarian; his wife, Sarah Cony Williams, was an orthodox Congregationalist. Their eldest daughter, Sarah, had on 9 August 1840 been one of nine persons confirmed as Episcopalians, the ceremony for that newly formed church taking place at the Unitarian church. The Williams family council-of-churches-in-miniature became the model for Judd's later and unsuccessful efforts to bring the Augusta churches together in harmonious relationships.

Judd's life became different from the one in which he had grown up; his father-in-law, Williams, could afford to be generous. He gave the couple a new house, built to their order, with stylish gothic gables. The Williams house nearby had a famous octagon room decorated with imported wallpaper showing scenes of Polynesian life, including dancing girls. The Judds' honeymoon was in Northampton, with excursions to the scenes of Judd's childhood in Westhampton and the traditional climb to the top of Mount Holyoke.

His parents did not succumb to Judd's influence, but his brother Hall later joined a communitarian society in Northampton, and his other three brothers became too liberal for their father's taste. During the spring of 1842 Judd's sister Apphia paid a long visit to the Judds in Augusta and within a few months married Joseph H. Williams, Jane's Unitarian brother, later a governor of Maine.

Despite the growing family harmony, Judd became embroiled in another controversy. On 13 March 1842 he gave a lecture at his church. With an impressive array of facts, he argued that even the American Revolution had been attended by the suppression of dissent and had not had entirely beneficial results. State legislators walked out in a huff and denounced Judd the next morning in the Capitol chambers; Judd was promptly dismissed from the group of chaplains used by the legislature. The town buzzed; Jane Judd fretted; and Judd published his lecture to show that he had attacked war in general, not the founding fathers. Newspapers all over New England commented, many of them in Judd's favor. The American Peace Society passed a resolution of support. From Washington, Reuel Williams wrote a letter to his family that criticized the legislature, not Judd, and all danger of losing his pulpit subsided.

Judd now began in earnest to write *Margaret.* He eavesdropped on his brothers playing cards, pulled out pieces of paper to write down scraps of people's dialect, and took Jane to Westhampton to drink in the scenery and gather folklore in rustic huts. The results of this research ended up in *Margaret. Margaret* also included Judd's flights of lyricism and his serious support for Transcendentalist idealism as opposed to Lockean empiricism. In his published lecture of 1836, Waterston had put the argument thus: "The mind of a child is not empty. . . . It is full of the seeds of things. The work of the teacher is not to pour in, but to draw out." Margaret expressed the idea this way:

all that is lies secretly coiled within our own breasts! All Beauty, I am persuaded, is within us. . . . A watermelon seed can say, "In me are ten watermelons, rind, pulp and seeds, so many yards of vine, so many pounds of

RICHARD EDNEY

AND

THE GOVERNOR'S FAMILY.

A RUS–URBAN TALE,

SIMPLE AND POPULAR, YET CULTURED AND NOBLE,

OF

MORALS, SENTIMENT, AND LIFE,

PRACTICALLY TREATED AND PLEASANTLY ILLUSTRATED

CONTAINING, ALSO,

HINTS ON BEING GOOD AND DOING GOOD.

[Sylvester Judd.]

BY THE AUTHOR OF

"MARGARET," AND "PHILO."

"MARGARET, A TALE OF THE REAL AND THE IDEAL," AND "PHILO, AN
EVANGELIAD."

BOSTON:
PHILLIPS, SAMPSON & COMPANY.
1850.

*Title page for Judd's novel about a country boy who
goes to the city to seek his fortune*

leaves." In myself seems sometimes to reside an infant Universe. My soul is certainly pistillate, and the pollen of all things is borne to me. The spider builds his house from his own bowels. I have sometimes seen a wood-spider let off a thread which the winds drew out for him and raised above the trees, and when it was sufficiently high and strong, he would climb up it, and sail off in the clear atmosphere. I think if you only begin, it will all come to you. As you drain off it will flow in.

Even Lowell condemned the crudity of the plot construction in *Margaret*. It includes such materials as a seduction and an attempted seduction, two unsuspenseful love stories, a missing heiress (Margaret), and a religious conversion. But Margaret's conversion by Charles Evelyn, her future husband, to a Transcenden-

talist version of Unitarianism was already nascent within her.

The most engaging parts of *Margaret* are Judd's dramatization of the heroine's childhood. At age nine Margaret encounters the repressive Calvinism of the village when she wanders barefooted into the church with a big bunch of wildflowers and is told to leave them outside. Flowers and Calvinism do not mix, and that is Judd's whole case in miniature. Margaret is a Wordsworthian nature maiden, an orphan. Her foster father, Pluck, scratches out an existence far from the village, drinks, swears, and blasphemes. Margaret says that her real parents are the pond and the beneficent hill: "Through me innumerable things went forth; the loons whooped me in the water, in my breath the midges sported, the Sun went down at my bidding. . . . In the darkest night, with our red tartarean links, Chilion [her foster brother] and I have rowed across the Pond, and sniggled for eels, and so we conquered the secrets of those depths."

William Dean Howells, in his review of *Margaret* for the *Atlantic Monthly* of January 1871, perhaps had such passages in mind when he called the book "this beautiful old romance," second only to Nathaniel Hawthorne's romances and "vastly better . . . than the best new novel of our generation." He said that "there is such sympathy with the inarticulate life of nature that the reader cannot help sharing the author's rapture. . . ." On 13 November 1854 Hawthorne had sent *Margaret* and some other books to R. Monckton Milnes as samples of new American writing, calling *Margaret* "intensely American" and implying that he valued it more than Henry David Thoreau's *Walden; or, Life in the Woods* (1854).

The unconventionality of *Margaret* is certainly intensely American. Judd prefered vulgarisms and irreverence to conventional utterance. "I be damned if it is," says one character. Brown Moll says to Pluck, her husband, "Don't deary me with your dish-cloth tongue." "Panguts!" she says another time, "what do you do? lazying about here like a mud-turtle nine days after it's killed." A boy at the bottom of a hill says, concerning his sledding, "I shall take it knee-bump next time," and another replies, "Try bellygut, you'll like that better." The sled race is described in a spray of imaginative verbs: "They skewed, brustled and bumped along, the crates wabbled and warped from side to side, the riders screamed, cross-bit, frumped and hooted at each other . . . one went giddying round and round. . . ." William B. O. Peabody, in *The North American Review* (January 1846), for whom the snowstorm scene of *Margaret* surpassed James Thomson's and William Cowper's, objected to "needless touches of coarseness," saying the words of Margaret's foster brother "never should have been written down."

The extravaganza at the end of *Margaret,* the utopian transformation of the town by heiress Margaret and her husband, eliminating Calvinism, prisons, capital punishment, military training, and the need for them, is intended to show that people will be as bad, or as good, as people think they are. In this ending the novel is similar to *Philo: An Evangeliad. By the Author of 'Margaret; A Tale of the Real and Ideal'* (1850), but that blank-verse drama has neither the freshness of *Margaret* nor its concreteness in describing the new society. Still, *Philo* has something of the grittiness of *Margaret,* its unconventionality. Unknown to Judd, the Devil is, like irreverent Pluck, the secret hero of *Philo.* He is "a travelling merchant of distress" who deals in bruised hearts, "gluttonies, / And jellied whoredoms." He is not "nice" like the "plumed ones" that "bang dove-bosomed girls as egg-shells smashed / And cackle of the deed." He has "muckered round in lanes, / Ditches, and garrets" where "maidens never smile, but glout, / And stare at you like stupid walruses." Enumerating the evils he has seen, he shouts, "I am excited; I go for reform." When the Devil speaks, people listen. Though the book is on the surface millennialist, ending with the second coming of Christ and the elimination of war, slavery, imprisonment, and poverty, it is really antimillennialist, designed to show that the second coming of Christ is occurring all the time, whenever Christ's love inspires people to reform the evils of the world.

In his review of *Philo* in the *National Anti-Slavery Standard* of 24 January 1850, Lowell says, "A more truly radical book has not been written, nor a more truly conservative. . . ." But in the *North American Review* of April 1850, Andrew Preston Peabody, who had preached at Judd's ordination, could find nothing to praise but Judd's most pallid and sentimental passages. He attacked Judd's "proficiency in the art of sinking," his leaping "from the clouds into the gutter," his use of words such as "soggy," "munch," "mucker," "dowse," "queachy," and "muzzy"—that is, anything in *Philo* that has life in it or the smell of damp dirt.

To protest the Mexican War, on Thanksgiving Day 1847 Judd read Lamentations, entire, to his congregation. A legislator commented, admiringly, "he is death against war." But in December 1852 Judd's lecture on "Non-resistance" included the following declaration, evidence of Judd's growing conservatism: "I am supremely a Christian, being neither pagan nor Jew, unbeliever nor transcendentalist." *Richard Edney* has no radicalism, and its pacifism is confined to a most improbable bolt of lightning that kills Clover, the town bully, who symbolizes the rule of force. The novel is determinedly cheerful, with even a Dickensian stage-

coach driver and the whimsy of a talking bridge. Richard, like Hawthorne's Robin in "My Kinsman of Major Molineux," goes to the city to seek his fortune but has better luck and all the pluck that Horatio Alger would have demanded. Richard saves the governor's daughter Melicent from a runaway horse, escapes the temptations of a designing woman and the misunderstandings that arise therefrom, does well in the world, does good among the less fortunate in the back lanes of the city, and, of course, marries Melicent.

Much attention is paid to the antics of Richard's nieces, Memmy and Bebby, less than six years old; Judd copied them from life, writing in his large study while his own children, Jane Elizabeth and Frances, played on the floor (Judd never saw his third daughter, Apphia). Emerson, who visited Augusta in 1852 and recorded the incident in his journal, asked Judd, "Who are your companions?" "Sunsets," replied Judd. He was a master of sunsets. In *Margaret* the sunset moment came as the cloud-fishes swam away with the sun, plunging down the cataract of light, and reluctant children were dragged inside. On Sundays children's playtime came only between sunset and dark, as a lone woodpecker "rapped and rattled over among the Chesnuts" and as clouds "like huge-breasted lions couchant" grew darker and grimmer.

In *Richard Edney,* Judd made his peace with limitation. He called his compromise "bordering": not the Infinite, the utopian, but the attainable—a good marriage and good children, a modest competence, and an improved city. Edward Everett Hale, a grandson of Enoch Hale, in the *Christian Examiner* of January 1855, defended the book against sneering critics, saying Judd "did not write it for reputation. He wrote it for country boys who have occasion to go to seek their living in large towns." He said Judd had asked his publisher to have part of the edition bound cheaply so that it might reach them. Hale, a friend, had written to Judd on 10 January 1850 that Emerson was enthusiastic about *Philo.* Hale had at first expected, reported his secretary later, that *Philo* would convert the world.

Judd failed to convert even the Unitarians. His last project was one of persuading Unitarians to form the child-centered church, with children admitted as a matter of right to full communion. He urged his parishioners to take communion and undergo baptism; but Reuel Williams would not bow to him, and he waited until after Judd's death to be baptized. Judd was on his way to Boston to deliver his most important lecture, on what he called "The Birthright Church," when he slept on damp sheets during a cold night in a hotel. He died three weeks later on 26 January 1853. His lecture was published; then his sermons on the subject were also published as *The Church*

(1854). His chief memorial, however, remained *Margaret*. After the first thousand copies were sold, a revised, two-volume edition on better paper appeared in 1851. That revision, reprinted several times, with many vulgarities of the first edition removed by Judd in response to the complaints of the genteel—among whom were Arethusa Hall—is the only version that survives outside of a few major libraries. The discreet, Flaxman-like illustrations of *Margaret* by Felix O. C. Darley, published separately in 1856, extended Judd's reputation. Margaret Fuller, Theodore Parker, Samuel Bowles, Carl Van Doren, VanWyck Brooks, and Kenneth Murdock gave *Margaret* high commendation. In 1986 Lawrence Buell, in *New England Literary Culture: From Revolution through Renaissance,* ranked Judd just behind Hawthorne, Harriet Beecher Stowe, and Elizabeth Stoddard among New England regionalists.

Biographies:

Arethusa Hall, *Life and Character of the Rev. Sylvester Judd* (Boston: Crosby & Nichols, 1854);

Richard D. Hathaway, *Sylvester Judd's New England* (University Park & London: Pennsylvania State University Press, 1981).

References:

Philip Judd Brockway, *Sylvester Judd (1813–1853): Novelist of Transcendentalism* (Orono: University of Maine Press, 1941);

Lawrence Buell, *New England Literary Culture: From Revolution through Renaissance* (Cambridge: Cambridge University Press, 1986), pp. 53, 296, 298, 310, 313–317, 341, 481;

Felix O. C. Darley, *Compositions in Outline . . . from Judd's Margaret* (New York: Redfield, 1856);

Francis B. Dedmond, *Sylvester Judd* (Boston: Twayne, 1980);

William Wallace Fenn, "Rev. Sylvester Judd and the Birthright Church 1813–53," *Proceedings of the Unitarian Historical Society,* 6 (Part 1, 1938): 13–30;

Margaret Fuller, *Papers on Literature and Art,* 2 volumes (London: Wiley & Putnam, 1846), II: 137;

Edward Everett Hale, "Life and Character of Sylvester Judd," *Christian Examiner,* 58 (January 1855): 63–75;

Gavin Jones, "The Paradise of Aesthetics: Sylvester Judd's *Margaret* and Antebellum American Literature," *New England Quarterly,* 71 (September 1998): 449–472;

S. Osgood, "The Real and the Ideal in New England," *North American Review,* 84 (April 1857): 535–559;

Vernon L. Parrington, *American Dreams: A Study of American Utopias* (Providence, R.I.: Brown University Press, 1947), pp. 27–34;

Sue W. Reed, "F. O. C. Darley's Outline Illustrations," in *The American Illustrated Book in the Nineteenth Century,* edited by Gerald W. R. Ward (Winterthur, Del.: Winterthur Museum, 1987), pp. 113, 123–135;

Bruce A. Ronda, "Sylvester Judd's *Margaret:* Open Spirits and Hidden Hearts," *American Transcendental Quarterly,* 39 (Summer 1978): 217–229;

"Sylvester Judd," *Fraser's Magazine for Town and Country,* 76 (July 1867): 45–60.

Papers:

The Sylvester Judd Papers at the Houghton Library, Harvard University, include his sermons and lectures, as well as most of his extant letters and other manuscripts.

Lucy Larcom

(5 May 1824 – 15 April 1893)

Beverly G. Merrick
New Mexico State University

See also the Larcom entry in *DLB 221: American Women Prose Writers, 1870–1920.*

BOOKS: *Similitudes* (Boston: Jewett, 1854);

Lottie's Thought-Book, anonymous (Philadelphia & New York: American Sunday-School Union, 1858);

Ships in the Mist; and Other Stories (Boston: Hoyt, 1859);

Leila Among the Mountains, anonymous (Boston: Hoyt, 1861);

Poems (Boston: Fields, Osgood, 1869);

Childhood Songs (Boston: Osgood, 1875);

An Idyl of Work (Boston: Osgood, 1875);

Snow Bloom and Other Poems (Newton, Mass.: Mrs. N. V. Walker, ca. 1880–1881);

Wild Roses of Cape Ann, and Other Poems (Boston: Houghton, Mifflin, 1881);

The Poetical Works (Boston: Houghton, Mifflin, 1885);

Wheaton Seminary: A Semi-Centennial Sketch (Cambridge, Mass.: Printed at the Riverside Press, 1885);

Easter Messengers, A New Poem of the Flowers (New York: White, Stokes & Allen, 1886);

A New England Girlhood, Outlined from Memory (Boston & New York: Houghton, Mifflin, 1889);

Easter Gleams (Boston & New York: Houghton, Mifflin, 1890);

The Governor's Tree. Original Poem . . . Arbor Day, 1890 (N.p., 1890);

As It Is in Heaven (Boston & New York: Houghton, Mifflin, 1891);

The Unseen Friend (Boston & New York: Houghton, Mifflin, 1892);

At the Beautiful Gate, and Other Songs of Faith (Boston & New York: Houghton, Mifflin, 1892);

Her Garden: A Memorial Poem (Cambridge, Mass.: Printed by L. F. Weston, 1909).

OTHER: "Elisha and the Angels" and "The Burning Prairie," in *The Female Poets of America,* edited by Rufus Wilmot Griswold (Philadelphia: Carey & Hart, 1849), pp. 360–361;

Lucy Larcom (Essex Institute, Salem, Massachusetts)

Breathings of the Better Life, edited by Larcom (Boston: Ticknor & Fields, 1867; London: Virtue, 1873; enlarged edition, Boston: Houghton, Osgood, 1879?; revised edition, Boston: Houghton, Mifflin, 1886);

Child Life: A Collection of Poems, edited by John Greenleaf Whittier, with assistance and contributions from Larcom (Boston: Osgood, 1872);

Child Life in Prose, edited by Whittier, with assistance and a contribution from Larcom (Boston: Osgood, 1874);

Songs of Three Centuries, edited by Whittier, with assistance and contributions from Larcom (Boston: Osgood, 1876; enlarged edition, Boston & New York: Houghton, Mifflin, 1890);

Roadside Poems for Summer Travellers, edited by Larcom (Boston: Osgood, 1876);

Hillside and Seaside in Poetry: A Companion to "Roadside Poems," edited by Larcom (Boston: Osgood, 1877);

Landscape in American Poetry, edited, with commentary, by Larcom (New York: Appleton, 1879);

"The Old Scholars," in *Fiftieth Anniversary of Wheaton Female Seminary: June 30th and July 1st, 1885. Commemorative Exercises, Addresses and Poem* (Norton, Mass.: Lane, 1885?), pp. 59–65;

"Letter from Lucy Larcom," in *Ossipee Mountain Park* (N.p., 1885), pp. 6–7;

Beckonings for Everyday, edited, with contributions, by Larcom (Boston & New York: Houghton, Mifflin, 1886; London: Ward, Lock, 1886); republished as *The Golden Calendar: A Birthday Book and Diary of Beautiful Thoughts* (London, New York, Melbourne & Sydney: Ward, Lock, Bowden, 1891);

The Cross and the Grail, edited, with contributions, by Larcom (Chicago: Woman's Temperance Publication Association, 1887).

PERIODICAL EDITED: *Our Young Folks: An Illustrated Magazine for Boys and Girls,* edited by Larcom, Gail Hamilton, and John T. Trowbridge, 1865–1873.

SELECTED PERIODICAL PUBLICATIONS–
UNCOLLECTED: "A Rose Enthroned," *Atlantic Monthly,* 7 (June 1861): 668–669;

"Hilary," *Atlantic Monthly,* 12 (August 1863): 159–160;

"Skipper Ben," *Atlantic Monthly,* 16 (July 1865): 84–85;

"The Red School-House," *Atlantic Monthly,* 19 (June 1867): 672–673;

"Mehetabel," *Atlantic Monthly,* 27 (June 1871): 671–672;

"Sylvia," *Atlantic Monthly,* 31 (January 1873): 86–88;

"A Gambrel Roof," *Atlantic Monthly,* 33 (February 1874): 141–144;

"Among Lowell Mill-Girls: A Reminiscence," *Atlantic Monthly,* 48 (November 1881): 593–612;

"In the Ossipee Glens," *New England Magazine* (October 1892): 192–207;

"Factory Life–Past, Present and Future," *American Journal of Social Science,* 16:141+.

Lucy Larcom, who as a child followed her mother into working in the New England mills, became an author, seminary teacher, magazine editor, and poet who transformed her common spiritual experiences into an uncommon American tapestry. As a child, she read *The Pilgrim's Progress* (1678–1684) and other English poetic works in a home that religiously studied the Bible. In addition, Larcom is said to have enjoyed most of the sermons of F. W. Robertson. She said of his *Sermons* (1861–1866) that scarcely anything she had read had been so inspiring and suggestive. This intensive training in religious studies was reflected in her writings throughout a life that spanned nearly three-quarters of a century. She is chiefly remembered for her recollections about this early life of discipline, documented in *A New England Girlhood, Outlined from Memory* (1889). Larcom writes, "Our parents considered it a duty that they owed to the youngest of us to teach us doctrines. And we believed in our instructors, if we could not always digest their instructions."

The American author and educator was born in rural Beverly, Massachusetts, to Benjamin and Lois (Barrett) Larcom, his second wife. Lucy Larcom's parents were part of an extended family in the rural area. The family was Huguenot by blood and Puritan by custom; the earlier spelling of the ancestral name was Larcum. Her home was close to the sea; her father had been a sea captain and a merchant. He died when she was young, leaving a wife and ten children without resources. The seventh daughter and ninth in the birth order, Lucy is said to have written stories and poems for her own amusement as early as the age of seven.

When Lucy Larcom was ten, her widowed mother moved to the regional business community of Lowell to find work. There the overburdened mother became the superintendent of a mill-run dormitory for girl workers. After several intermittent sessions of schooling, Lucy followed her mother into the mills, working from age eleven to twenty-two at various jobs, which she described as tedious but fulfilling. Years later, in 1881, Lucy wrote about her mill experience in "Among Lowell Mill-Girls," published in *The Atlantic Monthly* at a time when the magazine was a force for societal conscience. Lucy subsequently wrote verses and poems for the *Lowell Offering,* a mill publication featuring the literary efforts of mill girls.

David Baldwin notes that Larcom in the persona of "Esther" is one of three mill girls featured in her poetic narrative *An Idyl of Work* (1875). According to Baldwin, the narrative demonstrates that Larcom expressed little sympathy for those agitating for better working conditions in the mills. Larcom writes in her autobiography, *A New England Girlhood,* that an older sister once had told her when she was coming in from a snowstorm, "It doesn't make you any warmer to say you are cold." In a similar vein, Larcom said, in the preface of *An Idyl of Work,* "Labor, in itself, is neither elevating nor otherwise. It is the laborer's privilege to ennoble his work by the aim with which he undertakes it, and by the enthusiasm and faithfulness he puts into it."

Nor did Lucy Larcom climb on the bandwagon for women's rights. Still, she was the only one of the Larcom girls to remain single in a society that made marriage almost imperative. Baldwin writes of Larcom, "She illustrates the traits of small-town nineteenth-century women; conservative in customs, retiring, domestic, religious-minded, strong in sentiments, as well as self-reliant and somewhat ambitious intellectually."

Perhaps her philosophical slant toward the status of women is a matter of opinion. According to Margo Culley, Larcom's tendency to use *we* for *I* in her writing is explicitly grounded in gender. Larcom regards her writing as "drawing aside a veil." She writes in *A New England Girlhood:* "My audience is understood to be composed of girls of all ages, and of women who have not forgotten their girlhood. Such as have a friendly appreciation of girls–are also welcome to listen to as much of my narrative as they choose. All others are eavesdroppers, and of course, have no right to criticize."

Larcom, in *A New England Girlhood,* spoke about making the most out of the discipline of work:

It was a pity that we were expected to begin thinking on hard subjects so soon, and it is also a pity that we were set to hard work while so young. Yet these were both the inevitable results of circumstances then existing, and perhaps the two belonged together. Perhaps habits of conscientious work induce thought and habits of right thinking. Certainly right thinking impels people to work.

Her work at the mill had thwarted her ambition to obtain a higher education. She knew she would have to make a change. She met John Greenleaf Whittier in 1844, during his visit to Lowell, and a friendship developed. She was twenty; he, thirty-seven. Shortly thereafter, Larcom moved to Illinois, where she lived a nomadic and pioneer life, and several critics believe Whittier's influence guided her choice. Larcom taught for two years at a district school, where she earned $40 every three-month period. She was attempting to optimize her chance to further her own advanced education. She had traveled west with her married sister Emeline, and the two continued to bond closely for life.

Lucy lived in Illinois from 1846 to 1852. Her determination to extend her literary and spiritual growth was validated when she became one of the poets featured in Rufus Wilmot Griswold's *Female Poets of America* in 1849. During her last four years in Illinois, she attended Monticello Seminary at Godfrey. She deferred her expenses during her first year by teaching students aged fourteen and older in primary classes. Her role model at Monticello was the college president,

Larcom's father, Captain Benjamin Larcom (Beverly Historical Society, Beverly, Massachusetts)

Philena Fobes, to whom Larcom continued to write about their shared evangelical nonsectarian beliefs. The goal of the seminary was to provide a "symmetrical" education for its young women–training of the physical, mental, and spiritual. While Larcom was at the seminary, she founded the college newspaper, *The Rushlight.* Years later, in a special edition of *The Rushlight,* Fobes wrote that Larcom seemingly read and observed much at the seminary.

Fobes maintains that Larcom took especial delight in studies of natural history, sharing the enthusiasms of a teacher named Sara C. Eaton, daughter of the American pioneer in natural science Amos Eaton. "The Rose Enthroned," a poem subsequently appearing in the June 1861 issue of the *Atlantic Monthly,* was inspired by this experience, according to Fobes. "When I look back upon my life," Larcom writes, "I see it divided into epochs similar to geological ages, when by slow to sudden upheavals I have found myself the wondering professor of a new life in a new world. My years at Monticello were such an epoch."

Larcom reportedly did not write much poetry in the classroom. In English composition, she confined her writing mostly to the classroom exercises. Sometimes she was requested to furnish a poem for the paper published in-house once a month; she was, at the time, one of the two editors and readers. She was known to write narrative poems in blank verse, according to Fobes.

Larcom and a young teacher also led a debating society on Friday evenings. The poet's wry sense of humor sometimes was reflected in her early discourses. Larcom once said, referring to these gatherings and her general schooling at Monticello: "I think kindly of almost everybody, but it has been the uphill work of my life to be interested in many persons." Mentor Fobes said that even though Larcom was cheery, her manner was reserved, and that forbade familiarity. At the end of her seminary studies, she was invited to stay and teach. She had a great longing, however, to return to the home of her childhood. Larcom returned to Massachusetts. She formed only a few lasting friendships during this epoch of her life, but they were severed only by death. Larcom's correspondence with Fobes (housed now at the Essex Institute) includes a considerable number of published letters, dated from 1849 to 1893, the time of the poet's death. Larcom wrote to Fobes about her move back to Beverly and about how the sea drew her back: "Sometimes I think it is a pity that I have always been a waif, since it is so hard to bring myself back to any moorings. Certainly I am 'to nothing fixed, but love of change.'"

Upon her return, Larcom talked about the visit of Lucy Stone to one of the two weekly lyceum meetings, which she said usually supplied really good lectures. Larcom said that Stone delighted everyone: Even those who were conservative became converts to woman's rights. During that first winter of 1853 Larcom conducted a school for ten young ladies, several of them reading Virgil and Corinne, and all of them advanced as far as the second class at the seminary. She struck up a correspondence with Whittier; their relationship continued and was referred to by both of them in their correspondence.

In 1854 Larcom wrote *Similitudes,* a book of vignettes. That same year, she moved to Norton, Massachusetts, where she taught at Wheaton Seminary (now Wheaton College). Her major disciplines were rhetoric and English literature; she taught courses as well in history, biology, logic, and moral philosophy. She is said to have used the Socratic teaching method.

Among Larcom's lasting contributions to Wheaton was the founding of another college publication, a newspaper. She found herself cheering the men who marched off to the Civil War from Boston, but she vowed she had a pacifist nature as she sat among other women at Wheaton shortly thereafter, sewing flannel shirts for the soldiers. Her students from Georgia were temporarily orphaned by the conflict.

During this period, she had expressed doubts about whether or not teaching was her true mission. She wrote Fobes from Norton, after she had been there for two years, that teaching was her vocation but not her avocation: "I have spent a very pleasant year. I should be willing to stay here a long time if I knew this was my place, that teaching was my mission; but I have doubts of both." Larcom was worried that she had not challenged herself enough. She said about her life at Wheaton: "It is almost too easy a life. I have little to try me, little of really hard work to do, though all my time is occupied. And then I should so much prefer writing to teaching, if only I could earn a living that way."

In fact, she discovered during that critical time of re-evaluation that she was going through a preparatory process for some greater task and that study, travel, and her experience, including teaching, were only a preparation for her writing. Larcom resigned from Wheaton at the close of the 1862 school year. In November 1862 she commenced passing the winter at Waterbury, Connecticut, with an elderly woman. Whittier reportedly turned to Larcom for consolation following the death of his sister, Elizabeth, because Lucy had been her best friend. Whittier's poem *Snow-Bound* (1866) was written during this period as a tribute to his sister.

Larcom hoped that she would have time to write, declaring that the cares of teaching, reading to prepare her for class lectures, and grading papers had kept her from writing. The "clash of theories," she said, had stymied her writing, and she was suffering from "an overworked brain." She worked better in an atmosphere in which she could pursue her own private thinking "in some very retired situation."

Larcom later wrote to Fobes that she had left much of her vigor and her health behind her at Norton but did not regret it, nor did she regret that others had, according to her, "reaped where she sowed"—the legacy of a broader foundation for the education of women. Her self-assessment was on target, and time left for thinking resulted in creative pursuits. She worked part-time at lecturing, but she never let teaching overtake her writing pursuits. In 1865 she took a position in Boston, becoming the assistant editor, with Gail Hamilton and John T. Trowbridge, of a children's publication put out by the *Atlantic Monthly* called *Our Young Folks.* A year later Larcom became the chief editor of the publication, a position that lasted for eight years. This occupation led to her devoting even more time to her own writing. The publication also carried many of Whittier's poems. Eventually,

Wheaton Seminary in Norton, Massachusetts, where Larcom taught from 1854 until 1862 (Marion B. Gebbie Archives and Special Collections, Wheaton College)

many of her own poems that had appeared in *Our Young Folks* were published under the title *Childhood Songs* (1875). Larcom said during this time that writing gave her great pleasure: "Writing is my play. My verses mostly have written themselves."

In 1866 Larcom returned to Beverly, and according to a niece, Mary Larcom Dow, in *Old Days at Beverly Farms* (1921), the six or seven years following were the only ones in which her Aunt Lucy had a real home of her own. Dow said her aunt's income must always have been slender, but Mary could not remember a time that Larcom complained of it.

For the remainder of her years, Larcom pursued eclectic interests, as well as writing and editing–except for one year at Bradford Seminary (1872–1873). She painted flowers, studied French, and conducted her own literature class, but she did not continue to teach full-time. The rural environment of her youth inspired her to write works that romanticize her childhood days there, as she remembered long walks of up to five miles with a favored older brother.

Larcom and a niece apparently took several rooms near the railroad station, a house that was then owned by Captain Joseph Woodberry and almost opposite a local columnist, who wrote letters called "The Witty Autocrat." Dow believes the poem "By the Fireside" must have been written in those days. Larcom often engaged a neighbor named Josiah

Obear to hitch up the buggy and take her about the countryside. At that time, the woods and fields of Beverly Farms were accessible to all, and Dow said that her aunt knew where to find the first hepaticas and the rare spots where the linnea grew. The many wildflowers became the subjects of her paintings and poems. The New England fields were her essential habitat.

Dow describes Larcom, in her forties, as someone of a serene nature: "a beautiful, gracious figure, with flowing abundant brown hair, and a most benignant face." Larcom was still the editor of *Our Young Folks*. But her publishing interests grew after she won $50 for a poem called "Call to Kansas" from the New England Emigrant Aid Company, and her literary career was launched on a broader basis. To the Larcom home came such literary notables as Mary Livermore, Celia Thaxter, and, of course, Whittier. In 1867 she edited *Breathings of the Better Life,* writing in the prefatory note that the book was intended to bring the religious writings about Jesus under one cover. In 1869 she published her own work, called *Poems,* which revealed to the greater world for the first time her poetic philosophy that earth is "inhabited by heaven." She continued to publish her own poetry, and her prolific verse writing grew in time to four volumes of published work, which brought her more recognition from the literary center of Boston and from others on a national scale. Her verse was also in demand, published in *St. Nicholas,* the *Youth's Companion,* the *Atlantic Monthly,* and other literary magazines of the day.

Baldwin says that a false charge of plagiarism brought Larcom grief but ultimately fame. The charges concerned a poem called "Hannah Binding Shoes," which was first published in the *New York Crayon.* The poem curiously parallels the losses Larcom had experienced in life. He describes the poem as "a portrait of a lonely New England woman hopelessly awaiting the return of her lover lost at sea." Shortly after her retirement from *Our Young Folks,* Larcom published *An Idyl of Work,* which dealt largely with the life she had known in the cotton mills.

According to Albert Mordell, Larcom, as Whittier's prodigy, was "a martyr of love" for the renowned poet. During the later 1870s she compiled many anthologies of poetry, including most of the compilation of three anthologies that are credited to Whittier, the first of which is called *Child Life: A Collection of Poems* (1872). A companion volume of selections of prose for children followed in 1874. In the third volume, *Songs of Three Centuries* (1876), her name is listed in the preface; she had co-edited the volume with Whittier, who was credited with authorship. It is a telling tribute on his part that she belatedly received fuller credit when, upon his death, Whittier bequeathed the royalties for the three books to her.

In 1879 Larcom edited one critical work about poetry, *Landscape in American Poetry,* which included criticism of selected pastoral poetry of Whittier, Henry Wadsworth Longfellow, James Russell Lowell, William Cullen Bryant, and Ralph Waldo Emerson. As Baldwin has noted, she most valued nature poems that included references to divinity. Larcom's favorite English poet is said to have been William Wordsworth. She had written, however, to Fobes from Wheaton Seminary several years earlier that Emerson's works fascinated her and gave her much room to think, but that he was "a heathen to all intents and purposes."

Larcom was a student of the early history of Cape Anne. She capitalized on this knowledge in allusions to narratives of Captain John Smith and to the records of other historians writing about the settlements of the shore towns of Massachusetts, north of Salem. In her 1881 book of poetry *Wild Roses of Cape Ann, and Other Poems* she talked about a little brown cabin under a cliff, where the rose at the door was a sweetheart of a wife, who waited for the seafaring man to come home. She continued to write, even though illnesses postponed some of her best efforts. In 1885 Riverside Press of Cambridge published her semicentennial historical sketch of Wheaton Seminary. In 1889 *A New England Girlhood* appeared, a volume upon which she had labored for some time. Although this autobiography covered only the years up to 1852, it was the culmination of a life of small New England towns remembered.

Larcom's seminal work was of a religious nature. She spoke of religious transformation into her seventh decade. She discovered that she was distinctly not Calvinistic. Listening to the "Radicals" in Boston, she wrote, had driven her to the delusion that she would be a better Christian alone. She wrote Fobes in November 1890 that she would never be "churchy," explaining to her mentor, "I believe in the Holy Catholic Church of humanity." Shortly thereafter, *Easter Gleams* (1890) was published, a work that alludes favorably to the Puritan vision of the biblical concept of the resurrection. Larcom's *As It Is in Heaven,* published in 1891, refers to books as friends and to friends as books, as the author explores her vision about resurrection to an afterlife. It is a philosophical work about love, nature, God, and humanity. To expand on her view of the divine in nature, she turned to writers and poets, especially to E. H. Sears, J. H. Thom, and George MacDonald, quoting them extensively. She dedicated the book to Philena Fobes ("P.F."), who was uncertain concerning how to view the religious transmogrification in her former pupil and lifelong friend.

Larcom believed true friendship to be the most divine of all human relations, "a glimpse of God"–a theme on which she continued to expound in *The Unseen Friend* (1892), which was soon to be published. As Carol Holly writes, to Larcom's thinking, individuality is never achieved at the expense of relationship. Larcom believed that creatures were God's hieroglyphics and that persons are His Word. She writes, in one particularly revealing passage about friendship in *As It Is in Heaven:* "The soul itself is refreshed and enlarged by the stream of love that flows through it:–this is the true well of water springing up within unto everlasting life."

Larcom now advocated the religious teachings of the Episcopalian doctrine. She began what she called "another little book" in late summer of 1891. The death of Whittier and of her closest sister, Emeline, came during this lean season. She wrote to Fobes that she herself was nearing death and wanted to give a little book to others before she died. She worked on the manuscript, while enjoying the complexity in the writings of George Eliot. The result was *The Unseen Friend,* which was dedicated to her lifelong friend, Whittier, "the most beloved and most spiritual American poet, whose friendship to me was almost a life-long blessing." Larcom was chagrined to discover that her new book had been criticized in an Episcopalian publication in Philadelphia as a "substitutionary work" because there was "no Christ in the work." She wrote Fobes, "You see, it is not Calvinism alone that is intolerant of thought expressed in new forms."

Ill, Larcom worked on only what she thought must be done. She wrote to Fobes in December 1892, "I cannot afford to let my pen rest entirely, and there are words I want to say, very much, before I die . . . ." Right before her death, she was pleased to see that her last three works—*As It Is in Heaven, The Unseen Friend,* and the resulting seminal work, *At the Beautiful Gate, and Other Songs of Faith* (1892)—were going to be sold together—all bound in white, in a box.

Lucy Larcom was buried in Beverly, following services at Trinity Church in Boston. After her death, the literary community discovered in her posthumously published letters that she had the last word in the long relationship with Whittier. Larcom had felt hurt because Whittier did not allow her to have her name on the books they edited together. They also learned that Lucy Larcom had dedicated *At the Beautiful Gate* to her sister Emeline, who believed "that poetry and religion are one."

Letters:

Letters of Lucy Larcom to the Whittiers, edited by Grace F. Shepard (Portland, Me.: Southworth Press, 1930).

Biographies:

Daniel Dulany Addison, *Lucy Larcom: Life, Letters, and Diary* (Boston & New York: Houghton, Mifflin, 1894);

Caroline May, *The American Female Poets* (New York: Garrett, 1969);

Shirley Marchalonis, *The Worlds of Lucy Larcom, 1824–1893* (Athens & London: University of Georgia Press, 1989).

References:

William F. Abbot, "Genealogy of the Larcom Family," *Historical Collections of the Essex Institute,* 58 (January and April 1922): 41–48, 129–150;

Margo Culley, Introduction to *American Women's Autobiography: Fea(s)ts of Memory,* edited by Culley (Madison: University of Wisconsin Press, 1992);

Mary Larcom Dow, "Lucy Larcom, A Memory," in her *Old Days at Beverly Farms* (Beverly, Mass.: North Shore, 1921);

Carol Holly, "Nineteenth-Century Autobiographies of Affiliation: The Case of Catharine Sedgwick and Lucy Larcom," in *American Autobiography: Retrospect and Prospect,* edited by Paul John Eakin (Madison: University of Wisconsin Press, 1991), pp. 216–234;

Albert Mordell, *Quaker Militant: John Greenleaf Whittier* (Boston: Houghton Mifflin, 1933), pp. 191, 220–235;

Susan Hayes Ward, ed., *The Rushlight: Special Number in Memory of Lucy Larcom* (Boston: Ellis, 1894).

Papers:

The Lucy Larcom Collection in the Marion B. Gebbie Archives and Special Collections at the Madeleine Clark Wallace Library of Wheaton College includes letters, manuscripts for poems and lectures, copybooks, diaries, and artwork by Larcom. There are also letters at the Boston Athenaeum and the Essex Institute.

George Perkins Marsh

(15 March 1801 – 23 July 1882)

Ralph H. Orth
University of Vermont

See also the Marsh entries in *DLB 1: The American Renaissance in New England* and *DLB 64: American Literary Critics and Scholars, 1850–1880.*

BOOKS: *Address Delivered before the Burlington Mechanics Institute . . . April 5, 1843* (Burlington, Vt.: Burlington Free Press, 1843);

The Goths in New-England. A Discourse Delivered at the Anniversary of the Philomathesian Society of Middlebury College, Aug. 15, 1843 (Middlebury, Vt.: Printed by J. Cobb Jr., 1843);

Speech of Mr. G. P. Marsh, of Vermont, on the Tariff Bill; Delivered in the House of Representatives of the United States, April 30, 1844 (Washington, D.C.: Printed at Gideon's Office, 1844);

Address, Delivered Before the New England Society of the City of New-York, December 24, 1844 (New York: M. W. Dodd, 1845);

Speech of Mr. George P. Marsh, of Vermont, on the Annexation of Texas: Delivered in the House of Representatives, U.S., in Committee of the Whole on the State of the Union, Jan. 20, 1845 (Washington, D.C.: Printed by J. & G. S. Gideon, 1845);

Speech on the Bill for Establishing the Smithsonian Institution Delivered in the House of Representatives of the U. States, April 22, 1846 (Washington, D. C.: Printed by J. & G. S. Gideon, 1846);

Speech of Mr. G. P. Marsh, of Vermont, on the Tariff Question, Delivered in the House of Representatives of the U.S., June 30th, 1846 (Washington, D.C., 1846);

The American Historical School: A Discourse Delivered before the Literary Societies of Union College (Troy, N.Y.: Printed by J. C. Kneeland, 1847);

Human Knowledge: A Discourse Delivered Before the Massachusetts Alpha of the Phi Beta Kappa Society, at Cambridge, August 26, 1847 (Boston: Little & Brown, 1847);

Address Delivered Before the Agricultural Society of Rutland County, Sept. 30, 1847 (Rutland, Vt.: Printed at the Herald Office, 1848);

George Perkins Marsh, 1844 (portrait by George P. A. Healy; Dartmouth College)

Speech of Mr. G. P. Marsh, of Vermont, on the Mexican War, Delivered in the House of Representatives of the U.S., February 10, 1848 (Washington, D.C.: Printed by J. & G. S. Gideon, 1848);

Remarks of George P. Marsh, of Vermont, on Slavery in the Territories of New Mexico, California and Oregon; Delivered in the House of Representatives, August 3d, 1848 (Burlington: Free Press, 1848);

The Camel; His Organization, Habits, and Uses, Considered with Reference to His Introduction into the United States (Boston: Gould & Lincoln / New York: Sheldon, Blakeman, 1856);

An Apology for the Study of English Delivered . . . on Monday, November 1, 1858, Introductory to a Series of Lectures in the Post-graduate Course of Columbia College, New York (New York: Wynkoop, Hallenbeck & Thomas, 1859);

Lectures on the English Language (New York: Scribner, 1860); revised and enlarged as Lectures on the English Language: First Series (New York: Scribner, 1861; London: Murray, 1862);

The Origin and History of the English Language, and of the Early Literature It Embodies (New York: Scribner, 1862; London: Sampson Low, 1862; revised edition, New York: Scribners, 1885);

Man and Nature; or, Physical Geography as Modified by Human Action (New York: Scribner, 1864; London: Sampson Low, Son & Marston, 1864); revised and enlarged as The Earth as Modified by Human Action (New York: Scribner, Armstrong, 1874; London: Sampson Low, Marston, Low & Searle, 1874; revised again, New York: Scribners, 1885);

Mediæval and Modern Saints and Miracles, anonymous (New York: Harper, 1876).

Edition: Man and Nature, edited by David Lowenthal (Cambridge, Mass.: Harvard University Press, 1965).

OTHER: A Compendious Grammar of the Old-Northern or Icelandic Language: Compiled and Translated from the Grammars of Rask (Burlington, Vt.: Johnson, 1838);

Hensleigh Wedgwood, A Dictionary of English Etymology, volume 1 (A–D), notes and additions by Marsh (New York: Sheldon, 1862);

Johnson's New Universal Cyclopaedia, 4 volumes, includes forty articles by Marsh (New York: Johnson, 1874–1878).

SELECTED PERIODICAL PUBLICATIONS– UNCOLLECTED: "The Origin, Progress, and Decline of Icelandic Historical Literature, by Peter Erasmus Mueller," translated, with notes, by Marsh, American Eclectic, 1 (1841): 446–468; 2 (1841): 131–146;

"Old Northern Literature," American Review: A Whig Journal, 1 (1845): 250–257;

"The Principles and Tendencies of Modern Commerce: With Special Reference to the Character and Influence of the Traffic between the Christian States and the Oriental World," Hunt's Merchants' Magazine and Commercial Review, 33 (1855): 147–168;

"The Oriental Question," Christian Examiner, 64 (1858): 393–420;

"Oriental Christianity and Islamism," Christian Examiner, 65 (1858): 95–125;

"The Future of Turkey," Christian Examiner, 65 (1858): 401–419;

"The War and the Peace," Christian Examiner, 67 (1859): 260–282;

"Our English Dictionaries," Christian Review, 101 (1860): 384–415;

"The Study of Nature," Christian Examiner, 68 (1860): 33–62;

"Were the States Ever Sovereign?" Nation, 1 (1865): 5–8;

"State Sovereignty" [retitled "The Sovereignty of the States" after the first installment], Nation, 1 (1865): 554–556, 648–650, 715–716, 776–777, 810–812;

"Female Education in Italy," Nation, 3 (1866): 5–7;

"The Education of Women," Nation, 3 (1866): pp. 165–166;

"Notes on the New Edition of Webster's Dictionary," Nation, 3 (1866): 125–127, 147–148, 186–187, 225–226, 268–269, 288–289, 369, 408–409, 515–517; 4 (1867): 7–9, 108–109, 127–128, 312–313, 373, 392–393, 516–517; 5 (1867): 7–8, 88–89, 208–209;

"The Catholic Church and Modern Civilization," Nation, 5 (1867): 229–231;

"The Origin of the Italian Language," North American Review, 105 (1867): 1–41;

"The Proposed Revision of the English Bible," Nation, 11 (1870): 238–239, 261–263, 281–282;

"The Book of Marco Polo," Nation, 21 (1875): 135–137, 152–153.

George Perkins Marsh is known today primarily as the author of Man and Nature; or, Physical Geography as Modified by Human Action (1864), one of the most original and farsighted books of the nineteenth century. In an era devoted to the limitless exploitation of natural resources, it set forth in great detail the history and dangers of such exploitation, making it one of the earliest statements of the conservation ethic. Marsh, however, in his own day was known primarily as a philologist, and his various roles included those of public servant, legislator, and diplomat. He wrote on camels and religion, Turkey and trade, the Civil War, dictionaries, and the education of women. His questing mind and tireless energy insured a depth of research that conferred an aura of authority on any of the many subjects he chose to examine.

Marsh was born on 15 March 1801 in Woodstock, Vermont, to Charles Marsh, the leading lawyer of the town, and his wife, Susan (Perkins) Marsh. Charles Marsh, a strict Calvinist, believed in duty and hard work, and his son George learned early to measure up to the rigorous challenges set before him. A studious child, he damaged his eyesight by excessive reading and for four years was forbidden access to

Caroline Crane, whom Marsh married in 1839 (from David Lowenthal, George Perkins Marsh: Versatile Vermonter, *1958)*

books. Instead, he turned his attention to the countryside around Woodstock, roaming the hills and meadows with his friends and developing the keen sense of observation and sympathy with nature that characterized him throughout his life.

After a basic education in the local grammar school and a few months at Phillips Academy in Andover, Massachusetts, Marsh entered Dartmouth College at the age of fifteen. The old-fashioned curriculum—heavy with Greek, Latin (both of which he had already learned), moral philosophy, and metaphysics—had little appeal to him, and most of his education was self-derived from the books in the college library. He discovered that he had a gift for languages and taught himself French, Italian, Spanish, and Portuguese. After studying law for three years with his father, Marsh was admitted to the Vermont bar and in 1825 settled in Burlington, on Lake Champlain on the western side of the state, where he made his home for the next thirty-five years. His two-man law practice flourished, and on 10

April 1828 he married a local belle, Harriet Buell, with whom he had two sons, Charles Buell and George Ozias. But when his law partner died, the practice declined, and the death of his wife and older son in the fifth year of his marriage led to a long period of self-imposed isolation and despair. During this time he found solace by studying the Scandinavian languages, and his study led eventually to his first book, *A Compendious Grammar of the Old-Northern or Icelandic Language: Compiled and Translated from the Grammars of Rask* (1838), a translation of writings by the Danish linguist Rasmus Christian Rask with commentary by Marsh. On 25 September 1839 Marsh married Caroline Crane, who taught in a boarding school for young women; he was thirty-eight and she was twenty-three. Her youth and equable temperament brought Marsh tranquility and a return to an active social life.

Marsh's book and his other writings on and translations from Icelandic and Swedish established him as the premier authority on the Scandinavian languages in the United States. It also heightened his enthusiasm for the Goths—a term loosely used to describe the ancestors of the German, Scandinavian, and English peoples—who, he argued in an address at Middlebury College in 1843 (followed by one in New York City in 1844), were not "the savage and destructive devastators, that popular error has made them" but "the noblest branch of the Caucasian race." The Novanglians, or New Englanders, were their descendants: "It was the spirit of the Goth that guided the May-Flower across the trackless ocean; the blood of the Goth, that flowed at Bunker's Hill." Marsh contrasted the vigorous, plain, democratic, truth-seeking Goths with the sensuous, superficial, intolerant "Romans"—that is, with the Mediterranean peoples represented in ancient times by the Roman Empire and in modern times by the Roman Catholic Church. This attitude, derived in equal part from Marsh's Puritan heritage and his belief in republican principles, persisted throughout his life and was only partially mitigated later by his many years of residence in Turin, Florence, and Rome.

A different, strikingly prophetic note was sounded in Marsh's address on "The American Historical School," delivered at Union College in 1847. The writing of history, Marsh remarked, was invariably concerned with the doings of kings and popes, with battles and crusades and political intrigue, and seldom with the life of the people of a nation. "We require," Marsh insisted, "not so much the history of governments as the story of man; not a sketch of the outward relations of a people, but a picture of its social and domestic life, a revelation of its internal economy, and a philosophical investigation of the moral and political causes whose action and re-action have affected the personal liberties and the private interests and prosperity of its citizens." Several generations had to pass before anyone began to write the kind of history Marsh called for.

Marsh's interest in the practice of law had declined early, and he began a series of business ventures, most of which eventually ended in disaster. Sheep farming, a woolen mill, and later, investments in the Vermont Central railroad all succumbed to changing markets, lowered tariffs, or unscrupulous or ineffective partners. The financial losses resulting from these failures plagued Marsh for years. More auspicious was his election in 1842 as a Whig representative to Congress, where he fought for higher tariffs, opposed the annexation of Texas and the Mexican War, and did what he could to obstruct the power of the slave states. Just as significant, in Marsh's eyes, was his work on the Congressional committee that established the Smithsonian Institution, which insured the long-range involvement of the federal government in scientific and cultural endeavors. Shortly after his re-election to Congress in 1848, however, Marsh applied for a diplomatic appointment in Europe, hoping to alleviate his always precarious financial situation and the frustrations of political life in Washington while satisfying his long-standing desire to see the Old World. In May of 1849 President Zachary Taylor acceded to his request by appointing him minister not to Berlin, as he had hoped, but to Constantinople. In the fall he and his wife, accompanied by Marsh's son George and Caroline Marsh's sister Lucy, left to take up residence in the Turkish capital.

The post at Constantinople had its share of frustrations—inadequate accommodations, occasional extremes of climate, and the often trivial and irksome duties of his position. Marsh had to contend with refugees from various nationalist uprisings, many of whom wanted the safety of immigration to the United States; he was able, for instance, with a good deal of trouble, to arrange passage to the United States for the Hungarian patriot Lajos Kossuth. Nevertheless, there were compensations. His fellow ambassadors from the European countries were generally cultured, and Marsh could rely on a level of conversation not provided by everyday life among the politicians at home. Even more significant was the opportunity afforded Marsh and his wife to travel in Europe and the Near East. They had gone to Constantinople by way of Paris, Florence, Rome, and Naples, and later in 1852 made their way from Athens to Vienna and on to Munich and Dresden, returning in 1853 via Florence, where they met the American sculptor Hiram Powers (a boyhood friend of Marsh's) and Robert and Elizabeth Barrett Browning. In the winter of 1850–1851 the Marshes took their most adventurous trip when they left for an extended tour of Egypt and Palestine. Their route took them from Cairo up the Nile to Nubia and back, then by camel across the Sinai peninsula to Aqaba, Petra, Hebron, and Jerusalem, with a final leg to Nazareth and Beirut on the way back to Constantinople. On this journey Marsh's powers of observation and his wide-ranging interests stood him in good stead, and his journals and letters are full of details about the lands they passed through. He collected plants, small animals, insects, and fish in quantity, preserved them as best he could, and sent them back to Spencer Baird of the Smithsonian Institution. He also developed a great respect for the ungainly but highly serviceable camel, and in his book *The Camel; His Organization, Habits, and Uses, Considered with Reference to His Introduction into the United States* (1856), he made the case for its potential usefulness in other parts of the world: "That he will continue to spread . . . there can be little doubt, and we may therefore confidently expect his naturalization in South Africa, Australia, the desert of Atacama, Southern Chili and Buenos Ayres, and our own New Mexican and California territories"—a prophecy that, so far as the American territories were concerned, was actually being realized by Congressional authorization at the time.

With the election of Democrat Franklin Pierce as president in 1852, Marsh's career as ambassador came to an end, and he returned to the United States and to a host of troubles. The collapse of his railroad and real estate investments had left him about $50,000 in debt; he was owed back pay by the federal government for expenses he had incurred in the discharge of his official duties, but he had made enemies in Washington who accused him of neglecting his consular duties and taking long trips for his own pleasure. Only in 1860, when Marsh was fifty-nine, were his financial matters settled and his debts finally paid. In the intervening years, desperate for money, he had considered returning to the practice of law, despite his great distaste for it, or putting himself forward as a candidate for the U.S. Senate, although attaining the position would have meant involving himself once again in the repellent atmosphere of Washington politics. A partnership with a cousin-in-law quarrying marble from a vein near Burlington never showed a profit. Offers of a professorship in history at Harvard or the provostship at the University of Pennsylvania were appealing, but neither paid well enough to make acceptance worthwhile. From 1854 to 1857 Marsh undertook a series of lectures on his experiences in the Near East and on science and agriculture, venturing as far west as St. Louis, but the insufficient money he received and the miserable experience of traveling on American railroads were bitter disappointments.

A representative lecture from this period is one that Marsh delivered before the Mercantile Library

Marsh in 1861 (photograph by Mathew Brady)

Association in Boston on 15 November 1854, printed in 1855 in *Hunt's Merchants' Magazine and Commercial Review* as "The Principles and Tendencies of Modern Commerce: With Special Reference to the Character and Influence of the Traffic between the Christian States and the Oriental World" (1855). In this lecture Marsh fashions a role for trade appropriate to the era, stating that "The unobtrusive pursuits of Commerce . . . have had their heroes and their conquerors," and seldom "have the proudest structures of imperial munificence or enlightened national liberality . . . demanded a greater amount of intelligent physical activity than . . . commercial enterprise in the present day." The position of America is particularly noted: "America . . . is destined to be practically, what it is by nature geographically, the connecting link between the great oceanic basins–a middle term between the East and the West," and thus "Commerce will have conferred upon us a moral power in intellectual sway, mightier, wider, more durable, more beneficent, than fleets of armies have ever achieved."

In 1857 a chance to serve his home state arose when the governor of Vermont appointed Marsh to three posts–railroad commissioner, fish commissioner, and state house commissioner. In each of these Marsh was able to put his particular interests and knowledge to work. As a state house commissioner (one of three), Marsh, whose years abroad had given him a firsthand knowledge of classical architecture, was the guiding spirit in rebuilding the state capitol after a disastrous fire in 1857. He worked closely with the architect, Thomas Silloway, to achieve a sense of grandeur and harmony, rebuffing the efforts of the construction superintendent to economize by using cheaper materials. As fish commissioner, he submitted to the legislature a thorough report on the decline of many fish species in Vermont as a result of human disturbance of the land and rivers of the state, especially through dam building and siltation; it was another one of the studies that foreshadowed his later analysis of this phenomenon and similar phenomena in *Man and Nature*. As railroad commissioner, Marsh made what were quite radical recommendations. Because of his own disastrous railroad investments and his memories of the inadequate service he had experienced on his lecturing trips, he had become a bitter critic of the railroad companies, which, he maintained, supplied a vital public service in the most venal, fraudulent, and irresponsible manner. The problem was so great that Marsh felt the only solution was government ownership of the railroads, and indeed of all transport and communication facilities. His advice fell on deaf ears; in 1859 he was replaced as railroad commissioner by someone friendlier to the railroads.

A return to one of his enduring interests came with the opportunity to teach a postgraduate course of lectures on the English language at Columbia University in the winter of 1858–1859. In thirty installments he covered such subjects as the origin of English, the etymology of its words, its vocabulary (five lectures), its grammatical inflections (four lectures), the changes effected by the introduction of printing (three lectures), rhyme, synonymy, the principles of translation, and the English language in the United States. Like Noah Webster, whose *American Dictionary of the English Language* had appeared in 1828, and unlike most other philologists of the day, Marsh did not find this language necessarily inferior to that of the mother country. Moreover, he noted, since the vocabulary, syntax, and pronunciation of living languages undergo constant change that cannot and should not be stopped, it was only common sense to accept some divergence in the nature of the two national varieties of English–although not enough, the admirer of the "Goths" hoped, "to repudiate that community of speech, which, in spite of the keenly conflicting interests of politics and of commerce, makes us still one with the people of England."

When Marsh's observations were published as *Lectures on the English Language* (1860), the book was well received and so successful that it went through four printings in two years. A later series of twelve lectures in Lowell, Massachusetts, eventually resulted in another philological work, *The Origin and History of the English Language, and of the Early Literature It Embodies* (1862). After an extensive survey of the origin, vocabulary, literature, and grammar of Anglo-Saxon, Marsh dealt in detail with the period following the Norman Conquest when the language gained a French component, pausing especially to examine, among works by a host of writers well known or obscure, William Langland's *Piers Ploughman,* John Wycliffe's translation of the Bible, and Geoffrey Chaucer's works. From the "Babylonish confusion of speech" of the late Middle Ages in England, Marsh said, "the influence and example of Chaucer did more to rescue his native tongue than any other single cause," creating "a literary diction . . . which, in all the qualities required for the poetic art, had at that time no superior in the languages of modern Europe." Although Marsh's last lecture was titled "The English Language and Literature During the Reign of Elizabeth," William Shakespeare is mentioned only at the end, as a writer who was more fortunate than Chaucer because he "had been preceded by a multitude of skillful artists, who had improved and refined all the various special vocabularies which make up the totality of the English language" and thus found a fully formed "common dialect" ready for his use.

This second of Marsh's books on English did not do as well as the first, since it was too technical for a wide readership, but it was only one of the language projects he was involved in during this period. He was appointed the American secretary of the London Philological Society in its plan, subsequently suspended, to publish a New English dictionary, and he became the editor of the American edition of volume one of Hensleigh Wedgwood's *A Dictionary of English Etymology,* published in 1862, with many notes and additions by Marsh. This period of fruitful labor on language came to an end when, in March 1861, President Abraham Lincoln appointed Marsh as ambassador to the new Kingdom of Italy. Marsh was overjoyed, for the appointment meant that he would have a secure income (his philological labors had never earned him a living wage) and that he would return to Europe, with whose peoples and culture he had developed a deep affinity. Within six weeks, just after the outbreak of the Civil War, Marsh sailed from the United States, never to return.

As a diplomat at the court of King Victor Emmanuel at Turin (Rome was still under the rule of the Pope, and Venice under that of Austria), Marsh had a particularly delicate and important task—keeping the Italians well disposed toward the North during the Civil War. The fact that Italy had just emerged from centuries of disunion and was on the way toward complete unification made it naturally sympathetic to the Union cause; Marsh was able to persuade the government to close all Italian ports to Confederate shipping.

Marsh's tenure at Turin was, on the whole, intellectually and socially satisfying. Many prominent statesmen, scientists, and literary figures in Italy either lived in or frequently visited the capital; it was a magnet for other Europeans and for Americans passing through. The Marshes were able to take frequent trips into the nearby Alps, where Marsh continued the close observation and thoughtful interpretation of natural forces that was one of his enduring pleasures. During this time he also completed and sent off to his publishers in New York and London *Man and Nature,* the work that established securely his position in history.

To Marsh the book was not the capstone of his career but yet another inquiry into a topic of enduring interest to him and conceivably to others; he had made his reputation as a philologist and had produced works about such topics as Goths and camels. After *Man and Nature* he turned his restless intellect to other topics. He did, however, recognize the seriousness of the subjects. Sixty years of observation of mankind's effect on nature (beginning with his boyhood rambles about Woodstock and extending through his stay in the devastated hills and river valleys of the Mediterranean basin and his tours of the Alps, buttressed always by his extensive reading in natural history) convinced him that the prevailing idea about the formation of the landscape—that it was a natural process not seriously affected by man's presence—was seriously in error. In fact, man was often the determining factor in the landscape. The opening paragraph of his preface clearly states his purpose:

The object of the present volume is: to indicate the character and, approximately, the extent of the changes produced by human action in the physical conditions of the globe we inhabit; to point out the dangers of imprudence and the necessity of caution in all operations which, on a large scale, interfere with the spontaneous arrangements of the organic or the inorganic world; to suggest the possibility and the importance of the restoration of disturbed harmonies and the material improvement of waste and exhausted regions; and, incidentally, to illustrate the doctrine, that man is, in both kind and degree, a power of a higher order than any of the other forms of animated life, which, like him, are nourished at the table of bounteous nature.

Marsh in his library at Villa Forini in Florence, Italy, where he lived from 1864 until 1871

In six chapters, the first of which begins with an idyllic picture of the Mediterranean basin in Roman times, he deals in succession with the deleterious and the salutary effects of man's presence in nature. Among the negative effects are the introduction of exotic plant and animal species into new lands (chapter 2) and the removal of forests that are vital in protecting the earth from erosion and maintaining the health of the soil (chapter 3); among the beneficial ones are dams, reservoirs, canals, and irrigation used to produce a stable, fruitful landscape (chapter 4) and methods of stabilizing sand dunes to protect low-lying areas along the seacoast (chapter 5). The sixth chapter describes possible megaprojects such as the Suez and Panama Canals and the draining of the Zuider Zee. Marsh's enthusiasm for his views results in a style that frequently rises to the poetic, whether describing the "luxuriant harvests of cereals that waved on every field from the shores of the Rhine to the banks of the Nile" or the "melting snows and vernal rains [that], no longer absorbed by a loose and bibulous vegetable mould, rush over the frozen surface, and pour down the valleys seaward." Fundamen-

tal to his view is the belief that, while man feels entitled to change nature to suit his desires, he is as subject to the changes he produces as any other creature, and a wise husbandry will insure that what seem to be permanent gains are not actually long-term losses. Since the data available to Marsh about weather patterns, climatic changes, hydrology, the interrelation between animal and plant species, and a host of other topics was sparse, his intuitive grasp of his subject is astonishing. Marsh's solution to the ills often brought about by man's interference with nature—so obvious today but so novel in his own time—was the development of a conservation ethic. Man, he makes clear, can live on the planet indefinitely, but only as a respectful tenant, not as an imperious landlord.

Man and Nature sold surprisingly well. More than one thousand copies quickly sold, and a second printing was prepared; in 1874 a second, enlarged edition appeared; and in 1885 a third was published. The book was well received by critics and proved influential both in the United States and in Europe. But Marsh's life was inextricably tied to his diplomatic position, and when in 1864 the capital of Italy was moved from Turin to Florence, he, too, had to move. This move meant the end of his periodic trips into his beloved Alps, but there were compensations. Florence was a treasure house of Renaissance art and culture and the home of Hiram Powers and other artists; in addition, visitors ranging from Matthew Arnold to Admiral David Glasgow Farragut made Marsh's residence, the Villa Forini, a stop on their trips through the city. Marsh's diplomatic activities after the Civil War took a prosaic turn, involving trade and immigration treaties between Italy and the United States, and he busied himself by writing a series of articles on various topics for a new American journal of opinion, *The Nation*. Always the social progressive, Marsh was firm in his views; for instance, he believed regarding the education of women that "elevating the social and moral condition of women [is] in accordance with the democratic principles which constitute the true motive power of modern progress."

His last change of residence occurred in 1871, when Rome became part of united Italy and was established as its capital. Marsh had loved Turin; he had come to like Florence; he never felt entirely comfortable in Rome. It was hot and dusty, and its ruins could not make up for the loss of the elegance and artistic treasures of the other two cities. Moreover, it was the seat of the papacy, for which Marsh had an abiding distaste. He distrusted all ecclesiastical claims to spiritual authority, and none more so than those of the Pope. The promulgation of the doctrine of papal infallibility was only the latest and most egregious example of such presumption, he felt. In order to warn his fellow Americans of the dangers of Catholic immigration, he wrote *Mediæval and Modern Saints and Miracles* (1876), which, because of his diplomatic position, had to be published anonymously. The book was a fervent attack on all aspects of Catholicism, from miracles to Mariolatry, from the Inquisition to the rite of confession, to the writings of England's Cardinal Newman. Growing Catholic influence in the United States, Marsh warned, could only be baleful, since the church would never accommodate itself to the democratic principles upon which the United States was founded. He saw a restrictive immigration policy as the only answer. Stating that "The evidence respecting the real doctrines and history of the Romish Church is often to be found only in voluminous collections rare in Protestant countries, or in works existing only in foreign languages, and hence altogether inaccessible to the general reader," Marsh cited works—many in Latin, Italian, or French—by the defenders of the church to rebut what he saw as its pretensions. Compared to Marsh's other accomplishments in philology, politics, diplomacy, and the study of nature, the book is a minor performance, but, as always, written with conviction and based upon evidence designed to support his viewpoint.

Aside from a personal tragedy—his younger son, after a troubled life, had died in 1865 at the age of thirty-two—Marsh's last years were relatively tranquil. Administration after administration kept him in his post, and he became one of the longest-serving of all American ambassadors. As his energy gradually failed, he came to rely more and more on the services of his competent and hardworking secretary, George Washington Wurts, and as ever there were the satisfactions of a happy married life, many friends, and wide-ranging intellectual activity. He corresponded with museum curators, botanists, and architects on both sides of the Atlantic; his insistence that the Washington Monument be finished as an unadorned obelisk was decisive in giving it its final form. As always, he complained about lack of money, but that was less galling to a man in his seventies than it had been earlier. Perhaps most discouraging to him was what he saw as the lack of progress in human affairs: ignorance and corruption were as much the rule, and maybe more so, as they had been fifty years earlier.

Marsh's death, on 23 July 1882, came in the most appropriate of locales, a school of forestry established by one of his Italian friends at Vallombrosa in the Appenines. He was eighty-one and on the point of resigning because a consular shuffle had deprived him of the services of his irreplaceable secretary Wurts. His body was brought to Rome and laid to rest in the Protestant cemetery near the Porta San Paolo in the southwestern section of the city.

Bibliography:
H. L. Koopman, *Bibliography of George Perkins Marsh* (Burlington, Vt.: Free Press, 1892).

Biographies:
Samuel Gilman Brown, *A Discourse Commemorative of the Hon. George Perkins Marsh, LL.D.* (Burlington, Vt.: Free Press, 1883);

Caroline Crane Marsh, *Life and Letters of George Perkins Marsh* (New York: Scribners, 1888);

David Lowenthal, *George Perkins Marsh: Versatile Vermonter* (New York: Columbia University Press, 1958); revised as *George Perkins Marsh: Prophet of Conservation* (Seattle & London: University of Washington Press, 2000);

Jane Curtis and others, *The World of George Perkins Marsh, America's First Conservationist and Environmentalist: An Illustrated Biography* (Woodstock, Vt.: Countryman, 1982).

References:

Richard Beck, "George P. Marsh and Old Icelandic Studies," *Scandinavian Studies,* 17 (1943): 195–203;

Peter Bridges, "The Polymath from Vermont (George Perkins Marsh, 1801–1822)," *Virginia Quarterly Review,* 75 (1999): 82–94;

Catalogue of the Library of George Perkins Marsh (Burlington: University of Vermont, 1892);

Robert L. Dorman, *A Word for Nature: Four Pioneering Environmental Advocates, 1845–1913* (Chapel Hill: University of North Carolina Press, 1998);

Daniel W. Gade, "The Growing Recognition of George Perkins Marsh," *Geographical Review,* 73 (1983): 341–344;

Joseph Gustaitis, "George Perkins Marsh: The First Ecologist," *American History Illustrated,* 19 (1984): 42–43;

Marcus Hall, "George Perkins Marsh: Prophet of Conservation," *Environmental History,* 6 (2001): 118–122;

Hall, "Restoring the Countryside: George Perkins Marsh and the Italian Land Ethic (1861–1882)," *Environment and History,* 4 (1998): 91–103;

Samuel Kliger, "George Perkins Marsh and the Gothic Tradition in America," *New England Quarterly,* 19 (1946): 524–531;

David Lowenthal, "George Perkins Marsh on the Nature and Purpose of Geography," *Geographical Journal,* 126 (1960): 413–417;

Lowenthal, Introduction to *Man and Nature* (Cambridge, Mass.: Harvard University Press, 1965);

Lowenthal, *The Vermont Heritage of George Perkins Marsh* (Woodstock, Vt.: Woodstock Historical Society, 1960);

George Washington Moon, *Bad English Exposed: A Series of Criticisms on the Errors and Inconsistencies of Lindley Murray and Other Grammarians* (London, 1881);

Franklin Russell, "The Vermont Prophet: George Perkins Marsh," *Horizon,* 10 (Summer 1968): 16–23;

Edmund A. Schofield, "John Muir's Yankee Friends and Mentors: The New England Connection," *Pacific Historian,* 29 (1985): 65–89;

Mary Philip Trauth, *Italo-American Diplomatic Relations, 1861–1882: The Mission of George Perkins Marsh, First American Minister to the Kingdom of Italy* (Washington, D.C.: Catholic University of America Press, 1958).

Papers:

The main repository of George Perkins Marsh's papers is the Bailey-Howe Library at the University of Vermont; this collection includes notebooks, diaries, letters to and from Marsh, unpublished manuscripts, and drafts of published works. Material by Caroline Crane Marsh is also part of the collection. The Vermont Historical Society holds a significant collection of letters by Marsh; other letters are scattered in manuscript collections at many major Northeast libraries.

Donald Grant Mitchell

(12 April 1822 – 15 December 1908)

Brett Coker
University of California, Santa Barbara

See also the Mitchell entries in *DLB 1: The American Renaissance in New England* and *DLB Documentary Series 13: The House of Scribner, 1846–1904.*

BOOKS: *The Dignity of Learning. A Valedictory Oration . . . Pronounced Before the Senior Class of Yale College, July 7, 1841* (New Haven: Printed by B. L. Hamlen, 1841); also published in *Poem by Guy Bryan Schott, and The Valedictory Oration by Donald G. Mitchell. Pronounced Before the Senior Class of Yale College, July 7, 1841* (New Haven: Printed by B. L. Hamlen, 1841);

Fresh Gleanings: or, A New Sheaf from the Old Fields of Continental Europe, as Ik Marvel (2 parts, New York: Harper, 1847; 1 volume, 1847);

The Battle Summer: Being Transcripts from Personal Observations in Paris, During the Year 1848, as Ik Marvel (New York: Baker & Scribner, 1850);

The Lorgnette; or, Studies of the Town. By an Opera Goer, as John Timon (24 parts: nos. 1–13, New York: Henry Kernot, 1850; no. 14, New York: Stringer & Townsend, 1850; nos. 15–24, New York: Stringer & Townsend / Henry Kernot, 1850; republished in 2 volumes, New York: Printed for Stringer & Townsend, 1850); republished as *The Opera Goer: or, Studies of the Town* (London: Newby, 1852);

Reveries of a Bachelor: or, A Book of the Heart, as Ik Marvel (New York: Baker & Scribner, 1850; London: Bogue, 1852);

A Bachelor's Reverie: In Three Parts. I. Smoke–Signifying Doubt. II. Blaze–Signifying Cheer. III. Ashes–Signifying Desolation, as Ik Marvel (Wormsloe, Ga., 1850);

Dream Life: A Fable of the Seasons, as Ik Marvel (New York: Scribner, 1851; London: Nelson, 1853; Liverpool: Howell, 1853);

Fudge Doings: Being Tony Fudge's Record of the Same, as Ik Marvel, 2 volumes (New York: Scribner, 1855);

Donald Grant Mitchell, 1851 (portrait by Charles Loring Elliot; from Waldo H. Dunn, The Life of Donald G. Mitchell, Ik Marvel, *1922)*

Agricultural Address Delivered Before the Connecticut State Agricultural Society, at Bridgeport (N.p.: Published by the Society, 1858);

My Farm of Edgewood: A Country Book (New York: Scribner, 1863);

Seven Stories, With Basement and Attic (New York: Scribner, 1864; London: Sampson Low, 1884);

Wet Days at Edgewood: With Old Farmers, Old Gardeners, and Old Pastorals (New York: Scribner, 1865; London: Sampson Low, 1884);

Doctor Johns: Being a Narrative of Certain Events in the Life of an Orthodox Minister of Connecticut, 2 volumes (New

York: Scribner, 1866; London: Sampson Low, 1866);

Rural Studies With Hints for Country Places (New York: Scribner, 1867); republished as *Out-of-Town Places: With Hints for Their Improvement* (London: Sampson Low, 1884);

Pictures of Edgewood: In a Series of Photographs, by Rockwood, and Illustrative Text (New York: Scribner, 1869);

About Old Story-Tellers: Of How and When They Lived, and What Stories They Told (New York: Scribner, Armstrong, 1877);

Description of Lafayette College and Vicinity, Easton, Pa. (N.p., ca. 1880);

A Report to the Commissioners on Lay-out of East Rock Park (New Haven: Printed by L. S. Punderson, 1882);

Bound Together: A Sheaf of Papers (New York: Scribners, 1884; London: Sampson Low, 1884);

English Lands, Letters, and Kings from Celt to Tudor (New York: Scribners, 1889; London: Sampson Low, 1889);

English Lands, Letters, and Kings from Elizabeth to Anne (New York: Scribners, 1890; London: Sampson Low, 1890);

English Lands, Letters, and Kings: Queen Anne and the Georges (New York: Scribners, 1895; London: Sampson Low, 1895);

American Lands and Letters: The Mayflower to Rip-Van-Winkle (New York: Scribners, 1897; London: Dent, 1897);

English Lands, Letters, and Kings: The Later Georges to Victoria (New York: Scribners, 1897; London: Elkin Mathews, 1897);

American Lands and Letters: Leather-Stocking to Poe's "Raven" (New York: Scribners, 1899; London: Dent, 1899);

Looking Back at Boyhood, as Ik Marvel (N.p.: Academy Press, 1906);

Louis Mitchell: A Sketch, edited by Waldo H. Dunn (Claremont: Privately printed, 1947).

Collection: *The Works of Donald G. Mitchell*, Edgewood Edition, 15 volumes (New York: Scribners, 1907).

OTHER: *The Woodbridge Record: Being an Account of the Descendants of the Reverend John Woodbridge, of Newbury, Mass.*, edited by Donald G. Mitchell and Alfred Mitchell (New Haven: Privately printed, 1883);

Daniel Tyler: A Memorial Volume, edited by Mitchell (New Haven: Privately printed, 1883).

The name Donald Grant Mitchell remains virtually unknown today, though at the time of Mitchell's death in 1908 he was one of the most highly regarded American writers of the nineteenth century. If known at all today, he would most likely be recognized by his pseudonym, Ik Marvel. Mitchell's early essays were critical and popular successes, and two of his books, *Reveries of a Bachelor: or, A Book of the Heart* (1850) and its sequel *Dream Life: A Fable of the Seasons* (1851) were best-sellers at the height of what has come to be known as the American Renaissance. But with the twentieth century came a rapid decline in Mitchell's literary reputation. His writings were generally considered to be overly sentimental, hopelessly middle class, and lacking in the profundity of those of a Herman Melville, a Nathaniel Hawthorne, or a Ralph Waldo Emerson. During the last quarter of the twentieth century, only a handful of scholars have considered Mitchell's writings and their influence on nineteenth-century American society. But as twenty-first-century scholars immersed in cultural studies take more seriously the centrality of popular and sentimental writings in American life, Mitchell's works will deserve closer scrutiny.

Born on 12 April 1822 in the rural village of Norwich, Connecticut, Donald Grant Mitchell was the fourth of nine children of the Reverend Alfred Mitchell and Lucretia (Woodbridge) Mitchell. Both sides of Donald Mitchell's family were influential in the civil and spiritual affairs of New England. His paternal grandfather, Stephen Mix Mitchell, served as a U.S. Senator and was later appointed first chief justice of the Connecticut Supreme Court. The Reverend Alfred Mitchell was minister of the Second Congregational Church of Norwich. Although Mitchell had fond memories of his father, the strict Puritan discipline and rigorous religious instruction forced upon him as a child contributed to his later aversion to institutional religion. Indeed, as Mitchell himself wrote, the Mitchell children were more drawn to their spirited and less severe mother.

Although Mitchell's writings often stress the importance of close family ties in a child's upbringing, he himself experienced few years of uninterrupted home life. In 1830 he was sent away to a boarding school in Ellington founded by Judge John Hall, a graduate of Yale. Like Donald's father, Judge Hall was puritanical and a rigid disciplinarian. The curriculum at Hall's school was rigorous in classical studies, and Mitchell developed what a reviewer called his "trick of easy, high-bred quotation." During Mitchell's second year at Ellington his father died, leaving his mother alone with the burden of a large family. Lucretia Mitchell accepted the invitation of her uncle, Judge Elias Perkins, to reside at his home in New London. Throughout his seven years at boarding school, Donald spent vacations at relatives' homes alternately in Norwich, Salem, and New London. A cousin of Donald's, Mary Perkins, was taken into the Mitchell family after the death of her mother and the remarriage of her father, Henry. Although Mary was ten years Donald's senior, a close friendship developed between the two that lasted throughout their lives.

Over the next few years several members of the Mitchell family, including Donald himself, were stricken with tuberculosis. Donald's mother, his brother Stephen, and his sister Elizabeth were the most severely afflicted, and in the winter of 1836–1837, in an attempt to escape the harsh New England climate, they sought refuge in the milder region of Santa Cruz. The removal did not result in a cure, and consequently young Donald experienced great family tragedy over the next few years. On 29 March 1839 his mother died, followed a few weeks later by his brother Stephen. A little more than two years later, his sister Elizabeth also succumbed to the disease.

An old Norwich friend of the Mitchell family, General William Williams, took over as guardian of the remaining Mitchell children. General Williams was pragmatic and businesslike, and as guardian he took a close interest in Donald's studies. In 1837 Mitchell began attending Yale College, his father's alma mater. His college marks, however, were not unusually high, no doubt because of the staggering losses he had experienced and his own fragile health. The curriculum at Yale did not leave much room for Mitchell's creativity. Nevertheless, he found himself drawn to literature, especially to oratory and composition; he contributed heavily to the *Yale Literary Magazine* and was elected to its board of editors. At the age of nineteen he gave the class valedictory oration, "The Dignity of Learning." The oration showed Mitchell's early belief in literature as a tool for moral guidance. The no-nonsense General Williams, however, was not pleased with Mitchell's growing literary aspirations, as he felt the young man should devote himself to more practical studies, such as business or law.

With the settlement of his mother's estate, Mitchell inherited the "quiet farmhouse," later described in *Reveries of a Bachelor,* and nearly four hundred acres of adjoining land. Following his mother's death, he became drawn to the Connecticut countryside and shied away from society. Later he claimed a "native indisposition for society." After his graduation he moved into the home of his cousin Mary and her husband, Levi H. Goddard. Mitchell also took over general supervision of his farm, beginning a love affair with farming that lasted the rest of his life. In 1843 he was awarded the silver medal by the New York State Agricultural Society for his prizewinning plans of farm buildings. Yet, his growing reclusiveness and his failure to pursue a definite career worried General Williams. Williams decided to negotiate a deal with the newly

Mitchell's grandfather, Stephen Mix Mitchell, first chief justice of the Connecticut Supreme Court (portrait by Samuel F. B. Morse, 1827; from Waldo H. Dunn, The Life of Donald G. Mitchell, Ik Marvel, *1922)*

appointed consul to Liverpool, Joel W. White, to secure Mitchell a secretaryship in the consular office. Mitchell was not consulted in the matter and was quite surprised when he learned of the appointment. But he quickly became accustomed to the idea and later thanked General Williams for goading him into action. Mitchell sailed for Liverpool on 16 October 1844.

Mitchell's consulate position did not last long; the damp climate of London aggravated his lung condition, and he was forced to seek a milder climate to the south, on the island of Jersey. On 16 January 1845 his sister Lucretia succumbed to tuberculosis. Donald was deeply saddened, but he had been prepared for her death through correspondence with General Williams. He wondered if he would be the next family member to die. But the Jersey climate greatly improved his condition, and Mitchell was able to explore more of Europe, keeping extensive notebooks of his travels. While in Europe he began a series of letters to the *Cultivator,* an American monthly agricultural magazine, detailing his observations of European agricultural design and practices. Mitchell felt that America had much to learn from English landscape design, just as it had much to learn

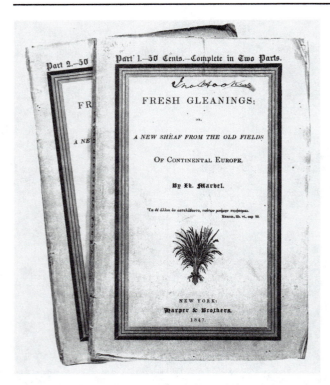

*Wrappers for the book published in parts that Mitchell based on the notebooks he kept during his 1845–1846 travels in Europe (*Bibliography of American Literature, *no. 13922)*

from English writers. He returned to America on 11 September 1846.

Following his return to the United States, Mitchell traveled to Washington in early December, apparently to learn something about the workings of government and to overcome his shyness in society. His initial impression of the capital was one of disgust. He found its streets and buildings dirty and its society vulgar. Eventually, however, he met people more to his liking, and although his general view of Washington did not change, his observations led him to publish a series of letters in the *New York Courier and Enquirer.* Called "Capitol Sketches," these writings were satirical letters that poked fun at certain ridiculous social types that he found around the capital. In these sketches Mitchell used the pseudonym Ik Marvel for the first time. He was always evasive about the derivation of the name, but presumably it was taken from two English rural writers he greatly admired, Izaak Walton and Andrew Marvell.

Mitchell's literary aspirations were always modest. He never intended to make a career of writing, but he did confess to "a most worrisome ambition to be the author of a good [book]." He proposed to Harper and Brothers the idea of publishing a collection of travel sketches that he had taken from his European note-

books. Harper and Brothers accepted the proposal, and in August 1847 *Fresh Gleanings: or, A New Sheaf from the Old Fields of Continental Europe* was published. The title was borrowed from James Fenimore Cooper's travel narrative, *Gleanings in Europe* (1837). Each of the five sections of the book deals with a particular culture or region, and descriptions are given in relation to historical facts and legends associated with the region. *Fresh Gleanings* sold moderately well, and Mitchell was content with its reception. Soon his restlessness led him to depart once again, this time to Canada with his youngest brother, Alfred.

After he returned to New York, Mitchell took up legal studies in the Wall Street offices of John Osborne Sargent. For a short time he threw himself into his law studies and put his travels behind him. Then on 24 February 1848 came the news of Louis Philippe's abdication in France and the establishment of a provisional government. Mitchell, desiring to witness firsthand this experiment in democracy, decided to return to Europe to serve as correspondent for the *Courier and Enquirer.* His "Marvel Letters from Abroad" appeared between 29 June 1848 and 10 February 1849. Initially, Mitchell was optimistic about the changes being brought about by the provisional government, but a bloody workers' insurrection against the National Assembly between 23 and 26 June dampened his hopes and led him to the conclusion that France was not yet ready for democracy. While still in Paris, Mitchell had the idea of turning his observations into a sort of "sketchy History of the summer at Paris." On returning to New York he put together his book *The Battle Summer: Being Transcripts from Personal Observations in Paris, During the Year 1848,* which was published in 1850. The volume, subtitled "The Reign of Blous," was originally meant to be the first of two volumes. But the projected second volume, to be subtitled "The Reign of Bourgeois," was shelved following the dismal public and critical reception of the first volume. Reviewers were put off by Mitchell's substitution of his usual detached and satirical personae in favor of what was considered a bald imitation of Thomas Carlyle.

The success of "Capitol Sketches" and the "Marvel Letters" and the subsequent failure of *The Battle Summer* led Mitchell to return to journalistic satire, but with a project that was more ambitious. He decided to publish a weekly pamphlet that would provide a humorous study of New York society. Wishing to keep the project a secret, he set aside his Ik Marvel pseudonym and adopted the name of John Timon instead. Twenty-four issues of *The Lorgnette; or, Studies of the Town. By an Opera Goer* were published between 20 January 1850 and 9 October 1850. In the initial pamphlet, Mitchell's Timon describes himself as a cosmopolitan and outsider who will focus his lorgnette on the foibles and excesses of New York society. The mystery surrounding the true identity of John Timon immediately became a topic of public debate. Mitchell himself added to the fray by commenting in one pamphlet on a list of persons who had been considered as possible authors, including in his list "Mr. Ik Marvell," whose name he purposely misspelled to divert attention. He further threw readers off the track by publishing a book that was an expanded form of a well-received article that appeared in the *Southern Literary Messenger* for September 1849, "A Bachelor's Reverie." The book *Reveries of a Bachelor* was published in December 1850 by Charles Scribner, and despite Scribner's doubts about the likelihood of its success, it brought Mitchell international fame, selling fourteen thousand copies in its first year of publication and remaining on best-seller lists in America throughout the 1850s.

Reveries of a Bachelor follows the musings of its bachelor narrator as he sits before a fire in his farmhouse with his dog, Carlo. The subjects of his fireside reveries range from love to marriage to the relative advantages and disadvantages of domestic life. Each of the four sections of the book is symbolically related to different stages of the bachelor narrator's fire. The book begins by providing a defense of bachelorhood, but the merits of married life, especially the shared sympathy it provides, eventually take precedence. A strain of melancholy also pervades the book, however, as the loss of loved ones mars the scenes of domestic bliss. The first-person point of view creates an autobiographical feeling, but as the bachelor's narrative moves from the first-person pronoun *I* to the second-person pronoun *you,* the barrier between narrator and reader collapses, and the reader is invited to imagine first-hand the emotions described in the bachelor's meditation. *Reveries of a Bachelor* is a highly sentimental and not terribly profound book. Yet, its ability to elicit identification through imagination and emotion is impressive and became a trademark of Mitchell's style. The great success of the book suggests the importance of such emotional investment to a nineteenth-century reading audience.

The publication of *Reveries of a Bachelor* opened doors for Mitchell in the literary world. He was offered an editorship at *Harper's New Monthly Magazine,* where in October 1851 he began a column titled "The Editor's Easy Chair," which was continued by subsequent editors of *Harper's* George William Curtis and William Dean Howells. Soon after, in 1851, Mitchell published a sequel to *Reveries of a Bachelor* called *Dream Life: A Fable of the Seasons,* which was prefaced with a dedicatory letter to Washington Irving. The four sections of the book follow its protagonist, Clarence, through boyhood, youth, manhood, and age, each corresponding to a different season. Some of the same themes found in *Rever-*

Mary Frances Pringle, whom Mitchell married in 1853

ies of a Bachelor resurface in *Dream Life,* such as the importance of family, the devastating loss of loved ones, and marriage as a means of displacing the loneliness of adult life. *Dream Life* also met with immediate success. Although it was these early, sentimental works that established Mitchell's fame, eventually he regretted that these youthful works overshadowed what he thought much better books, written later in his life.

In 1852 *Knickerbocker Magazine* serialized Mitchell's "Fudge Papers," a satirical look at a superficial New York family, published in book form in 1855 as *Fudge Doings: Being Tony Fudge's Record of the Same.* These articles, however, did not meet with the success of the earlier Ik Marvel satires. In July 1852 Mitchell was planning a trip to Europe when he heard that his idol, Washington Irving, was visiting the popular resort town of Saratoga Springs. Hoping to meet with Irving, a few days before leaving for Europe Mitchell rushed off to Saratoga Springs and unwittingly checked into a room just down the hall from Irving's. The two men struck up a friendship and spent much time together chatting and taking morning walks. At Saratoga Springs, Mitchell also met his future wife, Mary Frances Pringle, the daughter of a rice planter from Charleston, South Carolina, who was traveling with her family. The two spent some time together, and Mitchell was imme-

Mitchell in 1904 (portrait by Katharine Abbot Cox; from Waldo H. Dunn, The Life of Donald G. Mitchell, Ik Marvel, *1922)*

diately struck by her beauty, charm, and devotion to her family. He gave up thoughts of Europe and determined to win her heart instead. In the fall, unable to keep his mind on his literary tasks, Mitchell made a hurried journey to Charleston to propose marriage. He was disappointed to find Mary Pringle away from home. He traveled to Savannah and on 23 December sent her a letter proposing marriage, to which she returned an encouraging reply. Mitchell returned to Charleston, and on 1 February 1853 the two were engaged to be married.

Mitchell had given a lecture in 1851 on the history of Venice that his brother encouraged him to expand into a full-length study. The young couple had decided to take a trip to Europe following their wedding, so Mitchell traveled to Washington in hopes of securing an appointment as U.S. consul to an Italian city so that he could pursue his research of Venice. In Washington he chanced to meet Nathaniel Hawthorne, who had himself recently been appointed consul to Liverpool and who was close friends with President Franklin Pierce. Hawthorne introduced Mitchell to the president, and their interview led to a diplo-

matic appointment for Mitchell as consul to Venice. Donald and Mary were married in Charleston on 31 May 1853 and sailed for Liverpool on 25 June. Unfortunately, Mitchell disliked his position as consul because his diplomatic duties made pursuing his Venetian studies impossible. He resigned the position in February 1854, and he and Mary went to Paris, where on 5 June 1854 their daughter Hesse Alston was born.

As the Mitchells returned to the United States, they planned to have Mary and Hesse return to Charleston for a short time while Donald sought a residence for them. In May 1855 he placed an advertisement in New York newspapers seeking a farm of at least one hundred acres. Mitchell began receiving many responses on his return and made arrangements to inspect the most promising ones. Arriving in his college home of New Haven on 30 May 1855, Mitchell was swarmed by visitors and acquaintances, one of whom was the district member of Congress, Colin Ingersoll, who, along with his wife, offered to drive Mitchell on his search. The next morning Mitchell found a farm of two hundred acres overlooking New Haven and its valley. Mitchell later wrote about the purchase and improvement of the farm in his book *My Farm of Edgewood: A Country Book* (1863). Mitchell's literary output was significantly reduced immediately following the purchase of Edgewood, however, as he was forced to devote most of his time to his new family and the affairs of his farm. Between 1855 and 1861, six of the eleven Mitchell children were born, and Mitchell was able to publish only a handful of articles.

The early years at Edgewood were not profitable, and Mitchell was forced to look elsewhere to pay his mounting debt. He was turned down for a vacant professorship at Yale. In 1857 he proposed to Harper and Brothers to work as a columnist or editor for *Harper's Weekly Magazine* but was unsuccessful. His only recourse was the lecture circuit in New England, where he was paid $50 an appearance. Mitchell did not enjoy traveling and being away from his family for extended periods, but the venture did help to keep him out of debt. Then, in 1861, the Civil War broke out. The previous summer, Mary's parents had come from Charleston with their two daughters. They returned home, taking Hesse for an extended visit, but the outbreak of the war made Hesse's immediate return impossible. Communication between the Mitchells and the Pringles became difficult. Finally, tragedy struck in early January 1862 when a letter arrived announcing that Hesse had died of spinal meningitis. Adding to this blow were the deaths of two of Mary's five brothers who entered the Confederate army. The strain on the Mitchells' daily lives during this period was increased by Mary's being viewed with suspicion by local warmongers.

With the Civil War came a return to increased literary output for Mitchell. Although he made occasional critical comments on the destructiveness of the war and the profits being reaped by war manufacturers, the war was not the primary subject of his writings during this period. Instead, his works were largely devoted to promoting the value of country life, reforms in American rural architecture, farm management, and landscape design. Reviewers used to the dreamy and sentimental Ik Marvel were surprised by Mitchell's reappearance as a practical farmer dispensing sage agricultural advice. In 1863 James T. Fields suggested that Mitchell contribute a series of essays to *The Atlantic* that would discuss literature on agriculture and husbandry from Greco-Roman times to the present. The result was "Wet Weather Work," which appeared in eight installments between February 1863 and September 1864 and in 1865 was put into book form as *Wet Days at Edgewood: With Old Farmers, Old Gardeners, and Old Pastorals*. The essays were well received. Hawthorne told Fields of his admiration for them. During this time Mitchell also completed and published *My Farm of Edgewood: A Country Book* (1863). Developing out of an 1860 article, "Hints About Farming," the book was an immediate success and helped revive Mitchell's reputation in the 1860s. Mitchell himself considered it the best book he had written.

Mitchell also wrote two works of fiction during these years of increased literary output. From his European notebooks, Mitchell put together *Seven Stories, With Basement and Attic*, published in 1864, a series of stories that followed his earlier style of blending autobiography and fiction. The title plays on a pun for the structure of the book, with the introduction serving as the "basement" and the conclusion serving as the "attic"; the two parts frame seven stories relating to Mitchell's experiences in Europe. The book was not popular, perhaps because it came too closely on the heels of *My Farm of Edgewood* and perhaps because it was a return to an earlier, outmoded style. In February 1865 he began serial publication of a more ambitious work, *Doctor Johns: Being a Narrative of Certain Events in the Life of an Orthodox Minister of Connecticut* (published in book form, 1866). The story, set forty years in the past, tells of the conflicts between the puritanical Dr. Johns and his rebellious son, Reuben. Dr. Johns was no doubt based, at least in part, on Mitchell's memories of his father. Although Mitchell excelled in the essay form, fiction was not his true strength, as he had trouble sustaining the structure of a book-length narrative. Therefore, the book did not sell well.

By 1868 Mitchell was again desperate for funds and came close to selling his estate. Before he could do so, however, he was approached by two New York publishers who wanted to establish a journal for farm families and country residents called *Hearth and Home*. Mitchell accepted a position as editor of the magazine, where he worked in collaboration with Harriet Beecher Stowe. By 1870, however, the proprietors of the magazine had lost interest. They sold the magazine, and Mitchell was replaced as editor. Mitchell was not financially secure again until the mid 1880s, and then only marginally so.

Mitchell's later major writings consisted mostly of his thoughts on literature derived from college lectures he had given. In 1889 he published *English Lands, Letters, and Kings from Celt to Tudor*. This volume was followed by three subsequent volumes: *English Lands, Letters, and Kings from Elizabeth to Anne* (1890); *English Lands, Letters, and Kings: Queen Anne and the Georges* (1895); and *English Lands, Letters, and Kings: The Later Georges to Victoria* (1897). Mitchell decided to follow up these surveys with two volumes on American literature—*American Lands and Letters: The Mayflower to Rip-Van-Winkle* (1897), and *American Lands and Letters: Leather-Stocking to Poe's "Raven"* (1899). These surveys were not meant to be in-depth studies but surveys to whet readers' literary appetites and encourage them to pursue their own studies. Mitchell's last public appearance came at the dedication of Woodbridge Hall at Yale University in 1901. In 1907 Scribners published a collected edition of Mitchell's writings in fifteen volumes, *The Works of Donald G. Mitchell*. Omitted from this edition are *The Battle Summer*, *The Lorgnette*, and *Fudge Doings*. Mitchell remained physically active until his eighty-fifth year, but in August 1908 he suffered a severe hemorrhaging of the lungs. He died in his library on 15 December 1908.

Biography:

Waldo Dunn, *The Life of Donald G. Mitchell* (New York: Scribners, 1922).

References:

Ann Douglas, *The Feminization of American Culture* (New York: Noonday, 1998), pp. 234–243;

Wayne R. Kime, *Donald G. Mitchell* (Boston: Twayne, 1985);

David W. Pancost, "Donald Grant Mitchell's *Reveries of a Bachelor* and Herman Melville's 'I and My Chimney,'" *American Transcendental Quarterly*, 42 (Spring 1979): 129–136;

David S. Reynolds, *Beneath the American Renaissance* (New York: Knopf, 1988), pp. 32–35;

Arnold G. Tew and Allan Perkin, "The Disappearance of Ik. Marvel," *American Studies*, 33 (Fall 1992): 5–20;

Kathryn Whitford, "*The Blithedale Romance:* Hawthorne's *Reveries of a Bachelor*," *Thoth*, 15 (1974–1975): 19–28.

Papers:

A collection of Donald Grant Mitchell's manuscripts, letters, notebooks, and other papers is housed at the Beinecke Library, Yale University.

John Neal

(25 August 1793 – 20 June 1876)

Karen A. Weyler
University of North Carolina at Greensboro

See also the Neal entries in *DLB 1: The American Renaissance in New England* and *DLB 59: American Literary Critics and Scholars, 1800–1850.*

BOOKS: *Keep Cool, A Novel, Written in Hot Weather,* as Somebody, 2 volumes (Baltimore: Joseph Cushing, 1817);

Battle of Niagara, A Poem, Without Notes; and Goldau, or The Maniac Harper, as Jehu O'Cataract (Baltimore: N. G. Maxwell, 1818; enlarged, 1819);

A History of the American Revolution; Comprehending All the Principle Events Both in the Field and in the Cabinet, 2 volumes, by Neal, Paul Allen, and Tobias Watkins (Baltimore: Thomas Murphy, 1819);

Otho: A Tragedy, in Five Acts (Boston: West, Richardson & Lord, 1819);

Logan, a Family History, 2 volumes (Philadelphia: Carey & Lea, 1822; London: A. K. Newman, 1823);

Seventy-Six, 2 volumes (Baltimore: Joseph Robinson, 1823; London: Whittaker, 1823);

Randolph, a Novel, 2 volumes (Philadelphia: Published for Whom It May Concern, 1823);

Errata; or, the Works of Will. Adams, 2 volumes (New York: Published for the Proprietors, 1823);

Brother Jonathan: or, the New Englanders, anonymous, 3 volumes (Edinburgh: Blackwood / London: Cadell, Strand, 1825);

Rachel Dyer: A North American Story (Portland, Me.: Shirley & Hyde, 1828);

Address Delivered Before the Portland Association, For the Promotion of Temperance, February 11, 1829 (Portland, Me.: Day & Fraser, 1829);

City of Portland: Being a General Review of the Proceedings Heretofore Had, in the Town of Portland, on the Subject of a City Government (Portland, Me.: Printed by Shirley & Hyde, 1829);

Authorship, a Tale, as a New Englander Over-Sea (Boston: Gray & Bowen, 1830);

Our Country. An Address Delivered Before the Alumni of Waterville-College, July 29, 1830 (Portland, Me.: S. Colman, 1830);

John Neal, circa 1823 (portrait attributed to Sarah Miriam Peale; from Benjamin Lease, That Wild Fellow Neal, *1972)*

An Address Delivered Before the M. C. Mechanic Association, Thursday Evening, Jan. 13, 1831 (Portland, Me.: Printed by Day & Fraser, 1831);

The Down-Easters, 2 volumes (New York: Harper, 1833);

Banks and Banking: A Letter to the Bank-Directors of Portland (Portland, Me.: Printed at the Orion Office, 1837);

Man. A Discourse, Before the United Brothers' Society of Brown University, September 4, 1838 (Providence: Knowles, Vose, 1838);

Appeal from the American Press to the American People. In Behalf of John Bratish Eliovich, Late a Major General in the Service of Her Most Catholic Majesty, The Queen of

Spain . . . and Now an American Citizen (Portland, Me.: Printed at the Argus Office, 1840);

One Word More: Intended for the Reasoning and Thoughtful Among Unbelievers (Portland, Me.: Printed for the Author, 1854; Boston: Crocker & Brewster, 1854);

True Womanhood: A Tale (Boston: Ticknor & Fields, 1859);

The White-Faced Pacer: or, Before and After the Battle (New York: Beadle, 1863);

The Moose-Hunter; or, Life in the Maine Woods (New York: Beadle, 1864);

Little Moccasin; or, Along the Madawaska. A Story of Life and Love in the Lumber Region (New York: Beadle, 1866);

Account of the Great Conflagration in Portland, July 4th & 5th, 1866 (Portland, Me.: Starbird & Twitchell, 1866);

Wandering Recollections of a Somewhat Busy Life. An Autobiography (Boston: Roberts, 1869);

Great Mysteries and Little Plagues (Boston: Roberts, 1870);

Portland Illustrated (Portland, Me.: W. S. Jones, 1874);

American Writers. A Series of Papers Contributed to Blackwood's Magazine (1824–1825), edited by Fred Lewis Pattee (Durham, N.C.: Duke University Press, 1937);

Observations on American Art. Selections from the Writings of John Neal (1793–1876), edited by Harold Edward Dickson (State College: Pennsylvania State College, 1943).

Collection: *The Genius of John Neal: Selections from His Writings,* edited by Benjamin Lease and Hans-Joachim Lang (Bern: Lang, 1978).

OTHER: *General Index to the First Twelve Volumes, or First Series, of Niles' Weekly Register Being a Period of Six Years: From September, 1811, to September, 1817,* edited by Neal (Baltimore: Printed and Published by the Editor at Franklin Press, 1818);

"Otter-Bag, the Oneida Chief," in *The Token; A Christmas and New Year's Present,* edited by N. P. Willis (Boston: S. G. Goodrich, 1829), pp. 221–284;

"The Birth of a Poet," "Ode to Peace," and "The Sleeper," in *Specimens of American Poetry,* 3 volumes, edited by Samuel Kettell (Boston: S. G. Goodrich, 1829), III: 99–111;

"The Utilitarian," in *The Token; A Christmas and New Year's Present,* edited by S. G. Goodrich (Boston: Carter & Hendee, 1830), pp. 299–318;

Etienne Dumont, trans., *Principles of Legislation: From the Ms. of Jeremy Bentham,* translated into English, with a biographical notice of Bentham, by Neal (Boston: Wells & Lilly, 1830);

"The Haunted Man," in *The Atlantic Souvenir for MDCCCXXXII* (Philadelphia: Carey & Lea, 1832), pp. 221–246;

"Children—What are They?" in *The Token and Atlantic Souvenir. A Christmas and New Year's Present,* edited by Goodrich (Boston: Charles Bowen, 1835), pp. 280–298;

"The Young Phrenologist," in *The Token and Atlantic Souvenir. A Christmas and New Year's Present,* edited by Goodrich (Boston: Charles Bowen, 1836), pp. 156–169;

"The Unchangeable Jew" and "A War-Song of the Revolution," in *The Portland Sketch Book,* edited by Ann S. Stephens (Portland, Me.: Colman & Chisolm, 1836), pp. 168–184;

"Women," in *The Boston Book. Being Specimens of Metropolitan Literature,* edited by B. B. Thatcher (Boston: Light & Stearns, 1837), pp. 240–244;

"Elizabeth Oakes Smith," in *The Sinless Child, and Other Poems,* by Oakes Smith, edited by John Keese (New York: Wiley & Putnam / Boston: W. D. Ticknor, 1843), pp. xv–xxvi;

"My Child! My Child!" in *The Mayflower,* edited by Oakes Smith (Boston: Saxton & Kelt, 1847), pp. 112–113;

"Phantasmagoria," in *The Dew-Drop: A Tribute of Affection* (Philadelphia: Lippincott, Grambo, 1852), pp. 153–170;

"Battle Anthem," in *The Rebellion Record: A Diary of American Events,* edited by Frank Moore (New York: Putnam, 1861), p. 119.

SELECTED PERIODICAL PUBLICATIONS—UNCOLLECTED: "Yankee Notions," *London Magazine,* 4 (1826): 446–447;

Our Ephraim, or the New Englanders, New England Galaxy (16 May 1835 – 13 June 1835);

"Idiosyncrasies," *Brother Jonathan,* 5 (May 1843): 25; 5 (July 1843): 274–280;

Ruth Elder, Brother Jonathan, 5 (January–June 1843): 202–215, 361–363, 447–448, 475–477; 6 (July–December 1843): 1–4, 29–33, 132–135, 161–162, 172–175, 197–201, 253–258, 281–286, 337–343, 365–368, 393–396.

A staunch advocate of American literary nationalism, John Neal wrote fiction, poetry, and essays throughout a literary career that spanned nearly six decades. Neal was a contemporary of James Fenimore Cooper and, like Cooper, was one of the earliest American writers to experiment with historical fiction in the wake of Sir Walter Scott's popularity. Yet, after a meteoric rise to prominence based on his extravagantly plotted historical romances, Neal's notoriety gradually

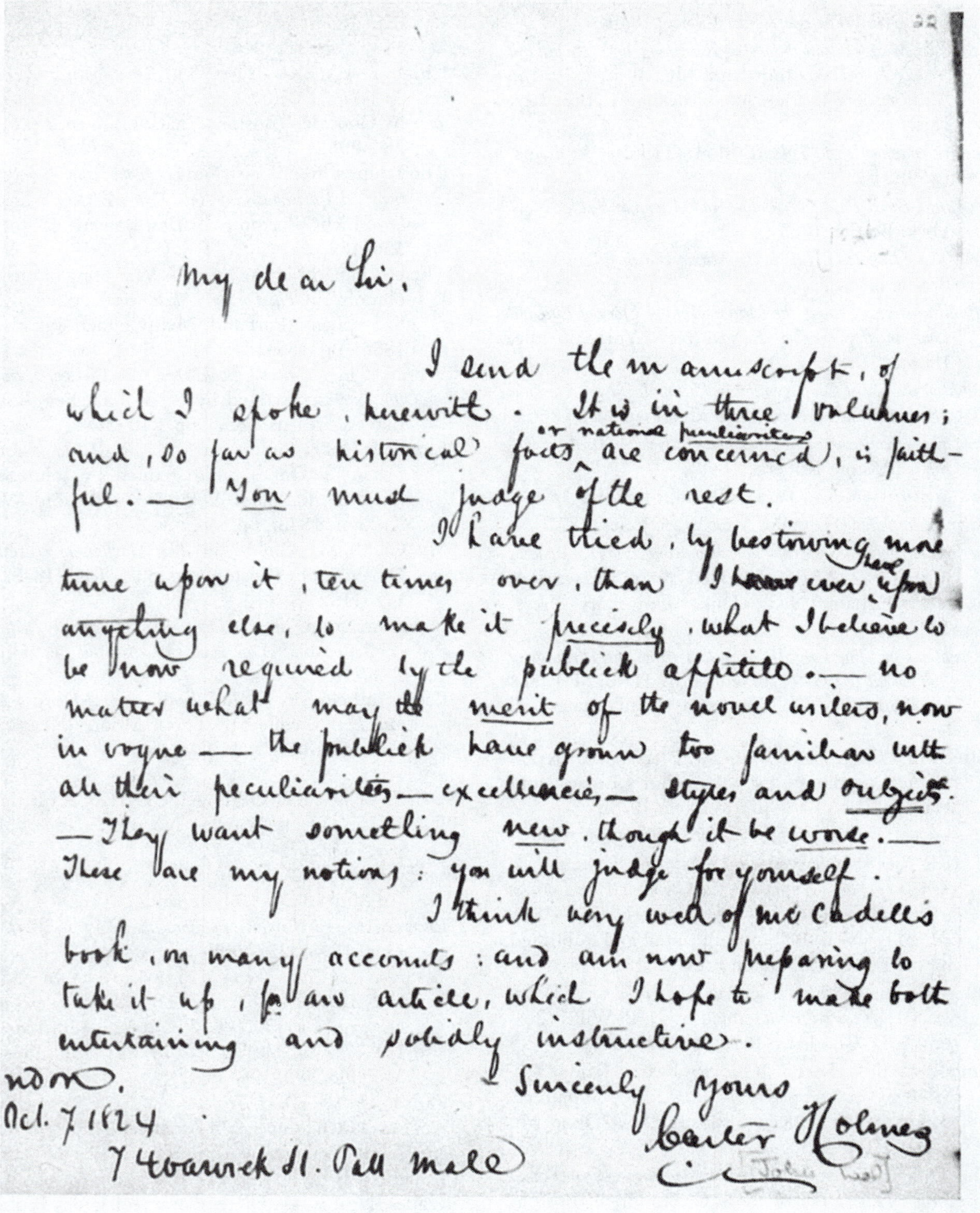

My dear Sir,

I send the manuscript, of which I spoke, herewith.— It is in three volumes; and, so far as historical facts, *or national peculiarities* are concerned), is faithful.— You must judge of the rest.

I have tried, by bestowing more time upon it, ten times over, than I *have* ever *upon* anything else, to make it precisely, what I believe to be now required by the publick appitite.— no matter what may the merit of the novel writers, now in vogue.— the publick have grown too familiar with all their peculiarities,— excellencies,— styles and subjects.— They want something new, though it be worse.— These are my notions: you will judge for yourself.

I think very well of McCadell's book, on many accounts: and am now preparing to take it up, for an article, which I hope to make both entertaining and solidly instructive.

Sincerely yours
Carter Holmes
(John Neal)

ndon.
Oct. 7 1824
7 Warwick St. Pall Mall

Letter to publisher William Blackwood that Neal, using the pseudonym Carter Holmes, sent with the manuscript for his 1825 novel,
Brother Jonathan *(National Library of Scotland)*

faded, prompting Nathaniel Hawthorne to observe somewhat disingenuously in 1845 in the sketch "P.'s Correspondence" from *Mosses from an Old Manse:* "How slowly our literature grows up! Most of our writers of promise have come to untimely ends. There was that wild fellow, John Neal, who almost turned my boyish brain with his romances; he surely has long been dead, else he never could keep himself so quiet." Neal's novels and poetry are seldom read today, but he remains important for his prescient literary criticism of other American authors, including his praise of Edgar Allan Poe early in Poe's career and his insightful assessments of the strengths and weaknesses of Washington Irving and a host of other writers.

Neal and his twin sister, Rachel, were born on 25 August 1793 in Falmouth, in what was then the District of Maine, to John and Rachel (Hall) Neal. The elder Neals were Quakers, and John Neal taught school. He died from a contagious fever less than a month after the birth of his children. Although Rachel Neal received some support from her family, after her husband's death she obtained a position as a schoolteacher in order to provide for her infant children. The younger John Neal was raised in poor circumstances and received formal education only through the age of twelve. In *Wandering Recollections of a Somewhat Busy Life. An Autobiography* (1869), written late in his life, Neal has little positive to say about his schooling and claims that he was chiefly self-educated. He was often taunted while in school by his classmates for his pacifistic Quaker heritage and recalls vowing as a nine-year-old "to bear these outrages no longer, and to take my own part against all the world, Quaker or no Quaker." Although he did not officially break with the Quakers until 1820, when he was read out of the Society for fighting, Neal from this time forward rejected the Quaker policy of nonresistance and soon gained a reputation for contentiousness—fostered by many public quarrels—that would last a lifetime.

Between 1805 and 1816 Neal worked in various mercantile endeavors in Portland, Boston, and Baltimore—beginning as a store clerk and working his way up to partnership with his close friend John Pierpont in a dry-goods wholesaling business. The end of the War of 1812, however, brought Neal's business to bankruptcy, and in 1816 he began the study of law; he was later admitted to the Maryland bar. During this same time he and Pierpont joined with other literary men in Baltimore to found the Delphian Club, which was modeled after eighteenth-century literary clubs such as the Tuesday Club of Annapolis. Founded in 1816, the Delphian Club met weekly through 1825 to allow its members to discuss their literary productions as well as published works by other writers. Each of the nine members was given a club name; Neal's was Jehu O'Cataract—Jehu inspired by a wild chariot driver in the Old Testament and Cataract inspired by his overflowing, torrent-like speech and prose. From January 1816 through June 1818, Neal published poetry, essays, and literary reviews in *The Portico,* a magazine produced by the Delphians.

Inspired by his success in writing for *The Portico* but seeking a means of writing that might be more financially lucrative, Neal turned to fiction. He gleefully recounts having sold for $200 in 1817 *Keep Cool, A Novel, Written in Hot Weather,* which he claims he wrote to discourage dueling. Neal took great pride in the amazing speed with which he wrote, and he intensely disliked revision. He valued the drama, intensity, and passion of first drafts—factors that he thought stimulated the blood of the reader. Neal's theory of reading effects was heavily influenced by August Wilhelm von Schlegel's theory in his *Über dramatische Kunst und Literatur* (1809–1811), translated by John Black as *Course of Lectures on Dramatic Art and Literature* (1815), a subject Benjamin Lease explores in detail in *That Wild Fellow John Neal and the American Literary Revolution* (1972). Although Neal's speedy composition and failure to revise did not benefit the structure of his novels, he was able to produce prodigious amounts of material, a fact he boasted of throughout the early portion of his career.

In 1818 Neal edited *The Portico* and published the *General Index to the First Twelve Volumes, or First Series, of Niles' Weekly Register Being a Period of Six Years: From September, 1811, to September, 1817* and *Battle of Niagara, A Poem, Without Notes; and Goldau, or The Maniac Harper.* In 1819 while continuing to study law, Neal wrote *Otho: A Tragedy, in Five Acts,* a verse drama that owes a large debt to *The Corsair* (1814) and *Manfred* (1817)—both by George Gordon, Lord Byron—and large portions of *A History of the American Revolution; Comprehending All the Principle Events Both in the Field and in the Cabinet* (1819), which appeared credited to Paul Allen, although it was actually written by Neal and Tobias Watkins. Neal's labors in writing history gave him sufficient knowledge to write *Seventy-Six* (1823) and *Brother Jonathan: or, the New Englanders* (1825), his historical romances set during the American Revolution.

Neal's desire to create truly American tales underlies much of his fiction. In the preface to *Rachel Dyer: A North American Story* (1828) Neal argues that the best writers the United States has produced "are English writers, not American writers. They are English in everything they do, and in everything they say, as authors—in the structure and moral of their stories, in their dialogue, speech, and pronunciation, yea in the very characters they draw. Not so much as one true Yankee is to be found in any of our native books:

BULLETIN EXTRA.

ARRIVED, at Portland, on Saturday evening last, in the Steam-Boat, in a short passage from London, via New-York, the celebrated author of "Keep Cool," "Randolph," "Errata," &c., &c., in a state of great bodily and mental exhaustion, owing to his excessive labors in furnishing matter for Blackwood's Edinburgh Monthly Magazine. It is said much of the elevation of the American character is owing to this distinguished author. Since his arrival in his native town, it has been recommended to put himself under the care of the Hon. STEPHEN JONES, M. D. an eminent Southern Physician. This has been done, and the Doctor reports favorably. On Wednesday afternoon he was walking with his Physician apparently much better. Dr. JONES, however, recommends his immediate removal to Baltimore, or some more Southern Climate, for his complete restoration.

July 12.

Broadside posted at Bowdoin College after Neal's return to the United States from England in 1827
(Houghton Library, Harvard University)

hardly so much as one true Yankee phrase." Disdaining to produce pale imitations of British fiction, for which he faulted Irving, Neal vowed to write a truly American book, with American characters and American dialect.

The labyrinthine plots of Neal's multivolume novels make simple summaries exceedingly difficult, but *Logan, a Family History* and *Seventy-Six,* published in 1822 and 1823 respectively, illustrate Neal's desire to mine the early history of the new Republic. Set in pre-Revolutionary British America and filled with multiple incidents of rape, murder, and incest, the Gothic plot of *Logan, a Family History* defies easy description. Based only loosely on the historical Native American Logan, Neal's novel traces the complex machinations of his fictional character Logan, an Englishman turned Mingo chief, and the struggle between his two sons, one raised as an Indian and the other raised as an Englishman. The central question of the novel, as Ter-

esa A. Goddu argues in *Gothic America: Narrative, History, and Nation* (1997) is "Who will inherit America? While the novel eventually resolves that the revolutionary American, not the Indian, is the rightful possessor, it also shows how that inheritance is an appropriation of Indian attributes as well as land." Essential for the creation of Americanness, the Indians in *Logan, a Family History* must nevertheless not only surrender the field to the new hybrid American but also disappear entirely to ensure the supremacy of this new American hybrid. As was typical with many of Neal's novels, reviews of *Logan, a Family History* were mixed, ranging from glowing praise in the *Columbian Observer* to a scathing review in the British *Monthly Review,* questioning the sanity of the author of *Logan, a Family History.*

Although similarly complicated in plot, *Seventy-Six* is far more coherent than *Logan, a Family History,* and Neal has better control over his material. An elderly

Jonathan Oadley narrates this novel of the American Revolution, tracing the fortunes of his family during his youth, as he, his brother, and his father all serve in General George Washington's army. Neal intertwines this tale of war with Oadley's and his brother's courtships of a pair of sisters in a neighboring family. Like Cooper's *The Spy* (1821), *Seventy-Six* has the thick historical description that marked a new era in fiction written by American writers. Neal further "Americanizes" his novel by striving for realistic dialogue; consequently, the dialogue includes oaths and profanity and Neal's experiments with the vernacular. Overall, reviews of *Seventy-Six* were positive, and Neal in *Wandering Recollections of a Somewhat Busy Life* labels it his personal favorite among his longer works. *Seventy-Six,* however, later prompted Poe to argue in "The Literati of New York City" (*Godey's Lady's Book,* May–October 1846) that despite Neal's admirable innovation and originality, "there is no precision, no finish about anything he does—always an excessive *force* but little of refined art. Mr. N. seems to be deficient in a sense of *completeness.* He begins well, vigorously, startlingly . . . but his conclusions are sure to be hurried and indistinct, so that the reader perceives a falling off, and closes the book with dissatisfaction."

Neal also published during this period *Randolph, a Novel* (1823) and *Errata; or, the Works of Will. Adams* (1823). In the epistolary novel *Randolph,* Sarah Ramsey tries to uncover the true nature of Edward Molton; the plot of the novel is interrupted, however, by lengthy digressions about British and American writers, periodicals, artists, and other subjects. In one such digression, Neal's disparaging comments about William Pinkney, a prominent Baltimore lawyer and statesman who died while the novel was in publication, led to a public quarrel with Pinkney's son, the poet Edward Coote Pinkney, who challenged Neal to a duel; Neal refused to fight and defended his comments. *Errata,* which Neal claims to have written in thirty-nine days, draws heavily on certain aspects of Neal's life, especially his Quaker boyhood and mercantile experience. Will Adams, the protagonist of *Errata,* murders a close friend out of unfounded jealousy and dies insane.

Seeking a larger audience and hoping to refute Sydney Smith's infamous 1820 taunt in the *Edinburgh Review,* "Who reads an American book?" Neal traveled to England, arriving there on 8 January 1824. He settled in London and published many newspaper articles and magazine essays. One of Neal's most interesting endeavors was a series of lengthy essays titled "American Writers," which he wrote for *Blackwood's Edinburgh Magazine* between 1824 and 1825. None of these essays was published under Neal's name, appearing instead unsigned or under a pseudonym, a strategy Neal pur-

John and Eleanor Neal with their son James and daughters Mary and Margaret, circa 1843

posefully adopted to deceive his British readership, although this strategy was not entirely successful. Neal sought to promote American literature under the guise of comprehensively surveying the literary history of the United States, including not only fiction and poetry but also belles lettres. One interesting highlight of "American Writers" is Neal's discussion of Charles Brockden Brown, whose complex plots may well have provided Neal himself with inspiration. Neal acknowledges Brown as one of the first professional authors of the United States and uses his discussion of Brown to attack the parsimonious American reader, who desires a native literary culture but is too cheap to pay for one. Neal includes himself in the fifth number of this literary survey, devoting several pages to his work and describing himself as a highly original writer and "one of those audacious, whimsical, obstinate, *self-educated* men." Neal composed his "American Writers" essays without notes or even primary texts at times; his essays are not always factually accurate (he tends to confuse dates and misspell names), but "American Writers" remains memorable for Neal's serious attempt to sketch out the boundaries of American literature during the early national period.

Neal in later years

An admirer of Jeremy Bentham and Utilitarianism, dating from the time of his study of law, Neal met Bentham during his sojourn in England. For part of 1825 and 1826, Neal resided in the Bentham household in London as he translated Bentham's *Traités de législation* (1802), which had been published first in a French translation by Etienne Dumont. Neal's English version appeared in the United States in 1830 as *Principles of Legislation: From the Ms. of Jeremy Bentham.* Neal also arranged for the British publication of his 1825 novel *Brother Jonathan: or, the New Englanders,* which was never published in the United States. Amid complicated subplots, *Brother Jonathan* follows a year in the life of Walter Harwood, who eventually joins the military under General Washington, fighting in the Battle of Brooklyn Heights. Like *Seventy-Six, Brother Jonathan* is marked by heavy use of the vernacular.

After visiting Paris in the spring of 1827, Neal returned to the United States, settling in Portland to practice law. He continued to write fiction, publishing in 1828 *Rachel Dyer,* an historical novel inspired by Robert Calef's *More Wonders of the Invisible World* (1700). In *Rachel Dyer* Neal explores the bigotry and injustices of the Salem witchcraft trials. The three central characters

are the preacher George Burroughs (only loosely based on the historical figure), who is loved by the Quaker sisters Rachel and Elizabeth Dyer, whose grandmother had earlier been executed for witchcraft. Burroughs and the Dyer sisters speak out on behalf of several others unjustly accused of witchcraft, until they themselves are accused. Burroughs is executed; Rachel, praying for and forgiving her accusers, dies before she can be executed. Their deaths break the spell of hysteria surrounding Salem and save Elizabeth Dyer from a death sentence.

On 12 October 1828 Neal married his cousin Eleanor Hall. Over the course of their marriage, they had five children—Mary, born 23 December 1829; James, born 6 January 1831; Margaret Eleanor, born 11 June 1834; Eleanor, born 17 October 1844, who died before her first birthday; and John Pierpont, born 29 November 1847.

Although Neal wrote *Authorship, a Tale* in 1830 and *The Down-Easters* in 1833, both minor novels set in New England, the majority of his published work from the late 1820s through the 1860s appeared in newspapers and the periodical press, as Irving T. Richards documents in his extensive bibliography of Neal's work. In addition to several brief stints as an editor—of *The Yankee and Boston Literary Gazette* (1828–1829); *The New England Galaxy* (1835); *The New World* (1840); *Brother Jonathan* (1843); and the *Portland Transcript* (1848)—Neal frequently published essays, reviews, sketches, and short stories in popular American periodicals such as *The Yankee, The Token, The Atlantic Souvenir, Godey's Ladies' Book,* and *The Atlantic Monthly.* Although most of his work was fictional, his nonfiction subjects were interesting and varied—including such diverse topics as the nature of children, phrenology, utilitarianism, and traveling.

A recurring and important topic for Neal's periodical publications was women's rights. Neal was a lifelong advocate of women's rights, most notably speaking three times at the Broadway Tabernacle of New York in 1843 on the "Rights of Women," focusing on property rights and suffrage. Neal's initial lecture and subsequent essays on the subject, which were published in *Brother Jonathan,* set off hostile public debate that continued throughout that year. Margaret Fuller was particularly taken with Neal's views and at one point had him speak to her school. Throughout his career, Neal frequently returned to the subject of women's rights in both his fictional and nonfictional works; Fritz Fleischmann explores in detail the relationship between Neal's fiction and his political beliefs in *A Right View of the Subject: Feminism in the Works of Charles Brockden Brown and John Neal* (1983).

As Neal grew older, his interest in formal religion increased. In 1851 he, along with his wife and his sister, joined the Congregational Church. He published a religious tract, *One Word More: Intended for the Reasoning and Thoughtful Among Unbelievers,* in 1854. The death of his son James in 1856 deeply grieved Neal and heightened his interest in religion. *True Womanhood: A Tale* (1859), Neal's first published novel in more than twenty years, focuses on the New York religious revivals of the 1850s.

Neal, who early in his career had identified himself as one of the most original American fiction writers, ended his literary career writing formulaic dime novels. Needing money, Neal in the mid 1860s wrote for the dime novel publisher Irwin P. Beadle and Company—*The White-Faced Pacer: or, Before and After the Battle* (1863); *The Moose-Hunter; or, Life in the Maine Woods* (1864); and *Little Moccasin; or, Along the Madawaska. A Story of Life and Love in the Lumber Region* (1866). Neal's other major publications in the decade before his death were his autobiography, *Wandering Recollections of a Somewhat Busy Life* (1869); *Great Mysteries and Little Plagues* (1870), a collection of essays, including one new piece and other previously published works for and about children; and *Portland Illustrated* (1874), a history of the city of Portland, Maine. Neal wrote *Wandering Recollections of a Somewhat Busy Life* at the urging of his old friend Henry Wadsworth Longfellow. Although *Wandering Recollections of a Somewhat Busy Life* was not published until 1869, Neal actually began composing this work in 1859. After the great Portland fire of 1866 burned down his law office, where he had stored the revised manuscript and many of his other papers, he had to begin anew. Focusing on Neal's early years in Baltimore and London and on the genesis of his literary career, *Wandering Recollections of a Somewhat Busy Life* is an important source of information about Neal, but it is digressive and as confusing in structure as are many of his novels.

Neal died on 20 June 1876 and was buried in Portland in the Western Cemetery. He was survived by his wife, Eleanor, his daughters Mary and Margaret Eleanor, and his son John Pierpont. Born almost a generation before most of the other writers of the American Renaissance, Neal's place in nineteenth-century American literary history has never been a secure one. Although David S. Reynolds in *Beneath the American Renaissance: The Subversive Imagination in the Age of Emerson and Melville* (1988) identifies Neal as one of the early leaders of the "subversive" school of writing, Neal's poetry and fiction were soon overshadowed by the productions of a younger generation of writers who rose to prominence during the central years of the American Renaissance. He nonetheless remained well-known by the literati of New England throughout his lifetime, many of whom either grew up with his fiction, as did Nathaniel Hawthorne, or were encouraged early in their careers by him, as were Edgar Allan Poe, John Greenleaf Whittier, and Elizabeth Oakes Smith. Further, Neal's work presaged in important ways the literary nationalism of Ralph Waldo Emerson, the historical fiction of Hawthorne, and the Gothic fiction of Poe. Neal remains notable today for his promotion of literary nationalism, for his contributions to the development of historical fiction based on the history of the British colonies in North America, and for his use of the vernacular to portray accurately the flavor of American life.

Bibliography:

Irving T. Richards, "John Neal: A Bibliography," *Jahrbuch fur Amerikastudien,* 7 (1962): 296–319.

Biographies:

Dane Yorke, "Yankee Neal," *American Mercury,* 19 (January–April 1930): 361–368;

Irving T. Richards, "The Life and Works of John Neal," 4 volumes, dissertation, Harvard University, 1932;

Benjamin Lease, *That Wild Fellow John Neal and the American Literary Revolution* (Chicago: University of Chicago Press, 1972).

References:

William Charvat, *The Origins of American Critical Thought, 1810–1835* (Philadelphia: University of Pennsylvania Press, 1936);

Alexander Cowie, *The Rise of the American Novel* (New York: American Book Company, 1948);

Edward Alfred Fiorelli, "Literary Nationalism in the Works of John Neal," dissertation, Fordham University, 1981;

Fritz Fleischmann, "'A Likeness, Once Acknowledged': John Neal and the 'Idiosyncrasies' of Literary History," in *Myth and Enlightenment in American Literature,* edited by Dieter Meindl and Friedrich W. Horlacher (Erlangen: Universitatsbund Erlangen-Nurnberg, 1985), pp. 161–176;

Fleischmann, *A Right View of the Subject: Feminism in the Works of Charles Brockden Brown and John Neal* (Erlangen: Palm & Enke, 1983);

Teresa A. Goddu, "Literary Nationalism and the Gothic: John Neal's *Logan,*" in her *Gothic America: Narrative, History, and Nation* (New York: Columbia University Press, 1997), pp. 52–72;

Gerald R. Grove Sr., "John Neal: American Romantic," dissertation, University of Utah, 1974;

Hans-Joachim Lang, "Critical Essays and Stories by John Neal," *Jahrbuch fur Amerikastudien,* 7 (1962): 204–288;

Benjamin Lease, "John Neal and Edgar Allan Poe," *Poe Studies,* 7 (1974): 38–41;

Lease, "Yankee Poetics: John Neal's Theory of Poetry and Fiction," *American Literature,* 24 (January 1953): 505–519;

Harold C. Martin, "The Colloquial Tradition in the Novel: John Neal," *New England Quarterly,* 32 (December 1959): 455–475;

Robert J. Menner, "Two Early Comments on American Dialects," *American Speech,* 13 (February 1938): 8–12;

Francesca Orestano, "The Old World and the New in the National Landscapes of John Neal," in *Views of American Landscapes,* edited by Mick Gigley and Robert Lawson Peebles (Cambridge: Cambridge University Press, 1989), pp. 129–145;

David S. Reynolds, *Beneath the American Renaissance: The Subversive Imagination in the Age of Emerson and Melville* (New York: Knopf, 1988);

Joseph J. Rubin, "John Neal's Poetics as an Influence on Whitman and Poe," *New England Quarterly,* 14 (June 1941): 359–362;

William J. Scheick, "Power, Authority, and Revolutionary Impulse in John Neal's *Rachel Dyer,*" *Studies in American Fiction,* 4 (Autumn 1976): 143–155;

Donald A. Sears, *John Neal* (Boston: Twayne, 1978);

Sears, "Portland, Maine, as a Cultural Center, 1800–1836," dissertation, Harvard University, 1952;

John J. Seydow, "The Sound of Passing Music: John Neal's Battle for American Literary Independence," *Costerus: Essays in English and American Language and Literature,* 7 (1973): 153–182;

John Earle Uhler, "The Delphian Club," *Maryland Historical Magazine,* 20 (December 1925): 305–346.

Papers:

Most of John Neal's papers were destroyed in the great Portland, Maine, fire of 1866. The Houghton Library at Harvard University owns several letterbooks and scrapbooks. Correspondence regarding his publishing career is held at the Historical Society of Pennsylvania and William Blackwood and Sons Limited of Edinburgh. Other useful collections may be found at the Pierpont Morgan Library, the Maryland Historical Society, the National Library of Scotland, the New York Public Library, the Maine Historical Society, the Library of Congress, and the Cooper Collection at Yale University.

Mary Gove Nichols

(10 August 1810 – 30 May 1884)

Arthur Wrobel
University of Kentucky

See also the Nichols entry in *DLB 1: The American Renaissance in New England.*

BOOKS: *Solitary Vice: An Address to Parents and to Those who Have the Care of Children* (Portland: Printed at the Journal Office, 1839);

Lectures to Ladies on Anatomy and Physiology (Boston: Saxton & Peirce, 1842); enlarged as *Lectures to Women on Anatomy and Physiology. With an Appendix on Water Cure* (New York: Harper, 1846);

Uncle John; or, "It Is Too Much Trouble," as Mary Orme (New York: Harper, 1846);

Experience in Water-Cure: A Familiar Exposition of the Principles and Results of Water Treatment in the Cure of Acute and Chronic Diseases, Illustrated by Numerous Cases in the Practice of the Author; with an Explanation of Water-cure Processes, Advice on Diet and Regimen, and Particular Directions to Women in the Treatment of Female Diseases, Water Treatment in Childbirth, and the Diseases of Infancy (New York: Fowler & Wells, 1849); republished as *A Woman's Work in Water Cure and Sanitary Education* (London: Nichols, 1868);

The Two Loves; or, Eros and Anteros (New York: Stringer & Townsend, 1849);

Agnes Morris; or, The Heroine of Domestic Life (New York: Harper, 1849);

Marriage: Its History, Character and Results; Its Sanctities, and the Profanities; Its Science and Its Facts. Demonstrating Its Influence, as a Civilized Institution on the Happiness of the Individual, and the Progress of the Race, by Mary Gove Nichols and Thomas Low Nichols (Cincinnati: Nicholson, 1854);

Mary Lyndon; or, Revelations of a Life (New York: Stringer & Townsend, 1855);

Nichols' Medical Miscellanies: A Familiar Guide to the Preservation of Health, and the Hydropathic Home Treatment of the Most Formidable Diseases, by Mary Gove Nichols and Thomas Low Nichols (Cincinnati: Printed for the Trade by T. L. Nichols, 1856; London: E. W. Allen, 1887);

Uncle Angus, 2 volumes (London: Saunders, Otley, 1864);

Jerry: A Novel of Yankee American Life (London: Sampson Low, Marston, Low & Searle, 1872);

The Clothes Question Considered in its Relations to Beauty, Comfort, and Health (London: Published by the Author, 1878);

Reminiscences of Edgar Allan Poe (New York: Union Square Book Shop, 1931).

SELECTED PERIODICAL PUBLICATIONS–
UNCOLLECTED: "Marrying a Genius," as Mary Orme, *Godey's Lady's Book,* 29 (September 1844): 104–107;

"The Artist," as Orme, *Godey's Lady's Book,* 30 (April 1845): 154–156;

"The Evil and the Good," as Orme, *Godey's Lady's Book,* 31 (July 1845): 36–38;

"The Gift of Prophecy," as Orme, *Broadway Journal,* 2 (4 October 1845): 187–188;

"Mary Pierson," as Orme, *Godey's Lady's Book,* 32 (January 1846): 39–41;

"Passages from the Life of a Medical Eclectic," anonymous, *American Review: A Whig Journal of Political, Literary, Art, and Science,* 3 (April 1846): 374–383; 3 (May 1846): 469–479; 4 (July 1846): 53–64; 4 (September 1846): 264–275;

"Minna Harmon or the Ideal and the Practical," as Mary Orme, *Godey's Lady's Book,* 37 (December 1848): 335–338;

"Maternity; and the Water-Cure of Infants," *Water-Cure Journal and Herald of Reform,* 11 (March 1851): 57–59;

"A Lecture on Woman's Dresses," *Water-Cure Journal and Herald of Reform,* 12 (August 1851): 34–36;

"Woman the Physician," *Water-Cure Journal and Herald of Reform,* 12 (October 1851): 73–75;

"On the Mississippi. From Cairo to Memphis," *All the Year Round,* 12 (27 August 1864): 58–62.

Were Mary Gove Nichols's posthumous reputation to rest solely on her literary output, her claim to fame would be, at best, minimal. Admittedly, she wrote a large

UNCLE JOHN;

OR,

"IT IS TOO MUCH TROUBLE."

BY

MARY ORME.

"I know not whether angels weep, but men
Have wept enough—for what?—to weep again."

NEW-YORK:
HARPER & BROTHERS, PUBLISHERS,
82 CLIFF STREET.
1846.

AGNES MORRIS;

OR,

THE HEROINE OF DOMESTIC LIFE.

[Mrs. Mary Sargeant (N.) G. Nichols (mrs.)

"Minds are of supernal birth;
Let us make a heaven of earth;
O! they wander wide, who roam
For the joys of life from home."

NEW YORK:
HARPER & BROTHERS, PUBLISHERS,
82 CLIFF STREET.
1849.

Title pages for two of Mary Gove Nichols's novels about women who bear illegitimate children (left: Vanderbilt University Library; right: University of Louisville Library)

number of reviews, several novels and short stories, and many articles, but these have slight intrinsic literary merit. Only her vivid and sympathetic sketches of Edgar Allan Poe at Fordham Cottage in 1846, where he lived in desperate poverty while his wife, Virginia, lay dying, have earned Nichols notice in recent years—an appreciative nod, however curt, among the cognoscenti of Poe scholarship. Nichols's work, however, as a medical reformer who focused primarily on women's health issues and proposed radically new definitions of women's rights and roles is, of late, rescuing her from neglect and obscurity. In these areas Nichols's contributions as an essayist, editor, lecturer, and unlicensed physician were significant and, in several ways, pioneering. Nichols's lectures on marriage were radical, and her views about the physiology of sex and its role in mental health, surprisingly frank. She advocated economic independence for women; attributed much of the ills of society and, more especially, the diseases of women—physical and spiritual—to indissoluble marriage vows; and

championed companionate marriage whereby women would have the right to choose their own sexual partners. She wrote sex manuals; spoke openly about the physiology of pregnancy, birth, and lactation; and endorsed a view of sexual union as a pleasurable and vitalizing encounter for both partners, rather than an unfortunate duty to which females were expected to submit. Pursuing the promptings of her own conscience, both in word and deed, earned her, however, unwanted notoriety and eventual alienation from contemporary feminist leadership.

Born on 10 August 1810 in Goffstown, New Hampshire, to working-class parents, Mary Sargeant Neal inherited from her mother, Rebecca, a capacity for hard work and learned from her father, William A. Neal—a freethinker, partisan Democrat, and a widely known lover of debate—a capacity for intellectual sparring. Between the ages of two and twelve, Mary attended a neighbor's school for six or seven months of the year but received only intermittent schooling after her family moved in 1822 to Craftsbury, Vermont. After undergoing a religious, mystical experience at age fifteen and reading a Quaker schoolbook that described the martyrdom suffered by members of this sect and the promise of peace that atonement would bring, she converted to Quakerism. Her spiritual needs taken care of, she read and studied on her own an eclectic assortment of books; these choices included forbidden medical literature her parents believed unsuitable for girls.

Mary also prepared for a teaching career in her local school district and, in the summer of 1828, assumed a teaching post. At this time, her first stories, poems, and essays appeared in the *Boston Traveler,* a New England weekly. That autumn an uncle introduced Mary to Hiram Gove of nearby Weare, New Hampshire—a pious Friend, widower, and hatter, ten years Mary's senior, whose mind was resolutely set on marriage. Under the assault of his persistent attentions and proposals, the intercession of his friends, and her parents' assent to the marriage, Mary consented to marry him despite her initial distaste for him. Her last-minute attempt to break the engagement failed, and on 5 March 1831 Mary reluctantly submitted to a marriage that in her later years she described as "martyrdom."

In March 1832 she gave birth to a daughter, Elma Penn, but lost four other children either to stillbirths or miscarriages during her eleven-year marriage to Gove. These were bleak times for her. Weakened in health, oppressed by the lack of economic security because of her husband's financial setbacks, tormented at being trapped in a loveless marriage to a husband who soon proved to be mean, ignorant, and tyrannical, and forced to give up teaching because he forbade her to work outside of the home, Mary contemplated suicide. Her only relief during these years came from her continuing studies in medical books, including those of John Mason Good, who elucidated the therapeutics of cold water. She used this system on herself and occasional women patients. After the couple's move to Lynn, Massachusetts, in 1837, she opened a girls' school with Hiram Gove's lukewarm approval, he having allowed himself to be swayed by the promise of more income for his support.

The epiphanic event that altered her life was an 1837 lecture she attended in Lynn given by the health reformer Sylvester Graham, whose works she was already familiar with. Graham advocated a vegetarian diet, whole wheat bread, exercise, and daily bathing as antidotes to disease and spoke out against sexual excesses, including masturbation and adultery. Caught up in the evangelistic fervor surrounding this hygienic crusade, she advertised in the *Graham Journal of Health and Longevity* of August 1838 a series of twelve weekly lectures to be given before the Ladies Physiological Society of Boston—an announcement that marked the first time a woman lectured publicly to members of her own sex on anatomy and physiology.

Despite opposition from some quarters regarding the propriety of a woman lecturing in public on controversial subject matter, Mary Gove's entrance into the lyceum movement proved successful. Equipped with drawings, a skeleton, an encouragement from some Harvard faculty and other physicians—and armed with an unshakable conviction that a knowledge of medicine and physiology could contribute to the emancipation of women from ignorance and ill-considered adherence to destructive practices—she drew audiences ranging in size from five hundred to six hundred. Disclaiming any pretense to originating new ideas, Gove fused elements of Grahamism with hydropathic principles garnered from William Andrus Alcott's *The House I Live In* (1834). She stressed, rather, her role as a disseminator of recent physiological knowledge, most particularly the prevention of illness through adherence to the natural laws of health. Her efforts to educate women about their anatomy belonged, in her mind, to the larger issue of the improvement of women's moral and intellectual beings, a theme that was to become more insistent and militant over time. Lecturing proved to be her calling; by January 1839 she had repeated her series in Boston, Lynn, Nantucket, Haverhill, Providence, Newark, and New York—frequently to capacity and appreciative audiences.

While Hiram Gove had sufficiently reconciled himself to his wife's career, others did not; the Quaker hierarchy excommunicated her after disciplining failed to deter her. The *New York Herald* censured her for speaking on matters more appropriate to trained and male physicians; and the editors of *The Lobelian, and Rhode Island Medical Review* judged her moral sense as "so blunted as to be incapable of seeing the difference between gratuitous obscenity and physiological truth." No doubt the publication of her pamphlet *Solitary Vice: An Address to Parents and to Those who Have the Care of Children* (1839) confirmed the views of her critics. Not only did Mary Gove treat a subject about which no woman should confess knowing, but she also identified the problem as being as prevalent among young females as among males. Horace Greeley, the editor of the *New Yorker* and an avowed Grahamite, "earnestly" recommended this "very guarded essay . . . [whose] subject . . . has recently attracted much attention."

In early 1840, after collapsing from a severe pulmonary hemorrhage, Mary Gove retired to Worcester, Massachusetts, to prepare her lectures for publication; but in need of income, she returned to lecturing. Oppressed by the knowledge that she had no rights to her own earnings as a married woman and inspired by her reading of Mary Wollstonecraft's *A Vindication of the Rights of Woman* (1792), her thoughts turned to women's rights. In an 1841 lecture in Baltimore she advocated property rights for married women and freedom from the tyrannies of both the law and tradition. Publication of her *Lectures to Ladies on Anatomy and Physiology* (1842) were met with formulaic, if not indif-

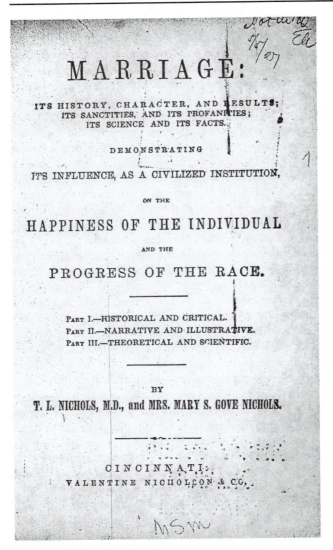

MARRIAGE:

ITS HISTORY, CHARACTER, AND RESULTS;
ITS SANCTITIES, AND ITS PROFANITIES;
ITS SCIENCE AND ITS FACTS.

DEMONSTRATING

ITS INFLUENCE, AS A CIVILIZED INSTITUTION,

ON THE

HAPPINESS OF THE INDIVIDUAL

AND THE

PROGRESS OF THE RACE.

PART I.—HISTORICAL AND CRITICAL.
PART II.—NARRATIVE AND ILLUSTRATIVE.
PART III.—THEORETICAL AND SCIENTIFIC.

BY

T. L. NICHOLS, M.D., and MRS. MARY S. GOVE NICHOLS.

CINCINNATI:
VALENTINE NICHOLSON & CO.

Title page for one of the books Nichols wrote with her husband, Thomas Low Nichols (New York Public Library, Astor, Lenox and Tilden Foundations). Some reviewers called the book licentious because it endorsed extramarital sex in some circumstances.

ferent, reviews: William Andrus Alcott concluded that the book had "merit enough, at any rate, to excite opposition," while the two reviews in the *Boston Medical and Surgical Journal* were equally muted. *Lectures to Ladies on Anatomy and Physiology* familiarly linked physiological education and reform as a means of freeing women, though Mary Gove's attack on the problem of tight lacing as emblematic of both women's slavish devotion to custom and women's social condition struck a more strident note: "Will not American females rise in the full vigor of intellectual majesty, and hunt from society constraint and compression, and the untold anguish they produce?"

For Mary Gove, her marriage to Hiram Gove was added anguish. Despite threats that he would destroy her

reputation and take her child, Mary Gove left her husband in late February 1842, convinced that "there could be no marriage where there was loathing instead of love."

Having experienced the plight common to many women—limited legal redress before the law, censure from religious quarters for pursuing one's intellectual or emotional needs, and limited educational opportunities—Mary Gove next turned her attention to the promise that utopian reform schemes offered. Albert Brisbane's theories in *The Social Destiny of Man; or, Association and Reorganization of Industry* (1840), founded on those of Charles Fourier, proposed a cooperative organization of society that included the restructuring of existing relations between the sexes and even an enlightened form of free love. Emanuel Swedenborg's concept of "Conjugal Love," a form of eternal, spiritual-physical love, was starkly different from her relationship with Hiram Gove. Where emotional coldness, aversion, and separation prevailed, Emanuel Swedenborg's doctrines permitted remarriage.

Such readings prepared Mary Gove emotionally and spiritually for the happiness of a brief, blissful love affair with English reformer Henry Gardiner Wright. A mystic, writer, and a teacher at Alcott House in London, Wright came to the United States to help Amos Bronson Alcott plan the community that became Fruitlands. After meeting Wright at a lyceum picnic, so Mary Gove later recounted in *Mary Lyndon; or, Revelations of a Life* (1855), love was "born in my heart, in a divine fullness." However emotionally enriching this new experience, she also needed financial security. To that end, in January 1843 she started *The Health Journal and Independent Magazine*. Its prospectus boldly announced that it would "discuss faithfully and fearlessly all questions and subjects that concern the great brotherhood of Man," including "the regenerating power of Love, the Pharisaism of the age, the Tyranny of Public Opinion, the right of Every Human Being to freedom of Thought and Action, the Divine nature of Marriage" as well as "the laws of Health, the Reorganization of Society or the Doctrine of Association and the restoration of all things to the Divine order." *The Health Journal and Independent Magazine* ceased publication, however, after one issue, despite (as one review in a sister reform journal described it) its "free spirit" and the "genius and talent" of the "earnest souls" who ran it.

A greater calamity, however, now preoccupied Gove—Wright's departure for England in July 1843 after a tumor in her breast, which Victor Priessnitz treated hydropathically, responded neither to water-cure methods nor surgery. Thereafter, Gove committed herself even more emphatically to the cause of associationism and the promise it offered of establishing a new society of equality between the sexes and of relationships based on emotional, not economic, attachments.

In March 1844, while visiting Ohio phalanxes, Hiram Gove kidnapped his twelve-year-old daughter, Elma, to gain custody. Without any legal right to her child, though she, not Hiram, had supported Elma for her twelve years, Mary Gove arranged a successful counterabduction three months later.

Lacking money, forced to live in boardinghouses where she was either shunned or patronized, and deteriorating in health, she apprenticed herself to Dr. Robert Wesselhoeft, at his Brattleboro, Vermont, water-cure establishment, where, to earn her board, she lectured to ladies about physiology and preventive medicine. After briefly serving as resident physician at a Lebanon Springs, New York, water-cure establishment, she moved in December 1845 to New York City. In May 1846 she founded her own water-cure house on Tenth Street, attending some patients at home and boarding others; using wax models, she also gave lectures four times a week to classes of ladies and engaged in medical consultations through correspondence. She specialized in obstetrics, preaching a program of health maintenance that extended from preparation for pregnancy through postpartum care based on a fusion of principles taken from Grahamism and water cure. Her focus on obstetrics widened to include a campaign against a misguided prudery that required doctors to protect a woman's modesty by delivering babies by touch alone and against those who wanted to restrict medical training to males alone.

Neither her various activities on behalf of women's rights and medical reform nor scandal dimmed her long-standing passion to pursue literary writing. Between September 1844 and December 1848 she published five short stories under the pseudonym "Mary Orme" in *Godey's Lady's Book;* its editor, Sarah Josepha Hale, said of Gove that "few among living women, deserve more respect." Didactic and moralistic, these stories all reflect Gove's own preoccupation with traditional marriage, particularly the pressures placed on women to choose economic security over love. In these stories the former are miserable in their attachments and the latter, happy. Some of her minor contributions appeared in John O'Sullivan's *United States Magazine and Democratic Review,* while a lengthy recounting of her reform efforts (with some gratuitous barbs directed at New York society), titled "Passages from the Life of a Medical Eclectic," appeared in more than four issues of *The American Review: A Whig Journal of Political, Literary, Art, and Science* between April and September 1846.

That same year Harper and Brothers published her first novel, *Uncle John; or, "It Is Too Much Trouble"* (1846), which portrayed the plight of a sympathetically treated Irish chambermaid confronting a harsh double standard after conceiving a child by a respectable member of society. Autobiographical outlines are faintly visible: though an outcast, the chambermaid—bolstered by loyal friends, a

job, good health, and her child—succeeds. Reviews were laudatory. *The American Review* declared that the novel was refreshingly free of the "aimless twaddle" of most contemporary fiction but found that it occasionally veered toward "ultraisms." *Godey's Lady's Book* noticed it as "a very entertaining and well-written story." In 1846 Mary Gove also republished *Lectures to Ladies on Anatomy and Physiology* with an appendix on water cure, and she started contributing to the *Water-Cure Journal.*

Her belletristic interests were such that her Tenth Street house became a meeting place on Saturday nights where "ultraists" mingled with literary people. Edgar Allan Poe and Herman Melville attended on occasion, as did the poets Richard Henry Stoddard and Frances Osgood, both her patients. She, in turn, attended others' literary soirees. At Anne Lynch's she met Poe, in whose *Broadway Journal,* in October 1845, she had pseudonymously published "The Gift of Prophecy," in which she had claimed the gift of clairvoyance through her exposure to mesmerism. Evidently, Mary Gove left a sufficient impression on Poe for him to include a sketch of her in a series on "The Literati of New York City" (*Godey's Lady's Book,* May–October 1846). He describes her as a minor novelist with a mystical bent but notes that she is better known for "her lectures on physiology to classes of females" and for her absorption in health reform: "She is, I think, a Mesmerist, a Swedenborgian, a phrenologist, a homoeopathist, and a disciple of Priessnitz."

Though honored, no doubt, to be counted by Poe as among New York's literati, Gove did Poe a greater service. Seeing the desperate poverty in which he was living at Fordham Cottage with his mother-in-law, Maria Clemm, as he faced the imminent death from tuberculosis of his wife, Virginia, Gove induced friends to come to Poe's relief with clothes and money. Gove's generous sympathy resulted in a memoir that appeared originally in *The Sixpenny Magazine* (February 1863), in which she gave a moving and vivid account of Poe's circumstances, especially the details surrounding his wife's dying. Gove also recorded Poe's love of fame: "I dote on it—I would drink to the very dregs of glorious intoxication." Her defense of him at a time after his death, when he had been tarred as a drunk, sustained his memory until his literary achievement could be rediscovered by a new generation of critics. In turn, the pamphlet, *Reminiscences of Edgar Allan Poe,* posthumously published in 1931, saved Gove's literary reputation.

The next significant event in her life came at a Christmas Eve party in 1847 when she met Thomas Low Nichols, a disaffected student of orthodox medicine and a Grahamite convert. After she struggled to reconcile her desire to retain her economic independence and pursue her profession in her own way, the two were soon bound together by love and, equally powerfully, by a commitment to health reform and to political and social reform.

The only remaining obstacle to their marriage—Hiram Gove—failed to materialize because he himself was considering remarriage. The Nicholses' marriage, conducted by a Swedenborgian minister, took place on 29 July 1848, but not before Thomas Nichols agreed to stipulations that Mary retain her "right to [her] soul," her name, and her own room, which only she could enter.

The marriage did not curtail Mary Nichols's productivity and activities over the next three decades. In 1849 she published two novels: *The Two Loves; or, Eros and Anteros* and *Agnes Morris; or, The Heroine of Domestic Life*. The plot details of the former were unusual for her—lovers, illegitimate children, adultery, contemplated suicide, pirates, kidnappings, violence, and druggings—while the latter is a more familiar domestic tale about vanity. Contrasting the responses of weak and strong women to calamity, it depicts the ostracism devolving on a woman who bears an illegitimate child. In the same year Nichols published *Experience in Water-Cure: A Familiar Exposition of the Principles and Results of Water Treatment in the Cure of Acute and Chronic Diseases, Illustrated by Numerous Cases in the Practice of the Author; with an Explanation of Water-cure Processes, Advice on Diet and Regimen, and Particular Directions to Women in the Treatment of Female Diseases, Water Treatment in Childbirth, and the Diseases of Infancy*, which ran concurrently in serialized form, from February through November 1849 in the *Water-Cure Journal and Herald of Reform* as "Mrs. Gove's Experience in Water Cure."

After Mary Nichols became pregnant—at age forty—she shared the details of her pregnancy and the birth of a daughter, Mary Wilhelmina, in late 1850, with readers of the *Water-Cure Journal and Herald of Reform*. In 1851, after Thomas earned a medical degree, the Nicholses announced the founding of the American Hydropathic Institute. The first water-cure medical college in the United States, the institute graduated its first class of twenty students in 1852. Among other topics, Mary Nichols lectured on dress reform at the institute, concurrently using the pages of the *Water-Cure Journal and Herald of Reform* between January 1852 and January 1853 to reach a wider audience on this subject. More independent than her sisters in the Bloomer movement, she resisted advocating any one outfit, urging women instead to choose outfits as occasions or fancy dictated.

Though happily married, Mary Nichols was not prepared to abandon her efforts to influence public thinking about current marriage laws and customs, charging that they conspired against women's freedom and equality. She also inveighed against perverted "amativeness," namely marriage without love, as a contributory factor in women's poor health. In an open letter that appeared in the columns of the New York *Daily Tribune* to her friend Stephen Pearl Andrews, a Fourierite and a liberal voice in the marriage debate, Mary Nichols stoutly declared: "The woman who is truly emancipate . . . this woman is pure, and a Teacher of Purity. . . . Such a Woman has a Heaven-conferred right to choose the Father of her babe." With that she placed herself squarely in the center of the free-love movement. The editor of the *Daily Tribune*, Horace Greeley, promptly closed his newspaper to any discussion on reconstituting the relationship of the sexes, declaring that the doctrines Andrews and his "lady correspondent" advocated were "offensive to the public sense of decency." Dr. Russell S. Trall similarly closed the pages of the *Water-Cure Journal and Herald of Reform* to the Nicholses.

Undeterred, they started their own journal, *Nichols' Journal of Health, Water-Cure, and Human Progress*, which reportedly had a monthly circulation of twenty thousand, and opened a larger facility in Port Chester, New York. The calm did not last long. An anonymous letter in late July 1853 in the *Daily Tribune* purported that students were fleeing the grounds of the American Hydropathic Institute, the "natural result of a practical application of such filthy doctrines as those inculcated by Messrs. Nichols and Andrews." Barely did they have time to defend themselves when another blow came, this time in the form of a novel, *Spiritual Vampirism: The History of Etherial Softdown, and Her Friends of the "New Lights"* (1853), by Charles Wilkins Webber, a former patient of Mary Nichols. The Nicholses and Marx Edgeworth Lazarus, a close friend and patron, appear in thinly disguised forms, with Mary Nichols as the spiritual vampire of the title.

Despite the slander, the Nicholses remained steadfast in promoting social change, now believing that the complete reorganization of society had to precede the emergence of regenerated individuals. To that end they founded the Institute of Desarrollo, organized around ideas taken from Fourier and Priessnitz, with a liberal dose of Andrews's Individual Sovereignty, but the scheme attracted neither subscribers nor financial support.

Their commitment to serve as the vanguard of the future remained steadfast, and they attempted to point the way for others in a co-authored volume, *Marriage: Its History, Character and Results; Its Sanctities, and the Profanities; Its Science and Its Facts. Demonstrating Its Influence, as a Civilized Institution on the Happiness of the Individual, and the Progress of the Race* (1854). Thomas Nichols wrote parts 1 and 3, and Mary Nichols wrote the middle section. In her section Mary Nichols redefined the traditional concepts of purity and adultery, proposing that true purity, whether within or outside of marriage, entailed "mutual love," while sexual intercourse without such love was adultery. Where love was absent, she bluntly counseled the unspeakable—women could enter into a relationship that the world commonly called adulterous.

Perhaps anticipating condemnation from reviewers of *Marriage* for encouraging licentiousness or desiring to strike a blow in the interests of women's rights, much as

Harriet Beecher Stowe did for slavery, Mary Nichols decided to present her ideas in a form that would give them their greatest immediacy and most dramatic impact—a novel. The ensuing work, *Mary Lyndon,* published serially in *Nichols' Journal* in 1855 and then in book form, generated considerable contemporary critical attention and is the only one of Nichols's fictions to attract ongoing scholarly analysis. A thinly veiled autobiography, it recounts the events of her protagonist's life—from childhood, to an unhappy and unfulfilling marriage, and to her confidently living alone—and explores the role various alternate therapies had in transforming her spiritually and strengthening her emotionally. The novel concludes with her determining her own future—as a physician and spiritual healer—and her joyful avowal of freedom and self-reliance: "I have only to be a law to myself, to do daily, and hourly, and momently the most urgent duty of the day, and hour, and moment. Whatever I feel in my best life is for me to do, that I will do and conquer my sphere, and compel the good opinion of the world, or live without it."

Mary Lyndon attracted a fair share of hostile reviews that bordered on the scurrilous. The *New-York Daily Times* summarized the novel as an attempt by Nichols to convince the world "of the advantages of hydropathy, the abominations of Christianity, and the reforming influence of fine art and fornication" and dismissed its author as "a coarse, sensual, and shamelessly immoral person." Most reviewers, however, distanced themselves from her ideas, offering more balanced assessments. Typically, the *Daily Tribune* repudiated her attacks on social institutions but applauded "the earnest feeling which animates almost every page, the frequent passages of powerful description, and the displays of a bold and even audacious spirit." *The Norton Literary Gazette,* more neutral, averred that "the volume is a powerful production what will create an excitement in literary circles." Despite the feminist message of the novel—the rights of women to be independent, to enjoy emotional and spiritual equality with men, and to control childbearing—the women's rights activists greeted the novel with silence, concerned lest its more radical views tar the larger movement.

Recent assessments of *Mary Lyndon* view it largely as a quasi-autobiographical novel written by a person deeply involved in various antebellum health and marriage reform movements, though some see that it has thematic and structural affinities with the domestic novel, the roman à clef, and the Quaker spiritual autobiography. Such scholarship concedes, however, that the novel also sharply veers from the familiar conventions of these forms; most notably, salvation in *Mary Lyndon* is achieved in the here-and-now by the protagonist's participation in the spiritualist sciences of phrenology, mesmerism, and water cure and in her retaining a high degree of independence.

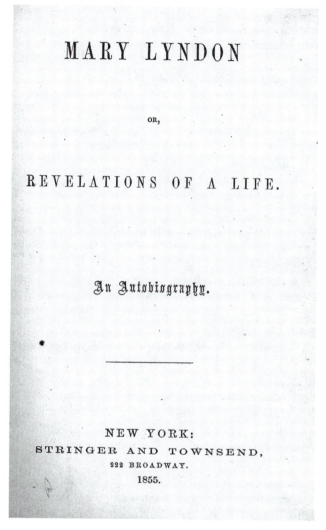

Title page for Nichols's most autobiographical novel, which includes barely fictionalized accounts of her efforts for health-care reform and women's rights (Duke University Library)

While waiting for matters related to the founding of Desarrollo to resolve themselves, the Nicholses' attention had been diverted by the spiritualist craze that was entrancing the country. Tutored by spirits (among them, that of Henry G. Wright) about the shortcomings of their former faith in Individual Sovereignty, they were instead encouraged to form a harmonic society in which the individual will would be submerged to the greater will of union members. To this end the Nicholses founded the Progressive Union, a Society for Mutual Protection in Right, and in the fall of 1855 they headed west to Cincinnati, where they gathered converts through lectures and solicited funds for a permanent site. They believed they had found such a site in Yellow Springs, Ohio, and on 1 April 1856 announced the founding of the Memnonia Institute: A School of Health, Progress, and Harmony. The president of Antioch

College, Horace Mann, considered Memnonia a spiritualist, anarchist, health reforming, free-love institute; yet, in fact, Memnonia taught ascetic self-denial, and the Nicholses severely condemned "discordant individualism" that would undermine discipline and self-control needed to prepare for "the dawn of a New Era for Humanity."

The community, however, failed within half a year, not only for economic reasons but also because the Nicholses and their immediate followers converted to Roman Catholicism—instructed in their conversion by the spirits of St. Ignatius Loyola and St. Francis Xavier. In a lengthy statement issued to their friends and followers, the Nicholses recounted the path that led them from "Protestantism and Infidelity and the pride of Science and Philosophy" to "the foot of the cross" and to "a Great Harmony already established." In the years that followed, the Nicholses returned to more-familiar health principles; they toured the Ohio and Mississippi River valleys, teaching nuns and priests preventive medicine and treating their pupils hydropathically.

Hoping to re-establish themselves as hydropathists, they returned to New York City in the late spring of 1860. But when President Abraham Lincoln called for volunteers a year later after the firing on Fort Sumter and curtailed civil liberties, the Nicholses lost heart. With the attention of the nation diverted from health and social reform to civil war, the Nicholses set sail for England in the fall of 1861.

Settling in London, they determined that publication was the least precarious means of livelihood. Mary Nichols wrote reviews and stories for the *Athenaèum, Fraser's,* and other journals. In February 1863 she published her reminiscences of Poe in *The Sixpenny Magazine,* and in the August 1864 issue of Charles Dickens's *All the Year Round* she published another domestic tale, "On the Mississippi: From Cairo to Memphis," about a woman's unfortunate choice in marriage. Mary Nichols reworked this theme in a two-volume novel, *Uncle Angus* (1864), though this time the ending is a happy one—the heroine marries both genius and wealth. In 1872 Mary Nichols published *Jerry: A Novel of Yankee American Life.* The Nicholses' London social circle and acquaintances included John Ruskin, William and Mary Howitt (pioneer English spiritualists), Robert Chambers, Charles Dickens, and Charles Kingsley.

With financial circumstances considerably less glittering, however, they once again responded to the call of health reform. In 1867 the Nicholses leased a large house at Malvern, where they boarded and educated students and treated the sick hydropathically. Mary Nichols completed several pamphlets, reiterating themes to which she had dedicated her life—the legal status of women in marriage, preventive medicine, the injustice of the double standard, and the despotism of customs that restricted women's choices in life. She also engaged in an extensive correspondence with people seeking medical advice. To establish her medical credentials, in 1868 she republished *Experience in Water-Cure,* retitling it *A Woman's Work in Water Cure and Sanitary Education;* new editions were published in 1869 and 1874.

Nichols was unable, however, to stay the infirmities of age and disease; she was successfully operated on for cataracts in 1875, but breast cancer and a painful neuralgia from an improperly healed fracture of the left femur debilitated her. She died on 30 May 1884 at the age of seventy-three and was buried in Kensal Green Cemetery, London.

Biography:

Janet Hubly Noever, "Passionate Rebel: The Life of Mary Gove Nichols, 1810–1884," dissertation, University of Oklahoma, 1983.

References:

Dorothy Eleanor Battenfield, "'She hath done what she could': Three Women in the Popular Health Movement: Harriot Kezia Hunt, Mary Gove Nichols and Paulina Wright Davis," M.A. thesis, George Washington University, 1985;

John B. Blake, "Mary Gove Nichols: Prophetess of Health," *Proceedings of the American Philosophical Society,* 106 (June 1962): 219–234;

Susan Steinberg Danielson, "Alternative Therapies: Spiritualism and Women's Rights in *Mary Lyndon: or, Revelations of a Life,*" dissertation, University of Oregon, 1990;

Danielson, "Healing Women's Wrongs: Water-Cure as (Fictional) Autobiography," in *Studies in the American Renaissance 1992,* edited by Joel Myerson (Charlottesville: University Press of Virginia, 1992), pp. 247–260;

Joel Myerson, "Mary Gove Nichols' *Mary Lyndon:* A Forgotten Reform Novel," *American Literature,* 58 (December 1986): 523–539;

Bertha-Monica Sterns, "Two Forgotten New England Reformers," *New England Quarterly,* 6 (March 1933): 59–84.

Papers:

Mary Gove Nichols's papers may be found at the American Antiquarian Society, the Boston Public Library, the Houghton Library at Harvard University, the Lynn Historical Society, the Alderman Library at the University of Virginia, and Vassar College.

Elizabeth Oakes Smith

(12 August 1806 – 15 November 1893)

Susan Belasco
University of Nebraska, Lincoln

See also the Oakes Smith entries in *DLB 1: The American Renaissance in New England* and *DLB 239: American Women Prose Writers, 1820–1870.*

BOOKS: *Riches Without Wings, of the Cleveland Family* (Boston: G. W. Light, 1838);

The Western Captive; or, The Times of Tecumseh (New York: J. Winchester, 1842);

The Sinless Child and Other Poems, edited by John Keese (New York: Wiley & Putnam / Boston: Ticknor, 1843);

The Poetical Writings of Elizabeth Oakes Smith (New York: J. S. Redfield, 1845);

The Dandelion (Boston: Saxton & Kelt / New York: Saxton & Miles, 1846);

The Moss Cup (Boston: Saxton & Kelt / New York: Saxton & Miles, 1846);

The Salamander: A Legend for Christmas, found amongst the Papers of the Late Ernest Helfenstein, edited by E. Oakes Smith (New York: Putnam, 1848); republished as *Hugo: A Legend of Rockland Lake, found amongst the Papers of the Late Ernest Helfenstein,* edited by E. Oakes Smith (New York: J. S. Taylor, 1851); republished again as *Mary and Hugo; or The Lost Angel, a Christmas Legend* (New York: Derby & Jackson, 1857);

The Keepsake: A Wreath of Poems and Sonnets (New York: Leavitt, 1849);

Rose Bud; or, The True Child (Buffalo: Derby, 1849);

Woman and Her Needs (New York: Fowler & Wells, 1851); republished in part as *The Sanctity of Marriage* (Syracuse: J. E. Master, 1853?);

Hints on Dress and Beauty (New York: Fowler & Wells, 1852);

Shadow Land; or, The Seer (New York: Fowler & Wells, 1852);

Old New York; or, Democracy in 1689. A Tragedy in Five Acts (New York: Stringer & Townsend, 1853);

Bertha and Lily; or, The Parsonage of Beech Glen. A Romance (New York: J. C. Derby / Boston: Phillips, Sampson / Cincinnati: H. W. Derby, 1854);

Elizabeth Oakes Smith

The Newsboy, anonymous (New York: J. C. Derby / Boston: Phillips, Sampson, 1854);

Bald Eagle; or, The Last of the Ramapaughs. A Romance of Revolutionary Times (New York: Beadle, 1867; London, 1870);

The Sagamore of Saco (New York: Beadle, 1868);

Selections from the Autobiography of Elizabeth Oakes Smith, edited by Mary Alice Wyman (Lewiston, Me.: Lewiston Journal Company, 1924);

"A Human Life: Being the Autobiography of Elizabeth Oakes Smith: A Critical Edition and Introduction," edited by Leigh Kirkland, dissertation, Georgia State University, 1994.

Edition: *Woman and Her Needs,* in *Liberating the Home* (New York: Arno, 1974).

OTHER: "Love Dead," "The Drowned Mariner," "Eros and Anteros," "Death and Resurrection," "Midnight," "The Seen and Unseen," "Stanzas," and "Regrets," in *The Female Poets of America: With Portraits, Biographical Notices, and Specimens of their Writing,* edited by Thomas Buchanan Read (Philadelphia: E. H. Butler, 1849 [i.e., 1848]), pp. 23–34;

Thomas Miller, *The Romance of Nature; or, the Poetical Language of Flowers,* edited by Oakes Smith (New York: J. C. Riker, 1852).

SELECTED PERIODICAL PUBLICATIONS—
UNCOLLECTED: "Stanzas," *New England Galaxy,* 18 (21 February 1835): 1;

"The Lover's Talisman; or, The Spirit Bride," *Southern Literary Messenger,* 5 (July 1839): 465–469;

"Shelley," *Southern Literary Messenger,* 6 (November 1840): 717–720;

"How to Tell a Story," *Graham's Magazine,* 22 (January 1843): 33–35;

"The Women of the May Flower," *May Flower for 1846,* edited by Robert Hamilton (Boston: Saxton & Kelt, 1845), pp. 148–159;

"Solitude," *Graham's Magazine,* 30 (January 1847): 27;

"April Rain," *United States Magazine of Science, Art, Manufactures, Agriculture, Commerce and Trade,* 1 (15 May 1854): 10;

"Women's Rights Convention," *Emerson's Magazine and Putnam's Monthly,* 3 (September 1856): 237–239.

Elizabeth Oakes Smith was among the most highly regarded and best-known literary women of mid-nineteenth-century America. In a chapter on Oakes Smith in his memoir, *Fifty Years Among Authors, Books, and Publishers* (1884), the influential editor J. C. Derby observed, "In the brilliant coterie of men and women who graced the literary circles of New York forty years ago, none excelled in intellectual capacity the subject of this sketch." Oakes Smith's poems, essays, and sketches were solicited by prominent magazines of the day, including *Godey's Lady's Book,* the *Home Journal,* and *Graham's Magazine.* Edgar Allan Poe greatly admired her poem in seven cantos, "The Sinless Child," and enthusiastically praised her work in print. The powerful critic Rufus W. Griswold edited the 1845 collection of her complete poems, and George Ripley reviewed her novels in the *New-York Tribune.* Herman Melville included lines from her poem "The Drowned Mariner" in the "Extracts" that preface *Moby-Dick* (1851). Ralph Waldo Emerson, Margaret Fuller, William Cullen Bryant, James Freeman Clarke, William Lloyd Garrison, Lucretia Mott, the artist Thomas Cole, and Paulina Wright Davis, editor of the feminist journal *Una,* all counted themselves as her friends. Horace Greeley commissioned her to do a series of feminist articles for his *New-York Tribune,* which were later published as *Woman and Her Needs* (1851). Among the first women to give public lectures, Oakes Smith toured the Northeast and as far west as Chicago, speaking on women's rights and abolition on the same platforms as Emerson, Henry David Thoreau, and Wendell Phillips. Her 1854 novel *The Newsboy* not only was a best-seller but also prompted a reform movement to protect young, orphaned boys living on the streets of New York. Oakes Smith was an important figure in the major literary circle of her day, well connected and well regarded as a prolific essayist, poet, speaker, editor, journalist, and novelist. However, in literary histories from the late nineteenth century on, her many accomplishments have generally been overlooked and, if mentioned at all, she is mainly noted as the young wife of Seba Smith, author of the popular political satire *The Jack Downing Letters* (1845). There is no contemporary biography of her life, and the only reliable reference guide to her extensive publications is in an unpublished dissertation.

Elizabeth Oakes Prince was born in North Yarmouth, Maine, on 12 August 1806, the second daughter of a sea captain, David Cushing Prince, and his wife, Sophia (Blanchard) Prince. In the unpublished "Autobiography" that Oakes Smith wrote near the end of her life, she explains that her father "belonged to the Pilgrim stock" and her mother "to Huguenot ancestry." These diverse backgrounds were important influences, especially as embodied in her two grandfathers and their households, both of which she knew well. On the one hand, her maternal grandfather, Seth Blanchard, was a colorful figure who had, among other adventures, run away to become a drummer boy in the Revolutionary War. Involved in the East India trade, he was a Universalist and a freethinker who owned land and a good library, and was fond of his many fine possessions and deeply interested in politics. In contrast, David Prince, a descendant of John Prince, a Massachusetts settler of the 1630s, was Puritanical in outlook and temperament. Although the young Elizabeth records a childhood spent outdoors with few restraints on her activities, her account of her early life reveals a temperament more drawn to the Puritan order and decorum of the Princes than to the more liberal worldview of the Blanchards. Referring to herself constantly as a "Puritan child" in

Page from a letter Oakes Smith wrote to her husband, Seba Smith, in 1837 (Manuscripts Division, University of Virginia Library)

"Autobiography," Elizabeth grew up with a strong sense of her duty and responsibility to others and reminisced in her later life about the rigid schedule of her childhood, with days divided into "stints" of sewing and specific times for reading, prayers, and other tasks.

Elizabeth was fond of reading and was permitted a wide range of choices. She records that she had read the Bible twice by the age of twelve and studied dictionaries when there was nothing else to read. She read *The Pilgrim's Progress* (1678), *Don Quixote* (1605), the novels of Samuel Richardson and Sir Walter Scott, Daniel Defoe's *Robinson Crusoe* (1719–1720), Henry Fielding's *Tom Jones* (1749), John Milton's *Paradise Lost* (1667), and John Foxe's *Book of Martyrs* (1563). Elizabeth also wrote poems, sketches, stories, and essays from an early age; in her "Autobiography" she reprints sentences and paragraphs from some of them, such as "Aim at Perfection," a revealing piece about the importance of cultivating virtue. When Elizabeth was still a child, her father's ship was lost at sea. Her mother eventually remarried to a widower with two children, and the family moved to Portland, Maine, in 1814. In Portland, Elizabeth joined the Congregationalist Church. She was sent to a private school run by a Quaker, Rachel Neal, the mother of John Neal, an editor and poet who later became editor of the *New England Galaxy* and encouraged Elizabeth and even published some of her poems. Elizabeth was a good student, was eager to learn, and won prizes for excellence in "study and correct morals." She met many famous people in Portland who were acquaintances of her mother and stepfather, among them Henry Wadsworth Longfellow and Robert E. Lee. By her own account, her girlhood, described in her "Autobiography" as the "most beautiful and the most suggestive period of a woman's life," was happy and contented. But as Elizabeth demonstrated an increasing interest in her reading and writing, her mother worried that she was becoming too bookish and possessed unsuitable ambitions for a woman. Fearing that her daughter would eventually become an old maid, she arranged for sixteen-year-old Elizabeth to marry Seba Smith on 6 March 1823, a cold spring day of strong rains and harsh winds. Elizabeth remembered in her "Autobiography" that one of the servants present commented on the ceremony: "A lowery day and a lowery bride."

The thirty-one-year-old Smith was a graduate of Bowdoin College and had worked briefly as a teacher in Portland before assuming the position of editor of the *Eastern Argus,* a newspaper that had published some of his poetry. As Seba Smith's wife, Elizabeth Smith left what she described as "the beautiful world that at once faded from my view." She swiftly passed from "a dreamy young girl" to a person responsible for the running of a large household that included printers and their apprentices and soon, children. After losing their first child, who died shortly after birth, the Smiths eventually had five sons, four of whom survived into adulthood. The young and overwhelmed Elizabeth had to learn quickly to meet the challenges of managing a large household on a small budget. There was little help from her husband, whom she described as "essentially a bachelor" with slight understanding of her concerns or interests. Although Elizabeth Smith had limited time to herself, she began reading William Shakespeare's plays and was especially fond of *Othello* (1622), *Hamlet* (1603), and the *Tempest* (1623). She also wrote a little poetry, publishing verses anonymously in her husband's *Eastern Argus.*

In 1826 Seba Smith sold his share in the newspaper, and in 1829 he started two papers, the *Family Reader* and his most successful venture, the first daily paper in Maine, the *Portland Courier.* Elizabeth Smith wrote verses, historical sketches, and articles about Maine in both, signing them "E." In 1830 Seba Smith began the series of articles that eventually became *The Jack Downing Letters,* the work for which he is best known. Entertainingly satiric of contemporary politics, these sketches invented a particularly American strain of humor in the form of the canny, self-made Yankee outwitting and influencing a staid establishment. Although Elizabeth Smith was pleased by her husband's success, the sketches were not to her taste, and she continued her writing of poems on childhood and sketches of women, such as Charlotte Corday and Madame Anne-Louise-Germaine de Staël.

Seba Smith, eager for financial independence and more time to write, gambled on one of the hundreds of land-speculation deals of the time and lost. In 1837 he was forced to sell his interest in the *Portland Courier.* Over the objections of his wife, Smith insisted on speculating on a new cotton gin being developed in the South. Their experiences in seeing plantations and the realities of slaveholding in South Carolina, however, reinforced Elizabeth Smith's growing interest in abolition. By 1839 the Smiths had returned to New York with sharply limited means and prospects.

The financial disasters proved to be a turning point for Elizabeth Smith. She began to write in earnest, and the next two decades were her most productive years. Her first book for children, *Riches Without Wings, of the Cleveland Family* (1838), was to her a "kind of Sunday School book." But it was with poetry that she made her first major contribution to the literary scene and gained a wider audience. Although she occasionally published works anonymously and sometimes with a pseudonym, she began to sign her work consistently as "Elizabeth Oakes Smith" from the early 1840s and clearly wished to identify herself separately from her well-known husband. (She eventually took legal action to change her sons' surnames to Oaksmith.)

The publication of her poem in seven cantos with prose headnotes, "The Sinless Child," in the *Southern Literary Messenger* in 1842 was a triumph and earned her almost immediate popularity. A strongly didactic work, the poem concerns the life of a young woman, Eva, who lives apart from the world, matures but maintains her innocence, and dies at the end, having converted a worldly young man, Albert Linne, to a better life. Wordsworthian in its theme of the purity of childhood and Emersonian in its promotion of self-reliance, "The Sinless Child" is also feminist and Christian in its presentation of Eva as a female Christ. With its evocation of mysticism and its treatment of death, the poem had wide appeal, and Oakes Smith revised and expanded it the next year and then published it again with her collected poems in 1845. Harriet Beecher Stowe likely had Oakes Smith's Eva in mind when she created Little Eva. Perhaps the greatest admirer of the poem, however, was Poe, who reviewed it and her other poems for *Godey's Lady's Book* in December 1845. He considered the poem one of the most original of long American poems and praised its "novelty of conception" and "grace and purity of style." Oakes Smith and Poe became friends, and after Poe's death, she wrote articles in the *United States Magazine* and in *Baldwin's Monthly* and played an important part in the efforts to salvage Poe's critical reputation after the publication of Rufus Griswold's devastating memoir of Poe in 1850.

Oakes Smith also wrote fiction during this time. Building on the contemporary popularity of Indian romance and drama, she published *The Western Captive; or, The Times of Tecumseh* (1842). This novel, available in an inexpensive paper-covered edition, sold well and was translated into German in 1847. Drawing on her interests in the occult and in German Romantic writers, she published *The Salamander: A Legend for Christmas* (1848) under her pseudonym Ernest Helfenstein with herself listed as an "editor." The novel, which Oakes Smith dedicated to James Fenimore Cooper, is set on the Hudson River in Rockland County and uses both Indian legends and supernatural events to develop a story about a central figure, Hugo, who settles a colony of ironworkers in the Ramapo Valley. Both Lydia Sigourney and Henry Wadsworth Longfellow admired the book.

At the same time that Oakes Smith was enjoying success as a poet and a fiction writer, she was becoming increasingly interested in reform movements, especially abolition and women's rights. As a girl in Portland she had attended a church that provided classes for escaped slaves (some of whom she taught), and she was strongly

antislavery. In her own life, however, rights for women became a pressing need, especially as her husband's career faltered and her large family needed strong economic support. A crucial experience for her in 1839 was attending a lecture by Fanny Wright, escorted by her unenthusiastic husband. Wright, a wealthy Scottish woman with strongly reformist views, had toured the United States in the 1820s and tried to establish a community for freed slaves and whites in western Tennessee along the lines of Robert Owen's New Harmony in Indiana. Among the first women to lecture publicly, Wright spoke frequently about her radical social ideas, including gradual emancipation for slaves, free public education for children, more-liberal marriage laws, and broader rights for women. Oakes Smith was deeply impressed by Wright, commenting in her "Autobiography" that "We have so few Sibyls and so much need of them." Throughout the 1840s Oakes Smith became increasingly engrossed in the question of women's prerogatives, and by the end of the decade she herself was speaking and writing about a variety of causes, especially broader individual rights for women. Horace Greeley, who had hired Margaret Fuller as the literary critic for his *New-York Tribune* in the mid 1840s, printed a series of Oakes Smith's articles, which were published in 1851 as a pamphlet, *Woman and Her Needs*.

Like Fuller's *Woman in the Nineteenth Century* (1845), *Woman and Her Needs* defends the intelligence of women and argues for expanded individual rights, more-liberal laws governing marriage (but not divorce), broader vocational opportunities for women, and women's right to vote. Unlike Fuller's more literary treatment of these themes, Oakes Smith's pamphlet is a straightforward argument that earned her praise from Emerson, Robert Owen, Lucretia Mott, Paulina Wright Davis, and James Freeman Clarke, but strong criticism from conservative family members and friends, such as Lydia Sigourney and especially Sarah Josepha Hale, who refused further contact with Oakes Smith after this book appeared. Throughout the 1850s Oakes Smith spoke and wrote about women's issues and sometimes took controversial stands. She thought that women needed their own outlets for their work on women's rights and encouraged her friend Davis to begin the *Una*, for which she occasionally wrote. Although her own marriage was a difficult one, she was opposed to divorce and extracted a section of *Woman and Her Needs* as a pamphlet, *The Sanctity of Marriage*, published in 1853. She was also at odds with many reformers on the issue of appropriate dress for women. Although she published *Hints on Dress and Beauty* in 1852, an advice book that promoted practicality over fashion, Oakes Smith herself evidently followed the taste of Fuller in this regard and dressed in a feminine style. In 1852, at the National Woman's Rights

Oakes Smith in the early 1890s

Convention, Oakes Smith earned the ire of Susan B. Anthony, who felt that Oakes Smith was inappropriately dressed for the meeting. Undeterred, Oakes Smith toured widely in the Northeast and the South, speaking on "Womanhood," "The Dignity of Labor," "Manhood," "Our Humanity," "Cleopatra," "Madame Roland," and even "Margaret Fuller." Her lectures were favorably received. When Oakes Smith spoke on "Womanhood" in Concord in 1851, Thoreau and Bronson Alcott were in her audience, and Alcott later consulted her about his daughter Louisa's future as a writer. Thoreau's response was more ambiguous and reveals some conflicting attitudes of his own. Although he noted in his journal for 31 December 1851 that "The most important fact about the lecture was that a woman said it—and in that respect it was suggestive," he also wrote that

> She was a woman in the too common sense after all. You had to fire small charges—I did not have a finger in once, for fear of blowing away all her works & so ending the game[.] You had to substitute courtesy for sense and argument. It requires nothing less than a chivalric

feeling to sustain a conversation with a lady. I carried her lecture for her in my pocket wrapped in her handkerchief—my pocket exhales cologne to this moment. The championness of womans rights still asks you to be a ladies' man.

Thoreau's opinion for his private journal notwithstanding, Emerson, Wendell Phillips, Nathaniel P. Willis, and John Neal were all enthusiastic in their opinions of her lectures and speaking abilities.

Despite her busy schedule of speaking engagements during this time, Oakes Smith also experimented with prose forms and even drama. Following her interest in psychic phenomena, she published *Shadow Land; or, The Seer* (1852), a book about the nature of dreams and her beliefs in the connections between the material and the spiritual worlds. Only the text of her play *Old New York; or, Democracy in 1689. A Tragedy in Five Acts* (1853) survives, but there are references to other plays in her "Autobiography." In 1854 she published two novels. *Bertha and Lily; or, The Parsonage of Beech Glen. A Romance* is a novel written in the form of a journal, which has as its heroine a fallen woman, Bertha, who has tried to establish an anonymous life in a small town. Known for her extraordinary goodness, virtue, and dedication to a Transcendentalist self-cultivation, Bertha is superior to all she meets and works with a young minister, Ernest Helfenstein, to educate two foundling children in an alms house. When her reformed former lover arrives to ask her to marry him, Bertha refuses, and he dies, griefstricken. Bertha is reunited with her child, who is revealed to be one of the foundlings, and marries Helfenstein, a character with the same name as a pseudonym that Oakes Smith had used occasionally in her early periodical publications and for *The Salamander*. The reviewer for *Putnam's Monthly* praised the strong feeling of the novel while George Ripley wrote in the *New-York Tribune* that her characterizations were excellent. More discursive than narrative, the novel was not a commercial success.

The other novel that Oakes Smith published in 1854, *The Newsboy*, emerged from her increasing interest in and involvement with (as an honorary member) the Young Men's Christian Union, which had been established in the early 1850s by a group of Unitarian men. The goal of the organization in part was to improve the condition of hundreds of young boys, orphaned and growing up on the streets of New York. In her "Autobiography" Oakes Smith noted that she wished to do something for them, and in her novel *The Newsboy* she did just that. The dense novel is filled with detailed descriptions of New York City slums and a large cast of characters (including Dickensian characters such as Flashy Jack, Maggie, and even an Aunt Beckey). Few novels of this time evoke the city as graphically and vividly as does *The*

Newsboy. The central story concerns Bob, an orphan who sells periodicals on the streets to earn a small living for himself and the other hapless children he supports. Through sheer effort, luck, and inherent goodness and intelligence, Bob earns the respect and patronage of Mr. Dinsmoor, whose daughter, Imogen, is kidnapped. The convoluted plot eventually takes Bob to Cuba, where he recovers Imogen, is rewarded by Dinsmoor, but in the end does not win the hand of Imogen, who instead marries a junior partner in her father's firm. Despite some negative reviews of the style and structure of the novel, it sold well, went through twelve editions during its first year, and drew widespread attention to the plight of homeless children in New York.

In 1860 Seba Smith moved his family to Long Island, and the couple gradually became less involved with the literary life of New York. The Civil War dramatically altered the literary marketplace, and then a series of family tragedies ensued, including Seba Smith's increasing deafness, the death of the Smiths' son Edward, and finally Seba Smith's death in 1868. During this time, Oakes Smith wrote regularly for *Beadle's Monthly* and also published two novels in the Beadle's Dime Novel series: *Bald Eagle; or, The Last of the Ramapaughs* (1867) and *The Sagamore of Saco* (1868), which had first appeared as a serial in *Graham's Magazine* in 1848. Another of the Smiths' sons died in 1869. Although Oakes Smith continued to contribute poetry and articles to the *Home Journal* and *Baldwin's Monthly,* she gradually began to retire from active literary life. She continued her extensive correspondence, however, with her literary friends—including Longfellow, Bryant, and Ripley. In 1877 she became the pastor of an Independent Congregation in Canastota, New York. Following that time she divided her time between the homes of two sons, one in Long Island and the other in North Carolina, and occasionally attended and spoke at women's rights meetings when she was in New York. The last several years of her life were spent in North Carolina, where she worked on her autobiography. She died on 15 November 1893 after a short illness.

Biography:

Mary Alice Wyman, *Two American Pioneers: Seba Smith and Elizabeth Oakes Smith* (New York: Columbia University Press, 1927).

References:

Nina Baym, *American Women Writers and the Work of History, 1790–1860* (New Brunswick: Rutgers University Press, 1995);

Paula Bernat Bennett, ed., *Nineteenth-Century American Women Poets: An Anthology* (Malden, Mass.: Blackwell, 1998);

Susan Phinney Conrad, *Perish the Thought: Intellectual Women in Romantic America, 1830–1860* (New York: Oxford University Press, 1976);

J. C. Derby, *Fifty Years Among Authors, Books, and Publishers* (New York: G. W. Carleton, 1884);

Ann Douglas, *The Feminization of American Culture* (New York: Knopf, 1977);

Rufus W. Griswold, Preface to *The Poetical Writings of Elizabeth Oakes Smith* (New York: J. S. Redfield, 1845);

Sarah Josepha Hale, *Women's Record; or, Sketches of All Distinguished Women,* second edition (New York: Harper, 1855), pp. 785–789;

Albert Johannsen, "Elizabeth Oakes Smith," in his *The House of Beadle and Adams and its Dime and Nickel Novels,* 2 volumes (Norman: University of Oklahoma Press, 1950), II: 259–261;

Kent Ljungquist and Cameron Nickels, "Elizabeth Oakes Smith on Poe: A Chapter in the Recovery of His Nineteenth-Century Reputation," in *Poe and His Times: The Artist and His Milieu,* edited by Benjamin Franklin Fisher IV (Baltimore: Edgar Allan Poe Society, 1990);

John Neal, Preface to *The Sinless Child and Other Poems* (New York: Wiley & Putnam, 1843);

Cameron Nickels and Timothy H. Scherman, "Elizabeth Oakes Smith: The Puritan as Feminist," in *Femmes de conscience: aspects du feminisme americain (1848–1975),* edited by Susan Goodman and Daniel Royot (Paris: Presses de la Sorbonne Nouvelle, 1994), pp. 109–126;

Robert E. Riegel, *American Feminists* (Lawrence: University of Kansas Press, 1963);

Ann Russo and Cheris Kramare, eds., *The Radical Women's Press of the 1850s* (New York: Routledge, 1991);

Cheryl Walker, *The Nightingale's Burden: Women Poets and American Culture Before 1900* (Bloomington: Indiana University Press, 1992);

Walker, ed., *American Women Poets of the Nineteenth Century: An Anthology* (New Brunswick: Rutgers University Press, 1992);

Emily Stipes Watts, *The Poetry of American Women from 1632 to 1945* (Austin: University of Texas Press, 1977);

Joy Wiltenberg, "Excerpts from the Diary of Elizabeth Oakes Smith," *Signs,* 9 (1984): 534–548.

Papers:

An extensive collection of papers, including the autobiography of Elizabeth Oakes Smith, is located at the New York Public Library.

Catharine Maria Sedgwick

(28 December 1789 – 31 July 1867)

Kathleen Healey
Colby-Sawyer College

See also the Sedgwick entries in *DLB 1: The American Renaissance in New England; DLB 74: American Short-Story Writers Before 1880; DLB 183: American Travel Writers, 1776–1864;* and *DLB 239: American Women Prose Writers, 1820–1870.*

BOOKS: *A New-England Tale; or Sketches of New-England Character and Manners,* anonymous (New York: Bliss & White, 1822; London: Miller, 1822); enlarged as *A New-England Tale and Miscellanies* (New York: Putnam, 1852);

Mary Hollis: An Original Tale, anonymous (New York: Unitarian Book Society, 1822);

Redwood: A Tale, anonymous, 2 volumes (New York: Bliss & White, 1824; London: Miller, 1824; revised edition, New York: Putnam, 1852);

The Travellers: A Tale Designed for Young People (New York: Bliss & White, 1825; London: Miller, 1825);

The Deformed Boy (Brookfield, Mass.: Printed by E. & G. Merriam, 1826);

Hope Leslie; or, Early Times in the Massachusetts, 2 volumes (New York: White, Gallaher & White, 1827; London: Miller, 1827; revised edition, New York: Harper, 1842);

A Short Essay to Do Good (Stockbridge, Mass.: Printed by Webster & Stanley, 1828);

Clarence; or, A Tale of Our Own Times, 2 volumes (Philadelphia: Carey & Lea, 1830; London: Colburn & Bentley, 1830; revised edition, New York: Putnam / London: Bogue, 1849);

Home (Boston & Cambridge: Munroe, 1835; London: Simpkin, Marshall, 1836);

The Linwoods; or, "Sixty Years Since" in America, 2 volumes (New York: Harper, 1835; London: Churton, 1835);

Tales and Sketches (Philadelphia: Carey, Lea & Blanchard, 1835);

The Poor Rich Man, and the Rich Poor Man (New York: Harper, 1836; London: Tegg, 1836);

Live and Let Live; or, Domestic Service Illustrated (New York: Harper, 1837; London: Green, 1837);

Engraving by F. Halpin after a portrait by Ingham

A Love Token for Children. Designed for Sunday-School Libraries (New York: Harper, 1838; London: Bentley, 1838);

Means and Ends, or Self-Training (Boston: Marsh, Capen, Lyon & Webb, 1839; London: Bogue, 1839);

Stories for Young Persons (New York: Harper, 1840; London: Tilt & Bogue, 1840);

Letters from Abroad to Kindred at Home, 2 volumes (London: Moxon, 1841; New York: Harper, 1841; revised edition, London: Moxon, 1841);

Tales and Sketches. Second Series. "Should Old Acquaintance Be Forgot?" (New York: Harper, 1844);

Morals of Manners; or, Hints for Our Young People (New York: Wiley & Putnam, 1846; London: Wiley, 1846; revised edition, New York: Putnam, 1854);

Facts and Fancies for School-Day Reading, A Sequel to "Morals of Manners" (New York & London: Wiley & Putnam, 1848);

The Boy of Mount Rhigi. "Do the Duty Nearest to You" (Boston: Charles H. Peirce, 1848);

Tales of City Life. I. The City Clerk. II. "Life IS Sweet" (Philadelphia: Hazard & Mitchell, 1850);

Married or Single? (1 volume, London: Knight, 1857; 2 volumes, New York: Harper, 1857);

Memoir of Joseph Curtis, A Model Man (New York: Harper, 1858; London: Sampson Low, 1858);

Life and Letters of Miss Sedgwick, edited by Mary E. Dewey (New York: Harper, 1871);

The Power of Her Sympathy: The Autobiography and Journal of Catharine Maria Sedgwick, edited by Mary Kelley (Boston: Massachusetts Historical Society, 1993).

OTHER: "Le Bossu," in *Tales of Glauber-Spa,* 2 volumes, edited by William Cullen Bryant (New York: J & J Harper, 1832), I: 25–108;

"A Memoir of Lucretia Maria Davidson," in *Lives of Sir William Phips, Israel Putnam, Lucretia Maria Davidson, and David Rittenhouse,* edited by Jared Sparks (Boston: Hilliard Gray / London: Kennett, 1837), pp. 219–294); revised as "Biography of Lucretia Maria Davidson," in *Poetical Remains of Lucretia Maria Davidson, Collected and Arranged by Her Mother: With a Biography by Miss Sedgwick* (Philadelphia: Lea & Blanchard, 1841; London: Tilt & Bogue, 1843), pp. 33–91;

Barbara Leigh Smith Bodichon, *Women and Work,* introduction by Sedgwick (New York: C. S. Francis, 1859);

Letters From Charles Sedgwick to His Family and Friends, edited by Catharine Sedgwick and Katharine Sedgwick Minot (Boston: Privately printed, 1870).

SELECTED PERIODICAL PUBLICATION–
UNCOLLECTED: "Slavery in New England," *Bentley's Miscellany,* 34 (1853): 417–424.

Catharine Maria Sedgwick's works were ranked in her time with those of her contemporaries James Fenimore Cooper and Washington Irving. Indeed, her lasting legacy is that, like Cooper, she brought the culture and flavor of an American region–in this case, New England–to life in the pages of her novels and short stories. Yet, she is also known for her popularity during her lifetime and her neglect following her death. While scholars have long celebrated writers such as Cooper, Irving, and William Cullen Bryant as among the founding authors of American literature, women writers such as Catharine Maria Sedgwick, who were as popular and prolific as their male contemporaries, have been ignored–their works perceived as lacking any literary merit. But there is renewed interest in Sedgwick's works as critiques of her society, expositions on morality and social ills, and the perspective of a woman living in a society that offered few options for women besides marriage and child rearing. Her works offer a glimpse of the regional color of New England and the culture of pre–Civil War America, and for this reason, in addition to their literary merit, her novels and short stories are finding a place next to those of her male counterparts.

Catharine Maria Sedgwick was born in Stockbridge, Massachusetts, on 28 December 1789. She spent most of her life living in or visiting Stockbridge and the surrounding Berkshire hills of Massachusetts. Of the surviving seven children born to Theodore Sedgwick and Pamela (Dwight) Sedgwick, Catharine Maria was the third daughter and sixth child. Her mother, Pamela, was descended from the politically and socially elite Dwight family of the Connecticut River valley. Theodore Sedgwick, in contrast, was an unknown lawyer, his background one of poverty and obscurity; therefore, Pamela's family at first objected to the marriage. Despite her family's objections, however, Pamela and Theodore were married on 17 April 1774. Theodore Sedgwick rose quickly socially and politically; he was actively involved in the American Revolution, was a member of the Provincial Congress, and served in both the U.S. Senate and the House of Representatives. A staunch Federalist who worked his way into the ranks of the American aristocracy, Theodore Sedgwick opposed Jefferson's egalitarian views and helped quell Shays' Rebellion. Pamela Sedgwick, like many women of her time, cared for her children and her home, yet she suffered most of her life with crippling depression. This depression was most likely compounded by the long absences of her husband, who was busy in Philadelphia with politics and the law. She died in 1807 after a particularly severe bout of depression. Two years later, Theodore married Penelope Russell. He died in January 1813, but not before converting, on his deathbed, from Calvinism to Unitarianism.

For Catharine, her mother's illness and her father's frequent absences were eased by her close relationships with the Sedgwicks' servant, a former slave named Mumbet, and Catharine's four brothers–Theodore II, Harry, Robert, and Charles. Her relationship with her brothers remained close throughout their lifetimes. She wrote that they shared "an intimate companionship and I think as true and loving a friendship as ever existed between brothers and sister." She considered them her "chiefest blessing in life." With-

The Sedgwick home in Stockbridge, Massachusetts

out their encouragement, she probably would not have become a writer.

Not surprisingly, Catharine was greatly influenced by the political and intellectual activity of her family, especially her brothers and father. She also had a strict Calvinist upbringing. She received the traditional education of her day for a well-to-do young woman, briefly attending the public schools of Stockbridge and later enrolling in boarding schools—including, when she was thirteen, Mrs. Bell's school in Albany and, when she was fifteen, Mrs. Payne's finishing school in Boston. She found her formal education inadequate, stating that she learned more from the intellectual environment of her home than from school. Her father read aloud to her works by authors such as David Hume, Samuel Butler, William Shakespeare, and Miguel de Cervantes, and he encouraged her to pursue challenging material on her own.

Sedgwick's religious, political, and social background became a shaping force for her fiction. As a member of the elite class, Sedgwick believed herself to have a moral responsibility to other members of society, a conviction that in part fueled the focus on morality and manners in her works. Before she wrote her first novel, she had converted from Calvinism to Unitarianism and from the Federalist Party to the Democratic Party. Her conversion to Unitarianism in 1821 precipi-

tated her first book, *A New-England Tale; or Sketches of New-England Character and Manners* (1822), which initially was to be a tract setting forth Unitarian beliefs. By the time of its publication, Sedgwick had developed the book beyond its original scope.

Set in a thinly disguised Stockbridge, *A New-England Tale* reveals the intolerance and oppression of strict Calvinism while presenting a more humane and tolerant form of Christianity. The heroine of the novel is Jane Elton, a meek and pious young woman who, like many protagonists in sentimental novels, faces great adversity with Christian fortitude and is rewarded with a happy marriage at the end of the novel.

Orphaned at the age of twelve, Jane Elton finds a home with her father's sister, Mrs. Wilson, who is a pillar of the Calvinist community. Despite her outward devotion to the church and her pronouncements of faith, Mrs. Wilson is a cruel and uncharitable woman who rigidly adheres to Calvinist doctrine. She makes clear that she does not want Jane and constantly finds fault with her. Two of Mrs. Wilson's children, Elvira and David, are morally corrupt and have no use for religion. Elvira becomes involved with immoral men, eventually running away with a debauched Frenchman. David seduces and impregnates a young woman who, with her baby, dies after he rejects them. He then steals from his mother and is involved with mail robbery.

After blaming his mother for his bad character, he escapes to the West Indies. Jane endures the abuse and accusations of her aunt and finally finds happiness with the kind and charitable Mr. Lloyd, a Quaker, who saves her from the machinations of a rake.

Sedgwick's juxtaposition of the piety and generosity of Mr. Lloyd and Jane Elton with the cruel hardness of Mrs. Wilson and the immorality of her children demonstrates Sedgwick's views about what constitutes true Christianity and exposes the hypocrisy of orthodox Calvinism. Mrs. Wilson's Calvinist God is one of wrath, while the God of Mr. Lloyd and Jane Elton is a God of mercy. As another criticism of Calvinism, Sedgwick presents a minister who, rather than offering comfort at the death of Jane's mother, reminds his congregation of their state of sinfulness. In addition to indicting Calvinism, *A New-England Tale* is concerned with both gender roles and issues of social class. While portraying traditional feminine behaviors such as passivity and self-effacement as positive traits, *A New-England Tale* at the same time questions these behaviors. Sedgwick also reveals the powerlessness and lack of options women of her time faced. For most single women, marriage or poverty were the only options available, and often of the two, marriage led to more misery. Furthermore, Sedgwick, despite her praise of the egalitarianism of America, draws a distinct line between the behavior and appearance of members of the social elite and those of the lower classes. Mr. Lloyd, a wealthy gentleman, finds fault with a peddler because of the unhealthy appearance of his home and family. Most of the characters embodying the ideal virtues that the novel promotes, however, are of the lower classes, while the members of the wealthy class, such as Jane's aunt, are criticized.

A New-England Tale was a popular novel in both America and England, with both the first and second editions selling well. Despite that the novel was published anonymously, Sedgwick earned the wrath of some of her neighbors because the book criticized New England Calvinism and depicted the Stockbridge community unfavorably. This controversy, however, only fueled the sale of the novel.

Sedgwick's next popular novel, *Redwood: A Tale* (1824), elevated her as author to the status of Cooper and Irving. Successful in England as well as America, it was translated into German, Swedish, Italian, Spanish, and French. In *The North American Review* William Cullen Bryant praised the novel for its exalted standard of morality and its depictions of American regions and life. Maria Edgeworth wrote to Sedgwick that the characters of *Redwood* are "to America what Scott's characters are to Scotland, valuable as original pictures, with enough of individual peculiarity to be interesting, and to give the feeling of reality and life as portraits. . . ."

Like *A New-England Tale*, *Redwood* portrays the virtues and vices evident in Sedgwick's society. The novel begins in Vermont, where Henry Redwood and his daughter, Caroline, are traveling from their home in the South. Redwood is injured in a carriage accident and recovers at the farm of the Lenox family. There he and Caroline meet a young woman named Ellen Bruce. While Caroline is a conceited, proud, and selfish woman, Ellen is virtuous and concerned with others around her. During their visit with the Lenoxes, the Redwoods are visited by another Southerner, Charles Westall, whom Redwood would like to have his daughter marry. Westall, however, falls in love with and eventually marries Ellen. The reader learns that Ellen is actually Redwood's daughter by a previous marriage to a servant who died when Redwood was traveling abroad; he was thus unaware that she had borne him a child. At the end of the novel Westall marries Ellen, and Caroline marries a fortune hunter.

Central to *Redwood* is the question of what constitutes true wealth and virtue. Sedgwick contrasts Ellen and Caroline in order to highlight the ideal characteristics of Ellen. Caroline, who has had every advantage throughout life and is descended from families of wealth and social standing, is vain, proud, and unable to care about those around her. Caroline's family has based its pride solely on wealth and social standing in Southern society. Ellen, on the other hand, reared in obscurity, has had only a basic education but is virtuous and caring of others. While Ellen's background is clearly not as distinguished as Caroline's, she is wealthy in Christian virtue and integrity, and her virtue is rewarded in the end with a happy marriage to a man with a character similar to her own.

Redwood is a novel about American life and character. Although the novel begins in Vermont, Sedgwick also places her characters in the South, Pennsylvania, New York, and a Shaker community in Hancock, Massachusetts. Rather than portraying virtuous characters as only from New England, Sedgwick demonstrates that virtue and vice can be found everywhere in America. *Redwood* won much praise from Sedgwick's contemporaries as a truly American novel that ranked with the sketches of American life found in the works of Cooper.

During the 1820s Sedgwick continued to develop within her profession, but she still found her family to be the most important part of her life. At this time, her brothers' interest in her work encouraged her to continue writing. Between *Redwood* (1824) and *Hope Leslie* (1827), she wrote two children's books—*The Travellers: A Tale Designed for Young People,* published in 1825, and *The Deformed Boy,* published in 1826. These works taught

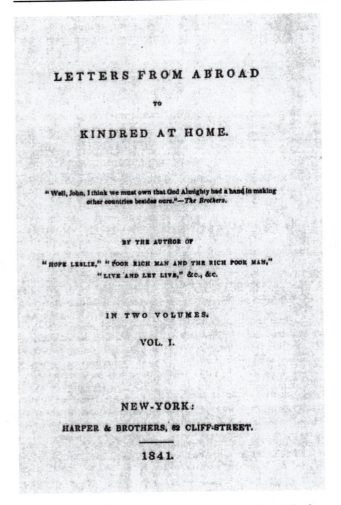

Title page for Sedgwick's observations on European society during her 1839–1840 tour of Great Britain and the Continent

forgets English, converts to Catholicism, and marries Oneco. She never returns to her family.

The latter part of the novel takes place in Boston, where Hope lives with Everell. During a secret meeting in which Magawisca brings Faith Leslie to meet Hope, the villainous Sir Philip Gardiner captures Magawisca, who is put on trial as an enemy. Sir Philip also hopes to abduct Hope. He dies, however, and Hope helps Magawisca escape from prison. At the end of the novel, Hope and Everell are married.

After the publication of *Hope Leslie,* a critic from the *Western Monthly Review* argued that Sedgwick's depiction of Magawisca was inaccurate: He believed no Indian woman could be so virtuous and "angelic." Throughout *Hope Leslie,* Sedgwick's depiction of Native Americans is more sympathetic than many portrayals before her time. In her description of the slaughter of the Pequots, for example, she makes clear that the act was especially brutal, a massacre of sleeping women and children. She also has Faith Leslie marry Oneco, even though these characters, with their tribe, conveniently disappear into the wilderness. Yet, Sedgwick's portrait of Magawisca was created to demonstrate that one does not need formal Christian training and doctrine in order to be a true Christian. Magawisca is good because her nature is to be so. Similarly, Hope Leslie is a true Christian, not because she adheres to doctrine but because she is naturally a Christian. Knowing that Magawisca's imprisonment is morally wrong, Hope frees her despite the legal ramifications of her action. Hope Leslie possesses the virtues embodied by Sedgwick's other heroines as well, for she is generous, charitable, and kind. As Sedgwick's earlier novels do, *Hope Leslie* examines the meaning of true virtue; yet, it also reveals that adherence to one's conscience can override adherence to the law, especially when that law is itself immoral.

As with *Redwood* and *A New-England Tale,* most reviewers praised the vivid, realistic delineation of character in *Hope Leslie.* The portrayal of Magawisca, especially as she risked her life to save Everell, captured the imaginations of many readers. Reviewers also lauded Sedgwick for writing a successful novel based on the early history of Massachusetts. The historical basis of the novel, the depiction of Native American characters, and its vivid descriptions of the Massachusetts landscape helped make *Hope Leslie* a distinctly American novel.

During the years following the publication of *Hope Leslie,* the Sedgwicks in Stockbridge received visits from famous people traveling in America, including Captain Basil Hall and his wife. Captain Hall traveled widely and wrote popular books of his travels. The attitude of the Halls toward Americans, especially the peo-

children virtues such as humility and sympathy with others. Besides writing novels for adults, Sedgwick became a prolific writer of didactic tales for children.

Sedgwick's third and best-known novel is *Hope Leslie,* based upon the colonial New England histories of John Winthrop, William Hubbard, Cotton Mather, and John Trumbull. This historical romance is set, initially, in Springfield, Massachusetts, where William Fletcher settles with his family after leaving England. Among the members of his household are Everell Fletcher and Hope and Faith Leslie, the daughters of an English friend. The children of the Indian sachem Mononotto—Magawisca and Oneco—are captive servants in the Fletcher household. Mononotto attacks the Fletcher home to retrieve his children, kills Mrs. Fletcher and her infant, and kidnaps Everell and Faith. Magawisca intervenes as her father tries to kill Everell and loses her arm. Faith Leslie remains with the Native Americans, ple of Stockbridge, was negative, and Captain Hall may have been the basis for a minor character, Mr. Stuart, in Sedgwick's fourth novel, *Clarence; or, A Tale of Our Own Times* (1830). Mr. Stuart writes scathing critiques of America and Americans while comparing them to England and English standards.

Central to *Clarence* is Thomas Jefferson's ideal of an agrarian utopia, in which farm and country life are the means by which one can achieve a virtuous republic. Mr. Clarence, who lives in New York City, inherits money and moves with his daughter, Gertrude, to the country town of Clarenceville. There they meet Mrs. Layton and her daughter, Emilie. Like Gertrude, Emilie is virtuous and well mannered, but Mrs. Layton is a social climber who longs for the fashionable life of New York. Mrs. Layton hopes to gain wealth by marrying her daughter to a rich but immoral man, Pedrillo, who abducts and attempts to seduce Emilie. Emilie later marries Randolph Marion, who helped save her from Pedrillo. Mr. Clarence taught Gertrude to choose companions based on moral character, not wealth, and so she eventually marries Gerald Roscoe, an upright individual.

In *Clarence,* Sedgwick examines not only the nature of virtue and vice but also the effects that country and city life can have on an individual's character. Life in New York City is fast paced and fashionable, while life in Clarenceville is quiet. In the country, an individual need not focus on fashion and social accomplishment, but can spend time acquiring knowledge and virtue. While the Clarences are aristocrats, they are true to the Jeffersonian ideal—they are well educated, well mannered, talented, and virtuous. Sedgwick contrasts this ideal aristocracy with that of aristocracy based only on wealth, in which good business is the sole aim. The novel suggests that character, not money, makes the true aristocrat. *Clarence,* like Sedgwick's earlier works, sold well, and once again she was praised for her accurate and sensitive depictions of the American character and life.

While Sedgwick was writing *Clarence,* her brother Henry suffered a mental collapse in 1827. Consequently, he quit his law practice in New York and moved to Stockbridge, where Theodore also lived. Henry struggled with mental illness until his death, late in 1831. In her journal Sedgwick notes her sense of loss at Henry's deteriorating condition. She was saddened at his "darkened mind" and his "troubled spirit," describing his once powerful intellect as "a broken instrument."

After *Clarence* was published, Sedgwick lived part of the year in New York with her brother Robert and the rest in Lenox with her brother Charles and his wife. In 1828 Charles's wife had opened a school for girls,

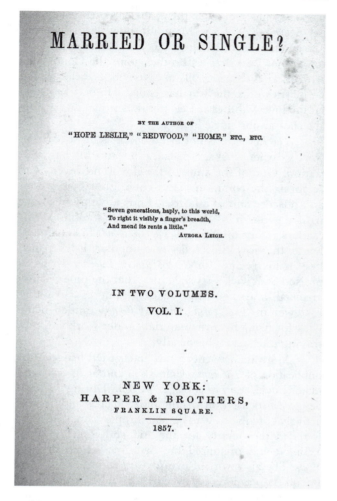

Title page for the first American edition of Sedgwick's last published novel, set in New York and New England during the 1850s

which came to be regarded as one of the best in America. During this period Sedgwick wrote some didactic tracts and continued to contribute short pieces to magazines and annuals. She also visited Washington during the 1830s, meeting with Vice President Martin Van Buren, President Andrew Jackson, and Chief Justice John Marshall. By this time her reputation as a novelist had reached its height.

In 1835 Sedgwick published *The Linwoods; or, "Sixty Years Since" in America,* another historical romance based on the American Revolution. The novel focuses on two families—the Linwoods, a Tory family from New York, and the Lees, a Republican family from New England. The Linwoods' son, Herbert, lives with the Lees in New England while he is at school, and during that time he becomes a Republican. At the start of the Revolutionary War, he joins the colonists and is disowned by his family. The Lees' daughter, Bessie, goes to school in New York and lives with the Linwoods; while living with them, she falls in love with Jasper Meredith, a Tory. Meredith, however, rejects her and pursues Isabella Linwood, heir to the family fortune. Eliot Lee, Bessie's brother, joins the Continental Army and eventually falls in love with Isabella, whom he marries once the war has ended. Herbert Linwood falls in love with Bessie Lee, but rather than marry him, she chooses the single life.

The Linwoods is not as complex as most of Sedgwick's earlier works, especially in terms of characterization. One of the aims of the novel, however, is to celebrate the common man. Thus, Eliot Lee, a poor and obscure son of a farmer, finds a happy marriage with a woman of a different social station. While readers today might find The Linwoods too melodramatic, the novel in its day was popular. Edgar Allan Poe in his review for The Southern Literary Messenger praised Sedgwick's style, stating that the plot was not artificial and kept the reader's interest. Another reviewer in The North American Review lauded Sedgwick for using historic materials in her work and portraying the past so heroically.

More than twenty years intervened between the publication of The Linwoods in 1835 and Sedgwick's last major novel, Married or Single? in 1857. During this time Sedgwick focused on writing didactic tales and became actively involved with philanthropic concerns. She founded the Society for the Aid and Relief of Poor Women and organized the first free school in New York. She also worked many years with the Women's Prison Association of New York, serving as its president from 1848 to 1863. Sedgwick was especially concerned with education, teaching for some time at her sister-in-law's school in Lenox. Most of her didactic tales attempted to teach morals and manners to children and members of the lower classes. Sedgwick's books indicate that the major problems in America, however, can be traced to bad manners and insufficient home life. In Home (1835), for example, Sedgwick praises life in New England and the country, but the focus of the book is to demonstrate that in order for democracy to succeed, education should come out of home life. At the same time, Home reveals Sedgwick's belief that if all Americans were to attain good manners, there would be true equality in America.

While Sedgwick was writing her didactic tales, she also was a prolific writer for magazines and collections of short stories, especially for children. She also wrote a biography of Lucretia Maria Davidson, a young Romantic poet. In 1841 she published Letters from Abroad to Kindred at Home, a collection of letters written while she was taking a fifteen-month tour of Europe in 1839 and 1840 with her brother Robert and other members of her family. In this work, Sedgwick observed British and European society from an American bias, often comparing what she saw to life in the Berkshires of Massachusetts. Although Letters from Abroad to Kindred at Home received criticism from English readers, it was popular and well reviewed in America.

Sedgwick's last major novel, Married or Single? examines the state of a woman who lives her life single rather than married. In this novel the socially elite and wealthy Grace Herbert is engaged to marry Horace Copley, who is unworthy of her. Grace does not marry Copley and chooses not to marry at all. She eventually falls in love, however, with Archibald Lisle, a moral man, and marries happily. While Sedgwick makes clear that women who choose to live their lives without marriage should be treated with respect, she also demonstrates her belief that being married is probably preferable to being single, a point that she makes about her own life. In a journal entry in 1828 Sedgwick wrote, "From my own experience, I would not advise any one to remain unmarried," although she admits that "my experience has been a singularly happy one." At the same time, the book celebrates the domestic life as ideal. Married or Single? however, was not a popular work. Sedgwick had not published a book in some time, and her reading public was dwindling. Furthermore, the sentimental literature she wrote was becoming less appealing to the public.

While some of Sedgwick's novels were still in print, she published no new works during the last nine years of her life. A year after she published Married or Single? Sedgwick was the last member of her immediate family alive. Theodore had died in 1839, Robert in 1841, and Charles in 1856. Considering the close relationship Sedgwick shared with her brothers, their deaths were extremely difficult for her. After Charles's death she found she could not leave their home in Lenox, at least for some time. Henry's wife died in 1859, and Robert's wife in 1861. Sedgwick's sister-in-law Elizabeth closed her school in 1861 and died three years later. Theodore's wife died in January 1867. Catharine Maria Sedgwick spent the last few years of her life at the home of her niece Kate Sedgwick Minot in West Roxbury, Massachusetts, where she died on 31 July 1867.

Letters:

Life and Letters of Catharine Maria Sedgwick, edited by Mary E. Dewey (New York: Harper, 1871).

Biographies:

Seth Curtis Beach, "Catharine Maria Sedgwick," in Daughters of the Puritans (Boston: American Unitarian Society, 1905), pp. 1–39;

Gladys Brooks, "Catharine Maria Sedgwick," in *Three Wise Virgins* (New York: Dutton, 1957), pp. 157–244.

References:

Victoria Clements, Introduction to *A New-England Tale; or Sketches of New-England Character and Manners,* edited by Clements (New York: Oxford University Press, 1995);

Edward Halsey Foster, *Catharine Maria Sedgwick* (New York: Twayne, 1974);

Susan K. Harris, "Preludes: The Early Didactic Novel. Narrative Control in *Charlotte Temple* and *A New-England Tale,*" in her *19th-Century American Women's Novels: Interpretive Strategies* (Cambridge: Cambridge University Press, 1990), pp. 39–59;

Mary Kelley, Introduction to *Hope Leslie; or Early Times in Massachusetts,* edited by Kelley (New Brunswick, N.J.: Rutgers University Press, 1987);

Kelley, "Negotiating Self: The Autobiography and Journals of Catharine Maria Sedgwick," *New England Quarterly,* 66 (September 1993): 366–398;

Kelley, *Private Woman Public Stage: Literary Domesticity in Nineteenth-Century America* (New York: Oxford University Press, 1984);

Dana Nelson, "Sympathy as Strategy in Sedgwick's *Hope Leslie,*" in *The Culture of Sentiment: Race, Gender, and Sentimentality in Nineteenth-Century America,* edited by Shirley Samuels (New York: Oxford University Press, 1992), pp. 191–202;

Sarah Cabot Sedgwick and Christina Sedgwick Marquand, *Stockbridge: 1739–1939: A Chronicle* (Great Barrington, Mass.: Berkshire Courier, 1939);

Carol J. Singley, "Catharine Maria Sedgwick's *Hope Leslie*: Radical Frontier Romance," in *The (Other) American Traditions: Nineteenth-Century Women Writers,* edited by Joyce Warren (New Brunswick, N.J.: Rutgers University Press, 1993), pp. 39–53;

Sister Mary Michael Welsh, *Catharine Maria Sedgwick, Her Position in the Literature and Thought of Her Time Up to 1860* (Washington, D.C.: Catholic University of America, 1937).

Papers:

The Massachusetts Historical Society houses the Catharine Maria Sedgwick papers. Other important holdings of Sedgwick's letters and manuscripts include the Houghton Library at Harvard University, the Butler Library at Columbia University, the Alderman Library at the University of Virginia, the Boston Public Library, the Beinecke Rare Book and Manuscript Library at Yale University, the Historical Society of Pennsylvania, and the Stockbridge Library Association, which holds a collection of the Sedgwick family papers.

Lydia Huntley Sigourney

(1 September 1791 – 10 June 1865)

Barbara Downs Wojtusik

See also the Sigourney entries in *DLB 1: The American Renaissance in New England; DLB 42: American Writers for Children Before 1900; DLB 73: American Magazine Journalists, 1741–1850; DLB 183: American Travel Writers 1776–1864;* and *DLB 239: American Women Prose Writers, 1820–1870.*

BOOKS: *Moral Pieces, in Prose and Verse* (Hartford: Sheldon & Goodwin, 1815);

The Square Table, anonymous (Hartford: Samuel G. Goodrich, 1819);

No. II. The Square Table, or the Meditations of Four Secluded Maidens Seated Around It, anonymous (Hartford, 1819);

Traits of the Aborigines of America. A Poem, anonymous (Cambridge, Mass.: University Press, 1822);

Sketch of Connecticut, Forty Years Since, anonymous (Hartford: Oliver D. Cooke, 1824);

Poems: By the Author of "Moral Pieces in Prose and Verse" (Boston: Samuel G. Goodrich / Hartford: H. & F. J. Huntington, 1827);

Female Biography: Containing Sketches of the Life and Character of Twelve American Women, anonymous (Philadelphia: American Sunday School Union, 1829);

Evening Readings in History: Comprising Portions of the History of Assyria, Egypt, Tyre, Syria, Persia, and the Sacred Scriptures; With Questions, Arranged for the Use of the Young, and of Family Circles, anonymous (Springfield, Mass.: G. & C. Merriam, 1833; London, 1834);

Memoir of Phebe P. Hammond, a Pupil in the American Asylum at Hartford (New York: Sleight & Van Norden, 1833);

Letters to Young Ladies, anonymous (Hartford: Canfield, 1833; revised edition, Hartford: William Watson, 1835; revised again, New York: Harper, 1837; revised again, London: Jackson & Walford / Edinburgh: W. Innes, 1841; New York: Harper, 1842);

How to Be Happy. Written for the Children of Some Dear Friends, anonymous (Hartford: D. F. Robinson, 1833);

Lydia Huntley Sigourney (The Connecticut Historical Society, Hartford, Connecticut)

Biography of Pious Persons; Abridged for Youth, 2 volumes, anonymous (Springfield, Mass.: G. & C. Merriam, 1833);

The Farmer and the Soldier. A Tale, as L. H. S. (Hartford: Printed by J. Hubbard Wells, 1833);

The Intemperate, and The Reformed. Shewing the Awful Consequences of Intemperance and the Blessed Effects of the Temperance Reformation, by Sigourney and Gerrit Smith (Boston: Seth Bliss, 1833);

A Report of the Hartford Female Beneficent Society (Hartford: Printed by Hanmer & Comstock, 1833);

Sketches (Philadelphia: Key & Biddle, 1834);

Poetry for Children (Hartford: Robinson & Pratt, 1834); enlarged as *Poems for Children* (Hartford: Canfield & Robbins, 1836);

Poems (Philadelphia: Key & Biddle, 1834; enlarged, 1836);

Lays from the West, edited by Joseph Belcher (London: Thomas Ward, 1834);

Tales and Essays for Children (Hartford: F. J. Huntington, 1835);

Memoir of Margaret and Henrietta Flower, anonymous (Boston: Perkins, Marvin, 1835); republished as *The Lovely Sisters: Margaret and Henrietta* (Hartford: H. S. Parsons, 1845); republished again as *Margaret and Henrietta* (New York: American Tract Society, 1852);

Zinzendorff, and Other Poems (New York: Leavitt, Lord / Boston: Crocker & Brewster, 1835);

History of Marcus Aurelius, Emperor of Rome (Hartford: Belknap & Hamersley, 1836);

Olive Buds (Hartford: William Watson, 1836);

The Girl's Reading-Book; in Prose and Poetry, for Schools (New York: J. Orville Taylor, 1838; revised, 1839); republished as *The Book for Girls* (New York: J. Orville Taylor, 1844);

Letters to Mothers (Hartford: Hudson & Skinner, 1838; London: Wiley & Putnam, 1839; revised edition, New York: Harper, 1839);

Select Poems (Philadelphia: F. W. Greenough, 1838; enlarged edition, Philadelphia: E. C. Biddle, 1842; enlarged again, 1845);

The Boy's Reading-Book; in Prose and Poetry, for Schools (New York: J. Orville Taylor, 1839); revised and enlarged as *The Boy's Book* (New York: Turner, Hughes & Hayden / Raleigh, N.C.: Turner & Hughes, 1843);

Memoir of Mary Anne Hooker (Philadelphia: American Sunday-School Union, 1840);

Pocahontas, and Other Poems (London: Robert Tyas, 1841; republished, with differing contents, New York: Harper, 1841);

Poems, Religious and Elegiac (London: Robert Tyas, 1841);

Pleasant Memories of Pleasant Lands (Boston: Munroe, 1842; revised, 1844);

Poems (Philadelphia: John Locken, 1842);

The Pictorial Reader, Consisting of Original Articles for the Instruction of Young Children (New York: Turner & Hayden, 1844); republished as *The Child's Book: Consisting of Original Articles, in Prose and Poetry* (New York: Turner & Hayden, 1844);

The Peace Series No. 3: Walks in Childhood (London: Gilpin, 1844);

Scenes in My Native Land (Boston: Munroe, 1845; London: Clarke, 1845);

Poetry for Seamen (Hartford: Munroe, 1845); enlarged as *Poems for the Sea* (Hartford: H. S. Parsons, 1850); republished as *The Sea and the Sailor* (Hartford: F. A. Brown, 1857);

The Voice of Flowers (Hartford: H. S. Parsons, 1846);

Myrtis, with Other Etchings and Sketchings (New York: Harper, 1846);

The Weeping Willow (Hartford: Henry S. Parsons, 1847);

Water-Drops (New York & Pittsburgh: Robert Carter, 1848);

Illustrated Poems . . . With Designs by Felix O. C. Darley, Engraved by American Artists (Philadelphia: Carey & Hart, 1849); republished as *The Poetical Works of Mrs. L. H. Sigourney,* edited by F. W. N. Bayley (London: Routledge, 1850);

Whisper to a Bride (Hartford: H. S. Parsons, 1850; enlarged edition, Hartford: Hamersley, 1851);

Letters to My Pupils: With Narrative and Biographical Sketches (New York: Robert Carter, 1851);

Examples of Life and Death (New York: Scribner, 1851);

Olive Leaves (New York: Robert Carter, 1852; London: Collins, 1853);

The Faded Hope (New York: Robert Carter, 1853);

Memoir of Mrs. Harriet Newell Cook (New York: Robert Carter, 1853);

The Western Home, and Other Poems (Philadelphia: Parry & McMillan, 1854);

Past Meridian (New York: Appleton / Boston: Jewett, 1854; London: Hall, 1855; enlarged edition, Hartford: F. A. Brown, 1856; revised and enlarged again, Hartford: Brown & Gross, 1864);

Sayings of the Little Ones, and Poems for Their Mothers (Buffalo: Phinney / New York: Ivision & Phinney, 1855);

Examples from the Eighteenth and Nineteenth Centuries (New York: Scribner, 1857);

Lucy Howard's Journal (New York: Harper, 1858);

The Daily Counsellor (Hartford: Brown & Gross, 1859);

Gleanings (Hartford: Brown & Gross / New York: Appleton, 1860);

The Man of Uz, and Other Poems (Hartford: Williams, Wiley & Waterman, 1862);

The Transplanted Daisy. Memoir of Frances Racilla Hackley (New York: Sanford, Harroun, 1865);

Letters of Life (New York: Appleton, 1866).

OTHER: *The Writings of Nancy Maria Hyde, of Norwich, Conn. Connected with a Sketch of Her Life,* edited anonymously, with commentary, by Sigourney (Norwich: Printed by Russell Hubbard, 1816).

Contemporaries considered Lydia Sigourney the most popular poet in America and the woman most respected and loved by the American people. Her fame rivaled that of Henry Wadsworth Longfellow and surpassed that of Ralph Waldo Emerson. Because of the financial success and quantity of her books, Sigourney became the first self-supporting American professional woman writer. Her renown was so great that her name became a commodity sought after by various publishers to advertise their periodicals and newspapers. Sigourney's fame was not limited to America. She was often referred to as the American Hemens, a reference to Felicia Hemens, the most popular female poet in England at the time. After Hemens's death in 1835 Sigourney was considered the only one who could fill the void left in the literary world and became the standard against which other women poets were judged. Sigourney's books had unprecedented sales and popularity throughout her long career. Her first book, *Moral Pieces, in Prose and Verse* (1815), which was sold by subscription, garnered the largest prepaid audience to that date. Her last endeavor, a posthumously published autobiography, *Letters of Life* (1866), was most recently printed in 1980. At the time of her death in Hartford, Connecticut, on 10 June 1865, church bells tolled for one hour. Two streets in Hartford are named for her, as is a town in Iowa.

Lydia Howard Huntley was born in the old town section of Norwich, Connecticut, the only child of Ezekiel and Sophia (Wentworth) Huntley. Her mother was descended from Tory governors of New Hampshire and the earl of Stafford, who was beheaded by Charles I of England. Her father was the son of a Scottish immigrant who died soon after participating in the French and Indian War. Ezekiel Huntley, as a young man, went to work for the household of Dr. Daniel Lathrop, a druggist and merchant in Norwich, and his wife, Jerusha (Talcott) Lathrop, daughter of a governor of Connecticut and the most socially prominent woman in town. After the death of Dr. Lathrop, who had attended medical school but never practiced medicine, Huntley took charge of managing Jerusha Lathrop's estate, where Lydia was born and raised. Jerusha Lathrop became Lydia's patron and was responsible for her being educated in the best schools of Norwich. At age thirteen Lydia left school to study domesticity with her mother. Two years later Jerusha Lathrop died, but her nephew, Daniel Wadsworth, and his wife, Faith Trumbull, of Hartford replaced Lathrop as protectors of the young Lydia Huntley.

In 1811 Lydia Huntley and her best friend, Nancy Maria Hyde, began a school in Norwich. Then, the Wadsworths financed schooling in Hartford, where the girls could learn drawing, painting, and embroidery in preparation for opening a school

Charles Sigourney, who married Lydia Huntley in 1819

for the daughters of the Wadsworths' friends. This school flourished in Hartford from 1814 until 1819. In 1815 Lydia Huntley's first book, *Moral Pieces, in Prose and Verse,* was published, also with the help of Daniel Wadsworth. The Wadsworths introduced Huntley to Charles Sigourney, a Hartford banker and merchant, whom she married in 1819. Charles Sigourney, a widower, had three sons by his previous marriage; he and Lydia had a daughter, Mary, born in 1827, and a son, Andrew, born two years later.

Lydia Sigourney believed that domesticity was the most important aspect of a woman's life. She was sincerely and adamantly religious and convinced that care of the home and children by women was God's will and a sacred duty. Sigourney confined her writing to spare time and devoted herself to being mother to five, wife to Charles, and nurse to her father and her husband's first wife's sister, while acting as her own press agent and secretary. She used domestic themes for her poetry but incorporated moral lessons into the poems to combat the issues of intolerance, intemperance, and war that she felt harmed domestic tranquility.

Each poem, written in language understandable to all ages and educational levels, had a lesson or was designed to promote love, duty, compassion, charity, and respect for God's creations. Her language is often sentimental, but she was fully aware that emotion could effect change. Often criticized for lack of care in revising composition, she claimed that her writings reflected spontaneous, sincere, unrestrained emotion. She also considered the healing power of language and wrote many words of comfort. She was a proponent of a national literature. Joining with other writers, clergymen, and teachers of the period in an attempt to stay what they considered increasing liberalism and fragmentation in the Christian church of America, Sigourney strongly supported the idea that America should develop its own literature designed to educate readers in Christian love that would take the country back to a time when its people were closer to God. To Lydia Sigourney, teaching was a divine calling.

In her autobiography, *Letters of Life,* Lydia Sigourney traces her literary career. She attributes the financial and popular success of her first book, *Moral Pieces, in Prose and Verse,* written when she was fifteen as teaching material in answer to the *New England Primer,* to the care of Daniel Wadsworth, although she does accept credit for the moral and religious tone of the work. Benefactors such as Wadsworth and Jerusha Lathrop exemplified for Sigourney the concept of loving thy neighbor. Later in life Lydia Sigourney, insisting that the Connecticut Valley produced the most moral society known to mankind, continued to assist those who were in financial, emotional, or moral jeopardy.

In 1816 Nancy Maria Hyde, began a school in Norwich, Connecticut. In 1816 Hyde died unexpectedly, leaving Huntley distraught. In order to grieve and reorder her life, Lydia Huntley retired to the Huntley homestead for three weeks. During this time she arranged and edited the notebooks and journals of Nancy Hyde for publication. The result was *The Writings of Nancy Maria Hyde, of Norwich, Conn. Connected with a Sketch of Her Life* (1816). Lydia Sigourney regarded publishing the book as solace to herself and financial assistance for Nancy Hyde's mother.

Being a housewife took over Sigourney's attention in 1819; it did not, however, dissuade her from a writing career. Because her husband disliked publicity, she allowed *The Square Table* (1819), a reply to a popular satirical work on King Arthur, to be printed anonymously. Nevertheless, sales were good for the pamphlet, and guessing the identity of the author became a social pastime.

Traits of the Aborigines of America. A Poem, composed in 1817 but not published until 1822, was not received by the public with such affection. This book deals with the unfair treatment of New England Native Americans, an injustice that Sigourney refers to in *Letters of Life* as "one of our greatest national sins." The poem, one of the earliest works to deal sympathetically with Native Americans, is narrated from their perspective and begins with the natives in peaceful possession of the continent. Soon, however, a series of European incursions occurs. Ostensibly, according to Sigourney, the Europeans come as Christians, but they do not behave in a Christian manner and because of their selfishness cannot convert the Native Americans. As more and more Europeans callously invade the land, the Native Americans become more hostile and defiant, thus leading to retaliation and warfare. Native distrust eventually extends to the religion of the whites, and Sigourney rues that instead of brotherhood, the Native Americans were offered betrayal. In *Letters of Life* Lydia Sigourney states that *Traits of the Aborigines* was her most unpopular creation because society rejected its subject matter and perspective, but she maintained her position throughout her lifetime. Critics such as Nina Baym see *Traits of the Aborigines* as an important precursor of modern anti-racist study and reform.

Another Sigourney work, *Sketch of Connecticut, Forty Years Since* (1824), includes native folklore and traditions of early New England meshed with fictionalized accounts. This sketch is a tribute to Jerusha Lathrop, Sigourney's initial benefactor. It is also a request for inclusion and community in America, particularly of the poor. Sigourney frequently uses examples from history to illustrate solutions to nineteenth-century issues. Her inspirations come from ancient and biblical history, the history of New England, and the condition of the Native Americans after the arrival of the settlers. By immortalizing Lathrop as the epitome of Christian charity, Sigourney furthers her conviction that America must atone for its iniquities toward the natives by including them in moral society as Lathrop included all classes of people in her charity and affection.

Since much of Sigourney's poetry was originally published in newspapers and periodicals, several of her books are gatherings of earlier produced pieces. Examples of collections covering her entire career are *Poems* (1827), *Selected Poems* (1838), *Illustrated Poems* (1849), *The Western Home, and Other Poems* (1854), *Gleanings* (1860), and *The Man of Uz, and Other Poems* (1862). That the works were often reprinted is a tribute to Sigourney's constant popularity, since merely having her name on a cover insured profits and sales. Profit, however, was not the sole motivation for Sigourney's production. Her books throughout her lifetime reflect her determination to model moral values and to encourage and inspire her readers to "good and distinguished examples of conduct."

The Hartford mansion where Lydia and Charles Sigourney lived from 1819 until 1838 (The Connecticut Historical Society, Hartford, Connecticut)

In 1829 Sigourney prepared *Female Biography: Containing Sketches of the Life and Character of Twelve American Women,* a book designed to inspire young ladies through the exemplary lives of other young women. This compilation was taken from essays Sigourney had written and read to her students. The initial volume featured twelve women; the immense popularity of the book led to the two-volume *Biography of Pious Persons; Abridged for Youth* (1833) with profiles of additional women. Other inspirational readings were presented for various groups. *Poems* (1842) is Christian in nature. *Poetry for Seamen* (1845) is poetry designed to accompany sailors aboard ship. *Examples from the Eighteenth and Nineteenth Centuries* (1857) is a collection of biographies of great and good people. In 1858 Sigourney produced *Lucy Howard's Journal,* the diary of a fictional girl whose life as reported in the journal reflects the traditional domestic position of proper and productive womanhood. As a companion and a positive influence for good, Sigourney's last virtuous reminder is *The Daily Counsellor* (1859). This text offers for each day of the year a poem based on a scripture reading; the purpose was to encourage meditation and good thoughts. So popular was this publication that the first printing was sold out in two weeks.

Admittedly always the teacher, Sigourney devotes many of her books to history, advice, and teaching.

Some of the historical pieces, such as *Evening Readings in History: Comprising Portions of the History of Assyria, Egypt, Tyre, Syria, Persia, and the Sacred Scriptures; With Questions, Arranged for the Use of the Young, and of Family Circles* (1833), combine all three. This book, based on stories of ancient history, gives brief readings and lessons to be shared with family members before bedtime in order to involve young and old in early education, of which Sigourney was an advocate. Between 1833 and 1846 she emphasized historical writing in such works as *Sketches* (1834), *History of Marcus Aurelius, Emperor of Rome* (1836), and *Myrtis, with Other Etchings and Sketchings* (1846). All three of these works were constructed to assist in home education. Besides teaching through history, Sigourney created other textbook pieces for use in home and school, including *How to Be Happy. Written for the Children of Some Dear Friends* (1833), advice to children on how to be good and obedient; *Letters to Young Ladies* (1833), words of encouragement for proper behavior; *Poetry for Children* (1834), truthful lessons in rhyme; *Tales and Essays for Children* (1835), an attempt to positively influence the minds of little children; *Letters to Mothers* (1838), words on child care that was in print for twenty-five years; *The Girl's Reading-Book; in Prose and Poetry, for Schools* (1838) and *The Boy's Reading-Book; in Prose and Poetry, for Schools* (1839), books using stories and poetry to instill principles in young people; *The Pictorial Reader,*

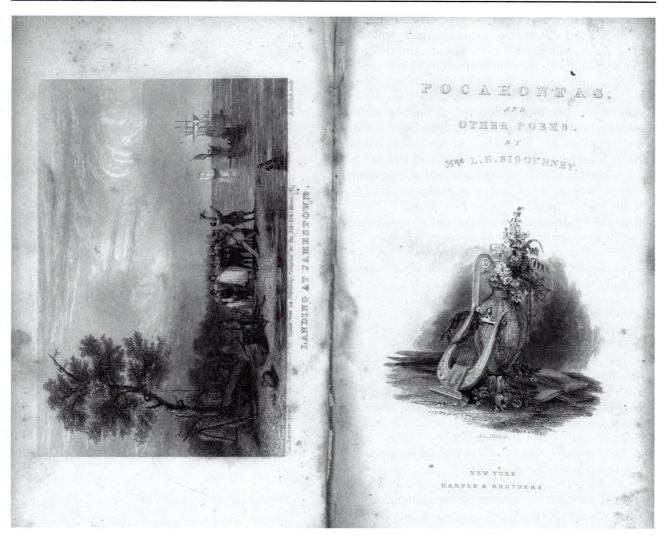

Frontispiece and decorated title page for a collection of poems inspired by Sigourney's visit to Jamestown, Virginia

Consisting of Original Articles for the Instruction of Young Children (1844), a work for those of varying reading ability, starting with chapters to read to an infant and progressing to those to read oneself; *Letters to My Pupils: With Narrative and Biographical Sketches* (1851), answers to students' letters and tributes to those who have died; *Olive Leaves* (1852), biography and history in prose and poetry for young people; and *Past Meridian* (1854), an appreciation of old age.

Even while Sigourney was producing instructional books, she was engaged in combating social ills. *The Farmer and the Soldier. A Tale* (1833), written to encourage pacifism in children, promotes the joy of a calm, peaceful spirit and reveals the ugliness and false glory of bloodshed and war. *Olive Buds* (1836) is of the same nature and appears to have been written as assistance to William Watson, in whose home she had

lived when beginning her teaching career and who had a small publishing firm. *Water-Drops* (1848), originally published by the Scottish Temperance League, admonished females to be vigilant and armed to protect their homes against the uncontrolled indulgence of the appetites.

Reflecting her earliest concerns with intolerance, particularly toward Native Americans, Sigourney published two more accounts on the subject. Both *Zinzendorff, and Other Poems* (1835) and *Pocahontas, and Other Poems* (1841) were inspired by Sigourney's visits to historical sites. A trip to the Moravian settlements in Bethlehem and Nazareth, Pennsylvania, motivated her to write about the life and work of their founder, Count Zinzendorff, who had gone to Wyoming in 1742 to Christianize the Native Americans. Sigourney's tale elaborates on Zinzendorff's bravery in remaining with them and persevering even though the Native Americans dislike and distrust him. After many attempts on his life, Zinzendorff appeals to the women and children of the tribe and wins their support through his peaceful persistence and kindness. In short, the poem is a somewhat embellished picture of how Sigourney thought the Native Americans could be saved–through peaceful missionary activities rather than through government action. The mood of *Pocahontas, and Other Poems* is less hopeful. Inspired by the Christian church in Jamestown where Pocahontas was baptized and later married, the poem recounts the life of the Native American princess. The story is told from the Native American perspective and begins by depicting the serene and natural life of the natives before the arrival of the English. Despite the intrusion of the settlers, Pocahontas convinces her father to spare John Smith and to attempt to co-exist peacefully with the English. Pocahontas's life proceeds through her capture, conversion, marriage, journey to England, and early death. Sigourney concludes that despite the goodwill of Native Americans such as Pocahontas, Americans have treated them abominably.

Yet, Sigourney's enthusiasm for her country never wavered. After nearly a year of travel in Europe, she wrote *Pleasant Memories of Pleasant Lands* (1842), a collection of poems and sketches concerning the people and places that most interested her during the trip. While ill and dependent on her daughter for copying, she produced *Scenes in My Native Land* (1845), a description of interesting places in her own country.

In the 1840s Sigourney began publishing some of her poems as miniature gift books, beginning with *The Voice of Flowers* (1846). Other miniatures include *The Weeping Willow* (1847), poems on death, and *Whisper to a Bride* (1850), marriage advice to brides. This book was followed by *Sayings of the Little Ones, and Poems for Their Mothers* (1855).

Earnestly helping others remained a quality of Sigourney throughout her career. In 1833 she was approached by the Reverend Thomas Gallaudet, founder and principal of the American Asylum for the Deaf and Dumb in Hartford, to transcribe the memoirs of Phebe P. Hammond, a pupil in the school. Since Sigourney had been instrumental in Gallaudet's opening the school and since he insisted the Hammond family was in great need of finances, she acquiesced. The result was *Memoir of Phebe P. Hammond, a Pupil in the American Asylum at Hartford* (1833). On other occasions, Sigourney edited and transcribed the papers of deceased people to console the bereaved. *Memoir of Mary Anne Hooker* (1840) is an example; the Reverend Horace Hooker and his wife, longtime friends of Sigourney, requested the book as a remembrance of Hooker. A similar situation arose in 1852 when another clergyman

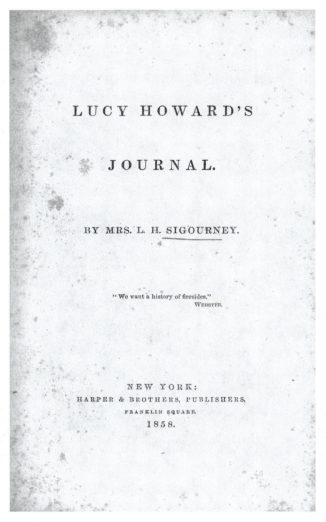

LUCY HOWARD'S

JOURNAL.

BY MRS. L. H. SIGOURNEY.

" We want a history of firesides."
WEBSTER.

NEW YORK:
HARPER & BROTHERS, PUBLISHERS,
FRANKLIN SQUARE.
1858.

*Title page for a novel in which Sigourney offered
her readers a model for female behavior*

pleaded for a book compiled of his wife's writings. Since the woman lived, as Sigourney notes in *Letters of Life,* "with a pen in her hand," Sigourney had no difficulty collecting material for *Memoir of Mrs. Harriet Newell Cook* (1853). Another memoir, written in 1852, is of a much more personal nature. *The Faded Hope* (1853) is Sigourney's memorial to her son, Andrew, who had drowned in the Connecticut River in 1850. Andrew was a student at Washington (now Trinity) College in Hartford at the time of his death.

Perhaps no topic more than Sigourney's consolation poetry has influenced current critics to consider her work sentimental and morose. As Baym states, however, Sigourney wrote different types of elegiac poetry. Baym sees three groups of death poems. The first she refers to as the memento mori poems, which deal with death as a part of life. The second consists of those poems Sigourney wrote to commemorate a lost way of life. The third comprises her most-common poems, those designed to offer immediate solace. Sigourney's career began in an era when society was still uncertain if to appreciate any poetry other than the Bible was sinful. She won respect and admiration by offering literature designed to encourage domesticity, devotion to God, moral guidelines, and healing. Her work was so acceptable to the populace that contemporary critics thought judging her poetry unnecessary. By 1902, however, Thomas Wentworth Higginson was referring to her as "Mrs. Sigourney, then famous." Her popularity did not dip immediately upon her death in 1865. In the first literary history published after her death, John Hart's *A Manual of American Literature* (1873), she was allotted a lengthy critical and biographical introduction. Hart saw her as a powerful moral influence during the first half of the nineteenth century and recognized her primarily for reformist prose rather than for poetry. Sigourney's poetry remained in anthologies in the nineteenth century, but during the twentieth century none of her work was anthologized until the 1930s, when there was a movement toward including authors who reflected national life in literary history. Once again Sigourney was represented as a reformer rather than a poet. Current critics praise Sigourney as a model for later writers but rue what they consider her maudlin preoccupation with death.

In *Letters of Life* Sigourney defends herself against the critics. She states that she composed her themes and stories while she was knitting stockings, fifteen to twenty pairs a year. She then corrected and rewrote them more than once. During this time she also attempted to honor requests for hymns to be written for churches, odes for festivals, poems for celebrations, lyrics for songs, and many elegies and epitaphs, as well as her signature for autograph hunters. Other requests were for dedication poems, investigative reports on schools, odes for weddings, rhymes for birthdays, help with manuscripts, advice on finding a teacher, preparation of memoirs, and correction of punctuation. She tried to comply with these requests. Some requests were

more bizarre. The owner of a canary that had accidentally been starved to death wanted some comforting verse. A father of a child who had drowned in a barrel of pig's food wanted an elegy. A baby show in New York City wanted her as a judge. A family in the South wanted an acrostic for a funeral urn. A person wanted a verse to accompany a gift of an embroidered piece of worsted. A farmer desired a poem to have on hand in case his wife and child died. According to her daughter, one of the last statements Sigourney made before her death was, "I love everybody."

Biography:

Gordon S. Haight, *Mrs. Sigourney: The Sweet Singer of Hartford* (New Haven: Yale University Press, 1930).

References:

Nina Baym, "Reinventing Lydia Sigourney," *American Literature,* 62 (September 1990): 385–404;

Betty Harris Day, "'This Comes of Writing Poetry': The Public and Private Life of Lydia H. Sigourney," dissertation, University of Maryland, 1992;

Alice Delano, *Lydia Huntley in the Bacon Collection* (Hartford: Hartford Public Library, 1986).

Papers:

Major collections of Lydia Huntley Sigourney's papers are at the Connecticut Historical Society and the Hartford Public Library. Other manuscripts and letters may be found at the Boston Public Library, the Butler Library at Columbia University, the Connecticut State Library, the John Hay Library at Brown University, the Haverford College Library, the Houghton Library at Harvard University, the Huntington Library, the Harry Ransom Humanities Research Center at the University of Texas at Austin, the Historical Society of Pennsylvania, the Massachusetts Historical Society, the New-York Historical Society, the Berg Collection at the New York Public Library, the Schlesinger Library at Radcliffe College, the Watkinson Library at Trinity College in Hartford, the Alderman Library at the University of Virginia, and the Beinecke Library at Yale University.

Seba Smith

(14 September 1792 – 28 July 1868)

Cameron C. Nickels
James Madison University

See also the Smith entries in *DLB 1: The American Renaissance in New England* and *DLB 11: American Humorists, 1800–1950*.

BOOKS: *The Life and Times of Major Jack Downing, of Downingville, Away Down East in the State of Maine. Written by Himself* (Boston: Lilly, Wait, Colman & Holden, 1833; enlarged, 1834);

John Smith's Letters with "Picters" to Match. Containing Reasons Why John Smith Should Not Change His Name; Miss Debby Smith's Juvenile Spirit; Together with the Only Authentic History Extant of the Late War in Our Disputed Territory (New York: Colman, 1839; London: Wiley & Putnam, 1839);

Powhatan: A Metrical Romance in Seven Cantos (New York: Harper, 1841);

May-Day in New York; or, House-Hunting and Moving; Illustrated and Explained in Letters to Aunt Keziah. By Major Jack Downing (New York: Burgess, Stringer, 1845); republished as *Jack Downing's Letters by Major Jack Downing* (Philadelphia: Peterson, 1845 [i.e., ca. 1859]);

New Elements of Geometry (New York: Putnam / London: Bentley, 1850; London: Bentley, 1850);

'Way Down East; or, Portraitures of Yankee Life (New York: J. C. Derby / Boston: Phillips, Sampson / Cincinnati: H. W. Derby, 1854);

My Thirty Years out of the Senate. By Major Jack Downing (New York: Oaksmith, 1859).

OTHER: *Dew-Drops of the Nineteenth Century Gathered and Preserved in Their Brightness and Purity,* edited, with contributions, by Smith and Elizabeth Oakes Smith (New York: Wellman, 1846).

Seba Smith

"Poet and Scholar" reads the epitaph on Seba Smith's gravestone in Patchogue, Long Island, where he died on 28 July 1868. Yet, if remembered at all, Smith would have been known—then and later—for his creation of Jack Downing, the first popular cracker-barrel philosopher, whose letters put both political shenanigans and lofty abstractions in homespun terms that informed while entertaining. Jack Downing's letters were widely reprinted and imitated, and with the addition of characterizations on stage, in cartoons, and in broadsides, as well as the original letters and their imitators for more than thirty years, he may well have been the most popular American literary character in the nineteenth century. He was certainly the forerunner of later cracker-barrel humorists, such as Thomas Chandler Haliburton's "Sam Slick," James Russell Lowell's "Hosea Biglow," Artemus Ward, Peter Finley Dunne's "Mr. Dooley," Marietta Holley's "Samantha," Will Rogers, and others. Seba Smith, however, aspired to literature of a higher sort and played down the worth of his Downing letters. They "were remarkable for their extensive circulation and very great popularity, which I conceive arose more from peculiar circumstances than from their intrinsic merit," he wrote in 1854. Nevertheless, throughout his life, in personal and economic crises, he turned again and again to the New England cracker-barrel humor that had proved so successful.

Seba Smith's early life was the stuff of the American Dream. The second child of twelve children of hardworking, pioneering parents, Seba and Apphia (Stevens) Smith, he was born on 14 September 1792 in the log cabin his father built in Buckfield, Maine, then the frontier. Later, in Bridgton, young Seba contributed to the family's income through his work in a grocery store, a brickyard, and an iron foundry. By necessity, his education was sporadic, taking place during the winters and "in the commonest of the common schools and the crudest schoolbooks of that day," he later wrote. At eighteen, however, he was qualified to teach in schools in the area.

Continuing his education when he could at North Bridgton Academy, he attracted the attention of a teacher who encouraged his desire for a college education, and with a loan from a benefactor, Smith, at twenty-three, joined the sophomore class at Bowdoin College in Brunswick, Maine, whose illustrious graduates in the next decade included Nathaniel Hawthorne, Franklin Pierce, and Henry Wadsworth Longfellow. Although in poor health and forced to live frugally—preparing his own meals and teaching when he could during school vacations—a surviving speech to his fellow students answered their charges of ostentation, defending himself against "the prejudices in college which would hinder the progress and development of genius." Driven to excel, he graduated at the head of his class of nineteen and delivered the valedictory address at commencement in September 1818.

Following graduation he tried private teaching in Portland and contributed poems to the *Portland Eastern Argus,* but, still plagued by ill health, he took a year off from work, traveling south as far as South Carolina, part of the way on foot, and took a ship to Liverpool in 1819. His future was uncertain, but he was drawn toward "the press," and with good fortune worthy of Benjamin Franklin, upon landing in Portland from his voyage abroad, he found a place as assistant editor of the *Eastern Argus* in 1820. In two years he purchased a half interest in the enterprise and became the editor.

His health sound, his career firmly established, on 6 March 1823, at the age of thirty, he married Elizabeth Oakes Prince. Sixteen, beautiful, and precocious, she aspired to an independent, intellectual life that her mother intended to thwart by urging the marriage. In time, however, as a writer in all genres, a lecturer, and a women's rights activist, Elizabeth Oakes Smith eclipsed her husband's achievements. Many years later, she wrote in her autobiography and often in her other writings of the profound loss of a woman's marrying young, but their years in Portland appear to have been happy. Their six sons, four of whom lived to adulthood (only one survived his father), were born there, and letters between Seba and Elizabeth during those years are loving, playful, and mutually supportive.

In 1826 Smith sold his interest in the *Argus* to pursue again (unsuccessfully) a career in belles lettres. In the fall of 1829, however, he became owner and editor of the weekly *Family Reader* and of the *Portland Courier,* the first daily newspaper north and east of Boston. In these journals in January 1830 appeared the first Jack Downing letters. Nearly thirty years later Smith said that he wrote them "partly for emolument, partly for amusement, and partly from a desire to exert a salutary influence upon public affairs and the politics of the country." A farm boy from the fictional Downingville, Maine, Jack Downing had come to Portland to sell a cartload of notions and stayed on to write home about the actions in the state legislature with a homespun style and innocence that gently satirized the political dickering and bickering there. The first letter, for example, reported the factional struggle to "seat" a Mr. Roberts. "And I thought it a needless piece of cruelty," Jack writes, "for they want crowded, and there was a number of seats empty."

With letters from others of the Downing clan, Smith, drawing upon recollections of family and friends from his boyhood village, soon created a local-color Downingville milieu that gave verisimilitude to Jack and his observations. Ignoring the warnings of his mother and cousin Nabby to return home (because of his dallying in Portland he has already lost his sweetheart to the schoolmaster), Jack stayed on in Portland to run for governor and in doing so became the satiric but good-natured embodiment of the perils of party politics that editor Smith deplored. Despite their parochial political concerns, the Downing letters entertained and were quickly reprinted in other papers. Then, in 1831, Smith gave Jack a national forum by sending him to Washington, D.C., to become the friend and adviser of President Andrew Jackson, closer even than the members of Jackson's famed Kitchen Cabinet. Unlike them, Jack had no apparent political agenda, and his letters appear as accurate, confidential accounts of what was really going on in Washington. As a result, they

Frontispiece by David Claypoole Johnston for Smith's first book,
The Life and Times of Major Jack Downing, of
Downingville *(1833)*

quickly gained a national audience and inspired letters by imitators who tried their hands as members of the far-flung Downingville family or even as Jack himself. Newspapers in the East, south to Kentucky and Georgia, and west to Indiana and Michigan reprinted these imitations, often on the same page as the originals. Throughout the decade, Jack became a popular phenomenon that appeared in many forms—in cartoons and broadsides, on stage, as editor of a songbook, and as author of a biography of Jackson. Newspaper editors printed anecdotal gossip about the fictitious Yankee, leading many readers to believe Downing was a real person.

Seba Smith did not invent the cracker-barrel philosopher (he tacitly acknowledged the work of George W. Arnold's "Joe Strickland" and Arnold's imitators in the mid 1820s), but he firmly established the tradition of that figure in American popular culture. The most popular imitation at the time was the work of Charles Augustus Davis, a New York Whig, whose letters signed "J. Downing" began to appear in the *New York Daily Advertiser* in July 1833. Davis's letters were more emphatically anti-Jackson than Smith's, and Davis did not write with Smith's good humor or attention to New England speech and character, but Davis more closely followed political events as they unfolded, and for that reason his letters rivaled the popularity of the originals.

Unable to copyright Jack's name or his original letters, appearing as they did in a newspaper, Smith could only protest against the "rascally counterfeiters," as Jack called them. To try to profit from the phenomenon he had created, Smith late in 1833 published a selection of his Downing letters as *The Life and Times of Major Jack Downing, of Downingville, Away Down East in the State of Maine. Written by Himself.* Illustrations by David Claypoole Johnston and a long introduction titled "My Life" gave Smith's own stamp to the book. Davis published his collection early the next year as *Letters of J. Downing,* and while both books went through many editions, Smith gained little profit, since his publisher's business failed late in 1834.

In *The Life and Times of Major Jack Downing,* Smith had treated President Jackson with good humor, at worst the weak-willed pawn of the Kitchen Cabinet, but in July 1834 Smith began another publishing venture, the weekly *Downingville Gazette,* to express his concern with Jackson's bold assertions of executive power. As editor, Downing declares his independence from the president and takes a stronger political position than he had in the earlier letters, but material such as schoolteacher Sarah Downing's history of the august family and Timothy Jones's local-color letters from a place called Wortleberry gave the popular *Downingville Gazette* the appearance of a true newspaper. Jack's cracker-barrel commentary, however, dwindled. After weeks of reporting Jack's mysterious, lingering illness, the *Downingville Gazette* (26 March 1836) graphically announced Smith's decision to drop the enterprise: a front page bordered in black reported Jack Downing's death at the age of forty-two, and a letter from Cousin Nabby dramatically recounted the deathbed scene.

The Smiths' relative prosperity and professional success in the early 1830s waned with the decade. Caught up in the fever of land speculation that swept much of the nation, Seba Smith had invested in a large tract of Maine land, but the property boom failed, forcing him to sell his Portland publications in 1837. The family moved to Boothbay, Maine, to live with Smith's parents, where Smith turned again to literature, completing and then discarding a novel and writing the first half of his book-length poem *Powhatan: A Metrical Romance in Seven Cantos* (1841) and other poems and stories that appeared later. The lure of quick riches still beckoned, but Seba Smith lacked the commercial acumen to be successful. Investing the last of his money in a machine invented by his brother-in-law to clean the fibers of Sea Island cotton, Smith and his family sailed to South Carolina to demonstrate the device in 1839, but it proved unaccept-

Jack Downing meeting an exhausted President Andrew Jackson, who is making an extended tour of the Northeast (illustration by David Claypoole Johnston in The Life and Times of Major Jack Downing, of Downingville*)*

able to the association that had offered a large reward for such a machine.

Sailing back north, the Smith family landed in New York, which became their permanent home and the place where Smith and his wife again sought their literary fortunes. Smith turned immediately to a genre he knew well, New England humor, writing in 1839 a series of letters for the *New York Mirror* as by John Smith, a cousin of Jack Downing. The series was published the same year as *John Smith's Letters with "Picters" to Match. Containing Reasons Why John Smith Should Not Change His Name; Miss Debby Smith's Juvenile Spirit; Together with the Only Authentic History Extant of the Late War in Our Disputed Territory.* In the *New World* the next year Smith brought back to life Jack himself, and although the description of the marvelous pills fleshing out Jack's skeleton is macabre, it affirms that this man is the "real" Jack Downing come to life, the one laid to rest by his original creator. Committed to establishing himself as a legitimate author of belles lettres, though, Smith found Jack something of a liability. He had worked long on *Powhatan,* his version of the Pocahontas–John Smith legend, and it received

generally good reviews that welcomed its contribution to a truly American literature. Edgar Allan Poe, however, dismissed it in *Graham's Magazine* (July 1841) with a review that surely rankled Smith, by referring to the author as "Jack Downing," who "never committed a greater mistake in his life than when he fancied himself a poet."

At first the family took in boarders to supplement an uncertain income from publishing, but by 1842 Smith reported that he and his wife could rely upon their writing for support, admittedly a precarious business. "It will do for a staff, but not for a crutch," he wrote to Rufus Griswold (11 August 1842). "However, since Mrs. Smith and myself have each a staff, if we walk together, I hope we may be able to keep from falling." Magazine publishing flourished in New York in the 1840s, and the Smiths found a ready market for the sentimental, romantic, and historical prose and verse that appealed to the popular taste of the time. Their work appeared in the best journals—including *The Knickerbocker, Graham's Magazine, Godey's Lady's Book,* and *The Southern Literary Messenger*—as well as in the many popular "giftbooks" in that day (beautifully bound, printed, and illustrated annual miscellanies of genteel, uplifting literature).

Although she had regretted leaving Portland, Maine, Elizabeth Oakes Smith, as she now began to call herself, found in New York the intellectual and literary fulfillment she had longed for since childhood, and, beginning with the popular and critical reception of *The Sinless Child and Other Poems* (1843), her literary reputation began to surpass her husband's. She enjoyed, although he did not, the active social and literary life that New York offered, and she held her own salon in their home, welcoming such writers as Edwin Forrest, Horace Greeley, William Cullen Bryant, Nathaniel Parker Willis, and Poe.

Upon arriving in New York, Seba Smith had sought an editorial position appropriate to his age and experience. He had approached Greeley, then the youthful editor of *The New Yorker,* who willingly published Smith's work but rejected the forty-nine-year-old as too old for a staff position. In March 1843, though, Smith found the place he wanted, editor of *The Rover,* a respectable "Weekly Magazine of Tales, Poetry, and Engravings," according to the subtitle. Much of the material consisted of reprinted work by well-known authors such as John Greenleaf Whittier, Bryant, and Longfellow, as well as the Smiths, who also contributed original works. Perhaps to distinguish his magazine from the hordes of similar publications and to attract readers to it, Smith turned again to Jack Downing, featuring his picture on the cover in March 1844 and then invoking his cracker-barrel voice in the cause of the Native American Party. Jack's homey, good-natured humor helped to undercut the often virulent opposition of the party (later known as the "Know Nothings") to Catholics and foreigners as voting blocs that nativists feared were too easily controlled by corrupt, urban Democrats. Many of Jack's letters were reprinted from the *Bunker Hill,* a political weekly ostensibly edited by Downing. Letters also appeared in a daily newspaper that Smith edited for a time, the *New York American Republican,* the journalistic voice of James Harper, the Native American Party candidate elected mayor in 1844.

For Smith the issues were not primarily political; from his early days as editor of the *Courier* he found party politics repellent and used the persona of Jack Downing as a comic, enthusiastic party loyalist to articulate in an ironic fashion Smith's broader concerns. Thus, whereas the outbreak of the Mexican War in 1846 led James Russell Lowell to create the cracker-barrel philosopher Hosea Biglow to challenge the morality of extending slavery into annexed territories, Smith used Jack Downing to expose the war in terms of the Democratic Party's expansionist version of Manifest Destiny, which Smith feared would overextend and weaken the power of the nation, leaving it open to foreign invasion. In the summer of 1847 the editors of the Washington, D.C., *National Intelligencer* accepted Smith's offer to make Jack their New York correspondent, and his letters appeared there intermittently to January 1856.

From July 1847 to December 1848 Jack appeared in his most effective role, as the intimate of a Democratic president, James K. Polk, providing a point of view on the chief executive "which that distinguished functionary had not thought necessary to confide to his most confidential friends," according to the editors of the *Intelligencer.* Jack's letters reporting his private talks with Polk portray him as the vain, weak leader of a party deeply divided, a president who admits to all of the accusations the Whig press leveled at him—that he failed to provide adequate support for the armies because he jealously resented the success of Generals Zachary Taylor and Winfield Scott, who as potential Whig presidential candidates posed a political threat; that he used the war to further his own political fortunes and those of the Democratic Party; and that he therefore temporized in making peace.

The election of Taylor in 1848 may have pleased Smith, but a Whig President did not provide the opportunity for Jack's type of wit. The next major series of letters, from 1852 to 1856, begins as the Democrats prepare for another presidential election. Jack reports the long struggle to choose a candidate in terms of a ploughing contest, each candidate representing a team and each of the interminable ballots a "pull." The winner, to the surprise of everyone, was the dark-horse nominee Franklin Pierce—who won the presidential election, giving Smith the opportunity to put Jack in the role he played so well—confidant of a Democrat president. Reporting the divisive party squabbling again provided a lively topic, but Smith's major concern was the administration's revival of an expansionist foreign policy. This time the prize was Cuba, and as Pierce's minister general and then president of the Ostend Congress and commander of naval forces ready to capture Cuba, Jack is in the thick of the jingoism and semisecret machinations to take the island from Spain that played perfectly to Smith's concerns. Jack's bellicose rhetoric of expansionism did not exaggerate the words of those who supported a foreign policy that ultimately proved embarrassing to Pierce and his party.

The letters in the *National Intelligencer* provided a political forum and some financial return for Smith in the late 1840s and 1850s, but he still sought what he

Sheet music for a march inspired by Smith's popular persona, circa 1834 (American Antiquarian Society)

considered a more legitimate legacy at the same time that he continued to struggle to make a living. To the end of his life he believed that his scholarly contribution to mathematics would do both, but the publication of *New Elements of Geometry* in 1850 was dismissed, despite his concerted efforts to promote it among educators and reviewers. Greater success came in 1854 with the publication of *'Way Down East; or, Portraitures of Yankee Life,* a collection of stories that had appeared in magazines over the years and that went through at least ten editions. The title page read "by Seba Smith, the original Jack Downing," a note that led some reviewers to conflate the author and the persona. The reviewer in *Putnam's* (February 1855) probed much closer to the complex ambiguities of that relationship

by referring to Jack as Smith's "straw auxiliary, or rather *doppelganger.*" For the most part, though, reviewers liked the intimate knowledge and quiet good humor of New England life that Smith brought to these tales. Indeed, if not for the overwhelming significance of his Jack Downing letters, scholars today might value them as foreshadowing the local-color movement later in the century.

Throughout most of the 1850s Smith also took on various editorial responsibilities. In 1858 he purchased *Emerson's Magazine and Putnam's Monthly,* and he, his wife, and their sons formed their own publishing firm, Oaksmith and Company. It published steel engravings, books by the Smiths, and attempted two magazines. Unable to pay for original contributions, however, the Smith family itself contributed most of the material. Both magazines failed by the end of 1859.

In *Emerson's Magazine* from October 1857 through June 1858, a series of Jack Downing letters appeared that had been selected from the 1833 *Life and Writings* and from the *National Intelligencer.* Published in 1859 as *My Thirty Years out of the Senate. By Major Jack Downing,* the title parodied *Thirty Years' View* (1854, 1856), the autobiography of Thomas Hart Benton, a powerful figure in the Democratic Party since Jackson's day. Jack Downing's book represented Seba Smith's own contribution to the political history of three decades. It marks as well his virtual retirement from a long literary career. Nearly seventy and in bad health, he moved to Patchogue, Long Island, in 1860. In a postscript to *My Thirty Years* Jack had written that he might contribute to a new magazine, the *Great Republic Monthly,* another Oaksmith and Company effort, but no further letters appeared. A series signed by Jack in the *New York Weekly Caucasian* from 1862 to 1864 (as a book it went through three editions) testified to the enduring appeal of the Yankee cracker-barrel philosopher that Seba Smith had created. These letters, however, were by another, anonymous, hand that paid no homage to the man who had pioneered cracker-barrel humor more than thirty years earlier. The nation scarcely noted Smith's death in July 1868. His wife wrote: "There is hardly a stone to his memory, except what was designed to be only a marking place where rest the ashes of a good and gifted man."

Biographies:

Mary Alice Wyman, *Two American Pioneers: Seba Smith and Elizabeth Oakes Smith* (New York: Columbia University Press, 1927);

Cameron C. Nickels, "Seba Smith Embattled," *Maine Historical Society Quarterly,* 13 (Summer 1973): 7–27.

References:

Walter Blair, *Horse Sense in American Humor* (Chicago: University of Chicago Press, 1942), pp. 55–65;

Cameron C. Nickels, *New England Humor from the Revolutionary War to the Civil War* (Knoxville: University of Tennessee Press, 1993), pp. 155–186;

Milton and Patricia Rickels, *Seba Smith* (New York: Twayne, 1977);

Constance M. Rourke, *American Humor: A Study of National Culture* (New York: Harcourt, Brace, 1931), pp. 23–27;

Daniel Royot, *L'Humour Americain, Des Puritans aux Yankees* (Lyon, France: Presses Universitaires de Lyon, 1980), pp. 256–273;

Jennette Tandy, *Crackerbox Philosophers in American Humor and Satire* (New York: Columbia University Press, 1931), pp. 24–37;

John William Ward, *Andrew Jackson, Symbol for an Age* (New York: Oxford University Press, 1955), pp. 79–91.

Papers:

The largest collection of Seba Smith's manuscripts and letters is in the Alderman Library at the University of Virginia.

Harriet Beecher Stowe

(14 June 1811 – 1 July 1896)

Barbara Ryan
University of Missouri, Kansas City

See also the Stowe entries in *DLB 1: The American Renaissance in New England; DLB 12: American Realists and Naturalists; DLB 42: American Writers for Children Before 1900; DLB 74: American Short-Story Writers Before 1880; DLB 189: American Travel Writers, 1850–1915;* and *DLB 239: American Women Prose Writers, 1820–1870.*

BOOKS: *Primary Geography for Children, on an Improved Plan* (Cincinnati: Corey & Fairbank, 1833);

Prize Tale: A New England Sketch (Lowell, Mass.: Gilman, 1834);

The Mayflower; or, Sketches of Scenes and Characters among the Descendants of the Pilgrims (New York: Harper, 1843); republished as *Tales and Sketches from Real Life* (London: T. Allman, 1845); enlarged as *The May Flower, and Miscellaneous Writings* (Boston: Phillips, Sampson, 1855); republished as *Tales and Sketches of New England Life* (London: Sampson Low, Son, 1855);

Uncle Tom's Cabin; or, Life among the Lowly, 2 volumes (Boston: Jewett / Cleveland: Jewett, Proctor & Worthington, 1852; London: Clarke, 1852);

Earthly Care, A Heavenly Discipline (Boston: John P. Jewett / Cleveland: Jewett, Proctor & Worthington, 1853 [i.e., 1852]);

The Two Altars; or, Two Pictures in One (Boston: Jewett, 1852);

A Key to Uncle Tom's Cabin; Presenting the Original Facts and Documents upon Which the Story is Founded. Together with Corroborative Statements Verifying the Truth of the Work (London: Sampson Low, Son, 1853; Boston: Jewett / Cleveland: Jewett, Proctor & Worthington / London: Sampson Low, Son, 1853);

Uncle Sam's Emancipation; Earthly Care, A Heavenly Discipline; and Other Sketches (Philadelphia: Hazard, 1853); enlarged as *Uncle Sam's Emancipation; Earthly Care, A Heavenly Discipline; and Other Tales and Sketches* (London: Nelson, 1853);

Sunny Memories of Foreign Lands, 2 volumes (London: Sampson Low, Son, 1854; Boston: Phillips, Sampson / New York: Derby, 1854);

Harriet Beecher Stowe

First Geography for Children, edited by Catharine E. Beecher (Boston: Phillips, Sampson / New York: Derby, 1855); revised as *A New Geography for Children: Revised by an English Lady* (London: Sampson Low, Son, 1855);

Dred: A Tale of the Great Dismal Swamp, 2 volumes (London: Sampson Low, Son / Edinburgh: Constable, 1856; Boston: Phillips, Sampson, 1856); republished as *Nina Gordon: A Tale of the Great Dismal Swamp,* 2 volumes (Boston: Ticknor & Fields, 1866);

Our Charley, and What To Do with Him (Boston: Phillips, Sampson, 1858; London: Routledge, 1859);

The Minister's Wooing (London: Sampson Low, Son, 1859; New York: Derby & Jackson, 1859);

The Pearl of Orr's Island: A Story of the Coast of Maine (2 parts, London: Sampson Low, Son, 1861, 1862; 1 volume, Boston: Ticknor & Fields, 1862);

Agnes of Sorrento (London: Smith, Elder, 1862; Boston: Ticknor & Fields, 1862);

A Reply to "The Affectionate and Christian Address of Many Thousands of Women of Great Britain and Ireland, to Their Sisters, The Women of the United States of America" (London: Sampson Low, Son, 1863);

House and Home Papers, as Christopher Crowfield (Boston: Ticknor & Fields, 1865; London: Sampson Low, Son & Marston, 1865);

Stories about Our Dogs (Edinburgh: Nimmo, 1865);

Little Foxes; or, The Insignificant Little Habits Which Mar Domestic Happiness (London: Bell & Daldy / Sampson Low, Son & Marston, 1866); republished as *Little Foxes,* as Crowfield (Boston: Ticknor & Fields, 1866);

Religious Poems (Boston: Ticknor & Fields, 1867); republished as *Light after Darkness: Religious Poems* (London: Sampson Low, Son & Marston / Bell & Daldy, 1867);

The Daisy's First Winter, and Other Stories (Edinburgh: Nimmo, 1867);

Queer Little People (Boston: Ticknor & Fields, 1867; London: Sampson Low, Son & Marston, 1867; enlarged edition, New York: Fords, Howard & Hulbert, 1867 [i.e., 1881]); republished as *Queer Little Folks* (London: Nelson, 1886);

The Chimney-Corner (London: Sampson Low, Son & Marston / Bell & Daldy, 1868; as Crowfield, Boston: Ticknor & Fields, 1868);

Men of Our Times; or, Leading Patriots of the Day: Being Narratives of the Lives and Deeds of Statesmen, Generals, and Orators (Hartford, Conn.: Hartford Publishing Co. / New York: Denison / Chicago: Stoddard, 1868); enlarged as *The Lives and Deeds of Our Self-Made Men* (Hartford, Conn.: Worthington, Dustin / Cincinnati: Queen City Publishing Co. / Chicago: Parker, 1872);

Oldtown Folks (3 volumes, London: Sampson Low, Son & Marston, 1869; 1 volume, Boston: Fields, Osgood, 1869);

The American Woman's Home; or, Principles of Domestic Science: Being a Guide to the Formation and Maintenance of Economical, Healthful, Beautiful, and Christian Homes, by Stowe and Beecher (New York: Ford / Boston: Brown, 1869);

Lady Byron Vindicated: A History of the Byron Controversy, from Its Beginning in 1816 to the Present Time (Boston: Fields, Osgood, 1870; London: Sampson Low, Son & Marston, 1870);

Little Pussy Willow (Boston: Fields, Osgood, 1870; London: Sampson Low, Son & Marston, 1870; enlarged edition, New York: Fords, Howard & Hulbert, 1880);

Pink and White Tyranny (London: Sampson Low, Son & Marston, 1871); republished as *Pink and White Tyranny: A Society Novel* (Boston: Roberts, 1871);

My Wife and I; or, Harry Henderson's History (New York: Ford, 1871; London: Sampson Low, Marston, Low & Searle, 1871);

Oldtown Fireside Stories (London: Sampson Low, Marston, Low & Searle, 1871; Boston: Osgood, 1872); enlarged as *Sam Lawson's Oldtown Fireside Stories* (Boston: Osgood, 1872; enlarged again, Boston: Houghton, Mifflin, 1881);

Palmetto-Leaves (Boston: Osgood, 1873; London: Sampson Low, Marston, Low & Searle, 1873);

Woman in Sacred History: A Series of Sketches Drawn from Scriptural, Historical, and Legendary Sources (London: Sampson Low, Marston, Low & Searle, 1874; New York: Ford, 1874; enlarged edition, New York: Ford, 1874); original edition republished as *Bible Heroines: Being Narrative Biographies of Prominent Hebrew Women* (New York: Fords, Howard & Hulbert, 1878);

We and Our Neighbors; or, The Records of an Unfashionable Street: A Novel (London: Sampson Low, Marston, Low & Searle, 1875; New York: Ford, 1875);

Betty's Bright Idea. Also, Deacon Pitkin's Farm, and the First Christmas of New England (New York: Ford, 1876 [i.e., 1875]; London: Sampson Low, Marston, Low & Searle, 1876);

Footsteps of the Master (New York: Ford, 1877; London: Sampson Low, Marston, Low & Searle, 1877);

Poganuc People: Their Loves and Lives (New York: Fords, Howard & Hulbert, 1878; London: Sampson Low, Marston, Low & Searle, 1878);

A Dog's Mission; or, The Story of the Old Avery House. And Other Stories (New York: Fords, Howard & Hulbert, 1880; London: Nelson, 1886);

Regional Sketches: New England and Florida, edited by John R. Adams (New Haven, Conn.: College & University Press, 1972).

Collection: *The Writings of Harriet Beecher Stowe,* Riverside Edition, 16 volumes (Boston & New York: Houghton, Mifflin, 1896).

Once feted as the author of the best-selling novel of the nineteenth century and among the best-paid writers of her day, Harriet Beecher Stowe fell into critical obscurity when literary modernists dismissed sentimental literature. More recently, Stowe's writings have been praised as leading exemplars of both sentimental and regional fiction, while Stowe herself has been designated a leading architect of what might be called "the New England myth." Her vision of Yankee village life, which rested on a beatific image of Connecticut, Massachusetts, and a Maine coast free of smoky factories and satanic mills, charmed a readership growing uneasily conscious of industrialization after the Civil War. Renewed attention to Stowe's regionalist interests has led to a new appreciation of this anxiety and of Stowe's significance for the Boston-based literary culture that dominated the later nineteenth century. Much of her capital, for the tastemaking group called the "Boston Brahmins," rested on the phenomenal success of *Uncle Tom's Cabin; or, Life among the Lowly* (1852). Though *Uncle Tom's Cabin* was not the first antislavery novel, it was incontrovertibly the most engaging, and it sold phenomenally well.

Born in Litchfield, Connecticut, on 14 June 1811 to well-known Presbyterian minister Lyman Beecher and his wife Roxana (Foote) Beecher, Harriet Elizabeth Beecher was raised in an atmosphere of unblinking Calvinist piety. Though she left home at the age of thirteen to attend her sister Catharine's school for teenaged girls, Harriet did not escape the effects of her demanding father and doctrinaire upbringing until she was well into middle age. That she wanted to escape both influences is a finding on which biographers concur, citing her neurotic mood swings, severe self-reproaches, and eventual admission to the Episcopalian Church. The consensus is that Stowe's father, who was one of the best-known preachers in America, set impossibly high standards that left most of his eleven children driven, self-doubting, and distraught. Despite these pressures, or because of them, several of Lyman Beecher's children became extremely successful. The eldest, Catharine, became known as an educator, an advocate of training schools for female teachers, author of the best-selling housekeeping guide of the century, and an innovative domestic architect; while Henry Ward Beecher, who was much younger, became the famous (and later perhaps notorious) pastor of Plymouth Church in Brooklyn. The family acquired a few scars along the way; one Beecher died of a self-inflicted gunshot wound that may not have been accidental, and another came to believe that she would lead the world after an imminent revolution in gender politics took place. The effects of rigid and patriarchal religious training were less obvious in Harriet's case, but modern scholars have conjectured that in her novels she tried to adapt and regender her father's ministerial authority.

As a teenaged member of Lyman Beecher's crowded household, Harriet was a voracious reader noted for her prodigious memory but a quiet girl who

Calvin Stowe, the widower who married Harriet Beecher in 1836

did not often impress outsiders as brilliant or witty. Her father saw her special qualities but had trouble appreciating them in a daughter. "Harriet is a great genius," he avowed, in a private letter. "I would give a hundred dollars if she was a boy & Henry a girl—She is as odd as she is intelligent & studious. . . ." Genius or not, Harriet was educated at minimal expense and in a manner that rested entirely on Catharine's devotion to her younger sister's gifts. As headmistress of the Hartford Female Seminary, Catharine was in a good position to set her sister a rigorous study schedule; it suited Harriet well and even left time for her to edit the *School Gazette*. An apt scholar, Harriet was soon engaged to teach religion and Latin to the other girls. Interested also in European languages, painting and drawing, and rhetoric and composition, she appeared set for a schoolteaching career when she and Catharine moved with their father to Cincinnati in 1832.

The move was made in the interests of Lyman Beecher's hopes of converting the West to Calvinism, but Catharine and Harriet soon established yet another school. Harriet turned spare moments to a modest authorial career—so modest, in fact, that her *Primary Geography for Children, on an Improved Plan* (1833) appeared under Catharine's name. Catharine returned the favor years later when she put Harriet's name on two domestic advice guides with which her sister had little or nothing to do. But even before then, strong sales of *Primary Geography for Children* led to reprints that acknowledged the younger sister's work. Other literary efforts of this period included a character essay that

Stowe with her twin daughters, Harriet (Hattie) and Eliza

Harriet based on Lyman Beecher's stories about his adoptive father; "A New England Sketch" (April 1834; later "Uncle Tim") won a local literary prize and an honorarium of $50. Reminiscences of old New England were popular with the members of the Semi-Colon Club, the Cincinnati literary society that gave Stowe a chance to hone her writing skills in a pleasantly social atmosphere. The club was also a haven when students at Lyman Beecher's seminary revolted and a large number decamped. The quarrel was over Lane Seminary's position on slavery, which was moderate rather than committed to abolition. When the rebels left Lane under the leadership of a fiery speaker named Theodore Weld, revenues dwindled; worse, Lane and Lyman were scorned as placatory toward slaveholders and intolerant of high-minded students' views. This debacle did not set Harriet against the fight to end slavery; on the contrary, she was soon swept into the partisanship that resulted when antiabolitionist mobs started rioting and deaths ensued. Though her most memorable publication of this period is an antimob satire rather than a statement of opposition to slavery per se, Harriet Beecher had begun to move in the direction that later made her a household name.

On 6 January 1836 she married Calvin Stowe, a childless widower who was a Bible scholar in her father's school; as his wife, she gave birth to seven children in fifteen years. Biographers question how much romance there was to Stowe's relationship with her husband, since the pair first grew close while they mourned his first wife, who had been Harriet's friend. Joan D. Hedrick suggests that Harriet was attracted by less dynamic and ambitious men, but Hedrick also acknowledges that the courtship was so restrained that newspapers were uncertain which of the Beecher sisters had been Calvin's choice. The newlyweds immediately parted so that Calvin could go to Europe on a book-buying tour; in his absence, Harriet grew more agitated about slavery but confined her literary efforts to venues such as *Godey's Lady's Book* and the *New-York Evangelist.* In 1843 she collected the best of her early work in *The Mayflower; or, Sketches of Scenes and Characters among the Descendants of the Pilgrims.* As the subtitle indicates, New England memories played a large part in this book; when she revised it, years later, Stowe asked readers to recall "the good old catechizing, churchgoing, school going, orderly times" of the New England past. She did not always dwell on recollections of her old home, however; she also wrote consolatory poetry, evangelical tracts, temperance fiction, so-called parables, and a few comments on the passing scene.

The profits from these efforts eked out her husband's professorial salary, and Calvin Stowe was proud of his wife's gifts: "You," he announced, "must be a *literary woman.*" His busy wife took this opportunity to make some demands. "If I am to write, I must have a room to myself, which shall be *my* room," she told her husband. "I can put a stove in it. I have bought a cheap carpet for it, and I have furniture enough at home to furnish it comfortably, and I only beg in addition that you will let me change the glass door from the nursery into that room and keep my plants there, and then I shall be quite happy." This letter suggests that while Stowe's early publications were a boost to the household budget, her short pieces also granted her time and space to ponder extradomestic issues. Family members agreed that Stowe was not much of a housekeeper and that servant management fretted her mercurial nature. "What shall we do?" Stowe's fictive homemaker wailed, in an early *Godey's Lady's Book* story. "Shall we go for slavery, or shall we give up houses, have no furniture to take care of—keep merely a bag of meal, a porridge pot, and a pudding stick, and sit in our tent door in real patriarchal independence?" Though Henry David Thoreau might have thought the latter suggestion worth pursuing, Stowe intended her readers to laugh ruefully at the real exigencies of managing the sorts of workers found even in less-wealthy homes. Decades later, in

The house in Brunswick, Maine, where Stowe wrote Uncle Tom's Cabin *(from Charles Edward Stowe,*
Harriet Beecher Stowe: The Story of Her Life, *1911)*

"The House and Home Papers," the best-known anti-slavery novelist of the nation put the longing for docile cooks and maids into other women's minds. "I have heard more than one lady declare," Stowe announced, "that she didn't care if it was unjust, she should like to have slaves rather than be plagued with servants who had so much liberty."

This sort of subterfuge always characterized Stowe's personal interactions, but letters from the 1840s indicate a burgeoning sense of authorship and growing certainty of her ability to contribute to the household income. The confidence suggested in these missives sustained Stowe during the tiring years of young motherhood; after the twins, Eliza and Hattie, were born in September 1836, Stowe gave birth to Henry (January 1838), Frederick (May 1840), Georgianna (July 1843), and Samuel Charles (January 1848). Caring for this brood was a full-time job, but this decade was also marked by grave religious uncertainty for Stowe. The most recent Stowe biography explains this uneasy period as a serious and imaginative woman's difficult trial of the perfectionist ideas that troubled American evangelicals in the antebellum

years. Finding perfectionism empty, Stowe grew depressed until her quest was relieved by a delayed but powerful religious conversion, in the orthodox Calvinist manner, which brought her to a deep belief in the doctrine of the soul's damnation and a just God's enormous mercy to a sinful world. "The will of Christ seems to me the steady pulse of my being," she told one of her half brothers. "I go because I can not help it. Skeptical doubt can not exist," she concluded, speaking of her late but ardent conversion. "My *all* changed."

Though this certainty was no transient product of religious enthusiasm, the daily grind sometimes could still leave Stowe depressed and tired. After a bad cholera scare in 1845 she set off for a long cure at a Vermont water spa. At this point Calvin Stowe recorded his views of his wife's troubles. One problem, he thought, was her own personality: "you are good, and kind, and devotional, with a rich and glowing soul," he told her, "but you are not one of the *resting sort*—some wheel must be buzzing where you are." The other problem he noted was Harriet's domineering sister: "I seriously think it to be just as much your duty to renounce Cate Beecher and all her school-marms, as it is to renounce the devil and all his work. . . ." Harriet laughed off the latter criticism but was soon waving Calvin off to a water cure of his own. He was still in Vermont when, amidst the summer sicknesses of 1849, his just-toddling youngest son caught cholera and died. Harriet was dazed with grief over the loss of her child. "At last it is over," she wrote to her spouse:

> and our dear little one is gone from us. He is now among the blessed. My Charley–my beautiful, loving, gladsome baby, so loving, so sweet, so full of life and hope and strength–never was he anything to me but a comfort. He has been my pride and joy. Many a heartache has he cured for me.

Stowe's mourning for this first Charley was intense and slow, but Calvin was soon able to provide a piece of extremely heartening news: he had been offered a post at his alma mater in Maine. The Stowes could return to the New England way of life that Harriet Stowe loved.

Established as a faculty wife at Bowdoin College, she bore her second Charley, Charles Edward, in July 1850. (This last child was the "Our Charley" who became nationally known, in fictive form; later, he was a Congregationalist minister and his mother's first biographer.) She also revived her literary career, although she did not plunge immediately into writing the novel that is still considered her greatest work. First, she started a small private school in her new home; only then did she become a regular contributor to the *National Era,* the weekly paper that soon ran installments of *Uncle Tom's Cabin.* In the meantime, Stowe revived her painting and drawing, started reading Sir Walter Scott's novels to her children, and developed a taste for the Maine seaside. Forrest Wilson calls this period the happiest in Stowe's life both before and after the publication of *Uncle Tom's Cabin,* though it was not the most prosperous; he notes, too, that Stowe left behind in Ohio no friends with whom she bothered to correspond. She was, Wilson observes, "what would be known today as a 'difficult' person. Richly as her nature was endowed, it lacked the gift of friendship. Respect, even veneration, came to her in full but never personal popularity." The usual explanation of Stowe's aloof demeanor is that it was an intense version of the family loyalty that characterized the Beecher progeny, but Stowe herself suggested that a natural reserve was the problem: "It costs me an effort to express feeling of any kind." Welcomed by the friendly Bowdoin faculty, she overcame enough of her watchfulness to make good friends and keep up a merry social round. By the spring of 1851 she began to shape the novel that she liked to recall as scrawled by her but written by the will of Almighty God. "The Lord Himself wrote it," Stowe said, of *Uncle Tom's Cabin,* "I was but an instrument in His hands."

Considering the pace at which Stowe composed, divine inspiration has seemed a likely explanation for the international appeal of her first novel. Its immediate political motivation was, however, to decry the federal legislation that forced Americans to confront the truth that two labor organizations existed in one nation. Most crucially, the Fugitive Slave Law was understood by opponents of slavery as forcing residents of the "free" states to act as accomplices to slaveholders' laws; certainly the law effected this result, since Boston papers noted a rash of court cases in which Northern judges remanded fugitives to slave catchers' custody. At the same time, abolitionists better versed than Stowe in the realities of American labor argued that the Fugitive Slave Law merely publicized a long-standing contradiction that those who did not actually own slaves had preferred to ignore. Denied this luxury with the passage of the new law, even nonradicals were outraged. "Hattie," a family member asserted at this time, "if I could use a pen as you can, I would write something that would make this whole nation feel what an accursed thing slavery is." In family memory, the result of this letter was a vow. "I *will* write something," Stowe declared; "I will if I live." This promise was rewarded by a vision that came to her at church; in it, Stowe reported, she saw a gentle and pious old man, a slave, being beaten to death by a low white man. The same day she wrote down the death scene that serves as the climax of *Uncle Tom's Cabin*–naming each character, describing Tom's Christian forgiveness, and concluding with the conversion of his slave companions who had seemed to be insensate brutes. When she read this sketch aloud to her children, they responded with the praise of tears– "Oh, mamma!" one is supposed to have wept, "slavery is the most cruel thing in the world!" Stowe never explained why, after getting this response, she put the brief vignette aside. The rest of the story is that her husband noticed her sketch a few weeks later and insisted that she carry it through. "Hattie, you must go on with it," he is reported to have said. "The Lord intends it so."

Stowe wrote to her editor in March 1851 with little sense of the novel that eventuated. "Dear Sir," she advised,

> I am at present occupied upon a story which will be a much longer one than any I have ever written, embracing a series of sketches which give the lights and shadows of the "patriarchal institution," written either from observation, incidents which have occurred in the sphere of my personal knowledge, or in the knowledge of my friends. I shall show the *best side* of the thing, and something *faintly approaching the worst.*

Uncle Tom

The cabin of Uncle Tom was a small log building close adjoining to "the house" — as the negro always par excellence designates the masters dwelling — In front it had a neat garden patch where strawberries rhaspberries & a variety of fruits flourished under careful tending — down The whole front of the dwelling was covered with a large big scarlet nonia & a native multiflora rose which entwisling & interlacing left scarce a vistage of the building to be seen & in the spring was redundant with its clusters of roses & in summer so too balious with the scarlet tubes of the honeysue Various brilliant annuals such as marigolds four oclocks & petunias found here and there a thrifty corner to vegetate unfold their glories & were the delight & pride of aunt Chloe's heart

Let us enter the dwelling — The evening meal at "the house" is over & Aunt Chloe who presides over its preparation as head cook has left to inferior officers in the kitchen the business of clearing away & washing dishes & come out into her own snug territory to "get her old man's supper" & therefore doubt not that it is her you see by the fire place presiding with anxious interest

Page from the manuscript for Uncle Tom's Cabin *(from Charles Edward Stowe,*
Harriet Beecher Stowe: The Story of Her Life, *1911)*

Describing herself as a "painter" whose "object will be to hold up in the most lifelike and graphic manner possible Slavery, its reverses, changes, and the negro character.... There is no arguing with *pictures,* and everybody is impressed by them, whether they mean to be or not." Stowe piqued enough interest to earn $300. This sum was good money for the pamphletlike tale that her editor envisioned, but not much for the thick two-volume novel that actually took shape over the coming year. Indeed, despite the gigantic sales that made *Uncle Tom's Cabin* a publishing marvel—ten thousand copies sold in the first week, and thirty times that number by the end of its first year—Stowe never made anything close to the profits of the book in its multiple new editions and translations. One reason was that the Stowes did not have enough spare cash to pay half the printing costs and thus receive the usual share of royalties; the second was that, as was common in the years before the United States passed a copyright law, this popular novel was pirated in Britain and Europe and even in some Western states.

Letters to the *National Era* were the first clue that Stowe was at work on a literary sensation. In addition to sending letters of praise and thanks to Stowe, readers expressed dismay if any issue of the *Era* appeared without a chapter of her story, for as one fan averred, "'Uncle Tom's Cabin' increases in interest and pathos with each successive number." Readers in the South were also enraptured at this early stage, and the *Era* was soon swamped by inquiries about Stowe's plans to publish the novel in book form. Yet, when Southern reaction began to turn against *Uncle Tom's Cabin*—after critics found that Stowe's story was fomenting sectionalist enmity—publishers balked at producing a book likely to affront many readers. The publisher who did take the plunge was said to have been persuaded by his wife; interestingly enough, John Jewett did not reap profits either; his firm went bankrupt only a few years after his greatest publishing coup. By the time three complete editions had sold out in a matter of weeks, the sales figures for *Uncle Tom's Cabin* had gone beyond record-breaking into astounding and unbelievable, as readers thronged to own Stowe's book.

One example of the emotional appeal in the novel is the scene in which a Kentucky household is threatened by the master's need to pay off pressing debts. Though Mr. Shelby does not want to sell his most fungible assets, he sees no option if he hopes to keep up his pleasant farm and comfortable way of life. Blind to all but his own interests and ignoring his wife's remonstrances, he resolves to sell the winsome young son of a beautiful and modest house slave named Eliza. Guided by morality and a loving heart, Mrs. Shelby helps Eliza run away, carrying young Harry in her arms. The intimation of loving bonds between mistresses and house slaves may

not always or often be borne out by the historical record, but the scene was a powerful statement of women's supposed moral power and an indictment of wrongheaded men's ability to endanger domestic bliss. The power is vaunted and the indictment affirmed when Eliza risks her own life to carry little Harry across a frozen river to Ohio, which was a free state. Eventually, the pair emigrate to Canada, abandoning "the land of the free." If, however, Eliza's race across the cracking ice floes is one of the early highlights of the novel, even it cannot match the scene in which Uncle Tom accepts that he is to be sold away from his wife and children as a sort of sacrificial lamb. His wife is not so quick to accept his submissive departure as the clear call of Christian duty. "Well, old man!" Aunt Chloe exclaims,

There's time for ye,—be off with Lizy,—you've got a pass to come and go any time. Come, bustle up, and I'll get your things together."

Tom slowly raised his head, and looked sorrowfully but quietly around, and said,—

"No, no,—I an't going. Let Eliza go,—it's her right! I wouldn't be the one to say no,—'t an't in natur for her to stay; but you heard what she said! If I must be sold, or all the people on the place, and everything go to rack, why, let me be sold. I s'pose I can b'ar it as well as any on 'em," he added, while something like a sob and a sigh shook his broad, rough chest convulsively. "Mas'r always found me on the spot,—he always will. I never have broke trust, nor used my pass no ways contrary to my word, and I never will. It's better for me alone to go, than to break up the place and sell all. Mas'r an't to blame, Chloe, and he'll take care of you and the poor"—

Here he turned to the rough trundle-bed full of little woolly heads, and broke fairly down.

Though Tom's meekness does not save him from the indignities of the slave coffle or the uncertainty of a public sale, it wins him the love of the angelic child he eventually serves in Louisiana. The victim of an irreversible and wasting disease, Little Eva begs her doting father to reconsider his slaveholding ways, and he agrees. Unfortunately, the well-intentioned Augustine St. Clare is dilatory in carrying out his promise and dies before signing the papers that will manumit his slaves. At that juncture Tom is sold away to a large plantation, where his preaching and piety enrage the superstitious and alcoholic Yankee who owns him and treats him as a thing. The scene in which Simon Legree beats Tom to death is the one that Stowe claimed to have seen while in church. Although Stowe made clear that not all slaves were as acquiescent to their unjust fates, nonetheless, her protagonist's Christ-like death gave rise to the scornful epithet "Uncle Tom."

From contemporaries, scorn had less to do with the idea of a pious slave and more to do with the charge that *Uncle Tom's Cabin* was a tissue of abolitionist lies. Probably President Abraham Lincoln did not greet Stowe with the words, "So this is the little lady who made this big war?" Yet, Stowe's novel did more than any other text, including narratives by former slaves, to incite the animus that erupted in civil war. Stowe emphasized that the most depraved slaveholding character is Northern born, while the most color-prejudiced is a Vermont woman presented as ridiculously stiff and prim. These portraits may seem at odds with the rest of Stowe's promotion of an idyllic New England past, but she never denied that a specifically Yankee fault was narrow-mindedness coupled with intolerance for those perceived as different.

Just how much readers noted Stowe's attempt at evenhanded characterizations is not known, but the publication of the book was followed by a tidal wave of commercial products that claimed some link to Uncle Tom. Not only was the novel abridged for children, illustrated, set to music, and dramatized, but it was also translated into forty-two languages—including Javanese, Hindu, Armenian, Welsh, Wallachian, Illyrian, Servian, Russian, and an Hungarian dialect. In addition, its most famous scenes were turned into decorative motifs for handkerchiefs, cutlery, statuary, wallpaper, and games. Even more popular in Great Britain than in the United States, *Uncle Tom's Cabin* delighted Queen Victoria and her family, though the British monarch could not say so openly for fear of roiling international relations. Queen Victoria found a way around this impasse when Stowe traveled to England to gain a British copyright on her next novel, *Dred: A Tale of the Great Dismal Swamp* (1856); though the meeting between Stowe and the Queen was staged to appear accidental, it was not. Hobnobbing with nobles and literary greats on each of her three trips abroad, Stowe found herself far more a literary lion than a target of criticism as she rode out the controversies that arose from her first novel with sangfroid and apparent ease. Her childhood training in articulate and pointed debate proved to her advantage, for Stowe never shied away from a confrontation as long as it was conducted in print.

Print was her weapon, for instance, when she published a compendium of atrocity stories called *A Key to Uncle Tom's Cabin; Presenting the Original Facts and Documents upon Which the Story is Founded. Together with Corroborative Statements Verifying the Truth of the Work* (1853) as a reply to critics who doubted the veracity of the scenes depicted in her novel. Scholars have learned that she did most of her research on actual conditions in the slave states after her

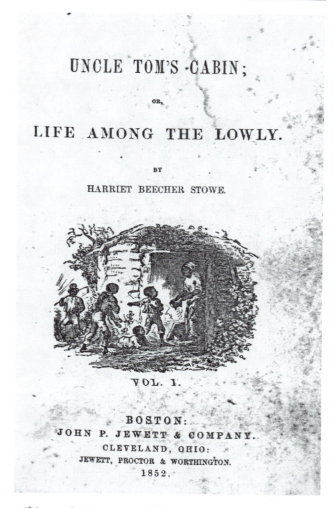

Title page for the novel in which Stowe attempted to depict slavery in "the most lifelike and graphic manner possible"

novel had proved a hit, but her attitude was that as long as *A Key to Uncle Tom's Cabin* supported her arguments, she could not be accused of spinning wild tales. Still, certain discrepancies between Stowe's recollections and the facts are worth pointing out. For instance, though she liked to say that Uncle Tom's character was based on a real man named Josiah Henson, who had been a slave, that story has been shown to be improbable at best because Stowe came to know Henson's story too late for it to serve as inspiration. Another sort of posturing appears in the now-famous self-description that she sent out to a friendly inquirer. "So you want to know something about what sort of woman I am," Stowe said, adding,

you shall have statistics free of charge.

To begin, then I am a little bit of a woman—somewhat more than 40—about as thin & dry as a pinch of snuff never very much to look at in my best days—& looking like a used-up article now.

Stowe in 1853 (portrait by George Richmond; from Charles Edward Stowe, Life of Harriet Beecher Stowe Compiled from Her Letters and Journals by Her Son, *1889)*

Despite the self-deprecation Stowe was far from "used-up" at this point. After her return from her first trip abroad–which included stays on ducal estates and sojourns in Germany, Switzerland, Italy, and France–she published her travel letters as *Sunny Memories of Foreign Lands* (1854). On trips to Europe, accompanied by family members, Stowe befriended Robert and Elizabeth Barrett Browning and George Eliot, with whom she discussed the popular topic of "spirit-rappings," a movement that was boosted as new proof of the soul's immortality. The possibility of communicating with the spirits of the dead was a lifelong interest about which Stowe commented in scattered essays and letters; she considered such communication one of the gifts lauded in the Bible, but recognized how easily appearances of such graces could be duplicated by charlatans anxious to prey on the weak. More immediately pressing in the 1850s was the ongoing conflict over slavery. Once back from her first trip to Europe, Stowe set to work on a second novel about slavery.

Critics agree that hasty composition spoiled *Dred,* the story of a faithful slave who knows himself to be his mistress's half brother. When she dies, still unaware of the bond, Harry Gordon becomes the property of an evil half brother who is driven by hatred of Harry's intelligence and industry. This plot begins to enact a shrewd critique of the idea that slaveholders lived in harmonious plantation "families" and brings up the topic of slave militancy, but its title character is a completely unbelievable amalgam of the way in which Stowe imagined Nat Turner and her image of a prophetic Jeremiah. More coherent, if stereotypical, is Tiff, a comic but still pious version of Uncle Tom, whose selfless concern for the young white children left in his care leads him to forego the chance at freedom that falls within his grasp. Tiff's loyalty is rewarded by the children's lifelong devotion, an affection that leaves unanswered the question of Tiff's eventual legal status.

Stowe was clearer about the status of the slave character Candace in *The Minister's Wooing* (1859), since this able but "uppish" cook is freed with an almost careless flick of her master's hand. More readers would have responded then, as now, to the knowledge that this novel was, in part, a product of Stowe's grief for her favorite son, Henry, who drowned in 1857. An undergraduate at Dartmouth College, Henry was caught in the strong currents of the Connecticut River just after his mother returned from her second trip overseas. The Stowes were heartbroken at the news of this tragedy, but the trauma of Henry's death was heightened by his family's not knowing whether or not he had undergone the conversion experience central to the old-line Congregationalist religion. Having experienced her own conversion after years of paying lip service to the idea, Stowe had hoped that her favorite son would find the same certainty. "Oh my darling," she had implored the laggard, "I want you to choose my Redeemer–your Father's & mother's God for your own." In her first New England novel Stowe addressed the conflict between rigid Calvinist tenets and the anxious maternal heart in the characters of Dr. Hopkins, a saintly but cold man of God, and the serving woman who knows how to comfort a mistress whose beloved son has died. The gender split is important, but so is Candace's being a just-manumitted slave whose wise solace affirms the racist idea of an all-loving chattel "mammy." Petting the woman who is on the verge of going mad with fear for her son's unshriven death, Candace adduces "dar's a dreful mistake somewhar" because

de Lord ain't like what ye tink–He *loves* ye, honey! Why, jes' feel how I loves ye,–poor old black Candace,– an' I ain't better'n Him as made me! Who was it wore de crown o' thorns, lamb?–who was it sweat great drops o' blood?–who was it said, "Father, forgive dem?" Say, honey! wasn't it de Lord dat made ye?—Dar, dar, now ye'r' cryin'—cry away, and ease yer poor little heart!

Candace turns out to be right that the son thought to have died will be "one o' de' lect"; at which point he is ready to marry the young heroine of the novel. "I do not need any arguments now to convince me that the Bible is from above," he tells the pretty young New Englander who turned his thoughts to the salvation of his soul,

> There is a great deal in it that I cannot understand, a great deal that seems to me inexplicable; but all I can say is, that I have tried its directions, and find that in my case they do work—that it is a book that I can live by; and that is enough for me.

For doctrinaire Calvinists, this revelation suggested that conversion could take place in ways hidden from loved ones at home; yet, the more obvious political point was that the wooing minister, who ended up jilted, did not know much about loving hearts. Within a few years of publishing this novel, Stowe began to attend Episcopalian services; she waited until the defection would not embarrass her father or her spouse. Since a kinder, gentler Christianity filled the spirit of the Civil War years and postbellum era, Stowe showed once again that she had a finger on the popular pulse.

As reformist theodicy or belletristic literature, *The Minister's Wooing* struck discerning readers as Stowe's finest work to date. John Ruskin praised it highly, and James Russell Lowell agreed. "What especially charmed me in the new story," Lowell told Stowe, "was, that you had taken your stand on New England ground." This praise did not guide all of Stowe's future works; her next book was a tale set in Italy. But *Agnes of Sorrento* (1862) was not her best work, and *The Pearl of Orr's Island: A Story of the Coast of Maine* (1861, 1862) was flawed as well. If, as is sometimes suggested, this story of the Northeast coast is the closest thing that Stowe wrote to a fictive autobiography, it opens fittingly with energy and grace, but it falters badly about one-third of the way through. Sarah Orne Jewett, who became famous for her own depictions of life in the coastal villages of Maine, praised the first few chapters of *The Pearl of Orr's Island* but mourned the novel that could have been if Stowe had been able to focus her energies.

One distraction was, of course, that a bloody war had been declared and, with a son of her own in the Union Army, Stowe chose to write less serious and sustained journalistic work. She kept busy during the war years with columns and articles for *The Atlantic Monthly* and for venues such as *Our Young Folks,* the *New York Ledger,* and the *Watchman and Reflector.* Though her work for *The Atlantic Monthly* was only columns of "spicy sprightly writing," Stowe pleased many readers as she affirmed

Stowe with her father, Lyman Beecher, and her brother Henry Ward Beecher

"the need of a little gentle household merriment & talk of common things." Both "The House and Home Papers" and "The Chimney-Corner" were collected and republished in book form. The latter appeared in two collections, the first titled *House and Home Papers* (1865), the second titled *Little Foxes; or, The Insignificant Little Habits Which Mar Domestic Happiness* (1866). *The Chimney-Corner* was published in book form in 1868. The book forms of both series were also written in an unwonted masculine guise. Though Stowe's publisher hinted that fans might have enjoyed a new novel from her, the occasional nature of a column suited the writer, who was busy moving into an elaborate new home after Calvin retired from teaching in 1863.

The enormous expense of designing, erecting, decorating, and maintaining the new house in Hartford, Connecticut, spurred Stowe to explicit financial negotiations with various editors and publishers and to a broader range of literary efforts as, over the next few years, she tried her hand at verse, short stories, essays, unofficial sermons, columns, recollections of old New England, hymns, domestic advice, biographies of women in the Bible and contemporary famous men, and children's books such as *Queer Little People* (1867) and *Little Pussy Willow* (1870). Earnings of this period were deftly elevated by a writer who knew her own powers, but money was in short supply even after Calvin scored a success with his magnum opus, *The Origin and History of the Books of the Bible* (1867). Several reasons accounted for the lack of funds: Stowe's openhanded generosity; the expensive new home (a showplace from the outset); the treatment for son Frederick's alcoholism, which the family traced to his war wound; the investment in a Florida cotton plantation that was intended to help this troubled son find a purpose in life; and Stowe's abrupt decision to buy a winter home for herself near Fred.

The pleasant retreat in Mandarin, Florida, led to the light but engaging travel stories collected as *Palmetto-Leaves* (1873); otherwise, it was for many years a distressing financial flop. Working under these pressures, Stowe did not produce much of lasting merit during the 1860s, though she did co-edit the magazine *Hearth and Home* for a year, starting in December 1868. She also dickered with Susan B. Anthony and Elizabeth Cady Stanton about putting her name on the masthead of their woman's-rights paper, *The Revolution,* though she eventually declined this connection. Stowe's flirtation with journalism delayed her next book, but probably to the benefit of the novel, for *Oldtown Folks* (1869) is one of the more polished books in her body of work. Ruminated over a period of several years ("I must dream and weave a while in peace and stupidity," Stowe told an impatient publisher), *Oldtown Folks* initiates Stowe's considered postbellum writings. She knew what she wanted to describe:

> New England life in the age after the revolutionary war & before rail roads had destroyed the primitive flavor of our life—the rough kindly simple religious life of a Massachusetts town in those days when the weekly mail stage was the only excitement. It is something I have been skimming & saving cream for for many years & I have a choice lot of actors ready to come onto the boards.

As Forrest Wilson recounts the development of this novel and its popular supplement, *Oldtown Fireside Stories* (1871), Stowe expressed so much enthusiasm about the manuscript that became *Oldtown Folks* that the publisher of the book, James T. Fields, proposed a new financial arrangement that would give him both serial rights for *The Atlantic Monthly* and the profits for the first year on the eventual book, all for the large sum of $6,000. Stowe declined Fields's offer in polite but positive tones, saying that this novel "is more to me than a story; it is my resume of the whole spirit and body of New England." In addition, she noted that recent satires of the good country people of the Northeast by writers such as Oliver Wendell Holmes had affronted the sort of readers most likely to esteem *Oldtown Folks.* Stowe argued that serialization would make matters worse because, as a result of the collaboration of

The Atlantic Monthly in those sophisticated gibes, few of "my people (i.e. the orthodoxy)" thought well of Fields's magazine. To circumvent their suspicions, Stowe decided to skip the serial stage entirely and unveil *Oldtown Folks* as a book, adding that she was confident of making much more money on this publication than the amount that her publisher had tendered. Despite the years that Fields had spent waiting for this novel, he could only acquiesce, after which Stowe realized that she had more material than the novel needed, anyway. Then she offered *The Atlantic Monthly* the additional tales, which were collected as *Oldtown Fireside Stories.* Both of the Oldtown books sold extremely well (*Oldtown Folks* was Stowe's most popular work since *Dred*), and many modern readers consider these New England stories her best-imagined and most realistic work.

Set in Natick, Massachusetts, which was Calvin Stowe's hometown, *Oldtown Folks* describes the childhoods and young adult years of Horace, Tina, and Harry. Horace resembles Calvin in at least one particular—he has psychic visions—but his greater significance is as a chronicler of a vanished New England that produces the sort of yeomanry on which a democracy may safely rely. A slight love plot ties the strands of the novel together (Horace and Tina marry after her giddiness has been chastened by long years of marriage to a cad), but the real interest of *Oldtown Folks* rests in its evocations of a way of life that many still read as nearly history. Stowe's rendering is not utopic, since characters betray religious bigotry, the intellectual barrenness of people forced to scratch livings from hardscrabble farms, and more than a little stiff-necked snobbery; yet, *Oldtown Folks* is crammed with affectionate recollections of the villagers who dozed through long Sunday sermons, twanged their pronunciation, and extended practical sympathy or cut capers at social "bees." The best-beloved character of the book in Stowe's day was the garrulous blacksmith, who spends most of his time serving as the chronicler of the local news. Absorbed in this unremunerated avocation, Sam Lawson is not much of a provider for his wife and children; yet, he has his merits:

> when a man gives himself seriously, for years, to the task of collecting information, thinking nothing of long tramps of twenty miles in the acquisition, never hesitating to put a question and never forgetting an answer, it is astonishing what an amount of information he may pick up. In Sam, a valuable reporter of the press has been lost forever.

A philosopher deeply versed in scriptural stories and long study of human nature, Sam loves to ruminate about the state of the world, though he never resolves his perplexities. "This 'ere world is cur'us," he says in a typical passage:

The house in Mandarin, Florida, where the Stowes spent the winter months from 1867 until 1884 (from Johanna Johnston, Runaway to Heaven: The Story of Harriet Beecher Stowe, *1963)*

"When we git to thinkin' about it, we think ef we'd ha' had the makin' on 't, things would ha' ben made someways diffurnt from what they be. But then things *is* just *as* they is, an' we can't help it. Sometimes I think," said Sam, embracing his knee profoundly, "an' then agin I dunno. There's all sorts o' folks hes to be in this 'ere world, an' I s'pose the Lord knows what he wants 'em fur; but I'm sure I don't. I kind o' hope the Lord'll fetch everybody out 'bout right some o' these 'ere times. He ain't got nothin' else to do, an' it's his lookout, an' not ourn, what comes of 'em all."

Many readers agreed with John Greenleaf Whittier, the Quaker poet who had done so much for abolition, that *Oldtown Folks* was every bit as good as *Uncle Tom's Cabin.* Stowe thought so, too.

Confident, or perhaps overconfident, of her standing in the wake of this popular and critical success, Stowe embarked on the publication that led to the biggest scandal of her long career and her gravest downfall with fans who had viewed her as a shining moral light. Stowe elected to publicize the "inside scoop" on a sexual liaison certain to rock literary circles in the western world. Revelation was Stowe's primary aim, and she foresaw some degree of the outrage that ensued. "I tremble at what I am doing & saying," she admitted, after sending "The True Story of Lady Byron's Life" to *The Atlantic Monthly,*

but she added, "I feel that justice demands it of me & I must not fail." The quest for justice should be borne in mind when evaluating Stowe's decision to expand on this essay and publish it as *Lady Byron Vindicated: A History of the Byron Controversy, from Its Beginning in 1816 to the Present Time* (1870), because both works declared what is now acknowledged as the simple truth.

The problem was that, in Stowe's day, the story of the incestuous relationship of George Gordon, Lord Byron, with his half sister, Augusta Leigh, was shockingly new, and the horrifying story of a frankly indecent *affaire* was too terrible to mention, much less broadcast. Readers sensitive to gender-based inequity might argue that the resultant silence forced Byron's widow (whom the poet deserted long before his death in 1824) to live in the shadow of the charge that her coldness had driven the wildest Romantic into the dissolute behavior for which he was both denounced and admired. Indeed, as a girl in Litchfield, Stowe herself had adored Byron, and even Lyman Beecher had noticed Byron's passing, opining that he might have saved the poet if he could have sat him down and outlined the true Christian faith. Forty years later Stowe's sympathies had shifted entirely to the wronged wife, whom she had befriended on her first trip to Britain and with whom she corresponded for years. An older and male-authored Stowe biography charges

THE ADVANCED WOMAN OF THE PERIOD.

"'You go for the emancipation of woman; but bless you, boy, you haven't the least idea what it means—not a bit of it, sonny, have you now? Confess!' she said, stroking my shoulder caressingly.

Illustration from My Wife and I *(1871), the novel in which Stowe indulged her "unsanctified hankering for 'slang'"*

that "a small, selfish voice" motivated the imprudent defense of Lady Byron as part of a self-aggrandizing announcement of the New England woman's intimacy with a peer. (A criticism published in the wake of the furor agreed, "Mrs. Stowe, as we all know, has a weakness for ladies of title.") In contrast, a more recent study written by a feminist historian suggests the political aspects of Stowe's decision to air a male poet's dirty linen adduces another motivation, too—Stowe's desire to attract readers uninterested in the rural portraiture of *Oldtown Folks*. The feminist argument is sound (the double standard at the heart of the Byron case roused support among women's-rights activists), but the titillating aspects of Stowe's revelation won many pages of angry response in the British and American press. "Startling in accusation," one reviewer declaimed:

barren in proof, inaccurate in dates, infelicitous in style, and altogether ill-advised in publication, her strange article will travel round the whole literary world and everywhere evoke against its author the spontaneous disapprobation of her life-long friends.

As the chorus of outraged displeasure rose, many charged that the tale had been fabricated, while others affirmed that even if the story were true, a lady would have refrained from publishing it and certainly should not have turned a profit on its sale. This second accusation dragged in Lady Byron, who was roundly condemned as, at best, jealously spiteful, if not deluded or insane. From a different angle, an old friend doubted Stowe's exposure, because he thought incest only took place "in lonely farmhouses," while the *Nation* dismissed the whole contretemps in coolly sarcastic tones: "We sincerely hope if anybody else has any dirty particulars about the Byron family or its branches in his possession, he will keep them to himself." Stowe's reaction to contemporaries' outrage was that "the world's people must have all lost their senses" on the vague assumption that "The proofs will probably eventually come out." Meanwhile, the brouhaha decimated the subscription list of *The Atlantic Monthly* and led to nasty cartoons of Stowe in British magazines.

Stowe survived the fuss by turning to her usual pursuits—wintering in Florida, enjoying the social and literary life of Hartford, and writing steadily. Her next novel was *Pink and White Tyranny* (1871), the story of a vain and foolish coquette who decides, after her charms fade, to marry a good and gentle but serious-minded New England man. Stowe subtitled the American publication "A Society Novel" but seemed to change her focus in the preface, for there she called her latest effort "a little common-place history, all about one man and one woman, living straight along in one little prosaic town in New England." The story line starts out like the Sarah Josepha Hale novels in which a woman trained only to lead fashion learns to run a home efficiently, except that Lillie never becomes the domestic angel in John's house. Only when her health is broken by an endless search for pleasure does Lillie understand her husband's quiet merits and steadfast love. After Lillie's repentance and consequent "good" death, her teenaged daughter becomes a loving homemaker who brings joy and comfort to her father's home. Noticeably spicier is *My Wife and I; or, Harry Henderson's History* (1871), a novel of newspaper life, in which Stowe let loose her "unsanctified hankering for 'slang,'" to readers' applause. Her decision to write in a livelier and more comically sarcastic style hit the public mood again, and *My Wife and I* led to a sequel, *We and Our Neighbors; or, The Records of an Unfashionable Street: A Novel* (1875). In 1877 a selection of her religious writings was published as *Footsteps of the Master*.

With the publication of the two novels *My Wife and I* and *We and Our Neighbors,* Stowe entered the twilight of her career. Though she continued to write and tried lecturing, her creativity was slowing. Age was one factor, but Stowe had also learned the burdens of celebrity. "On looking back," she told an importunate publisher:

> to the time when "Uncle Tom's Cabin" came forth, I see myself then a woman with no particular capital of reputation driven to write then, as now, by the necessity of making some income for family expenses. In this mood, with a mind burning with the wrongs of slavery, I undertook to write some loose sketches of slave life in the "National Era," and out of that attempt grew "Uncle Tom's Cabin." If there had been a grand preparatory blast of trumpets, or had it been announced that Mrs. Stowe would do this or that, I think it likely I could not have written; but nobody expected anything, nobody said anything, and so I wrote freely. Now what embarrasses me is to be announced as an attraction–to have eyes fixed on me and people all waiting.

Her expenses were reduced after she sold the lavish Hartford house; then, too, one daughter and one son had married and begun their adult lives. The twins, Hattie and Eliza, never wed. (Their lives of devoted service to aging parents may lie behind the portrait of a young homemaker that closes out *Pink and White Tyranny*.) To be a Beecher was, however, to wade joyfully into moral battle, and Stowe was roused from her happy home life by the next scandal to rock her world. This time she found herself an onlooker, since the longest and most divisive scandal that the Beecher clan endured was targeted at her adored younger brother, Henry Ward.

Renowned for dramatic preaching skills, or stunts, that drove the profits from the annual pew auction for his church into the tens of thousands of dollars, Henry Ward Beecher was the most famous minister in the United States when he was charged with committing adultery with a married member of his congregation. Spurred by Beecher's enemies, the charges could not be ignored. Newspapers around the United States printed daily transcripts of the long, drawn-out, and extremely confusing case. Today the thousands of pages of transcript, commentary, charges, and countercharges that resulted from the Beecher-Tilton trials reveal social, class, geographical, political, and personal implications having to do with Henry Ward Beecher's immense popularity and the jealousy it aroused–his showmanlike sermons and unorthodox doctrine; the religious, cultural, and political life of Brooklyn; and a certain carelessness about appearances that may have been a hint of other indiscretions. For the Beechers, though, the whole mess signaled the end of an era in which Lyman Beecher's children by his several wives had stuck together against all the world. The loudest dissenter was Isabella Beecher Hooker, a follower of Victoria Woodhull, the women's-rights activist who had a grudge against Henry Ward Beecher, but Isabella's full brother Thomas was not far behind; in response, Harriet

Stowe in 1884

defied both these half siblings by professing utter disbelief in reports of Henry Ward's sexual errancy. Recalling the uproar fifteen years later, Stowe's son charged that "the Rev. Henry Ward Beecher, was the victim of a most revolting, malicious, and groundless attack on his purity," a judgment with which scholars have not always agreed. Even if everyone who studies the Beecher-Tilton trial arrives at an opinion about Beecher's innocence or guilt, none can really know what took place between the minister, who liked to kiss married parishioners and even sit on their laps to show perfect love, and this woman of his congregation. What is known is that Henry Ward Beecher was eventually exonerated of all charges, after which, under the slogan "Cleanliness is next to godliness," he provided testimonials for Pears Soap, which continued to be used even after his death in 1887.

Not all of Stowe's final years were clouded by discord. In late 1872 she decided to buy a new house in Hartford, a residence that brought her into neighborly contact with Samuel Langhorne Clemens. In 1882 she was feted at a garden party for her seventieth birthday (though she was seventy-one) under the fond auspices of *The Atlantic Monthly*. The party was a gala affair, marked by paeans to

Stowe written by luminaries such as Whittier and Holmes, as well as family members. Whittier's tribute was especially graceful, as it gestured toward *Uncle Tom's Cabin, The Minister's Wooing, The Pearl of Orr's Island, Agnes of Sorrento, Oldtown Folks,* and Sam Lawson, too. He concluded,

> Ah, dearer than the praise that stirs
> The air to-day, our love is hers!
> She needs no guaranty of fame
> Whose own is linked with Freedom's name.

Guests at the party included a fair sampling of the Brahmin elite, from William Dean Howells and Thomas Bailey Aldrich to Franklin Sanborn and Bronson Alcott. Many more literary artists sent regrets, including Henry James, John Hay, Julia Ward Howe, Annie Fields, Thomas Wentworth Higginson, Edward Eggleston, Joel Chandler Harris, Louisa May Alcott, Rebecca Harding Davis, Wendell Phillips, George Washington Cable, and James Russell Lowell. Even Isabella Beecher Hooker attended, and Thomas Beecher sent a note. Elizabeth Stuart Phelps wrote a poem for the occasion and described the party in her memoirs: the only people not present, she avowed, those "of the school which does not call *Uncle Tom's Cabin* literature, were scarcely missed."

After this last highlight, Stowe's social activities dwindled. The Mandarin vacations stopped in 1884 when Calvin grew too weak to travel. He died in 1886; Catharine Beecher had died in 1878. Stowe asked her son Charles to compile a biography that included several recollections written by Stowe herself; she also enjoyed being a grandmother. In 1893 the first editions of both *Uncle Tom's Cabin* and *A Key to Uncle Tom's Cabin* were displayed at the hall honoring women's achievements at the Columbian Exposition. Stowe probably did not realize the honor, for her characteristic fits of absentmindedness were growing more frequent and prolonged. A grown daughter who cared for her wrote that "her mind is in a strange state of childishness and forgetfulness, with momentary flashes of her old self that come and go like falling stars." As the aging author visibly failed, her daughters hired a nurse-companion from whom Stowe liked to escape. The aged author was alone with this nurse when she died on 1 July 1896; her last words were, "I love you."

Despite Whittier's praise of enduring fame, Stowe's posthumous reputation was low for many years. Her sentimental effects were deemed mawkish and her greatest boosters were scorned as effete tastemakers of a bloodless genteel tradition. All the while, literary historians acknowledged that *Uncle Tom's Cabin* had been important; yet, the usual follow-up was that its literary style was so execrably vulgar that any reader who enjoyed it must be guilty of bad taste. When Stowe was rescued from critical scorn by scholars appreciative of sentimentality, women's history,

domestic issues, and antislavery propaganda, many were surprised to find that this neglected author had helped lay the groundwork for literary realism and the local-color school. Today Stowe's place in nineteenth-century literary and cultural studies is closer to the position she held in her own time and not just because of the novel that sold so extraordinarily well. Recognized as a gifted sentimental writer and an early regionalist, Stowe is accounted a writer of unusual breadth and a mythmaker whose talents continue to inform many Americans' perception of the national identity.

Biographies:

Charles Edward Stowe, *Life of Harriet Beecher Stowe Compiled from Her Letters and Journals by Her Son* (Boston & New York: Houghton, Mifflin, 1889);

Annie Fields, *Life and Letters of Harriet Beecher Stowe* (Boston & New York: Houghton, Mifflin, 1897);

Forrest Wilson, *Crusader in Crinoline: The Life of Harriet Beecher Stowe* (Philadelphia & New York: Lippincott, 1941);

Johanna Johnston, *Runaway to Heaven: The Story of Harriet Beecher Stowe* (Garden City, N.Y.: Doubleday, 1963);

Joan D. Hedrick, *Harriet Beecher Stowe* (New York: Oxford University Press, 1994).

References:

Jeanne Boydston, Mary Kelley, and Anne Margolis, eds., *The Limits of Sisterhood: The Beecher Sisters on Women's Rights and Woman's Sphere* (Chapel Hill: University of North Carolina Press, 1988);

Gillian Brown, *Domestic Individualism: Imagining Self in Nineteenth-Century America* (Berkeley & Los Angeles: University of California Press, 1990);

Josephine Donovan, *Uncle Tom's Cabin: Evil, Affliction, and Redemptive Love* (Boston: Twayne, 1991);

Ann Douglas, *The Feminization of American Culture* (New York: Knopf, 1977);

Lora Romero, *Home Fronts: Domesticity and Its Critics in the Antebellum United States* (Durham, N.C.: Duke University Press, 1997);

Jane P. Tompkins, *Sensational Designs: The Cultural Work of American Fiction, 1790–1860* (New York: Oxford University Press, 1985).

Papers:

Many of Harriet Beecher Stowe's papers are located among the Beecher Family Papers at the Schlesinger Library in Radcliffe College. Additional Stowe materials, including some of her letters, are at the University of Virginia, at the Beinecke Library at Yale University, and at the Stowe-Day Library in Hartford, Connecticut.

Frederick Goddard Tuckerman

(4 February 1821 – 9 May 1873)

Robert Bray
Illinois Wesleyan University

BOOKS: *Poems* (Boston: Privately printed, 1860; London: Smith, Elder, 1863; Boston: Ticknor & Fields, 1864);

The Sonnets of Frederick Goddard Tuckerman, edited by Witter Bynner (New York & London: Knopf, 1931);

Frederick Goddard Tuckerman: The Cricket, Printed from His Notebooks with Permission of His Granddaughter Margaret Tuckerman Clark (Cummington, Mass.: Cummington Press, 1950);

The Complete Poems of Frederick Goddard Tuckerman, edited by N. Scott Momaday (New York: Oxford University Press, 1965).

Frederick Goddard Tuckerman published only one book of poetry during his lifetime, and it was a commercial and critical failure. *Poems* (1860) included ninety-eight poems, mostly short lyrics, more than half of which were sonnets. Tuckerman paid for the printing of the first edition himself and sent copies to many famous New England and New York writers whose approval he sought but generally failed to obtain. (Most who bothered to acknowledge Tuckerman's gift responded with polite puzzlement; a few others advised him patronizingly to regularize his "unmusical" verse; only Nathaniel Hawthorne understood both the quality and complexity of the poetry and the difficulty Tuckerman faced in finding a readership). Tuckerman must have realized that, whatever the ultimate worth of his poems, they were not likely to be appreciated in his own time. Despite a few favorable critical responses (notably from Hawthorne) and support from Alfred Tennyson in England, Tuckerman's *Poems* did not have a discernible impact on literary history in either country.

After the appearance of *Poems,* Tuckerman continued to write, though sparingly, throughout the 1860s but published almost nothing of this new work. He wrote two occasional poems commemorating the Civil War, in which he did not participate (one, a private elegy for his friend, George D. Wells, who had died in battle; the other, a public dedicatory poem for the Greenfield, Massachusetts, soldiers' memorial), more

Frederick Goddard Tuckerman

sonnets (thirty-one of them), and "The Cricket," the Keatsian ode that some readers have regarded as his finest achievement.

These poems plus the earlier ones total scarcely 150, of which two-thirds appeared in a volume that had little impact upon publication. No reconfiguration of the American constellation of poets occurred. If anyone glimpsed Tuckerman at all, it was not as he saw himself—"indiscerptible" like "A star-point burning high, / Lit in the dark, and as alone / As Lyra in the sky"—but rather as flickering dimly, and he was noticed then only by a few of his contemporaries who had particularly excellent vision. Chief among these was Nathaniel

Hannah Lucinda Jones, whom Tuckerman married in 1847

Hawthorne, who presciently observed that Tuckerman's "great difficulty" in the 1860s and beyond would be "to get yourself read at all." And if by some miracle he might obtain a second reading (and Hawthorne had already given him one), then *Poems* "might be a success." Tuckerman's post-*Poems* sonnets and "The Cricket"—which, according to modernist Yvor Winters, is one of the finest lyrics in English of the nineteenth century—were not published until well into the twentieth century. Tuckerman in his last years did have the minor consolation of seeing both English (1863) and American (1864, 1869) commercial editions of *Poems* in print. But though the Ticknor and Fields imprint was also a cultural imprimatur, prestige did not mean a readership.

Born on 4 February 1821 into a wealthy Boston merchant family, Tuckerman grew up in the privilege of Beacon Street and attended an Episcopal boarding school and Boston Latin School before enrolling at Harvard at the age of seventeen. From an early age he was an avid reader of British and American literature and seems to have had an almost eidetic memory. According to Eugene England in *Beyond Romanticism: Tuckerman's Life and Poetry* (1991), Tuckerman read "with an incredibly retentive mind and long, careful study" that allowed him to summon up lines, stanzas, and even entire poems at will. Much of this reading was Romantic, and for a time he was a Romantic. At Harvard he was naturally drawn to Transcendentalism, particularly Ralph Waldo Emerson's Americanizing of German and British Romantic thought as well as his controversial Divinity School Address (1838), in which he called on his listeners "to go alone; to refuse the good models, even those which are sacred to the imagination of men, and dare to love God without mediator or veil."

But Romanticism, at least the Emersonian sort involving a platonic union with God, was not definitive for Tuckerman; another influence, both similar to and radically different from Transcendentalism, may have been more important. Tuckerman's tutor in Greek at Harvard was Jones Very, the sonneteer and Unitarian mystic who was just then (1838–1839) composing his most effective and "inspired" poetry. Very believed he was automatically taking down God's dictation. Tuckerman may have witnessed the shocking spectacle of Very urging his Greek students to stop reciting then and there and "flee to the mountains, for the end of all things is at hand." Very's evangelism (which he earnestly pressed upon anyone handy, including his pupils) was based in a conversion experience that required the utter surrender of self and will to God. But rather than Very's sonnets, which were always conventional in form and matter if sometimes intense in feeling, this immense emotional drama was what Tuckerman saw enacted by Very, and it affected him negatively. A key to Tuckerman's poetry, when the poems came in the 1850s, is likely a resistance of his integral mind and self to annihilation of any sort. Tuckerman's answer to Very was a tough-minded, pain-ridden look through time and nature that uncovered not Christian eternity or Romantic union with Nature but "life alone [circling] out flat and bare." Thus, though the sonnet became Tuckerman's most effective lyric form, too, the sonnets he wrote were anything but automatic. To Very's smooth, seamless "dictation" Tuckerman opposed a human angularity that left no doubt about who was doing the writing.

After finishing his law degree at Harvard in 1842, Tuckerman was admitted to the Massachusetts bar (1844) but scarcely practiced at all before giving up the profession entirely. Disliking commerce as much as law, and never sociable to begin with, he retreated, professionless, more and more into himself and natural solitude. He spent his days walking the river valleys around Greenfield, Massachusetts (whence he had retreated from Boston and Cambridge), and his nights watching the stars through a 4.6-inch refractor telescope. He "botanized" with his brother Edward (a noted "lichenologist"), brooded on the elusive meaning

X

An upper chamber in a darken'd house,
Where, ere his footsteps reach'd ripe manhood's brink
Terror & anguish were his cup to drink,—
I cannot rid the thought nor hold it close:
But dimly dream upon that Man alone;
Now though the autumn clouds most softly pass,
The cricket creaks beneath the doorstep stone,
And greener than the season grows the grass;
Nor can I drop my lids, nor shade my brows
But there he stands beside the lifted sash,
And with a swooning of the heart I think
Where the black shingles slope to meet the boughs,
And shattered on the roof like smallest snows,
The tiny petals of the mountain ash.

Manuscript for a poem in Tuckerman's first sonnet sequence (Houghton Library, Harvard University)

Tuckerman's lap desk

of life, and was generally unhappy and unfulfilled—though so privately that no one recognized his discontent. But he did not yet begin to write the poetry that eventually expressed his unsettled mind. Then, sometime in the mid 1840s, while living a country life in Greenfield, he met Hannah Lucinda Jones. In "Sonnet I: 14" Tuckerman deflected this momentous event into the third person, as if the poet were speaking of a self-contained, complacent "friend" ambushed by romantic love:

> Not proud of station, nor in worldly pelf
> Immoderately rich, nor rudely gay:
> Gentle he was and generous in a way,
> And with a wise discretion ruled himself.
> Blest Nature spread his table every day,
> And so he lived, to all the blasts that woo
> Responsible, as yon long locust spray
> That waves and washes in the windy blue.
> Nor wanted he a power to reach and reap
> From hardest things a consequence and use,
> And yet this friend of mine, in one small hour
> Fell from himself, and was content to weep
> For eyes love-dark, red lips, and cheeks in hues
> Not red, but rose-dim like the jacinth flower.

Hannah Jones (Tuckerman always called her Anna) "fell from herself" as well: "She turned to him as to a god of old, / Her smitten soul with its full strength and spring / Retaliating his love" (I: 15, 4–6).

The two married on 17 June 1847, settled in Greenfield, and began a family. Children came in 1848, 1853, and 1857. On 12 May 1857, a week after their last child was born (a son named after his father), Anna Tuckerman died, presumably of childbirth complications. Tuckerman's complete devotion to and passion for his wife caused intense grief, while the notion that he had fathered the child whose birth killed Anna led to racking feelings of guilt. Such emotions are evidenced in his later poetry. The voice of these later works is almost invariably one of loss and being lost in the world (even the natural world). The subject matter was the workings of, and then the working out of, grief and guilt personally and philosophically considered. The composition of poems may have exacerbated a guilt that was already present and active in the apprenticed but uncommitted poet of the late 1840s and earlier 1850s. After 12 May 1857 he became fully a man of guilty sorrows: He had not done what he might have while Anna lived, and now he could not. In two unpublished articles—"Frederick Goddard Tuckerman's *Prelude*: 'A Soul that out of Nature's Deep'" and "'O World-Sick Heart': Self-Portraiture in Four Poems of Frederick Goddard Tuckerman"—poet-critic James McGowan has located much of the power of Tuckerman's poetry in a probing dialectic that suited Tuckerman's restless mind. The emotional catastrophe of Anna's death provided the dialectical subject for much of Tuckerman's best poetry.

Tuckerman had, of course, written poems of value before his wife's death. Many poems in the 1860 volume were composed before 1857, and his infrequent publication of individual lyrics in magazines had begun as early as 1849 and continued throughout the 1850s. Two poems from these years, "Picomegan" (1854) and "A Soul that out of Nature's Deep" (circa 1855–1857), notably represent the kind of Romanticism Tuckerman received from William Wordsworth, transformed individually, and "Americanized" after the manner of the Hudson River School of landscape painting so popular between 1830 and the Civil War. A useful comparison can be made with Thomas Cole, artistic leader of the Hudson River School, in whose case both painting and poetry worked resonantly together to Romantic effect. For example, Cole's *The Oxbow* (1836), a "view" of the Connecticut River above Northampton, Massachusetts, not far from Tuckerman's Greenfield, and Cole's paean to the Hudson, "Lines Written after a Walk . . . ," are in a general way similar to Tuckerman's "Picomegan" and "A Soul that out of Nature's Deep." Tuckerman, like Cole, portrays the solitary romantic youth in a natural American landscape, the mature poet's mind identifying with a now-lost childhood bliss and innocence. Yet, while Cole employs a conventionally Romantic resolution—the union of the mind with Nature allowing imaginative recovery of "Eden" and a fitting grandeur of poetic and painterly effects, Tuckerman insists on a different hard-won truth about self and nature—that both are restlessly contradictory—a truth that leaves the poetic persona in a post-Romantic place, alienated rather than reconciled.

The familiar two-term aesthetic of the beautiful and the sublime of the Hudson River School is present in Tuckerman's poetic landscape, too, but Beauty and Sublimity conflict as irresolvably as do Mind and Nature. What Tuckerman was formulating in the 1850s was a post-Romantic aesthetic that denied even the ultimate powers of the imagination—synthesis, reconciling opposites, transcendence, and what Wordsworth in *The Prelude* (1850) deemed the highest human accomplishment, "the apocalypse of the mind." In his rebuttal of Wordsworth's "heroic argument," Tuckerman begins by agreeing with Wordsworth that "Nature never did

betray / The heart that loved her," but Tuckerman's dialectic insists on a "yes, but"; for there was, he thought, a betrayal. Only Tuckerman's weakness and guilt over his lack of Romantic perfection conduces him to say that the betrayal is his fault. In this respect he is closer to the Wordsworth of "The world is too much with us," who says "Little we see in Nature that is ours." At times he sees nothing in Nature that is his or through which he can recognize himself. His "Romantic upbringing" persuades him to accept the blame for the dissonance, cognitive and affective, while his singular mind urges that there may well be a problem of incomprehensibility residing at the heart of things.

"Picomegan" (the Native American name for the Green River, which flows through Greenfield), despite its distracting drumbeat meter, is an effective lyric. (The comparison with *The Song of Hiawatha* is inescapable, but in fact "Picomegan" was published nearly a year before Henry Wadsworth Longfellow's long narrative poem in 1855). Contributing to its force is the convincing sense that the voice is actually in Nature and knows what he sees. In the opening sixteen lines Tuckerman notes nine different plants and flowers along the river bank, some of them specifically, "Stars of gold . . . Clematis . . . Arrowhead . . . river-flags." Then, having established his credentials as a close noticer, the voice can look up from the flowers at his feet to the expansive river, and to the forest and distant mountains—in other words, from the beautiful to the sublime, in the best Hudson River School tradition:

> Dreamily, for perfect Summer
>   Hushed the vales with misty heat;
> In the wood a drowsy drummer,
>   The woodpecker, faintly beat.
> Songs were silent, save the voices
>   Of the mountain and the flood,
> Save the wisdom of the voices
>   Only known in solitude:
> But to me, a lonely liver,
>   All that fading afternoon
> From the undermining river
>   Came a burthen in its tune,
> Came a tone my ear remembers,
>   And I said, "What grief thee grieves,
> Pacing through thy leafy chambers,
>   And thy voice of rest bereaves?" (17–32)

The "lonely liver," rightly prepared by Nature, is the appropriate persona to ask the river what ails it. In American-landscape Romanticism, the river—or mountain or forest—would only answer if the pilgrim were worthy, but in that case it would always answer. In Cole's most famous poem, "The Lament of the Forest" (1838), the response to the query of what is wrong in Nature is a minor-key diapason of the choired trees, a

The Cricket

I.

The humming bee purrs softly o'er his flower,
    From lawn and thicket,
The dog-day locust singeth in the sun
    From hour to hour:
Each has his bard, and thou, ere day be done,
    Shalt have no wrong;
So bright that murmur mid the insect crowd,
Muffled and lost in bottom-grass, or loud
    By pale and picket:
Shall I not take to help me in my song,
    A little cooing cricket?

II.

The afternoon is sleepy; let us lie
Beneath these branches whilst the burden'd brook,
Muttering and moaning to himself goes by;
And mark our minstrels' card whilst we look
Toward the faint horizon swooning blue.
    Or in a garden bower
Trellised & trammel'd with deep drapery
    Of hanging green;
    Light glimmering thro —
There let the dull hop be
Let bloom, with poppy's dark refreshing flower:
Let the dead fragrance round our temples beat,
Stunning the sense to slumber, whilst between
The falling water and fluttering wind,
    Mingle & meet,
    Murmur & mix;
No few faint pipings from the glades behind,
    Or alder-thicks:
But louder as the day declines,
From tingling tassel, blade, & sheath,
Rising from nets of river vines,
    Winrows and ricks;
    Above, beneath,
    At every breath,
At hand, around, illimitably
Rising and falling like the sea,
    Acres of cricks!

III.

Dear to the child who hears thy rustling voice
Cease at his footstep, though he hears thee still,
Cease and resume with vibrance crisp & shrill,
Thou sittest in the sunshine to rejoice.
Night lover too; bringer of all things dark
And rest and silence; yet thou bringest to me
Always that burthen of the unresting Sea,
The moaning cliffs, the low rocks blackly stark;
These upland inland fields no more I view,
But the long flat seaside beach, the wild sea-mews
    And the overturning wave!
Thou bringest too, dim accents from the grave
To him who walketh when the day is dim,
Dreaming of those who dream no more of him,
With edged remembrances of joy and pain;
And heyday looks & laughter come again:
Forms that in happy sunshine lie & leap,
With faces where but now a gap must be,
Renunciations, and partitions deep
And final tears, and crowning vacancy!

And to thy poet at the twilight's hush,
No chirping touch of lips with starting blush,
But wringing arms, hearts wild with love and woe,
Closed eyes, and kisses that would not let go!

IV.

So wert thou loud in that old graceful time
    When Greece was fair;
While god and hero hearken'd to thy chime;
    Softly astir
Where the long grasses fringed Cayster's lip;
Long-drawn, with glimmering sails of swan & ship,
    And ship & swan;
    Or where
    Reedy Eurotas ran.
Did that low warble teach thy tender flute
Xenaphyle?
Its breathings mild? say! did the grasshopper
Sit golden in thy purple hair
    O Psammathe?
    Or wert thou mute,
Grieving for Pan amid the alders there?
And by the water and along the hill
That thirsty tinkle in the herbage still,
Though the lost forest wailed to horns of Arcady?

V.

Like the Enchanter old —
Who sought mid the dead water's weeds and scum,
For evil growths beneath the moonbeam cold,
Or mandrake or dorcynium;
And touched the leaf that open'd both his ears,
So that articulate voices now he hears
In cry of beast, or bird, or insect's hum, —
Might I but find thy knowledge in thy song!
    That twittering tongue,
Ancient as light, returning like the years.
    So might I be;
Unwise to sing. Thy true interpreter
Thro' denser stillness and in sounder dark,
Than ere thy notes have pierced to harrow me.
    So might I stir
    The world to hark
    To thee my lord & lawgiver,
    And cease my quest:
Content to bring thy wisdom to the world;
Content to gain at last some low applause,
    Now low, now lost
Like thine from mossy stone, amid the stem & straw,
    Or garden grave-mound tricked & drest —
    Powdered and pearl'd
    By stealing frost —
In rainbow beauty of euphorbias!
For larger would be less indeed, and like
The ceaseless summer in the summer grass
To him who toileth in the windy field,
    Or where the sunbeams strike,
Naught in innumerable numerousness.
    So might I much possess,
    So much must yield;
But failing this, the dell and grassy dike,
The water and the waste shall still be dear,
And all the pleasant plots and places
    Where thou hast sung, and I have hung
    To ignorantly hear.
Then Cricket, sing thy song! or answer mine!
Thine whispers blame, but mine has naught but praises,
It matters not. Behold! the Autumn goes,
    The Shadow grows,
The moments take hold of eternity;
Even while we stop to wrangle or repine
    Our lives are gone —
    Like thinnest mist,
Like you escaping colour in the tree;
Rejoice! rejoice! whilst yet the hours exist —
Rejoice or mourn, & let the World swing on
Unmoved by cricket song of thee or me.

                                        FGT

Manuscript for an ode Tuckerman wrote during the 1860s (Houghton Library, Harvard University)

univocal indictment of humankind's immoral depreda-
tions against its majesty—whole woods decimated by the
axe, rivers dammed to make mills, settlements crowding
the wilderness farther and farther west. Having heard the
forest's lament, and feeling it, Cole's version of Tuckerman's "lonely liver" returns to "civilization" with the
boon of exalted understanding and the charge to make
his fellow Americans understand as well, and therefore
desist.

In "Picomegan," however, no answer from the
river is forthcoming. The problem is twofold: Tuckerman, "lonely liver" and close noticer of Nature though
he is, is not a worthy seeker of Nature's truth, and he
knows it. He is out of tune. On the other hand, Nature
(the river) may turn out to be a force of Darwinian
indifference, singing the same song irrespective of
human expectations of teleology. On a second, autumnal walk by Picomegan's banks, Tuckerman—now an
older, less innocent, and more melancholy poet—
observes that the river "Babblest on of leaves and flowers" even though the season, like the poet's life, has
changed toward death:

I go mourning
O'er thy fallen banks and bowers;
O'er a life small grace adorning
With lost aims and broken powers
Wreck-flung, like these wavetorn beaches,
Tear-trenched, as by winter showers.

Though Tuckerman finally believes that in Nature life
lessons and a concomitant faith beyond rationality
remain to be learned, he does not expect to learn or to
achieve these: "Picomegan" concludes with its troubled
voice walking on and away from the river, "disturbed . . .
As a dream no reason yields," nothing gleaned from the
river song of triumph and of grief.

"Picomegan" indicates Tuckerman's Hudson
River School affinities; it also shows a distinction
between his early works and their Romantic forebears,
both American and British. Tuckerman's poetic voice,
however, was skeptical, pessimistic, and melancholy
before and during his life with Anna as well as after her
death. Skepticism and self-doubt were the givens of his
philosophy and personality. What Anna's death provided was the dramatic test on which everything in his
sonnets depended and from which hung the poetic salvation of a soul that wanted to believe (in a Christian
afterlife, for example, where he would see his wife
again) even against the evidence of science, but not at
the cost of forfeiting his knowing mind.

The five groups of sonnets are Tuckerman's
supreme achievement. These ninety-six poems represent much more than numbered individual lyrics.
Readers from Hawthorne to England and McGowan

have detected a larger informing at work, though its
nature and the poet's intention have remained elusive.
Even what to call the grouped sonnets has been a problem. In his manuscript Tuckerman titled the two groups
published in *Poems* "personal sonnets" and at first
intended them as one group; in *Poems,* however, the sonnets are divided into Parts I and II; and N. Scott Momaday, editor of *The Complete Poems of Frederick Goddard
Tuckerman* (1965), divided the collection into five series.
Almost uncritically, readers have come to regard what
Tuckerman was doing as composing sonnet sequences—
or perhaps even a kind of multisequence, since each of
the two sequences published during Tuckerman's lifetime, or the five sequences (which include the three
published after the poet's death), function as variations
on the theme of what to make of a life diminished if not
destroyed by Anna's death.

The sonnets may be known best as a nineteenth-
century forerunner of what M. L. Rosenthal and Sally
Gall term "modern lyric sequences"—"A grouping of
mainly lyric poems . . . which tend to interact as an
organic whole. . . . Intimate, fragmented, self-analytical,
open, emotionally volatile, meet[ing] the needs of modern sensibility even when the poet aspires to tragic or
epic scope." That Tuckerman had some such idea in his
sonnets is evident after even a cursory first reading.
One sonnet ends with a comma rather than a final stop,
but the next begins with a coordinate conjunction to
advance the dialectic. These markers indicate not only
that an "argument" is ongoing but also that the "burthen" is continuously turning on itself.

Tuckerman began his "personal sonnets" before
Anna died, but how far he got into the twenty-eight that
comprise "Part I" is impossible to tell with certainty. At
least the first nine are thematically and dramatically
consistent with "Picomegan" and "A Soul that out of
Nature's Deep"; the Child of Nature is discontented,
and the would-be poet is discouraged: "What avail / Is
the swan's voice, if all the hearers fail? / Or his great
flight, that no eye gathereth?" (I: 1, 10–12). With Sonnet I: 10, "An Upper Chamber in a Darkened House,"
the "matter of Anna" may make its first appearance; it
is Tuckerman's best-known and most-anthologized
poem:

An upper chamber in a darkened house,
Where, ere his footsteps reached ripe manhood's brink,
Terror and anguish were his cup to drink,—
I cannot rid the thought, nor hold it close;
But dimly dream upon that man alone;—
Now though the autumn clouds most softly pass;
The cricket chides beneath the doorstep stone,
And greener than the season grows the grass.
Nor can I drop my lids, nor shade my brows,
But there he stands beside the lifted sash;

The graves of Hannah and Frederick Tuckerman in Greenfield, Massachusetts

And, with a swooning of the heart, I think
Where the black shingles slope to meet the boughs,
And—shattered on the roof like smallest snows—
The tiny petals of the mountain-ash.

This sonnet is an epitome of Tuckerman's poetry at its finest and most characteristic. It just barely contains its image-powered "emotional volatility" within a traditional form (in this instance the Italian sonnet), whose line and stanza boundaries seem about to rupture and release tremendous anarchic force. Read outside its sequence, I: 10 relies entirely for effect not upon Romantic "high argument" but rather upon symbol, image, angular syntax, and a dramatic situation in which the "I" sees preternaturally a personal past and present that blend with the archetypal. Simultaneity resides in the surreal landscape: The season is autumn, but the grass grows "greener than the season"; the petal-fall of the mountain ash in May is happening again (or perhaps still happening); the poet is looking at himself in the third-person past as both himself and as the One undergoing a Passion—the Cup of the Last Supper in the Upper Chamber, the figurative Crucifixion Cup of responsibility he would rather pass but

knows he must drink (because he did). Even the ostensibly sentimental "swooning of the heart" fits with this November hallucination. For a swoon need not be a Romantic sign so much as an instance of "syncope," or a fainting disorientation in time and space that deprives the perceiver of his quotidian bearings. This reaction can occur either randomly or under the stimulus of repeating memory: Every time the poet drops his eyes (looks down and deliberately away) or shades his brows (looks up into bright light), the "swoon" recurs, and he is compelled to "think / Where the black shingles slope to meet the boughs," and the drama is replayed once more.

Many other sonnets in "Part I" (indeed in all five of the sequences) merit discussion, but Part I: 8 serves as an example. "As when down some broad River dropping" is a sonnet-long extended metaphor, and the extravagant grief over Anna's death is a mythology of godlike lovers:

And now,—to impulse cold, to passion dead,—
With the wild grief of unperfected years,
He kissed her hands, her mouth, her hair, her head;
Gathered her close and closer, to drink up

The odour of her beauty; then in tears,
As for a world, gave from his lips the cup! (I: 15, 9–14)

The dilemma of the sensitive and skeptical soul unprepared for eternity because unconvinced, despite the charged words of the preacher in the octave, ends with the line: "'Lo! Death is at the doors,' he crieth, 'with blows!'" The question is answered, typically, with another question in the sestet, though without the question mark:

But what to him, unto whose feverish sense
The stars tick audibly, and the wind's low surge
In the pine, attended, tolls, and throngs, and grows
On the dread ear,—a thunder too profound
For bearing,—a Niagara of sound! (I: 17, 9–14)

The poem of futile recollection—"By this low fire I often sit to woo / Memory to bring the days for ever done" (I: 24)—may be read in the company of William Shakespeare's "When to the sessions of sweet silent thought." The memorable concluding metaphor of the bird in the last of the sonnets in "Part I" appears to ground purpose and resolution of life in a passive Faith (until one reads the first sonnet of "Part II," which starts the dialectical variations all over again):

But, leaving straining thought, and stammering word,
Across the barren azure pass to God;
Shooting the void in silence, like a bird,—
A bird that shuts his wings for better speed! (I: 28, 11–14)

Tuckerman could never repose for long in any one conclusion about the meaning of human existence. In the five sonnet groups he oscillated between stoical faith and a sort of poetic protestantism: He doubted that he or anyone could know the truth under heaven, but then his mind was free, and he would know truth or at least pursue it until death. He cannot be said to have come to a conclusion so much as simply to have stopped writing sonnets after V: 16, yet another prayer to a God who he does not expect will answer. This last sonnet inverts its two parts: The opening sestet states the prayer ("Let me give something!—as the years unfold, / Some faint fruition, though not much, my most: / Perhaps a monument of labor lost."), while the octave recalls a rural scene from memory:

As once I saw at a houseside, a tree
Struck Scarlet by the lightning, utterly
To its last limb and twig: so strange it seemed,
I stopped to think if this indeed were May,
And were those windflowers? Or had I dreamed?
But there it stood, close by the cottage eaves,

Red-ripened to the heart: shedding its leaves
And autumn sadness on the dim spring day.

The blasted tree is an "icon" of Hudson River School landscape painting, "the memorial of some storm," as Cole said, standing both for and against time, defying the linear succession of seasons. May was the month of Anna's death—of the lightning that blasted Tuckerman's tree. Here again was the old pain. Yet, by the end of his sonnet writing, Tuckerman could almost forget for a time, almost be "surprised by joy," almost contemplate the ruined tree as himself, without bitterness, as "perhaps a monument of labor lost."

Frederick Goddard Tuckerman died in Greenfield of "heart trouble" on 9 May 1873 at the age of fifty-two, the man and the poetry already forgotten by his contemporaries. More than eighty years after the appearance of *Poems,* and then by the modernist aesthetic reckoning, Tuckerman received his necessary second reading. But even this rediscovery was periodic and brief. Such American modernists as Winters and Witter Bynner believed they discerned in Tuckerman their own precursor. Among them (Bynner in the 1930s, and then Winters and his student Momaday in the 1950s and 1960s), they used their considerable authority as poets and critics to bring Tuckerman's poetry to the attention of at least like-minded readers, if not the common reader. Indeed, throughout the twentieth century Tuckerman has never lacked for champions. Most recently, England has made a strong case for Tuckerman's originality and for admitting his poetry into the Anglo-American canon. But, as the poet himself understood—". . . of what avail, / I ask, are these dim fancies, cares, and fears?" (Sonnets, I: 1, 3–4)—until the poetry is available to whoever wants to read it, and read it again, he will remain in obscurity. The poems of Frederick Goddard Tuckerman are once again forgotten: Momaday's edition of 1965, the most comprehensive in a century, is long out of print.

References:

Eugene England, *Beyond Romanticism: Tuckerman's Life and Poetry* (Provo, Utah: Brigham Young University, 1991);

Samuel A. Golden, *Frederick Goddard Tuckerman* (New York: Twayne, 1966);

Thomas Patrick Lynch, "'Quick Fire for Frost': A Study of the Poetry of Frederick Goddard Tuckerman," dissertation, Columbia University, 1969.

Papers:

All known Frederick Goddard Tuckerman manuscripts are in the Houghton Library at Harvard University.

Jones Very

(28 August 1813 – 8 May 1880)

David M. Robinson
Oregon State University

See also the Very entry in *DLB 1: The American Renaissance in New England.*

BOOKS: *Essays and Poems,* edited by Ralph Waldo Emerson (Boston: Little & Brown, 1839);

Poems by Jones Very, edited, with a memoir, by William P. Andrews (Boston & New York: Houghton, Mifflin, 1883);

Poems and Essays, complete and revised edition, edited by James Freeman Clarke (Boston: Houghton, Mifflin, 1886);

Jones Very: The Complete Poems, edited by Helen R. Deese (Athens: University of Georgia Press, 1993).

Collection: *Poems by Jones Very: James Freeman Clarke's Enlarged Collection of 1886 Re-edited with a Thematic and Topical Index,* edited by Kenneth Walter Cameron (Hartford, Conn.: Transcendental Books, 1965);

Jones Very: Selected Poems, edited by Nathan Lyons (New Brunswick, N.J.: Rutgers University Press, 1966).

OTHER: Phyllis Cole, "Jones Very's 'Epistles to the Unborn,'" in *Studies in the American Renaissance 1982,* edited by Joel Myerson (Boston: Twayne, 1982), pp. 169–183;

Helen R. Deese, "Unpublished and Uncollected Poems of Jones Very," *ESQ: A Journal of the American Renaissance,* 30 (Third Quarter 1984): 154–162;

Deese, ed., "Selected Sermons of Jones Very," in *Studies in the American Renaissance 1984,* edited by Myerson (Charlottesville: University Press of Virginia, 1984), pp. 1–78.

Jones Very

Jones Very was one of the most accomplished poets among the New England Transcendentalists and is best known for his intensely pious religious sonnets describing the "new birth" and the nature of the "will-less existence," a state of absolute harmony with God that Very believed was the highest accomplishment of the religious life. Jones Very was born in Salem, Massachusetts, 28 August 1813, the eldest of the six children of Jones Very, a ship captain, and Lydia (Very) Very. Jones Very the son entered Harvard College as a sophomore in 1834 and distinguished himself as a scholar of the classics and an essayist, winning two consecutive Bowdoin Prizes for his essays, as a junior and as a senior. Very's outstanding scholarly achievement at Harvard was also accompanied, however, by a tumultuous religious struggle that eventually changed the course of his life

328

and resulted in an unusual and extraordinary poetic achievement. During his senior year Very underwent a transformative religious experience that he termed a "*change of heart*." This dramatic conversion led Very to see the world in completely new terms, as a struggle between the corrupt human will and the grace of God. He reacted to this profound experience of enlightenment or transformation by attempting to live a "will-less existence," in which he completely subdued any promptings from his own will or desire.

In Very's new conception of the world, the individual human will was a potentially corrupting force, standing as a barrier between the self and God. In a wholly transformed life, one must live without a private will, completely open to the commands of the Holy Spirit. "Thou wilt my hands employ," he declared in his 1839 sonnet "The Disciple," assuming a stance of utter humility before the promptings of God. "The life is all that He his sons has taught, / Obey within, and thou shalt see its light," he wrote in "To Him That Hath Shall Be Given," another poem from early 1839. These declarations express the internal struggle that Very was undergoing in the late 1830s to subdue himself completely to a rigorous and disciplined self-denial. They also suggest the burden of witness that this conversion had placed on him. Not only must he subdue himself, but he must also communicate this difficult message to a world dead to the reality of the spiritual life.

Very came to play a role in the Transcendentalist movement through the efforts of Elizabeth Palmer Peabody, an influential intellectual and educator in Unitarian and Transcendentalist circles. She heard Very lecture in 1837 on epic poetry and brought his work to the attention of Ralph Waldo Emerson, who was always on the lookout for promising young writers. Emerson hoped to cultivate a more fruitful literary atmosphere in New England. He was particularly intent on encouraging poets who might fulfill the promise of American democratic culture and provide new modes of expression for modern experience. Very's theory of epic poetry and his analysis of the nature of William Shakespeare's poetic method, subjects of the essays that Very published in the 1839 volume *Essays and Poems,* were of keen interest to Emerson. Emerson arranged for Very to lecture in Concord and afterward cultivated a friendship with him, though Emerson had to fend off Very's attempts to convert him. Nevertheless, the friendship was productive for each of them. Of particular importance was Emerson's help in encouraging, editing, and arranging publication for *Essays and Poems,* the only book Very published in his lifetime.

Very's developing relationships with Peabody and Emerson in 1837 and 1838 were occurring at a time of enormous turbulence in his life. He had remained at Harvard as a Greek tutor after his graduation in 1836, and his struggle to live out the meaning of his "change of heart" had gradually intensified, culminating finally in an outburst of religious fervor marked by strange and troubling behavior in September 1838. Very began to claim that he spoke the words of the Holy Spirit and told one of his classes to "flee to the mountains, for the end of all things is at hand." His behavior was so troubling that he was sent for recuperation to the McLean Asylum, where he stayed a month.

Very regained his stability, and many of his friends among the Transcendentalists retained their faith in his intellectual and creative power. In an October 1838 letter to Margaret Fuller, Emerson reported, in a worried tone, on "the calamity of poor Very" and also told of his receiving Very's essay on Shakespeare shortly before the incident. "The letter accompanying it betrayed the state of his mind; but the Essay is a noble production: not consecutive, filled with one thought; but that so deep & true & illustrated so happily & even grandly, that I account it an addition to our really scanty stock of adequate criticism of Shakspear. Such a mind cannot be lost."

The period surrounding Very's breakdown and recuperation was a remarkably rich one in literary productivity for him. He wrote poems at a remarkable pace, his spiritual intensity producing an unusual capacity for poetic work. Very's belief concerning his own state was that in this period he was open and attentive to the message given him by God. Emerson was genuinely interested in Very's work and felt it worthy of a published volume; however, he found interacting with Very difficult at times. One key point of contention was Very's resistance to Emerson's suggestions for revisions in his poetry. As Very saw them, his poems were dictation from the Holy Spirit, thus not to be tampered with by a mere mortal such as Emerson. Very's wrangling with Emerson over the editing of the poems provoked Emerson to retort, "Cannot the spirit parse and spell?"

Very's obsession with the idea that the Holy Spirit spoke through him and that he was only a conduit for the truth was, of course, a literary manifestation of his desire to achieve a "will-less existence." It was also a more literal enactment of the doctrine of poetic inspiration that Emerson had proposed in *Nature* (1836) and the Divinity School Address (1838) and developed in more detail in "The Poet" (1844). Under these circumstances Emerson's interest in Very is understandable, especially since Very's belief yielded quite impressive poetic results. Very had written poetry as early as 1833, the year before he entered Harvard, but around the time of his conversion in 1836 he began to pour out a stream of sonnets recounting his new birth. These poems, remarkable in both their formal command of the sonnet form and their vivid depiction of his religious vision, are among the most original literary products of the Transcendentalist movement.

One of the major purposes of Very's poems is to express the power and intensity of the religious experience that he has undergone. In "The New Life" he describes the state of mental excitement and intensity that his change of heart has produced:

'Tis a new life—thoughts move not as they did
With slow uncertain steps across my mind,
In thronging haste fast pressing on they bid
The portals open to the viewless wind.

Such a charged state of mind would of course put one out of step with others, and some of Very's most effective poems give voice to his perception of the darkness and corruption of a world that has not yet been spiritually transformed. In "The Dead" he described the seeming state of living death in which most individuals continue their lives, presenting ordinary life as a kind of surreal and disquieting spectacle: "I see them crowd on crowd they walk the earth / Dry, leafless trees no Autumn wind laid bare." The supposed life that most people enact in their ordinary pursuits is thus a strange and macabre masquerade, because it is cut off from the true life of spiritual realization. "They mimic life, as if from him to steal / His glow of health to paint the livid cheek."

The intense inner pressure that such a vision created in Very is evident not only from his nervous collapse and recuperation at the McLean Asylum but also in his poems. There is a distinctly millennial strand in them, in which Very envisions the return of Christ and the end of history (as in "The Coming" and "The Veil of the Temple," published in *Jones Very: The Complete Poems* [1993]), and he envisions for himself the role of a prophet, foretelling the end of the world and watching for the inevitable signs that the final conflagration had begun. "I place thee as a watchman on a tower, / That thou mayst warn the city of the dead," he wrote in "The Watchman." But there is also the admission, striking in "Night," that such vigilant attention is a burden or an affliction, exhausting in its stern demand: "I thank thee, Father, that the night is near / When I this conscious being may resign." The gift of sleep relieves the poet from

"Thy myriad-handed labors of the day" and "Thy words too frequent for my tongue to say."

While many of Very's poems, especially those sonnets written in the late 1830s under the sway of a profound religious experience, have a clearly otherworldly emphasis, there is also a strong sensitivity to nature in many of them. As Carl Dennis has pointed out in his study of Very's nature poetry, Very makes use of the Romantic concept of "correspondence," an important element in Emerson's first book, *Nature*. Dennis has argued that "like Emerson, Very sees nature as a source of analogues for the highest laws of the mind, as a language to be read by an inspired interpreter." Dennis links Very with the vision of nature associated with Emerson and other Romantics, who see "nature as a scroll or book to be read by the inquiring student." Very's passion for nature, one shared by all the Transcendentalists, is unquestionable, as the opening lines of "Nature" emphasize: "Nature, my love for thee is deeper far / Than strength of words though spirit-born can tell."

Of particular importance are Very's alterations and modifications of voice and persona in his poems, a literary method that is characterized in some poems when his assumption of the voice of prophetic authority becomes indistinguishable from the voice of the Holy Spirit. Who is speaking in these poems? Readers are intended to hear the voice of God through the poet, not hear the poet's voice. The merging of the personality of the author with that of God was a bold experiment, a form of writing in which the author's ego becomes so inflated, so to speak, that it disappears entirely, replaced by that of the Spirit. "The words I give thee they are not thine own," he writes in "The Promise." "Give them as freely as to thee they're given." These opening lines illustrate the complex workings of Very's poetics, when one considers the dramatic situation and dialogue they portray. Are these words a message from the poet to the reader, urging the reader to spread this message to others? Or are they an explanation of the source of the poet's inspiration, in which God charges him not to associate his own ego with the prophetic message of the poems and to spread that message as freely as it was given to him? Both these dynamics are working simultaneously in the poem, and, indeed, in many of Very's better poems. His poetic theory is one of self-extinguishment, in which he becomes only the conduit for the message that is given him. Through his sonnets, then, Very at times represents or enacts the merging of self with the larger spirit of God. This merger of self and spirit was at the core of his religious vision and was also an aspiration of other Tran-

John 1:4 In him was Life and the
life was the Light of men.

            Christianity is a life. It does
not consist in rites & forms, for these have
not in themselves a life-giving influence. Their
great object is not to appeal to and awaken
a life in man, but to restrain him from
transgressions, to fence him in from doing
evil. The laws of Moses regarded the overt
acts of men, and not their thoughts & motives. They served to keep men within certain bounds, and lead them to sigh
for something better. Thus the earth
lies bound in icy fetters through the
cold months of winter, the trees & shrubs
are stiff & dry, the rivers & brooks frozen
& mute, all waiting for the genial
breath of Spring to animate & set them
free. What spring is to nature, Chy was & is to man.
It is a quickening breath reaching our
inward nature awakening it to life &

Page from Very's sermon on "Christianity Not A Religion of Rites and Forms," which he preached on 10 February 1850 at the
First Church of Salem, Massachusetts, and several more times in other places
(Harris Collection of American Poetry, Brown University)

scendentalists such as Bronson Alcott, Emerson, and Henry David Thoreau.

Very's classification in literary history has been problematic. His reputation has always been tied to Emerson and the Transcendentalist movement, an association that is justified on several grounds. Emerson's friendship, advocacy, and editorial help for Very, and the publication of Very's work in the Transcendentalist periodicals *The Western Messenger* and *The Dial* all confirm his place in the Transcendentalist movement. Moreover, Very's apocalyptic sense of the coming of a new religious age accorded well with the expectation of the "newness" that informed the work of Transcendentalists such as Emerson, Alcott, Orestes Brownson, and Theodore Parker. Very also shared with Emerson and Thoreau a deep sense of the symbolic richness of nature and its spiritual quality, if rightly seen by the observer.

Some critics, such as Yvor Winters, have noted Very's more traditionally Christian outlook and terminology and argue that he is out of place among Emerson's more theologically liberal circle. Very's language is densely biblical in quality, and his poems are saturated with references to Christian concepts such as the crucifixion of Christ and his second coming. In this sense he differed from Emerson, whose religious vision, while grounded in Christian theology, discarded the supernatural aspects of Christian doctrine and developed a more universal perspective, incorporating insights, allusions, and symbols from other religious and philosophical traditions. The Christian elements of Very's religious vision and the elements of sensibility that he shared with Emerson and other Transcendentalists can be reconciled if the reader understands that Very entered the Unitarian ministry after leaving Harvard and adhered to a form of moderate liberalism that he regarded as "Channing Unitarianism," after the leading Unitarian preacher William Ellery Channing. Very can be understood within the tradition of "Unitarian pietism" as elucidated in Daniel Walker Howe's *The Unitarian Conscience* (1970). Each of these labels—Transcendentalist, Christian, and Unitarian—captures an aspect of this complex mind and personality, and all three have to be weighed in formulating a complete picture of his intellectual career and context.

To characterize with certainty the nature of Very's religious experience during his senior year at Harvard is similarly difficult. Several critics have applied the term "mystic" to Very, calling attention to the visionary qualities of his poetry and his desire to minimize the impact of the individual will in both ethical and aesthetic acts. In this sense his attempt to live a "will-less existence" during the period of his most intense religious fervor can be seen as part of a much larger tradition of mystical thought, in both Christian and Asian religious traditions, in which the self sought to merge with a larger spiritual consciousness. In an early assessment of his poetry and religious outlook, James Freeman Clarke, who published some of Very's essays in *The Western Messenger* in the 1830s and thus gave Very greater visibility among the Transcendentalists, described Very as "a genuine mystic." Clarke's characterization links Very to the larger phenomenon of the appearance of a mystical consciousness in many cultures and historical periods. "Mr. Very believed, with Madame Guion and others, that sin is self-will; and holiness, absolute obedience in all things, small and great, to the will of God made known in the soul. He believed himself led in all things by the Spirit of God, and so illuminated as not to think or conjecture or believe, but to know." Helen R. Deese, the editor of the definitive modern edition of Very's poetry, has written that Very's account of his religious experience "is a classic description of mystical experience" and has also called attention to his "To the Unborn," three prose "epistles" intended probably as a commentary and introduction to his *Essays and Poems* but unpublished in his life. These letters offer further evidence of Very's alignment with mystical thought, for in them "Very distinguishes between himself and the unregenerated world that has not passed through the stages of mystical rebirth as he has done; and he identifies himself with Christ." As Deese concludes, "If one concedes the possibility of the mystical state, Jones Very must surely be admitted to it."

In a reassessment of Very's achievement prompted by Deese's new edition of his poetry, Alan D. Hodder describes Very's account of his religious experience in different terms, arguing that it is in line with "traditional theological language and older New England conceptions of the way of salvation." From this perspective Very is best understood as an exemplar of a conception of salvation or regeneration consonant with that of the New England Puritans. He is in this view less a religious exotic than an extreme religious traditionalist, whose experience can be seen as an extension of New England religious tradition, not as a break with it. Whether Very is seen as a mystic struggling toward a unity with a transcendent spirit or an impassioned Christian convert attempting to live out the implications of his new birth (and these are not necessarily incompatible views), his remarkable sonnets must be read as the attempt to express and communicate the authority of his spiritual transformation. The expressive power of those poems marks one of the aesthetic high points of Transcendentalism and emphasizes the fusion of religious vision with artistic achievement so characteristic of that movement.

Very's later life presents something of a puzzle when compared with the drama of his religious enlightenment in the late 1830s. Deese calls his later work "anticlimatic." From late 1838 until his death on 8 May 1880, he lived a relatively quiet and uneventful life in Salem with his mother and his sisters Lydia (also a poet) and Frances. Very continued to write poetry, but he was also licensed to preach in 1843 and began to serve as a Unitarian preacher, supplying the pulpit occasionally for many Unitarian churches. Though he was never ordained and settled as the pastor of a church, Very identified himself primarily as a preacher in the last half of his life, his identity as a poet or man of letters becoming secondary to him. Very's extant manuscript sermons, most of which are preserved at the Houghton Library, Harvard University, suggest less an impassioned mystic or fervent convert than a thoughtful, moderately liberal Unitarian minister, whose ardor had perhaps cooled but whose sense of religious commitment remained deep. William P. Andrews offers a description of the quiet routine that characterized Very's later life. "His mornings were spent in study and a somewhat general course of scientific and literary reading; and his afternoons in rambles over the rocky hills and through the mossy dells of the wild pasture land surrounding the upper portion of his native city." Those who knew him recognized his saintly or spiritual mien, and Andrews quotes Very's friend E. A. Silsbee on this quality of spiritual absorption that Very retained throughout his life: "He moved in Salem like Dante among the Florentines: a man who had seen God; . . . and drew his inspiration from the Spirit itself, far away in the soul, where no ambition comes, but only lowliness, humility, and seeking."

Bibliographies:

David Robinson, "Jones Very: An Essay in Bibliography," *Resources for American Literary Study,* 5 (Autumn 1975): 131–146;

Robinson, "Jones Very," in *The Transcendentalists: A Review of Research and Criticism,* edited by Joel Myerson (New York: Modern Language Association, 1984), pp. 286–294.

Biographies:

William Irving Bartlett, *Jones Very: Emerson's "Brave Saint"* (Durham, N.C.: Duke University Press, 1942);

Edwin Gittleman, *Jones Very: The Effective Years, 1833–1840* (New York: Columbia University Press, 1967).

References:

Carlos A. Baker, "Emerson and Jones Very," *New England Quarterly,* 7 (March 1934): 90–99;

Warner Berthoff, "Jones Very: New England Mystic," *Boston Public Library Quarterly,* 2 (January 1950): 63–75;

Lawrence Buell, *Literary Transcendentalism: Style and Vision in the American Renaissance* (Ithaca, N.Y.: Cornell University Press, 1973);

L. H. Butterfield, "Come with Me to the Feast; or, Transcendentalism in Action," *M. H. S. Miscellany,* no. 6 (December 1960): 1–5;

James Freeman Clarke, *Events and Epochs in Religious History: Being the Substance of A Course of Twelve Lectures Delivered in the Lowell Institute, Boston, in 1880* (Boston: Osgood, 1881), pp. 291–298;

Helen R. Deese, "The Peabody Family and the Jones Very 'Insanity': Two Letters of Mary Peabody," *Harvard Library Bulletin,* 35 (Spring 1987): 218–229;

Deese, "The Posthumous Task of Editing 'The Holy Spirit': The Jones Very Edition," *Documentary Editing,* 11 (March 1989): 5–9;

Carl Dennis, "Correspondence in Very's Nature Poetry," *New England Quarterly,* 43 (June 1970): 250–273;

Margaret Fuller, "Chat in Boston Bookstores.—No. 1," *Boston Quarterly Review,* 3 (January 1840): 127–134;

Anthony Herbold, "Nature as Concept and Technique in the Poetry of Jones Very," *New England Quarterly,* 40 (June 1967): 244–259;

Alan D. Hodder, "Jones Very's Season in Heaven," *Harvard Divinity Bulletin,* 25 (1996): 14–17;

Daniel Walker Howe, *The Unitarian Conscience: Harvard Moral Philosophy, 1805–1861* (New Haven: Yale University Press, 1970);

Harry L. Jones, "The Very Madness: A New Manuscript," *CLA Journal,* 10 (March 1967): 196–200;

James A. Levernier, "Calvinism and Transcendentalism in the Poetry of Jones Very," *ESQ: A Journal of the American Renaissance,* 24 (First Quarter 1976): 30–41;

Perry Miller, ed., *The Transcendentalists: An Anthology* (Cambridge, Mass.: Harvard University Press, 1950);

William M. Moss, "'So Many Promising Youths': Emerson's Disappointing Discoveries of New

England Poet-Seers," *New England Quarterly,* 49 (March 1976): 46–64;

Joel Myerson, "A Calendar of Transcendental Club Meetings," *American Literature,* 44 (May 1972): 197–207;

Myerson, *The New England Transcendentalists and* The Dial: *A History of the Magazine and Its Contributors* (Rutherford, N.J.: Fairleigh Dickinson University Press, 1980);

Myerson, ed., *Transcendentalism: A Reader* (Oxford & New York: Oxford University Press, 2000);

Barbara L. Packer, "The Transcendentalists," in *The Cambridge History of American Literature. Volume Two: Prose Writing 1820–1865,* edited by Sacvan Bercovitch (Cambridge & New York: Cambridge University Press, 1995), pp. 329–604;

Paschal Reeves, "Jones Very as Preacher: The Extant Sermons," *ESQ: A Journal of the American Renaissance,* 57 (Fourth Quarter 1969): 16–22;

Reeves, "The Making of a Mystic: A Reconsideration of the Life of Jones Very," *Essex Institute Historical Collections,* 103 (January 1967): 3–30;

David Robinson, "The Exemplary Self and the Transcendent Self in the Poetry of Jones Very," *ESQ: A Journal of the American Renaissance,* 24 (Fourth Quarter 1978): 206–214;

Robinson, "Jones Very, the Transcendentalists, and the Unitarian Tradition," *Harvard Theological Review,* 68 (April 1975): 105–124;

Ralph L. Rusk, ed., *The Letters of Ralph Waldo Emerson,* 6 volumes (New York: Columbia University Press, 1939);

Yvor Winters, "Jones Very: A New England Mystic," *American Review,* 7 (May 1936): 159–168; republished in his *Maule's Curse* (Norfolk: New Directions, 1938), pp. 125–136.

Papers:

The major repository of Jones Very's papers is the Houghton Library at Harvard University. The Harris Collection of American Poetry at Brown University, the American Antiquarian Society, and the Essex Institute in Salem, Massachusetts, also hold important manuscript materials. The papers of the Very family are at the Massachusetts Historical Society.

Noah Webster
(16 October 1758 – 28 May 1843)

D'Ann Pletcher George
Bridgewater State College

See also the Webster entries in *DLB 1: The American Renaissance in New England; DLB 37: American Writers of the Early Republic; DLB 42: American Writers for Children Before 1900; DLB 43: American Newspaper Journalists, 1690–1872;* and *DLB 73: American Magazine Journalists, 1741–1850.*

BOOKS: *A Grammatical Institute, of the English Language, Comprising, an Easy, Concise, and Systematic Method of Education, Designed for the Use of English Schools in America. In Three Parts. Part I. Containing, a New and Accurate Standard of Pronunciation* (Hartford: Printed by Hudson & Goodwin, 1783);

A Grammatical Institute, of the English Language, Comprising, an Easy, Concise, and Systematic Method of Education, Designed for the Use of English Schools in America. In Three Parts. Part II. Containing, a Plain and Comprehensive Grammar . . . and an Essay Towards Investigating the Rules of English Verse (Hartford: Printed by Hudson & Goodwin, 1783; third edition, revised and amended, Philadelphia: Printed & sold by Young & M'Culloch, 1787; fourth edition, revised and amended, Hartford: Printed & sold by Hudson & Goodwin, 1787);

A Grammatical Institute, of the English Language, Comprising, an Easy, Concise, and Systematic Method of Education, Designed for the Use of English Schools in America. In Three Parts. Part III. Containing the Necessary Rules of Reading and Speaking, and a Variety of Essays (Hartford: Printed by Barrow & Babcock for the Author, 1783);

Sketches of American Policy. Under the Following Heads: I. Theory of Government. II. Governments on the Eastern Continent. III. American States; or the Principles of the American Constitutions Contrasted with Those of European States. IV. Plan of Policy for Improving the Advantages and Perpetuating the Union of the American States (Hartford: Printed by Hudson & Goodwin, 1785);

An American Selection of Lessons in Reading and Speaking. Calculated to Improve the Minds and Refine the Taste of Youth (Philadelphia: Printed & sold by Young &

Noah Webster in 1823 (portrait by Samuel F. B. Morse; from Harry R. Warfel, Noah Webster: Schoolmaster to America, *1936)*

M'Culloch, 1785; revised edition, New Haven: From Sidney's Press for I. Beers & I. Cooke, 1804)—a thorough revision of *A Grammatical Institute, of the English Language . . . Part III;*

The American Spelling Book, or First Part of the Grammatical Institute of the English Language (Philadelphia: Young & M'Culloch, 1787)—a thorough revision of *A Grammatical Institute, of the English Language . . . Part I;*

An Examination Into the Leading Principles of the Federal Constitution Proposed by the Late Convention Held at Philadelphia. With Answers to the Principle Objections That

Have Been Raised Against the System (Philadelphia: Printed & sold by Prichard & Hall, 1787);

Attention! Or, New Thoughts on a Serious Subject; Being an Enquiry into the Excise Laws of Connecticut; Addressed to the Freemen of the State. By a Private Citizen (Hartford: Printed & sold by Hudson & Goodwin, 1789);

Dissertations on the English Language: With Notes, Historical and Critical. To Which Is Added, By Way of Appendix, An Essay on a Reformed Mode of Spelling, with Dr. Franklin's Arguments on that Subject (Boston: Printed by Isaiah Thomas for the Author, 1789);

A Collection of Essays and Fugitiv Writings. On Moral, Historical, Political and Literary Subjects (Boston: Printed by I. Thomas & E. T. Andrews for the Author, 1790);

The Prompter; or A Commentary on Common Sayings and Subjects, Which are Full of Common Sense, the Best Sense in the World (Hartford: Printed by Hudson & Goodwin, 1790);

Effects of Slavery, on Morals and Industry (Hartford: Printed by Hudson & Goodwin, 1793);

The Revolution in France, Considered in Respect to Its Progress and Effects (New York: George Bunce, 1794);

A Letter to the Governors, Instructors and Trustees of the Universities, and Other Seminaries of Learning, in the United States, on the Errors of English Grammars (New York: Printed by George F. Hopkins for the Author, 1798);

An Oration Pronounced Before the Citizens of New-Haven on the Anniversary of the Independence of the United States, July 4th 1798 (New Haven: Printed by T. & S. Green, 1798);

A Brief History of Epidemic and Pestilential Diseases; with the Principal Phenomena of the Physical World, which Precede and Accompany Them, and Observations Deduced from the Facts Stated, 2 volumes (Hartford: Printed by Hudson & Goodwin, 1799; London: Printed for G. G. & J. Robinson, 1800);

Ten Letters to Dr. Joseph Priestly [sic], *in Answer to the Inhabitants of Northumberland* (New Haven: Printed by Read & Morse, 1800);

A Rod for the Fool's Back (New Haven? 1800);

A Letter to General Hamilton, Occasioned by his Letter to President Adams. By a Federalist (New York? 1800);

Miscellaneous Papers, On Political and Commercial Subjects (New York: Printed by E. Belden, 1802);

Elements of Useful Knowledge. Volume 1. Containing a Historical and Geographical Account of the United States: For the Use of Schools (Hartford: Printed & sold by Hudson & Goodwin, 1802);

An Oration Pronounced before the Citizens of New Haven, on the Anniversary of the Declaration of Independence; July,

1802 (New Haven: Printed by William W. Morse, 1802);

An Address to the Citizens of Connecticut (New Haven: Printed by J. Walter, 1803);

The American Spelling Book; Containing, the Rudiments of the English Language, for the Use of Schools in the United States (Philadelphia: Jacob Johnson, 1804)—a thorough revision of *The American Spelling Book, or First Part of the Grammatical Institute of the English Language; Elements of Useful Knowledge. Volume II. Containing a Historical and Geographical Account of the United States: For the Use of Schools* (New Haven: From Sidney's Press, for the Author, 1804);

Elements of Useful Knowledge. Vol. III. Containing a Historical and Geographical Account of the Empires and States in Europe, Asia and Africa, with Their Colonies. To Which Is Added, a Brief Description of New Holland, and the Principal Islands in the Pacific and Indian Oceans. For the Use of Schools (New Haven: Bronson, Walter, 1806);

A Compendious Dictionary of the English Language (Hartford: From Sidney's Press for Hudson & Goodwin and Increase Cooke, New Haven, 1806);

A Dictionary of the English Language; Compiled for the Use of Common Schools in the United States (Boston: Printed by Sidney's Press for John & David West; Brisban & Brannan, New York; Lincoln & Gleason and Oliver D. Cooke, Hartford; Increase Cooke, New Haven, 1807);

A Philosophical and Practical Grammar of the English Language (New Haven: Printed by Oliver Steele for Brisban & Brannan, 1807); republished as *An Improved Grammar of the English Language* (New Haven: Hezekiah Howe, 1831)—a thorough revision of *A Grammatical Institute, of the English Language . . . Part II;*

A Letter to Dr. David Ramsay, of Charlestown, (S.C.) Respecting the Errors in Johnson's Dictionary, and Other Lexicons (New Haven: Printed by Oliver Steele, 1807);

The Peculiar Doctrines of the Gospel, Explained and Defended (New York: J. Seymour, 1809);

History of Animals; Being the Fourth Volume of Elements of Useful Knowledge. For the Use of Schools, and Young Persons of Both Sexes (New Haven: Howe & Deforest and Walter & Steele, 1812);

An Oration Pronounced Before the Knox and Warren Branches of the Washington Benevolent Society, at Amherst, on the Celebration of the Anniversary of the Declaration of Independence, July 4, 1814 (Northampton, Mass.: Printed by William Butler, 1814);

A Letter to the Honorable John Pickering, On the Subject of His Vocabulary; or, Collection of Words and Phrases, Supposed to Be Peculiar to the United States of America (Boston: West & Richardson, 1817);

An Address, Delivered Before the Hampshire, Franklin and Hampden Agricultural Society, at Their Annual Meeting in Northampton, Oct. 14, 1818 (Northampton, Mass.: Printed by Thomas W. Shepard, 1818);

A Plea for a Miserable World. I. An Address Delivered at the Laying of the Corner Stone of the Building Erecting for the Charity Institution in Amherst, Massachusetts, August 9, 1820, by Noah Webster, Esq. II. A Sermon Delivered on the Same Occasion, by Rev. Daniel A. Clark, Pastor of the First Church and Society in Amherst. III. A Brief Account of the Origin of the Institution (Boston: Printed by Ezra Lincoln, 1820);

Letters to a Young Gentleman Commencing His Education: To which is Subjoined a Brief History of the United States (New Haven: Printed by S. Converse and sold by Howe & Spalding, 1823);

An American Dictionary of the English Language, 2 volumes (New York: S. Converse, 1828); revised by E. H. Barker as *A Dictionary of the English Language*, 12 parts (London: Printed for Black, Young & Young, 1830–1832); American edition revised and enlarged as *An American Dictionary of the English Language; First Edition in Octavo*, 2 volumes (New Haven: Printed by B. L. Hamlen for the Author, 1841);

The Elementary Spelling Book (New York: J. P. Haven & R. Lockwood, 1829)—a thorough revision of *The American Spelling Book; Containing, the Rudiments of the English Language, for the Use of Schools in the United States;*

Biography for the Use of Schools (New Haven: Printed by Hezekiah Howe, 1830);

A Dictionary of the English Language; Abridged from The American Dictionary, For the Use of Primary Schools and the Counting House (New York: White, Gallaher & White, 1830);

History of the United States: To Which Is Prefixed a Brief Historical Account of Our English Ancestors, from the Dispersion of Babel, to Their Migration to America; and of the Conquest of South America, by the Spaniards (New Haven: Durrie & Peck, 1832; revised edition, Cincinnati: Corey, Fairbank & Webster, 1835);

A Dictionary for Primary Schools (New York: N. & J. White / New Haven: N. & J. White, 1833);

Value of the Bible, And Excellence of the Christian Religion: for the Use of Families and Schools (New Haven: Durrie & Peck, 1834);

A Brief View 1. Of Errors and Obscurities in the Common Version of the Scriptures; Addressed to Bible Societies, Clergymen and Other Friends of Religion. 2. Of Errors and Defects in Class-Books Used in Seminaries of Learning; Including Dictionaries and Grammars of the English, French, Greek and Latin Languages; Addressed to Instructors of Youth, and Students, with a Few Hints to

Title page for Webster's first book, with which he began his lifelong attempt to standardize the spelling of American English (New York Public Library, Astor, Lenox and Tilden Foundations)

Statesmen, Members of Congress, and Heads of Departments. To Which Is Added, 3. A Few Plagiarisms, Showing the Way in Which Books May Be Made, by Those Who Use Borrowed Capital (New Haven, 1834?);

Instructive and Entertaining Lessons; With Rules for Reading With Propriety, Illustrated by Examples: Designed for Use in Schools and Families (New Haven: S. Babcock and Durrie & Peck, 1835)—a thorough revision of *An American Selection of Lessons in Reading and Speaking;*

The Teacher; A Supplement to The Elementary Spelling Book (New Haven: S. Babcock, 1836);

A Letter to the Hon. Daniel Webster, on the Political Affairs of the United States, as Marcellus (Philadelphia: Printed by J. Crissy, 1837);

Mistakes and Corrections. 1. Improprieties in the Common Version of the Scriptures; With Specimens of Amended Language in Webster's Edition of the Bible. 2. Explanations of Prepositions, in English, and Other Languages. These

Constitute a Very Difficult Part of Philology. 3. Errors in English Grammars. 4. Mistakes in the Hebrew Lexicon of Gesenius, and In Some Derivations of Dr. Horwitz. 5. Errors in Butter's Scholar's Companion and in Town's Analysis. 6. Errors in Richardson's Dictionary (New Haven: Printed by B. L. Hamlen, 1837);

Appeal to Americans. Fellow Citizens! (New York? 1838?);

A Manual of Useful Studies: For the Instruction of Young Persons of Both Sexes, in Families and Schools (New Haven: Printed & published by S. Babcock, 1839);

Observations on Language, and on the Errors of Class-books (New Haven: Printed by S. Babcock, 1839);

A Collection of Papers on Political, Literary and Moral Subjects (New York: Webster & Clark / Boston: Tappan & Dennett / Philadelphia: Smith & Peck, 1843);

Poems by Noah Webster, edited by Ruth Farquhar Warfel and Harry Redcay Warfel (College Park, Md.: Harruth Lefraw, 1936);

Noah Webster: Letters on Yellow Fever Addressed to Dr. William Currie, introduction by Benjamin Spector (Baltimore: Johns Hopkins University Press, 1947);

Noah Webster on Youth and Old Age, a Sophomore Latin Exercise Given at Yale College, May 4, 1776 (New York: New York Public Library, 1954);

The Autobiographies of Noah Webster: From the Letters and Essays, Memoir and Diary, edited by Richard M. Rollins (Columbia: University of South Carolina Press, 1989).

OTHER: *New England Primer, "Amended and Improved . . . ,"* edited by Webster (Philadelphia: Young & M'Culloch, 1787);

John Winthrop, *A Journal of the Transactions and Occurrences in the Settlement of Massachusetts and the Other New-England Colonies, from the Year 1630–1644,* edited by Webster (Hartford, Conn.: Printed by Elisha Babcock, 1790);

The Holy Bible, Containing the Old and New Testaments, in the Common Version. With Amendments of the Language, by Noah Webster, LL.D. (New Haven: Durrie & Peck, 1833).

Thirty years before Ralph Waldo Emerson argued that "Life is our dictionary," Noah Webster mined the U.S. trade, manufacturing, legal system, religious denominations, Indian heritage, and regional dialects for five thousand new words to add to his *A Compendious Dictionary of the English Language,* published in 1806. His best-known works—two dictionaries and a spelling book—signaled that Americans were becoming linguistically and culturally independent of England. In addition to his schoolbooks and dictionaries Webster wrote histories, biographies, essays, political pamphlets,

scientific treatises, and editorials. Often patriotic and pious, his influential writing encouraged Americans to improve and expand their literacy. Only after the people accomplished this goal, he believed, could the young country hope for a strong central government.

Born on 16 October 1758 to a middle-class farming family, the descendent of John Webster and William Bradford, Noah Webster grew up in the pious community of Hartford, Connecticut, on the eve of the American Revolution. His father, Noah Sr., held important positions in the Congregational church and the town government. At forty-eight years old, the elder Webster responded to the Boston Massacre by recruiting and training a volunteer militia. The company included his three young sons, who marched in the rear and played musical instruments. Mercy (Steele) Webster, Noah's mother, taught each child to play flute, sing the psalms of Isaac Watts, and read.

In contrast to the sympathetic education he received at home, Webster remembered his early schoolteachers as illiterate and too fond of the ferule. Though Connecticut required every town with more than fifty households to support a common school, materials were meager and lessons rudimentary at best. Students learned arithmetic by copying sums off of a blackboard and learned reading through study of a catechism, a Psalter, a Bible, and an English speller. Published in 1740, Thomas Dilworth's speller, which also taught religious doctrine and names of towns in England, remained the standard textbook until Webster's own superseded it.

Recognizing that his dreamy, bookish son was better suited to a profession than to farming, Noah Sr. mortgaged the family farm to send his second son to Yale College. In spite of a collapsing economy and hard times on the farm, Noah Sr. remained unswervingly devoted to his child's education, a commitment that Noah Jr. emulated later through a dogged commitment to establishing his own son, a spendthrift dullard who had no real interest in the publishing business.

At Yale, Webster studied the original languages of the Bible, including Greek, Hebrew, Latin, Syriac, and Chaldee. As a member of a debating society he honed his public speaking skills and discussed controversial topics, such as the proper relationship between government and its citizens. The society also provided him with a library, where he encountered the works of John Locke, Francis Bacon, and Sir Isaac Newton.

Drawing on his reading of Enlightenment philosophy, Webster wrote college essays that helped him to develop his political, religious, and pedagogical convictions. Rejecting the Puritan belief in original sin, he decided that man is a rational, educable creature who would respond well to a nurturing teacher. Universal access to education, furthermore, seemed essential for a strong republic, since ignorant people may fall prey to tyrants. Reasoning that women encourage the formation of a civil and stable society, Webster extended his argument for universal education to include women. Many ideas from these early writings appear in his later publications, such as "On the Education of Youth in America" (first published in 1788 in *American Magazine*).

News of the Revolutionary War, food shortages, and the absence of older students who left to become soldiers interrupted Webster's college education several times. At one point he and his classmates protested the attempt of the Continental Army to conscript them (the first draft protest in American history). Most students, however, supported the war, and after completing college, Webster joined the company led by his father, which never saw any fighting but camped on the Hudson River for three days to prevent two separate British companies from linking forces.

Webster's lifelong Yale friends included Joel Barlow, Josiah Meigs, Timothy Dwight, and Ezra Stiles, whom Webster met when Dwight became president of the college in 1778. In later years, praise from influential Yale friends helped Webster market his speller.

Unable to afford Litchfield Law School, where many of his classmates flocked after college, Noah settled on teaching at a common school in Hartford. Surprising himself, Webster flourished as a teacher, becoming deeply interested in how children learn, especially how they acquire their native language. Miserable conditions in schools, however, appalled him. Buildings were cold, furniture uncomfortable, and materials scarce. In a series of essays he critiqued the common school. One of his suggestions proved prophetic: children need interesting books that will make them like reading and learning.

While teaching, Webster found a way to study law by boarding with an attorney who possessed a vast law library. In a pattern that later repeated itself, Webster taught by day and read in the evenings, exhausting himself trying to do too much. He had to quit his teaching position and return home to recuperate. Turning his attention again in 1780 to the study of law, Webster clerked for a judge in Litchfield, where he could also attend lectures of Tapping Reeve, a prominent attorney. In 1781 Webster was admitted to the bar in Connecticut.

With a war going on, lawyers were not much in demand, so Webster turned again to teaching. This time he opened his own private academy, which attracted wealthy families who had fled war-torn New York. While teaching, Webster extended his writings on pedagogy, arguing that girls ought to learn speaking and writing as well as their legal rights.

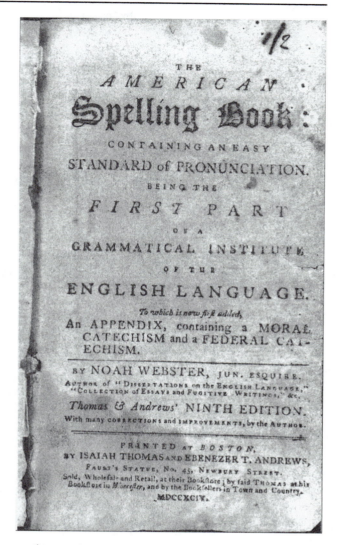

Title page for one of the 1794 editions of Webster's popular 1787 textbook. This ninth Boston edition was probably the thirtieth printed nationwide.

Though the school folded when students returned to New York, Webster had saved enough money to further his education. He spent the winter learning Italian, Spanish, and German, and reading the works of Jean-Jacques Rousseau and Thomas Paine. Webster came to believe that average Americans not only must become educated to ensure the stability of the republic, but they must also learn from American schoolbooks, which were virtually nonexistent.

When his savings ran out, Webster again donned the schoolmaster's robe, this time in Goshen, New York. On his way there, he spent a day in the camp of the Continental Army, awaiting disbandment. Instead of inspiring Webster with patriotic admiration, however, the colonial soldiers filled his heart with fear of anarchy at the hands of an uneducated mass whose lan-

Rebecca Greenleaf Webster in 1832 (portrait by Jared Flagg;
from Harry R. Warfel, Noah Webster:
Schoolmaster to America, *1936)*

guages and accents were so diverse that they could not understand each other, much less govern themselves. The answer to the problem, he decided, lay in teaching American children how to read, write, and speak uniformly—a "federal language," he later called it in the introduction to his speller, *A Grammatical Institute, of the English Language, Comprising, an Easy, Concise, and Systematic Method of Education, Designed for the Use of English Schools in America. In Three Parts. Part I. Containing, a New and Accurate Standard of Pronunciation* (1783).

Webster recognized that existing spellers, which taught reading through the alphabet method, included contradictory and confusing spellings, reflecting that the English language itself often had more than one acceptable spelling for a given word. Standardizing the spelling of American English and improving its teaching was a lifelong project for Webster that began with his speller and reached its climax forty-five years later with *An American Dictionary of the English Language* (1828).

By grouping together words that sound the same, Webster's speller made learning to read and pronounce the language easier for children, who love rhymes. Competing books grouped words of the same length and provided fewer clues to pronunciation. But what made *A Grammatical Institute* a peculiarly American book

was its emphasis on practical words, its sections on American geography and history, and its frequent lessons on morality and patriotism, which Webster taught as a kind of virtue. Literacy in a particularly American language, Webster believed, would strengthen the people's sense of their national identity and their ability to govern themselves.

Once Webster had completed a draft of his speller, he set out to copyright his work—a daunting task since the Continental Congress could only recommend that individual states grant an author copyright. After a failed attempt to win legislation in New Jersey, Webster concentrated on Connecticut and New York, where he had more influential friends. Gaining endorsements from former Yale professors, classmates, legislators whose children he had taught, and ministers who knew his family, the politically savvy Webster won the first state copyright laws, and in 1830, the first federal law.

From his experience working the political machinery to obtain copyright legislation, Webster learned the value of support from political, religious, and educational leaders. As he marketed his book to the public, he put this experience to work. In a book tour that was the first of its kind in the country, he discovered simple but highly effective ways to promote his writing and himself.

On arriving in a new town, Webster gathered endorsements from church ministers, college presidents, lawmakers, and war heroes, then repeated their praises in advertisements and essays published in the local press. His supporters included Samuel Adams, James Madison, and Benjamin Franklin, whose modified alphabet he shrewdly promised to incorporate into his own reforms. After Webster called on local schoolmasters to present them with a free copy and advise them of their patriotic duty to teach the American language, orders for the book almost always followed.

Occasionally Webster paid a price for his endorsements, as when he felt compelled to change the original title of his speller, "The American Instructor," to the ungainly *A Grammatical Institute* at the suggestion of Ezra Stiles, whose support Webster needed. After the first few publications, Webster renamed his book *The American Spelling Book, or First Part of the Grammatical Institute of the English Language* (1787). After 1804 the book was bound in blue paper, and it became known commonly as the "Blue-backed Speller," or "Old Blue Back," though Webster's title for that edition was *The American Spelling Book; Containing, the Rudiments of the English Language, for the Use of Schools in the United States.*

As Webster's reputation grew, he began to lecture on his ideas for reforming the English language and other topics as well, making extra money while continuing his book promotion. In another clever marketing move, he packaged his popular speller with two other books, a new grammar and a reader.

Webster's grammar book improved on previous books by eliminating unnecessary Latin terminology. Equally innovative, his reader was the first literary anthology produced specifically for children as well as the first to include a significant number of writings by Americans. In addition to several short stories of his own, Webster published an excerpt from Thomas Paine's *The Crisis* (1776–1783), an address by General George Washington, poetry by his Yale friends Dwight and Barlow, and Thomas Day's prediction of a national crisis over the slavery issue.

Of Webster's many publications, the speller and its companion textbooks proved most profitable. By his death in 1843, the book had been reprinted 388 times, and by one estimate, more than 100 million copies had sold, making the book one of the best-selling in American history. Though proceeds from the speller did not make Webster independently wealthy, royalties helped to finance his less lucrative publications, such as his dictionary.

Webster's book sales were also helped by his growing fame as an outspoken Federalist, whose essays were published in newspapers throughout the colonies. In 1782 Webster established his public voice with a series of essays titled "Observations on the Revolution of America" (*New York Packet,* 17 and 31 January and 7 February). Responding to a Tory publication suggesting that the colonies make peace with England, Webster asserted that "America is now an independent empire." Furthermore, he argued for religious freedom and complete separation of church and state.

At times Webster purposefully used his political writing to gain support for his speller. To help him make a pitch to Southerners, he drafted a description of the political philosophy underpinning his assertion that *A Grammatical Institute* would help unify the country by teaching an American language. After three weeks of writing, he unexpectedly produced enough material for *Sketches of American Policy. Under the Following Heads: I. Theory of Government. II. Governments on the Eastern Continent. III. American States; or the Principles of the American Constitutions Contrasted with Those of European States. IV. Plan of Policy for Improving the Advantages and Perpetuating the Union of the American States* (1785), a four-part pamphlet proposing a new constitution that would create a stronger federal government. Though most of his ideas can be traced to contemporary sources, Webster so eloquently and passionately stated his case that virtually every legislator who participated in the framing of the Constitution read Webster's sketches, which preceded *The Federalist* papers (1787–1788) by more than two years.

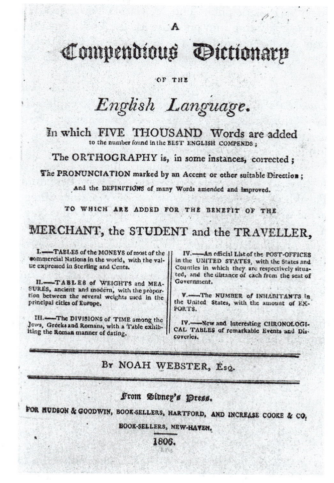

Title page for Webster's first attempt at lexicography, comprising 40,600 words, of which about 15 percent were not included in any previous dictionary (New York Public Library, Astor, Lenox and Tilden Foudations)

Webster's early writing envisioned a strong republic ruled by the common people. Soon, however, he changed his mind after he witnessed pitchfork-carrying farmers, financially ruined by postwar inflation, challenge the legitimacy of the government in Connecticut. If people wanted to displace a representative, they should do so through the election process, he believed. But as the behavior of many of his countrymen made increasingly clear that they were not content to wait for the electoral process to effect change, he abandoned his faith in government by the common people, believing that most were too ignorant and undisciplined to rule themselves. Ignoring the advice of friends, he published his views and ruined his chances for election to the Constitutional Convention.

Though Webster did not participate in the convention, he maintained close contact with many of its most prominent members throughout the proceedings in Philadelphia. The legislators rewarded his efforts by voting him publicist for the U.S. Constitution. Webster's address to the people of the United States, *An Examination Into the Leading Principles of the Federal Constitution Proposed by the Late Convention Held at Philadelphia. With Answers to the Principle Objections That Have Been Raised Against the System* (1787), explained how the various branches of government were designed to protect citizens from the tyranny of a monarch as well as political factions.

Exhilarated by the influence his work seemed to have, Webster was primed to listen to Benjamin Franklin's suggestion that Webster begin a newsmagazine of his own, *The American Magazine*. Using New York as his hub, Webster aggressively targeted a broader audience than many of his competitors, publishing, for example, articles written by and for women. At the same time he continued to air his own ideas concerning the need to improve education for the common people. The magazine enjoyed only modest success, however, and after three issues, at the age of thirty, Webster gave up the venture and devoted his energy to courting his soon-to-be wife, Rebecca Greenleaf.

In 1789 Webster turned his early lectures on language into a 410-page book, *Dissertations on the English Language: With Notes, Historical and Critical. To Which Is Added, By Way of Appendix, An Essay on a Reformed Mode of Spelling, with Dr. Franklin's Arguments on that Subject*. While his speller described methods for simplifying the teaching of spelling, *Dissertations on the English Language* simplified spelling itself through three broad changes to the language, all targeted to promote proper pronunciation. First, Webster dropped all silent letters, such as the *a* in bread and the *i* in friend. Second, he proposed some phonetic spellings, changing *speak* to *speek,* for example. Finally, he introduced pronunciation symbols for vowels. The new orthography, he argued, distinguished American English from that spoken and published in England, thus enhancing American cultural independence while saving paper. Despite its lofty intentions, the book received little notice and cost Webster $400.

Seeking a more stable income than publishing could provide, Webster moved with his new bride, whom he married on 26 October 1789, to Hartford, where he enjoyed great demand for his services as a writer, lawyer, and community leader. Street sanitation, inoculation against smallpox, and a publicly supported social safety net for the poor are only a few of the improvements he was able to effect through his writing. His works from this period also include a transcription of John Winthrop's journals and

twenty-eight issues of "The Prompter." Evoking the "Poor Richard" pseudonym of his mentor, Franklin, Webster as "The Prompter" wrote entertaining and edifying newspaper articles; first published in book form as *The Prompter; or A Commentary on Common Sayings and Subjects, Which are Full of Common Sense, the Best Sense in the World* (1790), it went through more than one hundred printings.

In 1793 Webster abandoned the success and comfort he enjoyed in Hartford to start a New York newspaper, *Minerva,* which he eventually renamed *Commercial Advertiser.* A shorter form of the paper, *Herald, a Gazette for the Country,* provided other states with headline news and eventually assumed the title *The Spectator.* This time Webster began his publication at the request of President George Washington's closest advisers, who wanted a pro-Federalist voice to answer the propaganda of the Jacobin-controlled media.

With the revolution in France spiraling out of control, the French were attempting to overthrow President Washington, who opposed American involvement in the French war with England. At a time when many Americans questioned the legitimacy of the federal government and sympathized with French emissaries, Webster supported the constitution and described the horrific excesses of the French Revolution. Those Americans who attempted to undermine elected officials outside of the electoral process, he argued, threatened freedom in the young republic.

In addition to political topics, Webster's paper addressed many social ills, such as child abandonment, slavery, and poor sanitation. In 1795, distressed at the lack of cooperation among physicians for addressing the yellow-fever epidemic, he devoted a section of the paper to a questionnaire designed to gather information about outbreaks and possible treatments. The response was so enormous that, with the help of Benjamin Rush, he published a book on the disease, *A Brief History of Epidemic and Pestilential Diseases; with the Principal Phenomena of the Physical World, which Precede and Accompany Them, and Observations Deduced from the Facts Stated* (1799), a two-volume work that became a standard medical textbook.

When Congress split into two political parties in 1798, the Federalist dream of an apolitical, centralized authority died, and Webster allowed his editorship of the newspaper to die with it, though he retained majority ownership until 1803. Moving to New Haven provided him the chance to devote himself to parenting his growing family (he and his wife had eight children in the course of their marriage) and increasing his public service. A stronghold of

Ch & Syr. אֲדֹנָי adone.

Adóniels n. [Heb. ...] Low, a scriptural title of the Supreme Being.
Among critics, a sect or party who maintain that the Hebrew points ordinarily annexed to the consonants of the word Jehovah, are not the natural points belonging to that word, & that they do not express the true pronunciation of it, but that they are the vowel-points belonging to the words Adonai & Elohim, applied to the ineffable name of Jehovah, which the Jews were forbid to utter, & the true pronunciation of which was lost; they were therefore always to pronounce the word Adonai, instead of Jehovah. These critics are opposed to the Jehovists. Encyc.

Adonéan. a. Pertaining to Adonis. "Fair Adonean Venus" Faber. 2.32

Adópt. v.t. [L. adopto, of ad & opto, to desire or choose. See option.] To take a stranger into one's family, as son & heir; to take one who is not a child, and treat him as one, — giving him a title to the privileges & rights of a child.

2. In a spiritual sense, to receive the sinful children of men into the invisible church, & into God's favor & protection, by which they become heirs of salvation by Christ. Brown.

3. To take or receive as one's own, that which is not naturally so, as to adopt the opinions of another; or to receive that which is new, as to adopt a particular mode of husbandry.

4. To select & take; as, which mode will you adopt?

Adopted. pp. Taken as one's own; received as son & heir; selected for use

Adoptedly. adv. In the manner of something adopted.

Adopter. n. One who adopts. In chemistry, a large round receiver, with two necks, diametrically opposite to each other, one of which admits the neck of a retort, & the other is joined to another receiver. It is used in distillations, to give more space to elastic vapors, or to increase the length of the neck of a retort.

Adopting. ppr. Taking a stranger as a son; taking as one's own.

Adoption. n. [L. adoptio.] The act of adopting, or the state of being adopted. — The taking & treating of a stranger, as one's own child. The receiving as one's own what is new or not natural. God's taking the sinful children of men into his favor & protection. Eph. 1. 5.

Page from the manuscript for An American Dictionary of the English Language *(1828), in which Webster included some 70,000 words (Webster Papers, New York Public Library, Astor, Lenox and Tilden Foundations)*

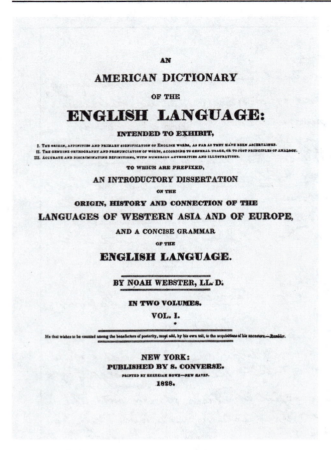

*Title page for the work to which Webster devoted
twenty years of his life*

Federalism and Calvinism, the community welcomed
Webster, electing him to city council and later the
state legislature, a post he held until 1807.

Webster also refocused his attention on education issues. While serving as president of a local
school, he again lamented the lack of good textbooks. Between 1802 and 1812 he wrote several new
schoolbooks in the areas of geography, history, biology, and civics. In addition, he began a project that
consumed much of his intellectual energy for the rest
of his life. Annoyed that American schoolchildren
still used English dictionaries to learn correct pronunciation, he determined to publish an American
dictionary to accompany his speller.

Webster soon realized, however, that his project
needed a broader market than schoolhouses. At the
time he set about gathering material for a new dictionary, several American dictionaries already existed.
They relied heavily on English pronunciations and
spellings, however, as Webster pointed out in an
1800 press release promoting his dictionary. Furthermore, they left out many new words coined in Amer-

ica. This omission made his new work "absolutely
necessary":

> New circumstances, new modes of life, new laws,
> new ideas of various kinds give rise to new words,
> and have already made many material differences
> between the language of England and America. . . .
> The differences in the language of the two countries
> will continue to multiply, and render it necessary
> that we should have *Dictionaries* of the *American Lan-
> guage.*

Though Webster originally intended to modify traditional spellings to make them more phonetic, he
abandoned his plan after facing ridicule from his
former political enemies. Instead, he published *A
Compendious Dictionary of the English Language,* a work of
40,600 words, most of which retained their traditional English spellings, and 5,000 of which were
new words not found in previous dictionaries.

Though his dictionary did not show a profit,
Webster so enjoyed lexicography that he decided to
attempt the largest, most complete dictionary of the
English language. The new reference not only would
supersede Samuel Johnson's but also would provide
the foundation for a "federal language." Subscriptions for the project, however, were few, leaving Webster to finance much of the work himself.

Moving to Amherst, where the cost of living
was lower, Webster began his difficult research by
restudying Greek, Latin, and Hebrew and learning
twenty different languages in all. He traveled to
Europe to consult dictionaries at the Bibliothèque du
Roi in Paris and the libraries at Oxford and Cambridge, where he impressed a renowned professor of
ancient languages with his project. Meanwhile, at
home he continued his devotion to public service,
convincing townspeople first to fund a local academy
and then to convert it to Amherst College, for which
Webster raised $50,000.

As he studied the origin of a word, Webster
read entries in up to thirty different dictionaries,
making careful notations as he went along. Perhaps
influenced by the religious revival movement of
1806, which touched his entire family deeply, he concluded erroneously that all languages have a common origin, a theory he thought was described in the
book of Genesis. Though much of Webster's etymology was misguided, the final volume of 70,000
words, completed in 1825 after twenty years of
study, was a remarkable piece of scholarship in its
day and commanded respect in the most prestigious
universities on both sides of the Atlantic. The work
of a single scholar, it was the last of its kind.

As 2,500 copies of the two-volume *An American Dictionary of the English Language* rolled off the press in 1828, Webster, now a seventy-year-old patriarch, received nothing but praise for his labor of love. Courts, common schools, universities, legislators, and foreign governments adopted Webster's dictionary as their standard of the English language. Even those Anglophiles who might have considered criticizing Webster's inclusion of so many new American words were quickly silenced by the patriotic and religious overtones of many entries.

Through his dictionary, which was more than just definitions of words, Webster argued for legislation, offered practical advice and entertainment, and modeled piety and civility. Furthermore, the introduction declared language to be of divine origin and paid homage to the great American authors on whose writing Webster had relied to discover the best uses and definitive spellings of words.

On 28 May 1843, just two years after the second edition of *An American Dictionary of the English Language,* Webster died in New Haven and was buried at a cemetery next to Yale College. His heirs sold the copyright for the dictionary to George and Charles Merriam. In 1859 the Merriam brothers hired a German philologist to correct Webster's etymologies and write more objective definitions, thus ensuring that "Webster's" dictionary would continue to be a standard reference.

Letters:

York Town. Letter from Noah Webster to George Washington and from George Washington to Noah Webster, from the Original in the Possession of Gordon L. Ford (Brooklyn: Privately printed, 1881);

Emily Ellsworth Fowler Ford, comp., *Notes on the Life of Noah Webster,* 2 volumes, edited by Emily Ellsworth Ford Skeel (New York: Privately printed, 1912);

Letters of Noah Webster, edited by Harry R. Warfel (New York: Library Publishers, 1953).

Bibliography:

Emily Ellsworth Ford Skeel, *A Bibliography of the Writings of Noah Webster,* edited by Edwin H. Carpenter (New York: New York Public Library, 1958).

Biographies:

Horace E. Scudder, *Noah Webster* (Boston & New York: Houghton, Mifflin, 1895);

Harry R. Warfel, *Noah Webster: Schoolmaster to America* (New York: Macmillan, 1936);

John S. Morgan, *Noah Webster* (New York: Mason-Charter, 1975);

Richard M. Rollins, *The Long Journey of Noah Webster* (Philadelphia: University of Pennsylvania Press, 1980);

Alan K. Snyder, *Defining Noah Webster: Mind and Morals in the Early Republic* (Lanham, Md.: University Press of America, 1990);

Harlow Giles Unger, *Noah Webster: The Life and Times of a Patriot* (New York: Wiley, 1998).

References:

David Micklethwait, *Noah Webster and the American Dictionary* (New York: McFarlan, 1999);

Richard J. Moss, *Noah Webster* (Boston: Twayne, 1984);

Richard M. Rollins, "Words as Social Control: Noah Webster and the Creation of the American Dictionary," *American Quarterly,* 28 (1976): 415–430;

Ervin C. Shoemaker, *Noah Webster: Pioneer of Learning* (New York: Columbia University Press, 1936).

Papers:

The New York Public Library has the largest collection of Noah Webster's personal and business papers. Other notable collections are in the Sterling Memorial Library at Yale University and at the Connecticut Historical Society.

John Weiss

(28 June 1818 – 9 March 1879)

Robert N. Hudspeth
University of Redlands

See also the Weiss entry in *DLB 1: The American Renaissance in New England.*

BOOKS: *An Address on Temperance Before the Watertown Washingtonian Society, November 10, 1844* (Boston: White, Lewis & Potter, 1844);

Our Private and Public Stewardship. A Discourse . . . In Watertown (Cambridge, Mass.: J. Owen, 1845);

Unity and Peace. A Sermon Preached Before the Church of the Unity, Worcester, Jan. 10, 1847 (Worcester, Mass.: Elihu Burritt, 1847);

Conscience the Best Policy. A Fast-Day Sermon, Preached on April 6, 1848 (New Bedford, Mass.: Press of H. Tilden, 1848);

The Modern Pulpit. A Sermon Preached At the Ordination of Samuel Longfellow, at Fall River, Mass., February 16th, 1848 (Fall River, Mass.: Printed by H. Pratt, 1848);

The Least of Two Evils; A Sermon, Preached On July 9, 1848 (New Bedford, Mass.: C. Taber, 1848);

The Claims of Seamen. An Address Delivered at the Annual Meeting of the New Bedford Port Society, Dec. 10, 1848 (Boston: B. H. Greene, 1849);

Shall We Kill the Body, or Save the Soul? A Sermon Upon Capital Punishment, Preached April 22, 1849 (New Bedford, Mass.: C. & A. Taylor, 1849);

Modern Materialism. A Discourse At the Ordination of Mr. Charles Lowe, As Associate Pastor Over the First Congregational Society, New Bedford, July 28, 1852 (New Bedford, Mass.: Press of B. Lindsey, 1852);

A Discourse Occasioned by the Death of Daniel Webster, Delivered in the Unitarian Church, New Bedford, November 14, 1852 (Boston: Munroe, 1853);

Sermon Upon the Late Disasters; Preached May 15, 1853 (New Bedford, Mass.: Privately printed, 1853);

Reform and Repeal, A Sermon Preached on Fast-Day, April 6, 1854, and Legal Anarchy, A Sermon Preached on June 4, 1854, After the Rendition of Anthony Burns (Boston: Crosby, Nichols, 1854);

A Discourse Occasioned by the Loss of the Arctic; Delivered in the Unitarian Church, New Bedford, October 22, 1854 (New Bedford, Mass.: B. Lindsey, 1854);

A Discourse Occasioned by the Death of Rev. Ephraim Peabody . . . Preached Before the First Congregational Society, New Bedford, December 7, 1856 (New Bedford, Mass.: Mercury Job, 1856);

A Discourse Upon Causes for Thanksgiving; Preached at Watertown, Nov. 30, 1862 (Boston: Printed by Wright & Potter, 1862);

The Four Necessities. A New-Year's Sermon (Boston: Walker, Wise, 1863);

Discourse Occasioned by the Death of Convers Francis, D.D. Delivered Before the First Congregational Society, Watertown, April 19, 1863 (Cambridge, Mass.: Privately printed, 1863);

Northern Strength and Weakness. An Address On Occasion of the National Fast, April 30, 1863. Delivered in Watertown (Boston: Walker, Wise, 1863);

Life and Correspondence of Theodore Parker, Minister of the Twenty-Eighth Congregational Society, Boston, 2 volumes (London: Longman, Green, Longman, Roberts & Green, 1863; New York: Appleton, 1864);

Co-Operation in the Father's Business. A Discourse Preached at the Installation of Rev. J. B. Marvin, Harrison Square, Jan. 25, 1865 (Boston: Walker, Wise, 1865);

The Political Exigencies of Political Submission; an Address Delivered on the Day of National Thanksgiving, Dec. 7, 1865, in the First Congregational Church, Watertown (Boston: Walker, Fuller, 1865);

American Religion (Boston: Roberts, 1871);

Address at the Funeral of Rev. Joseph Angier, Milton, April 15, 1871 (Boston: Printed by Rockwell & Churchill, 1871);

Theodore Parker. A Lecture Delivered in the Parker Fraternity Course, Nov. 19, 1872 (Boston: Roberts, 1873);

Poem, Read at the Annual Dinner of the Class of Eighteen Hundred and Thirty-Seven, February 26, 1874 (Boston: W. L. Deland, 1874);

The Bible and Science (Boston: Free Religious Association, 1875);

Wit, Humor, and Shakespeare. Twelve Essays (Boston: Roberts, 1876);

The Immortal Life (Boston: Lockwood, Brooks, 1880).

OTHER: Novalis (Friedrich, Freiherr von Hardenberg), *Henry of Ofterdingen,* translated by Weiss (Cambridge: J. Owen, 1842);

Johann Christoph Friedrich von Schiller, *The Philosophical and Aesthetic Letters and Essays of Schiller,* translated, with an introduction, by Weiss (Boston: Little & Brown, 1845; London: Chapman, 1845);

William Smith, *Memoir of Johann Gottlieb Fichte,* edited by Weiss (Boston: Munroe, 1846);

Schiller, "Upon Naive and Sentimental Poetry," translated by Weiss, in *The Prose Writers of Germany,* edited by Frederic Henry Hedge (Philadelphia: Carey & Hart, 1848), pp. 372–382;

Johann Wolfgang von Goethe, *Goethe's West-Easterly Divan,* translated, with an introduction and notes, by Weiss (Boston: Roberts, 1877).

SELECTED PERIODICAL PUBLICATIONS–UNCOLLECTED: "The German Catholic Movement," *Christian Examiner,* 42 (January 1847): 55–81;

"Germany, Religious and Political," *Christian Examiner,* 43 (November 1847): 394–427;

"Browning's *Poems,*" *Massachusetts Quarterly Review,* 3 (June 1850): 347–385;

"Thoreau," *Christian Examiner,* 79 (July 1865): 96–117;

"Woman Suffrage," *Radical,* 5 (June 1869): 445–462;

"The Task of Religion," *Radical,* 6 (September 1869): 177–190.

One of a group of radical Unitarian writers prominent in the 1860s and 1870s, John Weiss continued the work of Ralph Waldo Emerson and Theodore Parker well into a much-changed post–Civil War American society. He memorialized Parker in two volumes that are still read, and he wrote a challenging essay on his classmate Henry David Thoreau. But there was more to Weiss than a memorialist, for he was an original thinker about religion and science; he lectured widely on literary and historical topics, and he was an energetic advocate of social reform. A survey of his works reveals a man who was intellectually restless, probing, acerbic, and tenacious.

John Weiss was born on 28 June 1818 in Boston, the son of John and Mary (Galloupe) Weiss. His grandfather and great uncles were German political exiles, and his father was a barber. The family moved to Worcester and then sent John to Framingham to prepare for Harvard, where he became a member of the class of 1837, which included Thoreau, Charles Stearns Wheeler, and Richard Henry Dana. An indifferent student, the energetic Weiss became a leader in the "Dunkin rebellion" when students rioted against a punitive instructor. Everyone, from his classmates to those who wrote his obituaries, noted Weiss's high spirits, his energy, and his lively, often caustic humor. He was a thin man with a large head, black eyes, and, in his maturity, a dark beard and mustache. He spoke rapidly and intensely in a "thin, piping, penetrating voice." He is reputed to have been able to judge the character of a writer merely by holding a sealed letter in his hand.

After graduation Weiss taught school in Boston and Jamaica Plain, Massachusetts, then enrolled at the Divinity School in Cambridge in 1840 and graduated in 1843. In August 1842 he and Wheeler traveled to Germany, where they roomed together in Heidelberg. The trip sealed Weiss's attitudes about the importance of

German culture, which was his family heritage, and it led him to edit and translate German literature.

After returning to America, Weiss was ordained at the church in Watertown, Massachusetts, where he succeeded Convers Francis from October 1843 to October 1845. On 9 April 1844 Weiss married Sarah Fiske Jennison of Worcester (with whom he had five children). He found that he had trouble holding his parish, for undoubtedly his increasingly outspoken views of religion and politics were unsettling. He returned to his Watertown congregation from March 1846 to December 1847; he then accepted the pulpit at New Bedford, where he served until January 1859, the longest pastorate in his career.

During his residence in Watertown, Weiss undertook a series of projects to make German literature available to an American audience through reviewing, editing, and translating. At a time when German letters were increasingly important, especially in New England, Weiss worked in two directions. In his two essays on modern Germany in the *Christian Examiner* he traced the development of a "German" (as opposed to "Roman") Catholic Church and used that history as a basis for comments on the Protestant group "Friends of Light," which he thought was a German version of Anglo-American Unitarianism. Parallel to these essays he translated Novalis's *Heinrich von Ofterdingen* (1842) and Johann Christoph Friedrich von Schiller's *Aesthetic Letters and Essays* (1845). He edited William Smith's *Memoir of Johann Gottlieb Fichte* (1846), and he translated Schiller's *Über naive und sentimentalische Dichtung* (1795–1796) as "Upon Naive and Sentimental Poetry" for Frederic Henry Hedge's *The Prose Writers of Germany* (1848). The Schiller translations were important, for, according to Henry A. Pochmann, the translation of Schiller's letters "was one of the most difficult and demanding of all translation projects in German undertaken up to that time in America," and "Upon Naive and Sentimental Poetry" made available an important theoretical essay. Though Weiss had made public the work of three major German writers of that generation, he found, as Margaret Fuller had a few years earlier, that such labor, worthy as it was, could not provide a living.

In the pulpit Weiss was a brilliant, if undisciplined, speaker, "his whole being vibrant with the new gospel which he poured forth in a flood of literary, scientific, and classical erudition, and with a brilliance of figurative and epigrammatic expression." Though he stayed in New Bedford much longer than some of his friends stayed in their parishes, he was physically removed from the center of intellectual debate both in the church and outside it. This era was the time of the Compromise of 1850, of the freeing of Anthony Burns, and of Kansas and John Brown. Weiss was also in poor

Title page for the first British edition of one of the translations through which Weiss attempted to make German literature available to English-speaking readers (Thomas Cooper Library, University of South Carolina)

health, so he resigned his New Bedford pulpit in 1859 and moved to Milton. Three years later he returned to Watertown for a third time, lasting from 1862 to 1869, when he left the institutional church for good.

After he left Watertown for the last time little is known of Weiss's biography. He remained in the Boston area; he was widely known in literary and reform circles; he joined Bronson Alcott and others for "Conversations"; he lectured on William Shakespeare and on Greek religion, and he had opinions. Though ever lively and sharp-witted, Weiss has been elusive, for there is neither a bibliography of his work nor a full biography.

Weiss was present in May 1847 when a group of men met at Emerson's home to discuss a new journal, for he was consistently a part of the new-light, radical party in New England. Out of that meeting Theodore Parker became the editor of *The Massachusetts Review*, and Weiss was one of six potential contributors whom Parker named "certain and valuable." For the June 1850 issue Weiss wrote a long review of Robert Browning's new American two-volume edition of *Poems* (1850). He quoted liberally from the poems, summarizing their content, but his focus was more specific and more grounded in an aesthetic concern. He used *Sordello* (1840), which was not in the volumes he was reviewing, as an example of what goes wrong in Browning's work: It is metaphysical, not lyric; it is too compressed and depends too much on introspection. What interested Weiss was how Browning handled his materials and how the poetry and the ideas did or did not mesh. He judged the plays and poems as literary works, not as disguised metaphysical treatises.

Weiss's *Life and Correspondence of Theodore Parker, Minister of the Twenty-Eighth Congregational Society, Boston* (1863) is still a necessary source for scholars of the period. According to F. B. Sanborn in "Twelve Apostles of Heresy" in the *Independent* (27 January 1870), Parker wanted him to write his biography, but Lydia Parker chose Joseph Lyman to be literary executor, and Lyman chose Weiss to write the official biography. The *Life and Correspondence of Theodore Parker* is a typical nineteenth-century work. Weiss wrote a running narrative about Parker and included generous selections from the correspondence and the journals. As was the custom, he tried to let Parker's words speak for themselves, but much of the value of that principle is lost because the two volumes are not organized chronologically. Weiss devoted the first volume and the beginning of the second to theology and Unitarian controversy and then created a separate, long section on Parker's antislavery activities and closed with a return to theology. Still, since many of the letters he printed have been lost, the volumes remain indispensable.

Weiss wrote with his usual verve, even mixing his metaphors, when he described how Parker challenged the moderate Unitarians. "They were just baring their breasts with *abandon* to the universe," he wrote, "and calling to the 'over-soul' to come on, when Mr. Parker's sermon of 'The Transient and Permanent,' struck their bellying sails with a sudden dismay, and they were never hoisted more." Of course, Parker was heroic to Weiss, for the younger radical was willing to go even further in his rejection of historical Christianity. In both the pulpit and in politics Parker had stood for freedom, and he persisted in the face of adversity, even to the last days of his life, when Parker's "body, almost petulantly, dropped away, the members of his faith in that Infinite Perfection, Infinite Goodness,

Infinite Presence and Influence, which he had preached and obeyed, were one by one uncovered." Weiss might have written a better book had he not felt the need to defer to his materials, for he was up to the challenge of understanding Parker.

The contemporary reaction to the volumes mostly focused on Parker, not on Weiss's handling of Parker's life, but David Wasson more thoroughly and skeptically commented on Weiss. Wasson lamented that the book was first published in England, that the American edition was badly printed from those plates, and that it was published in New York, not Boston. He disliked the violation of privacy resulting from Parker's comments about living people, and he faulted the organization of the book. But Weiss the man drew Wasson's sharpest comments. He claimed that Weiss was so unlike Parker that Weiss could not bridge the gap between them. Whereas Parker was affable, Weiss was a separatist; whereas Parker was blunt, Weiss was "nice, curious, fanciful," an "intellectualist." Weiss writes with "point and brilliancy"; yet, he lacks "the capital merit of simplicity." Then, having thoroughly established his reservations, Wasson admitted that Weiss's mind "borders upon genius; and his intellect is so bright and vivid, his interest in his task so generous" that the pages "enchain even those whom they displease."

Wasson's reluctant admission that Weiss commanded his respect is similar to Weiss's essay on his classmate Henry David Thoreau. "Thoreau" (1865) ostensibly is a review of five Thoreau volumes, but it is more nearly a summing up of Thoreau the man contrasted with the Thoreau in print. Weiss spent a good deal of effort showing how cold and aloof he found Thoreau during their college years. He described Thoreau's habit of always looking down when walking; he called Thoreau dull, plodding, and, above all, complacent. In personality Thoreau and Weiss were opposites: Weiss, the class toastmaster at graduation and leader of the Dunkin rebellion, defined himself in social terms; the more meditative Thoreau separated himself from the class and never attended a postcollege gathering. Although Weiss's portrait is highly unflattering, he did see that Thoreau's personality was more than adequate to his genius, which, Weiss says, "was perfectly satisfied with its own ungraciousness, because that was essential to its private business." Weiss concluded that were Thoreau a different man, he would have been a worse writer.

Following the personal portrait, Weiss turned to Thoreau's writing, where he described Thoreau's love of nature, which is not to be separated from a deep religious sensibility. "No writer of the present day is more religious," said Weiss, "no one more profoundly penetrated with the redeeming power of simple integrity, and the spiritualizing effect of a personal consciousness of God." Aware that his harsh personal description might mislead readers, Weiss went out of his way to say that Thoreau was ever-faithful to his vocation and that he was more surely religious than the conventionally pious people whom both he and Weiss scorned. Weiss saw that Thoreau's habit of contradiction was necessary and inevitable, that it led him not to reject humanity but to offer a higher standard of living. Finally, Weiss is the source of the perhaps apocryphal scene in which "a friend" (Emerson) upon finding Thoreau in jail, asks "why are you here," to which Thoreau answers "why are you not here also?" Weiss had the advantage of a personal acquaintance with Thoreau, even if not a close one, but he had a better advantage of being a sympathetic and attentive reader who recognized the signal accomplishment in his "complacent" classmate.

As the Civil War neared its end, there emerged a new attack on institutionalized Unitarianism that continued Parker's earlier work. The younger Transcendentalists such as Weiss found coming together necessary to see where moral duty lay in a newly emerging American society. They found an outlet in a magazine that Sidney Morse founded in 1865, *The Radical,* which was devoted to reform and religion. Chief among its contributors were three "disciples" of Parker—Wasson, Samuel Johnson, and Weiss. Weiss in his 1869 essay "Woman Suffrage," published in *The Radical,* shows how he approached reform. He began with a withering denunciation of the practice of buying votes and of manipulating the ignorance and sloth of voters, especially among Irish immigrants. After showing how dear the act of voting is to those who learned the value of liberty by living as slaves, Weiss makes a case for extending the vote to women. He quickly puts aside the notion of "inferiority" in women by remarking that the idea is only cultural training, an "Oriental" attitude that is the legacy of the Greeks and St. Paul. Give women power, says Weiss, and men will begin to address questions of the teaching of children, of temperance, and of divorce—questions that they do not now consider worth discussion. His essay is marked by a willingness to treat women seriously and to look beyond the clichés that controlled discussions of women and public life.

When Weiss published his 1869 address to the graduating seniors at the Divinity School in Cambridge, "The Task of Religion," he was himself leaving the ministry for good. He had gone so far in his own thinking that he was beyond the ability to fulfill the vocation that he defined for the young men in his audience. He caustically dismissed the usual interests of young clergymen—church politics, aesthetics, scriptural authority, and social cohesion—mocking each in turn lest they "gain a parish, and lose your hold upon the vital exigency of the times." Instead, he says, he wants to address directly the "great mental disturbance" of his time, the conflict between science and religion. One of the most significant traits of Weiss's mind is his ability to take science seriously and yet to maintain its compatibility with religion. He unflinchingly accepts the method of science, its reliance on logical sequence and on the proofs of fossil records. Darwin gives him no pause, for the task, he says, is to use this method, to accept the mental discipline of science to incorporate the divine presence. Throughout his essay (and his later writing) runs the principle that God exists, that he has chosen to work in the material world, that there exist needs and longings in human consciousness that can be met only by "religion." Weiss claims that theologians have surrendered abjectly to the claims of the materialists, while in fact all theories of evolution "presume a divine presence," and each human soul "was derived from that Being who never paused during all the million years which have gone to make an earth." Instead of delivering homilies based on scriptural stories and faiths of the long dead, a minister, says Weiss, ought to enlist social science, which aims to "maintain the personal health which develops the highest amount of personal volition, and liberates it from bad births, bad education, and bad neighborhoods."

By this time Weiss had gone as far as he could in institutional religion. He and several like-minded radicals formed the "Free Religious Association," having become disgusted with Unitarianism. They also formed a "Radical Club," which met in Boston at the home of John T. Sargent; the group included women in its membership. Weiss was a founder and constant participant in the discussions that ranged over religious and social questions. *The Radical* became the Radical Club's de facto journal, and Sargent's wife, Mary, edited a volume that summarized the papers and quoted from the ensuing discussions. In these meetings, in the pages of *The Radical,* and on the lecture platform Weiss came to work out his vocation.

The line of thought he sketched for the Divinity School graduates developed into a major book, *American Religion* (1871). Well into that text, Weiss gave his definition of "religion," which governs the whole discussion: "religion is recognition of central facts, the confinement of effects to the lines of causality, the emancipation of mankind from ignorance and false habits, and the reconciliation of all knowledge to invisible Truth." In clear, concise terms Weiss named the activities that are "religious"—to see, to free, and to reconcile. His language aims to lead the reader to a recog-

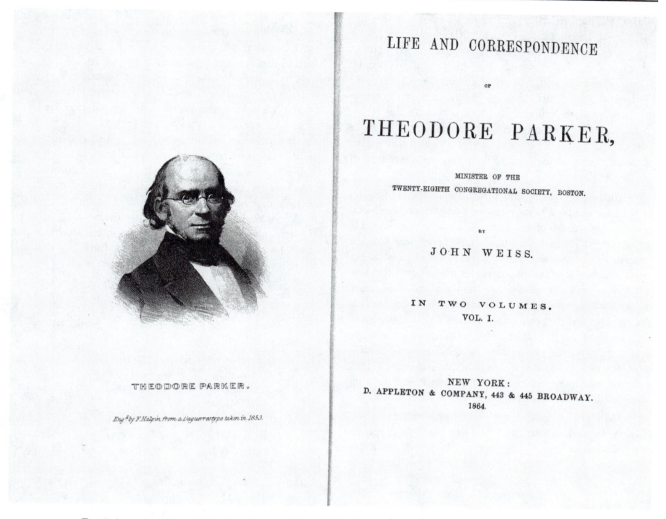

Frontispiece and title page for the first American edition of Weiss's biography of his Transcendentalist mentor and hero

nition that evolution defines all human growth. "The Divinity within the natural causes has assumed gradualism for its method."

Even more than had Parker before him, Weiss rejected any reliance on the past or on sacred scriptures. "It is a great benefit," he said, "to emancipate a mind from the habit of limping after its own truths on the crutch of mythological authority." Only when people can learn to look at nature for themselves, to see that all acts of the human mind are "texts of the continual Scripture" will humanity become truly free. Whether consciously or not, Weiss adopted the language that led to and flowed from the Civil War. He consistently aimed to "emancipate" an "enslaved" mind; he wanted to "reconcile" opposing points of view to end a paralytic hostility. The language suggests that, for Weiss, there was no distinction between what was "political" and what was "intellectual" or "religious." He argued from the premise that "God" exists

immanently as a "Divine Person," present to all individuals. By "Person" Weiss meant a divine consciousness, an "immeasurable Presence." That some people refuse to acknowledge this truth does not matter; for Weiss the divine presence is a fundamental reality that must be reconciled with intellectual activity.

Weiss knew that the American obsession with "individualism" can lead to either an egoism or a lonely rejection of social life, that it can be the excuse to ignore the plight of other people (all charges that had been leveled against Emerson in Weiss's youth). He claimed that the individual "is sacred by virtue of this organic fellow-feeling that moral and spiritual truth has for itself whenever it can be found." This belief led Weiss to proclaim "social science" as the major form of divine operation in life. "What a reconciler of man with God is Social Science, and what an atoner for every original taint! It directly attacks the evils which prevent mankind from becoming truly religious." He then listed several pages of reform, using the rights of women as the center, and concluded that, since poverty causes vice, "more shillings conceded to the making of a shirt would double the religion of mankind." Weiss takes his stand: Science does not destroy religion; God exists in the individual; social reform is religion in practice, for "bad living of all kinds nourishes this hypochrondiac of a feud between earth and heaven." America ought to be the leader in sweeping away the superstitions of the past and see itself as the daily renewing scripture of the Divine Person.

Although religion and reform were the topics that most often occupied Weiss, he had a deep interest in literature, as had many of his fellow Transcendentalists. He published his lectures on Shakespeare, and he chose the dramatist's humor as his subject. *Wit, Humor, and Shakespeare. Twelve Essays* (1876) has two introductory "theoretical" chapters followed by ten that analyze the use of humor in a variety of Shakespearean characters. At first Weiss observed that one wit produces only laughter and one produces thought. He carefully distinguished between a momentary relief from care (a human smile) and a moral revolt, which is not comic at all. Audiences come away from comedy refreshed, because wit has a "tonic quality and saves us from despair."

Weiss does not find his defining position until well into the second chapter, and it is one that has a specific echo of what he had said in *American Religion*. In coming to a definition of "humor," he noted that God cannot be comic, for he has no "consciousness of incongruities," having been the original creator of all life. Man alone can make a reconciliation between incongruous moments. In humor, man gets "relief by trying to discover the ideas which may effect a temporary reconcilement, to approach as far as we can to the temper of divine impartiality in which all circumstances must have been ordained."

In Shakespeare's work, Weiss found the humor of the comic characters woven into the logic of the plays themselves. They are not, he contended, extraneous; nor are they additions merely designed to amuse the oafish part of the audience. Because human beings make incongruities for themselves, the humor in the plays is a working out of human possibilities. For example, Weiss contrasted Touchstone and Jaques in *As You Like It*. Whereas Jaques's comedy is one of sour cynicism and unbelief, Touchstone "expresses the gladness of being a member of this inevitable world, and of tolerating himself with the other fools." Again, the reader hears an echo from Weiss's writing on religion: Humanity emerges most fundamentally (and most religiously) in a joining together such as Touchstone dramatizes; people fall farthest from their human possibility when they withdraw and rail, as does Jaques.

Weiss had always been tempted to be a Jaques, but "he was alternately angel and imp, yet not of mischief, there being no cruelty in him." He had a great and guiding faith in the human mind; he never wavered in his willingness to let thought take him where it might, for he had an even greater faith in the Divine Presence antecedent to human consciousness. Weiss faithfully pursued the possibilities Emerson and Parker had created in the youth of American Transcendentalism; he took further their assault on the past, on scripture, and on tradition; he even more radically joined nature and God: "There is dignity in dust that reaches any form," he said, "because it eventually betrays a forming power, and ceases to be dust by sharing it." Weiss shared Parker's hatred of slavery and went even further into calling for social reform. If his sharp tongue made him lose "part of the cipher of communication with his fellow-men," that wit made him "a flame of fire."

References:

Cyrus Augustus Bartol, "The Genius of Weiss," in his *Principles and Portraits* (Boston: Roberts, 1880), pp. 386–412;

Robert E. Burkholder, "John Weiss," in *The Transcendentalists: A Review of Research and Criticism,* edited by Joel Myerson (New York: Modern Language Association, 1984), pp. 295–298;

Catalogue of the Private Library of the Late John Weiss, to Be Sold by Auction, May 13th and Following Days in the Salesroom of Leonard & Co., Auctioneers (Boston: W. Richardson, 1879);

Octavius B. Frothingham, "John Weiss," *Unitarian Review,* 29 (May 1888): 417–429;

Edwin Stanton Hodgin, "John Weiss, Genius of the Pulpit: Brilliant, Brave, Scholarly, Whimsical," in his *One Hundred Years of Unitarianism in New Bedford, Massachusetts* (New Bedford: First Congregational Society, 1924), pp. 31–40;

Henry A. Pochmann, *German Culture in America: Philosophical and Literary Influences 1600–1900* (Madison: University of Wisconsin Press, 1957), p. 251;

Mary E. Sargent, *Sketches and Reminiscences of the Radical Club of Chestnut Street, Boston* (Boston: Osgood, 1880);

Minot J. Savage, "John Weiss," in *Heralds of a Liberal Faith,* edited by Samuel A. Eliot (Boston: American Unitarian Association, 1910), III: 376–380;

Henry Williams, "John Weiss," in his *Memorials of the Class of 1837 of Harvard University* (Boston: Ellis, 1887), pp. 58–63.

Papers:

John Weiss's letters are at the Houghton Library of Harvard University and at the Boston Public Library. His four-volume manuscript journal and a commonplace book are at the Massachusetts Historical Society.

Sarah Helen Whitman

(19 January 1803 – 27 June 1878)

John E. Reilly
College of the Holy Cross

See also the Whitman entry in *DLB 1: The American Renaissance in New England.*

BOOKS: *Poem Recited before the Rhode-Island Historical Society Jan. 13, 1847* (Providence, 1847);

Hours of Life, and Other Poems (Providence: George H. Whitney, 1853);

Edgar Poe and His Critics (New York: Rudd & Carleton, 1860);

Cinderella, by Whitman and Susan Anna Power (Providence: Printed by Hammond, Angell, 1867);

The Sleeping Beauty, by Whitman and Power (Providence: Printed by Hammond, Angell, 1868);

Poems by Sarah Helen Whitman (Boston: Houghton, Osgood, 1879);

Last Flowers: The Romance Poems of Edgar Allan Poe and Sarah Helen Whitman, edited by Brett Rutherford (Providence: Poet's Press, 1987).

OTHER: "The Blind Man's Lay," "Retrospection," "She Blooms No More," and "The Spirit of Poetry," in *The Ladies' Wreath,* edited by Sarah Josepha Hale (Boston: Marsh, Capen & Lyon / New York: Appleton, 1837), pp. 356–363;

The Rhode-Island Book: Selections in Prose and Verse, from the Writings of Rhode-Island Citizens, edited by Anne C. Lynch (Providence: H. Fuller, 1841; Boston: Weeks, Jordan, 1841), pp. 50–58, 126–130, 141–145, 278–279, 345;

The Female Poets of America, edited by Rufus W. Griswold (Philadelphia: Carey & Hart, 1849), pp. 167–176.

SELECTED PERIODICAL PUBLICATIONS–
UNCOLLECTED: "Character and Writings of Shelley," as Egeria, *Literary Journal, and Weekly Register of Science and the Arts,* 11 January 1834, pp. 252–253;

"On the Nature and Attributes of Genius," as Egeria, *Boston Pearl,* 14 (19 December 1835): 107–108;

Sarah Helen Whitman in 1869 (portrait by John G. Arnold; Brown University Library)

"Recollections of an Evening with Walter Savage Landor," *Providence Daily Journal,* 14 October 1864, p. 2;

"The Woman Question," *Providence Daily Journal,* 11 February 1868, p. 2;

"Woman's Suffrage," *Providence Daily Journal,* 10 December 1868, p. 2;

"Progressive Women and 'Average Young Men.'– Women of the Past versus Girls of the Period," *Providence Daily Journal,* 15 May 1869, p. 2;

"'Byronism,'" *Providence Daily Journal,* 18 October 1869, p. 2;

"Mrs. Davis and the New York Tribune," *Providence Daily Journal,* 11 July 1871, p. 2;

"Science and Spiritualism," *Providence Daily Journal*, 23 January 1874, p. 1;

"Immortality as Viewed by Scholars and Scientists," *Providence Daily Journal*, 20 March 1876, p. 2;

"Mr. Geo. W. Curtis on the 'True Mischief of Spiritualism,'" *Providence Daily Journal*, 29 September 1876, p. 1.

Edgar Allan Poe met Sarah Helen Whitman for the first time at her home in Providence, Rhode Island, on 21 September 1848. Both were widowed; he was in his thirty-ninth year, and she in her forty-fifth. Poe launched immediately into an intense and what proved to be a stormy courtship, pursuing her relentlessly until she consented late in December to an "immediate marriage." Two days later, however, the engagement was broken off, and Poe returned from Providence to New York, never to see her again. To these three months Sarah Whitman owes much of the recognition she enjoys even today, principally among Poe's biographers. They identify her as "Poe's Helen," as that eccentric Providence widow who came within a hairbreadth of marrying him and who subsequently stood almost alone defending his character against defamers who pounced upon him immediately following his death. But recognition of this nature has been a decidedly mixed blessing for Whitman, because it has reduced her to a single dimension, to a sort of aspect of Poe's life, at the expense of the multidimensional figure she was in her own right. One Poe biographer acknowledges that "she was undoubtedly the most 'civilized' woman whom Poe had ever approached," and another describes her as "the woman who, of all the women he [Poe] knew, came closest to being his peer."

Sarah Whitman was intelligent, gifted, witty, and warm. She was widely read: in one of her essays alone she cites thirty-three authors and three current periodicals. She was fluent in German, French, and Italian. She was acquainted with many prominent contemporaries—among them Bronson Alcott, Thomas Bailey Aldrich, Henry Ward Beecher, Park Benjamin, Orestes Brownson, General Benjamin Butler, Andrew Jackson Davis (the leading Spiritualist), Ralph Waldo Emerson, Margaret Fuller, Horace Greeley, Oliver Wendell Holmes, Fanny Kemble, Walter Savage Landor, Stéphane Mallarmé, John Neal, Frances Sargent Osgood, Richard Henry Stoddard, Henry David Thoreau, Walt Whitman, and Nathaniel Parker Willis. Sarah Whitman was a talented poet and an insightful critic of literature and art, as well as a perceptive commentator upon the contemporary scene, including politics; architecture; manners; fashions in ideas, clothing, and religion; and issues pertaining to her beloved city of Providence. She was independent, liberal, and unconventional—in her own way a model of Emerson's nonconformist. She clung faithfully and tenaciously to her beliefs in Spiritualism, in feminism, and in abolitionism. She stood staunchly in defense not only of Poe but also of Percy Bysshe Shelley, Johann Wolfgang von Goethe, and George Gordon, Lord Byron—all of whom were condemned by her contemporaries as moral pariahs.

Born in Providence on 19 January 1803, six years to the day before Poe, Sarah Helen Power was the daughter of Nicholas and Anna (Marsh) Power. She inherited her dominant character traits from her father rather than from her straitlaced and prosaic mother. Independent and unconventional, Nicholas Power was something of a free spirit. Personal business took him to St. Kitts in 1812, where he was captured by the British and held until the close of the war. Instead of returning directly to Providence, however, he remained absent for two decades, taking up residence apart from his family upon his return. Anna, the younger of his two children, celebrated her father's unexpected behavior in a quirky couplet:

> Mr. Nicholas Power left home in a sailing vessel bound for St. Kitts,
> When he returned, he frightened his family out of their wits.

At seventy-two years of age and following another protracted absence from Providence, Nicholas Power was swept up in "Dorr's Rebellion," an uprising in Rhode Island "fought" over the issue of suffrage. Not surprisingly, Power threw in his lot with Thomas Wilson Dorr, the leader of the movement to extend voting rights, and was incarcerated briefly upon being caught spiriting messages into Providence. Nicholas Power died in 1844 at the age of seventy-four.

An attractive, lively, and fun-loving young woman, Sarah Power married John Winslow Whitman on 10 July 1828. A young lawyer from Massachusetts whom she met when he was a student at Brown University, he was in some ways not unlike Nicholas Power—improvident and not entirely dependable. He and his bride settled in Boston where he practiced law and indulged an interest in belles lettres by serving as the editor of several short-lived literary magazines. He died in July of 1833, after which Sarah Whitman returned to live with her mother and sister, Anna, in Providence.

During the fifteen years following the death of her husband, Sarah Whitman began to establish a reputation as a poet and essayist. She also became active in the intellectual life of Providence, then a center of ferment only a little less heated than that taking place in the Concord and Boston area. As in Concord and Boston,

Transcendentalism as spelled out by Ralph Waldo Emerson was the dominant philosophy in Providence, and Emerson himself visited the city often and delivered lectures there from time to time. Whitman became personally acquainted with him early in the 1830s and even considered herself "A Disciple." Another prominent Transcendentalist with whom Whitman was acquainted was Margaret Fuller, who resided in Providence while teaching in the Greene Street School founded upon the educational theories of Bronson Alcott. Transcendentalism probably did not alter Whitman's outlook so much as it defined and confirmed convictions she had held all along—liberal convictions such as self-reliance, nonconformity, independence, intuition, and the dominance of spirit. Her liberalism led her to espouse both feminism and Spiritualism, two major movements that became popular in the area during the late 1840s.

Sarah Whitman was neither as strident a feminist as Margaret Fuller nor as militant as, for example, Susan B. Anthony, Lucretia Mott, and Paulina Wright Davis. She was, nonetheless, an active and prominent member of the movement. In an essay titled "The Woman Question" (1868) she asked, "How can woman ever hope to adapt herself to the masculine standard of perfection—a standard so capricious, so variable, so exacting?" and proceeded to chastise the masculine establishment for considering nineteenth-century women wicked because they were "seeking to transcend their natural, heaven-appointed sphere." In "Woman's Suffrage," an essay prompted by the "convention of the friends of woman's suffrage" held in Boston in 1868, Whitman celebrates, albeit prematurely, the success of the movement: "The wrongs of women are, to-day, too patent, their rights too palpable," she announces, "to be longer met by outworn platitudes and vapid sentimentalities about the 'home duties,' and 'the heaven-appointed sphere' of the 'true woman.' No *true man* to-day so ventures to meet them." Whitman becomes genuinely acerbic in still another essay, "Progressive Women and 'Average Young Men.'—Women of the Past versus Girls of the Period" (1869). Her target is Rebecca Harding Davis, a novelist who fashioned herself a champion of "the rights" and expectations of young men who, she alleged, were baffled by the behavior of those young women "alarmingly destitute of feminine purity." Why, Whitman asks, should "honest John," the typical young male, "mediocre in intellect, but well-meaning and industrious," be considered "a matrimonial prize worth securing, at any sacrifice of a young woman's progressive tastes and opinions"? No less acerbic is an old-fashioned verse satire Whitman composed for recitation at a suffragist banquet in Provi-

Whitman's mother, Anna Marsh Power (from Caroline Ticknor, Poe's Helen, *1916)*

dence in 1871. Titled "Woman's Sphere," the satire closes with the long view of man/woman relationships:

> Too long benighted man has had his way;
> Indignant woman turns and stands at bay.
> Old proverbs tell us when the world was new,
> And men and women had not much to do,
> Adam was wont to delve and Eve to spin;
> His work was out of doors and hers within.
> But Adam seized the distaff and the spindle,
> And Eve beheld her occupation dwindle.
> Must she then sit with folded hands and tarry,
> Till some fair sybil [*sic*] tell her "whom to marry?"
> Better devote her time to ward committees,
> To stumping States and canvassing the cities;
> Better no more on flimsy fineries dote,
> But take the field and claim the right to vote.

Modern Spiritualism sprang up suddenly in 1848 with the "spirit rappings" purportedly heard by Katherine and Margaret Fox, two young sisters living on a farm outside Rochester, New York, and the movement spread rapidly, particularly throughout New York and into New England. Sarah Whitman became caught up in it early and remained not only a faithful disciple to it throughout the remainder of her life, but also a steadfast, if not sometimes desperate,

Whitman's house in Providence, Rhode Island

defender of the faith as attacks upon it grew ever more virulent and defectors, including at least one of the Fox sisters, multiplied. At the invitation of her friend Horace Greeley, she submitted a series of letters (essays) to the *New-York Tribune* in the early 1850s explaining Spiritualism and alluding at one point, though covertly, to messages she had personally received from the spirit of Edgar Allan Poe shortly after his death. Thereafter, she contributed essays on the subject to publications such as the *Spiritual Telegraph* and the Spiritualist periodical *Shekinah* but above all to the pages of the *Providence Daily Journal,* essays bearing titles such as "Science and Spiritualism" (1878), "Immortality as Viewed by Scholars and Scientists" (1876), and "Mr. Geo. W. Curtis on the 'True Mischief of Spiritualism'" (1876)—the last, an especially virulent defense against an attack upon the faith by an old friend. Whitman persisted in her belief up to the close of her life, going so far as to assure that her funeral would be attended exclusively by her Spiritualist friends in Providence by directing that no public announcement of her death be made until she was safely interred.

The mystical disposition that made Spiritualism congenial to Whitman played no small part in the attraction Poe held for her. She confided to a friend after Poe's death that she had read his work with a strange fascination four or five years before meeting him: "I devoured with a half-reluctant and fearful avidity every line that fell from his pen and always experienced in reading them a singular pain & oppression about the heart which I am almost constrained to refer to some occult and mysterious influence." Her "conscious soul," she continued, "recoiled with an instinctive apprehension of the agonies it was destined to suffer through its strange union with his own." Whitman gave her destiny a nudge in February of 1848 by playfully addressing a valentine poem to Poe in the character of his raven. Playful though it is, her valentine recognizes the profound pessimism underlying Poe's work—a pessimism she interprets to be his sullen repudiation of the facile and foolish optimism of his contemporaries, especially those celebrants of progress through technology who promoted the absurdity that their Age of Iron would somehow be redeemed, a Golden Age somehow restored through the alchemy of steam and machinery. Whitman makes the point through the language of her bird metaphor: Poe is a grim and solemn raven among a flock of mere popinjays and parrots:

> Midst the roaring of machinery,
>   And the dismal shriek of steam,
> While each popinjay and parrot,
>   Makes the golden age his theme,
> Oft, methinks, I hear thee croaking,
>   "All is but an idle dream."
>
> While these warbling "guests of summer"
>   Prate of "Progress" evermore,
> And, by dint of *iron foundries,*
>   Would this golden age restore,
> Still, methinks, I hear thee croaking,
>   Hoarsely croaking, "Nevermore."

Whitman's relationship with Poe was doomed from the outset, principally by her mother's objections to a man of Poe's questionable reputation as well as by the hesitancy both Sarah Whitman and Poe themselves seem to have felt about going through with the marriage. Whatever the reason or reasons, their brief engagement came to a swift close late in December. Though Poe seems to have felt relief at breaking off with her, Whitman was regretful and recorded her regret in poems she addressed to him, a half dozen written before his death the following October and at least a dozen more over the four years immediately thereafter.

Much controversy swirled about Poe during the first decade following his death, and Whitman rose to his defense, a defense culminating in the publication in 1860 of *Edgar Poe and His Critics.* Scarcely more than an essay, her little book argues that Poe should not be condemned but appreciated, because he stood at the forefront of an illustrious company of contemporaries—including Emerson, Thomas Carlyle, Charles Fourier, Thomas De Quincey, Johann Wolfgang von Goethe, William Wordsworth, Byron, Shelley, and John Keats. "The unrest and faithlessness of the age culminated in him," she wrote of Poe. "Nothing so solitary, nothing so hopeless, nothing so desolate as his spirit in its darker moods has been instanced in the literary history of the nineteenth century."

Controversy surrounding Poe subsided as public interest turned to the Civil War and its immediate aftermath. But during the 1870s, the closing decade of Whitman's life, a new generation of biographers, bent upon rescuing his reputation from the defamation it had suffered immediately upon his death, led a revival of interest in Poe. Almost until her own death on 27 June 1878, Whitman generously and evenhandedly served these competing biographers, both as a living resource and as

a kind of research assistant, in spite of their efforts to draw her into the bitter quarrels among them.

Sarah Whitman's poetry appeared in newspapers, magazines, annuals, and gift books beginning in the 1820s. Sarah Josepha Hale in her *Ladies' Wreath* in 1837 republished four of Whitman's poems. Anne C. Lynch published six in her *The Rhode-Island Book* in 1841. And in 1849 the anthologist Rufus Griswold awarded Whitman's poems a prominent place in his *The Female Poets of America* and singled out her work for special mention in his preface. In 1853 George H. Whitney of Providence published a collection of her poems titled *Hours of Life, and Other Poems.* The collection opens with the lengthy title piece tracing the author's spiritual odyssey from the instinctive faith of her childhood through doubt and on to mature affirmation. This poem is followed by forty-one "Miscellaneous Poems," among which are scattered the verses she addressed to Poe, as well as fourteen sonnets, six poems translated from the German, and a final sonnet by way of envoi. In her will Whitman left funds for the publication of a posthumous collection that was issued by Houghton, Osgood, and Company of Boston in 1879 under the title *Poems by Sarah Helen Whitman.* This volume reprints all but four of the poems in the 1853 edition while adding several dozen composed thereafter. William Douglas O'Connor, a close friend of Sarah Whitman though far better known as a champion of Walt Whitman, selected and arranged the contents and furnished an introduction briefly surveying her life, literary career, and the critical reception of her work as well as identifying specifically those poems in the volume that Whitman devoted to Poe.

Sarah Whitman's contemporaries considered her an accomplished poet and singled out especially her "keen observation and delicate description of nature." As one critic remarked, however, her poems "contain occasional repetitions of sentiments, ideas, and favorite images, not only of her own, but those of other poets," especially Wordsworth, Edward Young, Alfred Tennyson, Felicia Hemans, Lydia Sigourney, Poe, and above all, William Cullen Bryant. Their conventionality and imitative character are principally responsible for the failure of Whitman's poetry to survive much beyond her own lifetime. Nonetheless, some of her poems may be attractive to the modern reader for their quality of idea, sentiment, and expression. Among them are her series (not strictly speaking a sequence) of six sonnets rehearsing her relationship to Poe, three sonnets addressed to Elizabeth Barrett Browning, passages in "Hours of Life," and a touching tribute to her sister, Anna Power, whose death preceded Whitman's by only six months.

Arcturus
Written in October
"Our star looks through the Storm."

Star of resplendent front! thy glorious eye
Shines on me still from out yon clouded sky —
Shines on me through the horrors of a night
More drear than ever fell oer day so bright —
Shines till the envious Serpent slinks away
And pales and trembles at thy steadfast ray.

Hast thou not stooped from heaven, fair star! to be
So near me in this hour of agony? —
So near — so bright — so glorious that I seem
To lie entranced as in some wondrous dream —
All earthly joys forgot — all earthly fear
Purged in the light of thy resplendent sphere:
Gazing upon thee till thy flaming eye
Dilates and kindles through the stormy sky,
While in its depths withdrawn — far, far away —
I see the dawn of a diviner day.

Manuscript for a poem Whitman sent to Edgar Allan Poe during their brief engagement in 1848 (from Caroline Ticknor, Poe's Helen, *1916)*

Whitman wearing a veil for a séance (Brown University Library)

Sarah Whitman was a prolific essayist. Her early essays, written during the 1830s and 1840s, cover a wide range of topics, from the "Nature and Attributes of Genius" to "The Scenery of Autumn." She composed most of her essays, however, after 1850, and the bulk, more than eighty in number, were carried in the pages of the *Providence Daily Journal* as letters to the editor, essay-length book reviews, travel correspondence, and simply essays. Some essays are reminiscences of deceased friends and of the halcyon days of intellectual life in Providence as well as descriptions of favorite locations in the city and its environs. Others promote feminism and defend Spiritualism. Still others are reports of lectures, art exhibits, performances of operas (including a matinee performance by the celebrated Italian soprano Marietta Piccolomini) that she attended in the course of frequent visits to New York City, an account of a ride through Central Park in 1860 while it was still a work in progress, and her description of the visit by the Japanese ambassadors to Manhattan, the same event celebrated by Walt Whitman in his "A Broadway Pageant." As a frequent traveler, she sent back to the *Journal* accounts of visits to Niagara Falls, Washington, Montreal, and in the summer of 1857, an extended trip to England and France, one of the highlights of which was an interview with the aging Walter Savage Landor at his home in Bath. In all these accounts, Whitman was a keen and witty observer and critic of manners, fashions, and settings.

With the exception of *Edgar Poe and His Critics*, none of Sarah Helen Whitman's work is in print. The last printing of her *Poems* was in 1916, and no effort has been made to collect her many essays.

Letters:

Poe's Helen Remembers, edited by John Carl Miller (Charlottesville: University Press of Virginia, 1979).

Biographies:

Caroline Ticknor, *Poe's Helen* (New York: Scribners, 1916);

John Grier Varner, "Sarah Helen Whitman: Seeress of Providence," dissertation, University of Virginia, 1940.

References:

James A. Harrison and Charlotte F. Dailey, "Poe and Mrs. Whitman—New Light on a Romantic Episode," *Century Magazine,* 55 (January 1909): 349–352;

Edgar Allan Poe, *The Last Letters of Edgar Allan Poe to Sarah Helen Whitman,* edited by James A. Harrison (New York & London: Putnam, 1909);

John E. Reilly, "Sarah Helen Whitman as a Critic of Poe," *University of Mississippi Studies in English,* 3 (1982): 120–127.

Papers:

Most of Sarah Helen Whitman's letters, private papers, and manuscripts can be found in the Harris Collection at Brown University, in the Poe-Ingram Collection at the University of Virginia, at The Lilly Library at Indiana University, and at the Harry Ransom Humanities Research Center at the University of Texas in Austin.

John Greenleaf Whittier

(17 December 1807 – 7 September 1892)

Albert J. von Frank
Washington State University

See also the Whittier entry in *DLB 1: The American Renaissance in New England.*

BOOKS: *Legends of New-England* (Hartford, Conn.: Hanmer & Phelps, 1831);

Moll Pitcher. A Poem, anonymous (Boston: Carter & Hendee, 1832);

Justice and Expediency; or, Slavery Considered with a View to Its Rightful and Effectual Remedy, Abolition (Haverhill, Mass.: Printed by C. P. Thayer, 1833);

Mogg Megone (Boston: Light & Stearns, 1836);

Poems Written During the Progress of the Abolition Question in the United States, Between the Years 1830 and 1838 (Boston: Isaac Knapp, 1837);

Poems (Philadelphia: Joseph Healy / Boston: Weeks, Jordan / New York: John S. Taylor, 1838);

Address Read at the Opening of the Pennsylvania Hall, on the 15th of Fifth Month, 1838, anonymous (Philadelphia: Printed by Merrihew & Gunn, 1838);

Moll Pitcher, and the Minstrel Girl (Philadelphia: Joseph Healy, 1840);

Lays of My Home, and Other Poems (Boston: Ticknor, 1843);

Ballads, and Other Poems (London: H. G. Clarke, 1844);

The Stranger in Lowell (Boston: Waite, Peirce, 1845);

Voices of Freedom (Philadelphia: Thomas S. Cavender / Boston: Waite, Pierce / New York: William Harned, 1846);

The Supernaturalism of New England (New York & London: Wiley & Putnam, 1847; London: Wiley & Putnam, 1847);

Poems (Boston: Mussey, 1849); republished as *The Poetical Works of John G. Whittier* (London: Routledge, 1850);

Leaves from Margaret Smith's Journal in the Province of Massachusetts Bay. 1678–9, anonymous (Boston: Ticknor, Reed & Fields, 1849);

Old Portraits and Modern Sketches (Boston: Ticknor, Reed & Fields, 1850);

Songs of Labor and Other Poems (Boston: Ticknor, Reed & Fields, 1850);

John Greenleaf Whittier, circa 1857

The Chapel of the Hermits and Other Poems (Boston: Ticknor, Reed & Fields, 1853; London: Sampson Low, 1853);

Literary Recreations and Miscellanies (Boston: Ticknor & Fields, 1854);

The Panorama, and Other Poems (Boston: Ticknor & Fields, 1856);

The Poetical Works of John Greenleaf Whittier, 2 volumes (Boston: Ticknor & Fields, 1857);

Home Ballads and Poems (Boston: Ticknor & Fields, 1860);

360

In War Time and Other Poems (Boston: Ticknor & Fields, 1864);

National Lyrics (Boston: Ticknor & Fields, 1865);

Snow-Bound. A Winter Idyl (Boston: Ticknor & Fields, 1866; London: Alfred W. Bennet, 1867);

The Tent on the Beach and Other Poems (Boston: Ticknor & Fields, 1867);

Among the Hills and Other Poems (Boston: Fields, Osgood, 1869);

Miriam and Other Poems (Boston: Fields, Osgood, 1871);

The Pennsylvania Pilgrim, and Other Poems (Boston: Osgood, 1872);

Hazel-Blossoms (Boston: Osgood, 1875);

Mabel Martin. A Harvest Idyl (Boston: Osgood, 1876);

The Vision of Echard and Other Poems (Boston: Houghton, Osgood, 1878);

The King's Missive, and Other Poems (Boston: Houghton, Mifflin, 1881);

The King's Missive, Mabel Martin, and Later Poems (London: Sampson Low, Marston, Searle & Rivington, 1881);

The Bay of Seven Islands, and Other Poems (Boston & New York: Houghton, Mifflin, 1883);

Saint Gregory's Guest and Recent Poems (Boston & New York: Houghton, Mifflin, 1886; London: Sampson Low, 1886);

The Writings of John Greenleaf Whittier, 7 volumes (Boston & New York: Houghton, Mifflin, 1888–1889; London: Macmillan, 1888–1889);

At Sundown (Cambridge: Privately printed at the Riverside Press, 1890; Boston & New York: Houghton, Mifflin, 1892; London: Longmans, Green, 1892);

Whittier on Writers and Writing: The Uncollected Critical Writings of John Greenleaf Whittier, edited by Edwin Harrison Cady and Harry Hayden Clark (Syracuse: Syracuse University Press, 1950).

Collection: *The Complete Poetical Works of John Greenleaf Whittier,* Cambridge Edition (Boston & New York: Houghton, Mifflin, 1895).

OTHER: *The Literary Remains of John G. C. Brainard,* edited, with an introduction, by Whittier (Hartford: P. B. Goodsell, 1832);

Narrative of James Williams, an American Slave, as told to Whittier (New York: American Anti-Slavery Society; Boston: Isaac Knapp, 1838);

The North Star: The Poetry of Freedom, edited anonymously, with contributions, by Whittier (Philadelphia: Printed by Merrihew & Thompson, 1840);

The Journal of John Woolman, edited, with an introduction, by Whittier (Boston: Osgood, 1871);

Child Life: A Collection of Poems, edited by Whittier, with the assistance of Lucy Larcom (Boston: Osgood, 1872);

Child Life in Prose, edited by Whittier, with the assistance of Larcom (Boston: Osgood, 1874);

Songs of Three Centuries, edited by Whittier, with the assistance of Larcom (Boston: Osgood, 1876);

Letters of Lydia Maria Child, introduction by Whittier (Boston & New York: Houghton, Mifflin, 1883).

Although John Greenleaf Whittier's reputation as a poet declined drastically in the twentieth century, his career is of continuing interest as an example of the writer functioning as a deeply committed reform activist. In the thirty-year struggle to abolish slavery Whittier played an important role as a poet, as a politician, and as a moral force; and yet, though he was among the most ardent of the antebellum reformers, he was saved from the besetting sin of that class—a narrowing and self-consuming zeal—by his equal insistence on tolerance, a quality he had come to cherish all the more through his study of the persecution of his Quaker ancestors. But if Whittier's life was dramatic for the moral, political, and, on occasion, physical conflicts it included, his poetry—the best of it—is of at least equal significance. Whittier was a highly regarded poet during the second half of the nineteenth century, enshrined in the pantheon of "Schoolroom Poets" along with William Cullen Bryant, Ralph Waldo Emerson, James Russell Lowell, Oliver Wendell Holmes, and Henry Wadsworth Longfellow. Whittier knew that he had written too much and that much of what he had written for the abolitionist movement had been hastily composed and for ends that were essentially political. Nevertheless, his collected poetry includes a core of excellent work, at the head of which stands his masterpiece, *Snow-Bound. A Winter Idyl* (1866), a lovingly imaginative re-creation of the good life in rural New England. This work—together with "Telling the Bees," "Ichabod," "Massachusetts to Virginia," "Skipper Ireson's Ride," "The Rendition," "The Double-Headed Snake of Newbury," and a dozen or so others—suggests not only the New England source of Whittier's finest achievements but also the predominant appeal that folk material had for his imagination.

Whittier's youth—indeed, his whole life—was deeply rooted in the values, history, and traditions of rural Essex County, Massachusetts. Born on 17 December 1807 near Haverhill, Massachusetts, in a farmhouse that his great-great-grandfather had built in the seventeenth century, John Greenleaf Whittier grew up in a poor but respectable household characterized by hard work, Quaker piety, and warm family affection. A more distinctive part of his background was the rich tradition of folklore in the region; tales of witches and ghosts told on winter evenings by the fire exercised the young Whittier's imagination. But his discovery of the

Whittier's birthplace in Haverhill, Massachusetts

Scottish poet Robert Burns, who could speak the beauty of the commonplace circumstances of a rural environment, made him wish to be a poet.

In 1829 at the age of twenty-two, too frail to be of much help on the farm, too poor to have given himself more than a year at the Haverhill Academy, and beginning already to doubt his abilities as a poet, Whittier accepted the editorship of *The American Manufacturer,* a political weekly in Boston. This position had been secured for him by William Lloyd Garrison, himself a young newspaper editor who was just then beginning his long career as an abolitionist. Whittier entered journalism for the opportunity to write. What he learned from the experience, however, were politics and polemics. His editorials, first in *The American Manufacturer* and later in the Hartford, Connecticut, *New England Review,* were at least as fierce in their denunciation of the Democrat Andrew Jackson as they were warm in support of the Whig Henry Clay.

In February 1831, while at Hartford, Whittier published a collection of tales and poems, *Legends of New-England.* Although the volume received little attention at the time, it is significant as a pioneering effort to render New England folklore, and in some respects it may be said to anticipate the works of Nathaniel Hawthorne. Whittier was never entirely comfortable with the Gothic mode, however, and suppressed the book in later life. On one occasion he paid five dollars for the privilege of destroying a copy of this rare early volume.

Toward the end of 1831 Whittier retired in ill health to Haverhill and spent the winter convalescing. He knew that he was at a crossroads in his life and wished to settle finally on a vocation. Poetry hardly paid at all, but he had come to like politics and found that his vociferous public support for Clay had made him a popular man in Massachusetts. The answer to Whittier's dilemma about his vocation arrived in the mail on 22 March 1833. His friend and patron, Garrison, who had begun publishing his *The Liberator* two years before, wrote to Whittier urging him to enlist in the gathering struggle against slavery. "Your talents, zeal, influence," he told Whittier, "all are needed." Whittier knew that to enlist in this cause, unpopular as it then was in New England, would be tantamount to giving up all hope of ever gaining elective office. To form such an alliance would also exclude him from influential literary circles and make publishing his poetry difficult, if not impossible. Still, Whittier had been slowly coming to the conclusion that Garrison now urged on him—that the evil of slavery had to be resisted actively.

Whittier responded in June 1833 with a privately printed pamphlet called *Justice and Expediency; or, Slavery Considered with a View to Its Rightful and Effectual Remedy, Abolition,* a closely reasoned and carefully documented attack on the Colonization Society. Widely supported by Northern and Southern churches, the Colonization Society was a conservative reform group that proposed to resolve the issue of slavery by sending American blacks, both slave and free, back to Africa. The society was, at the time of

Whittier's pamphlet, headed by Clay. An abolitionist group in New York republished the work and distributed hundreds of copies. Whittier's commitment to the cause was now sealed; as he expressed the experience many years later in "The Tent on the Beach" (1867), he

> Had left the Muses' haunts to turn
> 　　　The crank of an opinion-mill,
> Making his rustic reed of song
> 　　　A weapon in the war with wrong,
> Yoking his fancy to the breaking-plow
> That beam-deep turned to the soil for truth to spring and
> 　　　grow.

On the basis of this pamphlet and as a friend of Garrison, Whittier was chosen to be a delegate to the Philadelphia convention that in December 1833 founded the American Anti-Slavery Society. Accepting this position was an important moment in his life, and though his identification with the movement entailed many sacrifices throughout his career, he never regretted his decision. "I set a higher value on my name as appended to the Anti-Slavery Declaration of 1833," he later said, "than on the title-page of any book."

Though he could no longer hope to fulfill his dream of winning important political office, in 1835 he was able to gain a seat in the state legislature from his small home district of Haverhill. In the legislature he was an effective spokesman for his cause, winning over many to his views on the slavery question, sending petitions to the Congress, trying to get a bill through the state house granting trial by jury in cases involving the return of runaway slaves, and even organizing opposition to the death penalty. Whittier served only one term, having again jeopardized his always precarious health by hard work. He continued meanwhile to express his abolitionism in poems published in Garrison's *The Liberator* and in the columns of the *Essex Gazette,* which he now edited, but opposition to his moral stand was mounting. He was forced out of the *Essex Gazette* for failing to toe the orthodox Whig line and was threatened with violence in September 1835 by a mob in Concord, New Hampshire.

In 1836 Whittier sold the 148-acre family farm and moved with his mother and sister a few miles away to Amesbury in order that he and they might be closer to the Friends' meetinghouse. He was, however, frequently away. In 1837 he was in the New York office of the Anti-Slavery Society directing a nationwide petition campaign, and in the following year he moved to Philadelphia to edit the *Pennsylvania Freeman,* which he succeeded in turning into a vigorous organ of the abolitionist movement. During this period he was in close contact with all the most prominent American antislavery leaders, from Garrison and the Grimké sisters (Angelina Weld and

Whittier at age thirty

Sarah Moore) to Lydia Maria Child and John Quincy Adams.

Poems Written During the Progress of the Abolition Question in the United States, Between the Years 1830 and 1838—the first collection of Whittier's poetry—was brought out in 1837, without his knowledge, by some of his antislavery associates in Boston. In 1838 Whittier authorized an expanded and corrected edition, called *Poems,* which was published in Philadelphia. Included in these collections are some of his most heartfelt polemics, such as "Clerical Oppressors," a poem attacking the hypocrisy of the Southern clergy in lending the support of Christianity to the slave system:

> Feed fat, ye locusts, feed!
> And, in your tasselled pulpits, thank the Lord
> That, from the toiling bondman's utter need,
> Ye pile your own full board.

In such poems as "Stanzas" (later called "Expostulation") Whittier contrasted the apparent commitment of the United States to slavery with its historic dedication to freedom. He appealed to the regional pride of New England in "The Yankee Girl" and "Stanzas for the Times," but in these poems, as in most of the antislavery

Elizabeth Whittier, the poet's favorite sister (portrait by A. L. McPhail; from Samuel T. Pickard, Life and Letters of John Greenleaf Whittier, *1894)*

is indicated not only in the consistent advocacy of tolerance and brotherhood in the regional poems but also in the appeal to New England pride that so often forms the basis for his antislavery discourse. The finest poem of this sort, "Massachusetts to Virginia," was first published in this volume. After the overwhelming enthusiasm of the 1830s had dissipated in division and recrimination within the antislavery ranks, Whittier was able, during the next two decades, to maintain a healthier, maturer balance between his twin commitments to poetry and reform.

In 1846 Whittier published his last collection of antislavery poems, *Voices of Freedom,* and in 1847 brought out a collection of prose sketches titled *The Supernaturalism of New England.* A caustic review of the latter volume by Hawthorne, who pointed out its author's fundamental lack of sympathy with Gothic themes, may have contributed to Whittier's decision to suppress the book. In the same year he became a contributing editor with *The National Era,* a Washington-based antislavery journal that, until the founding of *The Atlantic Monthly* ten years later, served as his main publishing outlet. The most significant of Whittier's works to appear in *The National Era* was *Leaves from Margaret Smith's Journal in the Province of Massachusetts Bay. 1678–9* (published as a book in 1849). His only novel, *Leaves from Margaret Smith's Journal* is cast in the form of the letters and diary of a seventeenth-century New England Quaker, Margaret Smith. The story is sprightly and realistic, and the character of Margaret—"among the first of our native heroines," as Lewis Leary has observed—is carefully and sensitively portrayed.

On 7 March 1850 Massachusetts Senator Daniel Webster affirmed his support of compromise with the Southern slave power. Shocked and saddened by this unexpected defection, Whittier responded with his powerful protest "Ichabod." The poem is one of his best, its invective tightly controlled and deepened by the poet's acknowledgment of the frailties of all men, even the greatest:

> So fallen! so lost! the light withdrawn
>   Which once he wore!
> The glory from his gray hairs gone
>   Forevermore!
> Revile him not, the Tempter hath
>   A snare for all;
> And pitying tears, not scorn and wrath,
>   Befit his fall!
> . . . .
> Then, pay the reverence of old days
>   To his dead fame;
> Walk backward, with averted gaze,
>   And hide the shame!

Meanwhile, Whittier was busy trying to get a reluctant Charles Sumner to run for the other senatorial position

poems of the period, Whittier's anger swept everything before it, often including artistic control. The poems were meant to be, and indeed were, effective propaganda. During the late 1830s a split developed within the ranks of the abolitionists: some, such as Whittier, preferred to work through the political system for change and hoped to preserve the Union; others, such as Garrison, were less concerned with the Union and believed that slavery could not be abolished without also destroying the U.S. Constitution. While Garrison, working with the extreme "non-resistants," placed his reliance on moral suasion, Whittier was busy helping to organize the Liberty Party. He retired to Amesbury in 1840 but continued to work actively for Liberty Party candidates and for the election of others, regardless of party, who favored emancipation.

The publication in 1843 of Whittier's *Lays of My Home, and Other Poems* marked his return to the poetic treatment of regional materials. Included in this collection are poems such as "The Merrimack," treating the local scenery with the touch of the pastoral landscape artist; poems such as "The Ballad of Cassandra Southwick," exploring New England history; and poems such as "The Funeral Tree of the Sokokis," based on Indian lore. The near relation of Whittier's regional and abolitionist poetry

There are a great number of "Hicksites" in this vicinity — they have got possession of the Old Friends meeting houses all through the country. The "Orthodox" have meetings at Solebury 3 miles from Josephs — and at Buckingham 5 miles. We went yesterday to the latter place to meeting — The meeting house is within sight of the Hicksites' — it is a large new stone building beautifully situated in the midst of a fine grove of forest trees. — Some excellent remarks were made by Christopher Healy (Jos. uncle) who intends to visit N. E. Y. Meeting. I some expect, myself, to get back by way of Newport, although my health is not equal to a constant attendance of the meetings — I shall I think return to the city in a day a two, and after a short visit to Wilmington, go to New York —

Joseph & Rachel have a great deal of love to send thee. Rachel says thee must spend next summer with them. & keep the school. The School-House is only a few rods from the House.

With love to Mother & Aunt Mercy Mary & Lucii — Uncle Moses, & all the family. I am thy

aff. Bro.

Jno G. Whittier

Page from Whittier's 30 May 1840 letter to his sister Elizabeth (from John B. Pickard, ed.,
The Letters of John Greenleaf Whittier, *1975)*

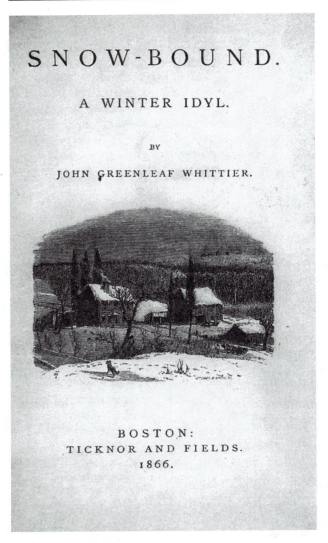

Title page for Whittier's poem about a snowstorm he experienced during his boyhood in New England

of Massachusetts. Whittier's maneuvers were successful and Sumner, with Whittier's advice and encouragement, became perhaps the most outspoken abolitionist in Washington.

Whittier's books of poetry were appearing at fairly regular intervals now that he had settled on the Boston publishing firm of Ticknor, Reed, and Fields (later Houghton, Mifflin). Sales, however, continued to be moderate at best. In 1850 appeared *Songs of Labor and Other Poems*, which, besides "Ichabod," included "Calef at Boston," "On Receiving a Quill . . . ," and the series of occupational poems that gives the volume its title. *The Chapel of the Hermits and Other Poems* was published in 1853, and *The Panorama and Other Poems* followed in 1856. The popular "Barefoot Boy," a sentimental tribute to the naturally free and unspoiled life of poor New

England children, was collected in the latter volume together with a fine antislavery poem, "The Haschich."

An important turn in Whittier's career occurred in 1857. The founding of *The Atlantic Monthly* in that year gave him a regular forum with all the most prominent writers of New England. His contributions to the earliest issues—including "Skipper Ireson's Ride" and "Telling the Bees"—were better poems than he had ever written. Symbolic of Whittier's entry into the literary establishment of Boston was the publication, also in 1857, of the "Blue and Gold Edition" of his poetry in a format to match Longfellow's. Toward the end of the year, Whittier's mother died and the poet himself turned fifty.

The poetry of this period shows Whittier's increasing disengagement from broadly political issues. His attention was turning more and more to his own personal past, as shown in the nostalgic, quasi-autobiographical poems "Telling the Bees" and "My Playmate"; he was also increasingly drawn to the larger but still personal past of New England history, as shown in the many fine ballads that he wrote at this time, such as "Skipper Ireson's Ride," "The Garrison of Cape Ann," "The Prophecy of Samuel Sewall," "The Double-Headed Snake of Newbury," and "The Swan Song of Parson Avery." All of these poems were first collected in *Home Ballads and Poems*, published in 1860. Almost the only hint of the impending Civil War that the volume included was the poem Whittier wrote in response to the raid on Harpers Ferry, "Brown of Ossawatomie."

Whittier's Quaker pacifism did not prevent him from being an ardent supporter of the Union cause when the Civil War broke out. He admired President Abraham Lincoln and was particularly proud of having voted for him four times, as a citizen and as an elector in 1860 and 1864. Whittier wrote many patriotic poems during the war, of which "Barbara Frietchie" is the most famous. *In War Time and Other Poems*, published in 1864, included several fine examples of Whittier's public poetry—"Thy Will Be Done" and "Ein Feste Berg. . . ," for example—in addition to several more "home ballads," including "Cobbler Keezar's Vision," "Amy Wentworth," and "The Countess." This volume was republished in 1865 under the title *National Lyrics* and included "Laus Deo," in which Whittier joyously recorded the death knell of slavery, the moment for which so much of his career had been a preparation.

With the Civil War over and the Thirteenth Amendment to the Constitution ratified, a part of Whittier's public life came to a close, just as, a year earlier, a part of his personal life had come to a close with the death of his beloved younger sister, Elizabeth. Whittier's whole mood was retrospective and memorial as he set to work on the "Yankee pastoral" that he had

The kitchen in Whittier's birthplace, setting for part of Snow-Bound *(from Samuel T. Pickard,*
Whittier-Land: A Handbook of North Essex, *1904)*

promised *The Atlantic Monthly* editor James Russell Lowell he would write. The result was *Snow-Bound,* his masterpiece.

The poem recalls a winter storm at the old Whittier homestead when the poet was a child. A day and a
night of driving snow had transformed everything:

We looked upon a world unknown,
On nothing we could call our own,
Around the glistening wonder bent
The blue walls of the firmament,
No cloud above, no earth below—
A universe of sky and snow!

The threat of isolation, of freezing or starving, is
countered by the family at the wood fire on the
hearth, the warmth of which is a symbol of life and
family affection.

Shut in from all the world without,
We sat the clean-winged hearth about,
Content to let the north-wind roar
In baffled rage at pane and door,
While the red logs before us beat
The frost-line back with tropic heat.

The physical and spiritual sufficiency of this besieged
family circle is the subject of Whittier's reminiscence
precisely because most of those who were then present

were now dead. By recalling each of them in turn,
Whittier substitutes the light of affectionate memory for
the light of the burning oaken log by which that night
they gathered together. The effect is to make the poem
itself stand witness to "The truth to flesh and sense
unknown, / That Life is ever lord of Death, / And Love
can never lose its own!"

Unlike many of Whittier's poems, *Snow-Bound*
has lost none of its appeal with the passing of time. A
large part of its charm is in its presentation of what
Whittier called "Flemish pictures of old days," composed of the common detail of rural life in early nineteenth-century New England: the few books, the
schoolmaster boarding with the family, the sounds to
be heard on windy winter nights ("We heard the loos-
ened clapboards toss, / The boardnails snapping in the
frost"), the importance of newspapers in gaining a sense
of the larger world outside, and especially the companionship of nature. In 1866 the kind of life that
Snow-Bound describes was as surely departed in fact as it
was present to the mellowed childhood memory of
thousands of readers. The poem was Whittier's first
genuine commercial success as well as his most complete artistic success. He realized $10,000 from the sale
of the first edition and never wanted for money again.

The Tent on the Beach and Other Poems, which followed in 1867, continued the success; twenty thousand

Whittier in about 1889

copies were sold in three weeks. "The Wreck of the Rivermouth," "The Changeling," "The Dead Ship of Harpswell," and "Abraham Davenport"—all first collected in this volume—show Whittier's abiding fondness for legendary and historical New England material, while "The Eternal Goodness" and "Our Master" indicate the new importance that the liberal religious tradition of the Quakers was coming to assume in his later poetry. If, after the Civil War, anything may be said to have taken on the personal importance that Whittier had before attached to the fight against slavery, it was his desire to see religion in America liberalized and the last vestiges of repressive Puritanism swept away. Oliver Wendell Holmes, who shared this hope, maintained that Whittier had done as much in America as Robert Burns had done in Scotland toward "humanizing" the hard theology of Calvinism. Whittier's edition of *The Journal of John Woolman,* published in 1871, gave new currency to that classic work of Quaker spiritual autobiography.

The remainder of the poet's long life was spent quietly and uneventfully in Amesbury and, after 1876, in a spacious home in Danvers, Massachusetts, called Oak Knoll, which he left only for his regular summer excursions into the lake and mountain region of New Hampshire. He continued to write almost up to the time of his death. *Among the Hills and Other Poems* (1869) is evidence that he knew of the darker and more solitary side of rural life in New England and can sustain comparison to some of the local-color realism then being written by female authors. The title poem in *The Pennsylvania Pilgrim, and Other Poems* (1872), one of Whittier's more successful long narratives, concerns the seventeenth-century German Pietist, Francis Daniel Pastorius, who founded Germantown near Philadelphia and who, after formally joining the Quakers, drafted one of the earliest American antislavery statements. The volume also includes "The Brewing of Soma," from which the popular hymn "Dear Lord and Father of Mankind" is taken. *The Vision of Echard, and Other Poems* (1878) includes, among other poems, "The Witch of Wenham," "In the 'Old South,'" and an astonishingly good courtly love lyric titled "The Henchman." Whittier's last book of poems, *At Sundown,* was privately printed in 1890 for close friends, and was republished for the public, with additions, at about the time of the poet's death on 7 September 1892. The last poem that Whittier wrote was a tribute to his friend Oliver Wendell Holmes on the occasion of Holmes's eighty-third birthday. They had outlived all their generation.

Whittier's reputation was never higher nor more apparently secure than at the time of his death. For years his birthdays had virtually been public holidays and were marked by celebrations throughout New England and the West. Whittier was essentially a public poet, a poet speaking to a large segment of the American people, including many who were not otherwise readers of poetry. They often came to his work to bask in the poet's moral tone, to attend to the heroic or prophetic voice in his poems, or to receive comfort from his characteristic optimism. Whittier, for better or worse, rarely challenged his audience. The popularity he enjoyed among his contemporaries seems to have been based largely on just those poems ("The Barefoot Boy" and "Barbara Frietchie," for example) that modern readers have rejected as sentimental. A reaction against the kind of soft-focus vision of the world that Whittier too often invoked set in during the early years of the twentieth century when a new, more astringent style of poetry was being established, in part by overturning the Victorian canons of taste that had elevated the work of Whittier's generation.

As critics today take a new look at the sentimental and local-color traditions in writings by Whittier's female contemporaries, however, Whittier may emerge in a somewhat fresher light. Some of his antislavery poems, such as "A Sabbath Scene," are especially con-

Whittier's funeral (from Samuel T. Pickard, Whittier-Land: A Handbook of North Essex, *1904)*

scious of gender issues and deploy an aesthetic rather similar to that found in Harriet Beecher Stowe's *Uncle Tom's Cabin* (1852), to which, indeed, the poem may be responding. Whittier's Quaker-derived acknowledgment of female equality surely formed a basis for his many friendships with such women authors of the period as Harriet Prescott Spofford, Celia Thaxter, the Cary sisters (Alice and Phoebe), Rose Terry Cooke, Lucy Larcom, Gail Hamilton, Ina Coolbrith, Annie Fields, and Sarah Orne Jewett. The personal and professional admiration that all of these authors expressed for Whittier and his poetry suggests that they may not, after all, have been working in dissimilar ways.

Letters:

The Letters of John Greenleaf Whittier, edited by John B. Pickard, 3 volumes (Cambridge, Mass.: Harvard University Press, 1975).

Bibliographies:

Thomas Franklin Currier, *Bibliography of John Greenleaf Whittier* (Cambridge, Mass.: Harvard University Press, 1937);

Annual bibliographies, *Whittier Newsletter* (1966–   );

Karl Keller, "John Greenleaf Whittier," in *Fifteen American Authors Before 1900: Bibliographical Essays on Research and Criticism,* edited by Robert A. Rees and Earl N. Harbert (Madison: University of Wisconsin Press, 1971), pp. 241–249;

Albert J. von Frank, *Whittier: A Comprehensive Annotated Bibliography* (New York: Garland, 1976);

John B. Pickard, *A Descriptive Catalogue of the John Greenleaf Whittier Collection* (Gainesville: Parkman Dexter Howe Library, University of Florida, 1987).

Biographies:

William Sloane Kennedy, *John Greenleaf Whittier: His Life, Genius and Writings* (Boston: S. E. Cassino, 1882);

Francis H. Underwood, *John Greenleaf Whittier: A Biography* (Boston: Osgood, 1884);

Annie Fields, *Whittier: Notes of His Life and Friendships* (New York: Harper, 1893);

Mary B. Claflin, *Personal Recollections of John Greenleaf Whittier* (New York & Boston: Crowell, 1893);

Samuel T. Pickard, *Life and Letters of John Greenleaf Whittier,* 2 volumes (Boston & New York: Houghton, Mifflin, 1894; revised, 1907);

Richard Burton, *John Greenleaf Whittier* (Boston: Small, Maynard, 1901);

Thomas Wentworth Higginson, *John Greenleaf Whittier* (New York: Macmillan, 1902);

George Rice Carpenter, *John Greenleaf Whittier* (Boston & New York: Houghton, Mifflin, 1903);

Frances Campbell Sparhawk, *Whittier at Close Range* (Brookline, Mass.: Riverdale Press, 1925);

Albert Mordell, *Quaker Militant: John Greenleaf Whittier* (Boston & New York: Houghton Mifflin, 1933);

Whitman Bennett, *Whittier: Bard of Freedom* (Chapel Hill: University of North Carolina Press, 1941);

John A. Pollard, *John Greenleaf Whittier: Friend of Man* (Boston: Houghton Mifflin, 1949);

Edward Wagenknecht, *John Greenleaf Whittier: A Portrait in Paradox* (New York: Oxford University Press, 1967);

Roland H. Woodwell, *John Greenleaf Whittier: A Biography* (Haverhill, Mass.: Trustees of the John Greenleaf Whittier Homestead, 1985).

References:

George Arms, *The Fields Were Green: A New View of Bryant, Whittier, Holmes, Lowell, and Longfellow* (Stanford, Cal.: Stanford University Press, 1953);

E. Miller Budick, "The Immortalizing Power of Imagination: A Reading of Whittier's *Snow-Bound*," *ESQ: A Journal of the American Renaissance*, 31 (1985): 89–99;

Joseph M. Ernest Jr., "Whittier and the American Writers," dissertation, University of Tennessee, 1952;

David Grant, "'The Unequal Sovereigns of a Slaveholding Land': The North as Subject in Whittier's 'The Panorama,'" *Criticism*, 38 (1996): 521–549;

Donald Hall, "Whittier," *Texas Quarterly*, 3 (Autumn 1960): 165–174;

Jayne K. Kribbs, ed., *Critical Essays on John Greenleaf Whittier* (Boston: G. K. Hall, 1980);

Lewis Leary, *John Greenleaf Whittier* (New York: Twayne, 1961);

Shirley Marchalonis, *Patrons and Protégées: Gender, Friendship, and Writing in the Nineteenth Century* (New Brunswick, N.J.: Rutgers University Press, 1994), pp. 94–121;

Roy Harvey Pearce, *The Continuity of American Poetry* (Princeton, N.J.: Princeton University Press, 1961);

John B. Pickard, "The Basis of Whittier's Critical Creed: The Beauty of the Commonplace and the Truth of Style," *Rice Institute Pamphlets*, 47 (October 1960): 34–50;

Pickard, "Imagistic and Structural Unity in 'Snow-Bound,'" *College English*, 21 (March 1960): 338–343;

Pickard, *John Greenleaf Whittier: An Introduction and Interpretation* (New York: Barnes & Noble, 1961);

Pickard, "Whittier's Ballads: The Maturing of an Artist," *Essex Institute Historical Collections*, 96 (January 1960): 56–72;

Pickard, ed., *Memorabilia of John Greenleaf Whittier* (Hartford, Conn.: Transcendental Books, 1968);

Frances M. Pray, *A Study of Whittier's Apprenticeship as a Poet* (Bristol, N.H.: Musgrove Printing House, 1930);

Donald A. Ringe, "The Artistry of *Margaret Smith's Journal*," *Essex Institute Historical Collections*, 108 (July 1972): 235–243;

James E. Rocks, "Whittier's *Snow-Bound:* 'The Circle of Our Hearth' and the Discourse on Domesticity," in *Studies in the American Renaissance 1993*, edited by Joel Myerson (Charlottesville: University Press of Virginia, 1993), pp. 339–353;

Louise C. Schaedler, "Whittier's Attitude toward Colonial Puritanism," *New England Quarterly*, 21 (September 1948): 350–367;

Winfield Townley Scott, "Poetry in America: A New Consideration of Whittier's Verse," *New England Quarterly*, 7 (June 1934): 258–275;

Leonard B. Trawick, "Whittier's Snow-Bound: A Poem About the Imagination," *Essays in Literature* (Western Illinois University), 1 (Spring 1974): 46–53;

Hyatt H. Waggoner, *American Poets from the Puritans to the Present* (Boston: Houghton Mifflin, 1967);

Robert Penn Warren, "Whittier," *Sewanee Review*, 79 (Winter 1971): 86–135.

Papers:

The largest collection of John Greenleaf Whittier manuscripts and correspondence is the Oak Knoll Collection at the Essex Institute in Salem, Massachusetts. Other notable collections include the Samuel T. Pickard–John Greenleaf Whittier Papers in the Houghton Library at Harvard University, the Roberts Collection at the Haverford College Library, the John Greenleaf Whittier–C. Marshall Taylor Papers at the Friends' Historical Library of Swarthmore College, the Berg Collection at the New York Public Library, and the Whittier Collection at the Haverhill Public Library.

Harriet E. Wilson

(1827/1828? – 1863?)

Andrew Smith
Lafayette College

See also the Wilson entries in *DLB 50: Afro-American Writers Before the Harlem Renaissance* and *DLB 239: American Women Prose Writers: 1820–1870*.

BOOK: *Our Nig; or, Sketches from the Life of a Free Black, In a Two-Story White House, North. Showing that Slavery's Shadows Fall Even There. By "Our Nig"* (Boston: George C. Rand & Avery, 1859).

Edition: *Our Nig; or, Sketches from the Life of a Free Black, In a Two-Story White House, North. Showing that Slavery's Shadows Fall Even There. By "Our Nig,"* edited by Henry Louis Gates Jr. (New York: Random House, 1983; London: Allison & Busby, 1984).

Harriet E. Wilson was perhaps the first African American to publish a novel in America. In Boston on 5 September 1859 Wilson published *Our Nig; or, Sketches from the Life of a Free Black, In a Two-Story White House, North. Showing that Slavery's Shadows Fall Even There. By "Our Nig,"* with the George C. Rand and Avery Company. The only work Wilson is known to have authored, *Our Nig* depicts the pernicious effects of slavery on a young, black indentured servant girl during her life with a white family in antebellum New England and, by extension, offers a critique of Northern abolitionist hypocrisy. The novel is significant for its blending of autobiographical elements with the conventions of slave narratives and sentimental fiction, for its unabashed and self-consciously direct appeal for readers to purchase the book, for its portrayal of an interracial marriage, and for its anticipation of crucial themes of later black American literature. Largely unknown, or at least unheralded, since its publication, *Our Nig* was reintroduced to scholarship, if not rediscovered, when Henry Louis Gates Jr. edited a facsimile edition of the book in 1983, along with a biographical reconstruction of the sparse details of its author's life.

What little is known about Wilson's life is confusing. Harriet E. Adams (the author's maiden name) may have been born in 1807 or 1808 in Fredericksburg, Virginia, or, more probably, in 1827 or 1828 in Milford,

New Hampshire. Harriet Adams spent her childhood living and working for a white family in Milford–likely the Nehemiah Haywards, who had strong connections with the New England abolitionist movement, or, possibly, with the family of Samuel Boyles, a carpenter. On 6 October 1851 Adams married a Virginian named Thomas Wilson. The couple's only child, George Mason Wilson, was born in Goffstown, New Hampshire, in May or June 1852 in the "County House," an establishment for the destitute, the mother having apparently been abandoned by her husband. Desperate financial straits led to Wilson's placing her son in a foster home and probably to her moving to the Boston area to seek work, where, on 18 August 1859, she registered the copyright of *Our Nig* with the district clerk's office. Although Wilson expressly states in the preface of the book that she was "forced into some experiment which shall aid me in maintaining myself and child without extinguishing this feeble life," Wilson apparently garnered little profit, and her seven-year-old son died less than six months later of "fever" in February 1860, in Milford. In chronic ill health herself, the last reference to Wilson may be an 1863 notation regarding a "Mrs. Wilson" at the Hillsborough, New Hampshire County Farm (poorhouse). No record of her death is known to exist.

Current understanding of Wilson's life depends mainly upon the archival research done by Gates and others; even so, the reconstruction of the events of her life is contingent upon incomplete and competing information. The 1807/1808 birth date in Fredericksburg is suggested by the record of a Mrs. Harriet E. Wilson, age fifty-two, in an 1860 Boston federal census. Conversely, an 1827/1828 date of birth is supported by the inclusion in the 1850 federal census in New Hampshire of a Harriet Adams, age twenty-two, a native of the state residing in Milford, whose race is recorded as "black." Indeed, the racial heritage of Wilson has historically been in question, since lacking clear details of her life, some critics before Gates's "rediscovery" assumed she was white. George Mason Wilson's death

OUR NIG;

OR,

Sketches from the Life of a Free Black,

IN A TWO-STORY WHITE HOUSE, NORTH.

SHOWING THAT SLAVERY'S SHADOWS FALL EVEN THERE.

BY "OUR NIG."

"I know
That care has iron crowns for many brows;
That Calvaries are everywhere, whereon
Virtue is crucified, and nails and spears
Draw guiltless blood; that sorrow sits and drinks
At sweetest hearts, till all their life is dry;
That gentle spirits on the rack of pain
Grow faint or fierce, and pray and curse by turns;
That hell's temptations, clad in heavenly guise
And armed with might, lie evermore in wait
Along life's path, giving assault to all."—HOLLAND.

BOSTON:
PRINTED BY GEO. C. RAND & AVERY.
1859.

Title page for Harriet Wilson's book, the first published novel by an African American woman (from Harriet E. Wilson, Our Nig, *edited by Henry Louis Gates Jr., 1983)*

certificate records the child's "color" as "Black" and says that he was the only son of "H. E. Wilson," the name, Gates notes—with the addition of "Mrs."—listed on the copyright page of *Our Nig.* Gates claims further biographical corroboration from the three supportive letters appended to the novel. These approbative epistles, a customary device of slave narratives, suggest that Wilson's text is largely autobiographical—that the experiences of Frado, the protagonist of *Our Nig,* are in no small part the tale of the author herself. A Margaretta Thorn, claiming to have known Wilson for years, describes the author as having endured a harsh childhood with absent parents and unrelenting, exploitative labor at the hands of her employers, a white family who made her "a slave, in every sense of the word." Thorn also notes Wilson's poor health since the age of eighteen, that she "has been married," and has a son she was forced to place into foster care. Another supporting epistle, signed by "Allida," an acquaintance of Wilson's

for some eight years, calls *Our Nig* "an Autobiography." Allida reports that Wilson was brought into Massachusetts around 1852 by "an itinerant colored lecturer" and subsequently found work as a maker of straw hats in either Ware or Walpole, Massachusetts. Soon after, Wilson met, fell in love with, and married a professed fugitive slave. Shortly after a return to New Hampshire, Allida continues, Wilson's husband abandoned her, forcing the expectant mother to flee to the county house to give birth. After a second move to Massachusetts, this time to Boston, Wilson was moderately successful in a hair-dying business, but because of failing health, resolved to write *Our Nig* in an attempt to support herself and her distant son. Allida's letter includes a sentimental poem written by Wilson—part of a letter to a Mrs. Walker (probably Allida's mother), for whom Wilson worked as domestic help when living in Massachusetts—the only extant piece of writing by Wilson besides the text of *Our Nig* proper. A "Chronology of Harriet E. Adams Wilson," by David A. Curtis, included in the Gates facsimile edition, suggests Wilson's residence in Boston before the publication of her novel is corroborated by 1855 and 1856 city directories, which list a Harriet Wilson, a "widow." Tangible evidence of Wilson's life after the 1860 death of her son, beyond the 1863 notation of the Hillsborough County Farm, has not been found.

Our Nig is the story of Frado, the mulatto daughter of Mag Smith, a poor, ostracized white woman and Jim, a free black cooper. Following Jim's death, Mag remarries and abandons six-year-old Frado to the Bellmonts, a white family living in a two-story white house near the New Hampshire village of Singleton. The child quickly assumes the role of servant and falls under the torments of Mrs. Bellmont, a racist "she-devil" who dominates the family and physically and emotionally abuses Frado. Blocked by Mrs. Bellmont from all but a minimum of formal schooling, Frado is severely overworked and treated as a virtual slave; she endures the despotic matriarch's repeated tortures and beatings for the slightest perceived infraction. Mrs. Bellmont is joined in her hatred of Frado—or "nig"—by her daughter Mary but opposed in mostly benign fashion by Mr. Bellmont, daughter Jane, sons James and Jack, and Aunt Abby, who befriend Frado. As Frado passes through adolescence, she becomes drawn to religion, growing close to the devout but deathly ill James. Frado wins a temporary victory over Mrs. Bellmont's arbitrary cruelty when she confronts her nemesis, staying her hand as she is about to beat Frado for a slight in her duties. When Frado reaches the age of eighteen, she is released from her servitude. Alone and her health broken from mistreatment, she must rely upon the charity of others to survive. Moving to Massachusetts, she supports herself by sewing straw bonnets and, returning to her studies, acquires a degree of self-consciousness about her position, along with the "new impulse" that she can elevate herself. Frado then marries Samuel, a black man posing as a fugitive slave and abolitionist lecturer, who quickly deserts his pregnant wife to go to sea. Frado gives birth back in Singleton but must leave the child in the hands of others as she feebly seeks a means of support. Moving again from New Hampshire to Massachusetts in her quest for sustainable work, the invalid's struggle becomes, at the end of the novel, a direct appeal to the reader to relieve her suffering.

Our Nig is both like and unlike the slave narratives and sentimental fiction from which it draws. As in the genre of the slave narrative, Wilson's protagonist is largely isolated in her struggle; she enjoys the meager succor of sympathetic friends, yet is continually frustrated in her hopes for release; she suffers under a central antagonist and, finally, wins (in result, somewhat like Frederick Douglass's battle royal with his tormentor Covey) a confrontation; and she possesses more devoutly religious and charitable impulses than whites who, to recall *The Interesting Narrative of the Life of Olaudah Equiano, or Gustavus Vassa, the African* (1791), are but "nominal Christians." In the end, she moves from bondage, in this case a punishing indentured servitude, to freedom. Similar to many slave narratives, Wilson's text begins with apologies for her inabilities as a writer and appends testimonial letters from those who knew her in order to confirm the veracity of the author's work. Like the genre of the sentimental novel, *Our Nig* employs direct address to the audience on behalf of an orphaned protagonist who is continually abused by those in power and must rely on the kindness of others to survive; it employs seductions and abandonments; it offers criticism of social practices and a protagonist well liked by those not twisted by hatred; and finally, rightness and inner strength carry the protagonist through her trials to a release from burden and into a better life. Gates, in his introduction to the facsimile edition of the novel, examines the similarities and contrasts of Wilson's story to women's fiction of the day by profitably employing what Nina Baym calls "overplot" taxonomy in *Woman's Fiction: A Guide to Novels by and about Women in America, 1820–1870.*

Yet, as Gates and others have suggested, the departures of *Our Nig* from the conventions of these genres are, if anything, more striking than its adherence. Unlike the stock protagonist of popular women's fiction, Frado has her escape and final reward dramatically qualified by the author. By the time of her release from the Bellmont house at age eighteen, Frado has had her health irreparably damaged. She is lame and physically unable to do the little work open to her. Instead of beginning a better life, Frado returns to the Bellmonts and is rejected, then is finally taken in by others in the community who charitably nurse her ailments. The novel ends with the mention of Mrs. Bellmont's offstage and "unspeakable" death, and Frado's intention—if not achievement—of "elevating herself" via the "merchandise" she prepares in hopes there will be customers to sell to. Even the possibility of spiritual reward for Frado is thwarted—she has longed for the release of death several times throughout the narrative—as she seems to reject her desire to enter Heaven if the Christian Mrs. Bellmont will be there waiting for her. While Frado does win a victory at the woodpile—getting Mrs. Bellmont to back down and even carry her own wood into the house—the act falls short of any lasting emancipatory reverberation. Also at odds with women's fiction, yet not dissimilar to some slave narratives, the mothers of *Our Nig* are decidedly antimaternal, muting the typically strong powers of motherhood. The power of racism to distort the soul is illustrated by Mrs. Bellmont's hatred, which leads not only to her torment of Frado but also to destructive meddling in the lives of her own children. Most significantly, Frado's mother, Mag, herself early deprived of parents, abandons her daughter at the age of six, an act Frado is forced to repeat with her own son, signaling no clear improvement from one generation to the next and no happy resolution of the story. Indeed, the final scene of the novel remains unwritten—the active support given to the destitute protagonist/author by the reader who, Wilson hopes, comes to provide aid by purchasing Frado's "merchandise."

Problems with the status of *Our Nig* as a novel are created by the conflation of Wilson the author and Frado the protagonist and the overlapping nature of their stories. In addition to the "Allida" testimonial that the book is an autobiography, the first three chapter headings—"Mag Smith, My Mother," "My Father's Death," and "A New Home for Me"—as well as the first line of the concluding chapter, "The Winding Up of the Matter," all drop the third-person narration used throughout the bulk of the story in favor of adopting first-person pronouns. Similarly, the admission of "H. E. W." in the preface that her writing "experiment" is an "appeal . . . for patronage" merges with the scene in the penultimate paragraph of the book: "And thus, to the present time, you may see her [Frado] busily employed in preparing her merchandise; then sallying forth to encounter many frowns, but some kind friends and purchasers." Even though *Our Nig* was published by a Boston printer, Wilson likely bore, as did her protagonist, the responsibility of distributing and selling her merchandise/book. At this point, then, the narrative voice of the book turns directly to the reader with a real-world appeal: "Still an invalid, *she* asks your sympathy, gentle reader. Refuse not. . . . Enough has been unrolled to demand your sympathy and aid." This explicit, sentimental appeal has prompted Gregory Eiselein to term the novel "unmistakably humanitarian" in its orientation and purpose. Moreover, the mixture of autobiography and sentimental fiction has led critics to refer to *Our Nig* as fictionalized or novelized autobiography, with still another possibility espoused by Hazel V. Carby, who sees the combination of conventions producing a rare form, an "allegory of a slave narrative, a 'slave' narrative set in the 'free' North."

Our Nig is largely allegorical in its central depiction of the Northern "shadows" cast by the Southern monster slavery. As Carby has noted, the Bellmonts' white, two-story house can be interpreted as the Southern plantation house, but, in the end, it is also an allegory of a nation divided over slavery. The mulatto Frado may be "free" in the North, yet she—just as heroes and heroines of slave narratives—must struggle to deliver herself from a white oppressor. The liberal and sympathetic Mr. Bellmont, as well as the religious son James, condemn Mrs. Bellmont's fanatical abuse of Frado; yet, like many abolitionists and religious leaders, they engage in no direct action to strike at the root of a problem typically understood to exist not at home, but "at the South." Additional allegorical resonance accrues in many scenes. Early in the novel, Frado's stepfather, Seth, speaks in a voice close to that of a slave dealer when he notes the girl would "be a prize somewhere," as he and Mag plan to dismantle their family. Fearing the separation, Frado temporarily disappears, paralleling the plight of the Southern slave who runs away for fear of being sold far from her family. Later, after a beating inflicted by Mrs. Bellmont, Frado takes refuge in the wilds of the countryside, just as fugitive slaves hid from their pursuers in swamps. In addition to these possibilities, the calamity of Frado's existence is, like that of slaves in the Southern states, determined by the realities of the existing economic system. Mag's nearly nonexistent economic prospects as a poor, seduced outcast lead to her union with the caring and employed cooper Jim, just as after his death she is forced to marry Seth and finally to abandon her children to improve her chances of survival. Mrs. Bellmont is pleased to have Frado enter her home as a six-year-old because she can train her from an early age and thus avoid her recent troubles with older servants; when, moreover, Frado later becomes drawn to religious study, Mrs. Bellmont, suspecting interference with the flow of "profit" Frado brings her because she does the work of two servants, seeks to prevent her from becoming "pious." Upon her release, Frado can find little work to sustain her and ultimately, as was the case with her downtrodden mother, must abandon her child to charity. All these problems speak to the severely restricted economic opportunities for black, mulatto, and, in the case

of Mag, lower-class white women in New England before the Civil War.

Wilson's own attempt at economic viability, the writing and publication of *Our Nig*, did little to relieve her desperate position. Friends or even Rand and Avery likely shouldered the expense of printing the book while leaving the sale of what was probably a printing of 100 to 150 copies to Wilson. Eric Gardner reports that most sales were in the three New Hampshire counties within twenty miles of Milford and that research into the distribution patterns (based on ownership of extant copies) of the novel suggests it may never have reached significant readership in Boston—the site of its publication and the heart of the abolitionist movement in New England, the one place where the book might reasonably be expected to have found an audience. Gardner, Gates, and others have speculated on possible motives for premeditated suppression—or at least deliberate decisions not to support or promote the book—by Boston abolitionists, but no hard proof exists to confirm such an effort. Still, the text of *Our Nig* provides a potential answer.

While the novel is clearly against slavery and its attendant evils, Wilson's book cannot easily be considered an abolitionist tract. To all appearances, the Bellmonts are a well-to-do, God-fearing, Northern white family. Yet, this appearance and this Northern white house mask a racist demon worthy of Harriet Beecher Stowe's Simon Legree in the person of Mrs. Bellmont, as well as passive family members who apparently know right from wrong when they see it but refuse to assert themselves in the defense of right and so prolong the injustices. Frado's husband, Samuel, supposedly a former slave now on the abolitionist lecture circuit, turns out to be a confidence man who has never even seen the South. Far from an admirable character, the duplicitous Samuel not only works the abolitionist crowd for personal gain, but he also abruptly abandons his wife and new child. Instead of a mythic site of comfort, the North is a place filled with people—including hypocritical abolitionists—who wish Frado ill:

> She passed into the various towns of the State she lived in, then into Massachusetts. Strange were some of her adventures. Watched by kidnappers, maltreated by professed abolitionists, who did n't want slaves at the South, nor niggers in their own houses, North. Faugh! To lodge one; to eat with one; to admit one through the front door; to sit next one; awful!

Such unflattering portrayals of abolitionists mark *Our Nig* as a novel focused on the tangled disease and parallel problem of white racism in the North rather than as a work seeking the abolition of slavery in the South. Northern abolitionists would not have heartily welcomed these negative scenes of the abolitionist movement. Indeed, Barbara

A. White argues that Wilson's early employers and probable models for the Bellmont family, the Haywards/Hutchinsons, were well known and active in abolitionist circles. If such was the case, Wilson's book may be in part a thinly veiled exposé of the hypocrisy of a liberal New England family active in the antislavery cause.

Certainly the author was mindful of the volatility of her subject matter. Wilson begins the preface to her book with a customary apology to the "refined and cultivated" for her poor abilities as a writer and ends it by imploring her "colored brethren" to refrain from condemning her for the attempt at erudition and, instead, to "rally around me a faithful band of supporters and defenders." While seeking an audience of free blacks, Wilson also admits she "purposely omitted what would most provoke shame in our good anti-slavery friends at home." That is, she cannily chose to edit even more-damning experiences of her life because of the damage their inclusion might cause "good" antislavery efforts in the North. This same note is struck again in the direct appeal near the end of the novel, when the narrative voice declares, "Refuse not, because some part of her history is unknown, save by the Omniscient God. Enough has been unrolled to demand your sympathy and aid." Indeed, Wilson's acknowledgment of the liminal quality of her project–her fear of the questionable appeal of the book to identifiable groups–indicates the difficulty of pleasing or even reaching an audience. Yet, there are still more reasons for which the book may have been shunned. The first chapter of the novel portrays the abandonment of the lonely Mag Smith, a white woman, by her own white community. Mag is completely alone until Jim, a "kind-hearted African" employed as a barrelmaker, suggests they marry: "'You's had trial of white folks, any how. They run off and left ye, and now none of 'em come near ye to see if you's dead or alive. I's black outside, I know, but I's got a white heart inside. Which would you rather have, a black heart in a white skin, or a white heart in a black one?'" The implication of Jim's offer and Mag's acceptance is clear enough–evil-hearted whites have deserted the helpless woman and a pure-hearted black man is more charitable than the entire white community. Thus, the specter of "amalgamation," an interracial marriage, is introduced within the first few pages of the novel. Yet, contemporary readers hardly needed to get even to the first chapter to find offense with the book. The audacity of the title–*Our Nig*–a vicious racial epithet repossessed and wielded as a pseudonym, undoubtedly induced reactions on its own.

Scholars have yet to locate any contemporary reviews or commentary on *Our Nig*. The 1983 reprinting of the novel, however, signified the beginning of a surge in critical attention and served as the catalyst for belated inclusion of Wilson's text into discussions of mid-nineteenth-century literary representations of race, class, and gender.

Dust jacket for the second edition (1983) of Wilson's novel, with an introduction that describes her book as "a 'missing link' . . . between the sustained and well-developed tradition of black autobiography and the slow emergence of a distinctive black voice in fiction"

Gates's call, at the end of his "A Note on the Text" in the facsimile edition, for further investigative work on the novel has been answered by many scholars. Among them and in addition to the works already mentioned are Julie Stern, who reads the novel as more Gothic than sentimental fiction; John Ernest, who focuses on the author's appeal for deliverance via commercial success in the marketplace; and Rafia Zafar, who suggests that Wilson's novel points to the difficulty of maintaining human relationships in a racially polarized America, while it anticipates the thematic concern of invisibility so important to later African American authors. Gates, in his own act of repossessing an expression with loaded racial meaning, has claimed for *Our Nig* the status of a "missing link" between African American autobiography and the emergence of a distinctive black voice in American fiction. Certainly many critics, from Gates on, acknowledge the power–perhaps threatening to Wilson's contemporary white neighbors, but heartening to others since—of the depiction in *Our Nig* of a detested Other's dramatic progression from a marginalized object to a literate, self-actualized subject. Although *Our Nig* is still far from a mainstream literary text, excerpts are now being included in some major literary anthologies—the *Norton Anthology of Literature by Women* (1985) and the *Heath Anthology of American Literature* (1990) among them. William L. Andrews has also chosen *Our Nig,* along with Douglass's *The Heroic Slave* (first published in *Autographs for Freedom,* 1854) and William Wells Brown's *Clotelle* (1864) as one of his *Three Classic African-American Novels,* published in 1990. The 1996 Project Gutenberg e-text of *Our Nig* is now available on-line at <http://www.gutenberg.net>. If the autobiographical intrusions of *Our Nig* are forgiven—or interpreted as the self-reflexivity of an author/protagonist engaged in literary production—Harriet E. Wilson did indeed write the first novel by an African American to be published in America. *Our Nig* is a valuable contribution to the diversity of voices in the American Renaissance.

References:

Katherine Clay Bassard, "'Beyond Mortal Vision': Harriet E. Wilson's *Our Nig* and the American Racial-Dream Text," in *Female Subjects in Black and White: Race, Psychoanalysis, Feminism,* edited by Elizabeth Abel, Barbara Christian, and Helene Moglen (Berkeley: University of California Press, 1997), pp. 187–200;

Nina Baym, *Woman's Fiction: A Guide to Novels by and about Women in America 1820–1870* (Ithaca, N.Y.: Cornell University Press, 1978);

Elizabeth Breau, "Identifying Satire: *Our Nig,*" *Callaloo,* 16 (Spring 1993): 455–465;

Hazel V. Carby, *Reconstructing Womanhood: The Emergence of the Afro-American Woman Novelist* (New York: Oxford University Press, 1987);

David A. Curtis, "Chronology of Harriet E. Adams Wilson," in *Our Nig; or, Sketches from the Life of a Free Black, In a Two-Story White House, North. Showing that Slavery's Shadows Fall Even There. By "Our Nig,"* edited by Henry Louis Gates Jr. (New York: Random House, 1983), pp. xii–xxvii;

Cynthia J. Davis, "Speaking the Body's Pain: Harriet Wilson's *Our Nig,*" *African American Review,* 27 (Fall 1993): 391–404;

Gregory Eiselein, *Literature and Humanitarian Reform in the Civil War Era* (Bloomington & Indianapolis: Indiana University Press, 1996);

John Ernest, "Economics of Identity: Harriet E. Wilson's *Our Nig,*" *PMLA,* 109 (May 1994): 424–438;

Gabrielle P. Foreman, "The Spoken and the Silenced in *Incidents in the Life of a Slave Girl* and *Our Nig,*" *Callaloo,* 13 (Spring 1990): 313–324;

Eric Gardner, "'This Attempt of Their Sister': Harriet Wilson's *Our Nig* From Printer to Readers," *New England Quarterly,* 66 (June 1993): 226–246;

Henry Louis Gates Jr., Introduction to *Our Nig; or, Sketches from the Life of a Free Black, In a Two-Story White House, North. Showing that Slavery's Shadows Fall Even There. By "Our Nig"* (New York: Random House, 1983);

Gates, "Parallel Discursive Universes: Fictions of the Self in Harriet E. Wilson's *Our Nig,*" in his *Figures in Black: Words, Signs, and the "Racial" Self* (New York: Oxford University Press, 1987), pp. 125–163;

Ronna C. Johnson, "Said but Not Spoken: Elision and the Representation of Rape, Race, and Gender in Harriet E. Wilson's *Our Nig,*" in *Speaking the Other Self: American Women Writers,* edited by Jeanne Campbell Reesman (Athens: University of Georgia Press, 1997), pp. 96–116;

Jill Jones, "The Disappearing 'I' in *Our Nig,*" *Legacy,* 13 (1996): 38–53;

Debra Walter King, "Harriet Wilson's *Our Nig:* The Demystification of Sentiment," in *Recovered Writers/Recovered Texts: Race, Class, and Gender in Black Women's Literature,* edited by Dolan Hubbard (Knoxville: University of Tennessee Press, 1997), pp. 31–45;

Angelyn Mitchell, "Her Side of His Story: A Feminist Analysis of Two Nineteenth-Century Antebellum Novels: William Wells Brown's *Clotel* and Harriet E. Wilson's *Our Nig,*" *American Literary Realism,* 24 (Spring 1992): 7–21;

Harryette Mullen, "Runaway Tongue: Resistant Orality in *Uncle Tom's Cabin, Our Nig, Incidents in the Life of a Slave Girl,* and *Beloved,*" in *The Culture of Sentiment: Race, Gender, and Sentimentality in Nineteenth-Century America,* edited by Shirley Samuels (New York: Oxford University Press, 1992), pp. 244–264;

Carla Peterson, *"Doers of the Word": African-American Women Speakers and Writers in the North (1830–1880)* (New York: Oxford University Press, 1995);

Shirley Samuels, ed., *The Culture of Sentiment: Race, Gender, and Sentimentality in Nineteenth-Century America* (New York: Oxford University Press, 1992);

Julie Stern, "Excavating Genre in *Our Nig,*" *American Literature,* 67 (September 1995): 439–466;

Barbara A. White, "'Our Nig'" and the She-Devil: New Information about Harriet Wilson and the 'Bellmont' Family," *American Literature,* 65 (March 1993): 19–52;

Rafia Zafar, *We Wear the Mask: African Americans Write American Literature, 1760–1870* (New York: Columbia University Press, 1997).

Checklist of Further Readings

The following selective list should be of value to those wishing to read more about the American Renaissance. Additional information may be obtained from Clarence Gohdes, *Bibliographical Guide to the Study of the Literature of the U.S.A.,* fourth edition (Durham, N.C.: Duke University Press, 1976); Lewis Leary, *Articles on American Literature, 1900–1930* (Durham, N.C.: Duke University Press, 1954); Leary, *Articles on American Literature, 1950–1967* (Durham, N.C.: Duke University Press, 1970); Joel Myerson, ed., *The Transcendentalists: A Review of Research and Criticism* (New York: Modern Language Association of America, 1984); the annual MLA bibliography; and *American Literary Scholarship: An Annual* (Durham, N.C.: Duke University Press, 1965–). Specialized bibliographies appear annually in the *Emerson Society Papers* and quarterly in the *Thoreau Society Bulletin.* Journals that regularly publish articles about the American Renaissance include *American Literature; American Transcendental Quarterly; ESQ: A Journal of the American Renaissance;* and *New England Quarterly.* The *Emerson Society Quarterly* was published from 1953 to 1971. See also *Studies in the American Renaissance,* edited by Joel Myerson (Boston: Twayne, 1977–1982 / Charlottesville: University Press of Virginia, 1983–1996).

Aaron, Daniel. *Men of Good Hope: A Story of American Progressives.* New York: Oxford University Press, 1951.

Aaron. *The Unwritten War.* New York: Knopf, 1973.

Adams, Grace, and Edward Hutter. *The Mad Forties.* New York: Harper, 1942.

Ahlstrom, Sydney E. "The Middle Period (1840–1880)," in *The Harvard Divinity School: Its Place in Harvard University and in American Culture,* edited by George Huntston Williams. Boston: Beacon, 1954, pp. 78–147.

Ahlstrom. *A Religious History of the American People.* New Haven: Yale University Press, 1972.

Ahlstrom and Jonathan S. Carey, eds. *An American Reformation: A Documentary History of Unitarian Christianity.* Middletown, Conn.: Wesleyan University Press, 1985.

Albanese, Catherine L. *Corresponding Motion: Transcendental Religion and the New America.* Philadelphia: Temple University Press, 1977.

Allen, Joseph Henry. *Our Liberal Movement in Theology.* Boston: Roberts, 1882.

Allen. *Sequel to "Our Liberal Movement."* Boston: Roberts, 1897.

Allen and Richard Eddy. *A History of the Unitarians and Universalists in the United States.* New York: Christian Literature Company, 1894.

Anagnos, Julia R. *Philosophiae Quaestor; or, Days in Concord.* Boston: Lothrop, 1885.

Anderson, Quentin. *The Imperial Self: An Essay in American Literary and Cultural History.* New York: Knopf, 1971.

Ando, Shoei. *Zen and American Transcendentalism.* Tokyo: Hokuseido, 1970.

Andrews, William L., ed. *Literary Romanticism in America.* Baton Rouge: Louisiana State University Press, 1981.

Asselineau, Roger. *The Transcendentalist Constant in American Literature.* New York: New York University Press, 1980.

Bacon, Edwin M. *Literary Pilgrimages in New England.* New York: Silver, Burdett, 1902.

Baker, Paul R. *The Fortunate Pilgrims: Americans in Italy 1800–1860.* Cambridge, Mass.: Harvard University Press, 1964.

Barbour, Brian M., ed. *American Transcendentalism: An Anthology of Criticism.* Notre Dame, Ind.: University of Notre Dame Press, 1973.

Barbour, James, and Thomas Quirk, eds. *Romanticism: Critical Essays in American Literature.* New York: Garland, 1986.

Bartlett, George B. *Concord: Historic, Literary and Picturesque,* third edition. Boston: Lothrop, 1885.

Bartlett, Irving H. *The American Mind in the Mid-Nineteenth Century.* New York: Crowell, 1967.

Bauerlein, Mark. *The Pragmatic Mind: Explorations in the Psychology of Belief.* Durham, N.C.: Duke University Press, 1997.

Baym, Max I. *A History of Literary Aesthetics in America.* New York: Ungar, 1973.

Baym, Nina. *American Women Writers and the Work of History, 1790–1860.* New Brunswick, N.J.: Rutgers University Press, 1995.

Baym. *Novels, Readers, and Reviewers: Responses to Fiction in Antebellum America.* Ithaca, N.Y.: Cornell University Press, 1984.

Baym. *Woman's Fiction: A Guide to Novels by and about Women in America, 1820–1870,* second edition. Urbana: University of Illinois Press, 1993.

Bell, Michael. *The Development of American Romance: The Sacrifice of Relation.* Chicago: University of Chicago Press, 1980.

Bercovitch, Sacvan. *The American Jeremiad.* Madison: University of Wisconsin Press, 1978.

Bercovitch. *The Puritan Origins of the American Self.* New Haven: Yale University Press, 1975.

Bercovitch. *The Rites of Assent: Transformations in the Symbolic Construction of America.* New York: Routledge, 1993.

Bercovitch, ed. *The Cambridge History of American Literature. Volume 2: Prose Writing, 1820–1865.* Cambridge: Cambridge University Press, 1995.

Bercovitch and Myra Jehlen, eds. *Ideology and Classic American Literature.* Cambridge: Cambridge University Press, 1986.

Berlin, James A. *Writing Instruction in Nineteenth-Century American Colleges.* Carbondale: Southern Illinois University Press, 1984.

Bickman, Martin. *The Unsounded Centre: Jungian Studies in American Romanticism.* Chapel Hill: University of North Carolina Press, 1980. Republished as *American Romantic Psychology: Emerson, Poe, Whitman, Dickinson.* Dallas: Spring, 1988.

Blasing, Mutlu Konuk. *American Poetry: The Rhetoric of Its Forms.* New Haven: Yale University Press, 1987.

Blau, Joseph L. *Men and Moments in American Philosophy.* Englewood Cliffs, N.J.: Prentice-Hall, 1952.

Bloom, Harold. *Agon: Towards a Theory of Romanticism.* New York: Oxford University Press, 1982.

Bloom. *The Breaking of the Vessels*. Chicago: University of Chicago Press, 1982.

Bloom. *Figures of the Capable Imagination*. New York: Seabury Press, 1976.

Bloom. *Poetry and Repression: Revisionism from Blake to Stevens*. New Haven: Yale University Press, 1976.

Blumenthal, Henry. *American and French Culture, 1800–1900: Interchanges in Art, Science, Literature, and Society*. Baton Rouge: Louisiana State University Press, 1975.

Boas, George, ed. *Romanticism in America*. Baltimore: Johns Hopkins University Press, 1940.

Bode, Carl. *The American Lyceum*. New York: Oxford University Press, 1956.

Boller, Paul F., Jr. *American Transcendentalism, 1830–1860: An Intellectual Inquiry*. New York: Putnam, 1974.

Branch, Douglas E. *The Sentimental Years 1836–1860*. New York: Appleton-Century, 1934.

Brantley, Richard E. *Coordinates of Anglo-American Romanticism: Wesley, Edwards, Carlyle & Emerson*. Gainesville: University Press of Florida, 1993.

Brooks, Paul. *The People of Concord: One Year in the Flowering of New England*. Chester, Conn.: Globe Pequot Press, 1990.

Brooks, Van Wyck. *The Dream of Arcadia: American Writers and Artists in Italy 1760–1915*. New York: Dutton, 1958.

Brooks. *The Flowering of New England 1815–1865*. New York: Dutton, 1936.

Brown, Herbert Ross. *The Sentimental Novel in America 1789–1860*. Chapel Hill: University of North Carolina Press, 1940.

Brown, Jerry Wayne. *The Rise of Biblical Criticism in America, 1800–1870: The New England Scholars*. Middletown, Conn.: Wesleyan University Press, 1969.

Brown, Mary Hosmer. *Memories of Concord*. Boston: Four Seas, 1926.

Buell, Lawrence. *The Environmental Imagination: Thoreau, Nature Writing, and the Formation of American Culture*. Cambridge, Mass.: Harvard University Press, 1995.

Buell. *Literary Transcendentalism: Style and Vision in the American Renaissance*. Ithaca, N.Y.: Cornell University Press, 1973.

Buell. *New England Literary Culture from Revolution through Renaissance*. New York: Cambridge University Press, 1986.

Buell. "The Transcendentalists," in *Columbia Literary History of the United States,* general editor Emory Elliott. New York: Columbia University Press, 1988, pp. 364–378.

Burton, Katherine. *Paradise Planters: The Story of Brook Farm*. London: Longmans, Green, 1939.

Cain, William E. *F. O. Matthiessen and the Politics of Criticism*. Madison: University of Wisconsin Press, 1988.

Calverton, V. F. *The Liberation of American Literature*. New York: Scribners, 1932.

Cameron, Kenneth Walter. *Transcendental Climate*, 3 volumes. Hartford: Transcendental Books, 1963.

Capper, Charles, and Conrad Edick Wright, eds. *Transient and Permanent: The Transcendentalist Movement and Its Contexts*. Boston: Massachusetts Historical Society/Northeastern University Press, 1999.

Carafiol, Peter. *The American Ideal: Literary History as a Worldly Activity.* New York: Oxford University Press, 1991.

Carpenter, Frederic I. *American Literature and the Dream.* New York: Philosophical Library, 1955.

Carter, Everett. *The American Idea: The Literary Response to American Optimism.* Chapel Hill: University of North Carolina Press, 1977.

Carton, Evan. *The Rhetoric of American Romance: Dialectic and Identity in Emerson, Dickinson, Poe, and Hawthorne.* Baltimore: Johns Hopkins University Press, 1985.

Cavell, Stanley. *Conditions Handsome and Unhandsome: The Constitution of Emersonian Perfectionism.* Chicago: University of Chicago Press, 1990.

Cavell. *In Quest of the Ordinary: Lines of Skepticism and Romanticism.* Chicago: University of Chicago Press, 1988.

Cavell. *This New Yet Unapproachable America: Lectures after Emerson and Wittgenstein.* Albuquerque, N.Mex.: Living Batch Press, 1989.

Chai, Leon. *The Romantic Foundations of the American Renaissance.* Ithaca, N.Y.: Cornell University Press, 1987.

Chapin, Sarah. *Concord, Massachusetts.* Dover, N.H.: Arcadia, 1997.

Charvat, William. *Literary Publishing in America: 1790–1850.* Amherst: University of Massachusetts Press, 1993.

Charvat. *The Origins of American Critical Thought 1810–1835.* Philadelphia: University of Pennsylvania Press, 1936.

Charvat. *The Profession of Authorship in America, 1800–1870,* edited by Matthew J. Bruccoli. Columbus: Ohio State University Press, 1968.

Chase, Richard. *The American Novel and Its Tradition.* Garden City, N.Y.: Doubleday, 1957.

Christy, Arthur. *The Orient in American Transcendentalism.* New York: Columbia University Press, 1932.

Colacurcio, Michael J. *Doctrine and Difference: Essays in the Literature of New England.* New York: Routledge, 1997.

Cole, Phyllis. *Mary Moody Emerson and the Origins of Transcendentalism: A Family History.* New York: Oxford University Press, 1998.

Conrad, Susan P. *Perish the Thought: Intellectual Women in Romantic America 1830–1860.* New York: Oxford University Press, 1976.

Cooke, George Willis. *Unitarianism in America.* Boston: American Unitarian Association, 1902.

Cooke, ed. *The Poets of Transcendentalism: An Anthology.* Boston: Houghton, Mifflin, 1903.

Cowen, Michael H. *City of the West: Emerson, America, and Urban Metaphor.* New Haven: Yale University Press, 1967.

Cowie, Alexander. *The Rise of the American Novel.* New York: American Book Co., 1948.

Crawford, Mary Caroline. *Romantic Days in Old Boston.* Boston: Little, Brown, 1910.

Cunliffe, Marcus. *The Literature of the United States.* London: Penguin, 1954.

Curtis, Edith Roelker. *A Season in Utopia: The Story of Brook Farm.* New York: Nelson, 1961.

Day, Martin S. *History of American Literature from the Beginning to 1900*. Garden City, N.Y.: Doubleday, 1970.

Decker, William Merrill. *Epistolary Practices: Letter Writing in America before Telecommunications*. Chapel Hill: University of North Carolina Press, 1998.

Dekker, George. *The American Historical Romance*. Cambridge: Cambridge University Press, 1987.

Delano, Sterling F. *The Harbinger and New England Transcendentalism: A Portrait of Associationism in America*. Rutherford, N.J.: Fairleigh Dickinson University Press, 1983.

Dickens, Charles. *American Notes for General Circulation*. London: Chapman & Hall, 1842.

Douglas, Ann. *The Feminization of American Culture*. New York: Knopf, 1977.

Duyckinck, Evert A., and George L. Duyckinck, eds. *Cyclopaedia of American Literature,* 2 volumes. New York: Scribner, 1856.

Eakin, Paul John. *The New England Girl: Cultural Ideals in Hawthorne, Stowe, Howells and James*. Athens: University of Georgia Press, 1976.

Ekirch, Arthur A., Jr. *Man and Nature in America*. New York: Columbia University Press, 1963.

Eliot, Samuel A., ed. *Heralds of a Liberal Faith,* 3 volumes. Boston: American Unitarian Association, 1910.

Elliott, Emory, gen. ed. *Columbia Literary History of the United States*. New York: Columbia University Press, 1988.

Emerson, Edward Waldo. *The Early Years of the Saturday Club 1855–1870*. Boston: Houghton Mifflin, 1918.

Falk, Robert. *The Victorian Mode in American Fiction*. East Lansing: Michigan State University Press, 1965.

Feidelson, Charles, Jr. *Symbolism and American Literature*. Chicago: University of Chicago Press, 1953.

Fellman, Michael. *The Unbounded Frame: Freedom and Community in Nineteenth Century American Utopianism*. Westport, Conn.: Greenwood Press, 1973.

Fenn, William W. *The Religious History of New England*. Cambridge, Mass.: Harvard University Press, 1917.

Ferguson, Robert A. *Law & Letters in American Culture*. Cambridge, Mass.: Harvard University Press, 1984.

Fiedler, Leslie A. *Love and Death in the American Novel,* revised edition. New York: Stein & Day, 1966.

Fischer, David Hackett, ed. *Concord: The Social History of a New England Town 1750–1850*. Waltham, Mass.: Brandeis University, 1983.

Fish, Carl Russell. *The Rise of the Common Man 1830–1850*. New York: Macmillan, 1927.

Floan, Howard R. *The South in Northern Eyes 1831 to 1861*. Austin: University of Texas Press, 1958.

Flower, Elizabeth, and Murray G. Murphey. "Transcendentalism," in their *A History of Philosophy in America,* 2 volumes. New York: Putnam, 1977, I: 397–435.

Foerster, Norman. *American Criticism*. Boston: Houghton Mifflin, 1928.

Foster, Edward Halsey. *The Civilized Wilderness: Backgrounds to American Romantic Literature, 1817–1860*. New York: Free Press, 1975.

Francis, Richard. *Transcendental Utopias: Individual and Community at Brook Farm, Fruitlands, and Walden*. Ithaca, N.Y.: Cornell University Press, 1997.

Freidel, Frank, ed. *Harvard Guide to American History,* revised edition, 2 volumes. Cambridge, Mass.: Harvard University Press, 1974.

Frothingham, Octavius Brooks. *Transcendentalism in New England: A History*. New York: Putnam, 1876.

Fussell, Edwin. *Frontier: American Literature and the American West*. Princeton: Princeton University Press, 1965.

Gardiner, Harold C., ed. *American Classics Reconsidered: A Christian Appraisal*. New York: Scribners, 1958.

Gelpi, Albert. *The Tenth Muse: The Psyche of the American Poet*. Cambridge, Mass.: Harvard University Press, 1975.

Gilmore, Michael T. *American Romanticism and the Marketplace*. Chicago: University of Chicago Press, 1985.

Gittleman, Edwin, ed. *The Minor and Later Transcendentalists: A Symposium*. Hartford, Conn.: Transcendental Books, 1969.

Goddard, Harold Clarke. *Studies in New England Transcendentalism*. New York: Columbia University Press, 1908.

Gohdes, Clarence. *American Literature in Nineteenth Century England*. New York: Columbia University Press, 1944.

Gohdes. *The Periodicals of American Transcendentalism*. Durham, N.C.: Duke University Press, 1931.

Goodman, Russell B. *American Philosophy and the Romantic Tradition*. New York: Cambridge University Press, 1991.

Gougeon, Len. *Virtue's Hero: Emerson, Antislavery, and Reform*. Athens: University of Georgia Press, 1990.

Green, Martin. *The Problem of Boston: Some Readings in Cultural History*. New York: Norton, 1966.

Green. *Re-appraisals: Some Commonsense Readings in American Literature*. London: Hugh Evelyn, 1963.

Greer, Louise. *Browning and America*. Chapel Hill: University of North Carolina Press, 1952.

Grey, Robin. *The Complicity of Imagination: The American Renaissance, Contests of Authority, and Seventeenth-Century English Culture*. New York: Cambridge University Press, 1995.

Griffin, C. S. *The Ferment of Reform, 1830–1860*. New York: Crowell, 1967.

Gross, Theodore L. *The Heroic Ideal in American Literature*. New York: Free Press, 1971.

Grusin, Richard. *Transcendentalist Hermeneutics: Institutional Authority and the Higher Criticism of the Bible*. Durham, N.C.: Duke University Press, 1991.

Guarneri, Carl J. *The Utopian Alternative: Fourierism in Nineteenth-Century America*. Ithaca, N.Y.: Cornell University Press, 1991.

Gura, Philip F. *The Crossroads of American History and Literature*. University Park: Pennsylvania State University Press, 1996.

Gura. *The Wisdom of Words: Language, Theology, and Literature in the New England Renaissance.* Middletown, Conn.: Wesleyan University Press, 1981.

Gura and Joel Myerson, eds. *Critical Essays on American Transcendentalism.* Boston: G. K. Hall, 1982.

Gustafson, Thomas. *Representative Words: Politics, Literature, and the American Language, 1776–1865.* New York: Cambridge University Press, 1992.

Habich, Robert D. *Transcendentalism and the* Western Messenger: *A History of the Magazine and Its Contributors, 1835–1841.* Rutherford, N.J.: Fairleigh Dickinson University Press, 1985.

Haralson, Eric L., ed. *Encyclopedia of American Poetry: The Nineteenth Century.* Chicago: Fitzroy Dearborn, 1998.

Haraszti, Zoltan. *The Idyll of Brook Farm as Revealed by Unpublished Letters in the Boston Public Library.* Boston: Trustees of the Public Library, 1937.

Harbert, Earl N., and Robert A. Rees. *Fifteen American Authors Before 1900: Bibliographical Essays on Research and Criticism,* revised edition. Madison: University of Wisconsin Press, 1984.

Harris, Susan K. *Nineteenth-Century American Women's Novels.* Cambridge: Cambridge University Press, 1990.

Hart, James D. *The Popular Book: A History of America's Literary Taste.* New York: Oxford University Press, 1950.

Hendrick, George, ed. *The American Renaissance: The History and Literature of an Era.* Berlin: Diesterweg, 1961.

Herreshoff, David. *American Disciples of Marx.* Detroit: Wayne State University Press, 1967.

Hertz, David Michael. *Angels of Reality: Emersonian Unfoldings in Wright, Stevens, and Ives.* Carbondale: Southern Illinois University Press, 1993.

Higginson, Thomas Wentworth, and Henry Walcott Boynton. *A Reader's History of American Literature.* Boston: Houghton, Mifflin, 1903.

Hochfield, George. "New England Transcendentalism," in *American Literature to 1900,* edited by Marcus Cunliffe. New York: Peter Bedrick, 1987, pp. 135–168.

Hochfield, ed. *Selected Writings of the American Transcendentalists.* New York: New American Library, 1966.

Hoffman, Daniel G. *Form and Fable in American Fiction.* New York: Oxford University Press, 1961.

Horton, Rod W., and Herbert W. Edwards. *Backgrounds of American Literary Thought.* New York: Appleton-Century-Crofts, 1952.

Howard, Leon. *Literature and the American Tradition.* Garden City, N.Y.: Doubleday, 1960.

Howe, Daniel Walker. "'At Morning Blessed and Golden Browed,'" in *A Stream of Light: A Sesquicentennial History of American Unitarianism,* edited by Conrad Wright. Boston: Beacon, 1975, pp. 3–61.

Howe. *Making the American Self: Jonathan Edwards to Abraham Lincoln.* Cambridge, Mass.: Harvard University Press, 1997.

Howe. *The Unitarian Conscience: Harvard Moral Philosophy, 1805–1861.* Cambridge, Mass.: Harvard University Press, 1970.

Howe, Irving. *The American Newness: Culture and Politics in the Age of Emerson.* Cambridge, Mass.: Harvard University Press, 1986.

Howells, William Dean. *Literary Friends and Acquaintance: A Personal Retrospect of American Authorship* (1900). Edited by David F. Hiatt and Edwin H. Cady. Bloomington: Indiana University Press, 1968.

Hutchison, William R. *The Transcendentalist Ministers: Church Reform in the New England Renaissance.* New Haven: Yale University Press, 1959.

Huth, Hans. *Nature and the American: Three Centuries of Changing Attitudes.* Berkeley: University of California Press, 1957.

Irwin, John T. *American Hieroglyphics: The Symbol of the Egyptian Hieroglyphics in the American Renaissance.* New Haven: Yale University Press, 1980.

Jackson, Carl T. *The Oriental Religions and American Thought: Nineteenth-Century Explorations.* Westport, Conn.: Greenwood Press, 1981.

Jarvis, Edward. *Traditions and Reminiscences of Concord, Massachusetts, 1779–1878,* edited by Sarah Chapin. Amherst: University of Massachusetts Press, 1993.

Johnson, James L. *Mark Twain and the Limits of Power: Emerson's God in Ruins.* Knoxville: University of Tennessee Press, 1982.

Jones, Howard Mumford. *American and French Culture 1750–1848.* Chapel Hill: University of North Carolina Press, 1927.

Jones. *Belief and Disbelief in American Literature.* Chicago: University of Chicago Press, 1967.

Jones. *The Theory of American Literature.* Ithaca, N.Y.: Cornell University Press, 1965.

Kaplan, Harold. *Democratic Humanism and American Literature.* Chicago: University of Chicago Press, 1972.

Kaplan, Nathan, and Thomas Katsaros. *The Origins of American Transcendentalism in Philosophy and Mysticism.* New Haven: College and University Press, 1975.

Kateb, George. *The Inner Ocean: Individualism and Democratic Culture.* Ithaca, N.Y.: Cornell University Press, 1992.

Kaufman, Paul. "The Romantic Movement," in *The Reinterpretation of American Literature,* edited by Norman Foerster. New York: Harcourt, Brace, 1928, pp. 114–138.

Kazin, Alfred. *An American Procession: The Major American Writers from 1830 to 1930–The Crucial Century.* New York: Knopf, 1984.

Kazin. *God and the American Writer.* New York: Knopf, 1997.

Kelley, Mary. *Private Woman, Public Stage: Literary Domesticity in Nineteenth-Century America.* New York: Oxford University Press, 1984.

Kern, Alexander. "The Rise of Transcendentalism, 1815–1860," in *Transitions in American Literary History,* edited by Harry Hayden Clark. Durham, N.C.: Duke University Press, 1954, pp. 247–314.

Knight, Denise D., ed. *Nineteenth-Century American Women Writers: A Bio-Bibliographical Critical Sourcebook.* Westport, Conn.: Greenwood Press, 1997.

Knight, Grant C. *American Literature and Culture*. New York: Ray Long & Richard R. Smith, 1932.

Kolb, Harold H., Jr. *A Field Guide to the Study of American Literature*. Charlottesville: University Press of Virginia, 1976.

Kopley, Richard, ed. *Prospects for the Study of American Literature: A Guide for Scholars and Students*. New York: New York University Press, 1997.

Koster, Donald N. *Transcendentalism in America*. Boston: Twayne, 1975.

Kramer, Michael P. *Imagining Language in America: From the Revolution to the Civil War*. Princeton: Princeton University Press, 1992.

Kreymborg, Alfred. *Our Singing Strength: An Outline of American Poetry, 1620–1930*. New York: Coward-McCann, 1929.

Kronick, Joseph G. *American Poetics of History: From Emerson to the Moderns*. Baton Rouge: Louisiana State University Press, 1984.

Kuklick, Bruce. *Churchmen and Philosophers: From Jonathan Edwards to John Dewey*. New Haven: Yale University Press, 1985.

Lader, Lawrence. *The Bold Brahmins: New England's War against Slavery, 1831–1863*. New York: Dutton, 1961.

Layman, Richard, and Joel Myerson, eds. *The Professions of Authorship: Essays in Honor of Matthew J. Bruccoli*. Columbia: University of South Carolina Press, 1996.

Leary, Lewis. *American Literature: A Study and Research Guide*. New York: St. Martin's Press, 1976.

Lease, Benjamin. *Anglo-American Encounters: England and the Rise of American Literature*. Cambridge: Cambridge University Press, 1981.

Lehmann-Haupt, Hellmut, Lawrence C. Wroth, and Rollo G. Silver. *The Book in America: A History of the Making and Selling of Books in the U.S.*, second edition, revised and enlarged. New York: R. R. Bowker, 1952.

Leighton, Walter L. *French Philosophers and New-England Transcendentalism*. Charlottesville: University of Virginia, 1908.

Leisy, Ernest Erwin. *The American Historical Novel*. Norman: University of Oklahoma Press, 1950.

Leisy. *American Literature*. New York: Crowell, 1929.

Leverenz, David. *Manhood and the American Renaissance*. Ithaca, N.Y.: Cornell University Press, 1989.

Lewis, R. W. B. *The American Adam: Innocence, Tragedy and Tradition in the Nineteenth Century*. Chicago: University of Chicago Press, 1955.

Lewisohn, Ludwig. *Expression in America*. New York: Harper, 1932.

Lieber, Todd M. *Endless Experiments: Essays on the Heroic Experience in American Romanticism*. Columbus: Ohio State University Press, 1973.

Loving, Jerome. *Emerson, Whitman, and the American Muse*. Chapel Hill: University of North Carolina Press, 1982.

Loving. *Lost in the Customhouse: Authorship in the American Renaissance*. Iowa City: University of Iowa Press, 1993.

Madden, Edward H. *Civil Disobedience and Moral Law in Nineteenth-Century American Philosophy.* Seattle: University of Washington Press, 1968.

Marchalonis, Shirley, ed. *Patrons and Protégées: Gender, Friendship, and Writing in Nineteenth-Century America.* New Brunswick, N.J.: Rutgers University Press, 1988.

Marr, David. *American Worlds since Emerson.* Amherst: University of Massachusetts Press, 1988.

Martin, Terence. *The Instructed Vision: Scottish Common Sense Philosophy and the Origins of American Fiction.* Bloomington: Indiana University Press, 1961.

Martin. *Parables of Possibility: The American Need for Beginnings.* New York: Columbia University Press, 1995.

Marx, Leo. *The Machine in the Garden: Technology and the Pastoral Ideal in America.* New York: Oxford University Press, 1964.

Matthiessen, F. O. *American Renaissance: Art and Expression in the Age of Emerson and Whitman.* New York: Oxford University Press, 1941.

Maxwell, D. E. S. *American Fiction: The Intellectual Background.* New York: Columbia University Press, 1963.

McDowell, Deborah E., and Arnold Rampersad, eds. *Slavery and the Literary Imagination.* Baltimore: Johns Hopkins University Press, 1989.

McKinsey, Elizabeth R. *The Western Experiment: New England Transcendentalists in the Ohio Valley.* Cambridge, Mass.: Harvard University Press, 1973.

McWilliams, Wilson Carey. *The Idea of Fraternity in America.* Berkeley: University of California Press, 1973.

Mead, David. *Yankee Eloquence in the Middle West: The Ohio Lyceum, 1850–1870.* East Lansing: Michigan State College Press, 1951.

Michaels, Walter Benn, and Donald E. Pease, eds. *The American Renaissance Reconsidered.* Baltimore: Johns Hopkins University Press, 1984.

Miller, Perry. *Nature's Nation.* Cambridge, Mass.: Harvard University Press, 1967.

Miller. *The Raven and the Whale: The War of Words and Wits in the Era of Poe and Melville.* New York: Harcourt, Brace, 1956.

Miller, ed. *The Transcendentalists: An Anthology.* Cambridge, Mass.: Harvard University Press, 1950.

Minnigerode, Meade. *The Fabulous Forties 1840–1850.* New York & London: Putnam, 1924.

Minter, David L. *The Interpreted Design as a Structural Principle in American Prose.* New Haven: Yale University Press, 1969.

Mitchell, Charles E. *Individualism and Its Discontents: Appropriations of Emerson, 1880–1950.* Amherst: University of Massachusetts Press, 1997.

Mitchell, Donald G. *American Lands and Letters: Leather-Stocking to Poe's "Raven."* New York: Scribners, 1899.

More, Paul Elmer. *Paul Elmer More's Shelbourne Essays on American Literature,* edited by Daniel Aaron. New York: Harcourt, Brace & World, 1963.

Mott, Frank Luther. *Golden Multitudes: The Story of Best Sellers in the United States.* New York: Macmillan, 1947.

Mott. *A History of American Magazines,* 5 volumes. Cambridge, Mass.: Harvard University Press, 1938–1968.

Mott, Wesley T., ed. *Biographical Dictionary of Transcendentalism.* Westport, Conn.: Greenwood Press, 1996.

Mott, ed. *Encyclopedia of Transcendentalism.* Westport, Conn.: Greenwood Press, 1996.

Mott and Robert E. Burkholder, eds. *Emersonian Circles: Essays in Honor of Joel Myerson.* Rochester, N.Y.: University of Rochester Press, 1997.

Mumford, Lewis. *The Golden Day: A Study in American Experience and Culture.* New York: Boni & Liveright, 1926.

Myerson, Joel. *Brook Farm: An Annotated Bibliography and Resources Guide.* New York: Garland, 1978.

Myerson. *The Brook Farm Book: A Collection of First-Hand Accounts of the Community.* New York: Garland, 1987.

Myerson. *The New England Transcendentalists and The Dial: A History of the Magazine and Its Contributors.* Rutherford, N.J.: Fairleigh Dickinson University Press, 1980.

Myerson, ed. *The American Transcendentalists.* Detroit: Gale, 1988.

Myerson, ed. *Transcendentalism: A Reader.* New York: Oxford University Press, 2000.

Myerson, ed. *The Transcendentalists: A Review of Research and Criticism.* New York: Modern Language Association, 1984.

Nash, Roderick. *Wilderness and the American Mind.* New Haven: Yale University Press, 1967.

New, Elisa. *The Regenerate Lyric: Theology and Innovation in American Poetry.* New York: Cambridge University Press, 1993.

Newbury, Michael. *Figuring Authorship in Antebellum America.* Stanford, Cal.: Stanford University Press, 1997.

Newfield, Christopher. *The Emerson Effect: Individualism and Submission in America.* Chicago: University of Chicago Press, 1996.

Newton, Annabel. *Wordsworth in Early American Criticism.* Chicago: University of Chicago Press, 1928.

Nilon, Charles H. *Bibliography of Bibliographies in American Literature.* New York: R. R. Bowker, 1970.

Novak, Barbara. *Nature and Culture: American Landscape and Painting, 1825–1875,* revised edition. New York: Oxford University Press, 1995.

Nye, Russel Blaine. *Society and Culture in America 1830–1860.* New York: Harper, 1974.

Nye. *The Unembarrassed Muse: The Popular Arts in America.* New York: Dial, 1970.

O'Connell, Shaun. *Imagining Boston: A Literary Landscape.* Boston: Beacon, 1990.

Oelschlaeger, Max. *The Idea of Wilderness from Prehistory to the Age of Ecology.* New Haven: Yale University Press, 1991.

Orians, G. Harrison. "The Rise of Romanticism, 1805–1855," in *Transitions in American Literary History,* edited by Harry Hayden Clark. Durham, N.C.: Duke University Press, 1954, pp. 161–244.

Packer, Barbara. "The Transcendentalists," in *The Cambridge History of American Literature,* edited by Sacvan Bercovitch, volume 2: *Prose Writing, 1820–1865.* Cambridge: Cambridge University Press, 1995, pp. 329–604.

Papasvily, Helen Waite. *All the Happy Endings.* New York: Harper, 1956.

Parini, Jay, ed. *The Columbia History of American Poetry.* New York: Columbia University Press, 1993.

Parrington, Vernon Lewis. *The Romantic Revolution in America 1800–1860.* New York: Harcourt, Brace, 1927.

Parrington, Vernon Lewis, Jr. *American Dreams: A Study of American Utopias.* Providence: Brown University Press, 1947.

Pattee, Fred Lewis. *The Development of the American Short Story.* New York: Harper, 1923.

Pattee. *The First Century of American Literature 1770–1870.* New York: Appleton-Century, 1935.

Patterson, Anita Haya. *From Emerson to King: Democracy, Race, and the Politics of Protest.* New York: Oxford University Press, 1997.

Patterson, Mark R. *Authority, Autonomy, and Representation in American Literature, 1776–1865.* Princeton: Princeton University Press, 1988.

Payne, Edward F. *Dickens Days in Boston.* Boston & New York: Houghton Mifflin, 1927.

Peach, Linden. *British Influence on the Birth of American Literature.* London: Macmillan, 1982.

Pearce, Roy Harvey. *The Continuity of American Poetry.* Princeton: Princeton University Press, 1961.

Pease, Donald E. *Visionary Compacts: American Renaissance Writings in Cultural Context.* Madison: University of Wisconsin Press, 1987.

Pease, Jane H., and William H. Pease. *Bound Them in Chains: A Biographical History of the Antislavery Movement.* Westport, Conn.: Greenwood Press, 1972.

Perry, Bliss. *The American Spirit in Literature.* New Haven: Yale University Press, 1918.

Perry, Lewis. *Boats against the Current: American Culture between Revolution and Modernity 1820–1860.* New York: Oxford University Press, 1993.

Persons, Stow. *American Minds: A History of Ideas.* New York: Holt, 1958.

Persons. *Free Religion: An American Faith.* New Haven: Yale University Press, 1947.

Pochmann, Henry A. *German Culture in America: Philosophical and Literary Influences, 1600–1900.* Madison: University of Wisconsin Press, 1956.

Pochmann. *New England Transcendentalism and St. Louis Hegelianism.* Philadelphia: Carl Schurz Foundation, 1948.

Poirier, Richard. *Poetry and Pragmatism.* Cambridge, Mass.: Harvard University Press, 1992.

Poirier. *The Renewal of Literature: Emersonian Reflections.* New York: Random House, 1987.

Poirier. *A World Elsewhere: The Place of Style in American Literature.* New York: Oxford University Press, 1966.

Porte, Joel. *Emerson and Thoreau: Transcendentalists in Conflict.* Middletown, Conn.: Wesleyan University Press, 1966.

Porte. *In Respect to Egotism: Studies in American Romantic Writing.* Cambridge: Cambridge University Press, 1991.

Power, Julia. *Shelley in America in the Nineteenth Century.* Lincoln: University of Nebraska Press, 1940.

Pritchard, John Paul. *Criticism in America.* Norman: University of Oklahoma Press, 1956.

Quinn, Arthur Hobson. *American Fiction: An Historical and Critical Survey.* New York: Appleton-Century, 1936.

Quinn, ed. *The Literature of the American People: An Historical and Critical Survey.* New York: Appleton-Century-Crofts, 1951.

Railton, Stephen. *Authorship and Audience: Literary Performance in the American Renaissance.* Princeton: Princeton University Press, 1991.

Rayapati, J. P. Rao. *Early American Interest in Vedanta: Pre-Emersonian Interest in Vedic Literature and Vedantic Philosophy.* London: Asia Publishing House, 1973.

Rees, Robert A., and Earl N. Harbert, eds. *Fifteen American Authors before 1900: Bibliographic Essays on Research and Criticism,* revised edition. Madison: University of Wisconsin Press, 1984.

Reising, Russell J. *The Unusable Past: Theory and the Study of American Literature.* New York: Methuen, 1986.

Reynolds, David S. *Beneath the American Renaissance: The Subversive Imagination in the Age of Emerson and Melville.* New York: Knopf, 1988.

Reynolds. *Faith in Fiction: The Emergence of Religious Literature in America.* Cambridge, Mass.: Harvard University Press, 1981.

Reynolds, Larry J. *European Revolutions and the American Literary Renaissance.* New Haven: Yale University Press, 1988.

Richardson, Robert D., Jr. *Myth and Literature in the American Renaissance.* Bloomington: Indiana University Press, 1978.

Riegel, Robert E. *Young America 1830–1840.* Norman: University of Oklahoma Press, 1949.

Riley, Woodbridge. *American Thought from Puritanism to Pragmatism and Beyond.* New York: Holt, 1915.

Robinson, David. *The Unitarians and the Universalists.* Westport, Conn.: Greenwood Press, 1985.

Rose, Anne C. *Transcendentalism as a Social Movement 1830–1850.* New Haven: Yale University Press, 1981.

Rosenthal, Bernard. *City of Nature: Journeys to Nature in the Age of American Romanticism.* Newark: University of Delaware Press, 1980.

Rourke, Constance. *American Humor: A Study of the National Character.* New York: Harcourt, Brace, 1931.

Rowe, John Carlos. *At Emerson's Tomb: The Politics of Classic American Literature.* New York: Columbia University Press, 1997.

Rowland, William G., Jr. *Literature and the Marketplace: Romantic Writers and Their Audiences in Great Britain and the United States.* Lincoln: University of Nebraska Press, 1996.

Ruland, Richard. *The Rediscovery of American Literature: Premises of Critical Taste, 1900–1940.* Cambridge, Mass.: Harvard University Press, 1967.

Sams, Henry W., ed. *Autobiography of Brook Farm*. Englewood Cliffs, N.J.: Prentice-Hall, 1958.

Saum, Lewis O. *The Popular Mood of Pre-Civil War America*. Westport, Conn.: Greenwood Press, 1980.

Schlesinger, Arthur M., Jr. *The Age of Jackson*. Boston: Little, Brown, 1945.

Schneider, Herbert W. *A History of American Philosophy*. New York: Columbia University Press, 1946.

Scudder, Townsend. *Concord: American Town*. Boston: Little, Brown, 1947.

Sealts, Merton M., Jr. *Beyond the Classroom: Essays on American Authors*. Columbia: University of Missouri Press, 1996.

Seldes, Gilbert. *The Stammering Century*. New York: John Day, 1928.

Sellers, Charles. *The Market Revolution: Jacksonian America 1815–1846*. New York: Oxford University Press, 1991.

Serafin, Steven R., gen. ed. *Encyclopedia of American Literature*. New York: Continuum, 1999.

Shi, David. *The Simple Life: Plain Living and High Thinking in American Culture*. New York: Oxford University Press, 1985.

Shucard, Alan. *American Poetry: The Puritans through Walt Whitman*. Boston: Twayne, 1988.

Shumway, David R. *Creating American Civilization: A Genealogy of American Literature as an Academic Discipline*. Minneapolis: University of Minnesota Press, 1994.

Simon, Myron, and Thornton H. Parsons, eds. *Transcendentalism and Its Legacy*. Ann Arbor: University of Michigan Press, 1966.

Simpson, David. *The Politics of American English, 1776–1850*. New York: Oxford University Press, 1986.

Sizer, Lyde Cullen. *The Political Work of Northern Women Writers and the Civil War, 1850–1872*. Chapel Hill: University of North Carolina Press, 2000.

Slotkin, Richard. *Regeneration through Violence: The Mythology of the American Frontier, 1600–1860*. Middletown, Conn.: Wesleyan University Press, 1973.

Smith, Bernard. *Forces in American Criticism: A Study in the History of American Literary Thought*. New York: Harcourt, Brace, 1939.

Smith, Henry Nash. *Democracy and the Novel: Popular Resistance to Classic American Writers*. New York: Oxford University Press, 1978.

Smithline, Arnold. *Natural Religion and American Literature*. New Haven: College and University Press, 1966.

Spencer, Benjamin. *The Quest for Nationality: An American Literary Campaign*. Syracuse, N.Y.: Syracuse University Press, 1957.

Spengemann, William C. *A Mirror for Americanists: Reflections on the Idea of American Literature*. Hanover, N.H.: University Press of New England, 1989.

Spiller, Robert E. *The American in England during the First Half Century of Independence*. New York: Holt, 1926.

Spiller. *The Cycle of American Literature*. New York: Macmillan, 1956.

Spiller and others. *Literary History of the United States,* 2 volumes, fourth edition, revised. New York: Macmillan, 1974.

Stafford, John. *The Literary Criticism of "Young America": A Study in the Relationship of Politics and Literature 1837–1850.* Berkeley: University of California Press, 1952.

Stange, Douglas C. *Patterns of Antislavery among American Unitarians, 1831–1860.* Rutherford, N.J.: Fairleigh Dickinson University Press, 1977.

Stapleton, Laurence. *The Elected Circle: Studies in the Art of Prose.* Princeton: Princeton University Press, 1973.

Stauffer, Donald Barlow. *A Short History of American Poetry.* New York: Dutton, 1974.

Stearns, Frank Preston. *Sketches from Concord and Appledore.* New York: Putnam, 1895.

Steele, Jeffrey. *The Representation of the Self in the American Renaissance.* Chapel Hill: University of North Carolina Press, 1987.

Stern, Madeleine B. *Imprints on History: Book Publishers and American Frontiers.* Bloomington: Indiana University Press, 1956.

Stewart, Randall. *American Literature and Christian Doctrine.* Baton Rouge: Louisiana State University Press, 1958.

Stoehr, Taylor. *Nay-Saying in Concord: Emerson, Alcott, and Thoreau.* Hamden, Conn.: Archon Books, 1979.

Stovall, Floyd. *American Idealism.* Norman: University of Oklahoma Press, 1943.

Stovall, ed. *The Development of American Literary Criticism.* Chapel Hill: University of North Carolina Press, 1955.

Sundquist, Eric. *Home as Found: Authority and Genealogy in Nineteenth-Century American Literature.* Baltimore: Johns Hopkins University Press, 1979.

Swayne, Josephine Latham. *The Story of Concord Told by Concord Writers,* second edition, revised. Boston: Meador, 1939.

Swift, Lindsay. *Brook Farm: Its Members, Scholars, and Visitors.* New York: Macmillan, 1900.

Tanner, Tony. *The Reign of Wonder: Naivety and Reality in American Literature.* Cambridge: Cambridge University Press, 1965.

Taylor, Walter Fuller. *The Economic Novel in America.* Chapel Hill: University of North Carolina Press, 1942.

Teichgraeber, Richard F., III. *Sublime Thoughts/Penny Wisdom: Situating Emerson and Thoreau in the American Market.* Baltimore: Johns Hopkins University Press, 1995.

Thompson, G. R., and Eric Carl Link. *Neutral Ground: New Traditionalism and the American Romance Controversy.* Baton Rouge: Louisiana State University Press, 1998.

Trent, William P. *A History of American Literature 1607–1865.* New York: Appleton, 1903.

Turner, Lorenzo Dow. *Anti-Slavery Sentiment in American Literature Prior to 1865.* Washington, D.C.: Association for the Study of Negro Life and History, 1929.

Unitarianism: Its Origin and History: A Course of Sixteen Lectures Delivered in Channing Hall, Boston, 1888–89. Boston: American Unitarian Association, 1890.

Vanderbilt, Kermit. *American Literature and the Academy: The Roots, Growth, and Maturity of a Profession.* Philadelphia: University of Pennsylvania Press, 1986.

Van Nostrand, A. D. *Everyman His Own Poet: Romantic Gospels in American Literature.* New York: McGraw-Hill, 1968.

Versluis, Arthur. *American Transcendentalism and Asian Religions.* New York: Oxford University Press, 1993.

Vogel, Stanley M. *German Literary Influences on the American Transcendentalists.* New Haven: Yale University Press, 1955.

Von Frank, Albert J. *The Sacred Game: Provincialism and Frontier Consciousness in American Literature.* New York: Cambridge University Press, 1985.

Von Frank. *The Trials of Anthony Burns: Freedom and Slavery in Emerson's Boston.* Cambridge, Mass.: Harvard University Press, 1998.

Wagenknecht, Edward. *A Pictorial History of New England.* New York: Crown, 1976.

Wager, Willis. *American Literature: A World View.* New York: New York University Press, 1968.

Waggoner, Hyatt H. *American Poets from the Puritans to the Present.* Boston: Houghton Mifflin, 1968.

Walls, Laura Dassow. *Seeing New Worlds: Henry David Thoreau and Nineteenth-Century Natural Science.* Madison: University of Wisconsin Press, 1995.

Warren, Joyce W. *The American Narcissus: Individualism and Women in Nineteenth-Century American Fiction.* New Brunswick, N.J.: Rutgers University Press, 1984.

Warren, ed. *The (Other) American Traditions: Nineteenth-Century Women Writers.* New Brunswick, N.J.: Rutgers University Press, 1993.

Webber, Everett. *Escape to Utopia: The Communal Movement in America.* New York: Hastings House, 1959.

Weisbuch, Robert. *Atlantic Double-Cross: American Literature and British Influence in the Age of Emerson.* Chicago: University of Chicago Press, 1986.

Welter, Barbara. *Dimity Convictions: The American Woman in the Nineteenth Century.* Athens: Ohio University Press, 1976.

Welter, Rush. *The Mind of America 1820–1860.* New York: Columbia University Press, 1975.

Wendell, Barrett. *A Literary History of America.* New York: Scribners, 1900.

West, Cornel. *The American Evasion of Philosophy: A Genealogy of Pragmatism.* Madison: University of Wisconsin Press, 1989.

West, Michael. *Transcendental Wordplay: America's Romantic Punsters & the Search for the Language of Nature.* Athens: Ohio University Press, 2000.

Westbrook, Perry D. *A Literary History of New England.* Bethlehem, Pa.: Lehigh University Press, 1988.

Westbrook. *The New England Town in Fact and Fiction.* Rutherford, N.J.: Fairleigh Dickinson University Press, 1982.

Wheeler, Ruth R. *Concord: Climate for Freedom.* Concord, Mass.: Concord Antiquarian Society, 1967.

Whicher, George F., ed. *The Transcendentalist Revolt against Materialism.* Boston: Heath, 1949; revised as *The Transcendentalist Revolt,* edited by Gail Kennedy. Boston: Heath, 1968.

White, Barbara A. *American Women's Fiction: 1790–1870: A Reference Guide.* New York: Garland, 1990.

White, Morton. *Science and Sentiment in America.* New York: Oxford University Press, 1972.

Whiting, Lilian. *Boston Days.* Boston: Little, Brown, 1911.

Wider, Sarah Ann. *Anna Tilden, Unitarian Culture, and the Problem of Self-Representation.* Athens: University of Georgia Press, 1997.

Williams, Stanley T. *The Beginnings of American Poetry (1620–1855).* Uppsala, Sweden: Almquist & Wiksells, 1951.

Wilmerding, John, ed. *American Light: The Luminist Movement, 1850–1875. Paintings, Drawings, Photographs.* New York: Harper & Row, 1980.

Wilson, R. Jackson. *Figures of Speech: American Writers and the Literary Marketplace, from Benjamin Franklin to Emily Dickinson.* New York: Knopf, 1989.

Wilson, Rufus Rockwell. *New England in Letters.* New York: A. Wessels, 1904.

Winsor, Justin, ed. *The Memorial of Boston.* 4 volumes. Boston: Osgood, 1881.

Wolf, Brian Jay. *Romantic Re-Vision: Culture and Consciousness in Nineteenth-Century American Painting and Literature.* Chicago: University of Chicago Press, 1982.

Wright, Conrad. *The Beginnings of Unitarianism in America.* Boston: Starr King Press, 1955.

Wright. "The Early Period (1811–1840)," in *The Harvard Divinity School: Its Place in Harvard University and in American Culture,* edited by George Huntston Williams. Boston: Beacon, 1954, pp. 21–77.

Wright. *The Liberal Christians: Essays on American Unitarian History.* Boston: Beacon, 1970.

Wright. *The Unitarian Controversy: Essays on American Unitarian History.* Boston: Skinner House, 1994.

Wright, ed. *A Stream of Light: A Sesquicentennial History of American Unitarianism.* Boston: Unitarian Universalist Association, 1975.

Wright, Conrad Edick, ed. *American Unitarianism, 1805–1865.* Boston: Northeastern University Press, 1989.

Ziff, Larzer. *Literary Democracy: The Declaration of Cultural Independence in America.* New York: Viking, 1981.

Contributors

Susan Belasco . . . . *University of Nebraska, Lincoln*

Michael Berthold . . . . *Villanova University*

Alan D. Brasher . . . . *East Georgia College*

Robert Bray . . . . *Illinois Wesleyan University*

Larry A. Carlson . . . . *College of Charleston*

Deborah P. Clifford . . . . *New Haven, Vermont*

Brett Coker . . . . *University of California, Santa Barbara*

John W. Crowley . . . . *Syracuse University*

Mathew David Fisher . . . . *Ball State University*

D'Ann Pletcher George . . . . *Bridgewater State College*

Richard D. Hathaway . . . . *State University of New York at New Paltz*

Kathleen Healey . . . . *Colby-Sawyer College*

Robert N. Hudspeth . . . . *University of Redlands*

Judy Logan . . . . *Eastern Washington University*

Larry R. Long . . . . *Harding University*

Beverly G. Merrick . . . . *New Mexico State University*

Christopher L. Nesmith . . . . *University of South Carolina*

Cameron C. Nickels . . . . *James Madison University*

Patricia Okker . . . . *University of Missouri, Columbia*

Ralph H. Orth . . . . *University of Vermont*

Sandra Harbert Petrulionis . . . . *Pennsylvania State University, The Altoona College*

John E. Reilly . . . . *College of the Holy Cross*

Susan L. Roberson . . . . *Alabama State University*

David M. Robinson . . . . *Oregon State University*

Barbara Ryan . . . . *University of Missouri, Kansas City*

James Emmett Ryan . . . . *Auburn University*

Nancy Craig Simmons . . . . *Virginia Polytechnic Institute and State University*

Andrew Smith . . . . *Lafayette College*

Roger Thompson . . . . *Virginia Military Institute*

Patricia Dunlavy Valenti . . . . *University of North Carolina at Pembroke*

Albert J. von Frank . . . . *Washington State University*

Karen A. Weyler . . . . *University of North Carolina at Greensboro*

Sarah Ann Wider . . . . *Colgate University*

Barbara Downs Wojtusik . . . . *Bristol, Connecticut*

Guy R. Woodall . . . . *Tennessee Technological University*

Arthur Wrobel . . . . *University of Kentucky*

Anne Zanzucchi . . . . *University of Rochester*

Cumulative Index

Dictionary of Literary Biography, Volumes 1-243
Dictionary of Literary Biography Yearbook, 1980-2000
Dictionary of Literary Biography Documentary Series, Volumes 1-19
Concise Dictionary of American Literary Biography, Volumes 1-7
Concise Dictionary of British Literary Biography, Volumes 1-8
Concise Dictionary of World Literary Biography, Volumes 1-4

Cumulative Index

DLB before number: *Dictionary of Literary Biography,* Volumes 1-243
Y before number: *Dictionary of Literary Biography Yearbook,* 1980-2000
DS before number: *Dictionary of Literary Biography Documentary Series,* Volumes 1-19
CDALB before number: *Concise Dictionary of American Literary Biography,* Volumes 1-7
CDBLB before number: *Concise Dictionary of British Literary Biography,* Volumes 1-8
CDWLB before number: *Concise Dictionary of World Literary Biography,* Volumes 1-4

C

F

L

N

ISBN 0-7876-4660-1

90000

9 780787 646608